THE POLITICS OF THE PRESIDENCY

THE POLITICS OF THE PRESIDENCY

REVISED FOURTH EDITION

NORMAN C. THOMAS
University of Cincinnati

JOSEPH A. PIKA
University of Delaware

 A DIVISION OF CONGRESSIONAL QUARTERLY INC.
PRESS WASHINGTON, D.C.

Book design by Kachergis Book Design, Pittsboro, North Carolina.
Cover photo: Michael McMullan, AP.

Printed and bound in the United States.

Permissions for copyrighted materials are listed on page 500, which is
to be considered an extension of the copyright page.

LIBRARY OF CONGRESS
CATALOGING-IN-PUBLICATION DATA

Thomas, Norman C.
    The politics of the presidency / Norman C. Thomas, Joseph A. Pika.
    — Rev. 4th ed.
        p.   cm.
    Includes bibliographical references and index.
    ISBN 1-56802-316-2   2029788
    1. Presidents — United States. I. Pika, Joseph August, 1947– .
II. Title.
JK516.T46   1997   97-20161
352.23'0973—dc21

TO MARILYN AND MARY

CONTENTS

    CENTURY'S END   443
    The Presidency Since Midcentury   444
    The Clinton Presidency   449
    The Presidency at Century's End   452
    The Presidency at Century's End: An Assessment   458
    Readings   464

    APPENDIXES   467
    INDEX   481

PREFACE

AFTER MORE THAN TWO CENTURIES of change and development, the presidency stands not only as the nation's preeminent public office but also its most problematic. Because presidents today are far more important for peace and prosperity than were their nineteenth-century counterparts, ensuring the selection of qualified candidates and enhancing the winner's effectiveness in office are major concerns of specialists and citizens alike. In the post–World War II period, however, few presidents have left office with a record of unqualified success. In fact, academic and media observers have labeled each presidency since Lyndon Johnson's as "failures."

Johnson enjoyed unparalleled success in getting his Great Society legislative program through Congress, but he could not extricate himself or the country from the Vietnam War. Richard Nixon managed to bring the war to an end, but Watergate cost him the confidence of the country. Gerald Ford and Jimmy Carter failed to convince voters that they could exercise effective leadership. Like Johnson, Ronald Reagan succeeded in getting Congress to approve his program of economic reforms, but the budgetary consequences of those policies and his mishandling of the Iran-contra affair tarnished his reputation. George Bush and Bill Clinton were threatened by the same difficulties that beset Ford and Carter—a perception of ineffectiveness. Clinton had an additional problem—a perception of inconstancy. But given the inflated expectations of performance held by the public and political elites, it is reasonable to wonder if any president can be considered a success.

Our focus in *The Politics of the Presidency* is on how presidents govern—in the country and in Washington. The book views the presidency as essentially a political office; that is, the chief executive must govern more through skilled political leadership than through the assertion of constitutional prerogatives. We also examine how effectiveness in office varies with the character, personality, and political style of the incumbent. Major political developments in society, the U.S. political system, and the international arena also affect how well or poorly a president does in office. By examining this full range of influences, *The Politics of the Presidency* provides a comprehensive treatment of the nation's most important political office.

Part I begins with an analysis of the origins and development of the presidency as well as changing conceptions of the office. It then explores the president's relationships with the public in electoral politics and in the process of governing. Next, it examines the kinds of people who have become president and the interactions between them and the office. Part II analyzes the president's relations with other government elites—members of Congress, the bureaucracy, and the judiciary. In Part III the focus shifts to how presidents formulate and implement domestic, economic, and national security policies. The book concludes with an assessment of the condition of the presidency as the twentieth century comes to a close.

In the revised fourth edition of *The Politics of the Presidency*, Joseph Pika updated Chapters 1–4 and is primarily responsible for them. Norman Thomas updated and accepts major responsibility for Chapters 5–10. The concluding chapter is a joint effort. The imprint of Richard Watson, who originally conceived of the book, is present throughout.

Many extensive studies of the presidency have appeared since publication of the third edition. We have incorporated findings from them as well as from scholarly and journalistic analyses, historical and legal materials, and, where appropriate, behavioral and quantitative research. In addition to discussing the results of the 1994 and 1996 nomination and election contests, we consider the major developments during the first four years of the Clinton presidency, including the enactment of much of his economic program in 1993 followed by the failure in 1994 of his major policy initiative (health care reform); the consequences of the Republican capture of Congress in the 1994 elections; and the president's reluctant acceptance of the imperatives of presidential leadership in foreign policy.

A note on the language: in writing about the people who have served as president we have followed the convention of using male pronouns. There are several reasons. So far only men have held the office, use of the plural is not always accurate, and "he or she" is cumbersome when repeated many times. We are confident that in the not too distant future the nation will elect a woman president or vice president, and we hope that when the time comes we will be skillful enough to make the appropriate linguistic adjustments.

We have benefited from manuscript reviews by Professors Michael Grossman of Towson State University, Mary Stuckey of the University of Mississippi, an anonymous reviewer, and other colleagues who have used the previous edition.

We are grateful to Brenda Carter and Christopher Karlsten of CQ Press for their contributions to the revised fourth edition. We also appreciate research assistance provided by Joseph Liberti, Jennifer Marrone, and Tim Dudderar.

PART I

THE PRESIDENT AND
THE PUBLIC

1 THE CHANGING PRESIDE

The White House—nerve center of the executive branch and home of its chief.

FOR MOST AMERICANS THE president is the focal point of public life. Almost every night they see the president on television newscasts interpreting the day's events, meeting with foreign dignitaries, or grappling with national problems. This person appears to be in charge, and such recurrent images of an engaged leader are reassuring. But the reality of the presidency rests on a very different truth: presidents are seldom in command and usually must negotiate with others to achieve their goals. In short, politics is inescapable, and it is only by exercising adroit political skill in winning public and elite support and knowing how to use it that a president can succeed in office. For more than three decades this lesson has dominated scholarly accounts of the presidency, but it has not always been fully appreciated either by the public or the presidents themselves, as reflected in constantly changing conceptions of the office.

Conceptions of the Presidency

When Harry S. Truman and Lyndon Baines Johnson assumed office from the vice presidency, the public rallied to support them. But both left office repudiated by their own parties after they involved the country in controversial military conflicts abroad. Richard Nixon, reelected by a landslide in 1972, resigned two years later after congressional investigations revealed his abuse of power. Neither president who followed Nixon, Gerald R. Ford nor Jimmy Carter, was reelected, and the reputation of Ronald Reagan's presidency was damaged by the Iran-contra controversy. George Bush, praised as the architect of American victory in the Persian Gulf War, was defeated in his bid for a second term. Almost every modern president has experienced such a decline in public approval.

Dramatic changes in presidential fortunes are not new to American politics, nor are the alternative interpretations offered to explain their meaning. Scholars' conceptions of the presidency have varied substantially over the past fifty years and are likely to be recast as the office continues to change in the future. Students of the modern presidency have identified three conceptions of the office: the heroic, the imperial, and the post–imperial.

The Heroic Presidency

The 1950s and 1960s were the era of what has been termed the *heroic* presidency. Writing about the office in 1960, at the end of Dwight D. Eisenhower's second term, Clinton Rossiter expressed his belief that the American presidency is "one of the few truly successful institutions created by men in their endless quest for the blessings of free government." [1] His book clearly glorifies the office and the "great" presidents who have shaped it—George Washington, Thomas Jefferson, Andrew Jackson, Abraham Lincoln, Theodore Roosevelt, Woodrow Wilson, Franklin D. Roosevelt, and Harry Truman. Rossiter concluded his analysis with a poetic celebration of the institution:

It is, finally, an office of freedom. The Presidency is a standing reproach to those petty doctrinaires who insist that executive power is inherently undemocratic; for, to the exact contrary, it has been more responsive to the needs and dreams of giant democracy than any other office or institution in the whole mosaic of American life. It is no less a reproach to those easy generalizers who think that Lord Acton had the very last word on the corrupting effects of power, for, again, to the contrary, his doctrine finds small confirmation in the history of the Presidency. The vast power of this office has not been "poison," as Henry Adams wrote in scorn; rather, it has elevated often and corrupted never, chiefly because those who held it recognized the true source of the power and were ennobled by the knowledge.[2]

Also appearing in 1960 was the first edition of Richard E. Neustadt's *Presidential Power: The Politics of Leadership,* considered by many to be the most perceptive analysis of the office ever written. Like Rossiter, Neustadt is a great admirer of the American presidency. He expressed concern, however, that the limitations of the office, especially those stemming from a "government of separated institutions *sharing* power," threaten to make the president a clerk rather than a leader.[3] To rectify this situation, Neustadt proposed, chief executives seek their political power by bargaining with other political actors—members of Congress, bureaucrats, and party leaders, for example—persuading them that "what he wants of them is what their own appraisal of their own responsibilities requires them to do in their interest, not his."[4] Neustadt's analysis of three modern presidents—Franklin Roosevelt, Truman, and Eisenhower—convinced him that FDR's temperament and understanding of political power made him by far the most successful: "No modern President has been more nearly master in the White House."[5] Toward the end of the book Neustadt made a sweeping statement that epitomizes his glorification of the office:

The contributions that a President can make to government are indispensable. Assuming that he knows what power is and wants it, those contributions cannot help but be forthcoming in some measure as by-products of his search for personal influence. In a relative but real sense one can say of a President what Eisenhower's first Secretary of Defense once said of General Motors: what is good for the country is good for the President and vice versa.[6]

In 1965, during the Johnson administration, yet another study appeared celebrating the heroic American presidency—James MacGregor Burns's *Presidential Government: The Crucible of Leadership.* Analyzing the performance of the presidency in history, Burns chose as his model a man who never served as president. Alexander Hamilton was an influential member of the Washington administration who "succeeded in 'turning government high,' so high that Washington's administration stands as one of the truly creative presidencies in American history."[7] Burns's analysis of the characteristics of a Hamiltonian president (he includes Washington, Lincoln, and the two Roosevelts) parallels that espoused by Neustadt: they are heroic leaders who build a loyal personal political organization and expediently use their reputations, prestige, patronage, power, and political friendships, as well as tactics of co-opting and disorganizing the opposition party leadership, to achieve the results they want.[8] Unlike Neustadt, however, who made no mention of the ends for which presidential power is to be used, Burns examined the performance of the presidency to determine whether it has served the basic values of American society. His conclusion affirms the concept of the heroic president:

For in presidential government Americans have established one of the most powerful political institutions in the free world. They have fashioned, sometimes unwittingly, a weapon that has served them well in the long struggle for freedom and equality at home and in the search for stable and democratic politics abroad. They have grasped the uses of power, and as Harold Laski said, great power makes great leadership possible.[9]

These three important presidential scholars of the 1950s and 1960s agreed on the existence and value of a heroic institution. Writing in 1970, Thomas E. Cronin labeled this perspective the "textbook presidency" because it was adopted not only by presidential scholars but also by writers of general American government textbooks of the era, who described the presidency in glowing terms. Underlying their view of the office was a common assumption: the national government should be the leader in solving the problems of an increasingly interdependent world and of U.S. domestic society as well. These authors were political liberals who saw the office as the only institution in the political system that can understand the needs of all Americans, including the disadvantaged, and that has a nationwide constituency providing the political support to meet those needs.

Cronin went on to note that conditions in the late 1960s, in particular the inability of President Johnson to end the Vietnam War, were beginning to tarnish the heroic image of the presidency.[10] As the following section indicates, the 1970s did indeed usher in a radically different version of the nation's highest office.

The Imperial Presidency

Studies appearing between 1970 and 1973 characterized the office as the "imperial presidency," a term coined by Arthur Schlesinger, Jr., who served in John F. Kennedy's White House, in his 1973 book by that name. Before Schlesinger, however, in 1970 George Reedy, a White House aide under President Johnson, described the office as "the American monarchy." The thesis of Reedy's book, *The Twilight of the Presidency*, is that, far from ennobling its occupants, the office creates "an environment in which men cannot function in any kind of decent and human relationship to the people whom they are supposed to lead." [11] At fault are presidential "courts" composed of sycophants who tell presidents what they want to hear and who thereby isolate them from the harsh facts of political life. Denied the presence of peer pressure and of people who tell them when they are wrong, presidents exaggerate their own importance and competence.

Schlesinger's study benefited not only from the insights gained from the Vietnam War but also from the Watergate scandal. He found the origins of the imperial presidency in foreign policy, "from the capture by the Presidency of the most vital of national decisions, the decision to go to war." [12] Tracing presidential arrogation of the war power from Congress, with which the Founders intended it be shared, Schlesinger noted that the trend became more pronounced after World War II, especially under Johnson and Nixon. Presidential imperialism spread into the domestic sphere as Nixon employed a number of measures to deal with those who opposed him: he impounded funds appropriated by Congress, dismantled the Office of Economic Opportunity without congressional authorization, made excessive claims of executive privilege to withhold vital information from Congress, and used a special investigative unit to conduct illegal surveillance of U.S. citizens. In fact, Schlesinger described the Nixon presidency not only as "imperial" but also as "plebiscitary," a concept borrowed from Napoleon and, more recently, from former French president Charles de Gaulle. When a plebiscitary leader is elected, "he personifies the majority and all resistance to his will is undemocratic," at least until the next election.[13] Nixon's presidency renewed traditional American concerns about the threat of tyranny associated with a powerful executive.

In 1975, the year after Nixon was forced to resign, Sen. Walter F. Mondale, D-Minn., analyzed the contemporary presidency in his book, *The Accountability of Power: Toward a Responsible Presidency.* He stated that Vietnam burst "the bubble of Presidential ascendancy and omniscience" and that Watergate initiated a "wholesale decline in Americans' belief in the viability and honesty of their governmental institutions." [14] Mondale blamed the imperial presidency not only on the occupants of that office but also on Congress, which regularly voted appropriations for U.S. military involvement in Vietnam, and the American people, who knew what their tax money was buying.

The message of presidency analysts writing in the first half of the 1970s was, therefore, precisely the opposite of those who wrote about the office in the 1950s and 1960s. As William Andrews describes the transformation, "Hallowed Be the Presidency" became "Deliver Us from Presidents." [15] The radical change in viewpoint cannot be attributed to a different type of analyst. Reedy, Schlesinger, and Mondale shared the same political philosophy as those who examined the presidency in the earlier period: all were liberals. Over time, these writers came to appreciate that the vast powers of the presidency, which could be used for purposes such as ameliorating domestic social and economic problems and winning World War II, also could be used to wage a futile, costly conflict in Southeast Asia and launch an all-out attack on political "enemies," which led to the abuses of Watergate. Just when it seemed, however, that presidential scholars agreed upon the true nature of the presidency, a new conception of the office began to develop.

The Post–Imperial Presidency

In 1978, Fred Greenstein noted another change in the contemporary American presidency. Observing the rapid turnover in presidents—from 1961 to 1978, five chief executives had served, three of them since 1974—Greenstein suggested that such a short tenure in office had required the chief executive

to have a hurried approach to the making of policy ... to engage in activities that are politically risky: simply to win office he needs to raise aspirations about what he will be able to contribute to the nation; once in office, the difficulty of meeting those aspirations opens up the temptation to cut corners— for example, to rush legislation through Congress and leave considerations of political implementation for later on.[16]

Greenstein went on to outline "the intractable political environment of the post–imperial presidency," which includes a Congress whose leaders cannot serve as "effective intermediaries between their Congress and the president"; a weakened party system over which the president is no longer chief; aggressive media that initially idealize new presidents and then "quickly search out their warts"; and a presidential bureaucracy that "has expanded to the point where the president is victimized rather than helped by members of a staff whom he cannot begin to supervise." [17] He also noted the "presidency-curbing legislation" passed by Congress in the 1970s. New laws required the president to consult Congress "in every possible instance" before committing troops to combat and to report to Congress all executive agreements made with foreign powers; limited the power of the president to reorganize executive departments and to impound funds appropriated by Congress; and made the appointment of the director and deputy directors of the Office of Management and Budget subject to Senate confirmation. Greenstein's analysis demonstrates that the presidency of the late 1970s was anything but imperial.

In 1980 the British journalist Godfrey Hodgson presented similar conclusions about the office in *All Things to All Men: The False Promise of the American Presidency*. In Hodgson's view, presidents are isolated from other elements of the U.S. political system through which they could make the system work: the bureaucracy, Congress, their own political party, the media, and even the American people. Presidents also face social and economic problems so difficult and complex that they "have little chance of making any real progress in the direction of solving them within their first term of office. Moreover, they have virtually no hope of making *visible* progress toward solving them in time to have a positive effect on their own prospects of being reelected." [18] As Hodgson summarized the situation, "Never has so powerful a leader been so impotent to do what he wants to do, what he is pledged to do, what he is expected to do, and what he knows he must do." [19]

The presidency of the last half of the 1970s bore little resemblance to the imperial presidency of the first half. Some observers, like Hodgson, thought the office was "impotent." Others, like Cronin, asked whether it was "imperiled." [20] Cronin maintained that the experiences of the post–imperial presidency led many political liberals, who had feared the office in the mid-1970s, to conclude that Congress was incapable of leading the nation's affairs and to call for a resurgent and vigorous presidency. Indeed, part of Ronald Reagan's appeal to the voters in the 1980 election was a pledge to restore the strength of the office.

The Reagan presidency was characterized several different ways. In 1983 Richard Nathan noted approvingly Reagan's use of administrative rather than legislative means to accomplish presidential policy objectives whenever it is possible to do so.[21] Others pointed out, however, that such maneuvers politicized the federal bureaucracy and weakened the civil service by increasing the number of policy-sensitive positions filled by political appointees instead of career civil servants.[22] In 1984 Bert Rockman suggested in his thought-provoking book, *The Leadership Question*, that answers lay not in more "presidentialism"—efforts to strengthen presidential leadership—but in "making the whole of government more effective." [23] A year later Theodore Lowi argued that a plebiscitary presidency, entailing a direct relationship between the president and the American people, had been developing since 1933 and had come to maturity under Reagan. The result, Lowi asserted, is the pathological growth of big government and the eclipse of Congress and the party system.[24] Others described the plebiscitary presidency in favorable terms: along with institutional restraints, it is the answer to the problem of presidential accountability.[25]

Other books published in the late 1980s expressed further concerns arising from domestic and foreign affairs. Lester Seligman and Cary Covington point to presidents' inability to translate their winning electoral coalition into a "core governing coalition [that] constitutes a working majority in each relevant policymaking and implementing arena." [26] Failure to form a stable coalition requires presidents to govern on the basis of ad hoc coalitions fashioned to deal with specific issues and problems. Presidential leadership is increasingly problematic: some presidents may not be effective at organizing issue-specific coalitions and those who do so successfully in one policy arena may fail in others. Richard Rose argues that the end of America's hegemonic position in international relations and the growth of worldwide economic interdependence have transformed the presidency.[27] Although the international responsibilities of the United States remain substantial, the president's resources for meeting them have diminished. The president can no longer dominate foreign governments and their leaders but must bargain with them and win their support through persuasion, as George Bush did in 1991 during the Persian Gulf War.

Reflecting on developments since 1973, Schlesinger sees the Reagan administration as passing two of the three essential tests that determine the existence of an imperial presidency.[28] Much like Nixon, Reagan defended " 'almost royal' prerogatives" in exercising presidential war-making power.[29] He also reasserted the need for government secrecy through aggressive use of the document classification system and by exercising an unconditional claim of executive privilege, the president's supposed right to deny information to Congress. The combination of secrecy and expansive interpretation of presidential war powers led Reagan, like many of his predecessors in the post–World War II period, to rely heavily on covert action to project American influence in the world. The Iran-contra affair revealed an administration operating on the basis of "secret laws," "secret decrees," and "White House indifference to legal and constitutional standards." [30]

But Schlesinger finds an important difference between Nixon and Reagan. "Unlike Nixon ... Reagan did not bring the imperial Presidency into its final stage—the policy of stigmatizing opponents of the president as traitors to the republic." [31] Therefore, while it might be tempting to describe the Reagan experience as "the imperial presidency revitalized," Schlesinger seems to suggest that another description is more appropriate: "the indestructible presidency." [32] Placing the post–Nixon era in perspective, one can see that those who feared the presidency would be brought to its knees by an assertive Congress and an aggressive media failed to recognize the fundamental strength of the institution both under the Constitution and in the minds of the public. What had been lacking were presidents who could provide the nation with a sense of direction and the ability to persuade the nation to follow their vision. [33] Schlesinger returns, in short, to emphasizing the need for heroic leadership.

George Bush seemed to raise the presidency to new heights when he won virtually universal acclaim for his handling of the military crisis in the Persian Gulf triggered by Iraq's invasion of Kuwait in 1990. Yet, twenty months after registering the highest public approval rating in the history of the Gallup Poll, Bush was voted out of office. His successor, Bill Clinton, encountered immediate resistance to his proposals for change from an ideologically unified Republican opposition, a critical media, and portions of his own Democratic Party. Two years after his own victory, Clinton confronted a situation unfamiliar to any president from the last four decades: a Republican majority in both the House and the Senate. On the heels of this dramatic reversal of party fortunes, Newt Gingrich, the new Speaker of the House, seemed to usurp roles previously reserved for presidents: he claimed an electoral mandate, pledged to adopt provisions of the House Republicans' "Contract with America" within the 100-day time period traditionally associated with new presidents, conducted daily briefings with the press, and presented a prime-time address to the nation.

Gingrich's sudden ability to eclipse President Clinton seemed to usher in a new era—the "preempted presidency." It prompted an unexpected question: Had the era of presidential preeminence come to a close? For the first four months of 1995, at least, this seemed to be the case as Clinton appeared irrelevant to the debates swirling in Washington and throughout the nation. Even before the midterm election, Stephen Skowronek concluded his sweeping historical analysis of the presidency by suggesting that the presidency's traditional capacity periodically to reconstruct relations between the government and society had come to an end. Ronald Reagan, the most recent "president of reconstruction" in Skowronek's classification scheme, had successfully repudiated the old order of government programs but been unable to create a new one. He foresaw the need for a new "politics of preemption" in which presidents would cut themselves loose from old coalitions, establish independent political identities, and exploit ad hoc coalitions, a reasonable description of what Clinton was forced to do.[34] Skowronek, however, had seen the president as needing to preempt his opposition, not the reverse. We return to the question of the president's role in this new era in our concluding chapter.

The Presidency: Changeable and Political

In our view, it is inaccurate to describe the presidency as heroic, imperial, post–imperial, imperiled, indestructible, or preempted. Such characterizations fall short because they treat temporary conditions as though they were permanent—they mistake a snapshot for a portrait. The rapidity with which conceptions of the office and the office itself have changed over the past thirty years testifies to the error of this approach.

The presidency is variable for several reasons. First, in no other public office do the personality, character, and political style of the incumbent make as much difference as in the presidency. As an institution, the presidency exhibits important continuities across administrations, but the entry of each new occupant has an undeniably pervasive effect on the position's operation. The presidency also is heavily influenced by changes outside the office and throughout the U.S. political system— whether in the formal political structure (Congress, the executive branch, the courts), in the informal political institutions (political parties and interest groups), in society at large, in the mass media, or in conditions surrounding substantive issues, particularly national security and the economy. Because of their extensive responsibilities, presidents must contend with all of these influences. Furthermore, although the Constitution and historical precedents give structure to the office, the powers of the presidency are so vast and vague that incumbents have tremendous latitude in shaping the office to their particular desires.

The presidency is not only highly *changeable* but also essentially *political*. Although on occasion, especially in times of crisis, presidents rule by asserting their constitutional prerogatives, they usually are forced to govern by political maneuvering, by trying to convince and persuade the many participants in the political process. While Americans were held hostage in Iran, for example, President Carter invoked a number of constitutional prerogatives, but they did not help him handle the problems of the domestic economy or alter the perceived decline of U.S. power and prestige in the world—conditions that contributed substantially to his defeat in the 1980 election. Moreover, the changes that occurred in the first year of the Reagan administration resulted not from the president's exercising constitutional prerogatives but from his successful maneuvering with executive officials, members of Congress, political party and interest group leaders, representatives of the media, and the American public. Since then, these same political actors have effectively limited the changes in domestic and economic policy that Presidents Reagan, Bush, and Clinton wanted to make. On the eve of ordering American forces into combat, a power that administration spokespersons had steadfastly asserted was the president's to exercise, Bush sought congressional authorization. He recognized that the political costs of using force unilaterally could be devastating. Clinton proposed a major reform of health care that faltered on opposition from Congress and organized interests. He then faced a challenge to his preeminent leadership position mounted by a Republican Congress.

The presidency is likely to assume still other forms as the office and the concerns of scholars develop. This book does not claim, however, to provide a comprehensive theory of the American presidency or of presidential behavior. Rather, it maintains that greater understanding of the presidency and the actions of presidents can be gained by keeping in mind the true character of the office.

Those who invented the presidency in 1787 did not expect the office to become the nation's central political institution. In fact, Article II of the Constitution, which deals with the executive branch, is known for its brevity and lack of clarity, particularly in comparison with the carefully detailed description of the legislative branch found in Article I. But within the presidency's vague constitutional description lay the seeds of a far more powerful position, one that has grown through elaboration of its explicit, *enumerated* powers as well as interpretation of its implied, *inherent* powers. Moreover, over the years Congress and the public have caused the range of responsibilities associated with the presidency to expand, particularly in response to changes in society and America's position in the world. What has developed over two centuries is the office that now stands at the center of American government and American politics.

It is ironic that the presidency has come to play such a central and complex role in national life. Invented at the Constitutional Convention by delegates unsure of what they wanted, the position gained stature and a set of precedents from its initial occupant, George Washington. During the nineteenth century, however, the office languished, so much so, in fact, that Lord Bryce, the British chronicler of American government, felt compelled to explain in 1890 that great men do not become president because of the institution's weaknesses. Government during this period centered on Congress and political parties, an American invention that the Founders did not anticipate. A few presidents— most notably Jefferson, Jackson, and Lincoln—seemed to suggest the future, but most receded quickly from history.

How, then, did the presidency come to assume its exalted position? The answer is complex and involves a variety of factors. At one level, the original design of the office—its structure, mode of selection, and powers—continues to exercise important influence on its operation today. The office has changed over time, however, partly in response to the influence of its occupants, partly in response to changing expectations in Congress and the public, and partly in response to internal dynamics of institutional development. A comprehensive view of the office and its occupants requires that we address all of these influences while recognizing their interrelatedness.

Constitutional Design

When they convened in Philadelphia, delegates to the Constitutional Convention had little sense of what the executive in the new or revised scheme of government would look like. Nor did they devise solutions to the major design issues, leaving several of the most critical questions to be dealt with by the Committee on Postponed Matters just before adjourning in September 1787. If James Madison, commonly credited as the chief architect of the Constitution, had prevailed, today's president would be a ceremonial head of state, doing the bidding of Congress. The Virginia Plan, offered by Madison on the convention's first working day, provided for an executive of unspecified size and tenure, selected by the legislature, and with unclear powers.[35] What emerged was an office quite different from Madison's design and with far greater potential in the scheme of government.

Throughout its deliberations, the convention vacillated between two disparate concepts of a national executive.[36] The weak model foresaw an executive whose primary function would be to carry out the will of the legislature. This task was to be accomplished through a plural executive or, if only one man headed the branch, a strong council that would share his powers and hold him in check. Congress would choose the chief executive for a limited term; moreover, he could not be reappointed immediately and would even be subject to removal by the legislative body during his term of office. The executive's powers would be limited and delegated to him by Congress, which would also make appointments to the executive branch and hold the authority to make treaties and declare war. There would be no executive veto of laws passed by Congress.

At the other extreme was the idea of a strong executive, independent of Congress and responsible for important functions in the new government. Under this concept, a single chief executive, chosen by some means other than legislative appointment, would have no limit placed on tenure. If the president was removable at all, it would be only for definite, enumerated reasons, and then only after impeachment and conviction by a judicial body or the legislature. Presidential powers would be derived from the Constitution and not be subject to legislative interference. He would appoint judicial and diplomatic officials and participate in the execution of foreign affairs, including the making of treaties. He would have a veto (preferably absolute) over legislation passed by Congress, a power that he would exercise either alone or in conjunction with the judiciary. There would be no executive council at all, or, if one did exist, it would be a purely advisory body whose actions would not bind the chief executive.

Credit usually goes to a small group of delegates who used their strategic positions within the convention's working committees to fashion an office that more closely corresponds to the strong model. James Wilson, delegate from Pennsylvania, was probably the most persistent exponent of a strong national executive and deserves to be called the father of the presidency. Wilson fought hard for a unitary rather than a plural executive. (One proposal would have had an executive committee of three people, one from each geographic region.) Wilson also argued against creating a council of revision to be entrusted with power to veto legislation. He preferred giving the president an absolute veto, a battle he lost when the decision was for a veto that the legislature could override. In the same way, after a losing effort to establish direct popular election of the president, Wilson proposed a selection procedure much like the one eventually adopted, the electoral college, which introduced the possibility of popular participation. Wilson was able to exact several of these concessions while serving on the Committee of Detail, which also pushed for a constitutional grant of powers rather than relying on the legislature to establish responsibilities for the executive.[37]

In addition to Wilson, several other delegates influenced the design of the presidency. Gouverneur Morris, also from Pennsylvania, used his position on two working committees—Style and Unfinished Business—to strengthen the executive. The Style Committee provided the president with the basis for broadly construed discretionary powers with the ambiguous wording that begins Article II: "The executive Power shall be vested in a President of the United States of America." The Unfinished Business Committee proposed selection through an electoral college, an explicit rejection of selection by the legislature, a position that had earlier been adopted by votes of the convention on several occasions.[38] Alexander Hamilton of New York advocated the need for executive authority, although he did so by endorsing the British model; that is, he advocated an elected American king. Washington, the leading candidate for president, calmed delegates' concerns about creating an office with powers that might be abused, providing behind-the-scenes rather than vocal support. Finally, Madison was persuaded to accept an executive stronger than he had originally envisioned in his draft plan.[39]

Tyranny Versus Effectiveness

These five delegates and their fifty colleagues brought two conflicting attitudes to the task of designing an executive office: a healthy skepticism for executive power and a new appreciation of its necessity. Most commentators stress the distrust of executive authority derived from the prerevolutionary period when colonial governors implemented edicts from London that colonists regarded as violations of their fundamental rights. After many decades of relative neglect by the mother country, the colonists were outraged at being forced to pay new taxes designed to support British troops sent to America for the French and Indian Wars. The resulting rebellion was justified in the Declaration of Independence as a fitting response to the arbitrary actions of King George III. (Although Parliament was the real source of the pressure, the king was an easier target.) This bout with tyranny produced a healthy distrust of executives that was mirrored in the state governments created during the Revolutionary War and under the Articles of Confederation. State constitutions during this period typically had weak governors chosen by the legislature for a single brief term, usually one year. Governors often shared powers with a council.

The Articles of Confederation, a compact among the thirteen colonies adopted in 1781, had provided for a national legislative body with a single house in which each state had an equal vote. There was no provision at all for independent executive and judicial branches. In time, however, a reaction set in against this type of legislative democracy. Attempts to administer laws through ad hoc committees, councils, or conventions proved unsuccessful; and it was ultimately necessary for Congress to create permanent departments of diplomacy, war, and finance and to appoint eminent men, such as Robert Livingston, John Jay, and Robert Morris, to head their activities.[40] Calling the constitutional convention signaled a desire for more effective central government, and there was growing awareness of how executives could contribute to improved efficiency. New York's constitution, a striking exception to general practice, provided for a governor chosen by direct election to a three-year term with unlimited reeligibility. Massachusetts voters adopted a constitution that included a popularly elected governor (who could be reelected) with substantial powers, including that of vetoing legislative acts.

The ambivalence over executive power exhibited by the convention has become a permanent feature of American political culture. Like the delegates in 1787, Americans have had to confront the tradeoff between tyranny and effectiveness, the one to be feared and the other to be prized. The antifederalists, who opposed ratification of the Constitution, frequently pointed to the risks inherent in a national executive, a post some considered even more threatening than its British counterpart. George Mason argued, "We are not indeed constituting a British monarchy, but a more dangerous monarchy, an elective one." [41] But others saw the newly created presidency as essential to effective government, the source of energy, dispatch, and responsibility in the conduct of domestic and foreign affairs. These differing views are found in the three conceptions of the office already reviewed.

The presidency created by the convention most closely resembles the strong executive model *(see Table 1-1)*. The president is chosen by the electoral college, which will be discussed in Chapter 2. The process is national in scope, providing for a unique perspective on problems. Originally, no limit was placed on a president's eligibility to run for another term, and the removal process was made difficult: presidents may be removed only for specific causes (treason, bribery, high crimes, and misdemeanors), and then only by an impeachment charge brought by the House of Representatives and conviction by vote of two-thirds of the members of the Senate. Specific powers are granted by the Constitution, and, thanks to the efforts of Gouverneur Morris, the president is given a basis for claiming broad, undefined authority.

At the same time, the president does not enjoy all the prerogatives of the strong executive model. The veto power is not absolute: a veto can be overridden by a two-thirds vote in each of the two houses of Congress. Moreover, the appointment power is subject to the advice and consent of the Senate, as is the authority to negotiate treaties. Thus, although the Founders did not create a council that shares all the chief executive's powers, they did grant the upper chamber a check on specified presidential actions.

Several amendments to the Constitution changed aspects of the original design: the Twelfth provided an important clarification in the selection of the president and vice president; the Twentieth moved the beginning of their term to January from March; and the Twenty-second limited the tenure of the chief executive to no more than two terms— probably the most significant change from the original design.[42] The Twenty-fifth Amendment dealt with one of the problems left unresolved by the convention, presidential disability and succession. Nevertheless, the essential constitutional framework of the presidential office remains just as it was created two centuries ago.

But what did the Founders intend for the president to do? George Mason was not the only observer struck by the near-monarchical nature of the office designed in Philadelphia. Henry Jones Ford, reflecting on the office's evolution on the eve of the twentieth century, described it in similar terms. "The truth is that in the presidential office, as it has been constituted since Jackson's time, American democracy has revived the oldest political institution of the race, the elective kingship."[43] What Ford stressed was the president's special relationship with the people, which carries with it the ability to mobilize public support behind their government. Only the barest outlines of this powerful position are visible in the enumerated powers of the chief executive.

Constitutional Roles: Complexity and Ambiguity

A time-honored way for political scientists to think about the president's powers and responsibilities is to concentrate on the multiple roles discernible in the constitutional design.[44] Most frequently, observers

Table 1-1   Models of Executive Considered by the Constitutional Convention

Elements of executive	Weak-executive model	Strong-executive model	Decision by convention
Relation to Congress	To put into effect will of Congress	Powers independent of Congress	Powers independent of Congress but with checks and balances
Number of executive	Plural or single individual checked by council	Single individual with no council or only advisory one	Single individual with Senate advisory on some matters
Method of choosing	By Congress	By means other than congressional selection	Electoral college
Tenure	Limited term; not immediately renewable	No limitation	Unlimited
Method of removal	By Congress during term of office	Only for definite, enumerated reasons after impeachment and conviction by judicial body or Congress	For treason, bribery, high crimes and misdemeanors, by impeachment by majority of House and conviction by two-thirds of Senate
Scope and source of powers	Limited powers delegated by Congress	Broad powers from Constitution, not subject to congressional interference	Broad powers delegated by Constitution
Appointment and foreign policy and war-making powers	None—province of Congress	Would appoint judicial and diplomatic officials and participate in foreign policy and war-making powers, including making of treaties	Appoints executive and judicial officials with consent of Senate; shares foreign policy and war-making powers with Congress; Senate must approve treaties negotiated by president
Veto	None	Veto over legislation passed by Congress, exercised alone or with judiciary	Qualified veto, may be overridden by two-thirds vote of House and Senate

Source: Joseph E. Kallenbach, *The American Chief Executive: The Presidency and the Governorship* (New York: Harper & Row, 1966), chap. 2.

identify five roles found in Article II, Sections 2 and 3, that comprise the central elements of a presidential job description *(see Appendix C)*.

Commander in Chief. Article II, Section 2, set forth the first enumerated executive power, but did it merely confer a title on the president or imply wide-ranging powers in times of emergency? From this germ of constitutional power has grown the enormous control that modern presidents exercise over a permanent military establishment and its deployment. The Constitution stipulates that the legislative and executive branches share the war power, but the pressure of events and the presidency's institutional advantages in taking decisive action have led Congress to give greater discretion to the executive. Nor was this delegation of power completely unexpected. Recognizing the need to repel attacks when Congress was not in session, the convention altered language describing the role of Congress in armed hostilities from "make" war to "declare" war, thereby expanding the president's realm of discretionary action. Over time, presidents have invoked the commander-in-chief clause to justify military expenditures without congressional authorization, emergency powers to suppress rebellion, the internment of American citizens of Japanese descent during World War II, and the seizure of domestic steel mills during the undeclared armed conflict in Korea.[45] Moreover, presidents have initiated the use of force far more frequently than they have awaited congressional authorization.

Chief Administrator. This role for the president is more implicit than explicit as set forth in the Constitution. It rests on the executive power clause as well as passages dealing with the right to require opinions from the heads of government departments and the power to make personnel appointments subject to whatever approval Congress may require. As the national government has grown, so too has the significance of these powers, but Congress has jealously guarded its own appointment and oversight powers, thereby denying the president anything approximating a monopoly of administrative power.

Chief Diplomat. When combined with the president's expanded war power, constitutional primacy in the conduct of foreign affairs establishes the office's claim to being the government's principal agent in the world if not its "sole organ." Presidents are not only authorized to make treaties "by and with the Advice and Consent of the Senate," but also they are empowered to nominate ambassadors, subject to Senate approval, and to receive diplomatic emissaries from abroad. Presidents have varied in how closely they collaborated with the Senate in making treaties, most waiting until after negotiations have been concluded before allowing any Senate participation. More significant, the conduct of foreign affairs has come to rely on executive agreements between heads of state in place of treaties. These agreements are not subject to Senate approval.[46]

Chief Legislator. A nascent constitutional role that stressed negative (the veto) rather than positive leadership, this feature of the job did not fully develop until the twentieth century. Today, the president's power to provide leadership for Congress rests primarily on the ability to shape the legislative agenda. Now considered a task for all presidents to fulfill, it stems from language in Article II, Section 3, that obliges the president to give "the Congress Information of the State of the Union," and to recommend such other measures for its consideration as deemed "necessary and expedient." Presidents now routinely develop extensive legislative agendas and present them to Congress and the nation at the beginning of each year. Moreover, the development of an activist national government has led presidents, their aides, and cabinet secretaries to submit detailed proposals for legislative consideration rather than await congressional reaction to their ideas. During an era of divided government—when one party controls the presidency and the other party controls Congress—the veto power has once again come to the fore. Surprisingly, a Republican Congress approved a proposal to give President Bill Clinton, a Democrat, a line-item veto; it then hesitated to make it operational, however, until key elements of the party's programmatic reforms were enacted. *(See Chapter 5.)*

Chief Magistrate. Perhaps the least clearly recognized area of presidential activity, but one that was important to the Founders' conception of executive power, was the general charge that "he shall take Care that the Laws be faithfully executed." Eighteenth-century conceptions of executive power did not draw sharp distinctions with judicial power: each type of official interpreted and applied the laws in the process of enforcing them. In addition, relations between these two branches of the new government were less distant during the 1790s than is the case today.[47] Presidents, in short, play a complementary role to that of the courts in the enforcement of federal laws; the executive branch helps by apprehending criminals and exercising responsibility for prosecution.

Despite being enumerated in the Constitution, what is most striking about these presidential responsibilities is their ambiguity. As a consequence, their effect on behavior—*what* presidents should do and *how* presidents should behave—is limited. Multiplicity provides presidents with the opportunity to select among a range of activities, and ambiguity gives them maximum flexibility in deciding how to go about the job. The constitutional job description is permissive rather than confining, providing presidents with great freedom in deciding how to invest energy but leaving them open to criticism for failing to fulfill tasks of lesser interest.

Functional Roles and Inherent Powers

Political scientists have described a set of functional roles that may be thought of as bundles of activities associated with a formal position. Fred Greenstein has argued that one distinguishing feature of the American executive is the combination of two functional roles that are separated in many other political systems. Presidents serve as both head of state and prime minister, positions that are separate and occupied by different people in most other Western political systems. Obvious examples are the British system with its monarch and prime minister and the German system with an elected president and chancellor. Typically, heads of state perform ceremonial tasks in their capacity of symbolizing the entire nation. Prime ministers are charged with partisan political leadership—proposing agendas, formulating policies, addressing potentially divisive national issues.[48] Greenstein suggests that several consequences flow from this "condensation" of roles, the most significant of which is "role strain." "As head of state the president needs to be a national unifier, much like a constitutional monarch; yet as politician he must also be responsive to the intrinsically divisive demands made of prime ministers in other democracies. This conjunction can enhance the president's influence by reinforcing policy appeals with patriotic emotions, but it can also have the reverse effect of holding presidents to unrealistically idealized standards of comportment and performance."[49]

Finally, the convention accepted John Locke's idea that executive power provided for a largely undefined grant of *inherent* power derived from the nature of government itself. As Locke wrote, "prerogative" authorized executives "to act according to discretion for the public good, without prescription of the law and sometimes even against it."[50] Since Washington's first term in office, generations of American political elites have struggled over the claims made by presidents and their supporters based on the indefinite grant of executive power found in the opening phrases of Article II. Although such claims may be based on very different justifications, their effects are the same if resolved in the president's favor—expansion of the office, which has happened steadily throughout our history.[51]

Expansion of the Presidency

A number of influences have reshaped the American presidency since its constitutional beginnings, perhaps none more than the occupants of the office. Some expanded their powers according to coherent conceptions of the office, and others responded to the needs of the moment. Not surprisingly, several of these latter presidencies coincided with crises facing the nation arising from either domestic or foreign sources. Rather than being inhibited by the ambiguities of power, these presidents shaped the office in which they served by adopting broad interpretations of their responsibilities. In addition, changes in the presidency have been established by Congress through statute, as a result of presidential actions that later became customary practices, and through institutional development.

Expansion by Individual Presidents

In a number of cases, presidents have significantly expanded the office and its powers, but there is no guarantee that every incumbent will have such an enduring effect. The constitutional scholar Edward S. Corwin wrote in 1957, "Taken by and large, the history of the presidency is a history of aggrandizement, but the story is a highly discontinuous one." [52] At the time of his landmark study, Corwin estimated that one of every three presidents "has contributed to the development of [the presidency's] powers; under other incumbents things have either stood still or gone backward." [53]

Many of the expansions have occurred when presidents claimed "the silences of the Constitution"; that is, they sought to exploit the ambiguity or absence of constitutional clarification in their own favor.[54] It is customary for political histories of the presidency to examine precedents established by a small group of notable officeholders who provided their successors with an institutional legacy that left the office more powerful than before. As Corwin explained, "Precedents established by a forceful or politically successful personality in the office are available to less gifted successors, and permanently so because of the difficulty with which the Constitution is amended." [55] Which presidents qualify for such select company? Corwin's classic analysis focused on seven: Washington, Jefferson, Jackson, Lincoln, Wilson, and the two Roosevelts.[56] Other scholars and historians have selected the same group.[57]

George Washington. Because he was the first person to occupy the presidency, Washington was conscious that his actions could establish precedents for his successors. Soon after his inauguration he expressed the opinion that "many things which appear of little importance in themselves ... may have great and durable consequences from their having been established at the commencement of a new general government." [58] Consequently, Washington often turned to his group of department heads for advice on political matters. In doing so, he went beyond the constitutional provision to gather their written opinions on subjects relating to the duties of their offices and solicited their oral judgments as a group on any matter he put before them. Washington established the precedent that department heads should support the president's policies; he forced Secretary of State Edmund Randolph to resign because of his failure to back the administration's foreign policy. With the president's blessing, Secretary of the Treasury Hamilton created and steered through Congress a broad economic program, setting the stage for later liaison between the executive and legislative branches.

In foreign policy Washington quickly established the prerogatives of the president by receiving an emissary from the new French government, making it clear that presidents have the right to receive ambassadors and to grant diplomatic recognition to foreign countries. When he sought the Senate's advice on treaty negotiations with certain Indian tribes, and the Senate delayed by referring the matter to committee, Washington stalked out of the chamber in anger, vowing never again to bring such a matter to the Senate. Since then, no president has sought that body's counsel on the negotiation of a treaty, despite the constitutional instruction that presidents "shall make such treaties with its advice." [59] When the House of Representatives demanded that he present papers pertaining to the negotiation of the Jay Treaty, Washington refused to do so on the grounds that the Constitution granted the lower chamber of Congress no authority in such matters.

Thomas Jefferson. Jefferson epitomized the president who could stretch the powers of the office when the occasion demanded it. When Napoleon unexpectedly offered French lands (the Louisiana Purchase) at a favorable price, Jefferson reconsidered his narrow interpretation of the national government's powers and chose direct action, becoming the first of many presidents who decided to respond to political rather than legal considerations. Jefferson also was the first president to govern through personal leadership of a political party. Using members of the Democratic-Republican Party in Congress as his medium, he dominated the political affairs of the legislature. His control extended to decisions of the party caucus (which, unlike today's counterpart, exercised significant powers over legislation) and to the appointment and removal of standing committee members, as well as party officials in Congress. So strong was his leadership that he pushed the drastic Embargo Act of 1807 through both houses in one day. But his control was not restricted to crises. It is a testament to Jefferson's domination that he did not veto a single piece of legislation: no law he seriously opposed was reported out of the Congress during his eight years in office.

Andrew Jackson. In contrast to Jefferson, Jackson became a strong president by asserting his independence of the legislative branch as well as virtually all other centers of government authority. His administration was characterized by conflicts with Congress over issues large and small, including appointments to diplomatic and judicial posts and creation of a national bank, which was supported by the legislature but opposed and undermined by Jackson. The full range of Jackson's disputes with Congress is reflected in his use of the veto; with twelve, he was the first president to use this power to any significant degree. Jackson asserted that the president's right to judge the constitutionality of legislation was no less than that of the Supreme Court, and on one occasion he dared Chief Justice John Marshall to enforce a ruling that went against the president's view. He acted decisively to protect the rights of the national government against the states when South Carolina threatened to secede from the Union. Jackson declared the action treasonous and pushed a bill through Congress giving him the power to use force to prevent it.

Jackson succeeded in these defiant actions because he was the first president whose authority rested on a popular constituency. Chosen not by a congressional caucus but by a national convention reflecting grassroots party support *(see Chapter 2)*, Jackson considered himself the "tribune of the people." When he had disagreements with members of Congress, he went over their heads and appealed to the population for support of his policies; to keep control of his administration, he instituted the spoils system (so named for the idea that "to the victor belong the spoils") to reward his political friends and punish his enemies. Jackson transformed the presidency from an elitist to a popular office.

Abraham Lincoln. The nineteenth-century presidency reached the zenith of its powers during the Civil War administration of Abraham Lincoln. He stretched the executive's emergency powers further than ever before during the eleven weeks from the outbreak of hostilities at Fort Sumter, South Carolina, on April 12, 1861, until he called Congress into special session July 4. This period has been described as a time of "quasipresidential dictatorship." [60] Lincoln unilaterally authorized a series of drastic actions: he called up the militia and volunteers, blockaded Southern ports, expanded the army and navy beyond the limits set by statute, pledged the credit of the United States without congressional authority to do so, closed the mails to "treasonous" correspondence, arrested persons suspected of disloyalty, and suspended the writ of habeas corpus in areas around the nation's capital. Admitting that most of these matters lay within the jurisdiction of Congress rather than the president, Lincoln asserted that they were done because of popular demand and public necessity, and with the trust "that Congress would readily ratify them." But he deliberately chose not to call the national legislature into special session until he was ready to do so, and then he presented it with *faits accomplis.*

Although Lincoln's presidency was most dramatic in those early days of hostilities, he continued to exercise firm control over the war during the entire time he was in the White House. He controlled the mails and newspapers, confiscated property of people suspected of impeding the conduct of the war, and even tried civilians in military courts in areas where the regular courts were operating. To justify such actions, he appealed to military necessity, asserting that the commander-in-chief clause and the take-care (that the laws be faithfully executed) clause combined to create a "war power" for the president that was virtually unlimited. Lincoln's success in defending that position is demonstrated by the fact that neither Congress nor the courts placed any significant limits on his actions.

Theodore Roosevelt. In contrast to the domestic crisis that shaped Lincoln's presidency, Roosevelt's took its impetus from the emergence of the United States as a world power at the beginning of the twentieth century. Concerned over the rise of Japan as a threat to American interests in the Pacific, Roosevelt sought and obtained a major role in negotiating the Portsmouth Treaty, which terminated the Russo-Japanese War of 1905. Closer to home he intervened in the affairs of neighbors to the south when he considered it vital to the national interests of the United States, sending troops to the Dominican Republic and Cuba. Even more blatant was Roosevelt's role in fomenting the rebellion of Panama against Colombia so that the United States could acquire rights to build a canal. An avowed nationalist with the desire to expand U.S. influence in international affairs, Roosevelt ordered the navy to sail around the world as a demonstration of American military might. When Congress balked at the expense, he countered that there were sufficient funds to get the navy halfway there; if the lawmakers wanted the fleet back home, they would have to provide the money for the return trip.

Roosevelt also responded vigorously to the rapid industrialization of American life. He had charges pressed against corporations that violated antitrust laws, and he pushed legislation through Congress that gave the Interstate Commerce Commission power to reduce railroad rates. When coal mine operators in Colorado refused to agree to arbitration of a dispute with their workers, Roosevelt threatened to have troops seize the mines and administer them as a receiver for the government. He was the first American chief executive to intervene in a labor dispute who did *not* take management's side. Roosevelt also championed major reclamation and conservation projects, as well as meat inspection and pure food and drug laws.

Perhaps most important, Roosevelt did much to popularize the presidency after three decades of lackluster leaders. (Of the eight men who served from Lincoln through William McKinley, only Grover Cleveland is considered at all significant.) A dynamic personality, an attractive family, and love of the public spotlight enabled Roosevelt "to put the presidency on the front page of every newspaper in America." [61] Considering himself (as did Jackson) the "tribune of the people" and seeing the office as a "bully pulpit" from which the incumbent should set the tone of American life, Roosevelt was the first president to provide meeting rooms for the members of the press and to hold informal news conferences to link the presidency with the people.

Roosevelt was the first president to rely on broad discretionary authority in peacetime as well as in crisis.[62] His style of leadership depended upon extensive use of popular rhetoric, a distinctive reinterpretation of statesmanship that ushered in the era of the "rhetorical presidency." [63] Roosevelt explained after leaving office that his concept of the president as "steward of the people" held that "it was not only his right but his duty to do anything that the needs of the nation demanded unless such action was forbidden by the Constitution or by the laws." He continued, "Under this interpretation of executive power I did and caused to be done many things not previously done by the president and the heads of the departments. I did not usurp power, but I did greatly broaden the use of executive power." [64]

Woodrow Wilson. While Theodore Roosevelt laid the groundwork for use of popular appeals, Wilson linked inspirational rhetoric to a broad program of action in an effort to address domestic and foreign affairs in much the same way as a British prime minister. Jeffrey Tulis has argued that this effort rested on a systematic, ambitious reinterpretation of the president's role in the constitutional order.[65] A skilled public speaker, Wilson was the first president since John Adams to go before Congress in person to give his State of the Union message, a practice we now take for granted.[66] Like Jefferson, he was a powerful party chief who worked through congressional leaders and the Democratic caucus to influence legislation. Nor did he hesitate to take his case to the people, casting himself as the interpreter as well as the representative of their interests.

During his first term in office Wilson pushed through a vast program of economic reform that lowered tariffs, raised taxes on the wealthy, created a central banking system, regulated unfair trade practices, provided low-interest loans to farmers, and established an eight-hour day for railroad employees. When the United States became involved in World War I during his second term, rather than prosecute it through unilateral executive action, Wilson went to Congress and obtained authority to control the economic as well as the military aspects of the war. This grant gave him the power to allocate food and fuel, to license trade with the enemy, to censor the mail, to regulate the foreign language press of the country, and to operate railroads, water transportation systems, and telegraph and telephone facilities. At the end of the war he made a triumphant trip to Europe, where he assumed the leading role in the writing of the Versailles peace treaty.

Wilson also provided a lesson in how *not* to work with Congress: his adamant refusal to accept any reservations proposed by the Senate for the League of Nations Covenant of the Treaty of Versailles ensured that the United States would not participate. Wilson's archenemy, Sen.

Henry Cabot Lodge, R-Mass., calculated that the president's intransigence and personal hatred of him would be so intense that he would reject all compromises proposed to the treaty. Lodge was right: Wilson, spurning the advice of his wife and of close friends such as Col. Edward House, avowed it "better a thousand times to go down fighting than to dip your colors to dishonorable compromise." A trip to win popular support for the league ended in failure and a personal breakdown; as a result, the country whose leader proposed the League of Nations ended up not belonging to the organization at all.

Franklin D. Roosevelt. Confronted by enormous domestic and international crises, Franklin Roosevelt began a program of action and innovation unmatched by any chief executive in our history. In most respects, his service is now used as a yardstick against which the performance of his successors is measured.[67] When he came into office in March 1933, business failures were legion, 12 million people were unemployed, banks all over the country were closed or doing business under restrictions, and Americans had lost confidence in their leaders as well as in themselves. Counseling the nation in his inaugural address—the first of four—that "the only thing we have to fear is fear itself," the new chief executive swung into action: a four-day bank holiday was declared, and an emergency banking bill was prepared within a day's time. During Roosevelt's first hundred days in office, the nation witnessed a social and economic revolution in the form of his New Deal. Congress adopted a series of far-reaching government programs insuring bank deposits; providing crop payments for farmers; establishing codes of fair competition for industry; granting labor the right to organize; providing relief and jobs for the unemployed; and creating the Tennessee Valley Authority, a government corporation, to develop that region. With these measures and others such as Social Security, public housing, unemployment compensation, and the like, Roosevelt established the concept of the "positive state" in America—a government that had the obligation to take the lead in providing for the welfare of all the people.

Internationally, Roosevelt extended diplomatic recognition to the Soviet Union, embarked on the Good Neighbor policy toward South America, and pushed through the Reciprocal Trade Program, which lowered tariffs with other nations. In his second term, FDR began the slow and difficult task of preparing the nation for its eventual entry into World War II: he funneled aid to the Allies; traded fifty "over-age" destroyers to Britain for naval and air bases in the British West Indies, Argentia (Newfoundland), and Bermuda; and obtained the passage of the nation's first peacetime draft. After Pearl Harbor, in his own words, "Dr. New Deal" became "Dr. Win-the-War." He took over the economic control of the war effort granted him by Congress and established the victorious strategy of concentrating on defeating Germany before Japan. While hostilities were still going on, he took the lead in setting up the United Nations. Unfortunately, he died before he could see the organization established in 1945.

Roosevelt was an innovator whose actions reshaped the presidential office. He was not only an effective legislative leader but also a skilled administrator responsible for a thorough reorganization of the executive branch, including the creation of the Executive Office of the President (see Chapter 6). Even more important, FDR was probably the most effective molder of public opinion the nation has ever known. He pioneered the use of "fireside chats" over radio to explain his actions to the people. In addition, he raised the presidential press conference to new heights as a tool of public persuasion. As a man who could take idealistic goals, reduce them to manageable and practical programs, and then sell them to Congress and the American people, Roosevelt has no peer.

Expansion Through Statute

Congress is another major source of change in the presidency. Legislators have mandated activities that earlier presidents exercised on a discretionary basis or have formally delegated responsibility for activities that traditionally resided with Congress. One of the contemporary presidency's major responsibilities—serving as the nation's economic manager—is nowhere suggested in the Constitution.[68] Most observers trace this added presidential duty to passage of the Employment Act of 1946. As James Sundquist explains, the act "compels the president to maintain a continuous surveillance of the nation's economy, to report on the state of its health at least annually, and if there are signs of pathology—inflation, recession, stagnation—to recommend corrective action."[69] To assist with this task, the president was given a staff of professional economists, the Council of Economic Advisers, to prepare the Economic Report, one of the three formal communications submitted annually by the president to Congress (the State of the Union and Budget messages are the other two).

This statutory expansion of presidential responsibilities formalized activities that had gravitated to the White House under FDR, with the significant difference that government intervention in the economy was to precede (and prevent) depressions rather than come after the fact. The principle of presidential leadership, however, had been established with Roosevelt's activism of 1933, which stood in such sharp contrast to the inaction of his predecessor, Herbert Hoover. Although it gave the president new tasks to fulfill, Congress did not surrender its traditional right to alter presidential proposals, thereby ensuring that tax rates and spending proposals would remain a mainstay of partisan politics as well as legislative-executive relations. (The politics of economic policy making are examined in detail in Chapter 9.)

Congress has taken comparable action in other areas as well. During the same period, following World War II, the president was charged with the task of coordinating national security policy—foreign policy, intelligence collection and evaluation, and defense policy—through the mechanism of the National Security Council (NSC). Harry Truman resisted the newly created NSC as an intrusion on his powers and was slow to use it. In fact, no president can be *required* to use such a structure, but the more conflictive setting of the cold war saw one president after another establish administrative machinery designed to achieve the same goal, coordination of American foreign policy *(see Chapter 10)*. Thus, we find that Congress may encourage presidents to provide leadership in areas that are either wholly absent from the original constitutional design, or encourage executives to devise new ways to exercise their traditional responsibilities.

Expansion Through Custom and Practice

Across a wide range of presidential activities, "action based on usage may acquire legitimacy." [70] Nowhere in the Constitution did it say that presidents would serve as leaders of their party, but that task has been associated with the office since Thomas Jefferson first established his dominance of the Democratic-Republicans' congressional caucus. Enormous variation may be found in how presidents pursue such activities and in how successful they are. At times, they have been virtually abandoned by their partisan allies (Rutherford B. Hayes) and at other times seemed to derive greater influence by appearing to serve "above" party (Eisenhower). If the political parties continue to weaken or have difficulty reasserting themselves as structures vital to democracy, this informal part of the president's job description might disappear.

A second example of precedent and custom can be found in Theodore Roosevelt's attempt to mediate a labor-management dispute.

Earlier presidents had intervened on the side of company owners, but Roosevelt put his prestige on the line when he sought to resolve the anthracite coal strike of 1902, a struggle that had paralyzed a vital industry. Other presidents followed suit: Wilson intervened in eight major disputes, Harding in two, FDR in eleven, and Truman in three.[71] The response of one president to emergency conditions had become an accepted precedent for his successors, if they wished to pursue it.

Institutional Sources of Change

Finally, it needs to be recognized that the modern presidency is no longer a one-person job, a reality that may have significant consequences for the office's evolution. Although designed to be unitary rather than plural, the modern presidency has become a working collectivity in order to dispatch the many responsibilities placed at the president's door. This new, complex institution employs nearly 1,600 full-time assistants in the White House and in the specialized units of the Executive Office of the President, an administrative structure created in 1939 to accommodate Franklin Roosevelt's many aides. Bradley Patterson points out that within the White House one can identify twenty policy and political staff specializations, supplemented by another seven professional staff units. Another six to eight staff units operate outside the White House proper as part of the Executive Office of the President.[72]

Given this bureaucratic structure, it is reasonable to expect the presidency to be susceptible to some of the same developmental dynamics as other organizations, including tendencies toward highly refined divisions of labor and staff specialization. One notable change in the modern presidency is the emergence of a highly professional team of public relations experts charged with portraying presidents in the most favorable light and projecting their influence on public life.[73] Other changes in the presidency's environment, such as inflated public expectations and expanded media coverage, help account for much of this development, but so does a staff system designed to help presidents reach new parts of the public in ever more effective ways. By the late 1970s, more than 30 percent of the White House staff was specifically assigned to deal with media relations or policy, but a more realistic estimate would find somewhere between 60 percent and 85 percent of the president's aides engaged in promotional operations.[74] Little has changed in the intervening years. With such a mammoth effort afoot, it is hardly surprising to find commentators expressing concern about the concentration on image and style rather than reality and substance.

Students of the presidency commonly divide the institution's development into two major periods: traditional and modern. In this view, the presidency of Franklin Roosevelt was the turning point. FDR's long tenure in the office, combined with his dramatically activist style, placed a distinctive imprint on the position with which his successors have had to contend. Fred Greenstein argues that the modern presidency, as shaped by FDR, is distinguished by four features: (1) the president is expected to develop a legislative program and to persuade Congress to enact it; (2) presidents regularly engage in direct policy making through actions not requiring congressional approval; (3) the presidential office has become an extensive bureaucracy designed to enable presidents to undertake points 1 and 2; and (4) presidents have come to symbolize the nation and to personify its government to such an extent that the public holds them primarily responsible for its condition and closely monitors their performance through intensive coverage carried in the media.[75]

A number of scholars recently have sought to resuscitate our appreciation of presidents from the traditional period and to erase the impression that they were highly forgettable.[76] Their efforts have reawakened interest in the historic dimensions of the office and its development, a sensitivity reflected throughout this book. But like most other political scientists, we will concentrate our discussion on the modern period while recognizing that important precedents were established much earlier.

Understanding the presidency's institutional development provides an important perspective on roles played by the office, but one also needs to address a less concrete question: What does the presidency *mean* to Americans? The final section of this chapter focuses on the office's emotional and psychological significance.

Presidential Culture

The presidency has always been important in American civic life, but it may have assumed even greater proportions in the modern era, assisted by new technologies and resting on new conceptions of the office. The office acquired mythic dimensions when it was filled by the country's first true hero. George Washington, argues Seymour Martin Lipset, supplied the virtues of a charismatic leader who serves as "symbol of the new nation, its hero who embodies in his person its values and aspirations. But more than merely symbolizing the new nation, he legitimizes the state, the new secular government, by endowing it with his 'gift of grace,' " the near magical qualities such leaders supposedly possess.[77] A cult of personality grew up around Washington so that well into the nineteenth century citizens displayed his likeness in their homes, named their children after him, and paid him endless tributes.

In the process of contributing stability and identity to the new nation, Washington also endowed the presidential office with a special meaning that has become part of our collective heritage. Bruce Buchanan refers to this as *presidential culture,* "widely held meanings of the presidency, derived from selected episodes in the history of the institution and transmitted from one generation to the next by political socialization." [78] Buchanan explains that families, teachers, and the media sustain this view of the presidency as an office with the ability to deliver the nation from danger as a result of its occupants' greatness. Somehow, it is widely believed, the institution "has the potential to make extraordinary events happen" and the incumbent "should be able to realize that potential." [79] Occupants of the position, then, are expected to live up to these levels of performance and are roundly criticized when they fall short.

Why have such unrealistic expectations taken hold? One reason is that we have glorified the memories of past presidents. The "great" presidents, particularly those who took decisive action and bold initiatives, and even some of the "not so great" are treated as folk heroes and enshrined in a national mythology—figures whose births we celebrate, whose virtues we are urged to emulate, whose achievements we memorialize, and whose sex lives continue to interest us long after their deaths. Schoolchildren throughout America are regaled with stories of Washington and Lincoln every February while looking at bulletin boards featuring their silhouettes. Every summer, thousands of vacationers make the pilgrimage to visit shrines located along the Potomac in Washington, D.C., or scattered throughout the nation in presidential libraries and museums. But historical and popular glorification do not constitute the full story.

A number of political scientists have pointed to the importance of the presidency in meeting the emotional and psychological needs of the populace. In particular, it is argued that citizens have expressive needs for confidence, security, reassurance, and pride in citizenship.[80] In the view of Murray Edelman, citizens suffer from a "general sense of anxiety about the comprehensive function played in human affairs by chance, ignorance, and inability to comprehend, plan, and take responsibility for remote and complicated contingencies." The natural response is to seek emotional comfort through attachment to reassuring symbols, "and what symbol can be more reassuring than the incumbent of a high position who knows what to do and is willing to act, especially when others are bewildered and alone?" [81] We know that American children develop a highly idealized image of presidents that emphasizes both their power and benevolence, a source of reassurance that may be transferred from childhood to adulthood.

Fred Greenstein suggests additional psychological needs that are met through the presidency. Citizens seeking to sort through the complexity of political life turn to presidents for cognitive assistance. Presidents personify the government and make it possible to become engaged by what would otherwise be an impersonal abstraction. By following the president's activities, citizens may also experience a sort of vicarious participation in public affairs, giving them a sense of power and control that ordinarily would be unavailable. As a symbol of stability, predictability, and national unity, the president soothes fears and enables us to proceed with our daily lives.[82]

Symbols, in fact, are central to the character of the presidential office, which has become particularly "potent as a symbol of the public welfare, built-in benevolence, and competence to lead." [83] Barbara Hinckley points out that "symbols evoke ideas the society wants to believe are true . . . [they] can substitute for something that does not exist otherwise." [84] In fact, Hinckley argues, because the Constitution failed to clarify the presidency's nature and responsibilities, symbols have become enormously significant: "The office is undefined; thus presidents become what people want them to be." [85] And the people want them to be many things. The list of desirable personal attributes is impressive, as Ray Price, an aide to Richard Nixon during the 1968 campaign, pointed out in a memo to the staff:

People identify with a President in a way they do with no other public figure. Potential presidents are measured against an ideal that's a combination of leading man, God, father, hero, pope, king, with maybe just a touch of the avenging Furies thrown in. They want him to be larger than life, a living legend, and yet quintessentially human; someone to be held up to their children as a model; someone to be cherished by themselves as a revered member of the family, in somewhat the same way in which peasant families pray to the icon in the corner. Reverence goes where power is.[86]

The problem for Nixon as a candidate was how to project an image that would match these public expectations.

Hinckley's research reveals that incumbents as well as candidates seek to project desirable images and that the terms used by presidents to depict themselves and their office have been remarkably consistent. Over a forty-year period, presidents from Truman to Reagan have portrayed themselves in speeches as "alone in the government, equivalent to the nation, religious and cultural leaders who shun politics and elections."[87] In other words, the self-image presidents project to the nation reinforces the mystique and majesty that are integral features of the modern presidency and confirms the confidence that citizens have placed in the leader on whom they depend to contend with distant sources of pain and uncertainty. The underlying message in these accounts is clear: *presidents tell the public what it wants to hear.*

Many unsettling implications flow from this line of analysis. What if presidents compensate for their failure to achieve real success in managing the economy or in conducting foreign policy by projecting the *appearance* of policy success? Would the press or the public be capable of seeing through such deception? Probably not, suggests Theodore Lowi. Instead, modern presidents must function in the face of a dangerous imbalance: "the expectations of the masses have grown faster than the capacity of presidential government to meet them."[88] Modern presidents, argues Lowi, resort to illusions to cover failures and seek quick fixes for their flagging public support in foreign adventures. Such pathological behavior—portrayed by Lowi as rooted in the presidential institution, not in individual presidents' personalities—is ultimately self-defeating because it does nothing more than further inflate expectations and ensure public disappointment.

Part of this dynamic can be traced to advances in the means of communication. Television, argues Bruce Miroff, gives the president an unequaled vehicle "to display his leadership qualities" through presidential spectacles.[89] As Miroff explains, a spectacle is

the utilization of modern media, especially television, to present the president in visible and highly dramatic actions designed to establish a favorable public identity. It is the presentation of the president in actions that minimize the potential for public interruption and treat citizens as passive spectators. Most important, it is the presentation of actions which are meaningful less for what they accomplish, in the sense of substantive outcome, than for what they signify. Actions in a presidential spectacle serve as gestures rather than as means.[90]

Military intervention in Grenada, he suggests, was a prime example of such a spectacle, the effectiveness of which was enhanced by the high level of secrecy maintained about the military operation. Vivid images of Ronald Reagan as a decisive and determined opponent of communist expansion were etched in the minds of Americans while the reality was considerably less impressive. Reagan's favorable image endured even the debacle of the Iran-contra incident (discussed further in Chapter 10), but Miroff makes clear his successors were not so fortunate. The Persian Gulf War provided George Bush with the setting for an enormously powerful spectacle, but domestic problems revealed him to be a drifting, out-of-touch leader. Clinton's image underwent a similar transformation. Clinton entered office with the aura of "populist intimacy," established through news reports of interaction with the people and televised town meetings. This populist image was tarnished as first-year battles with Congress converted the crusading outsider into a bargaining insider, and the new president came to be regarded as just another member of the political elite. Although spectacles derive their power from the emotional and psychological needs of the populace, they cannot be counted upon to replace effective governing. An appreciation of the emotional and psychological roles the president assumes makes us realize that spectacles may meet not only the president's needs but also the public's.

Conclusion

There can be little doubt that today's presidency is a far cry from the office designed by the Constitutional Convention. Responsibilities have grown enormously as have means to fulfill them, although probably not at the same pace. Unlike the office that was launched in 1789, today's presidency is firmly rooted in the national consciousness as the consequence of childhood socialization and a secular mythology whose idealized images are magnified with the passage of time. There is no way to determine whether today's office means more to Americans than it did two centuries ago in terms of the emotional and psychological needs it meets, but certainly it occupies a more central—some would argue excessive—place in the public consciousness.

The presidency is not a static construct, however. As this overview of institutional development demonstrates, how Americans see the office and what they want from it can and will change over time. In this continuing process, features of the past will be carried forward and continue to shape the institution and its occupants, while more immediate forces provide new twists to the definition, sometimes through law, constitutional amendments, and other formal means, but more often through informal means. At the formal level, individual presidents enjoy considerable freedom in determining what they will do and how they will do it, but they also must respond to informal expectations if they hope to be successful.

Even with powers grounded in the Constitution, expanded through practice, and enhanced by powerful public expectations, presidents remain preeminently political beings. Moreover, their political tasks are unusually complex; not only must they perform on the public stage of mass politics, but they also must master the intricacies of elite politics, a game played among skilled insiders. In the following chapters, we first examine "public politics" (Chapters 2, 3, and 4) and then turn to the skills that presidents bring to relations with other public elites (Chapters 5, 6, and 7). These separate dimensions are linked in discussions of major policy areas (Chapters 8, 9, and 10).

NOTES

1. Clinton Rossiter, *The American Presidency*, rev. ed. (New York: Harcourt, Brace, 1960), 15.

2. Ibid., 260–261.

3. Richard E. Neustadt, *Presidential Power: The Politics of Leadership* (New York: Wiley, 1960), 33.

4. Ibid., 46.

5. Ibid., 161.

6. Ibid., 195.

7. James MacGregor Burns, *Presidential Government: The Crucible of Leadership* (Boston: Houghton Mifflin, 1965), 28.

8. Ibid., 113–114.

9. Ibid., 351.

10. Thomas E. Cronin, "The Textbook Presidency" (Paper presented at the annual meeting of the American Political Science Association, Los Angeles, Calif., Sept. 8–12, 1970). Reprinted in *Perspectives on the Presidency: A Collection*, ed. Stanley Bach and George T. Sulzner (Lexington, Mass.: D. C. Heath, 1974), 54–74.

11. George Reedy, *The Twilight of the Presidency* (New York: New American Library, 1970), x.

12. Arthur M. Schlesinger, Jr., *The Imperial Presidency* (Boston: Houghton Mifflin, 1973), ix.

13. Ibid., 254.

14. Walter F. Mondale, *The Accountability of Power: Toward a Responsible Presidency* (New York: David McKay, 1975), 4.

15. William G. Andrews, "The Presidency, Congress, and Constitutional Theory," in *The Presidency in Contemporary Context*, ed. Norman C. Thomas (New York: Dodd, Mead, 1973), 13, 17.

16. Fred I. Greenstein, "Change and Continuity in the Modern Presidency," in *The New American Political System*, ed. Anthony King (Washington, D.C.: American Enterprise Institute, 1978), 65.

17. Ibid., 70–75.

18. Godfrey Hodgson, *All Things to All Men: The False Promise of the American Presidency* (New York: Simon & Schuster, 1980), 225.

19. Ibid., 13.

20. Thomas E. Cronin, "An Imperiled Presidency?" in *The Post–Imperial Presidency,* ed. Vincent Davis (New Brunswick, N.J.: Transaction Books, 1980).

21. Richard P. Nathan, *The Administrative Presidency* (New York: Wiley, 1983).

22. Chester A. Newland, "A Mid-Term Appraisal—The Reagan Presidency, Limited Government and Political Administration," *Public Administration Review* 43 (January/February 1983): 1–21; and Edie N. Goldenberg, "The Permanent Government in an Era of Retrenchment and Redirection," in *The Reagan Presidency and the Governing of America,* ed. Lester M. Salamon and Michael S. Lund (Washington, D.C.: Urban Institute Press, 1984), 381–404.

23. Bert A. Rockman, *The Leadership Question: The Presidency and the American Political System* (New York: Praeger, 1984), 236.

24. Theodore J. Lowi, *The Personal Presidency: Power Invested, Promise Unfulfilled* (Ithaca, N.Y.: Cornell University Press, 1985).

25. Bert A. Rockman, "The Modern Presidency and Theories of Accountability: Old Wine and Old Bottles," *Congress and the Presidency* 13 (Autumn 1986): 135–156.

26. Lester G. Seligman and Cary R. Covington, *The Coalitional Presidency* (Chicago: Dorsey, 1989), 12.

27. Richard Rose, *The Postmodern President: The White House Meets the World,* 2d ed. (Chatham, N.J.: Chatham House, 1991), 28.

28. Arthur M. Schlesinger, Jr., *The Imperial Presidency,* 2d ed. (Boston: Houghton Mifflin, 1989), 441.

29. Ibid., 443.

30. Ibid., 453.

31. Ibid., 457.

32. Ibid., 431, 436.

33. Ibid., 438.

34. Stephen Skowronek, *The Politics Presidents Make: Leadership from John Adams to George Bush* (Cambridge, Mass.: Harvard University Press, 1993), 444.

35. Sidney M. Milkis and Michael Nelson, *The American Presidency: Origins and Development, 1776–1993,* 2d ed. (Washington, D.C.: CQ Press, 1994), 13–14, chap. 2. Also see chap. 1, n. 34, where it is suggested that the Pinckney Plan may actually have provided considerable guidance for designing the presidency.

36. Joseph E. Kallenbach, *The American Chief Executive: The Presidency and the Governorship* (New York: Harper & Row, 1966), chap. 2.

37. Edward S. Corwin, *The President: Office and Powers, 1787–1984,* 5th ed. (New York: New York University Press, 1984), 11.

38. Ibid., 11–13.

39. Michael Nelson, "Constitutional Beginnings," in *Guide to the Presidency,* 2d ed., vol. I, ed. Michael Nelson (Washington, D.C.: Congressional Quarterly, 1996), 3–22. Much of the same material also can be found in Milkis and Nelson, *The American Presidency,* chap. 1.

40. C. C. Thach, Jr., *The Creation of the Presidency, 1775–1789: A Study in Constitutional History* (Baltimore: The Johns Hopkins University Press, 1922), chap. 3.

41. Nelson, *Guide to the Presidency,* 30.

42. Although presidents are limited to two elected terms, it is possible to serve for as many as ten years. A vice president who became president because of death, impeachment, or resignation and served no more than two years could be elected to two terms.

43. As cited in Corwin, *The President,* 28. Original from Henry Jones Ford, *The Rise and Growth of American Politics* (New York: Macmillan, 1898).

44. The term *role* often has been criticized by social scientists for lacking analytic rigor; nonetheless, *role* remains a powerful metaphor for understanding human behavior. During the 1960s analysts seemed almost to compete in developing an ever-lengthening list of roles filled by the president. See David L. Paletz, "Perspectives on the Presidency," in *The Institutionalized Presidency,* ed. Norman Thomas and Hans Baade (Dobbs Ferry, N.Y.: Oceana, 1972), 8–18.

45. Louis Fisher, *Constitutional Conflicts Between Congress and the President,* 3d ed. (Lawrence: University Press of Kansas, 1991), chap. 9.

46. Ibid., chap. 8.

47. Robert Scigliano, "The Presidency and the Judiciary," in *The Presidency and the Political System,* 3d ed., ed. Michael Nelson (Washington, D.C.: CQ Press, 1990), 473–476.

48. Fred I. Greenstein, "In Search of a Modern Presidency," in *Leadership in the Modern Presidency,* ed. Fred I. Greenstein (Cambridge, Mass.: Harvard University Press, 1989), 3, 346. Also see Fred I. Greenstein, *The Hidden-Hand Presidency* (New York: Basic Books, 1982), 4–5. In the latter, Greenstein (252 n. 4) attributes the initial functional role treatment to Clinton Rossiter in his classic text, *The American Presidency.*

49. Greenstein, "In Search of a Modern Presidency," 3.

50. John Locke, *Two Treatises of Civil Government* (New York: Dutton, 1924), 199.

51. For a thoughtful discussion of many of these incidents see Christopher H. Pyle and Richard M. Pious, *The President, Congress, and the Constitution: Power and Legitimacy in American Politics* (New York: Free Press, 1984). The varying grounds for claiming inherent power are reviewed on pages 76–78.

52. Corwin, *The President,* 30.

53. Ibid.

54. Richard M. Pious, *The American Presidency* (New York: Basic Books, 1979), 333. Also cited in Milkis and Nelson, *The American Presidency,* 70.

55. Corwin, *The President,* 30.

56. Ibid., chap. 1.

57. Clinton Rossiter selected the same seven and added Harry Truman. See Rossiter, *The American Presidency,* chaps. 3, 5. Four separate polls of historians, evaluating the leadership skills of all the presidents, rate highest Corwin's original seven chief executives. See Chapter 4 for further discussion. In *The Politics Presidents Make,* Skowronek classifies Jefferson, Jackson, Lincoln, and Franklin Roosevelt as presidents of reconstruction. He also includes Reagan in this group. Woodrow Wilson came close to the same achievement by probing for reconstructive possibilities. Theodore Roosevelt did not break with existing commitments, but he did usher in a new set of techniques that ultimately strengthened the presidency.

58. Leonard White, *The Federalists: A Study in Administrative History* (New York: Macmillan, 1967), 99.

59. As a matter of political strategy presidents now often seek the advice of influential individual senators. Woodrow Wilson's failure to consult with prominent Republican senators about the Treaty of Versailles probably contributed to his failure to get it approved, a lesson for his successors.

60. Alfred Kelly and Winfred Harbison, *The American Constitution: Its Origins and Development,* 4th ed. (New York: Norton, 1970), 424.

61. Rossiter, *The American Presidency,* 102.

62. Milkis and Nelson, *The American Presidency,* 208.

63. Jeffrey K. Tulis, *The Rhetorical Presidency* (Princeton, N.J.: Princeton University Press, 1987), chap. 4.

64. From *The Autobiography of Theodore Roosevelt,* excerpted in *Classics of the American Presidency,* ed. Harry Bailey (Oak Park, Ill.: Moore Publishing, 1980), 35.

65. Tulis, *The Rhetorical Presidency,* chap. 5. Also see Jeffrey K. Tulis, "The Two Constitutional Presidencies," in *The Presidency and the Political System,* 4th ed., ed. Michael Nelson (Washington, D.C.: CQ Press, 1995).

66. Thomas Jefferson had discontinued the practice as an undesirable indication of monarchist tendencies.

67. William E. Leuchtenberg, *In the Shadow of FDR: From Harry Truman to Ronald Reagan,* rev. ed. (Ithaca, N.Y.: Cornell University Press, 1985).

68. James L. Sundquist uses the term "economic stabilizer" and earlier, Clinton Rossiter had used the term "Manager of Prosperity." See Sundquist, *The Decline and Resurgence of Congress* (Washington, D.C.: Brookings, 1981), chap. 4.

69. Ibid., 66–67.

70. Fisher, *Constitutional Conflicts,* 24.

71. Corwin, *The President,* 175–177.

72. On White House staffing, see Bradley H. Patterson, Jr., *The Ring of Power: The White House Staff and Its Expanding Role in Government* (New York: Basic Books, 1988); Charles E. Walcott and Karen M. Hult, *Governing the White House from Hoover Through LBJ* (Lawrence: University Press of Kansas, 1995). On the larger development of presidential staffing, see John Hart, *The Presidential Branch,* 2d ed. (Chatham, N.J.: Chatham House, 1995).

73. For an essay that challenges the desirability of such a manifest presence, see Bruce Miroff, "Monopolizing the Public Space: The President as a Problem for Democratic Politics," in *Rethinking the Presidency,* ed. Thomas E. Cronin (Boston: Little, Brown, 1982).

74. Michael B. Grossman and Martha J. Kumar, *Portraying the President: The White House and the News Media* (Baltimore: Johns Hopkins University Press, 1981), 83–84.

75. Greenstein, "Change and Continuity in the Modern Presidency," 45–46.

76. See especially Milkis and Nelson, *The American Presidency,* chaps. 4–7; Tulis, *The Rhetorical Presidency*; and Skowronek, *The Politics Presidents Make.*

77. Seymour Martin Lipset, *The First New Nation: The United States in Historical and Comparative Perspective* (New York: Norton, 1979), 18.

78. Bruce Buchanan, *The Citizen's Presidency: Standards of Choice and Judgment* (Washington, D.C.: CQ Press, 1987), 25.

79. Ibid., 28.

80. See especially Murray Edelman, *The Symbolic Uses of Politics* (Urbana: University of Illinois Press, 1964); and Fred I. Greenstein, "What the President Means to Americans: Presidential 'Choice' Between Elections," in *Choosing the President,* ed. James David Barber (Englewood Cliffs, N.J.: Prentice-Hall, 1974).

81. Edelman, *The Symbolic Uses of Politics,* 76–77.

82. Greenstein, "What the President Means to Americans," 144–147. It should be noted that in this later essay Greenstein de-emphasized the likelihood that children socialized to a positive feeling about the president as an authority figure would extend this reliance on an "unconscious symbolic surrogate of childhood authority figures" into adulthood (142).

83. Murray Edelman, "The Politics of Persuasion," in *Choosing the President,* 172.

84. Barbara Hinckley, *The Symbolic Presidency: How Presidents Portray Themselves* (New York: Routledge, 1990), 5.

85. Ibid., 8.

86. As cited in Michael Novak, *Choosing Our King: Powerful Symbols in Presidential Politics* (New York: Macmillan, 1974), 44.

87. Hinckley, *The Symbolic Presidency,* 133.

88. Theodore J. Lowi, *The Personal President: Power Invested, Promise Unfulfilled* (Ithaca, N.Y.: Cornell University Press, 1985), xii.

89. Bruce Miroff, "The Presidency and the Public: Leadership as Spectacle," in *The Presidency and the Political System,* 4th ed., 273–296.

90. Bruce Miroff, "Secrecy and Spectacle: Reflections on the Dangers of the Presidency," in *The Presidency in American Politics,* ed. Paul Brace, Christine B. Harrington, and Gary King (New York: New York University Press, 1989), 157. Also see Miroff, "Monopolizing the Public Space," in *Rethinking the Presidency.*

READINGS

Burns, James MacGregor. *Presidential Government: The Crucible of Leadership.* Boston: Houghton Mifflin, 1965.

Corwin, Edward S. *The President: Office and Powers, 1789–1984.* 5th ed. New York: New York University Press, 1984.

Heclo, Hugh, and Lester M. Salamon, eds. *The Illusion of Presidential Government.* Boulder, Colo.: Westview, 1981.

Kallenbach, Joseph E. *The American Chief Executive: The Presidency and the Governorship.* New York: Harper & Row, 1966.

Lowi, Theodore J. *The Personal President: Power Invested, Promise Unfulfilled.* Ithaca, N.Y.: Cornell University Press, 1985.

Nelson, Michael, ed. *The Presidency and the Political System,* 4th ed. Washington, D.C.: CQ Press, 1995.

Neustadt, Richard E. *Presidential Power and the Modern Presidents: The Politics of Leadership from Roosevelt to Reagan.* New York: Free Press, 1990.

Rockman, Bert A. *The Leadership Question: The Presidency and the American Political System.* New York: Praeger, 1984.

Rose, Richard. *The Postmodern President: George Bush Meets the World,* 2d ed. Chatham, N.J.: Chatham House, 1991.

Rossiter, Clinton. *The American Presidency,* rev. ed. New York: Harcourt, Brace, 1960.

Seligman, Lester G., and Cary R. Covington. *The Coalitional Presidency.* Chicago: Dorsey, 1989.

Skowronek, Stephen. *The Politics Presidents Make: Leadership from John Adams to George Bush.* Cambridge, Mass.: Harvard University Press, 1993.

2   ELECTION POLITICS

For almost a century Americans have delighted in expressing their preferences in primary campaigns, symbolized by this collage of historical buttons.

THE FOCAL POINT OF AMERI-can political life is the presidential election. More citizens participate in this process than in any other aspect of civic life, and their choice has enormous significance for the nation and, indeed, for the world. Historians use presidential terms to break history into four-year blocks of time, and policy making at the federal level follows the same rhythm. The election also serves as a unifying event, a collective celebration of democracy coming at the conclusion of an elaborate pageant replete with familiar rituals, colorful characters, and plot lines that capture attention despite their repetition every four years.

Today's selection process bears little resemblance to what the Founders outlined in the original Constitution. Most of the changes have been extra-constitutional; that is, they result from the evolution of political parties, the media, and citizen expectations rather than constitutional amendments. There has been almost constant tinkering with the rules governing this aspect of American politics, with the movement consistently toward greater democratization. Most dissatisfaction with the process centers on the remnants of indirect democracy that persist, particularly the national party conventions and the electoral college, but some argue that democratization may have gone too far. The most important question that can be asked about U.S. presidential elections is whether they produce winners with the requisite abilities and skills.

At the conclusion of this chapter, we review recommendations for reform intended to improve system performance and provide for a greater degree of direct democracy. To appreciate the current selection process and suggestions for reform, it is necessary to gain an understanding of the major transformations the system has undergone.

Evolution of the Selection Process

In 1789 and 1792 electing a president was simple. Each member of the electoral college cast two votes, one of which had to be for a person outside of his state. Both times George Washington was elected by unanimous votes.[1] And both times John Adams received the second highest number of votes to become the vice president. In 1789 the process took only three months to complete: electors were chosen on the first Wednesday of January, met in their respective states to vote on the first Wednesday in February, and the votes were counted on April 6. In 1792 the procedure took even less time. The contrast with today's process could not be sharper: candidates now launch nomination campaigns up to two years before the general election, spending millions of dollars in pursuit of the office.

Consensus support for Washington ensured smooth operation of the selection procedure during the first two elections: there was widespread confidence that the nation's wartime hero would govern in the interest of all the people. The erosion of that consensus triggered the development of a separate nomination procedure. Policy differences in Congress created the basis for an important institution not mentioned in the Constitution—the political party. By the early 1790s the Federalist Party had formed around the economic policies of Secretary of the Treasury Alexander Hamilton, and his supporters in Congress backed his programs.[2] Resigning as secretary of state in 1793, Thomas Jefferson joined James Madison, then serving in the House of Representatives, as a critic of Hamilton's policies, and they formed the rival Republican Party.[3] By the mid-1790s cohesive pro- and antiadministration blocs had formed in Congress, and congressional candidates were labeled Democratic-Republicans or Federalists.[4] Washington's retirement at the end of his second term opened the presidential election to party politics.

The rise of parties fundamentally altered presidential selection by creating a separate nomination stage: the parties had to devise a method for choosing their nominees. Influence over presidential selection shifted from the local notables who had served as electors to party elites whose character has continued to evolve over time. In 1796 the Federalists' leaders chose their candidate, John Adams, and the Democratic-Republicans relied on their party members in Congress to nominate Jefferson as their standard-bearer. Four years later the Federalists adopted their opponents' idea, and the congressional caucus became the nominating mechanism for both parties, a practice that continued until 1824.

Political parties also had an almost immediate impact on the electoral college. Electors became party loyalists whose discipline was apparent in 1800, when Jefferson, the Democratic-Republicans' candidate for president, and Aaron Burr, the party's candidate for vice president, tied in the electoral college voting. Loyal to their party, the electors had cast their ballots for both candidates, but the Constitution had no provision for counting the ballots separately for president and vice president. Jefferson and Burr each received seventy-three votes to President Adams's sixty-five. The election was decided in the House of Representatives, where Jefferson won, but only after thirty-six ballots. Hamilton broke the tie by throwing his support behind Jefferson, his longtime rival. Party loyalty, with infrequent exceptions, has prevailed in electoral college balloting ever since. The Twelfth Amendment to the Constitution, ratified in 1804, provided for separate presidential and vice presidential balloting in the electoral college to prevent a similar deadlock.[5]

The congressional caucus allowed members of Congress, already assembled in the nation's capital and facing minimal transportation problems, to select a nominee. Because legislators were familiar with potential presidential candidates from all parts of the new country, they were the logical agents for choosing candidates for an office with a nationwide constituency. Caucuses provided a peer review of candidates' credentials, with one group of politicians assessing another's skills, abilities, and political appeal. But the congressional caucus had serious flaws. It violated the constitutional principle of separation of powers by giving members of the legislative body a routine role in choosing the president rather than only in the event of an electoral college deadlock. The caucus could not represent areas in which the party had lost the previous congressional election, a problem quickly encountered by the Federalists. Moreover, interested and informed citizens who participated in grass-roots party activities, especially campaigns, had no means to participate in congressional caucus deliberations.

The 1824 election brought an end to nomination by congressional caucus. First, the Democratic-Republicans in Congress insisted on nominating Secretary of the Treasury William Crawford, who had suffered a debilitating stroke. Then, in the general election Andrew Jackson, proposed by the Tennessee legislature, won more popular votes and more electoral votes than any other candidate but failed to achieve a majority in the electoral college. The election had to be decided by the House, where John Quincy Adams emerged victorious after he agreed to make Henry Clay, another of the five contestants, secretary of state in return for his support. These shenanigans permanently discredited King Caucus, as its critics called it. "Favorite sons" nominated by state legislatures and conventions dominated the 1828 campaign, but this method proved too decentralized to select a national official. A device was needed that would represent party elements throughout the country and at the same time facilitate the nomination of a candidate.

National Party Conventions

What developed was the party convention, an assembly made truly national by including delegates from all the states. Rail transportation made such meetings feasible, and the expanding citizen participation in presidential elections made the change necessary. Influence over selection of the party nominee therefore shifted to state and local party leaders, particularly those able to commit large blocs of delegate votes to a candidate.

Two minor parties with no appreciable representation in Congress, the Anti-Masons and National Republicans, led the way with conventions in 1831.[6] The Democrats, under President Andrew Jackson (elected in 1828), also held a convention in 1832 to rally support. Major political parties have nominated their presidential and vice presidential candidates by holding national conventions ever since. National committees composed of state party leaders call the presidential nominating conventions into session to choose nominees and to adopt a platform of common policy positions.[7] Delegates are selected by states and allocated primarily on the basis of population.

Although today's conventions in some ways resemble those of 150 years ago, the nomination process has undergone drastic revision, especially since 1968. Just as influence over selection of the party nominee shifted from Congress to party leaders, it has moved within the party from a small group of organization professionals to a broad base of activists and voters. This shift, the origins of which can be traced to the development of presidential primary elections early in the twentieth century (Florida passed the first primary election law in 1901), accelerated rapidly after 1968. Modern conventions serve as ratifying assemblies for a popular choice rather than deliberative bodies, and candidates with popular appeal have the advantage over those whose appeal is primarily with party leaders.

Under the system that operated from roughly 1850 to 1950, party leaders from the largest states could bargain over presidential nominations. Most influential were those who controlled large blocs of delegates and would throw their support behind a candidate for the right price. These power brokers—hence the term *brokered conventions*—might seek a program commitment in the platform, a place in the president's cabinet, or other forms of federal patronage in return for support. To be successful, candidates had to curry favor with party and elected officials before and during the national convention. An effective campaign manager might tour the country selling the candidate's virtues and securing delegate commitments prior to the convention, but about half the conventions began with no sense of the likely outcome. Protracted bargaining and negotiation among powerful state and local party leaders were often the result; the Democrats needed 103 ballots cast over seventeen days to nominate John W. Davis in 1924, an effort that must have seemed pointless when he attracted only 29 percent of the popular vote. Nevertheless, the convention was a deliberative body that reached decisions on common policy positions as well as on nominees. Providing a way to accommodate the demands of major elements within the party established the base for a nationwide campaign.

In this respect, modern conventions are quite different. Not since 1952, when the Democrats needed three ballots to nominate Gov. Adlai Stevenson of Illinois for president, has it taken more than one ballot to determine either party's nominee.[8] Raucous floor battles over procedures and delegate credentials have given way to a stream of symbols and speakers whose appearance is carefully choreographed to appeal to a prime-time television audience. Although much of the convention's business is still conducted in backroom meetings, the most important business—determining who the presidential nominee will be—already has been decided through the grueling primary and caucus process used to select convention delegates. Compared with their forerunners, modern conventions conduct their business in a routinized fashion, adhere to a set of enforceable national party standards for delegate selection and demographic representation, and are more heavily influenced by rank-and-file party supporters than by the party organization's leaders.[9] These changes, however, appeared gradually through a process often fraught with conflict that centered on the rules governing delegate selection.

The Contemporary Selection Process

The pace of change accelerated when the Democratic Party adopted a set of internal reforms following its loss in 1968. In addition to the actions already noted, rules adopted by a variety of actors—100 state political parties and fifty legislatures, the national political parties, and Congress—reformed the process. Sometimes individuals even turn to the courts to interpret provisions of these regulations and reconcile conflicts among them. In addition, the rules were adjusted so drastically and so often, particularly in the Democratic Party, that candidates and their supporters found it difficult to keep up with them.

Reform has been especially pervasive in the nomination process. Following their tumultuous convention in 1968, when Vietnam War protesters clashed with police in the streets of Chicago, the Democrats adopted a set of guidelines that reduced the influence of party leaders, encouraged participation by rank-and-file Democrats, and expanded convention representation of previously underrepresented groups, particularly women and African Americans. The result was a pronounced shift of influence within the party from *party professionals* toward *amateurs,* a term encompassing citizens who become engaged in the presidential contest because of a short-term concern such as an attractive candidate (candidate enthusiasts) or an especially important issue (issue enthusiasts).

States, seeking to conform to the party's new guidelines on participation, adopted the primary as the preferred means to select delegates to the national convention. In 1968 only seventeen states chose delegates through primaries; in 1996, forty-one states and the District of Columbia did so.[10] Because of these changes, nominations are more apt to reflect the voters' concerns. Conventions changed accordingly: nominations are now determined by the party supporters who selected delegates during the preceding primaries and caucuses.

But abandoning the convention's traditional deliberative role, some argue, has come at a heavy cost. By transferring power to amateurs and by sacrificing the peer review exercised by professionals, Democrats, in particular, feared they had been weakened organizationally and chosen less capable nominees. Moreover, the changes have enhanced the importance of the media. By operating as the principal source of information about the candidates and by emphasizing the "horse race"—who is ahead—the media have become enormously influential during the delegate selection process. So not everyone is satisfied with the general movement toward a more democratized selection process, and several counter-reforms appeared during the 1980s.

Now that the historical context has been set and some of the current concerns about the nomination process have been previewed, the discussion focuses on how the contemporary selection process operates. Despite the seemingly perpetual flux that characterizes presidential elections, it is possible to identify four stages in the process: (1) the pool of eligible candidates is defined; (2) following the primaries and caucuses, the parties nominate their candidates at the national conventions; (3) the general election campaign is waged, culminating in election day; and (4) the electoral college validates the results.

No two presidential election cycles are identical, but the customary time line is relatively predictable *(Figure 2-1)*. Potential candidates maneuver for position during the one or two years preceding the election year. Selection of convention delegates begins in January and February of the election year, with conventions typically scheduled first for the out party followed by the party that controls the presidency: in 1996, August 11 through August 16 in San Diego for the Republicans and August 26 through August 29 in Chicago for the Democrats. Traditionally, the general election campaign begins on Labor Day and runs to election day, the first Tuesday following the first Monday in November, but the planning for modern campaigns begins once the identity of major party nominees becomes clear. Electors cast ballots in their state capitols in mid-December. Finally, those ballots are officially tabulated during the first week in January during a joint session of the U.S. Congress, which is presided over by the incumbent vice president. The duly elected president is inaugurated on January 20, a date set in the Twentieth Amendment to the Constitution.

Figure 2-1 The 1996 Presidential Contest Time Line

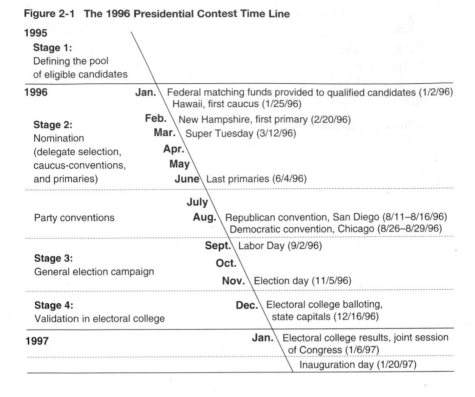

1995		
Stage 1: Defining the pool of eligible candidates		
1996	**Jan.**	Federal matching funds provided to qualified candidates (1/2/96) Hawaii, first caucus (1/25/96)
Stage 2: Nomination (delegate selection, caucus-conventions, and primaries)	**Feb.**	New Hampshire, first primary (2/20/96)
	Mar.	Super Tuesday (3/12/96)
	Apr.	
	May	
	June	Last primaries (6/4/96)
	July	
Party conventions	**Aug.**	Republican convention, San Diego (8/11–8/16/96) Democratic convention, Chicago (8/26–8/29/96)
Stage 3: General election campaign	**Sept.**	Labor Day (9/2/96)
	Oct.	
	Nov.	Election day (11/5/96)
Stage 4: Validation in electoral college	**Dec.**	Electoral college balloting, state capitals (12/16/96)
1997	**Jan.**	Electoral college results, joint session of Congress (1/6/97)
		Inauguration day (1/20/97)

Defining the Pool of Eligibles

Who is eligible to serve as president? The formal rules relating to the candidates' qualifications are minimal and have been remarkably stable over time. Individuals need to meet only three requirements, which are set forth in Article II, Section 1, of the Constitution. One must be a "natural born" citizen, at least thirty-five years of age, and a resident of the United States for fourteen years or longer.[11] More than 90 million Americans meet these constitutional requirements, but the pool of plausible candidates is far smaller than that of possible candidates.

The informal requirements for the presidency are less easy to satisfy than the formal. People who entertain presidential ambitions must have what is generally called "political availability"; that is, they must have the political experiences and personal characteristics that make them attractive to political activists and to the general voting public. Potential candidates accumulate these credentials through personal and career decisions made long before the presidential election year.

There is no explicit checklist of job qualifications for the presidency. The closest that one can come to determining what particular political experiences and personal characteristics put an individual in line for a presidential nomination is to look at past candidates. Even this approach poses some difficulties because the attitudes of political leaders and the American public change over time.

Political Experience of Candidates

Who is nominated to run for president? Overwhelmingly, the answer is people with experience in one of a few civilian, elective, political offices. Since 1932, with only two exceptions, nominees have been drawn from one of four positions: the presidency, the vice presidency, a state governorship, or a U.S. Senate seat.[12] *(See Appendix A.)* Candidates with other backgrounds are seldom successful. For example, in 1988 three aspirants who lacked experience in elected office unsuccessfully sought the Republican nomination. In 1992 H. Ross Perot, a billionaire businessman, sought election without a party nomination and did so again in 1996 as nominee of the Reform Party. Before he withdrew from consideration in November 1995, considerable speculation also centered on whether retired general Colin Powell would seek the presidency either as a Republican or as an independent.

Nominees' backgrounds have changed very little since the last half of the nineteenth century.[13] Moreover, since 1932 the party controlling the presidency has turned to the presidency or vice presidency for candidates, while the out party has turned first to governors and then to the Senate.

Presidents and Vice Presidents. In only one of the last seventeen elections from 1932 to 1996 has the name of an incumbent president or vice president not been on the ballot. Thirteen times, the incumbent president was renominated, and in three of the four instances when the incumbent president was either prohibited by the Twenty-second Amendment from running again (Eisenhower in 1960 and Reagan in 1988) or declined to do so (Truman in 1952 and Johnson in 1968), the incumbent vice president won his party's nomination. The exception occurred in 1952, when President Harry Truman chose not to run for reelection and Adlai Stevenson became the nominee rather than the vice president, seventy-five-year-old Alben Barkley. The presidency itself has been the major source of candidates for the office, and the principal variation in recruitment has occurred in the out party.

There are no guarantees that an incumbent president or vice president will win the party's nomination, but it is enormously difficult for the party in power to remove these leaders from the national ticket. Incumbents have considerable advantages when it comes to winning renomination, as demonstrated by Gerald Ford in 1976 and Jimmy Carter in 1980. Party leaders are reluctant to admit that they made a mistake four years earlier; incumbents can direct federal programs toward politically important areas or make politically useful executive branch appointments; and presidents enjoy far greater media exposure than others seeking the nomination. As a result, even unpopular presidents tend to be renominated. The Republicans chose Ford again despite an energy crisis and slow economy, and the Democrats renominated Carter when both inflation and unemployment were high, Americans were being held hostage in Iran, and Soviet troops occupied Afghanistan.

Incumbent vice presidents are more likely to win their party's nomination today than in the past.[14] Recent presidential candidates have chosen running mates who are arguably more capable than their predecessors, which makes these individuals more viable prospects for the presidency, although Bush's selection of Sen. Dan Quayle of Indiana raised questions concerning his experience and maturity. Moreover, presidents now assign their vice presidents meaningful responsibilities, including political party activities (especially campaigning in off-year elections), liaison assignments with social groups, and diplomatic missions to foreign countries. As the position's visibility and significance have increased, so have the political chances of its occupants improved.[15]

If it was an asset in securing the party's nomination, the vice presidency seemed to be a liability in winning the general election until Bush broke a 152-year-old tradition of losing campaigns. Richard Nixon and Hubert Humphrey lost as incumbent vice presidents in 1960 and 1968. Dan Quayle, widely mentioned as a likely candidate in 1996, surprised most observers when he chose not to seek the nomination.

Senators and Governors. From 1932 through 1996 the party out of power nominated nine governors, four senators, two former vice presidents, one general (Dwight Eisenhower), and one businessman (Wendell Willkie). *(See Table 2-1.)* Both major parties have looked to governors as promising candidates except for the period from 1960 to 1972, when Sens. John Kennedy (D-1960), Barry Goldwater (R-1964), and George McGovern (D-1972), as well as former vice president Nixon (R-1968), won the nomination. Governorships later regained prominence

Table 2-1   Principal Experience of In- and Out-Party Candidates
Before Gaining Nomination, 1932–1996

Election year	In party	Out party
1932	President (R)	Governor (D)
1936	President (D)	Governor (R)
1940	President (D)	Businessman (R)
1944	President (D)	Governor (R)
1948	President (D)	Governor (R)
1952	Governor (D)	General/educator (R)
1956	President (R)	Governor (former) (D)
1960	Vice president (R)	Senator (D)
1964	President (D)	Senator (R)
1968	Vice president (D)	Vice president (former) (R)
1972	President (R)	Senator (D)
1976	President (R)	Governor (former) (D)
1980	President (D)	Governor (former) (R)
1984	President (R)	Vice president (former) (D)
1988	Vice president (R)	Governor (D)
1992	President (R)	Governor (D)
1996	President (D)	Senator (R)

with the nomination of former governors Carter (D-1976) and Ronald Reagan (R-1980) as well as sitting governors Michael Dukakis (D-1988) and Bill Clinton (D-1992). Only twice in the last six elections did the party out of power not turn to a governor: former vice president Mondale was the Democratic nominee in 1984, and Senate Majority Leader Robert Dole in 1996. Mondale, out of office when he sought the nomination, enjoyed the freedom to run a full-time campaign. Dole resigned from the Senate effective June 11, 1996, in order to pursue his long-time goal.

It is possible to argue that these patterns understate the importance of the Senate as a recruiting ground for president. Certainly, many senators have sought their parties' presidential nomination since the early 1950s. Senators share the political and media spotlight focused on the capital, enjoy the opportunity to address major public problems and develop a record in foreign affairs, and usually can pursue the presidency without giving up their legislative seat. Nonetheless, only twice in American history have senators been elected directly to the White House (Harding in 1920 and Kennedy in 1960).[16] Hoping to register another exception in 1996, four Republican senators vied for the nomination and only one former governor entered the primaries.

Instead of serving as a steppingstone to the presidency, the Senate has often been one to the *vice presidency,* which then gave its occupants the inside track either to assume the presidency through succession or to win nomination on their own. This role of the Senate can be seen in the careers of vice presidents Truman, Nixon, Johnson, Humphrey, and Mondale, who served as senators immediately before assuming their executive posts. Gerald Ford, who succeeded to the presidency when Nixon resigned in 1974, had moved into the vice presidency from the House of Representatives. Service in the Senate, therefore, *has* been an important source of experience for presidents since 1932, but almost all have needed seasoning in the vice presidency.

Although the office regained prominence during the 1970s and 1980s, governors seeking the presidency confront major obstacles. It is difficult for them to gain national publicity unless they serve in states with large cities that function as national media centers. Governor Clinton of Arkansas was an exception to this rule. Nor do governors have responsibilities of consequence in foreign affairs; instead, they are more closely tied to their home states, particularly when the state legislature is in session, than are senators. Their terms are often limited by law or they are defeated for reelection because of public disappointment at their failure to solve major domestic problems without increasing taxes. Becoming sufficiently well known to be a viable presidential candidate is a major task.

Carter's election in 1976 and Reagan's bid for the nomination that year and election in 1980 indicate, however, that governors may enjoy some advantages as candidates, particularly if they are *not* in office when they seek the presidency, a point driven home by Dukakis's defeat in 1988. Unlike Dukakis, Carter and Reagan were free to devote themselves full time to the demanding task of winning the nomination, an opportunity not available to the senators who sought the presidency in both of those years. Clinton, however, secured the nomination and the presidency in 1992 while serving as governor. Governors can claim valuable executive experience in managing large-scale public enterprises and thousands of state government employees in contrast to a senator's essentially legislative duties and direction of a small personal staff. Moreover, the public's concern with foreign affairs has declined since 1976 and been replaced by anxiety over the domestic economy, taxes, and the budget. This shift in public attitudes was evident in 1992 when Clinton benefited from the cold war's reduced prominence.

Among those who pursued the 1996 Republican presidential nomination, senators outnumbered governors by 2 to 1. Four Republican senators—Robert Dole (Kan.), Phil Gramm (Texas), Richard Lugar (Ind.), and Arlen Specter (Pa.)—announced their candidacies during the first half of 1995. The two governors were Pete Wilson, a former senator who had been reelected as governor of California in 1994 and was the sole sitting chief executive to pursue the nomination, and Lamar Alexander, a former governor of Tennessee. Beyond these six candidates, five others launched campaigns: Rep. Robert Dornan (Calif.); Patrick Buchanan, a political commentator and former White House speechwriter; Alan Keyes, a talk show host; Malcolm (Steve) Forbes, Jr., a magazine publisher; and Maurice Taylor, a tire manufacturer. No Democrat challenged President Clinton for the nomination.

Personal Characteristics of Candidates

Although millions meet the formal requirements for president, far fewer meet the informal criteria that have guided choices in the past. Most constraining have been the limits imposed by social conventions on gender and race. So far only males of European heritage have been nominated for president by either of the two major parties, although several women and African Americans have waged national campaigns since 1972, and former representative Geraldine Ferraro of New York was the Democrats' 1984 nominee for vice president. Presidential aspirants also have had to pass other "tests" based on personal characteristics, although these informal requirements have undergone change in the past three decades.[17]

Until 1960 it seemed that candidates had to meet unspoken demographic and religious requirements—that they hail from English ethnic stock and practice a Protestant religion. These tests have weakened in the intervening years. John Kennedy's successful candidacy in 1960 challenged the traditional preference for Protestants; Alfred Smith, also a Catholic, was nominated by the Democrats in 1928 but lost the general election. Today, little is made of the fact when Catholics pursue the nomination. The Republican senator Barry Goldwater was the first nominee from a partly Jewish background. Other recent candidates have come from Irish, Norwegian, and Greek heritage, suggesting that the traditional preference for English stock has weakened.

Representing an idealized version of home and family life also seemed to be essential to winning a party's nomination. These criteria have undergone modest change, but other considerations may have taken their place. Nelson Rockefeller's divorce in 1963 from his wife of more than thirty years and his rapid remarriage virtually ensured the failure of his efforts to win the Republican nomination in 1964 and 1968. The marital status of several later candidates was an issue, but in

1980 Ronald Reagan became the country's first president to have divorced and remarried.

Public attitudes about other moral and ethical questions have become important. Gary Hart's widely reported extramarital affair ended his presidential hopes for 1988, even though he began the campaign as the clear front-runner. Bill Clinton's alleged extramarital relationships and drug use also became an issue in 1992. Sen. Joseph Biden's 1987 campaign foundered on charges that he had plagiarized campaign speeches and misrepresented his record. Although traditional moral and ethical tests regarding divorce may have changed, it is not clear which standards will continue to receive media attention and elicit public response, particularly in an era when religion and political activism seem to mix more readily than in the past.

Thus, several of the informal qualifications applied to the presidency have altered with the passage of time, probably in response to changes in the nomination process itself as well as broader currents in U.S. society. One observer suggests that the proliferation of presidential primaries "provides a forum in which prejudices can be addressed openly." [18] The vice presidential nomination offers a way to confront traditional social views indirectly, as was the case with Ferraro. We might expect something similar to happen with an African American candidate in the near future.

The development of a more common culture and the nationalization of American life in general, brought about by modern communication and transportation, have reduced the importance of parochial concerns—the candidates' religious, ethnic, or geographical background—and increased the emphasis on their experience in the national political arena and their association with national issues. Moreover, as other groups that are still socially or politically disadvantaged—African Americans, women, and immigrants from Asia, Mexico, and eastern and southern Europe—begin to occupy governorships and seats in the U.S. Senate, they will enhance their chances of becoming serious candidates for the presidency.[19]

Competing for the Nomination

Once the pool of eligible candidates is established, the selection process begins. This phase has two major components: choosing delegates to the two parties' national conventions and selecting the nominees at the conventions. By far the more complicated of these steps, the selection of delegates has been the principal focus of party reform efforts since 1968. As already mentioned, these reforms have fundamentally altered the convention's role: once a deliberative assembly, it now anoints the winner of the primary and caucus contests as the party's standard-bearer and serves as a backdrop for launching the ticket's general election campaign. Should the convention begin without a distinct front-runner, deliberation would once again be possible, a situation made more likely if many candidates pursue the nomination.

Prior to the conventions, candidates crisscross the country in pursuit of delegates, who then attend the convention to select the party's nominee. Delegates are chosen by three methods: they can be named by party leaders such as members of the party's state committee; be elected by a state convention attended by delegates themselves selected at caucuses (party meetings) held in precincts, wards, counties, or congressional districts; or be chosen by direct election in presidential primaries. Although Hawaii, Alaska, and Louisiana held caucuses in 1996 that preceded Iowa, both candidates and the media continued to stress the midwestern contest.

The first presidential primary of 1996 was held in New Hampshire on February 20. Delegate selection extended into June, when four states held primaries, the last of forty-one Republican and thirty-five Democratic primary contests that chose convention delegates, including those from the District of Columbia. Through this complex structure, the Republicans chose 1,990 delegates to attend their national convention, and the Democrats selected 4,289 for theirs. Consistent with post-1968 reforms, most of these delegates were chosen through primaries—nearly two-thirds of the Democratic delegates and more than three-fourths of the Republican delegates (see Table 2-2). Millions of Americans participate in primaries: in 1996, for example, 10.9 million voted in Democratic primary elections, and another 15.3 million in Republican primaries.[20] Caucus participation is less easily calculated, but in 1996 nearly 200,000 attended seven Republican caucuses.[21]

In truth, the nomination contest begins much earlier than January of the election year. For example, in pursuing the 1988 nomination, former Delaware governor Pierre "Pete" DuPont officially declared his candidacy in September 1986; thirteen others followed suit in 1987, nine before the Fourth of July. By starting their campaigns early, candidates hope to amass the financial backing, attract the media attention, and generate the popular support necessary to ensure eventual victory. There was only one "early bird" in 1992, but in 1995 nine can-

Table 2-2   Delegates to 1996 Presidential Conventions by Selection
Procedure

Selection method		Delegates (N)	Percentage of convention
Democrats			
	Primaries	2,572	60.0
	Caucuses	949	22.1
	Superdelegates	768	17.9
	Total	4,289	
Republicans			
	Primaries	1,665	83.7
	Caucuses	325	16.3
	Total	1,990	

Sources: Democratic National Committee; Republican National Committee; Federal
Election Commission.

didates launched campaigns before May 1995, probably because Clinton appeared highly vulnerable.

The Nomination Campaign

The nomination campaign is a winnowing process in which each of the two major parties eliminates from the pool of potential candidates all but the one who will represent the party in the general election. As the political scientist Austin Ranney points out, the nomination phase of the campaign is more important than the election stage, because "the parties' nominating processes eliminate far more presidential possibilities than do the voters' electing processes." [22] A nomination campaign is long, arduous, and relatively unstructured: aspirants typically do not know how many opponents they will face or who they will be; candidates start up to two years early and drop out along the way; and, instead of a simultaneous nationwide campaign, the competition takes place in stages with candidates hopscotching the nation in pursuit of votes. Planning and conducting such a campaign are enormously difficult tasks. Most first-time candidates must organize a nationwide political effort, a chore that dwarfs the campaign required to win a Senate seat or governorship in even the largest states.

Preliminary planning is essential, and presidential hopefuls spend considerable time before January of the election year laying the groundwork for their effort. The journalist Arthur Hadley calls this period the "invisible primary," a testing ground for the would-be president waged behind the scenes to determine whether his or her candidacy is viable.[23] Candidates must assemble a staff to help raise money, develop campaign strategy, hone a message, and identify a larger group of people willing to do the advance work necessary to organize states for the upcoming primaries and caucuses. Visits are made to party organizations throughout the country, but especially in pivotal states such as Iowa and New Hampshire, to curry favor with activists. Competition often takes on the trappings of a full-fledged campaign with candidates broadcasting television ads, engaging in debates, and seeking to finish well in prenomination popularity contests or "straw polls."

Because their coverage provides name recognition and potentially positive publicity, developing a favorable relationship with the media is crucial during this phase of the contest. Those who are ignored because reporters and commentators do not regard them as serious contenders find it almost impossible to become candidates. Adverse publicity can seriously damage a candidacy: Hart's and Biden's 1988 campaigns were scuttled during the "invisible primary" stage.

Financing Nomination Campaigns

It is now more important than ever that candidates for the nomination begin raising funds early. Candidates can qualify to receive federal funds that match individual contributions of $250 or less if they can raise $100,000 in individual contributions, with at least $5,000 collected in twenty different states. By checking a box on their federal income tax forms, taxpayers authorize the government to set aside $3.00 of their tax payments for public financing of campaigns. Candidates who accept public financing—and since 1976 only John Connally, Malcolm (Steve) Forbes, Jr., and Maurice Taylor, all Republicans, have chosen not to do so—must also accept limitations on total expenditures and a cap on spending in individual states that is based on population. For 1996 the national expenditure ceiling for the prenomination campaign was $37.1 million.

By providing partial funding of nomination campaigns, reformers sought to establish a system based on citizen contributions and replace the financial support of a small number of "fat cats," who previously bankrolled candidates.[24] In 1996, eleven candidates qualified for $55.95 million in matching funds, up from $42.9 million in 1992. The federal government also provided $12.4 million to the Democratic and Republican parties to finance their nominating conventions. The Federal Election Commission (FEC), a bipartisan body of six members nominated by the president and confirmed by the Senate, oversees the administration of these provisions.

Despite the establishment of a new public financing system, loopholes remain. One of the largest in 1988 was the precandidacy political action committee (PAC). Nine candidates remained undeclared for as long as possible and established a PAC to finance their pre-announcement activities. They collectively spent $25.2 million, with Vice President Bush leading the way with $10.8 million, followed by Sen. Robert Dole, R-Kan. ($6.54 million) and Rep. Jack Kemp, R-N.Y. ($4.16 million).[25] Once candidacy is officially announced, the statutory restrictions apply.

In 1996 personal money played an unprecedented role in the prenomination stage of the campaign. Steve Forbes loaned his campaign $37.5 million, and Maurice Taylor spent $6.5 million of his own resources. Neither was ultimately successful, but Forbes dramatically influenced the Republican nomination process by outspending his rivals in several early contests. Because he received no public funds, Forbes was not subject to the state spending limits imposed on his competitors. He launched a $12.5 million media blitz during the last three months of 1995 that concentrated on Iowa, New Hampshire, and other early events. Even Dole, who led all candidates in fund raising, could not match such an expenditure since he had to observe federal limits.[26]

Although the 1996 election process focused public attention on campaign finance loopholes more than ever before, fewer questions surround the prenomination phase. The 1970s legislation radically changed sources and techniques for raising money. Most candidates continue to raise funds from a large number of individual contributors, often through direct mail solicitation.[27] Public funds open the door for people who formerly could not afford to mount a nomination campaign because large contributors would not support them. Even some third party candidates, such as Lenora Fulani of the New Alliance Party in 1988 and 1992 and John Hagelin of the Natural Law Party in 1996, qualified for federal funds at the nominating stage. Even though financial disparities among candidates may not be as great as once was the case, candidate resources are still highly unequal. In 1988 and 1992 George Bush easily outdistanced the financing of his competition, and Bob Dole did the same in 1996. Eventual nominees Michael Dukakis and Bill Clinton led the Democratic fields in fund raising in the same years.[28] Superior financial resources enable candidates to compete in more of the early nomination contests, help them expand their fund-raising lead, enable them to survive poor results, and make them stronger in later primaries. Failing to do well in early caucus and primary contests means more than losing delegates to opponents; it also means that contributions stop. Moreover, under the campaign finance law, federal matching funds must be cut off within thirty days if a candidate receives less than 10 percent of the votes in two consecutive primaries. Leading Republican candidates in 1995 worked aggressively to reach the target of $20 million in contributions by year's end, the consensus target among political consultants on what it would take to run a "serious" campaign.[29]

Candidates must decide not only how to raise funds but also how to spend them. In the face of overall campaign spending limits as well as expenditure limits in each state, money must be carefully allocated. Because they want to win the first primaries and caucuses, candidates are inclined to spend heavily in the very early stage of the campaign, which can create problems in later competition, an especially pressing problem for Dole in 1996 when he nearly reached the spending limit by April, fully three months before the convention.

Dynamics of the Contest

Candidates who begin the election year as leaders in the public opinion polls frequently go on to win nomination. This pattern prevailed from 1936 through 1968. In four more recent contests, however, the front-runner among Democrats ultimately was replaced by a dark horse. George McGovern defeated front-runner Edmund Muskie in 1972; Jimmy Carter likewise surpassed Hubert Humphrey in 1976; Michael Dukakis won the 1988 nomination over the early leader, Gary Hart. Bill Clinton trailed Jerry Brown in January 1992 and stood in fifth place among Democratic contenders two months earlier. Both Robert Dole and Bill Clinton led the field by wide margins in 1996. Leaders in the polls must guard against verbal slips, personal indiscretions, and the assumption that early popularity is permanent; the final choice of the nominee depends on presidential primaries and caucus-convention contests.

When deciding which contests they should emphasize in their nomination campaigns, candidates take into account the premium placed on competing in as many locations as funds will allow. This is especially true for Democrats, whose rules call for proportional allocation of delegates: so long as candidates achieve at least 15 percent of the vote, they are awarded a share of delegates proportional to the vote share.[30] A critical consideration, however, is the date of the primary. The earliest contest, traditionally the New Hampshire primary, usually attracts most of the major contenders because it is the first test of rank-and-file voter sentiment. Although the number of New Hampshire delegates is small—in 1996, only 26 of 4,289 Democratic delegates, and 16 of 1,990 Republican delegates—victory ensures immediate attention, as it did for Kennedy in 1960 and Carter in 1976. Pat Buchanan was the surprise winner in 1996 with a slim 1 percent victory margin over Dole based on a consolidated conservative vote, while moderates split between the Kansas senator and Lamar Alexander. The relatively small New Hampshire electorate also enables candidates with modest financial resources to conduct labor-intensive campaigns.[31]

A new twist in the 1988 campaign was the round of primaries held on Tuesday, March 8—Super Tuesday. Twenty states selected delegates, sixteen through primaries and four through caucuses. In 1992 only eleven states participated in Super Tuesday, but the Democratic designers accomplished their goal of boosting the chances of a moderate candidate when Clinton won all six of the southern primaries and two caucuses, while Tsongas, his principal rival, claimed victories in just two primaries and one caucus. Texas and Florida, with the largest delegate totals, went to Clinton; in 1988 they had gone to the non-southerner Dukakis. Bush, who swept all sixteen of the 1988 Super Tuesday primaries, repeated this success on March 10, 1992, by winning all of the contests against Patrick Buchanan and David Duke. Likewise, Dole won all seven Super Tuesday primaries in 1996 and 349 of the 362 delegates at stake.

Although smaller in 1992 than in 1996, Super Tuesday contests selected 783 Democratic delegates and 403 Republican delegates, roughly 18 percent of their respective convention totals. Because of these large stakes, observers have termed the process *front-loaded*, meaning that a significant number of delegates is chosen early. In all, twenty-three states selected delegates between March 3 and March 10, and nearly one-half of all Democratic convention delegates were named by March 18. The process was even more concentrated in 1996. Twenty-eight states held primaries by the end of March, including New York and California, which had moved to earlier positions in the process. In fact, an increasing number of states sought to increase their impact on the nomination process by moving their primary or caucus up in the calendar. New Hampshire had to defend its privileged position of holding the nation's first primary at least one week before anyone else against challenges from Arizona and Delaware. Hawaii, Alaska, and Louisiana Republicans upstaged Iowa as the first caucus. Most candidates succumbed to pressure from Iowa and New Hampshire to boycott these upstart contests, once again giving these states the lion's share of media coverage.

Later primaries once played an important role. California formerly scheduled its primary on the final day, giving Golden State voters the chance to determine a party's nominee, as with Goldwater in 1964 and McGovern in 1972. After the experience of 1996, Republican rules will encourage states to schedule their primaries later in 2000 by providing them with bonus delegates.[32]

State caucuses operate in the shadow of the primaries, although they remain important for candidates able to mobilize an intensely motivated group of supporters. The Iowa caucuses, long the initial delegate selection contest, diminished in importance as a launching pad for presidential contenders in 1988 and 1992. The 1988 winners, Richard Gephardt and Robert Dole, dropped out of the nomination contest by the end of March; in 1992, Democrats chose not to compete against Tom Harkin, the home-state senator. The state was again hotly contested in 1996, with Dole narrowly defeating Buchanan. When primaries do not produce a clear victor, candidates devote more attention to delegates chosen in caucus-convention states, as in the 1976 Republican contest and the 1984 Democratic race.

Media Influence and Campaign Consultants

The media play an enormous role in the nomination campaign. They interpret results and serve as the principal vehicle for candidates to make appeals, both paid and unpaid. As the nomination process has grown in complexity, the influence of the media also has grown. Candidates who must campaign in a score of states within two weeks, as they did in 1992 and 1996, necessarily rely on the media to communicate with large numbers of potential voters. Televised advertisements, network- and station-sponsored debates, and prime-time news coverage are critical to candidates' efforts. Talk show appearances were an important communication link in 1992, though less so in 1996.

The media tend to focus on the game aspects of the pre-election year maneuvering and the early contests. As candidates begin to emerge, journalists concentrate on the race for financial contributions, the quality of professionals enlisted to work on a campaign, and speculations about the candidates' relative chances of success based on polls and nonbinding straw votes in various states. Once the delegate selection contests begin, the media focus on political tactics, strategy, and competitive position more than the candidates' messages and issue stands, particularly in their coverage of Iowa, New Hampshire, and the compressed schedule of contests in March. In general, the media use a winner-take-all principle that, regardless of how narrow the victory or the number of popular votes involved, gives virtually all the publicity to the victorious candidate. In the 1976 Iowa caucuses, for example, Carter was declared the "clear winner" and described as leading the pack of contenders even though he received only about 14,000 votes, 28 percent of the 50,000 cast; he actually trailed the "uncommitted" group.[33] A surprise showing by a runner-up may garner the most attention: after winning a mere 16 percent of the votes to finish an unexpected second in the Iowa caucuses in 1984, Hart got as much publicity as Mondale, who captured three times as many votes.[34]

Presidential nominating campaigns are highly complex operations that call for a variety of specialists. Pollsters help candidates assess their nomination prospects and provide vital feedback on voters' reactions to the candidates and their campaigns, on the issues that concern people, and on the attitudes of social and economic groups about such issues. Media consultants help candidates develop a favorable image, write their speeches, and plan their television appearances; and direct-mail specialists raise money and get out the vote. Beginning with the 1952 presidential election, candidates have increasingly turned to political consultants, rather than party officials, to organize these diverse operations, develop strategy, and manage the overall campaign.

As the fate of presidential candidates passed from a small group of party professionals to rank-and-file voters, media-based appeals grew in importance. Voter attitudes evolve during the course of the nomination contest, in large part because of the media's influence. The media help determine who the viable candidates are, label the "winners" and "losers," and influence the results of future contests as voters as well as contributors gravitate toward the winners and desert the losers. Public opinion polls reflecting voters' presidential preferences are a fixture of media coverage. Favorable polls impress media representatives as well as political activists and many rank-and-file voters, leading to more victories for the poll leaders in both nonprimary and primary contests. The result of this reinforcement process is that by the time the delegates gather for their party's national convention, one candidate usually has enough delegates to receive the nomination.[35] The last remaining hurdle for the front-runner to navigate is for the most part automatic—the party's national convention.

The National Convention

No part of the selection process has undergone more dramatic change than the presidential nominating conventions. Long the province of kingmakers, today's conventions are largely media extravaganzas carefully choreographed to project images designed to reawaken party loyalty, appeal to contemporary public concerns, and project the most desirable aspects of the newly anointed presidential ticket. In short, the national convention is important to presidential candidates for two reasons. First, whatever may have happened during the long search for delegates, the actual nomination occurs at the convention. Second, a well-run convention can help candidates win the general election.

Nominating the Ticket

Since the early 1950s, conventions have offered little drama about the choice of the presidential nominee. In the twenty-six conventions held by the two major parties since World War II, only two nominees—Thomas Dewey in 1948 and Adlai Stevenson in 1952—failed to win a majority of the convention votes on the first ballot. In all other cases, victory has gone to the candidate who arrived at the convention with the largest number of pledged delegates.

Selecting the vice presidential nominee is the convention's final chore and the only chance to create any suspense. Although in theory the delegates make the choice, it has been a matter of political custom since 1940 to allow presidential nominees to pick their own running mates after conferring with leaders whose judgment they trust. Parties traditionally attempt to balance the ticket—that is, broaden its appeal by selecting a person who differs in certain ways from the presidential nominee. Bush's links to the eastern establishment and moderate wings of the Republican Party complemented the conservative, western Reagan in 1980. Ferraro balanced the 1984 Democratic ticket geographically and in other ways: the first woman to serve as a major party candidate in a presidential contest, she was also the first Italian American.

In 1988 Dan Quayle brought generational balance to the ticket, and he was enthusiastically supported by the party's conservative wing. But the media raised questions about Quayle's ability to perform as president should the need arise, his service in the National Guard during the Vietnam War, and his modest academic performance. Quayle remained on the Republican ticket in 1992 despite speculation about his replacement. Clinton violated political tradition by selecting Al Gore, a fellow southerner and baby boomer, rather than balancing the ticket, but the choice was well received by the party faithful and probably helped Clinton erode Republican support in this crucial region. Dole chose Jack Kemp as his running mate in 1996, a one-time presidential candidate who was highly popular with Republican activists. Clinton retained the faithful Gore.

The final night of the convention is devoted to acceptance speeches. The presidential nominee tries to make peace with former competitors and to reunite various party factions that have confronted one another during the long campaign and the hectic days of the convention. Major party figures usually come to the stage and pledge their support for the winner in the upcoming campaign.

Conducting Party Business

The convention's location may boost the chances of a favorite son candidate—for example, Chicago for Adlai Stevenson in 1952—or prove an insurmountable disadvantage, such as the Democrats' 1968 debacle in the same city. Fear was expressed by some Democrats that a return to Chicago in 1996 would remind television viewers of the 1968 divisiveness more than the 1952 unity. At times credentials committees have had to resolve disputes between contending delegations; their decisions on who would be considered the official delegates could influence the outcome, as in 1972 with George McGovern's nomination. Candidates trailing the front-runner sometimes use a rules question as their last-ditch effort to derail the nomination, a ploy attempted by Reagan in 1976 and Sen. Edward Kennedy in 1980.

Parties continue the writing and adopting of a convention platform, although participants acknowledge that winning presidential candidates may disavow planks with which they disagree. Because delegates, party leaders, and major groups affiliated with the party have strong feelings about some issues, the platform provides an opportunity to resolve differences and find a politically palatable position.[36] Civil rights and the Vietnam War once prompted major disagreements within the Democratic Party; civil rights, foreign policy, and abortion have been major bones of contention among Republicans.

Despite intraparty differences, conventions provide strong incentives for compromise, to bring back to the fold a disgruntled segment of the party that might otherwise offer only lukewarm support during the fall election or launch a third party effort. To avoid such damage, almost every presidential candidate decides to provide major rivals and their supporters with concessions in the platform and a prime-time speaking opportunity during the convention. In 1988 Dukakis accepted modified versions of nine of Jesse Jackson's platform positions in exchange for Jackson's acceptance of a shorter, less-detailed party statement. At the Republican convention in 1992, Pat Buchanan was given an opportunity to address a national audience, but his address proved so controversial that the invitation was not extended in 1996.

National nominating conventions have become so predictable that network television coverage was dramatically reduced in 1996 to one hour for each of the first three nights and two hours for the final night's acceptance speech. This was a far cry from the traditional "gavel to gavel" coverage that ushered in the television age, and some observers predicted no network would cover the next round of conventions in 2000. Instead, CNN and other cable networks would assume the job. Parties may have become so adept at scripting these quadrennial gatherings that their very existence is jeopardized.[37]

The General Election

With nominees selected, the nation moves into the general election period. Candidates must develop new political appeals for this stage of the process, which is a one-on-one contest that pits the nominees of the two major parties against each other (although a strong independent candidate like Ross Perot may also run). The campaign's audience increases greatly—more than twice as many people vote in the general election as participate in the nomination process. Candidates and staff members therefore must decide how they can win the support of these new voters as well as appeal to people who identify with the other party and partisans who backed losing candidates for the nomination. A further complication is time: this nationwide phase of the presidential contest is compressed into a mere ten weeks, traditionally running from Labor Day to election day.

The general election phase differs from the nomination phase for two reasons: the way the electoral college works and the distinctive provisions of the campaign finance laws. Compared with changes effected in the nomination stage, the constitutional requirements surrounding the president's election have been remarkably stable over time, but campaign finance laws have undergone significant change since 1972. Both are critical considerations in how the campaign is waged.

The Electoral College

To understand how candidates plan and carry out their general election strategies, it is necessary to keep in mind the ultimate goal, which is to win a majority of electoral college votes. Two hundred years ago delegates to the constitutional convention rejected the two most popular plans for choosing the president. They felt that selection by Congress violated the separation of powers principle, but they did not have enough confidence in the people's wisdom to approve direct popular election.[38] The newly devised plan was complicated: each state legislature would choose electors, by whatever means it desired, equal to its total number of senators and representatives in Congress (but none of the electors could be members of Congress or hold other national office); the individual electors would assemble at a fixed time in their respective state capitals and cast two votes each for president; the votes would be transmitted to the seat of government and opened and counted during a joint session of Congress. Whoever received the largest number of electoral votes, provided a majority—one more than half—had been obtained, would be declared the winner. If no candidate received a majority, the House of Representatives, voting by states (one state delegation, one vote), would choose the president from among the five candidates receiving the highest number of electoral votes. After the president was chosen, the person with the next highest number of electoral votes became the vice president. If two or more of these contenders received an equal number of electoral votes, the Senate would choose the vice president from among them. As noted, these procedures were modified in 1804 by the Twelfth Amendment, which established separate balloting for president and vice president and reduced the field to three candidates if the House and Senate had to vote.

This method of selection resolved the struggle between large and small states, upheld states' rights by allowing the state legislatures to decide how the electors should be chosen, and left open the possibility that electors could reflect the popular vote for president in their state. With the rapid expansion of popular participation, state legislators began giving the right to choose electors to the general electorate; by 1836 all states except South Carolina had adopted such rules, and the latter did so in 1860.

At first, electoral votes were determined by congressional districts—the winner of a popular vote plurality in each district would receive the associated electoral vote, with the statewide winner of the popular vote getting the two electoral votes representing senators. Legislatures soon, however, began to adopt the "unit" or "general-ticket" rule, whereby all the state's electoral votes went to the candidate who received the plurality of the statewide popular vote. This rule benefited the state's majority party and maximized the state's influence in the election by permitting it to throw all its electoral votes to one candidate. By 1836 the district plan had vanished and the unit system had taken its place. Since then two states have returned to the old plan: Maine has followed the district plan since 1969, and Nebraska adopted it for 1992.

The final product is a strange method for choosing a chief executive. Although most Americans view the system as a popular election, it is not. When voters mark their ballots, the vote actually determines which slate of electors pledged to support the party's presidential candidate will have the opportunity to vote. In a few states, electors' names appear on the ballot either with or without the presidential candidate's name. The electors are party loyalists, chosen in primaries, at conventions, or by state committees. In mid-December the electors associated with the winning candidate meet in their state capitals to cast ballots. (About one-third of the states attempt by law to bind the electors to vote for the winner of the popular vote, but there is some question whether such laws are constitutional.) The electoral votes are transmitted to Washington, D.C., and counted early in January of the following year. Next, the presiding officer of the Senate, who is the incumbent vice president, announces the outcome before a joint session of Congress. If, as usually happens, one candidate receives an absolute majority of the electoral votes, currently 270, the vice president officially declares that candidate to be president. Because the winner of the popular vote usually wins in the electoral college as well, we call this final stage of the selection process the "validation" of the popular vote outcome.

Financing the General Election

The financial resources needed to mount a nationwide campaign are significantly greater than those required to win the nomination. For the general election, complete public financing is provided to nominees of the major parties, and any party that won 25 percent or more of the popular vote in the last presidential election is considered a major party. In the 1996 presidential election, the federal government gave each major party candidate $61.8 million, up from $55.24 million in 1992. Ross Perot sought no federal funds in 1992, but spent an estimated $63 million of his own money to mount a major campaign effort. In 1996, however, he accepted $29 million in federal funds and was limited to using only $50,000 of his own money in the general election. To qualify for federal funds, nominees must not accept other direct contributions to their campaign. Candidates of minor parties, those that won between 5 percent and 25 percent of the vote in the previous election, receive partial public financing. Candidates of parties that won less than 5 percent of the vote in the previous election can be partially reimbursed after the current election if they receive at least 5 percent of that vote.

Campaign expenditures other than those from public funding may be made from two sources. There is no limit on *independent campaign expenditures*, which are made by individuals or political committees that advocate the defeat or election of a presidential candidate but are not made in conjunction with a candidate's campaign. In addition, state and local party organizations may spend money for any purpose except campaign advertising and the hiring of outside personnel. Until 1996, these funds, commonly called *soft money*, had largely been used for grass-roots activities such as distributing campaign buttons, stickers, and yard signs; registering voters; and transporting voters to the polls. Spending from both these sources has varied: between 1988 and 1992, independent expenditures declined from $10.1 million to about $4 million and soft money expenditures remained steady at $42.5 million.[39] But in 1996 the Democratic and Republican parties enormously expanded their use of soft money to fund *issue advocacy* campaigns, media advertisements that do not expressly support or oppose a candidate but educate the public about an issue or a candidate's position on an issue. The Democratic National Committee launched an aggressive series of such ads in mid-1995 designed to help Clinton even before the nomination contests began; when Dole ran short of money in late spring 1996, the Republican National Committee stepped in with a similar campaign to help their expected standard-bearer. The combined result was unprecedented spending under a campaign finance loophole that led the parties to raise a combined $263.5 million in soft money contributions that are not subject to size limitations. The result was a return to "fat cat" contributions from wealthy individuals, corporations, and labor unions. Included among these were millions collected by the DNC from foreign sources that became a source of major controversy during the final weeks of the campaign and the topic of congressional inquiries in 1997.[40]

The introduction of public financing in the 1976 election has generally been viewed as a success: major party candidates no longer depended on wealthy contributors and other private sources to finance their

Figure 2-2   State Size by Number of Electoral Votes, 1992 and 1996

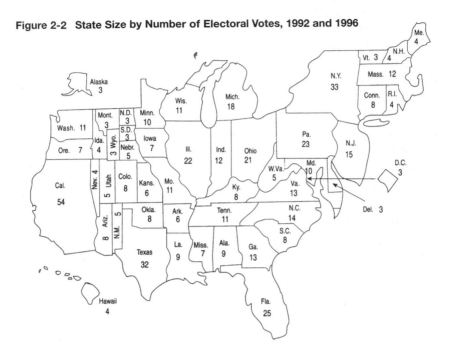

campaigns; expenditures of the two major party candidates were limited and equalized, an advantage for Democrats who were historically outspent by their opponents.[41] On the other hand, the law clearly benefits the candidates of the two major parties, whose candidates receive full public financing of their general election campaigns, while minor party candidates are entitled to only partial financing, if any at all.[42] More important, however, the 1996 experience with soft money has called into question the adequacy of current legislation and its future. In the absence of further reform, financing the election in 2000 looms as an enormous unknown.

Targeting the Campaign

As in the nomination process, presidential candidates must decide which states will be the focus of their efforts in the fall campaign. By far the most important consideration is the electoral college. The candidate's task is clear: to win the presidency, he or she must win a majority—270—of the 538 electoral votes.[43] This fact places a premium on carrying the states with the largest number of electoral votes *(see Figure*

2-2). In 1996, by winning the eleven largest states—California, New York, Texas, Florida, Pennsylvania, Illinois, Ohio, Michigan, New Jersey, North Carolina, and Georgia—a candidate could win the presidency while losing the other thirty-nine states. Naturally, candidates from both major political parties concentrate their personal visits on the most populous states.[44]

Another element that affects candidates' decisions on where to campaign is the political situation in a particular state—that is, whether the state generally goes to one party's candidate or whether it swings back and forth from one election to the next. Distinctly one-party states are likely to be slighted by the major party candidates—both will think it a waste of time, although for different reasons. Swing states with large populations naturally draw a good deal of attention from presidential candidates of both parties.

In formulating campaign strategy, therefore, candidates and their advisers start with the electoral map as modified by calculations of probable success. The electoral college creates fifty-one separate presidential contests—fifty states plus the District of Columbia—primarily following the winner-take-all principle, the goal of which is a popular vote victory in each, no matter how small the margin of victory may be. The winner in a large state benefits from the unit or general-ticket system by getting all of the state's electoral votes. In 1992 Bill Clinton won California, an electoral prize with fifty-four votes, 20 percent of the total needed for election, but the combined total of popular votes for George Bush and the independent candidate Ross Perot exceeded Clinton's total by more than 800,000. Clinton's total in 1996, however, easily exceeded his rivals' combined votes.

Electoral votes were reapportioned for the 1992 presidential election, reflecting the results of the 1990 census. Eight states gained seats in the House of Representatives, and thirteen lost seats; the states' electoral vote totals were adjusted accordingly, with political influence moving (along with the population) from the Northeast/Midwest to the South/Southwest. The biggest gains were recorded in California—its delegation increased by seven seats—Florida (four seats), and Texas (three seats). On the other end, New York lost three seats, while Illinois, Michigan, Ohio, and Pennsylvania lost two seats each, and several other states lost one seat.[45]

The regions that have been important in recent presidential contests are the Middle Atlantic states of New Jersey, New York, and Pennsylvania and the Midwest states of Illinois, Michigan, Missouri, and Ohio.

These seven highly industrial states control 143 electoral votes and also tend to be highly competitive, which means that campaign efforts there can be very important in deciding which candidate prevails. Because they are so often the focus of campaign efforts, analysts refer to them as the "battleground" states.

Before 1992 the Democrats had confronted a particularly difficult strategic situation: in looking at presidential balloting between 1968 and 1984, some commentators felt the Republicans had constructed an "electoral lock" on the presidency because twenty-three states with 202 electoral votes had gone for the Republican candidate in each of the five elections. Democratic candidates had won only the District of Columbia with the same level of consistency.[46] West Coast, Rocky Mountain, and Midwest states comprised this staunchly Republican cohort along with a few surprises such as Illinois, New Jersey, and Virginia.

A good part of the Democrats' problem can be traced to the historic realignment of the South in presidential politics. Long a bastion of solid Democratic support and critical to their candidates' success—until 1992 no Democrat had ever won the White House without carrying a majority of southern states—southern voters had not supported the party's nominee since 1976, when they helped to elect Jimmy Carter, the first southern presidential nominee other than Lyndon Baines Johnson, who had succeeded to the office, since before the Civil War. Even that support evaporated in 1980, when only Georgia supported its favorite son. No southern state voted for the Democratic ticket in 1984 or 1988. The Solid South was a Republican stronghold until Clinton cut into Bush's support in 1992 by winning four states: Arkansas, Georgia, Louisiana, and Tennessee. Clinton added support from the West, Midwest, and the Mountain States to the Democratic strongholds in the Northeast. In 1992 the Democrats won each state that had voted for Dukakis and added all but one of the twelve where he had won at least 45 percent of the vote in 1988, a significant part of the thirty-two states carried by Clinton.[47] He won twenty-nine of the same states in 1996 and added two longtime Republican strongholds—Florida and Arizona—while narrowly losing in Colorado, Georgia, and Montana, states carried in 1992.

Electoral college considerations are fundamental to every campaign's strategy for victory. Clinton's broad strength in 1996 meant that Dole's options were limited. The Republican's original plan to contest most of the Midwest battleground states while holding Texas and Florida was altered as polls revealed little headway in narrowing the president's lead. Pennsylvania, New Jersey, Connecticut, and Ohio became the focus until just three weeks before the election, when the decision was made to redirect resources and effort to California. In the end, Texas was the only large state that supported Dole. Ross Perot's popularity complicated strategy in 1992, when he won 19 percent of the popular vote, but was far less significant in 1996, when he won only 8 percent. In neither election did Perot garner any electoral votes.[48] *(For 1996 election results, see Appendix A.)*

Appealing for Public Support

Presidential campaigns spend millions of dollars and untold hours of effort pursuing two goals: to motivate people to vote on election day and to win their support for a particular candidate. Several factors other than campaign appeals determine who votes and how. Voters' choices depend on their long-term political predispositions, such as political party loyalties and social group affiliations, and their reactions to short-term forces, such as the particular candidates and issues involved in specific elections. Candidates and their teams of campaign professionals try to design appeals that activate these influences, attract support, and counter perceived weaknesses.

Because the general election audience is larger and the time shorter, presidential candidates use their resources primarily for mass media appeals. Advertising expenditures have risen accordingly, with campaigns spending half their public funding on radio and primarily television advertising. Since 1952, television has been the chief source of campaign information for most Americans. In addition, polls indicate that people are more inclined to believe what they see on television than what they read in the newspapers or hear on the radio. Increasingly, however, advertising is targeted on selected markets in key electoral college states rather than being national in scope.

Long-Term Influences. Students of elections have categorized influences on voter decisions as either long-term or short-term. Long-term influences include partisanship and group membership, while the short-term ones include issues, candidate image, and campaign incidents.

Partisan loyalty, although still important for a large part of the public, has become less significant as a determinant of election outcomes. Conditions have changed considerably since a group of researchers studying presidential elections in the 1950s concluded that the single most important determinant of voting at that time was the *party identification* of the voter.[49] This general psychological attachment, shaped by family and social groups, tended to intensify with age. For the average person looking for guidance on how to vote amid the complexities of personalities, issues, and events of the 1950s, the party label of the candidates was the most important reference point. At that time partisanship was also fairly constant—about 45 percent of Americans in 1952 and 1956 said they thought of themselves as Democrats, and about 28 percent viewed themselves as Republicans, for a combined total of nearly three-fourths of the electorate. When asked to classify themselves further as "strong" or "weak" partisans, both Republicans and Democrats tended to divide equally between those two categories. Independents in 1952 and 1956 averaged about 23 percent of the electorate.

In the mid-to-late 1960s, however, partisan affiliation in the United States began to change (see Table 2-3). Beginning with the 1968 election, the number of independents started to increase, primarily at the expense of the Democrats, until they constituted one-third of the electorate in 1972. Even those voters who stayed with the Democrats were more inclined than formerly to say they were weak rather than strong party members. Since 1968, more people also identify themselves as independents than as Republicans. This trend progressed one step further in 1988, when some polls found that independents outnumbered Democrats for the first time. The rise in the number of independents has occurred primarily among young people, particularly those who entered the electorate in 1964 or later. Voters who have come of age since that time are much more likely to be political independents than are voters of earlier political generations, a development that has been linked to the influence of Vietnam and Watergate.

Partisanship fell to its lowest level between 1972 and 1976 and sank again to that level in 1992, with a modest uptick in 1996. Although the trend away from party affiliation seemed to stop, the parties have been unable to lure the public back. After 1980, Republicans scored modest gains of roughly 5 to 10 percent, which offset Democratic losses of the same size. The picture remained remarkably stable until 1992, with just under two-thirds of citizens expressing a party identification. Considered in light of their enormous success in winning presidential elections, Republican gains were more limited than one might expect until apparent gains in 1994 and 1996.

Given the patterns of party identification, it is not surprising to find that Democrats designed appeals to reinforce traditional party loyalties, while Republicans, as the minority party, urged voters to ignore party labels. Moreover, Republicans associated themselves with the memories

Table 2–3 Party Identification, 1952–1996 (Percent)

Party	1952	1956	1960	1964	1968	1972	1976	1980	1984	1988	1992	1994	1996
Strong Democrat	22	21	20	27	20	15	15	18	17	18	18	15	19
Weak Democrat	25	23	25	25	25	26	25	23	20	18	18	19	19
Total	47	44	45	52	45	41	40	41	37	36	35	34	38
Strong Republican	14	14	16	11	10	10	9	9	10	14	11	16	13
Weak Republican	13	15	14	14	15	13	14	14	15	14	14	15	15
Total	27	29	30	25	25	23	23	23	25	28	26	31	28
Independent	22	24	23	23	30	35	37	34	34	36	38	35	33

Source: *Statistical Abstract of the United States, 1994*, Table 446 (Washington, D.C.: Government Printing Office, 1994). 1996 figures based on preliminary analysis by author of national election studies data from Center for Political Studies at the University of Michigan's Institute for Social Research.

of former Democratic leaders; Ronald Reagan, who before his political conversion in the 1960s had been a lifelong Democrat, used this technique effectively. Party appeals are not as powerful today, however, as they were in the past.

Social group membership is another potentially important influence on voting that candidates try to tap. Patterns of group support established during the New Deal have persisted during succeeding decades, although with decreasing vibrancy. In the 1940s Democrats received most of their support from southerners, blacks, Catholics, and people with limited education, lower incomes, and a working-class background. Republican candidates were supported by northerners, whites, Protestants, and people with more education, higher incomes, and a professional or business background. Table 2-4 shows how various groups voted in selected presidential elections from 1952 through 1996. The support of many groups for their traditional party's candidates declined over the forty-year period. The most significant drop for the Democrats came in the southern white vote: by 1988 only one in three white votes in the South went to Dukakis, and only 26 percent of white males supported the Democrat.[50] The only group that significantly increased its support for its traditional party candidate over this period was nonwhites, whose support for Democrats strengthened between 1964 and 1988 but has now returned to the 1952 level.[51]

Table 2-4 also shows that group preferences can vary greatly from election to election. In 1964, when the very conservative Barry Goldwater was the Republican standard-bearer, all the groups, including those that typically support the GOP, supported the Democratic candidate, Lyndon Johnson. In 1972 the opposite occurred; when the very liberal George McGovern ran on the Democratic ticket, all the groups that usually sympathize with that party, except for nonwhites, voted for Richard Nixon, the Republican candidate. In 1992 Bush's support declined from 1988 levels in virtually every category, but the decline was especially marked among men, the college-educated, and baby boomers, the voters between thirty and forty-nine. Dole rebounded among men and the college-educated but not enough for victory in 1996.

The weakening of party loyalties means that candidates must target many groups. Organized labor, far from a monolithic entity, has been seriously divided in recent elections, and ethnic groups have been openly courted by both camps. Moreover, new groups have emerged as critical factors: women, fundamentalist Christians, young voters, and His-

Table 2-4 Group Voting Patterns in Presidential Elections, Selected Years (Percent)

| | 1952 | | 1960 | | 1964 | | 1968 | | | 1972 | |
| | | (R) | | (R) | | (R) | | (R) | | | (R) |
Group	Stevenson	Eisenhower	Kennedy	Nixon	Johnson	Goldwater	Humphrey	Nixon	Wallace	McGovern	Nixon
Sex											
male	47	53	52	48	60	40	41	43	16	37	63
female	42	58	49	51	62	38	45	43	12	38	62
Race											
white	43	57	49	51	59	41	38	47	15	32	68
nonwhite	79	21	68	32	94	6	85	12	3	87	13
Education											
college	34	66	39	61	52	48	37	54	9	37	63
high school	45	55	52	48	62	38	42	43	15	34	66
grade school	52	48	55	45	66	34	52	33	15	49	51
Occupation											
professional, business	36	64	42	58	54	46	34	56	10	31	69
white collar	40	60	48	52	57	43	41	47	12	36	64
manual	55	45	60	40	71	29	50	35	15	43	57
Age											
under 30	51	49	54	45	64	36	47	38	15	48	52
30–49	47	53	54	46	63	37	44	41	15	33	67
50 and older	39	61	46	54	59	41	41	47	12	36	64
Religion											
Protestant	37	63	38	62	55	45	35	49	16	30	70
Catholic	56	44	78	22	76	24	59	33	8	48	52
Region											
East	45	55	53	47	68	32	50	43	7	42	58
Midwest	42	58	48	52	61	39	44	47	9	40	60
South	51	49	51	49	52	48	31	36	33	29	71
West	42	58	49	51	60	40	44	49	7	41	59
Members of labor union families	61	39	65	35	73	27	56	29	15	46	54
National	45	55	50	50	61	39	43	43	14	38	62

Sources: Excerpted from *Gallup Report,* November 1988, 6, 7; *The Gallup Poll Monthly,* November 1992, 9; 1996 data provided by Gallup Organization from poll conducted November 3 to November 4, 1996.

Note: NA = Not available.

Table 2-4 (Continued)

1976		1980			1988		1992			1996		
	(R)		(R)			(R)	(R)				(R)	
Carter	Ford	Carter	Reagan	Anderson	Dukakis	Bush	Bush	Clinton	Perot	Clinton	Dole	Perot
53	45	38	53	7	44	56	37	39	19	45	39	11
48	51	44	49	6	48	52	36	48	10	53	34	6
46	52	36	56	7	41	59	40	40	15	44	41	9
85	15	86	10	2	82	18	12	76	4	78	9	4
42	55	35	53	10	42	58	39	43	14	44	44	6
54	46	43	51	5	46	54	37	45	12	52	30	11
58	41	54	42	3	55	45	35	43	15	NA	NA	NA
42	56	33	55	10	NA	NA	NA	NA	NA	NA	—	—
50	48	40	51	9	NA	NA	NA	NA	NA	NA	—	—
58	41	48	46	5	NA	NA	NA	NA	NA	NA	—	—
53	45	47	41	11	37	63	44	38	14	54	27	13
48	49	38	52	8	45	55	35	43	17	49	36	10
52	48	41	54	4	49	51	37	46	11	48	39	6
46	53	39	54	6	42	58	NA	NA	NA	NA	—	—
57	42	46	47	6	51	49	NA	NA	NA	NA	—	—
51	47	43	47	9	51	49	33	47	15	59	26	9
48	50	41	51	7	47	53	35	45	13	47	39	8
54	45	44	52	3	40	60	42	40	13	45	39	9
46	51	35	54	9	46	54	36	43	15	48	38	8
63	36	50	43	5	63	37	NA	NA	NA	NA	—	—
50	48	41	51	7	46	54	37	44	14	49	36	9

panics have attracted particular attention. But because many American voters have lost their partisan anchor, short-term influences—such as candidates, issues, events—and presidential performance are now more important to them.

Short-Term Influences. What are voters looking for in a president? Pollsters working with presidential campaigns try to project their candidate's most attractive features and direct voter attention to the opponent's least attractive features. During the 1984 campaign, for example, the Michigan Center for Political Studies asked citizens to evaluate Reagan and Mondale on twelve specific personal traits, combined into four summary measures: (1) leadership (commands respect, is inspiring, provides strong leadership); (2) competence (is hard-working, intelligent, and knowledgeable); (3) integrity (is decent, is moral, sets a good example); and (4) empathy (is compassionate, is kind, "really cares about people like you"). In contrast to some expectations, Reagan was favored over Mondale on only two of those four measures, leadership and integrity. Mondale prevailed on competence and empathy, and only on leadership was Reagan's margin substantial.[52]

In a 1988 election day poll, voters concerned with experience and competence overwhelmingly supported Bush, while those who wanted a more caring president and one more likely to introduce change disproportionately supported Dukakis. Those who saw Dukakis as too liberal predictably supported Bush, but those worried about dirty campaigns leaned toward Dukakis.[53] In a 1992 exit poll that asked voters what qualities mattered most in deciding how they voted, more than one-third cited the ability to bring about change, with Clinton winning 67 percent of those votes. Clinton also led among voters concerned about which candidate had the best plan for the nation, cared about people, and had the best vice presidential candidate. Bush led among voters concerned with experience, trustworthiness, and good judgment in a crisis.[54] In 1996 Dole won 84 percent of those mentioning honesty and trustworthiness (20 percent of respondents), but Clinton won 72–89 percent of those who mentioned caring, having a vision for the future, and being in touch with the 1990s, more than one-third of the voters.[55]

Because the public focuses so much attention in a presidential campaign on the candidates themselves, the personality and character the aspirants project are particularly important. Each campaign organization strives to create a composite image of its candidate's most attractive features. To do this sometimes means transforming liabilities into assets:

age becomes mature judgment (Dwight Eisenhower); youth and inexperience become vigor (John Kennedy). Alternatively, a candidate can direct attention to the opponent's personal liabilities, a move that has proved beneficial even though some voters see such an effort as dirty campaigning and beneath the dignity of the office.

The 1988 and 1992 campaigns provide better examples of how candidates try to shape each other's image than 1996. Bush succeeded in creating a negative portrait of Dukakis in 1988, but the tactic proved less successful against Clinton. Dukakis enjoyed a largely favorable image before the summer conventions, but Bush's pollsters discovered it was based on very little information.[56] Interviews conducted with small groups of Democrats who had supported Reagan in 1980 and 1984 determined which features of Dukakis's record they found most upsetting. The Bush campaign then portrayed the Democrat as sympathetic to criminals, weak on defense, opposed to saying the pledge of allegiance in school, and a liberal who favored high taxes and big government. Dukakis's effort to paint an unflattering image of Bush was far less successful.[57] Bush launched a similar effort against Clinton in 1992 when he focused on trust and taxes in the final weeks. Earlier efforts to picture Clinton as the failed governor of a crime-filled state with environmental problems and as an unpatriotic antiwar activist had not proved successful. In contrast to the situation in 1988, observers demanded more supporting evidence, and Clinton met all negative charges with broadcast rebuttals and attacks of his own that focused on Bush's role in the Iran-contra incident, pro-Iraq actions of his administration prior to the Persian Gulf War, and Bush's violation of 1988 campaign promises. By leaving no charge unanswered, Clinton succeeded where Dukakis had faltered. In 1996 Clinton's ads blended positive portrayals of himself with unflattering, black and white accounts of Dole's long public career (during which he aged perceptibly), including his original opposition to Medicare and votes for tax increases. The Republican was often pictured with Newt Gingrich to suggest his link to extreme views. Dole's criticism of Clinton was unfocused but included the president's record on crime, teenage drug use, administration corruption, and taxes. "Trust" was a positive trait that Dole claimed for himself and contrasted with Clinton's shaky integrity. Even though Clinton's ads seemed more critical in content, the public viewed the Dole campaign as more negative.[58]

Issues are the other major short-term influence on voting behavior. University of Michigan researchers in the 1950s suggested that issues influence a voter's choice only if three conditions are present: the voter is aware that an issue or a number of issues exist; issues are of some personal concern to the voter; and the voter perceives that one party represents his or her position better than the other party does.[59] When the three conditions were applied to U.S. voters in the 1952 and 1956 presidential elections, researchers found that these criteria existed for relatively few voters. About one-third of the respondents were unaware of *any* of the sixteen principal issues about which they were questioned. Even the two-thirds who were aware of one or more issues frequently had no personal concern about them. Finally, many of those who were aware and concerned about issues were unable to perceive differences between the two parties' positions. The analysts concluded that issues *potentially* determined the choice of, at the most, only one-third of the electorate. (The proportion who *actually* voted as they did because of issues could have been, and probably was, even less.)

Studies of political attitudes in the 1960s and 1970s demonstrate a change: the number and types of issues of which voters were aware increased.[60] Voters during the Eisenhower years had exhibited some interest in traditional domestic matters, such as welfare and labor-management relationships, and in a few foreign policy issues, like the threat of communism and the danger of the atomic bomb. Beginning with the 1964 election, however, voters' interests broadened to include concerns such as civil rights and the Vietnam War. The war in particular remained an important consideration in the 1968 and 1972 contests and was joined by new matters such as crime, disorder, and juvenile delinquency—sometimes referred to collectively along with race problems as "social issues." Naturally, the issues that are salient vary from election to election.

Incumbency. Incumbency may be viewed as a candidate characteristic that also involves issues. Service in the job provides experience that no one else can claim. Incumbency also provides concrete advantages in conducting a campaign: an incumbent already has national campaign experience (true for all incumbents in U.S. history except Gerald Ford), can obtain media coverage more easily, and has considerable discretion in allocating benefits selectively. As noted earlier, incumbency has been especially important since World War II because of the pattern of recruitment. Until Bush's victory in 1988 incumbency seemed to provide advantages solely to presidents and not to incumbent vice presidents.

Of the five incumbent presidents who ran for reelection between 1976 and 1996, only Reagan and Clinton succeeded, and of the last three incumbent vice presidents who sought the presidency, only Bush was elected. The defeats of Ford, Carter, and Bush demonstrate the disadvantages of incumbency, particularly if service in the presidency coincides with negative economic developments such as recession and high inflation or an unresolved foreign crisis for which a president is blamed, even if erroneously. Experience in the job, then, is not a political plus if a sitting president's record is considered weak or national conditions seem to have deteriorated under the incumbent's stewardship. The president may be held accountable by voters who cast their ballots *retrospectively* rather than *prospectively;* in other words, these voters evaluate an administration's past performance rather than try to predict future performance.

Retrospective voting has been suggested as the major explanation for Carter's defeat in 1980 and Bush's in 1992. To illustrate the problem, one can contrast what many perceived as Carter's failure to resolve the hostage crisis in Iran with the respect that many believed the nation enjoyed after Reagan's first term. Bush's foreign policy success in the Persian Gulf War made his apparent inaction in dealing with the slowing economy all the more vivid. In the 1996 election, Clinton benefited from the conditions of peace and prosperity during his first term.

Presidential Debates. Voters have the opportunity to assess the issue positions and personal characteristics of presidential and vice presidential contenders during nationally televised debates. Debates were staged first in 1960 and then each year since 1976, and they quickly became the most important and most widely watched campaign events. Candidates recognize the danger of making a mistake or an embarrassing gaffe on live television, a particular danger for incumbents. Ford misspoke in 1976 when he suggested that countries of Eastern Europe were not under Soviet domination; Reagan appeared to be confused and out of touch during his first debate with Mondale in 1984 but rallied in the second encounter. Challengers try to demonstrate their knowledge of issues and their presidential bearing to a nationwide audience. Kennedy in 1960 and Reagan in 1980 seem to have benefited the most from debating a more experienced opponent, in part because they exceeded performance expectations and dispelled negative impressions. Most candidates prepare carefully prior to the meeting and follow a conservative game plan of reemphasizing themes already made prominent during the campaign. As a result, the exchanges often seem wooden rather than extemporaneous, an impression heightened by the cautious rules approved by the respective camps.

In 1992 the first three-way presidential debates in history included Ross Perot, who met the two party nominees in three different formats: questions posed by the traditional panel of journalists, by citizens at a town meeting, and by a single moderator. The formats allowed for greater interaction and extemporaneous exchange among the contestants rather than triggering the patented responses that have characterized so many of these meetings in the past. Perot's humor and homespun one-liners spiced up the first debate; Clinton's ease and command of issues shone forth in the second town meeting format; Bush was most aggressive and effective in the third meeting, although his advantage was not overwhelming. Perot did not get the same chance in 1996, however. The Commission on Presidential Debates concluded that the Reform Party candidate could not win the election, and he was excluded from participating, much to the relief of the Dole campaign which feared a split in the anti-Clinton vote. The result was a pair of relatively lackluster encounters before an audience half the size of that in 1992.[61] Clinton fended off Dole's criticism in both the single moderator and town meeting formats; Dole acquitted himself better than many had expected and avoided personal attacks, but Clinton was judged the winner of both encounters.

Single vice presidential debates were held in 1988, 1992, and 1996. Dan Quayle's performance was the focus of the first two encounters. Much younger than Lloyd Bentsen, his 1988 opponent, Quayle was repeatedly asked what he would do if forced to assume the duties of president. When Quayle compared himself to former president John F. Kennedy, Bentsen pounced with withering directness: "Senator, I served with Jack Kennedy. I knew Jack Kennedy. Jack Kennedy was a friend of mine. Senator, you're no Jack Kennedy." Quayle never recovered. In 1992 Quayle debated Al Gore, the Democrat, and James Stockdale, Perot's running mate, who watched as his younger opponents struggled to dominate one another. Gore's encounter with Jack Kemp in 1996 could have been a preview of the presidential contestants in 2000. Gore was so focused on the campaign message that he appeared even more wooden than usual, while Kemp disappointed fellow partisans who had hoped he would repeat Quayle's 1992 aggressiveness.

Table 2-5 Participation of General Public In Presidential Elections, 1932–1996

Year	Estimated population of voting age (in millions)	Number of votes cast (in millions)	Number of votes as percentage of population of voting age
1932	75.8	39.7	52.4
1936	80.2	45.6	56.0
1940	84.7	49.9	58.9
1944	85.7	48.0	56.0
1948	95.6	48.8	51.1
1952	99.9	61.6	61.6
1956	104.5	62.0	59.3
1960	109.7	68.8	62.8
1964	114.1	70.6	61.9
1968	120.3	73.2	60.9
1972 [a]	140.8	77.6	55.1
1976 [a]	152.3	81.6	53.6
1980 [a]	164.6	86.5	52.6
1984 [a]	174.5	92.7	53.1
1988 [a]	182.8	91.6	50.1
1992 [a]	189.0	104.4	55.2
1996 [a]	196.5 (est.)	96.46	49.1

Sources: U.S. Bureau of the Census, *Current Population Reports*, Series P-25, No. 1085 (Washington, D.C.: U.S. Government Printing Office, 1994). 1996 data from Federal Election Commission Web site *(www.fec.gov)*.

[a] Elections in which persons eighteen to twenty years old were eligible to vote in all states.

Televised debates enable even the least engaged citizen to develop an impression of the major party contenders. However, candidates have become more adept at staging, and the public may now expect more than just a polite exchange of policy challenges.

Election Day

One of the ironies of U.S. presidential elections since 1960 is that, although more citizens have acquired the right to vote, a smaller proportion of them have exercised that right. As Table 2-5 indicates, the estimated number of people of voting age has more than doubled since Franklin Roosevelt was first elected in 1932. After reaching a peak in 1960, however, the percentage of people who voted declined in the next five presidential elections and resumed its decline in 1988 after a modest increase in 1984. Only 50.1 percent of the eligible voting age population went to the polls in 1998, but this pattern was reversed dramatically in 1992 when 55.2 percent of the eligible voters went to the polls.[62] The resurgence was short-lived; only 49.08 percent of eligible voters showed up in 1996, the lowest turnout since 1924.

The decline in voter participation runs counter to most theories of why people do not vote. Laws pertaining to registration and voting, said to prevent citizens from going to the polls, have been eased in most states. Federal laws have made it much easier for a person to register and to vote for president in 1996 than it was in 1960. A person's lack of education is often put forward as a reason for not voting, but the level of education of U.S. citizens rose as participation declined. Lack of political information is yet another frequently cited explanation, but more Americans than ever are aware of the candidates and their views on public issues, thanks to media coverage and the debates. Finally, close political races are supposed to stimulate people to get out and vote because they think their ballot will make a difference in the outcome. Pollsters predicted that the 1964 and 1972 elections would be landslides and that the 1968, 1976, and 1980 elections would be close contests, but a smaller percentage of people voted in 1968 than in 1964, and participation also declined in 1976 and 1980 despite close contests. In 1984 there was a slight (0.5 percent) increase in participation, even though the outcome was hardly in doubt, while participation declined in 1988, a closer contest. From early in 1996 polls showed Clinton comfortably ahead, and many reports suggested voters expected the eventual outcome.

Why did voting decline in recent years, surge in 1992, and decline again in 1996? Paul Abramson, John Aldrich, and David Rohde link the longterm decline to the erosion in political party identification and to lower political efficacy, the belief that citizens can influence what government does.[63] But neither party identification nor political efficacy changed significantly in 1992 and 1996. There is evidence that Ross Perot's presence contributed to the 1992 turnout increase; 14 percent of Perot voters (which translates into nearly 3 million voters, a substantial portion of the increased turnout) indicated in exit polls that they would not have voted if the Texan had not been on the ballot. Neither major party made a concerted effort in 1992 to register new voters, although there were some nonpartisan turnout efforts, including MTV's "Rock the Vote" feature aimed at youth voters, the group with the lowest turnout rates. By 1996 the Motor Voter bill had increased registration, and Democrats made a concerted effort to register newly naturalized citizens. As both the 1992 and 1996 elections came to a close, national polls indicated that Clinton's lead was narrowing, and the outcome was uncertain in 1992. Yet, one year had an upsurge in turnout and the other a decline. Thus, we cannot be certain what caused the changes. It is important to note, however, that the 1992 turnout was still well below that for 1960 and that neither of the long-term causes noted above has been reversed.[64]

Validation

Translating the popular vote into the official outcome is the final stage of the selection process, in which the electoral college produces the true winner. It has been more than a century since the constitutionally prescribed process failed to do so or produced a winner who was not also the "people's choice," but we have been dangerously close to electoral college *misfires* on a number of occasions.

Three possible problems remained even after presidential and vice presidential balloting were separated. The electoral college does not ensure that the candidate who receives the most popular votes wins the presidency: John Quincy Adams in 1824, Rutherford B. Hayes in 1876, and Benjamin Harrison in 1888 became president even though they finished second in total popular vote to their respective political opponents, Andrew Jackson, Samuel Tilden, and Grover Cleveland. The same thing would have happened in 1976 if some 9,000 voters in Hawaii and Ohio had shifted their ballots to President Ford, giving him a victory even though Carter had won the popular vote.

Candidates also may fail to win an electoral college majority, thereby throwing selection into the House of Representatives. This situation occurred in the elections of 1800, 1824, and 1876. In 1948 Harry S. Truman defeated Thomas Dewey by more than 2 million popular votes, but if some 12,000 people in California and Ohio had voted for Dewey rather than the president, the election would have been thrown into the House of Representatives. The same thing could have happened in 1960 and 1968 with the shift of a few thousand votes in close states.

The 1968 election illustrates another danger of the electoral college system: an elector need not cast his or her ballot for the candidate who wins the plurality of votes in the elector's state. This problem of the *faithless elector* has occurred seven times in the twentieth century, most recently in 1988, when an elector from West Virginia cast her vote for Bentsen as president rather than Dukakis. It is not particularly dangerous when isolated electors refuse to follow the result of their state's popular vote, but the possibility of widespread desertion from the popular choice is another matter, a scenario that could have occurred in 1968.[65]

The electoral college as it operates today violates some of the major tenets of political equality that are central to our contemporary understanding of democracy. Each person's vote does not count equally: one's influence on the outcome depends on the political situation in one's state. For the many Americans who support a losing candidate, it is as though they had not voted at all, because under the general-ticket system all the electoral votes of a state go to the candidate who wins a plurality of its popular votes. Thus, although Perot received 19,741,048 votes, 18.9 percent of the total votes cast nationally in 1992, he won no electoral votes because he finished first in no states nor in any of the House districts in Maine and Nebraska. Citizens who live in populous, politically competitive states have a premium placed on their vote because they are in a position to affect how large blocs of electoral votes are cast. Similarly, permitting the House of Representatives, voting by states, to select the president of the United States is not consistent with the "one person, one vote" principle that has become a central tenet of modern American democracy.

Proposals to reform the electoral college system promise to remove the possibility of system failures and uphold a more modern understanding of democracy. They range from the rather modest suggestion to prohibit faithless electors—votes would be cast automatically—to scrapping the present system altogether and moving to direct popular election. Intermediate suggestions would nationalize the district plan used in Maine and Nebraska, divide electoral votes proportionally between (or among) the contenders, or provide the popular vote winner with 100 bonus votes, enough to ensure his or her victory in the electoral college. No proposal is foolproof; most have to develop means to guard against new problems. Moreover, any change requires passage of a constitutional amendment by Congress, which is problematic because national legislators will calculate how the new system would affect their state's influence on the outcome (or affect their own chances to pursue the office) and vote accordingly. Therefore, prospects for change are not especially good until the system actually misfires or comes so close that the public demands action.

Is the electoral college a constitutional anachronism that should no longer be preserved? Why not move to direct popular election? Defenders of the current system note that the most serious misfires occurred during periods of intense political divisiveness (for example, 1824 and 1876), when alternative selection systems would have been just as severely tested. Several of the close calls in the twentieth century, such as in 1948 and 1968, occurred when political parties were suffering serious internal divisions. An examination of the historical conditions surrounding the misfires shows that only 1888 offers a clear example of a popular vote winner who lost, but even in this case the loser, Cleveland, had failed to meet one of the other requirements for success in the electoral college: broad distribution of support. Cleveland won fewer states than Harrison, receiving huge majorities in several while losing by slim majorities in even more. With this pattern of support, it is an open question which candidate was truly the people's choice.[66]

Defenders of the present system argue that far from having performed badly, the system has been remarkably successful in producing peaceful resolutions even in years of unusual turmoil. The system's virtues include the requirement that candidates not only receive sufficient popular support but also that support is sufficiently distributed geographically to enable the winner to govern. Ethnic minority groups, it is argued, receive special leverage under the present system because they are concentrated in states with large electoral vote totals and receive attention because their support might make the difference between a candidate's winning all of the electoral votes or none of them. Finally, there is concern that a system of direct election would encourage the development of minor parties based on regional or ideological interests that might organize in hopes of denying any candidate a majority or winning plurality and thereby force a runoff. Two-party stability, it is suggested, would be threatened.[67]

Thus, analysts of the American political system differ over the wisdom of retaining the present electoral system, a difference of opinion echoed by the authors of this book. Both of us are concerned with legitimacy, but we view the dangers differently. One of us believes that the present system, flawed as it may be, offers the advantage of continuity, something that yet another electoral reform following those initiated after 1968 is likely to endanger. The other fears that a misfire would dangerously imperil system legitimacy and, therefore, endorses reforms more consistent with direct popular election. As this brief review indicates, the debate is likely to continue.

Transitions to Governing

For the individual and election team that prevail in this long, grueling process, victory requires a change in focus. Successful candidates suddenly realize that winning the election is the means to an end, not an end in itself. Making that transition is sometimes difficult. It involves putting together a team of political executives to staff the new administration as well as establishing a list of program and policy priorities. Much of this is accomplished during the *transition*, the period between election and inauguration. Many other tasks are tackled during the first six months of the new administration. Governing, however, offers a new set of problems. Frequently, the techniques that proved successful during the election are simply transferred over to help meet the new challenges, but such methods are seldom sufficient to ensure success. In the modern presidency, governing involves some of the same activities as getting elected, but the two are far from identical, a lesson that some incumbents are slow to learn.

The burning question for everyone is how effective will the president be in leading the nation. Presidents vary along a wide range of dimensions—abilities, interests, personality—even as the office exhibits certain commonalities over time. In Chapter 4, we turn to the problem of understanding the ways that a president's personal characteristics influence performance in office, and subsequent chapters focus on presidents' political success. First, however, we examine their relationship with the public *between* elections, a relationship that has grown increasingly important in modern times.

NOTES

1. Besides George Washington, James Monroe is the only candidate to approach this distinction; he won all but one electoral college vote in 1820. *Guide to the Presidency,* 2d ed., vol. II, ed. Michael Nelson (Washington, D.C.: Congressional Quarterly, 1996), 1638.

2. William Chambers, *Political Parties in a New Nation: The American Experience, 1776–1809* (New York: Oxford University Press, 1963), chap. 2.

3. In the early 1820s the Republican Party became known as the Democratic-Republicans and in 1840 was officially designated as the Democratic Party. Paul David, Ralph Goldman, and Richard Bain, *The Politics of National Party Conventions* (New York: Vintage, 1964), chap. 3.

4. Joseph Charles, *The Origins of the American Party System* (New York: Harper Torch, 1956), 83–94.

5. Other constitutional amendments dealing with presidential selection have expanded participation (Amendments 15, 19, 24, 26), set the term of office (20, 22), or sought to cope with death or disability (20, 25).

6. David, Goldman, and Bain, *National Party Conventions,* 50. The National Republican Party was soon to give way to the Whigs, with many Whig supporters joining the Republican Party when it was formed in the 1850s (pp. 57–59).

7. Ibid., 61.

8. First-ballot convention decisions have been surprisingly prevalent. Through 1996, the two major parties selected their candidates on the first ballot at fifty-three

of seventy-nine conventions. Many of the multiballot conventions were held from 1840 to 1888, when sixteen of the twenty-two went past the first ballot. What distinguishes the post-1952 era is that *none* of the twenty-two conventions has gone past one ballot.

9. Richard C. Bain and Judith H. Parris, *Convention Decisions and Voting Records,* 2d ed. (Washington, D.C.: Brookings, 1973), 1–6.

10. In three states, one party chose delegates through the primary method, and the other used a caucus. The Republicans used primaries in Idaho and North Dakota, and the Democrats did so in South Carolina.

11. Naturalized citizens (such as former secretary of state Henry Kissinger, who was born in Germany) do not meet this requirement. There is some question whether persons born abroad of American citizens (one such is George Romney, former governor of Michigan and 1968 presidential contender, who was born of American parents in France) are also legally barred from the presidency by this stipulation.

12. The two exceptions were Wendell Willkie, the president of a public utility company, who was nominated by the Republicans in 1940, and Dwight D. Eisenhower, a career military man and World War II hero, who became the successful GOP candidate in 1952.

13. John Aldrich, "Methods and Actors: The Relationship of Processes to Candidates," in *Presidential Selection,* ed. Alexander Heard and Michael Nelson (Durham, N.C.: Duke University Press, 1987).

14. Before Richard Nixon's selection in 1960, the last incumbent vice president to be nominated was Martin Van Buren in 1836.

15. Joseph A. Pika, "Bush, Quayle, and the New Vice Presidency," in *The Presidency and the Political System,* 3d ed., ed. Michael Nelson (Washington, D.C.: CQ Press, 1990).

16. Ronald D. Elving, "The Senators' Lane to the Presidency," *Congressional Quarterly Weekly Report,* May 20, 1989, 1218.

17. For a statement of informal expectations from three decades ago, see Sidney Hyman, "Nine Tests for the Presidential Hopeful," *New York Times,* Jan. 4, 1959, sec. 5, 1–11.

18. Michael Nelson, "Who Vies for President?" in *Presidential Selection,* 144.

19. For example, Jesse Jackson finished third behind Walter Mondale and Gary Hart for the 1984 Democratic nomination and second for the 1988 nomination. Jackson was again mentioned prominently in 1995 as a possible nominee, as was Colin Powell, another African American.

20. Federal Election Commission Web site *(www.fec.gov).*

21. Harold W. Stanley, "The Nominations: Republican Doldrums, Democratic Revival," in *The Elections of 1996,* ed. Michael Nelson (Washington, D.C.: CQ Press, 1997), 22.

22. Austin Ranney, "Changing the Rules of the Nominating Game," in *Choosing the President,* ed. James David Barber (Englewood Cliffs, N.J.: Prentice-Hall, 1974), 71.

23. Arthur Hadley, *The Invisible Primary* (Englewood Cliffs, N.J.: Prentice-Hall, 1976). For a valuable update see Emmett H. Buell, Jr., "The Invisible Primary," in *In Pursuit of the White House,* ed. William G. Mayer (Chatham, N.J.: Chatham House, 1996).

24. Individuals are limited to contributions of $1,000 to a presidential candidate for each election (the nomination and general election are considered separate contests), $5,000 to a political action committee (one that contributes to more than one candidate), $20,000 to the national committee of a political party, and a total contribution of no more than $25,000 a year. Presidential candidates are free to spend

an unlimited amount of their own and their immediate family's money on their campaigns, but if they accept public financing, their contributions to their own campaign are limited to $50,000 per election.

25. Herbert E. Alexander and Monica Bauer, *Financing the 1988 Election* (Boulder, Colo.: Westview, 1991), table 2.5.

26. Anthony Corrado, "Financing the 1996 Elections," in *The Election of 1996*, ed. Gerald M. Pomper (Chatham, N.J.: Chatham House Publishers, 1997).

27. Not all individual contributions are small, and it is legal for political action committees to help finance nomination campaigns, but their contributions are not matched by federal funds as in the case of individuals. Vice President Bush, for example, received $1,000 contributions (the maximum) from 16,500 individuals in 1988 for a total of $16.5 million. Cumulatively, PACs contributed $3.114 million during the 1988 prenomination campaign, but that sum represented only 1.4 percent of total funding. Alexander and Bauer, *Financing the 1988 Election*, 23, 25.

28. At the time of writing, only the 1988 figures are complete. Bush raised $18.7 million in 1988 to Dole's $14.0 million and Pat Robertson's $14.0 million. Dukakis raised $10.6 million, with Richard Gephardt ($4.4 million), Al Gore ($3.8 million), and Paul Simon ($3.8 million) trailing badly. Alexander and Bauer, *Financing the 1988 Election*, 20.

29. Richard Berke, "In G.O.P. Presidential Field, a Race to Raise Money Is On," *New York Times*, Feb. 2, 1995, 1.

30. In 1984 the minimum was 20 percent, a rule that favored the front-runner, Walter Mondale. Complaints from the defeated candidates Jesse Jackson and Gary Hart resulted in lowering the qualifying level to 15 percent for the 1988 contest and that rule was continued in 1992 and 1996. Most Republican contests have been conducted under "winner-take-all" rules, although some states use proportional rules for both parties.

31. Only about 120,000 Democrats were registered in New Hampshire in 1976, and the Carter organization stated that it contacted about 95 percent of them. The state was therefore ideal for the former governor in the early stages of the nomination contest: he had not yet acquired substantial financial resources for media expenditures, and his contingent of Georgia volunteers could conduct an effective door-to-door campaign.

32. Alan Greenblatt and Rhodes Cook, "Nominating Process Rules Change," *Congressional Quarterly Weekly Report*, Aug. 17, 1996, 2299.

33. C. Anthony Broh, *A Horse of a Different Color: Television's Treatment of Jesse Jackson's 1984 Presidential Campaign* (Washington, D.C.: Joint Center for Political Studies, 1987), 4.

34. Ibid., 44.

35. Exceptions to this pattern can be found when two candidates end the preconvention period fairly even, which Ford and Reagan did in 1976, McGovern and Humphrey did in 1972, and Mondale and Hart did in 1984; in each case, however, the preconvention leader took the nomination.

36. Judith Parris, *The Convention Problem: Issues in Reform of Presidential Nominating Procedures* (Washington, D.C.: Brookings, 1972), 110.

37. Edwin Diamond, Gregg Geller, and Chris Whitley, "Air Wars: Conventions Go Cable," *National Journal*, Aug. 31, 1996, 1859.

38. Max Farrand, *The Framing of the Constitution of the United States* (New Haven, Conn.: Yale University Press, 1913), 160. There is some question whether it was doubt in the public's ability or concern about the natural tendency to support a "favorite son" that motivated delegates to reject direct election. See William C. Kim-

berling, "Electing the President: The Genius of the Electoral College," *FEC Journal* (Fall 1988): 12.

39. Alexander and Bauer, *Financing the 1988 Election,* table 2.1. Herbert Alexander and Anthony Corrado, *Financing the 1992 Election* (Boulder, Colo.: Westview, 1995), chap. 5, table 5.1; Federal Election Commission, *The Presidential Public Funding Program* (Washington, D.C., 1993), 31.

40. Corrado, "Financing the 1996 Elections," 145–155.

41. Although presidential candidates are free to refuse public funds, no major party nominee has done so in the general election, perhaps because the maximum contribution limitations have made raising money from individuals and groups more difficult. Candidates may also think the public favors the use of public rather than private funds.

42. Perot was eligible to match the major parties' spending by raising additional contributions, but was able to raise less than $1 million. He had spent more than $8 million of his own money during the prenomination phase to get on state ballots and fund his own nomination efforts. Corrado, "Financing the 1996 Elections," 140, 150.

43. The Twenty-third Amendment, ratified in 1961, gave the District of Columbia the right to participate in presidential elections. Previously, District residents were excluded. Their inclusion accounts for there being three more electoral votes (538) than the total number of senators and representatives (535).

44. In 1992 Bill Clinton won eight of the eleven most populous states. In contrast, George Bush won ten of these states in 1988.

45. Reapportionment was complex following the 1990 census. Because of widespread criticism, the Census Bureau agreed to conduct a post-census survey to determine the extent to which some population groups had been undercounted. The results of that study would have called for further changes in congressional representation. However, the secretary of commerce recommended following the initial census findings rather than the adjusted figures.

46. For a general discussion of this pattern, see Michael Nelson, "Constitutional Aspects of the Elections," in *The Elections of 1988* (Washington, D.C.: CQ Press, 1990), 192–195. Also see Everett Carll Ladd, "On Mandates, Realignments, and the 1984 Presidential Election," *Political Science Quarterly* 100:1 (Spring 1985): 17ff.

47. Dukakis won electoral votes from the District of Columbia and ten states in 1988: Hawaii, Iowa, Massachusetts, Minnesota, New York, Oregon, Rhode Island, Washington, West Virginia, and Wisconsin. He won 45 percent or more of the vote in California, Colorado, Connecticut, Illinois, Maryland, Michigan, Missouri, Montana, New Mexico, Pennsylvania, South Dakota, and Vermont. Of these states, only South Dakota did not support Clinton in 1992. Clinton won four southern states plus Kentucky and trailed Bush in the region's popular vote, as well.

48. Perot's share of the popular vote was the second best by an independent or third-party candidate in the twentieth century, surpassed only by Theodore Roosevelt's 27 percent in 1912. In comparison, George Wallace received nearly 14 percent of the popular vote in 1968, and John Anderson received 6 percent in 1980. Wallace's support was concentrated in the South, and he won forty-six electoral votes. Like Perot's support, Anderson's was scattered nationwide, and he also won no electoral votes.

49. Angus Campbell, Philip Converse, Warren Miller, and Donald Stokes, *The American Voter,* abr. ed. (New York: Wiley, 1964).

50. Gerald M. Pomper, "The Presidential Election," in *The Elections of 1988: Reports and Interpretations,* ed. Gerald Pomper (Chatham, N.J.: Chatham House, 1989), 136.

51. Offsetting gains in nonwhite voting, white fundamentalist or evangelical Christians have gained significance in national politics. This group has become solidly Republican and in 1988 comprised nearly as large a proportion of the voting population as blacks (9 percent versus 10 percent). See poll results reported in Pomper, "The Presidential Election," 134.

52. J. Merrill Shanks and Warren Miller, "Policy Direction and Performance Evaluation: Complementary Explanations of the Reagan Elections" (Paper delivered at the annual meeting of the American Political Science Association, New Orleans, Aug. 29–Sept. 1, 1985), 60, 69.

53. Pomper, "The Presidential Election," 143. The results of this CNN/*Los Angeles Times* poll also can be found in *National Journal*, Nov. 12, 1988, 2854.

54. Voter Research and Surveys exit polls as reported in Paul J. Quirk and Jon K. Dallager, "The Election: A 'New Democrat' and a New Kind of Presidential Campaign," in *The Elections of 1992*, ed. Michael Nelson (Washington, D.C.: CQ Press, 1993), 81.

55. Exit poll conducted by Voter News Service and reported in Michael Nelson, "The Election: Turbulence and Tranquillity in Contemporary American Politics," in *The Elections of 1996*, ed. Nelson, 57.

56. Marjorie Randon Hershey, "The Campaign and the Media," in *The Elections of 1988*, 78.

57. Ibid., 80–83; Paul J. Quirk, "The Election," in *The Elections of 1988*, 76.

58. Nelson, "The Election: Turbulence and Tranquillity," 58. Marion R. Just, "Candidate Strategies and the Media Campaign," in *The Elections of 1988*, ed. Pomper, 91–96.

59. Campbell et al., *The American Voter*, chap. 7.

60. For 1960s data, see Gerald Pomper, *Voters' Choice: Varieties of American Electoral Behavior* (New York: Dodd Mead, 1975), chap. 8. For 1970s data, see Norman Nie, Sidney Verba, and John Petrocik, *The Changing American Voter* (Cambridge, Mass.: Harvard University Press, 1979), chap. 7.

61. Michael Nelson, "The Election: Turbulence and Tranquillity," 71.

62. The 1992 turnout represented an increase of about 13 million voters over the 1988 total. Twenty-three candidates shared the votes, although only four, Bush, Clinton, Perot, and the Libertarian Party candidate, Andre Marrou, were on ballots in all fifty states. Federal Election Commission, press release, Jan. 14, 1993.

63. Paul R. Abramson, John H. Aldrich, and David W. Rohde, *Change and Continuity in the 1980 Elections* (Washington, D.C.: CQ Press, 1982), chap. 4.

64. Paul R. Abramson, John H. Aldrich, and David W. Rohde, *Change and Continuity in the 1992 Elections* (Washington, D.C.: CQ Press, 1994), 120.

65. In 1960, 1968, 1972, 1976, and 1988 single electors in Oklahoma, North Carolina, Virginia, Washington, and West Virginia failed to cast their ballots for the candidate receiving the popular vote plurality in their state. For complete results of electoral college voting, see *Guide to the Presidency*, 1634–1658; see 1634 for a list of faithless electors.

66. Kimberling, "Electing the President," 16.

67. Ibid., 19–20.

READINGS

Abramson, Paul R., John H. Aldrich, and David W. Rohde. *Change and Continuity in the 1980 Elections*. Washington, D.C.: CQ Press, 1982.

____. *Change and Continuity in the 1984 Elections*. Washington, D.C.: CQ Press, 1986.

___. *Change and Continuity in the 1988 Elections*. Washington, D.C.: CQ Press, 1990.

___. *Change and Continuity in the 1992 Elections*. Washington, D.C.: CQ Press, 1994.

Alexander, Herbert E., and Anthony Corrado. *Financing the 1992 Election*. Boulder, Colo.: Westview, 1995.

Bartels, Larry M. *Presidential Primaries and the Dynamics of Public Choice*. Princeton, N.J.: Princeton University Press, 1988.

Campbell, Angus, Philip Converse, Warren Miller, and Donald Stokes. *The American Voter*, abr. ed. New York: Wiley, 1964.

Heard, Alexander, and Michael Nelson, eds. *Presidential Selection*. Durham, N.C.: Duke University Press, 1987.

Mayer, William B., ed. *In Pursuit of the White House: How We Choose Our Presidential Nominees*. Chatham, N.J.: Chatham House, 1996.

Nelson, Michael, ed. *The Elections of 1996*. Washington, D.C.: CQ Press, 1997.

Pomper, Gerald M., ed. *The Election of 1996:* Reports and Interpretations. Chatham, N.J.: Chatham House, 1997.

Rose, Gary L., ed. *Controversial Issues in Presidential Selection*. 2d ed. Albany, N.Y.: SUNY Press, 1994.

Shafer, Byron E. *Quiet Revolution: The Struggle for the Democratic Party and the Shaping of Post-Reform Politics*. New York: Russell Sage Foundation, 1983.

Wayne, Stephen J. *The Road to the White House 1996: The Politics of Presidential Elections*. New York: St. Martin's Press, 1997.

3   PUBLIC POLITICS

FOR NEARLY A CENTURY, students of the presidency have argued that the chief executive's continuing relationship with the American public is a major factor in governing the nation. Writing in 1900 Henry Jones Ford concluded that only presidents can "define issues in such a way that public opinion can pass upon them decisively."[1] Woodrow Wilson, anticipating his own approach to the office, echoed that sentiment: "His [the president's] is the only national voice in affairs. Let him once win the admiration and confidence of the country and no other single force can withstand him; no combination of forces will easily overpower him."[2]

Ever since President William Howard Taft threw out the first baseball of the 1910 major league season in Washington, most presidents have observed the tradition.

If anything, the president's preeminent position has been strengthened during the last half of this century. In 1960 Richard Neustadt explained how the president's "public prestige"—in other words, the president's "standing with the public outside Washington"—influences the decisions of other government officials and nongovernmental elites—members of Congress, the bureaucracy, state governors, military commanders, party politicians, journalists, and foreign diplomats.[3] By the mid-1980s Samuel Kernell argued that "going public," issuing campaign-like appeals for citizen support, had become the key to presidential success in the modern era, rather than the traditional strategy of bargaining with other elites.[4] In short, presidents cannot afford to stop courting voters after the returns are in on election day; modern chief executives must woo the American public between elections just as they do during elections.

In courting support, presidents must take into account existing public attitudes, especially citizens' attitudes toward the institution of the presidency and the incumbent. Presidents hope to secure the public support they need for governing the nation by triggering favorable predispositions and building their own attractiveness as leaders. But success in this endeavor is far from automatic. Even an able president like Bill Clinton—blessed with a nimble mind and impressive rhetorical skills—failed to generate high levels of public support during his first three years.[5]

This chapter begins with an analysis of enduring public attitudes toward the presidency and then considers the ways chief executives try to hold the support of the American people. The third principal section examines an important element in the between-elections campaign, the relationship between the president and the media. The fourth section analyzes the president's relationship with one particular segment of the broader American public—members of his own political party.

Public Attitudes Toward the Presidency

Citizens relate to the presidency on both conscious and subconscious levels. At the conscious level, people develop attitudes toward three major components of a political system: the political community of which they are a part; the regime, or formal and informal "rules of the game" followed in the constitutional system; and the authorities, or public officials who hold positions in the government structure.[6] If these attitudes are sufficiently strong and positive, the public may follow its leaders even if it does not like the particular incumbent or the policies that leader advocates.

The president, it can be argued, is the focus of public attitudes in each of these three areas. Like the British monarch, the U.S. chief executive is the symbol of the nation, a personification of government capable of inspiring feelings of loyalty and patriotism, particularly in times of crisis when the leader becomes the rallying point for national efforts. For example, Franklin D. Roosevelt's political friends and foes alike turned to him for leadership when the Japanese attacked Pearl Harbor in December 1941. The same support arose when Ronald Reagan decided to invade the Caribbean island of Grenada in 1983 and Bill Clinton directed that cruise missiles strike Iraq in 1993. Calls to support the president quickly drown out critical voices.

Because presidents are central figures in the constitutional system, they can benefit from upholding the accepted rules of the game or suffer from violating them. Many Americans felt that Richard Nixon violated his constitutional obligations as well as basic democratic values by placing himself above the law during the Watergate incident; evidence indicated that he participated in a cover-up designed to hide the truth about an illegal break-in directed by White House aides. Finally, presidents are major actors in the policy-making process; the positions they adopt elicit support or opposition, and their overall performance in office becomes the object of citizen evaluations.

Fred Greenstein has suggested that presidents meet a variety of psychological needs held by the citizenry. As a *cognitive aid*, the president can make government and politics comprehensible; by focusing on the president's activities, citizens simplify a distant and complex world. The president also provides an *outlet for feelings* experienced by supporters and opponents, giving citizens the opportunity to develop and express emotions about politics. On the subconscious level, some citizens may seek *vicarious participation*, a desire to identify with a powerful political figure much as people do with fictional figures and entertainment personalities. Presidents symbolize *national unity* as well as *stability* and *predictability*, providing citizens with psychologically satisfying feelings that may meet fundamental needs for membership and reassurance. Finally, presidents serve as a *lightning rod* within the political system, a figure to blame for bad times and to credit for good times.[7] Because presidents play a central role in the nightly dramas communicated on television news, their importance as objects of psychological feelings may be greater today than ever before.

Beyond basic beliefs and psychological needs, the public also has views about the day-to-day operation of the political system—in particular, the major issues of the day and the policies the government should follow in dealing with them. These views, which are generally assumed to be less stable and enduring than beliefs about the political culture, are often described as matters of "public opinion." A citizen's attitudes on policy issues and presidential performance depend on his or her identity with a particular group, such as a political party, and his or her social, economic, and geographical background. As the nation's leading political figure, the president is expected to develop and help put into effect controversial policies that are binding on the entire populace. People respond favorably or unfavorably to the president's particular personality and political style and to the events that occur while he is in office. They also assess the president by the way he relates to particular groups—their political party or the opposition, as well as social (religious, ethnic, racial), economic (business, labor), and geographical divisions of the population.

Thus, many diverse attitudes affect public opinion toward the president. At times, people see him as the embodiment of the nation; on other occasions people link him with a particular issue or policy they favor or oppose. After examining the symbolic importance accorded the presidency, we analyze the ways children and adults view presidents and the factors that affect their thinking about chief executives.

Symbolic Dimensions of the Presidency

The Ronald Reagan Presidential Library opened on November 4, 1991, a day marked by speeches from five presidents (Nixon, Ford, Carter, Reagan, and Bush—the largest number of former and current chief executives alive at the same time since 1861) and appearances by six first ladies (including Lady Bird Johnson) as well as offspring from two other presidents. It was perhaps the largest assemblage of presidents and presidential families in history.[8] The library cost $60 million to construct and devotes 22,000 of its 153,000 square feet to exhibits commemorating the Reagan years. Each of the presidents from Hoover through Bush has had a library erected in his name to house the papers of his administration and his prepresidential career, explain his record to the public, and define his legacy to the nation. Like all the others, the Reagan structure combines commemoration with facilities for research. Most visitors choose only to view relics from a president's life, items drawn from childhood through retirement, and to reexperience personal memories and moments of drama through museum-like displays, many of which are interactive.

The presidential libraries, therefore, have a significance that extends beyond their ostensible purposes. In many respects, they can be viewed as shrines constructed to commemorate the lives and achievements of the most recent heroes in the nation's collective memory, a veritable presidential pantheon whose most sacred shrines, the Washington Monument and Lincoln Memorial, are located in Washington, D.C. Presidents stand at the center of what might be termed an "American mythology," a collection of stories and interpretations loosely linked to historical events but serving larger purposes in our collective experience—to celebrate basic values held in common, extol national virtues, and maintain unity in the face of enormous national diversity. In addition to the commemorative sites, Americans have created national holidays, public rituals, and icons, as well as a collection of stories, some of them apocryphal, that are passed on to our children. All attest to the presidency's symbolic importance.

Ceremony and pomp surround the presidency, another indication of the importance of the office in national life. A presidential inauguration resembles the coronation of a king, complete with the taking of an oath in the presence of notables and "the hailing by the multitudes." [9] Public appearances are accompanied by a display of the special presidential seal and the playing of "Hail to the Chief" as the president arrives. News conferences are conducted under a set of rules designed to communicate deference and respect as much as elicit hard news.

Particular occasions have been elevated to ritualistic status. The State of the Union message, for example, allows the president to outline an agenda for Congress and the nation. This ceremony was resurrected by Woodrow Wilson after a century of disuse; today it is an annual occasion for high drama and solemn pronouncements aimed as much at the prime-time television audience as the political elites in attendance. Members of Congress, the cabinet, and the diplomatic corps as well as distinguished visitors gather in the House chamber and chatter expectantly until the sergeant-at-arms solemnly announces the president's arrival, at which point the audience respectfully rises to its feet and applauds. Following a formal introduction from the Speaker of the House, there is another standing ovation. After the speech, a phalanx of congressional leaders accompanies the president as he leaves the hall, and members reach out along the way to shake hands or just to touch the presidential person.

These outward manifestations of respect, made part of recurrent governing rituals, indicate the near-reverence accorded the position of president. Respect for the *presidency* as distinct from the *president*, the current officeholder, is deeply ingrained in American political culture. George Washington and his advisers gave the office dignity by enhancing its ceremonial functions and designing a set of "republican rituals" for which no direct precedents existed, based on their exclusive experience with monarchy.[10] But Washington's major contribution to the presidency was to imbue the office with nearly mythical stature. The hero worship lavished on Washington during his lifetime and the subsequent cult that developed in commemorating his service to the nation ensured that the presidency will always be associated with the nation's own sense of moral virtue and collective destiny.[11]

Washington's birthday became a day of national celebration second only to the Fourth of July. Abraham Lincoln's birthday also was celebrated as a holiday until the two were combined into Presidents' Day. Every February American schoolchildren are taught stories about these presidents whose youthful endeavors illustrate the fundamental virtues of truthfulness ("Father, I cannot tell a lie"), honesty (walking miles to return change), and hard work (wilderness surveyor and railsplitter). At one time, Washington's likeness was so widely displayed that it became a virtual icon, the picture of a venerated saint displayed by fervent believers in hopes of deriving blessings.[12] In like ways, we celebrate the lives of Washington's successors, but we also expect them to live up to the heroic qualities of their predecessors during service in this most sacred of America's political positions.

Consistent with this symbolic role, the nation routinely turns to the president to perform a variety of ceremonial chores, many of which are minor, such as lighting the national Christmas tree and issuing proclamations on the observance of special days. But Americans also call upon presidents to perform more important symbolic tasks, such as helping citizens deal with their collective grief when disaster strikes. For example, President Reagan expressed the feelings of millions when he publicly mourned the crew lost in the explosion of the space shuttle *Challenger* in 1986 and President Clinton provided solace and reassurance in the face of sudden, inexplicable death after the federal building in Oklahoma City was bombed on April 19, 1995.

The presidency, more than any other aspect of political life, links Americans with both the past and the future. In focusing on the current White House occupant, citizens simultaneously derive a sense of fulfillment from past accomplishments and reassurance about the future. But presidential symbolism is not necessarily static; that is, its content may reflect contemporary changes in those qualities Americans expect from the chief executive and may be altered in the future as the public sees fit. Barbara Hinckley argues that presidents and their speechwriters are highly attuned to the public's expectations of a president. In turn, the White House projects "a symbolic presentation of the presidential office" expressed through the chief executive's public actions and statements.[13] With remarkable consistency, the picture portrayed to the public from Truman through Reagan (and we can safely assume through Clinton) has emphasized several common themes: the president, the American people, and the nation are indistinguishable from each other and together carry out most of the work of "government"; Congress, when mentioned, usually is dismissed rather than recognized as an equal branch of government; identifiable population groups share in the larger purposes that unite the nation; political and electoral activity is far less prominent in presidential discourse than references to religious objects like God and the Bible; presidents are without peers and enjoy a unique relationship with the public.[14]

As Hinckley suggests, the public might be able to reshape the presidency and its position in the constitutional order by altering expectations of the office and its occupants. But this possibility may be more theoretical than real. As we have seen, enormous pressures for continuity have developed around the presidential office; expectations of heroic performance and belief in the identity between presidents and the nation are attitudes that are deeply embedded in the political culture. Collectively, these beliefs about the presidency provide the incumbent with a remarkably durable base of popular support. Moreover, through their actions and speeches, presidents may directly and indirectly play on these symbolic meanings and benefit from an additional upsurge in public support. Some of these efforts are strained, as when presidents associate themselves with other popular heroes by phoning the locker room of the winning team in the World Series or the Super Bowl, or pose for a group picture with members of the championship National Hockey League or National Basketball Association teams. Other efforts to boost support may be less innocuous. Paul Brace and Barbara Hinckley note that presidential symbolism is especially potent in foreign policy initiatives. Thus, Carter's approval ratings rose after leaders from Israel and Egypt signed the Camp David Accords; the Reagan administration's decision to invade Grenada distracted public attention from the Marines who had been killed by a terrorist bombing in Lebanon; and the gulf war waged to drive Iraqi military forces out of Kuwait was one of several foreign policy moves that maintained high approval ratings for George Bush. As Brace and Hinckley conclude, "Rightly or wrongly, people worry that the treaty or the secret arms deal or the use of force might have been decided less because of long-range national interest and more because of public-opinion polls." [15]

Symbolism is not the only factor shaping public attitudes toward the presidency, but it would be wrong to ignore its impact. Symbols are likely to be no less important in American culture than in the foreign cultures where we are more accustomed to recognize their significance.

Developing Children's Attitudes Toward the Presidency

Cultural attitudes like those discussed in the preceding section are transmitted to new generations through a process social scientists call "political socialization." Considerable attention has been devoted to the attitudes that children develop toward the presidency. Major studies have shown the importance of the president in a child's world.[16] For younger children, presidents share the spotlight with the local mayor and police officers as visible political officials, but as children grow older the president becomes more prominent, and children place more emphasis on his power. Not until they are teenagers are children aware that the president shares the running of the government with Congress and the Supreme Court. In the *cognitive* (knowing) world of the young child, therefore, the president personifies the government. Studies also underscored the *affective* (emotional) dimension of children's attitudes toward the president. Not only are they aware of the president's importance, but they also think of him as a "good" person who cares about people, wants to help them, and wants to "get things done." For the young child the president is both powerful and benevolent; only when the child grows older does he or she view the president less favorably.

Why do young children develop these favorable attitudes? Parents who view the president favorably pass on these views to their children; those who do not, often tend to suppress their unfavorable views for fear of undermining the child's respect for authority. Children's favorable attitudes toward other authority figures, particularly their fathers, might carry over into their respect for the president, who becomes a kind of family figure "writ large." A third explanation for children's favorable views emphasizes their sense of vulnerability—they want to believe the president is a good person who will protect rather than threaten them. But it was discovered that children are able to distinguish between the person temporarily occupying the office and the presidency itself. They therefore can respect the institution without respecting the incumbent, an attitude that could carry over into their adult years and provide a solid basis of support for the U.S. political system.

Subsequent research found that not everyone experiences the same socialization. Poor children in Kentucky were found to be much less favorably disposed toward the president, regarding him as less honest, less hard working, less caring, and less knowledgeable than had the urban middle-class children of previous studies.[17] Nearly a quarter of these children viewed the president as a malevolent rather than a benevolent leader. After revelations of the Watergate scandal, a group of middle-class children were less likely to idealize the chief executive than their earlier counterparts, nor did they assign the president as important a role in running the country or in making its laws.[18] Children interviewed at the time of the Watergate hearings, which were televised, had a much less idealized view of the president than another group studied in 1969 and 1970, at the height of the Vietnam War. Fred Greenstein concluded that children had been more insulated from the political turmoil of the 1960s and its subsequent effects than they were from the Watergate scandal of the 1970s.[19]

Can we expect socialization experiences during the 1960s and 1970s to have lingering effects? Most findings suggest not. Studies have found a less benevolent image of the president among both middle-class and Appalachian students, but there is evidence that by early 1975, some of the extremely negative feelings revealed in 1973 had moderated.[20]

Thus, children's attitudes may be shaped by their social and economic backgrounds, norms from the geographic area in which they live, and by salient political events, such as Watergate. Children may have different affective and cognitive views of the president: they may dislike a president but still think he is an important and powerful political leader. They also can distinguish between the personal qualities of a president and his performance in office. Finally, because children as a group do not necessarily regard all presidents favorably, this research casts doubt on the view that a base of presidential support *automatically* carries over into the adult years. Rather, as following sections will indicate, presidents must exert considerable effort to win support from American citizens.

Attitudes of Adults

Although the president does not dominate the political world of adults the way he does that of young children, he is still by far the most visible person in the American political system. Not surprisingly, the president is the public official most likely to be correctly identified in surveys. He also enjoys general respect and admiration; in Gallup polls asking Americans to name the man, living anywhere in the world, whom they most admire, the president of the United States is almost always the first choice.[21] The first lady usually heads the list of most admired women.

Favorable attitudes are expressed toward the "generalized abstract" president rather than toward any specific incumbent.[22] In one survey, most persons agreed that the president "stands for our country" and that they sleep better when a president they trust is watching over the country. They also tended to believe that the president should be given a chance to work out his policies before he is criticized and that, even if the president is wrong, once he has committed the nation to action, people should be supportive. Most respondents also believed that in time of crisis in domestic or foreign affairs, all citizens should rally to support the president.

The public also develops attitudes toward particular occupants of the office. Since the end of World War II, the Gallup organization periodically has polled a cross-section of Americans on whether they approve or disapprove of the way the president is handling the job. The emphasis of the question is on performance in office rather than personal qualities, a virtual "continuing monthly referendum" on how he is handling the job.[23]

A study based on analysis of the answers to that Gallup question from 1946 to 1970 shows that all the presidents of that period, except for Dwight Eisenhower, declined in popularity over the course of their term in office.[24] They typically start with a high level of support, as the public accords them a measure of trust that they will do well in the job. As presidents undertake various actions, however, they antagonize more and more groups. John Mueller explains that a "coalition of minorities" forms as different groups respond unfavorably to presidential decisions, as businesses did when President Kennedy forced them to roll back a steel price rise in 1962, and as southerners did when he sent federal officials to the South to enforce integration. Although the various groups become unhappy with the president for different reasons, the result is a progressive decline in the president's popularity.[25]

In addition to this overall downward trend, public opinion of the presidency is affected by certain kinds of events. A downturn in the economy, particularly if it increases the rate of unemployment, harms presidential popularity. (A decrease in unemployment, however, does not improve the president's popularity.) International events can affect public opinion either way. A dramatic event, involving national and presidential prestige, may inspire Americans to "rally 'round the flag" and support their chief executive. They do so even if things turn out badly, as they did at the Bay of Pigs in 1961, when the U.S. effort to help ex-Cuban forces invade the island and overthrow Fidel Castro ended in a fiasco. But wars that drag on and involve significant casualties, such as those in Korea and Vietnam, ultimately harm the president's popularity. Jimmy Carter's inability to solve the 1979–1980 hostage crisis in Iran had a similar effect.

Finally, the party affiliation of adults in the United States affects their opinion of the president's performance. Those who identify with the party out of power start with much less support for the president than members of the president's party. In addition, those in the out party are more easily alienated by the president's policies or by unfavorable events; they also tend to resume criticism sooner after the temporary favorable effect of an international crisis. As a result, presidents enjoy far less support at the end of their term from out-party identifiers than from in-party identifiers.

The chief executive's prestige is generally high at the beginning of a term as the public grants him the opportunity to establish successful relationships with other public officials.[26] One study found that wars and military crises affect public support for an average duration of five months.[27] Another found that some events during the years from 1953 to 1980 substantially increased the president's approval rating—for example, U.S. action against the Soviet Union during the 1962 missile crisis in Cuba and the ending of the Vietnam War—while others, such as the Bay of Pigs and the ending of the Korean War, did not.[28] George Edwards concludes that events that generate sudden increases in presidential popularity are "highly idiosyncratic and do not seem to significantly differ from other events that were not followed by significant surges in presidential approval." [29]

Economic factors affect presidential popularity. In addition to the rate of unemployment, the rate of inflation also influences the public attitude toward the president.[30] Edwards found that in assessing President Carter, Democrats were strongly affected by unemployment statistics, while Republicans were more concerned with inflation.[31] Another analyst has determined that increases in both unemployment and inflation convince the public that things are getting worse economically and therefore depress the president's popularity. Ultimately,

Clinton benefitted from the opposite situation, economic growth and less inflation, but not until late in the first term.[32]

Scholars have challenged the theory that a coalition of minorities causes a steady, long-term decline in presidents' popularity. Instead, the decline may be cyclical, reaching a low point the third year of a president's term and then rising again in the fourth year as the president who is seeking reelection manipulates events to his advantage.[33] The president who does not stand for reelection also benefits in the fourth year in office because, as he is retiring, his motives are less open to cynical interpretation. The decline in popularity results not from the president's alienating various groups but from the public's becoming disillusioned with presidential performance, as the unrealistic expectations about what the chief executive can accomplish are not fulfilled.

Recent research similarly attributes the "decay of support" to the deflation of unrealistically high expectations of performance that typically bottoms out near the thirtieth month of an initial term. The decay occurs "irrespective of the economy, the president, or outside events." If a president is fortunate enough to be reelected, an uncertain prospect at best, the decline begins earlier and follows a steeper path. As Brace and Hinckley conclude, "all presidents, quite literally, are set up for a fall." Beyond this cycle, however, events that capture the public's attention may diminish or decrease presidential support. In general, events that "dramatize conflict in the nation," even if the president has taken no action to trigger them, are likely to reduce support. Events that "unify the nation around its symbols"—for example, an international crisis or attempted assassination—are likely to increase support. Some presidents may simply have better luck than others; domestic or international events beyond their control conspire to increase public support. Others may be responsible for their own good or bad fortune by taking actions that trigger positive or negative public responses. After reviewing fifty-nine dramatic events that had an impact on the public support of seven presidents, Brace and Hinckley found that Kennedy, Eisenhower, and Reagan benefited from more positive than negative events; Truman, Johnson, and Ford suffered through more negative than positive events; and Carter confronted a balance.[34]

Others contend that events rather than time in office affect a president's prestige.[35] Moreover, it is not presidents' decisions that determine their popularity, as the coalition-of-minorities factor suggests; rather, presidents are judged by real conditions and events that occur on their

Figure 3-1   Presidential Approval, 1977–1996

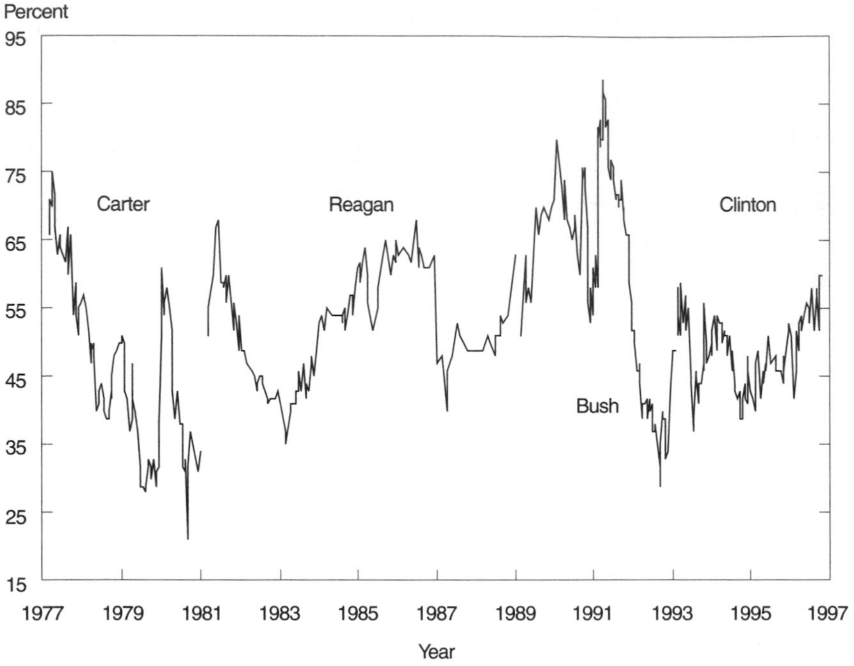

Percent

Note: Question: "Do you approve or disapprove of the way _____ (last name of president) is handling his job as president?"

Source: The Gallup Opinion Index as analyzed by Harold W. Stanley and Richard G. Niemi, *Vital Statistics on American Politics*, 5th ed. (Washington, D.C.: CQ Press, 1995), Figure 8-2.

watch. They also are held accountable by the American public for what they *do not* do: if a president does not attempt to deal with a major problem, such as the energy crisis, or a declining economy, and it persists, his popularity declines.

Figure 3-1 shows results of the Gallup Poll on presidential performance during the Carter, Reagan, Bush, and Clinton administrations. Reagan and Bush began with initial approval ratings of only 51 percent, low compared with Jimmy Carter's 66 percent rating and Bill Clinton's 58 percent. Carter's rating declined as the Iranian hostage crisis remained unresolved and took a dramatic nose dive following the unsuccessful hostage rescue attempt in 1980. He left office with barely a third of the citizenry approving his performance.

Both Reagan and Bush enjoyed significant improvements from their initial low ratings. Reagan's rating rose to 68 percent following the unsuccessful attempt on his life by John Hinckley, Jr., in late March 1981. His popularity began to decline in mid-1981 and continued to do so as the economy worsened, reaching its lowest point in early 1983. When the economy began to improve, so did Reagan's approval ratings, which increased steadily in 1983 and ended on a high note late that year following the invasion of Grenada. His approval ratings remained constant during the first half of 1984 and then rose at the time of the summer Olympics and the fall election campaign. President Reagan's ratings plummeted by sixteen percentage points after the revelation of the Iran-contra affair, the largest single monthly decline in the history of Gallup surveys on presidential approval ratings. Nonetheless, Reagan's low point never rivaled Carter's. Reagan's ratings gradually recovered and by the end of 1988 had returned to a healthy level.

Bush's approval ratings also went through dramatic changes. From the initial low, they rose to 70 percent by June 1989, hit 80 percent in January 1990, increased to nearly 90 percent following the Persian Gulf War, and plunged to less than 50 percent at the beginning of 1992. During his first year in office Bush was the beneficiary of favorable foreign policy developments: the disintegration of communism in Eastern Europe and the highly popular U.S. invasion of Panama to seize Manuel Noriega. In 1989 alone, U.S. military force was used on four occasions. Bush traveled extensively abroad and focused on foreign policy when addressing the American people.[36] His ratings declined in the early fall of 1990 because of conflict with Congress over the budget and concerns about the American military response to Iraq's invasion of Kuwait. Bush's approval ratings went into the stratosphere, however, following the successful war in the gulf, hitting 89 percent during the week of February 28–March 3, 1991, the highest Gallup Poll rating in history. Declines from that level were inevitable but began to accelerate late in 1991 as the recession lingered and questions were raised about the president's lack of a game plan. Going into the 1992 election year, momentum was decidedly against Bush.

Although Bill Clinton's initial approval ratings exceeded those of Reagan and Bush, they fell to 37 percent by June of his first year in office and have never achieved the heights of his immediate predecessor. The result, of course, is that Clinton's ratings have been less volatile (modest highs make the lows less startling), but they have been persistently anemic, usually ranging narrowly between 40 and 50 percent approval. Each year until 1996, his high point was reached after delivering the State of the Union message, but that high became progressively lower, declining from 59 percent to 58 percent to 50 percent. Moreover, his disapproval ratings were consistently high, reaching nearly 55 percent in late summer 1994. *(See Figure 3-1.)* Clinton received his strongest approval in 1996 when it remained above 50 percent from late January until the election.

Blessed with a growing economy, low inflation, and international peace, Clinton might have expected better. Moreover, his White House was particularly sensitive to the need to build public support. Elected with only 43 percent of the popular vote in 1992, Clinton and his aides recognized the need to expand his base of support. Toward this end, he spent far more on public opinion polls and public relations efforts than did Bush—by one account, $2 million in his first year, whereas Bush had spent a little over $200,000 in his first two years.[37] According to George Edwards, several factors explained Clinton's consistently weak support: the public's reluctance to credit him with success, as in the case of the economy; the perception that he was unable to get things done; the continuance of the public's first impression of an inept White House; the belief that he was evasive and waffling on policy decisions as well as inattentive to foreign policy; and, an "almost visceral level of mistrust and dislike."[38] Clinton's support got a boost when cruise missiles were used against Iraq in 1993 (+ 14 percent) and when American military forces intervened in Haiti (+ 5 percent), but the rally effects were short-lived and modest, respectively.[39]

The public also judges presidents by their *policies*. As Edwards put it, "Evidently the public evaluates the president more on the basis of how it thinks the government is performing on economic policy than how it thinks the economy itself is performing."[40] Moreover, people assess economic policy by how it affects the entire nation, not just their personal situation. He finds a similar pattern in public judgments of presidents' handling of war, with the nation's welfare rather than an individual's own experience considered most important.

Thus, it is not just events that determine how a president is regarded but how the public *perceives* those events. The perception, in turn, depends on how the mass media report the news. If there is a discrepancy between the balance of good and bad news and the way the president was regarded before the reporting of that news, his popularity moves in the direction of the discrepancy.[41] It has also been determined that a relationship exists between the amount of television news time accorded the president, as well as the proportion of positive coverage, and how the public views him.[42] Negative coverage also affects the president's opinion ratings.[43] A similar connection exists between the number of nationwide radio or television broadcasts a president makes and the amount of support received from the American public.[44]

Public views toward presidents, therefore, reflect long-term attitudes on the office as an institution as well as short-term responses to a particular incumbent based on international and domestic events, the state of the economy, policies of the president, news reports on events, and the president's use of the media. The next section analyzes how chief executives consciously use such influences to enhance their popularity with the American public.   .

Projecting a Favorable Image

Presidents are not passive objects of public attitudes. Rather, presidents and their aides take the initiative in shaping public perceptions. Over time, the White House has developed several specialized staffs devoted to maintaining favorable public relations. The modern presidency includes staff members to oversee press relations, communications strategy, presidential speeches and messages, and travel.[45] In performing their tasks, aides take actions and fashion appeals designed to win the support of different kinds of audiences, including the general public and particular segments of that public, represented primarily by interest groups.

Appealing to the Public

Consistent with the positive attitudes that Americans hold toward the presidency's symbolic roles, chief executives seek to present themselves in those terms, that is, to personalize the American political system and to embody American ideals. They do this through conscious choices about what they do, where they travel, and what they say.

There are ample opportunities for presidents to emphasize the ceremonial aspects of the office. Each year the president receives innumerable invitations to appear at national conventions, public gatherings, and celebrations, as well as requests to endorse various worthwhile causes. Responses vary widely. Important groups may garner a visit and speech. If the project is deemed worthy, the president may make an appearance to dedicate a new hospital, dam, or library. At times, he may even make a televised appeal or merely lend his name in behalf of a cause. Dwight Eisenhower, for example, began the practice of pro-claiming a "national day of prayer" in coordination with Catholics, Jews, and major Protestant denominations.

Major holidays offer the opportunity to stir the public's patriotic sentiments. For example, on his first Fourth of July in the White House, Ronald Reagan held a picnic complete with a gigantic fireworks display. Five years later, he helped commemorate the restoration of the Statue of Liberty, again on the Fourth of July, in a televised celebration with appearances by big name entertainers.

With the onset of jet travel, presidential trips have become more feasible. A foreign trip emphasizes the president's role as head of state because the chief executive becomes the representative of the United States and the American people. Nixon made historic visits to mainland China and the Soviet Union. Reagan met with the leaders of major Western nations during his first year in office and later in his first term visited China, the Normandy beaches of France (which became the backdrop for dramatic reelection ads), and his family's ancestral home in Ireland.[46] One study found evidence that foreign trips are especially frequent as reelection campaigns near—that is, they are timed for their strategic benefit.[47]

Domestic trips may also enhance the image of the president as a national leader. George Washington initiated a "grand tour" of two-months' duration by visiting the South in 1791, a region where suspicions of central authority had run strong during the constitutional ratification campaign.[48] Travel to special locations frequently is used to highlight particular themes. In 1985, for example, Reagan kicked off his tax reform proposal in Williamsburg, Virginia, calling it the "new American Revolution." [49] Bush traveled to Arizona in 1991 to use the Grand Canyon as a spectacular prop for a message on the environment.

Not all presidential trips turn out well, however. Woodrow Wilson's ill-fated attempt to take his case for the Versailles peace treaty to the American people ended in failure. He collapsed near the end of his tour, was disabled for a long period, and probably changed not a single senator's vote by this difficult journey. Reagan's trip to West Germany in 1985 was intended to symbolize reconciliation between the United States and its former enemy, but many people criticized him for visiting a cemetery that included the graves of former Nazi officials associated with the Holocaust. Finally, during his trip to the Far East in late 1991, George Bush was personally embarrassed when a stomach virus attacked at the worst possible time—during a state dinner with the

Japanese prime minister, which was captured on videotape. Based on their analysis of presidential travel from Truman through Reagan, Brace and Hinckley conclude that foreign trips seem to make no difference to a president's public approval rating, and domestic trips may actually have a small negative impact. By traveling abroad, presidents may benefit by drawing public attention briefly away from divisive domestic issues, but such trips are unlikely to be major rallying events. In contrast, domestic trips are often made for more explicit political purposes, particularly as the time approaches for midterm congressional campaigns and their own reelection efforts.[50]

Although their occurrence cannot be planned, crises and a president's responses to them may improve his standing when opinion rallies 'round the flag. What is most important is that the president appear to be decisive, as Kennedy did in the Cuban missile crisis and as Ford did in the *Mayaguez* incident with Cambodia after the Vietnam War, and that Americans perceive the president as defending the interests of the nation from foreign or domestic threats. To the extent possible, therefore, the White House works to project the right kind of image. Bruce Miroff suggests that during the Grenada invasion of 1983, effective management of stories and pictures about the president's handling of a sudden crisis and a news blackout of the invasion enabled Reagan to reap substantial rewards in public support.[51] The president portrayed the Grenada invasion as an end to "our days of weakness," a successful rescue of endangered American students, and the liberation of peaceful islanders from a communist plot. Miroff calls the deliberate projection of images "to shape public understanding and gain popular support" a "spectacle." [52] And although he traces the roots of such White House efforts to the Kennedy administration, Miroff suggests that they are becoming more frequent.

Unlike basic attitudes of political culture, which link the chief executive with the country, the constitutional system, and the presidential office, attitudes relating the president to less stable matters of public opinion are much more likely to be unfavorable. People may respect the presidency as an institution but may not like the personality or political style of the incumbent, as suggested earlier in regard to Clinton. They may agree with the broad, general rules of the game and the basic values that the president embodies but disagree with his positions on controversial issues of public policy. They may also feel that the president is unsympathetic with certain economic, social, or political groups with which they identify or that he is partial to groups they oppose.

One tactic presidents use to overcome negative views is to try to create a favorable impression of themselves as individuals. This approach may take the form of emphasizing their "down-to-earth" qualities, the traits that make them "ordinary" people. Much was made of the fact that Gerald Ford toasted his own English muffins for breakfast. At his swearing-in ceremony, Carter wore a dark business suit rather than the traditional morning coat, and then he walked up Pennsylvania Avenue to the White House rather than riding at the head of the inaugural parade as his predecessors had done. Reagan saw to it that he was frequently photographed in informal western attire, often astride his favorite horse or chopping wood on his ranch. Bush made it known that he loves country music and pork rinds, hates broccoli, plays baseball, enjoys fishing, and drives his speed boat as fast as possible. Clinton jogs, loves to eat fast foods, and is a rabid fan of his home state university's basketball team. Presidents also like to be pictured as family men, surrounded by an adoring wife and respectful children. These images are stressed during election campaigns and continue to be seen throughout the White House years.

Perhaps the president's most difficult task in fostering favorable public attitudes is assuaging opposition to his stands on public policy issues, some of which may be controversial. They pay close attention to the results of public opinion polls reported in the media and, starting with Franklin Roosevelt, have hired their own pollsters to probe public attitudes more deeply on the issues in which the chief executives are particularly interested. Although presidents may not choose to follow the sentiments of a majority of Americans, a knowledge of public attitudes helps a president measure how effectively he is getting his message across to the public and determine when the mood of the country is amenable to his proposals. Clinton's extensive polling is only the latest in a long line of presidential attempts to learn what is on the public's mind.[53]

Targeted Communications: Presidents and Interest Groups

Just as scholars discovered that political socialization may vary by subgroups, we also know that opinions vary by group. People who organize to advocate a particular interest are highly attentive to public issues that affect their members. These groups also have ongoing links with Congress and the bureaucracy that provide them with policy-making influence. The president, therefore, must also communicate with these specific populations. Presidents give major public addresses on business to conventions of the National Association of Manufacturers or the Chamber of Commerce of the United States, and on labor relations to meetings of the American Federation of Labor–Congress of Industrial Organizations (AFL-CIO). Chief executives also dispatch surrogates, such as cabinet officers, to speak on their behalf and in support of the administration's programs. White House aides serve as a channel for private communications with group representatives and will sometimes arrange meetings with the president.

Interest groups want to hear about current matters of public policy, but they also want to be reassured that the president is sympathetic to the problems group members face. Not surprisingly, chief executives pay particular attention to the groups that helped them get elected. They hope to convert their electoral coalition into one that helps them govern, as well. Democratic presidents typically have focused on labor unions and civil rights organizations; Republicans have concentrated on business and professional organizations. Presidents also know that as the leader of the nation, they are supposed to represent *all* the people, not just those who supported their election. Chief executives cannot afford to ignore prominent interest groups, even those that are politically opposed to them.

Presidents also have established channels for routine communication with particular groups through systematic White House liaison. Truman used David Niles, formerly on FDR's staff, as a liaison with blacks and Jews.[54] Eisenhower, who cultivated an image of being above politics, de-emphasized, but did not completely ignore, group relations, and the Kennedy and Johnson administrations designated White House staff members to work with Jews, Catholics, and other groups. Gradually, however, the range of group ties became more predictable so that the Nixon, Ford, Carter, Reagan, Bush, and Clinton administrations assigned aides to work full-time with eight population groups: business, labor, Jews, consumers, blacks, women, Hispanics, and the elderly.[55] Most of these ties are pursued through the Office of Public Liaison, a White House staff unit first conceived in the Nixon administration and consolidated in one unit under Ford. The office has continued to be a part of each subsequent administration and has sometimes played an important role in promoting administration policies.

Thus, the official representation of interest groups in the White House has become institutionalized in the administrations of both political parties. People who serve in the liaison office articulate the demands of interest groups inside White House circles and rally the support of interest groups behind the president's programs. Despite this dual purpose, there is little doubt that the office exists primarily to further the president's wishes rather than those of interest groups; aides who reverse these priorities encounter difficulties.[56]

Although many regularities in relations between the White House and interest groups carry across administrations, significant differences still occur. Bill Clinton, for example, was far more responsive to the goals of groups that had recently joined the Democratic coalition.[57] One of the new president-elect's first public policy statements was a commitment to change the government's policy on gays in the military. After both the military and influential members of Congress opposed such changes, the president retreated to a policy of "don't ask, don't tell" which angered gay groups at the same time that it made him appear weak. Clinton was more successful in opposing the policy goals of two powerful groups, the AFL-CIO and the National Rifle Association (NRA). Organized labor had been a member of the Democratic Party's core coalition since Franklin Roosevelt's New Deal, but Clinton found himself opposing it when he sought congressional approval of the North American Free Trade Agreement (NAFTA). Ultimately, Clinton triumphed with substantial Republican support in the House, but created dissension within his own coalition of support, and many liberal Democrats joined labor in opposing the new treaty. Clinton also won the battle against the NRA when the Brady Bill, which required a waiting period before purchasing a handgun, and limits on assault weapons were passed by Congress. In contrast, powerful organized groups were successful in their opposition to the president's proposal for universal health care. One coalition of insurance interests financed a $60 million ad campaign featuring a middle-class couple, Harry and Louise, pondering the impact of Clinton's reforms. Although the administration may have made many mistakes that contributed to the demise of health care reform, it clearly was never able to create a stable coalition of groups favoring reform.[58]

Presidents, then, attempt to shape the attitudes of both the general public and specific publics as a way to garner favor and support. Their success in that endeavor depends to a considerable extent upon the ability to communicate their appeals through the media, the subject of the following section.

The President and the Media

Historically, the most important link between the president and the American public has been the press. In the early years of the Republic the press was as partisan as it is in many European countries today. The partisan press reached its peak during the presidency of Andrew Jackson, when federal officeholders were expected to subscribe to the administration organ, the *Washington Globe*, which was financed primarily by revenues derived from the printing of official government notices.[59]

The partisan press began to decline during the presidency of Abraham Lincoln. The establishment of the Government Printing Office in 1860 destroyed the printing-contract patronage that had supported former administration organs.[60] The invention of the telegraph led to the formation of wire services, which provided standardized and politically neutral information to avoid antagonizing the diverse readerships of the various subscribing newspapers. Advertising provided newspapers with a secure financial base independent of the support of presidential administrations. By the end of the nineteenth century "news about the White House was transmitted to the public by independent, nonpartisan news organizations," a factor that continues to affect relationships between the president and the press today.[61]

In this century, two new media, radio in the 1920s and television in the 1950s, took their place beside newspapers as channels between the chief executive and citizens, and those media continue to undergo evolution; for example, the development of cable television provides citizens with far more potential sources of news and commentary.[62] Electronic media made it possible for presidents to establish direct contact with people rather than having their message relayed (and interpreted) by journalists.

The Presidential Media

Today, the words and actions of the U.S. president are covered by an enormous variety of media. These media differ in the way they deal with executive branch developments and in their target audience. They also vary in importance to chief executives and their programs. Over the last four decades the way Americans get information has undergone a fundamental change. In 1959, 57 percent of the public claimed to get most of their news from newspapers and 51 percent from television (more than one response was allowed in the survey); but by 1994 only 38 percent cited newspapers as a principal source and 72 percent cited television.[63] This pattern developed with the spread of television ownership: only 9 percent of households had television sets in 1950, a figure that grew to 87 percent by 1960 and 98 percent by 1980.[64] As one would expect, White House attention to television coverage rose over the same period.

In addition, the White House must be attentive to the most influential media figures—a select group of columnists, elite reporters, anchors of the broadcast news, and executives of the media organizations. There is substantial evidence that the stated views of news commentators and experts have a greater impact on citizens' policy preferences than the president's own comments.[65] Although popular presidents are more likely to have an impact on public approval and attitudes than unpopular presidents, even these effects are limited and substantially less than those of the highly credible commentators and experts. Columnists deal in matters of opinion rather than just factual developments affecting the presidency. "They are guaranteed space, they have no assigned topics, they are freed from the pressure of breaking news stories at deadline, and they have the opportunity to introduce their own perspectives into their stories." [66] George Will epitomizes this sort of columnist, and he appears regularly on television. Elite reporters cover current developments affecting the presidency, explain why certain events have occurred, and examine the effect they are likely to have on the president's program and the governing of the country. David Broder, another member of the elite corps, is both chief political reporter and a columnist for the *Washington Post*.

Syndicated columnists and elite reporters earn White House attention because they reach powerful audiences outside government, including business and labor leaders, lobbyists, and academics, as well as top officials in government—members of Congress, members of the bureaucracy, judges, governors, and mayors. These reporters and columnists influence views on the political feasibility of a president's proposed programs.

Television anchors, such as Dan Rather, Peter Jennings, and Tom Brokaw, are important to the president because of the size of the audience they reach, more than 26 million people each weekday night.[67] Because far more people watch television than read newspapers, the information the ordinary citizen receives about the presidency depends on what is included in the nightly broadcasts. Bureau chiefs and other media executives determine which stories are covered, how they are handled, which reporters are assigned to cover the White House, and who should be represented in "pools" that travel with the chief executive to cover significant events.

The basic task of the presidential press corps is to wait around the White House to see if any of the daily events merit coverage. Their importance to the president and their prestige with fellow reporters depend on the organization to which they belong. Reporters with the *New York Times* and *Washington Post* are considered the most influential by virtue of their readership—besides public officials and important people in the private sector, their readers are the other Washington reporters.[68] These publications (particularly the *Times*) influence decisions on which news stories will be carried on network television broadcasts.[69]

Reporters for the three major television networks loom large in the presidential media because most viewers tend to believe what they see on television; that is, it helps to determine reality for them. At the same time, television coverage of the presidency has serious limitations: very little time is devoted to the most important stories (about seventy-five seconds on the average); emphasis is placed on events that are visually exciting; a focus on the president personalizes complex developments; and broadcasts usually lack in-depth reporting and analysis.[70]

The nation's three major news magazines, *Time*, *Newsweek*, and *U.S. News and World Report*, bring national news to a broad readership throughout the country; their reporters benefit from having weekly rather than daily deadlines and from combining their efforts into a single, in-depth account. Also significant are the reporters for the wire services—Associated Press (AP) and United Press International (UPI)—because they provide coverage of the president for newspapers across the country that subscribe to their services. Wire service reporters cover "hard news" rather than analysis and focus on the official and personal activities of the president—what Michael Grossman and Martha Kumar refer to as "body-watching." [71] Because they often prepare several stories a day for client newspapers with different deadlines and must cater to the diverse interests of this broad clientele, they have little opportunity for in-depth or interpretative reporting.

Beyond this inner circle of Washington reporters are the many other national journalists who work for a wide variety of news organizations.[72] In addition are the reporters who provide coverage for radio stations around the country (including those that belong to commercial networks as well as those affiliated with the National Public Radio system) and photographers who provide a pictorial record of the presidency.

Channels of Presidential Communication

Because the media interested in the presidency differ in prestige and influence, the chief executive and members of the administration use different techniques and channels of communication to manage the flow of information about the president. Formal communications are provided to all members of the presidential media through different individuals and units within the executive branch.

The Press Secretary. The most important person in the executive branch for day-to-day contact with the presidential media is the White House press secretary. Typically holding two daily briefings, the press secretary provides routine information on executive branch appointments and resignations, on presidential actions and policies, and on the president's schedule—visits, meetings, and travel plans. By the end of an administration there may have been more than 2,000 such briefings. In addition, the press secretary holds private meetings with select reporters to provide background information to explain the president's actions on a particular problem or program.

Press secretaries serve three constituencies. They try to balance serving the interests of the president, members of the White House staff, and members of the media.[73] The secretary can perform well only if granted continuous access to and the confidence of the president so that journalists may assume that the news comes from the chief executive. If a president tries to be his own press secretary, as may have been true of Lyndon Johnson, even a capable and influential person like Bill Moyers will not succeed in managing the message.[74] When secretaries are excluded from White House decisions, as appeared to be the case with Dee Dee Myers in the Clinton administration, their credibility suffers.

The modern era's press secretaries have varied in effectiveness. Among those considered successful are Stephen Early from Franklin Roosevelt's staff, James Hagerty from Eisenhower's, and Jody Powell, who served under Carter. Hagerty and Powell benefited from the fact that their presidents kept them informed on virtually everything that was going on in the White House. Not all press secretaries have garnered praise. Some have been unpopular with their White House colleagues, and others were openly disdained by reporters. Larry Speakes, press spokesman for Ronald Reagan, provoked cries of outrage when he admitted in his memoirs that he had manufactured quotes during the president's Iceland summit meeting with the Soviet general secretary Mikhail Gorbachev in November 1985. Fearing that Reagan was being upstaged, Speakes created a public relations solution to the problem, and the fabricated quotes were given prominent attention back home. But Speakes generally lacked clout; he learned of the administration's plan to invade the Caribbean island of Grenada in October 1985 just as the troops were landing.[75]

The Presidential Press Conference. Beginning with the administration of Woodrow Wilson, presidents have held press conferences to try to influence public opinion and to gauge what is on people's minds as revealed by the questions put to them. Over the years, however, each president has used the institution in his own way. Some required that questions be submitted in advance. Beginning with FDR, presidents have permitted spontaneous questioning, but required careful rules concerning attribution. Press conferences were televised live under Kennedy (Eisenhower had allowed taping, but the White House controlled which clips could be broadcast), and presidents found other ways to minimize risks. Members of the president's staff draw up a list of questions likely to be asked by reporters, together with suggested answers and supporting information. Some presidents have held full-scale mock news conferences for practice. Reagan, for example, liked two-hour practices, dividing the time between foreign policy and domestic policy. Errors would be pointed out, and the president's performance critiqued by staff. On the day of the news conference, photos of the reporters expected to attend were fixed to their likely places on a seating chart, and difficult questions were reviewed.[76]

Overall, presidents control the interchange. At times, the White House limits questions to domestic policy or foreign policy, and presidents can always refuse to answer certain questions on the grounds that the subject matter is too sensitive for public discussion, a frequent response to foreign and military questions.

The success of a press conference depends on the skills of the president. Harry Truman, who enjoyed the give and take of exchanges with reporters, performed poorly in formal encounters. Dwight Eisenhower also came across badly. He appeared to have trouble expressing himself clearly and grammatically and displayed meager knowledge about many vital issues of the day. It has since been revealed that he may have used this as a tactic to avoid sensitive issues.[77]

Franklin Roosevelt and John Kennedy were masters of the press conference. FDR had a keen sense of what was newsworthy and even suggested reporters' lead stories to them. He also prepared members of the press for actions he took on controversial problems by educating them initially with confidential background information; consequently, reporters tended to support his decisions because they understood his reasoning. Kennedy, who had served a brief stint as a newspaperman and enjoyed the company of reporters, used his press conferences to great advantage; his ability to field difficult questions impressed not only the members of the press but also the public. Although Jimmy Carter was not as effective as either Roosevelt or Kennedy, he came across as calm, well prepared, frank, and articulate.

Despite differences among presidents on how well they handle the press conference, there are some similarities in its use by all chief executives, such as scheduling frequency. Since the advent of television, press conferences have been held less often.[78] Presidents also are less likely to schedule press conferences during periods of international crisis, especially when major policy options are being weighed. After an important decision has been made (such as entering the Korean War or invading Cambodia), a president may schedule a conference or televised address to present the nation with a *fait accompli* and magnify the rally effects on his public approval.[79] Also, news conferences are more likely to be held when the president's standing in the polls is declining rather than rising; perhaps they are considered a way to improve the president's public image, but no one wants to rock the boat when things are going well.[80]

Most people who have studied or been involved in the press conference have concluded that it serves primarily the interests of the president rather than the media. As George Reedy, press secretary to Lyndon Johnson, has pointed out, a president rarely receives an unexpected question on an important issue in a press conference, and, should that happen, the president could respond with a witty or a noncommittal remark.[81] Grossman and Kumar summarize the president's advantage as follows: "The President decides when to hold a conference, how much notice reporters will be given, who will ask the questions, and what the answers will be." [82]

Despite these advantages, presidents approach press conferences in different ways. Although Clinton and Bush maintained more press interaction than Reagan *(see Table 3-1)*, Clinton has shied away from prime-time press conferences and has frequently appeared in joint sessions with visiting heads of state. Perhaps in the television age each conference is regarded as a more newsworthy and potentially dangerous event.

Bill Clinton followed George Bush's example by returning to a more informal exchange with the media, achieved by holding most of his sessions during mid-day rather than prime-time evening hours. As a result, the press conferences are less widely viewed (CNN is the princi-

Table 3-1   **Presidential News Conferences with White House Correspondents, 1929–1997**

President	Average number of press conferences per month	Total number of press conferences
Hoover (1929–1933)	5.6	268
Roosevelt (1933–1945)	6.9	998
Truman (1945–1953)	3.4	324
Eisenhower (1953–1961)	2.0	193
Kennedy (1961–1963)	1.9	64
Johnson (1963–1969)	2.2	135
Nixon (1969–1974)	0.6	37
Ford (1974–1977)	1.3	39
Carter (1977–1981)	1.2	59
Reagan (1981–1989)	0.5	44
Bush (1989–1992)	3.0	142
Clinton (1993–1997) [a]	2.8	145

Sources: Harold W. Stanley and Richard G. Niemi, *Vital Statistics on American Politics,* 5th ed. (Washington, D.C.: CQ Press, 1995), Table 2-4, 53, for Hoover and Roosevelt. The figures for Truman through Clinton compiled by Martha Joynt Kumar, *Guide to the Presidency,* 2d ed., vol. I (Washington, D.C.: Congressional Quarterly, 1996), Table 19-3, 862. Additional Clinton data compiled by the authors.

[a] As of May 10, 1997.

pal source of coverage), but the president earns points with the press for his accessibility.

Other Presidential Channels of Communication. In some instances presidents may want to communicate directly with the American people without having their remarks filtered by reporters or columnists. Although he held relatively few press conferences, Richard Nixon appeared more often on prime-time television during his first eighteen months in office than did presidents Eisenhower, Kennedy, and Johnson combined during their first eighteen months. In this way, a president can avoid searching questions from the press, a strategy Nixon adopted in the 1968 presidential campaign. The television networks responded by having reporters and columnists analyze Nixon's remarks immediately after a speech; the administration complained that some of these comments— dubbed "instant analysis"—were excessively critical and biased. Vice President Spiro T. Agnew launched a major administration assault on the media with a pair of speeches written by Patrick Buchanan, then a White House assistant, deriding the critics as members of a self-styled elite that should be made more responsive to majority opinion. Subsequent administration actions included challenges filed by Nixon supporters to the license renewals of several television stations owned by the *Wash-*

ington Post, among the administration's harshest critics; personal visits paid by Charles Colson, another White House aide, to television network executives, intended to intimidate them into providing less critical coverage; antitrust complaints filed by the Justice Department against the television networks; and attempts to get one White House reporter (Dan Rather) reassigned and to embarrass another (Daniel Schorr) through an FBI investigation. In short, the Nixon administration sought to use intimidation as a strategy for dealing with the press.[83]

Even presidents who enjoy and do well in regular press conferences turn to other means of communicating directly with citizens. FDR made effective use of radio for his famous "fireside chats," a technique that enabled him to create the feeling that he was coming directly into American homes and speaking personally to each of his millions of listeners. Carter used the same approach in his first television address to the nation: seated before an open hearth and wearing a cardigan sweater, the new president sought to project an image of informality and to underscore his concern with the nation's energy crisis.

During its first six months, the Clinton White House aggressively sought to bypass the national press corps by continuing many of the techniques it had successfully employed during the election campaign. Town Hall meetings, appearances on nontraditional outlets (Clinton's first exclusive television interview was on MTV), e-mail connections, and aggressive use of satellite links to local news outlets were supposed to replace the traditional reliance on the White House press corps. These avenues promised enhanced White House control of unmediated communication. The changes did not go unnoticed and occasioned considerable criticism by the established media. It did not help that many of the aides overseeing these alternative channels were young, inexperienced in the ways of Washington, and occasionally arrogant. Even though many features of Clinton's relations with the media were distinctive, they fell within the general trend toward White House pursuit of greater control over the president's message.[84]

In managing their relationships with the media, presidents must take into account their particular strengths and weaknesses. Nicknamed the Great Communicator, Reagan benefited enormously from his previous professional experience in radio, films, and television. To take advantage of those skills, the president frequently addressed the nation on prime-time television and used a series of Saturday radio broadcasts to explain and justify his administration's policies. The administration also avoided or restricted its use of other media formats that President Reagan did not handle as well as prepared speeches, specifically those that required him to give spontaneous answers to questions. He did not participate in call-in shows and seldom invited reporters to the White House for informal, on-the-record question and answer sessions. Reagan seldom would answer impromptu questions from reporters at photo sessions, and he held fewer press conferences in eight years than President Carter did in four.

Nationally televised speeches became "the basic mode of public communication during his [Reagan's] presidency." [85] It was not that Reagan gave substantially more major addresses than his predecessors,[86] but he seemed to use the occasions to greater effect. Reagan thus used the natural drama of appearances before joint sessions of Congress to launch his economic plan in 1981 and the Strategic Defense Initiative, which became known as Star Wars, in 1983.

Even presidents less skilled in public speaking than Reagan might think seriously about expanding their use of major addresses. Brace and Hinckley found that major addresses to the nation from Truman through Reagan added 6 percentage points, on average, to presidential approval ratings. Moreover, they found that these speeches were more frequent during the reelection year and more likely to be given the month after a drop in the approval ratings. Thus, the timing indicates that presidents have used them strategically as a way to boost their reelection efforts and combat criticism.[87]

Clinton has made effective use of addresses to the nation but could have done better. Probably the most widely anticipated and best received was his address on health care delivered on September 22, 1993. The speech laid out broad goals of health care reform and contributed to a rise in his approval ratings. But the reform plan was not submitted to Congress for another month, and formal proposals were not introduced until yet another month had passed and the battle for NAFTA had been concluded. The tactical error was serious: "Like a World War I general who ended the artillery barrage hours before the infantry advanced, Clinton's masterful speech on health-care reform was given long before the administration's plan was ready." [88] Although elaborate steps were taken to develop the capacity to plan communications strategy, the administration floundered in communicating a clear, consistent message.

Director of Communications. Since the administration of Lyndon Johnson, the White House has assigned someone to oversee the general message and symbolism projected to the public, a position known as director of communications. In concrete terms, the communications director oversees "HPCQ": headlines, pictures, captions, and quotes. The goal is "to structure the White House and Cabinet activities today [so] that tomorrow's headlines will be positive to the president, the photos and television shots will portray him attractively, the captions will be laudatory, and the quotes will encapsulate his policies." [89]At times, more than one person takes on this job. For example, in his first term, President Reagan benefited greatly not only from the skill and experience of Director of Communications David Gergen, but also from that of James A. Baker III and Michael Deaver, other members of the White House staff who carefully managed his media and public image.

This team was especially adept at selecting the "line of the day," based around a story or "photo opportunity" featuring the president that would dominate the evening news, as well as a "theme for the week," selected to coordinate communication throughout the entire administration. Managing these undertakings required sensitivity to media rhythms, an eye for the dramatic, and a sense of politics. The absence of this team was keenly felt in Reagan's second term when the images were not nearly so favorable. One explanation for the slump in Bush's popularity in mid-1990 and mid-1991 was the absence of a senior White House official with extensive political experience to manage the communication message.[90]

After a rocky beginning to his presidency, Bill Clinton coaxed David Gergen, the former aide to Reagan and two other Republican presidents, to join the White House staff in May 1993. It was hoped that this consummate Washington insider would improve relations with the press corps, develop a better coordinated communications strategy, and provide beneficial "spin," or flattering interpretations of administration actions. Early in Clinton's term, several administration missteps garnered extensive negative media coverage that led his young, inexperienced staff to become bitter and accusatory toward the press. Two botched nominations for attorney general, a $200 haircut that tied up air traffic in Los Angeles, a mini-scandal over staff dismissals in the White House travel office, and compromises over budget details drew critical coverage and produced a siege mentality in the White House even earlier than it usually develops. Gergen's credibility and inside knowledge of the communications process helped to stabilize relations with the press corps. But Gergen's moderate political views and partisan background reportedly triggered White House friction. He worked most heavily on NAFTA and developed strategies for the first economic summit, the 1994 State of the Union message, and Clinton's comments at the funeral of former president Nixon. He was less closely involved, either by choice or exclusion, with health care, defending the president on allegations about Whitewater, and preparing for the 1994 midterm elections. Gergen was given credit by some for the administration's improved standing in the polls during the last half of 1993, but his presence was less welcome and possibly less needed in 1994, and he transferred to the State Department in late June in the midst of a major White House staff shake-up.[91] Gergen finally left the administration at the end of the year, when Clinton's ratings had again fallen substantially.

Regardless of how carefully the White House plans, the nature and timing of events also influence how the media and the American people view the president. The potentially damaging effects of the bombing of the Marine barracks in Lebanon in late 1983 were mitigated by stories, shortly following, on the successful invasion of Grenada. In contrast, there was no mitigating development in late 1986: the story on the Iran arms shipment was followed immediately by another on the alleged diversion of profits from the arms sale to assist the contras in Central America. Moreover, the complexity and long-term nature of the Iran-contra affair meant that media and public attention focused on the matter for a protracted time as one revelation after another was released.

Relations Between the President and the Media: Conflict or Collusion?

It is common for presidents to view the press unfavorably. George Washington, whom journalists treated rather well, was inclined not to run for a second term because of what he considered a critical press.[92] From that beginning, virtually all presidents have expressed outrage, indignation, resentment, or consternation over their treatment in the media.

In turn, members of the press have criticized the way presidents handle media relations. Typically, chief executives are accused of "managing" the news and, as their terms in office progress, of becoming increasingly "isolated" from the media and the American people. Some, such as Lyndon Johnson and Richard Nixon, also were charged with deliberately lying to the media and the public.

There is little question that a built-in conflict exists between the president and the media. Chief executives want to suppress information they feel will endanger the nation's security or put their administrations in a bad light. Members of the media are eager for news, however sensitive it may be, and they have an interest in criticizing the president and his associates as a means of getting the public's attention and thereby creating a demand for their services.

Despite the potential for conflict, there is a basis for cooperation between presidents and the press that ultimately produces a collusive relationship.[93] Quite simply, the two are mutually dependent: neither presidents nor the press can perform their jobs without the assistance of the other, and cooperation is, therefore, mutually beneficial. The president must be able to communicate with the public through the media, and the media must have the administration's cooperation if they are to cover the most important official in the national government and give the public an accurate assessment of presidential activities. Moreover, the White House offers a range of media services designed to seduce reporters into favorable coverage. The product is an *exchange relationship*, a set of negotiated terms for the interaction between media and the president that favors the White House and disadvantages the public.[94] As David Broder has argued, "We have been drawn into a circle of working relationships and even friendships with the people we are supposed to cover. The distinction between press and government has tended to become erased." [95]

Grossman and Kumar's analysis of the media's treatment of six presidents over a twenty-five-year period shows that, for the most part, coverage has been favorable.[96] From 1953 to 1978, positive stories on the president outnumbered negative stories in *Time* magazine and the *New York Times* and the same finding held for the "CBS Evening News" from 1968 to 1978. Pictures, particularly those appearing in newspapers, tended to be favorable even when they accompanied a negative story. The number of unfavorable stories rose during the Vietnam War and the Watergate scandal, but after 1974 the treatment of the president became more favorable again.[97]

Grossman and Kumar argue that the general relationship between the president and the media goes through certain predictable phases.[98] During the initial period of "alliance," both parties agree that the focus should be on the new administration's appointees and its proposed goals and policies—the presidency is "open"; reporters are likely "to have their phone calls answered, to be granted interviews, and to get information that has not been specifically restricted." [99] During the second phase, "competition," the president wants to concentrate on portraying members of his administration as part of a happy team, committed to common goals and policies, while the media focus on conflicts among personalities in the administration and controversies over policies.[100] Presidents restrict access to themselves and others in the administration and may even go on the attack against especially critical reporters or organizations. The final phase of presidential-media relationships is "detachment." Surrogates manage the news, and presidents appear only in favorable settings scheduled to coincide with major events. The media, in turn, engage in more investigative reporting and seek information from sources other than the White House.

The Clinton administration's relationship with the press did not seem to follow the typical phases identified by Grossman and Kumar. There was an unusually brief period of "alliance," relations becoming obviously strained within a matter of months. The period of "competition" set in early with the president offering outspoken criticism on several occasions, including a bitter public exchange with Brit Hume of ABC News on June 12, 1993, and a first-year-ending interview with *Rolling Stone* magazine that blamed the media for giving a false impression of his administration.[101] Moreover, one study found that television news coverage provided, on balance, more negative than positive comments for all but one of the administration's first sixteen months in office. In fact, nearly three-quarters of all network reporters' assessments of Clinton were found to have been negative.[102] Administration spokespersons quickly latched onto the report as a way to explain why the president was getting no credit for the good economic conditions (Lichter found that 60 percent of the network stories on the economy were negative),[103] and there was an upsurge in stories considering whether the press had been too harsh in its treatment of the president. Although the precise content of coverage may be debated, it is clear that Clinton was the darling of neither establishment nor nonestablishment (such as talk radio) media.[104]

Many people in the executive branch help presidents deal with the media, but the media also have their share of resources. A large number of reporters cover the White House, many of whom have expertise in substantive areas such as law, science, welfare, and defense policy.[105] Nonetheless, members of the media may not use their skills to full advantage. Journalists covering the presidency generally lack confidence in dealing with the substance of policies and consequently focus their coverage on four areas where they feel most comfortable: administration scandals, internal dissension, a public gaffe or tactical blunder, and the ebb and flow of electoral contests and public opinion polls.[106] The result is unintended collusion between the presidency and the media that keeps the public less rather than more informed about American government. This line of criticism, focused on journalistic norms and practices, goes beyond those who believe that particular presidents received less vigorous scrutiny than they deserved. For example, some have suggested that Reagan's vaunted "Teflon coating" was the product of poor journalism.[107]

As we have seen, presidents are not powerless to influence the impressions that the public develops of them and their programs. One segment of the public is most likely to be supportive—members of the president's political party, the subject of the final section of this chapter.

Presidents and Parties

Parties have been important to presidents since 1796, but this relationship has undergone dramatic change throughout American history, particularly over the past fifty years. As reviewed in Chapter 2, political parties emerged early in American history despite concern that they represented a potentially divisive influence. Since the election of 1796, when Washington retired from office, parties have been central structures in the presidential selection process, nominating candidates, helping diverse social and economic interests to coalesce under a common banner, mobilizing voters, organizing campaigns, raising funds, recruiting personnel for the winning administration, mediating relations with interest groups, and helping to develop programmatic appeals. In modern times, however, responsibility for most of these activities has been transferred elsewhere. With the advent of "personalized politics"—electoral competition that concentrates on candidates more than traditional party loyalties—the link between presidents and their political parties has changed. Campaign staffs are personal constructs almost wholly independent of party structures, and televised ads are the principal means of mobilizing voters. Once in office, presidents use White House aides to recruit personnel, maintain liaison with interest groups, and develop program ideas. In short, presidents are now less dependent on their parties both for winning elections and for governing. Modern presidents largely preempt the services traditionally performed by party leaders.[108]

Thus, the relationship between presidents and their parties has undergone significant change. On the one hand, today's presidents are less constrained by party leaders and structures than in the past. After thirty years of decline, American parties are less powerful organizations, run by leaders who are considerably less independent than in earlier days. On the other hand, presidents no longer rely exclusively on these broadly based public structures to muster support behind presidential initiatives.

Altering the Traditional President-Party Relationship

Thomas Jefferson, once a staunch critic of political parties, became the most powerful party leader to occupy the presidency. By exercising control over fellow partisans in Congress, he used the party as a means to govern the nation.[109] Throughout the nineteenth century, parties were the means to effectively link political elites with the public and then bridge the institutional distances so carefully created under the Constitution.[110] The relationship between presidents and party became even more critical with the emergence of an activist conception of the presidency, a change usually associated with Theodore Roosevelt and Woodrow Wilson. When harnessed by a program-minded executive, parties could serve as agents of change and progress, an instrument to facilitate presidential leadership much as Jefferson had demonstrated. But the central concerns of American parties were customarily focused on far more mundane and parochial pursuits—patronage jobs, public contracts, and subsidies—that made them close allies of Congress and resistant to presidential control. As decentralized structures reflecting local conditions and concerns, parties acted far more often as impediments to change and enemies of central leadership than they did as instruments of such efforts. This posed minimal difficulty to most nineteenth-century presidents but became a serious hindrance to the kind of heroic leadership routinely expected in the twentieth century.

Franklin Roosevelt's actions ultimately altered the nature of American political parties. Roosevelt abandoned the usual practices of filling administration vacancies with party loyalists, turning instead to committed New Dealers. He attempted to unseat uncooperative members of his own party by supporting challengers to conservative Democrats in primary elections in twelve states during 1938. Party rules governing the presidential nomination were changed to weaken the influence of southern leaders. Roosevelt forged a direct, personal relationship with citizens through the radio to replace the mediated relationship via political parties. And, by creating administrative machinery subject to presidential control, it was made feasible for "the president [to] govern in the absence of party government."[111]

Subsequent presidents, particularly Johnson and Nixon, introduced changes that were consistent with the path of development set in motion by Roosevelt.[112] Johnson ran party affairs from the White House, weakening national and local party organizations. Nixon created the wholly autonomous Committee for the Reelection of the President (CREEP), which hastened the decline of not only Republican Party organizations, but also his own presidency. Republican fortunes hit their low point after Nixon resigned from the presidency in disgrace on August 9, 1974; many Republican members of Congress suffered defeat in the November 1974 elections, and Republican identification dropped precipitously. By the mid-1970s, these developments had combined with other trends in American politics (post-1968 reforms in the nomination process, the development of single-issue interest groups, the rise of the professional campaign consultant) to leave the party system largely irrelevant. Presidents Ford and Carter had the misfortune of serving when party fortunes were at their nadir.

Today, the situation may have changed once again. Presidents Reagan and Bush took actions that may not only have revitalized but also reconstructed the Republican Party. Both raised large sums of money in behalf of party candidates, an activity other presidents have undertaken but which Reagan and Bush pursued with special vigor. Bush, in particular, brought an extensive history of party service to the White House, having served as a county chairman in Texas during the 1960s and as chairman of the Republican National Committee during the Watergate crisis. The result has been a renewal of national party organizations, based on raising funds, providing important services to local and national candidates, and serving as a stimulus for policy debate. Republican revitalization occurred first, with the Democrats following suit.

But party revitalization was not enough to save George Bush. Only months after registering nearly 90 percent approval ratings, his support crashed; he experienced the worst election loss by an incumbent since William Howard Taft in 1912. Without the firm base of party, presidential support is dangerously volatile, and despite the new services provided through the national party offices, the parties' connection to the public remains remarkably weak.

Into this setting stepped Bill Clinton, who, perhaps dangerously, presented himself to the American public as a "New Democrat," a member of the party's minority, moderate wing. The Democrats' dominant, liberal wing remained in control of Congress, however, and Clinton found himself inexorably drawn to embrace a Democratic agenda frustrated by earlier Republican presidents and pushed forward by congressional Democrats and their principal interest group allies. (This leaves open, of course, the question of Clinton's own core beliefs, a subject addressed in Chapter 4.) As a moderate, Clinton might have hoped to win limited Republican support on a wide range of issues, but congressional Republicans were solidly opposed to most presidential proposals, leaving Clinton dependent on his own fragmented party. During his first year in office, Clinton broke dramatically with his fellow Democrats over NAFTA when a majority of congressional Democrats opposed the treaty and success depended on Republican votes. Following the Republican takeover of the House and Senate in the 1994 midterm elections, the distance between Clinton and congressional Democrats increased. The party was in disarray with uncertain prospects for the 1996 election year. The president ordered a review of the effectiveness and desirability of affirmative action programs, a mainstay of Democratic platforms for a quarter century. Again in 1995, Clinton ignored the advice of most congressional Democrats and offered a budget compromise that agreed to substantial spending cuts in existing programs and a balanced budget in ten years rather than rejecting outright Republican proposals for even larger cuts and a balanced budget in seven years. Although Clinton's relationship with his fellow Democrats had been strained, his prospects of working with congressional Republicans, who remained remarkably united despite several presidential candidates, were even worse. As the battle over the 1996 budget intensified, Clinton hardened his position in negotiations with Republicans and most elected Democrats rallied behind him. This development reduced the likelihood of a 1996 challenge to his renomination from the party's liberal wing.

Public officials, party leaders, and party activists still look to the president to serve as chief of the party that helped to put him in the White House. However, presidents have not wanted to share influence within the party for fear of endangering their short-term needs. So long as parties are useful as a vehicle to organize and manage the government, we might expect presidents to continue supporting revitalization efforts, but once their helpfulness comes into question, presidents will begin to question the value of party building. This is especially true for Clinton.

Presidents, Party, and Elections

Presidents also try to boost their party by influencing the outcome of elections. As the head of the national ticket, most presidential candidates work to get their party's candidates elected to Congress. Such support is especially valued if it comes from a popular incumbent who is expected to win in November. But it is possible for a chief executive to have little to do with the party's congressional candidates, a strategy Nixon followed in 1972 in his quest to win support from traditionally Democratic voters. Alternatively, congressional candidates may choose to avoid too close an association with an unpopular president.

Most presidents also try to influence the outcome of midterm congressional elections, those held between presidential elections, in hopes of minimizing the loss of seats that the president's party customarily experiences in these contests.[113] Assistance in the form of joint campaign appearances, fund raising, and televised speeches cannot be provided to everyone, and the decisions about where to concentrate efforts are often difficult. Should help be channeled to candidates in crucial competitive contests, to close political friends, or important party figures? What about legislators who have voted against the administration's proposals? Of the presidents who have served since Eisenhower, only Johnson chose not to campaign actively in 1966 in the midst of the Vietnam War. Given his background in party affairs, it is not surprising to discover that Bush pursued an aggressive strategy of presidential support during the 1990 midterm election, recruiting some candidates, raising money, and committing at least one day a week to campaign-related visits after Labor Day and three or four days a week as election day approached.[114] Clinton also sought to help Democrats in 1994, although some chose to stay arm's length from a president with declining approval ratings.

But it is surprising how seldom presidents attempt to pick their party's nominees for Senate and House seats. An early study of approximately 1,200 congressional nomination campaigns from 1943 to 1960 found that presidents endorsed only thirty-seven candidates, only seventeen of whom won both the nomination and the general election.[115] Franklin Roosevelt had only partial success in 1938 when he endorsed twelve nominees. Only six got to Congress, but by violating traditional norms, the president suffered a more serious setback. There is a long tradition of such contests being exclusively state or district business, and presidents are reluctant to make an enemy in Congress by endorsing the wrong candidate.

There are limits to what a president can accomplish, especially in elections for the House of Representatives. For one thing, the sheer number of contests (435 every two years) precludes participation in many of them. For another, there is good evidence that the off-year House elections are primarily local, not national, events. Scholars who have examined off-year congressional elections report the same basic finding: how people vote has more to do with their evaluations of the congressional candidates than with their assessment of the president.[116] Moreover, incumbency is a valuable asset for congressional candidates; they benefit from previous campaign experience, close relationships with voters, greater knowledge of issues, and superior financial resources, which give them a considerable advantage over their opponents.[117] Presidents who attempt to campaign against sitting members of Congress therefore face almost insurmountable odds. In 1994, some observers suggest, Clinton's last-week efforts in behalf of Democrats may have helped nationalize the process, making it more of a referendum on the incumbent and offsetting his candidates' local advantages.[118]

Midterm election outcomes depend on the condition of the national economy and the president's standing in public opinion polls at the time of the elections.[119] Voting in these contests tends to be *negative*; that is, those who disapprove of the president's performance in office are more likely to cast their ballot in such elections than those who approve of his performance.[120] Gary Jacobson contends that the president's role in congressional elections is essentially indirect: the state of the economy and the president's ratings in the public opinion polls influence the caliber of candidates who run in congressional elections. If, for example, these are not favorable, the opposition party will be able to field an unusually large proportion of formidable challengers with well-financed campaigns, and the president's party in Congress may lose a considerable number of seats.[121]

Senatorial midterm elections offer a somewhat more encouraging opportunity for presidents who wish to influence results. Approximately one-third of the Senate's 100 seats are at stake every two years, so the chief executive can concentrate on these contests in a way that is not possible for House races. Although sitting senators are in the same position as House members in being able to bring their name to the attention of constituents, incumbency is not as advantageous for a senator as it is for a House member, because most Senate races are hard fought. Challengers are much more visible to the electorate than are those who run against House incumbents. Popular presidents, therefore, are better able to help candidates who challenge incumbent senators of the opposite party by increasing the challengers' visibility through public association.

Senate elections since the early 1960s demonstrate the combined effect of these factors. In 1962, when John Kennedy was president, his party lost five seats in the House but picked up two in the Senate; in

Table 3-2 Gains and Losses of President's Party in House and Senate Off-Year Elections, 1942–1994

Year	President	President's party	Change in House seats	Change in Senate seats
1942	Roosevelt	Democratic	−50	−8
1946	Truman	Democratic	−54	−11
1950	Truman	Democratic	−29	−5
1954	Eisenhower	Republican	−18	−1
1958	Eisenhower	Republican	−47	−12
1962	Kennedy	Democratic	−5	+2
1966	Johnson	Democratic	−48	−4
1970	Nixon	Republican	−12	+1
1974	Ford	Republican	−48	−5
1978	Carter	Democratic	−16	−3
1982	Reagan	Republican	−27	+1
1986	Reagan	Republican	−5	−8
1990	Bush	Republican	−8	+1
1994	Clinton	Democratic	−52	−8

Source: *Statistical Abstract of the United States* (Washington, D.C.: Government Printing Office, 1986), 247. Data for 1986, 1990, and 1994 are from *Congressional Quarterly Weekly Report,* Nov. 8, 1986, 2803; Nov. 10, 1990, 3796; and Nov. 12, 1994, 3232.

Note: Data represent the difference between the number of seats held by the president's party in present and preceding Congress.

1974, when Gerald Ford succeeded to the presidency after Nixon's forced resignation, Republicans lost forty-eight House seats but only five Senate seats. Republicans lost eight House seats in 1990 but gained one seat in the Senate. Once again in 1994, the president's party lost seats in the House and in the Senate, as well. But even more important, the election dramatically reshaped the American political landscape. The outcome was, in the words of Walter Dean Burnham, a "seismic event," producing Republican majorities in the House for the first time in forty years while restoring a majority in the Senate which had been lost in the 1986 midterms. To Burnham, it was the "most consequential off-year election in (exactly) one hundred years." [122] While thirty-five Democratic House incumbents were being defeated, not a single Republican House incumbent lost. Republicans were also far more successful in competing for open House seats. The result was a dramatic loss of fifty-two House seats for the president's party. No Republican Senate incumbents lost, whereas two Democratic incumbents did, and the president's party failed to defend open seats, producing a net Democratic loss of eight. The Republican sweep extended beyond Congress with net losses by Democrats in gubernatorial and state legislative elections, as well (*see Table 3-2*).

At times the president avoids playing party leader. Because voting in the U.S. Congress does not follow strict party lines, presidents often need support from members of the other party. (Chapter 5 examines this matter further.) Carter won passage of the Panama Canal Treaty only because of Republican support; Reagan's budget victories in 1981 rested on a coalition of Republicans and Southern Democrats in the House, and Clinton was able to win passage of NAFTA only because of Republican votes. In such circumstances, it is not surprising to find presidents reluctant to engage in aggressive partisan conflict. Campaign rhetoric can be taken personally by members of the opposition party, making it more difficult for the president to win their future support on legislation.

The President and Party Programs

One area of partisan activity the president clearly dominates is the preparation of party programs for dealing with major national problems. A president seeking reelection has the greatest influence in the writing of the party platform at the national convention. The incumbent also has the opportunity to identify party issues and programs during the course of the presidential campaign and may choose to emphasize certain parts of the platform, ignore others, or even take stands at variance with those contained in the document.

Traditionally, students of American politics have concluded that party platforms and presidential campaign speeches are not to be taken seriously. (The platform planks are for candidates to "run" on, not to "stand" on; campaign promises are merely rhetoric and do not constitute commitments on the candidate's part.) Other studies revealed that presidents took the pledges seriously, and that they worked with Congress or issued executive orders to enact most of their campaign commitments.[123] Johnson and Nixon acted on more than half of the promises they made in campaign speeches in 1964 and 1968, respectively.[124] Eisenhower and Kennedy took action on about three-fourths of their campaign promises.[125] Looking at the period Kennedy through Reagan, Jeff Fishel concluded that these presidents acted on some two-thirds of their campaign promises.[126]

Although George Bush was one of the most party-oriented presidents in the modern era, he encountered surprising criticism from Republican members of Congress when he entered into an agreement with congressional Democrats on a package of spending cuts and revenue increases for the 1991 fiscal year budget. His acceptance of tax increases broke a campaign pledge to oppose new taxes. When the budget agreement was announced just a month before the midterm election, House Republicans, led by the minority whip Newt Gingrich, abandoned the president and voted against the plan. The resulting chain reaction defeated the proposal. Not only did the president lose the immediate battle, but for a time he also lost the leadership on programs within his party.[127] Although presidents do not automatically exercise this type of leadership in their parties, there is a strong expectation that they will do so. Violation of this expectation by leaders who get too far out in front of their followers can exact a heavy price.

The extent to which presidential programs become reality depends to a considerable degree on the president's influence over the party within the government, the officials in the legislative and executive branches who are either elected under a partisan label or appointed primarily because of their party activities or because it is expected that they will implement party views on public policy matters. A president usually has little control over party activities in Congress. Most senators and representatives are elected independently of the president. Moreover, the president has comparatively little influence over the organization of his party in Congress. Although Thomas Jefferson determined who his party's leaders would be, for the most part American chief executives have been chary of interfering with the right of Congress to choose its own people. Dwight Eisenhower was forced to work with Senate Republican leader William Knowland, whose views on foreign policy were quite different from his own. During part of John Kennedy's administration, the Democratic Speaker of the House was John McCormack, a political rival from Kennedy's home state.

The president has more influence over the party in the executive branch. (Chapter 6 examines the president's relations with the executive branch.) The chief executive can make appointments to policy-making posts that both reward individuals for their service to the party and permit them to influence the administration of government programs. In particular, his closest political advisers on the White House staff constitute what is, in effect, the president's personal party: individuals who have labored in the presidential campaign want to protect their chief's interests and promote the administration's policies after they assume their new posts.[128] Ronald Reagan demonstrated the potential influence that a president can exercise over the bureaucracy by carefully selecting political appointees in accordance with ideology as well as shared party affiliation.

The Rhetorical Presidency

The president's relationship with the American people between elections has undergone significant changes. Kernell contends that presidents used to promote their programs primarily by negotiating with other political elites in Congress and the executive branch, but today they more often choose to "go public"; that is, a president resorts to promoting "himself and his policies in Washington by appealing to the American public for support." [129] He does this by means of public addresses, public appearances, and political travel. James Ceaser and his associates refer to this development as "the rise of the rhetorical presidency," and argue that "presidential speech and action increasingly reflect the opinion that speaking is governing. Speeches are written to become the events to which people react no less than the 'real' events themselves." [130]

There are several reasons for this development. The mass media—first radio, and then television—enabled the president to communicate directly with the American people and to reach the public instantaneously. In addition, the tactics of the campaign are now carried into the governing process: Washington "outsiders"—Carter, Reagan, and Clinton are examples—used the same approaches in governing as they used in winning the nomination and the election. As Ceaser and his associates explain, "So formative has the campaign become of our tastes for oratory and of our conception of leadership that presidential speech and governing have come more and more to imitate the model of the campaign." [131] They also contend that beginning with Woodrow Wilson, presidents changed their view of leadership: a president now employs "oratory to create an active public opinion that, if necessary, will pressure the Congress into accepting his program." [132] Kernell sees this development as a somewhat more recent one, a practice presidents use because the elites with whom they must bargain are more numerous, fragmented, and politically independent than before.[133]

Although these new developments undoubtedly have affected the presidency, the fact remains that public opinion cannot be transformed directly into public policy. If the president wants to see his programs adopted and implemented, he must use the powers and institutional arrangements of his office, and he must work with Congress, the executive branch, and the courts to accomplish his purpose. In Chapter 4 we examine the personality traits and skills that presidents bring to this task.

NOTES

1. Henry Jones Ford, *The Rise and Growth of American Politics: A Sketch of Constitutional Development* (New York: Macmillan, 1900), 283.

2. Woodrow Wilson, *Constitutional Government in the United States* (1908; reprint, New York: Columbia University Press, 1961), 68.

3. Richard Neustadt, *Presidential Power: The Politics of Leadership* (New York: Wiley, 1960), 86–107.

4. Samuel Kernell, *Going Public: New Strategies of Presidential Leadership*, 3d ed. (Washington, D.C.: CQ Press, 1997).

5. George C. Edwards III, "Frustration and Folly: Bill Clinton and the Public Presidency," in *The Clinton Presidency: First Appraisals*, ed. Colin Campbell and Bert A. Rockman (Chatham, N.J.: Chatham House, 1996).

6. David Easton, *A Systems Analysis of Political Life* (New York: Wiley, 1965), chaps. 10–13.

7. Fred I. Greenstein, "What the President Means to Americans: Presidential Choice Between Elections," in *Choosing the President*, ed. James David Barber (Englewood Cliffs, N.J.: Prentice-Hall, 1974), 144–146.

8. *New York Times*, Nov. 5, 1991.

9. Joseph E. Kallenbach, *The American Chief Executive: The Presidency and the Governorship* (New York: Harper & Row, 1966), 275.

10. Barry Schwartz, *George Washington: The Making of an American Symbol* (Ithaca, N.Y.: Cornell University Press, 1987), 58–63.

11. Ibid., esp. part 2.

12. Schwartz's discussion of the various public portrayals of Washington and their iconography is especially valuable. It may be of interest to students to note which figures' portraits appear on the most widely circulated coins and currency of the time.

13. Barbara Hinckley, *The Symbolic Presidency: How Presidents Portray Themselves* (New York: Routledge, 1990), 130.

14. Ibid., 131–133.

15. Paul Brace and Barbara Hinckley, *Follow the Leader: Opinion Polls and the Modern Presidents* (New York: Basic Books, 1992), 92.

16. Fred Greenstein, *Children and Politics* (New Haven, Conn.: Yale University Press, 1965); Robert Hess and Judith Torney, *The Development of Political Attitudes in Children* (Chicago: Aldine, 1967); David Easton and Jack Dennis, *Children in the Political System: Origins of Political Legitimacy* (New York: McGraw-Hill, 1969).

17. Dean Jaros, Herbert Hirsch, and Frederick J. Fleron, Jr., "The Malevolent Leader: Political Socialization in an American Subculture," *American Political Science Review* (June 1968): 564–575.

18. Jack Dennis and Carol Webster, "Children's Images of the President and Government in 1962 and 1974," *American Politics Quarterly* (October 1975): 398.

19. Greenstein, "What the President Means to Americans."

20. Christopher Arterton, "The Impact of Watergate on Children's Attitudes Towards Political Authority," *Political Science Quarterly* (June 1974): 269–288; Christopher Arterton, "Watergate and Children's Attitudes Towards Political Authority Revisited," *Political Science Quarterly* (Fall 1975): 477–496; Dean Jaros and John Shoemaker, "The Malevolent Unindicted Co-conspirator: Watergate and Appalachian Youth," *American Politics Quarterly* (October 1976): 483–505.

21. Findings of the Survey Research Center at the University of Michigan in the mid-1960s indicated that of all the occupations in the United States, including "famous doctor," "president of a large corporation like General Motors," "bishop or

other church official," "Supreme Court justice," and "senator," more than half the adults named the president as the most respected.

22. Samuel Kernell, Peter Sperlich, and Aaron Wildavsky, "Public Support for Presidents," in *Perspectives on the Presidency*, ed. Aaron Wildavsky (Boston: Little, Brown, 1975), 148–181.

23. Brace and Hinckley, *Follow the Leader*, 19.

24. John Mueller, *War, Presidents and Public Opinion* (New York: Wiley, 1973).

25. Ibid. Mueller attributes Eisenhower's continued high popularity ratings in office to a number of reasons, including his personal appeal, the credit he received for ending the Korean War, his "amateur" political status, which allowed him to appear "above the battle," and the fact that he made few changes in domestic policy and so did not antagonize groups as much as other presidents.

26. Samuel Kernell, "Explaining Presidential Popularity," *American Political Science Review* (June 1978): 506–522.

27. Jong Lee, "Rallying Around the Flag: Foreign Policy Events and Presidential Popularity," *Presidential Studies Quarterly* (Fall 1977): 252–256.

28. George C. Edwards III, *The Public Presidency: The Pursuit of Popular Support* (New York: St. Martin's Press, 1983), 239–247.

29. Ibid., 247.

30. Henry Kenski, "The Impact of Economic Conditions on Presidential Popularity," *Journal of Politics* (August 1977): 764–773; Kristen Monroe, "Economic Influences on Presidential Popularity," *Public Opinion Quarterly* (Fall 1978): 360–369.

31. Edwards, *The Public Presidency*, 235.

32. Robert Shapiro, "Politics and the Federal Reserve," *Public Interest* (Winter 1982): 119–139; Edwards, "Frustration and Folly."

33. James Stimson, "Public Support for American Presidents: A Cyclical Model," *Public Opinion Quarterly* (Spring 1976): 1–21. Another possible reason the incumbent president's performance ratings tend to rise in the fourth year is that when potential political opponents begin to appear on the scene, citizens compare the president with these real people rather than with an abstract ideal of a chief executive.

34. Brace and Hinckley, *Follow the Leader*, 23–24, 32, 24, 27, 28.

35. Kernell, "Explaining Presidential Popularity."

36. Ibid., chap. 7.

37. James M. Perry, "Clinton Relies Heavily on White House Pollster to Take Words Right Out of the Public's Mouth," *Wall Street Journal*, March 23, 1994, A16, as cited in Edwards, "Frustration and Folly," 232.

38. Edwards, "Frustration and Folly," 240.

39. Ibid., 243.

40. Edwards, *The Public Presidency*, 233.

41. Richard Brody and Benjamin Page, "The Impact of Events on Presidential Popularity: The Johnson and Nixon Administrations," in *Perspectives on the Presidency*.

42. Donald Singleton, "The Role of Broadcasting in Presidential Popularity: An Exploration in Presidential Power" (Paper delivered at the 1976 annual meeting of the International Communication Association).

43. Fred Smoller, "The Six-O'Clock Presidency: Patterns of Network Coverage of the President," *Presidential Studies Quarterly* (Winter 1986): 42–43.

44. Timothy Haight and Richard Brody, "The Mass Media and Presidential Popularity: Presidential Broadcasting and News in the Nixon Administration," *Communications Research* (Spring 1977): 41–60.

45. Bradley H. Patterson, Jr., *The Ring of Power: The White House Staff and Its Expanding Role in Government* (New York: Basic Books, 1988), chaps. 11, 12, 13, 19.

Also see Charles E. Walcott and Karen M. Hult, *Governing the White House: From Hoover through LBJ* (Lawrence: University Press of Kansas, 1995), chaps. 3 and 10.

46. Foreign trips have other benefits as well. Not only are they flattering to the people of the visited country, but they also appeal to ethnic groups at home with ties to those nations.

47. Brace and Hinckley, *Follow the Leader*, 54.

48. Louis Koenig, *The Chief Executive*, rev. ed. (New York: Harcourt, Brace and World, 1968), 188.

49. Kernell, *Going Public*, 119.

50. Brace and Hinckley, *Follow the Leader*, 56–57. Also see Paul Brace and Barbara Hinckley, "Presidential Activities from Truman Through Reagan: Timing and Impact," *Journal of Politics* (May 1993): 382–398.

51. Bruce Miroff, "The Presidency and the Public: Leadership as Spectacle," in *The Presidency and the Political System*, 4th ed., ed. Michael Nelson (Washington, D.C.: CQ Press, 1995).

52. Ibid., 290.

53. Edwards, *The Public Presidency*, 16–17.

54. Joseph A. Pika, "Interest Groups and the White House under Roosevelt and Truman," *Political Science Quarterly* (Winter 1987–88): 647–668.

55. Joseph A. Pika, "Interest Groups and the Executive: Presidential Intervention," in *Interest Group Politics*, ed. Allan J. Cigler and Burdett A. Loomis (Washington, D.C.: CQ Press, 1983), 318. Also see Joseph A. Pika, "Opening Doors for Kindred Souls: The White House Office of Public Liaison," in *Interest Group Politics*, 3d ed., ed. Allan J. Cigler and Burdett A. Loomis (Washington, D.C.: CQ Press, 1991); Martha Joynt Kumar and Michael Baruch Grossman, "Political Communications from the White House: The Interest Group Connection," *Presidential Studies Quarterly* (Winter 1986): 92–101; Walcott and Hult, *Governing the White House*, chap. 6; and Patterson, *The Ring of Power*, chap. 14.

56. Kumar and Grossman, "Political Communications," 98.

57. Graham Wilson, "The Clinton Administration and Interest Groups," in *The Clinton Presidency: First Appraisals*.

58. In addition to the essay by Wilson, "The Clinton Administration and Interest Groups," see Barbara Sinclair, "Trying to Govern Positively in a Negative Era: Clinton and the 103rd Congress," and Paul J. Quirk and Joseph Hinchliffe, "Domestic Policy: The Trials of a Centrist Democrat," in *The Clinton Presidency: First Appraisals*.

59. James Pollard, *The Presidents and the Press* (New York: Macmillan, 1947), chap. 1.

60. William Rivers, *The Opinion-Makers* (Boston: Beacon Press, 1967), 7.

61. Michael Baruch Grossman and Martha Joynt Kumar, *Portraying the President: The White House and the News Media* (Baltimore: Johns Hopkins University Press, 1981), 19.

62. Austin Ranney, "Broadcasting, Narrowcasting, and Politics," in *The New American Political System*, 2d ed., ed. Anthony King (Washington, D.C.: American Enterprise Institute, 1990).

63. Harold W. Stanley and Richard G. Niemi, *Vital Statistics on American Politics*, 5th ed. (Washington, D.C.: CQ Press, 1995), table 2-12, 68.

64. Ibid., table 2-1, 47.

65. Benjamin I. Page, Robert Y. Shapiro, and Glenn R. Dempsey, "What Moves Public Opinion?" *American Political Science Review* (March 1987): 23–43; and Donald L. Jordan, "Newspaper Effects on Policy Preferences," *Public Opinion Quarterly* (1993): 191–204. Page, Shapiro, and Dempsey examined television reports, whereas Jordan concentrated on newspaper effects.

66. Grossman and Kumar, *Portraying the President*, 209–210.

67. Stanley and Niemi, *Vital Statistics on American Politics*, 5th ed., table 2-2, 48–49.

68. Stephen Hess, *The Washington Reporters* (Washington, D.C.: Brookings, 1981), chap. 2; Leon Segal, *Reporters and Officials* (Lexington, Mass.: D.C. Heath, 1973), chap. 1.

69. Hess, *The Washington Reporters*, 31.

70. There are some notable exceptions to this rule. The "News Hour with Jim Lehrer," broadcast nightly by the Public Broadcasting Service (PBS), takes an hour to examine two or three topics in depth; ABC's "Nightline" looks at one topic for half an hour. PBS's "Washington Week in Review" uses major political reporters to analyze the significant news developments of the previous week; CNN provides continuing coverage as well as expanded focus on Washington, as on "Inside Politics."

71. Grossman and Kumar, *Portraying the President*, 43.

72. Worthy of note are reporters who write high-quality, in-depth pieces for the *Wall Street Journal*—a weekday publication available throughout the United States, with a large daily circulation. Other skilled journalists work for elite publications with specialized readerships, such as *Business Week, Congressional Quarterly, National Journal,* and *New Republic*; for large, regional, daily newspapers, such as the *Los Angeles Times, Baltimore Sun,* and *Chicago Tribune*; and for the chains, such as Knight-Ridder or Scripps-Howard, that provide service to many newspapers.

73. Grossman and Kumar, *Portraying the President*, chap. 5.

74. M. L. Stein, *When Presidents Meet the Press* (New York: Julian Messner, 1969), 166.

75. Larry Speakes, *Speaking Out: Inside the Reagan White House* (New York: Scribners, 1988), 136, 153.

76. Patterson, *The Ring of Power,* 174.

77. Fred I. Greenstein, *The Hidden-Hand Presidency: Eisenhower as Leader* (New York: Basic Books, 1982), 66–70.

78. William Lammers, "Presidential Press Conference Schedules: Who Hides and When?" *Political Science Quarterly* (Spring 1981): 261–278.

79. See especially the discussion of George Bush in Brace and Hinckley, *Follow the Leader,* chap. 7.

80. Jarol Manheim and William Lammers, "The News Conference and Presidential Leadership of Public Opinion: Does the Tail Wag the Dog?" *Presidential Studies Quarterly* (Spring 1981): 177–188.

81. George Reedy, *The Twilight of the Presidency* (New York: New American Library, 1970), 164.

82. Grossman and Kumar, *Portraying the President*, 244.

83. Richard S. Salant, "Agnew Plus Ten," in *Views on the News: The Media and Public Opinion,* ed. Michael P. Beaubien and John S. Wyeth, Jr. (New York: New York University Press, 1994), 10–37.

84. Thomas B. Rosenstiel, "Potus and the Posties," *Los Angeles Times Magazine,* May 16, 1993, 20ff; Martha Joynt Kumar, "President Clinton Meets the Media: Communications Shaped by Predictable Patterns," in *The Clinton Presidency: Campaigning, Governing, and the Psychology of Leadership,* ed. Stanley A. Renshon (Boulder, Colo.: Westview, 1995).

85. Lou Cannon, *President Reagan: The Role of a Lifetime* (New York: Simon & Schuster, 1991), 118.

86. Barbara Hinckley found that during his first four years in office, Reagan averaged 5.5 major addresses per year compared with a low of 4.0 for Truman, Johnson, and Carter; 5.0 for Eisenhower, Kennedy, and Ford; and 6.0 for Nixon. Only Eisen-

hower, Nixon, and Reagan had as many as 7 such addresses in a single year, and Reagan ranked second to Nixon in total addresses, 24 to 22. Hinckley, *The Symbolic Presidency*, table 1.1, 19.

87. Brace and Hinckley, *Follow the Leader*, 53–56.

88. Graham Wilson, "The Clinton Administration and Interest Groups," in *The Clinton Presidency: First Appraisals*, 225. Also see discussions in the same volume by Sinclair, "Trying to Govern Positively," and Edwards, "Frustration and Folly."

89. Patterson, *The Ring of Power*, 177. Patterson attributes the quotation to John R. (Tex) McCrary.

90. Colin Campbell, S.J., "The White House and Presidency Under the 'Let's Deal' President," in *The Bush Presidency*, 214.

91. Thomas B. Rosenstiel, "Media Focus on Insiders Misses Big Picture," *Los Angeles Times*, Feb. 12, 1994, A18; Thomas B. Rosenstiel and David Lauter, *Los Angeles Times*, Feb. 12, 1994, A18; Richard L. Berke, "With Boss Besieged, Gergen Minds Himself," *New York Times*, Mar. 10, 1994, A1; Ann Devroy, "For Gergen, Bipartisan Goals Unfulfilled," *Washington Post*, July 15, 1994, A1; Kumar, "President Clinton Meets the Media."

92. Pollard, *The Presidents and the Press*, 14.

93. Grossman and Kumar, *Portraying the President*, chap. 1.

94. Michael Grossman and Francis Rourke, "The Media and the Presidency: An Exchange Analysis," *Political Science Quarterly* (Fall 1976): 455–470. Also see Timothy E. Cook and Lyn Ragsdale, "The President and the Press: Negotiating Newsworthiness at the White House," in *The Presidency and the Political System*.

95. David Broder, as quoted by Patterson in *The Ring of Power*, 170.

96. Grossman and Kumar, *Portraying the President*, chap. 10.

97. A more recent analysis of the "CBS Evening News" from 1968 to 1985 found that in eleven of the seventeen years studied, the president received more negative than positive coverage; in addition, negative stories became more numerous with each year of a president's term as well as from one administration to the next. See Smoller, "The Six-O'Clock Presidency." It should be noted that Smoller's analysis is based on transcripts of the CBS broadcasts, while Grossman and Kumar used films of the broadcasts.

98. Grossman and Kumar, *Portraying the President*, chap. 11.

99. Ibid., 178.

100. This tendency first became apparent during the second year of the Reagan administration when reporters began to ask him more embarrassing questions (for instance, why he did not set an example by making more generous donations to private charities). They also appeared not to take seriously the president's statement that members of his administration were one big happy family.

101. Kumar, "President Clinton Meets the Media," 167–171.

102. Study conducted by Robert Lichter of the Center for Media and Public Affairs as reported in Howard Kurtz, "The Bad News About Clinton," *Washington Post*, Sept. 1, 1994, D1.

103. James Risen, "Clinton Gets Little Credit for Economic Turnaround," *Los Angeles Times*, Sept. 5, 1994, A2.

104. Godfrey Sperling, " 'Clinton Bashing' and the Liberal Press," *Christian Science Monitor*, Sept. 20, 1994, 19.

105. Stephen Hess showed that in 1978, 73 percent were college graduates and 33 percent had graduate degrees (*The Washington Reporters*, 83); Leo Rosten reported that in 1936, 51 percent were college graduates and 6 percent had an advanced academic degree. See *The Washington Correspondents* (New York: Harcourt, Brace, 1937), 159–160.

106. James Fallows, "The Presidency and the Press," in *The Presidency and the Political System*, 3d ed. (Washington, D.C.: CQ Press, 1991).

107. Mark Hertsgaard, *On Bended Knee* (New York: Farrar, Straus & Giroux, 1988).

108. See the discussion by Sidney M. Milkis, "The Presidency and Political Parties," in *The Presidency and the Political System*, 4th ed.

109. James MacGregor Burns, *The Deadlock of Democracy: Four-Party Politics in America* (Englewood Cliffs, N.J.: Prentice-Hall, 1963), 36.

110. Stephen Skowronek argues that along with the court system, political parties proved essential to the survival of the new political system by linking governments at center and periphery, reducing the effects of socioeconomic divisions, and bridging constitutional separations. See *Building a New American State: The Expansion of National Administrative Capacities, 1877–1920* (Cambridge: Cambridge University Press, 1982), esp. 3–46. Also see Sidney M. Milkis, *The President and the Parties: The Transformation of the American Party System Since the New Deal* (New York: Oxford University Press, 1993).

111. Milkis, "The Presidency and Political Parties," 352.

112. Milkis devotes little attention to Eisenhower. It might be argued that Ike contributed to the pattern of change in numerous ways. By cultivating the image of being "above politics," Ike made parties seem less relevant to presidential leadership. This conduct was consistent with his appeal to ticket-splitters, those who crossed over from the Democratic Party to vote for Eisenhower while still supporting other Democratic candidates. Finally, Eisenhower set up a number of campaign committees outside the Republican Party at least partly to encourage Democratic support. Milkis, *The President and the Parties*, 161–169.

113. Losses by the president's party in midterm elections have been remarkably predictable. In the thirty-four midterm elections between 1862 and 1994, the president's party lost seats in the House of Representatives in thirty-two (1902 and 1934 are the exceptions) and in the Senate in twenty-one of the elections. Stanley and Niemi, *Vital Statistics on American Politics*, 5th ed., table 7-4, 189.

114. Burt Solomon, "Bush Takes to the Campaign Trail ... But Are Voters Paying Attention?" *National Journal*, Oct. 27, 1990, 2614–2615.

115. William Riker and William Bast, "Presidential Action in Congressional Nominations," in *The Presidency*, ed. Aaron Wildavsky (Boston: Little, Brown, 1969).

116. Thomas Mann presents his findings on the 1974 elections in *Unsafe at Any Margin: Interpreting Congressional Elections* (Washington, D.C.: American Enterprise Institute, 1978), 92; Lyn Ragsdale presents her findings on the 1978 elections in "The Fiction of Congressional Elections as Presidential Events," *American Politics Quarterly* (October 1980): 375–398.

117. David Leuthold, *Electioneering in a Democracy: Campaigns for Congress* (New York: Wiley, 1968).

118. Charles O. Jones, "Campaigning to Govern: The Clinton Style," in *The Clinton Presidency*, 44.

119. Edward Tufte, "Determinants of the Outcomes of Midterm Congressional Elections," *American Political Science Review* (September 1975): 812–826.

120. Samuel Kernell, "Presidential Popularity and Negative Voting: An Alternative Explanation of the Midterm Decline of the Presidential Party," *American Political Science Review* (March 1977): 44–66.

121. Gary Jacobson, *The Politics of Congressional Elections* (Boston: Little, Brown, 1983),138ff.

122. Walter Dean Burnham, "Realignment Lives: The 1994 Earthquake and Its Implications," in *The Clinton Presidency: First Appraisals*, 363.

123. Gerald Pomper with Susan Lederman, *Elections in America: Control and Influence in Democratic Politics*, 2d ed. (New York: Longman, 1980), chap. 8.

124. Fred Grogan, "Candidate Promises and Presidential Performance" (Paper delivered at the annual meeting of the Midwest Political Science Association, Chicago, Apr. 21–23, 1977).

125. Arnold Muller, "Public Policy and the Presidential Election Process: A Study of Promise and Performance" (Ph.D. diss., University of Missouri-Columbia, 1986), 351.

126. Jeff Fishel, *Presidents and Promises: From Campaign Pledge to Presidential Performance* (Washington, D.C.: CQ Press, 1985), 38.

127. For discussions of these events see portions of the following essays included in *The Bush Presidency*: Paul J. Quirk, "Domestic Policy: Divided Government and Cooperative Presidential Leadership"; Barbara Sinclair, "Governing Unheroically (and Sometimes Unappetizingly): Bush and the 101st Congress"; and Anthony King and Giles Alston, "Good Government and the Politics of High Exposure."

128. Lester Seligman, "The Presidential Office and the President as Party Leader," *Law and Contemporary Problems* (Autumn 1956): 724–734.

129. Kernell, *Going Public*, 2.

130. James Ceaser, Glen Thurow, Jeffrey Tulis, and Joseph Bessette, "The Rise of the Rhetorical Presidency," *Presidential Studies Quarterly* (Spring 1981): 159.

131. Ibid., 167.

132. Ibid., 163. Also see Jeffrey Tulis, *The Rhetorical Presidency* (Princeton University Press, 1987).

133. Kernell, *Going Public*, esp. chap. 2.

READINGS

Brace, Paul, and Barbara Hinckley. *Follow the Leader: Opinion Polls and the Modern Presidents*. New York: Basic Books, 1992.

Cornwell, Elmer. *Presidential Leadership of Public Opinion*. Bloomington: Indiana University Press, 1965.

Edwards, George C., III. *The Public Presidency: The Pursuit of Popular Support*. New York: St. Martin's Press, 1983.

Grossman, Michael Baruch, and Martha Joynt Kumar. *Portraying the President: The White House and the News Media*. Baltimore: Johns Hopkins University Press, 1981.

Hess, Stephen. *The Washington Reporters*. Washington, D.C.: Brookings, 1981.

Hinckley, Barbara. *The Symbolic Presidency: How Presidents Portray Themselves*. New York: Routledge, 1990.

Kernell, Samuel. *Going Public: New Strategies of Presidential Leadership*. 3d ed. Washington, D.C.: CQ Press, 1997.

Milkis, Sidney M. *The President and the Parties: The Transformation of the American Party System Since the New Deal*. New York: Oxford University Press, 1993.

Mueller, John. *War, Presidents and Public Opinion*. New York: Wiley, 1973.

Schwartz, Barry. *George Washington: The Making of an American Symbol*. Ithaca, N.Y.: Cornell University Press, 1987.

Tulis, Jeffrey K. *The Rhetorical Presidency*. Princeton, N.J.: Princeton University Press, 1987.

4 PRESIDENTIAL CHARACTER AND PERFORMANCE

Whether campaigning or jogging along the White House grounds, Bill Clinton displays the high energy of both "active-positive" and "active-negative" personalities.

WHAT KIND OF PEOPLE HAVE served as president, and how have their personal qualities shaped their conduct? These are the broad questions addressed in this chapter. We are especially concerned with the backgrounds, skills, psychological traits, and management styles of presidents and how these factors influence their performance in office. We therefore examine the abilities and attitudes that presidents develop before entering office, ways in which their personalities affect how they do the job, and habitual modes of working. We also look at the way presidents interact with their staffs, those assistants whose positions were created to extend presidents' personal capabilities. To conclude, we take a close look at Bill Clinton in an effort to understand the factors that shaped a particular president's performance in office.

Determinants and Evaluations of Performance

For generations, historians and political scientists have argued among themselves about just how important a leader's characteristics are for understanding and explaining events. Does one, for example, place great significance on the intelligence, stature, and wisdom of Abraham Lincoln in explaining the Union's ultimate victory over the Confederacy? Or was victory the product of forces beyond Lincoln's control, such as the changing nature of modern warfare in an industrial age, which favored the North? Did America and the Soviet Union avert nuclear war during the Cuban missile crisis of 1962 because of the decision style adopted by John F. Kennedy? Or was the outcome the result of organizational routines for crisis management and other random occurrences perhaps not even intended by either side during the confrontation? The larger questions, then, are just what importance should one ascribe to the president's personal characteristics, and are these elements powerful predictors of performance in office?

Although specialists have not reached agreement on the importance of these factors, there is widespread belief that it does indeed matter—and probably a great deal—just who is president. Certainly the time, effort, and money devoted to selecting the president suggest that this is the case. This confidence in the difference that an individual can make is revealed when citizens proudly explain that they "voted for the person, not the party." Believing in the ultimate importance of individuals in shaping events is consistent with deeply held American attitudes. These cultural orientations have been underlined by the treatment accorded presidents in the mass media, particularly during the television era, when political problems and their attempted solutions have become highly personalized. Public attention focuses on the president, and this individual has come to embody the larger political process. Moreover, presidents and their media advisers encourage personalization when it emphasizes traits that the public regards as highly desirable, such as decisiveness and strength of character.

There is broad consensus among students of the presidency that each chief executive brings to the job a combination of attitudes, skills, strengths, and shortcomings that will influence his or her performance in office and may at times have an enduring effect on the nation's history. There is less agreement, however, on the relative significance of these causal factors and exactly how they are related to job performance and policy outcomes. A number of analysts have suggested ways to concep-

Figure 4-1   Relationship of Background to Performance

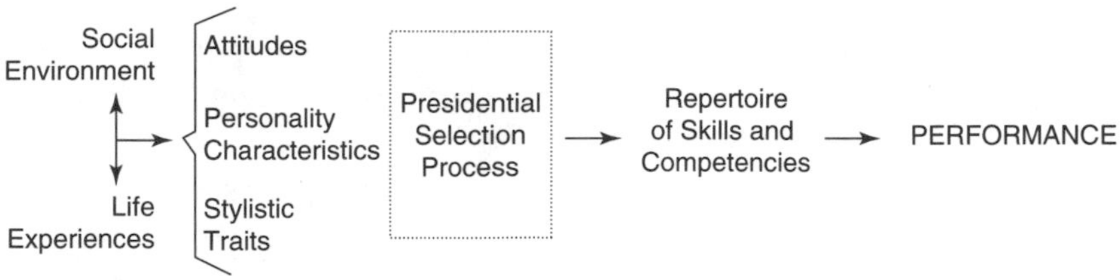

Social Environment → Life Experiences

Attitudes / Personality Characteristics / Stylistic Traits → Presidential Selection Process → Repertoire of Skills and Competencies → PERFORMANCE

Sources: Bert Rockman, *The Leadership Question* (New York: Praeger, 1984), 189; Fred I. Greenstein, *Personality and Politics* (New York: Norton, 1975), 27.

tualize these issues; a modified, considerably simplified diagram based on two of the most prominent treatments is presented in Figure 4-1.

As well as enduring personality traits, all presidents develop attitudes toward the full array of political structures, institutions, and relationships. Their characteristics and attitudes take shape within a social context. In addition, their professional experiences prior to entering office, particularly as they relate to role demands of the presidency, produce a personal style that may be more or less congruent with the demands of serving as chief executive. This personal style, translated into a repertoire of skills and competencies, is brought to the presidency after first being filtered by the selection process. Ultimately, presidents may be more or less likely to produce successful outcomes as these individual traits interact with the situations they confront. In concentrating on the importance of leaders' individual characteristics, one recognizes that presidents are in the position to have potentially momentous impacts on political events. Even if the environment, forces beyond the control of the individual leader, has a determinative effect on events, "environments are always mediated by the individuals on whom they act." [1]

Just as analysts disagree over the determinants of presidential behavior, there is no consensus on how to evaluate a president's performance, although the general public and professional presidency watchers engage in evaluations at the time. Polls provide current, short-term assessments of public approval *(discussed in Chapter 3)*, and journalists are constantly assessing the administration's record in dealing with Congress or in addressing particular areas of public policy. Certain evaluation points have become institutionalized: the end of an administration's first 100 days in office (a carry-over from Franklin D. Roosevelt's first term) always produces a spate of articles. Other evaluation points are mid-term (the end of two years) and departure from office. In other words, the public, journalists, and academics are constantly engaged in *contemporary evaluation* of performance.

Scholars and others use a variety of criteria in reaching these evaluations. Bruce Buchanan has drawn broad distinctions between subjective and objective criteria. Judgments based on subjective grounds emphasize the "appearance and demeanor" of leadership, including success in projecting the image of integrity and charisma; the "moral desirability of a president's means or ends"; and the pragmatic test of self-interest—the extent to which the president contributed to a citizen's well-being. Objective criteria, on which professionals make their evaluations, focus on presidential skill in making things happen, especially short-term successes, or on the lasting results produced for the nation.[2] For example, in reflecting on the record of achievements by the administration of Ronald Reagan, a number of works adopted the long view in assessing the administration's legacy. As Bert Rockman put it, politicians can "leave greater or lesser footprints. Assessing the depth and durability of those marks is hazardous while the administration under evaluation is still in power. The real answers will come later—much later."[3]

Since 1948, various scholars, primarily historians, have been asked on several occasions to "rate" American presidents. In essence, they were to assess the "depth and durability" of presidential footprints and provide a *historical evaluation*. The results from five of these efforts are reported in Table 4-1. Each poll was structured a bit differently and surveyed a different panel of "experts."[4] Even so, one finds considerable consensus among participants on the top ten and the bottom ten, a result that led Robert Murray and Tim Blessing to conclude that historians "had in mind more than vague and uncritical generalities when they evaluated presidential performances."[5] Assessments of recent presidents are particularly susceptible to change with the passage of time. Note how Dwight D. Eisenhower moved up from twentieth place in 1962 to ninth in the *Chicago Tribune* poll in 1982. Harry S. Truman's standing among professionals was already strong by 1962 and has remained so.

In addition to 846 completed surveys, Murray and Blessing conducted sixty in-depth interviews with historians to determine their evaluative criteria. The most important personal trait contributing to presidential achievement, in the view of these historians, was decisiveness; intelligence, particularly the capacity for growth, and integrity were close behind.[6] Greatness, many seemed to feel, is achieved by those leaders able to exercise moral, inspirational leadership, who have "a

Table 4-1   Ratings of U.S. Presidents

Schlesinger poll (1948)	Schlesinger poll (1962)	Maranell-Dodder poll (1982)	*Chicago Tribune* poll (1982)	Murray-Blessing poll[a] (1982)
Great	Great	Accomplish-ments of administration	Ten best presidents	Great
	1. Lincoln		1. Lincoln	1. Lincoln
1. Lincoln	2. Washington	1. Lincoln	(best)	2. F. Roosevelt
2. Washington	3. F. Roosevelt	2. F. Roosevelt	2. Washington	3. Washington
3. F. Roosevelt	4. Wilson	3. Washington	3. F. Roosevelt	4. Jefferson
4. Wilson	5. Jefferson	4. Jefferson	4. T. Roosevelt	
5. Jefferson		5. T. Roosevelt	5. Jefferson	Near great
6. Jackson	Near great	6. Truman	6. Wilson	5. T. Roosevelt
	6. Jackson	7. Wilson	7. Jackson	6. Wilson
Near great	7. T. Roosevelt	8. Jackson	8. Truman	7. Jackson
7. T. Roosevelt	8. Polk	9. L. Johnson	9. Eisenhower	8. Truman
8. Cleveland	Truman (tie)	10. Polk	10. Polk (10th	
9. J. Adams	9. J. Adams	11. J. Adams	best)	Above average
10. Polk	10. Cleveland	12. Kennedy		9. J. Adams
		13. Monroe	Ten worst presidents	10. L. Johnson
Average	Average	14. Cleveland	1. Harding	11. Eisenhower
11. J. Q. Adams	11. Madison	15. Madison	(worst)	12. Polk
12. Monroe	12. J. Q. Adams	16. Taft	2. Nixon	13. Kennedy
13. Hayes	13. Hayes	17. McKinley	3. Buchanan	14. Madison
14. Madison	14. McKinley	18. J. Q. Adams	4. Pierce	15. Monroe
15. Van Buren	15. Taft	19. Hoover	5. Grant	16. J. Q. Adams
16. Taft	16. Van Buren	20. Eisenhower	6. Fillmore	17. Cleveland
17. Arthur	17. Monroe	21. A. Johnson	7. A. Johnson	
18. McKinley	18. Hoover	22. Van Buren	8. Coolidge	Average
19. A. Johnson	19. B. Harrison	23. Arthur	9. Tyler	18. McKinley
20. Hoover	20. Arthur	24. Hayes	10. Carter (10th	19. Taft
21. B. Harrison	Eisenhower	25. Tyler	worst)	20. Van Buren
	(tie)	26. B. Harrison		21. Hoover
Below average	21. A. Johnson	27. Taylor		22. Hayes
22. Tyler		28. Buchanan		23. Arthur
23. Coolidge	Below average	29. Fillmore		24. Ford
24. Fillmore	22. Taylor	30. Coolidge		25. Carter
25. Taylor	23. Tyler	31. Pierce		26. B. Harrison
26. Buchanan	24. Fillmore	32. Grant		
27. Pierce	25. Coolidge	33. Harding		Below average
	26. Pierce			27. Taylor
Failure	27. Buchanan			28. Reagan
28. Grant				29. Tyler
29. Harding	Failure			30. Fillmore
	28. Grant			31. Coolidge
	29. Harding			32. Pierce
				Failure
				33. A. Johnson
				34. Buchanan
				35. Nixon
				36. Grant
				37. Harding

Source: Harold W. Stanley and Richard G. Niemi, *Vital Statistics on American Politics,* 5th ed. (Washington, D.C.: CQ Press, 1995), Table 8-2, 240–241.

Note: These ratings result from surveys of scholars and range in number from 49 to 846.

[a] The rating of President Reagan was obtained in a separate poll conducted in 1989.

capacity for creative innovation and an imagination that was fired by a clear vision of the future."[7] James MacGregor Burns's discussion of leadership emphasizes similar abilities as the source of "transformational" leadership, where presidents appeal to the higher goals and motives of followers to achieve true change.[8]

In assessing performance, it is also necessary to factor in an additional consideration: modern presidents no longer govern alone. Since the 1930s they have been assisted by a large number of aides appointed to serve in the Executive Office of the President, who may prove a genuine asset in helping presidents exercise their responsibilities. A president's personal capabilities may be amplified by careful selection and use of these aides.

In examining the importance of individual characteristics, we turn first to a discussion of the backgrounds from which presidents have been drawn. As depicted in Figure 4-1, a president's life and occupational experiences are distant from the actual service in office and should therefore have only limited power to explain performance. Nonetheless, the patterns uncovered tell us something about leadership in America.

What Manner of Person?

Each president brings to the office a cumulation of experience derived from a position in American society and previous professional experience. The selection process, rather than producing a random sampling of Americans, favors some backgrounds over others. After reviewing the historical pattern for social background and education, it is not surprising to find that presidents have disproportionately been drawn from traditionally dominant groups in American society. It is less clear, however, just what this has meant for their performance in office.

Social Background

Although there is no single indicator of social status upon which all Americans would agree, occupation is probably the most important criterion for social ranking in the United States.[9] Moreover, the occupation of a person's father provides a reasonably accurate picture of his or her class origins. By analyzing such origins, one can determine the extent to which presidents have achieved their positions of power as a result of their own ability or thanks to the advantages of family background.[10] The presidency has long been cited as an example of how ability can enable individuals to overcome disadvantages and rise to positions of power. But the reality of presidents' personal histories, argues Edward Pessen, contradicts "the log cabin myth" and demonstrates that "the political race here as elsewhere has usually been won by those who had the advantage of starting from a favorable position." [11] Pessen uses a complex conceptualization of class in characterizing the family background of each president through Reagan in terms of six basic groupings: upper-upper and lower-upper, upper-middle and lower-middle, upper-lower and lower-lower.[12] In making his evaluations, Pessen compared the presidents' family backgrounds to the economic and social conditions that existed at the time.

Four distinguished American families alone produced eight American presidents, nearly one-fifth of the total. Included were John Adams and his son John Quincy Adams; James Madison and Zachary Taylor, who had grandparents in common; William Henry Harrison and his grandson Benjamin Harrison; and cousins Theodore and Franklin Roosevelt. All four families meet Pessen's criteria for upper-class status as depicted in Table 4-2. It is also not uncommon to find that presidents come from politically prominent families, a background that, more often than not, is also upper class. John Tyler was the son of a Virginia governor; William Howard Taft's father served as secretary of war, attorney general, and ambassador to Austria and Russia; and John Kennedy's father was the chairman of the Securities and Exchange Commission and ambassador to Great Britain. Franklin Pierce's father was governor of New Hampshire, but Pessen locates the family between the lower-upper and upper-middle classes. One would also expect to find George Bush (unranked by Pessen) among those with upper-class backgrounds; Bush's father accumulated a considerable fortune working on Wall Street before he was elected to the Senate from Connecticut.

Several chief executives had upper-class origins, but their fathers did not hold high political office. George Washington, Thomas Jefferson, and James Monroe were sons of wealthy farmers who were not in politics. Rounding out Pessen's upper-class group is James K. Polk, whose family was notably more prosperous than its neighbors, and Woodrow Wilson, whose father was a minister, a profession of considerable social prestige. The fathers of Chester Arthur and Grover Cleveland also were ministers, but Pessen ranks them as upper-middle and lower-upper, respectively. Pessen locates a number of presidents, including Pierce, Hayes, Harding, Coolidge, and Truman, in a special bridge category between upper-class and middle-class origins. Altogether, Pessen con-

Table 4-2 Pessen's Analysis of Presidential Social Class

Social Class	President
Upper-Upper	G. Washington, T. Jefferson, J. Madison, J. Q. Adams, W. H. Harrison, J. Tyler, Z. Taylor, B. Harrison, T. Roosevelt, W. H. Taft, F. D. Roosevelt
Middle-Upper	J. Polk, J. Kennedy
Lower-Upper	J. Adams, J. Monroe, W. Wilson
Lower-Upper/ Upper-Middle	F. Pierce, R. Hayes, G. Cleveland, W. Harding, C. Coolidge, H. Truman
Upper-Middle	A. Jackson, M. Van Buren, J. Buchanan, U. S. Grant, C. Arthur, W. McKinley, H. Hoover, L. Johnson, G. Ford, J. Carter
Middle	A. Lincoln, D. Eisenhower, R. Reagan
Lower-Middle	M. Fillmore, J. Garfield, R. Nixon
Upper-Lower	A. Johnson
Lower-Lower	None

Source: Edward Pessen, *The Log Cabin Myth: The Social Backgrounds of the Presidents* (New Haven, Conn.: Yale University Press, 1984), 68.

siders sixteen presidents to be drawn from upper-class roots and six more as bordering on this exclusive group—a total of twenty-two (Bush would make twenty-three), more than half of those who have served in the White House.

Another ten presidents fall within Pessen's upper-middle category, leaving only seven who can be regarded as drawn from middle- or lower-class roots, although Bill Clinton would make an eighth. The presidents who were most socially disadvantaged include Andrew Johnson, whose father held a variety of jobs, including janitor and porter at an inn; Millard Fillmore, who was probably the only president truly born in a log cabin as the son of a dirt farmer; and James Garfield, whose father pulled the family into prosperity through manual labor as a canal worker in the Midwest. Despite the many schoolbook stories about Lincoln's modest background, his father owned more property and livestock at the time of Abraham's birth than the majority of his neighbors, and his prominence in the community continued to grow. Three more recent presidents—Eisenhower, Nixon, and Reagan—were the sons of poor men who tried numerous jobs without much success. Eisenhower's father was a mechanic in a creamery for a time after an investment failed; Nixon's father was a streetcar conductor in Columbus, Ohio, before trying his luck as a painter, carpenter, glass worker, and sheep rancher; and Reagan's father worked on and off as an itinerant shoe salesman. Bill Clinton's father, a traveling salesman, died before his son was born, and Clinton's mother became a nurse anes-thetist. His grandfather, with whom he lived until age six, was first the town iceman and later a neighborhood grocer, and his stepfather was a car salesman.

Four chief executives—Jackson, Hayes, Hoover, and Clinton—were born after their fathers died; all but Clinton were reared by relatives who were better off than their own parents. Jackson's condition was sufficiently comfortable to afford him an education at a private school. Hoover's uncle, who reared him, headed a private academy that later became Pacific University. An upper-middle-class background was eco-nomically secure and sometimes prosperous: Van Buren's father kept a tavern; Buchanan's was a successful merchant; and Grant's did well as a tanner. McKinley's father manufactured pig iron and invested in min-ing. The fathers of three recent presidents—Johnson, Ford, and Carter—met mixed success in business; Johnson's father traded in com-modities and livestock; Ford's stepfather (the president was born Leslie King and adopted as Gerald R. Ford, Jr.) operated a paint and lumber business; Carter's father founded a successful peanut warehouse.

Although presidents have come from diverse backgrounds, those with upper-class origins have been the most prevalent, while most others were drawn from prosperous and socially respected backgrounds. Even so, one can discern some changes over time. The first six chief executives came from socially, and in many cases politically, prominent families. Not wholly by coincidence, they served during the period when presi-dential candidates were nominated by congressional caucus. After both political parties adopted the national nominating convention in the early 1830s, the picture changed, with some presidents continuing to come from prominent families (John Tyler and Zachary Taylor, for example), while others from less-privileged backgrounds also began to make it to the White House. Fillmore, Lincoln, Andrew Johnson, and Garfield— four presidents with the humblest origins—are concentrated in the peri-od 1850–1880. Few generalizations can be made, however, about twen-tieth-century presidents, who come from distinctly upper-class families (the two Roosevelts, Taft, Wilson, Kennedy, and Bush) as well as more modest circumstances (Eisenhower, Nixon, Reagan, and Clinton).

Education

Education is often closely correlated with social class, a pattern that holds true for the presidency. Most U.S. presidents have been well edu-cated. Only nine of the forty-one individuals (Cleveland served two, nonconsecutive terms, making Clinton the forty-second president) did not have any formal instruction at a college or university. Moreover, the trend has been toward chief executives with greater college training. Of the eighteen who have occupied the presidency in this century, only one, Harry Truman, did not attend an institution of higher learning.[13] The universities and colleges that presidents attended are among the most highly regarded in the nation. Harvard University leads the list with five chief executives as alumni—the two Adamses, the two Roosevelts, and Kennedy. Alma maters of other presidents include major private universities such as Princeton (Madison and Wilson), Yale (Taft and Bush), Stanford (Hoover), Georgetown (Clinton), and a wide variety of prestigious, smaller private colleges, such as Allegheny (McKinley), Amherst (Coolidge), Bowdoin (Pierce), Dickinson (Buchanan), Hampden-Sidney (W. H. Harrison), Kenyon (Hayes), Union (Arthur), and Williams (Garfield). Although less prevalent than private institutions, well-known public universities also figure among the alma maters of the presidents: Miami University of Ohio (B. Harrison), the University of Michigan (Ford), the University of North Carolina (Polk), William and Mary (Jefferson, Monroe, and Tyler), and two service academies, Annapolis (Carter) and West Point (Grant and Eisenhower). Twentieth-century presidents hailing from families with more modest social standing attended less prestigious institutions: Johnson attended Southwest Texas State Teachers College; Nixon graduated from Whittier College in California before attending Duke University Law School; Reagan majored in economics and sociology at Eureka College in Illinois.

The fact that so many presidents attended prestigious institutions of higher learning probably has less to do with their innate abilities or career aspirations than with family status or their desire to improve their economic and social positions through education. A classic example is James Garfield, the son of a canal construction worker, who died when Garfield was two. Garfield managed, after a long struggle for education, to graduate from Williams College and then become principal of a church school before being admitted to the bar and eventually going into politics. More presidents attended private than public schools because private schools were established earlier, particularly in the northeastern states, such as New York and Massachusetts, which have produced ten presidents, and the Midwestern states, such as Ohio, which has produced six presidents. Several postwar presidents, including Eisenhower, Johnson, Ford, and Carter, attended public institutions, a trend that may become more pronounced in the future. The selection of more presidents from states in which there are more public than private universities (such as the western states) would contribute to this trend. Although most citizens today would probably agree that a college education is essential if presidents are to understand the many complex problems confronting the nation, there is no direct correlation between quality of institution or years of training and performance.

Career Experience

Although the family occupational backgrounds of the presidents are fairly broad, their own careers prior to and outside politics have been much less diverse. Twenty-five of the forty-one chief executives practiced law at some time in their lives. Other occupations include the military (W. H. Harrison, Taylor, Grant, and Eisenhower), education (Wilson and Lyndon Johnson), journalism (Harding and Kennedy), engineering (Hoover), and entertainment (Reagan). Two presidents, Washington and Madison, were gentleman farmers. Carter combined farming with his family peanut business after he gave up his career as a navy engineer to return home to Georgia when his father died. Two presidents who pursued less prestigious careers before entering public life were Truman, who, in addition to trying his hand at farming, was a haberdasher and a railroad timekeeper, and Andrew Johnson, who was a tailor. It is not surprising that so many presidents were lawyers because that profession is closely linked with a political career. Law is a prestigious occupation, rewards skill in interpersonal negotiation and conciliation as well as verbal and argumentative facility, and enables its practitioners to return to private life more readily than is true of medicine or engineering, for example.[14] Although the law is a natural profession for presidents, in recent years fewer chief executives have come from that occupation. Of the ten presidents since World War II, only three, Nixon, Ford, and Clinton, were lawyers. As increasing numbers of people from nonlegal backgrounds—business and teaching, in particular—become senators and governors, the positions from which today's presidents often are recruited, still more presidents without legal training may occupy the White House.

As noted in the discussion of presidential selection, most candidates have little difficulty meeting the formal requirements of office, but informal requirements, although changing in content, are far more restrictive. The most pervasive of these informal requirements is previous experience in elective or appointive public office. The only exceptions to this rule have been three career military officers, Zachary Taylor, Ulysses S. Grant, and Dwight D. Eisenhower, whose heroic exploits in the Mexican War, Civil War, and World War II, respectively, thrust them suddenly into the vortex of presidential politics. Not only did these three presidents lack experience in civilian office, but as professional military men they had not even been involved in partisan activities. Taylor, elected as the Whig candidate in 1848, had never voted before in a presidential election and had no party affiliation.[15] Grant, the Republican Party candidate elected in 1868, had voted for James Buchanan, the Democratic standard-bearer in 1856, and had political views that have been described as "obscure." [16] Even more perplexing for party leaders was Eisenhower, the Republican Party candidate in 1952 and 1956, whom a number of liberal Democratic leaders had tried to draft for their party's nomination in 1948.[17]

For most U.S. chief executives, the road to the presidency involved a long apprenticeship in public office with careers usually beginning at lower levels of the political system when they were in their twenties or thirties. Andrew Johnson and Calvin Coolidge began their public careers as city aldermen or councilmen. Others were first elected to county offices: John Adams was a highway surveyor; Truman was a member of the county court, an administrative, not a judicial, position. Some presidents, including Andrew Jackson, James Buchanan, Grover Cleveland, William McKinley, and William Howard Taft, entered public service as prosecuting or district attorney; others, such as Rutherford B. Hayes and Benjamin Harrison, served as city solicitor or attorney. Bill Clinton began his career in 1976 as Arkansas's attorney general. Several chief executives, Jefferson, Lincoln, and the two Roosevelts among them, began their public careers as state legislators.

The typical career pattern for these presidents was to move up the political ladder by winning offices representing progressively larger constituencies. Approximately two-thirds of the presidents served in either the House of Representatives or the Senate or both. There are, of course, exceptions. Woodrow Wilson spent most of his adult life as a professor of government and later as president of Princeton University; in 1910, at age fifty-four, he was elected governor of New Jersey, just two years before he won the presidency. Ronald Reagan was primarily a radio, movie, and television performer until his fifties, when he became active in national politics in the 1964 presidential campaign in behalf of Barry Goldwater. In 1966 he was elected to the first of two terms as governor of California; in 1980 he was elected president. Neither William Howard Taft nor Herbert Hoover held any elective office before being chosen as president. Taft served as a judge at the county, state, and federal levels, and later became governor general of the Philippines and secretary of war. Hoover chaired the Commission for Relief in Belgium; oversaw prices, production, and distribution of food during World War I as U.S. food administrator; and later served as secretary of commerce in the Harding and Coolidge administrations.

Most presidents come to the White House directly from another high public office. *(See the discussion in Chapter 2.)* Typical positions include the vice presidency, appointive executive office, state governorships, and Senate seats. From one era to the next in U.S. political history, these offices have varied in the extent to which their occupants have been favored or disfavored in their pursuit of the presidency.

How is experience related to performance? Most observers assume that experience can make a president more or less familiar with the problems confronting the nation as well as with the institutions and people who must collectively address these problems. Moreover, an earlier career in elective office may enable individuals to develop the skills necessary for exercising leadership—bargaining skills, facility in public speaking, and the capacity to inspire others. Candidates, therefore, usually argue that their particular blend of experience—whether in state, national, or non-public sectors—has made them best qualified for the position.

Background-Performance Links

How have scholars linked these biographical characteristics to presidential performance? Are there systematic patterns that would enable the public to predict which candidates will enjoy greatest success in office? Unfortunately, there are no simple answers.

As noted, most presidents achieved political success with a substantial boost from their family circumstances, advantages that included political and social standing as well as educational and professional opportunities unavailable to most of their fellow citizens. Edward Pessen finds that this pattern of recruitment has had important implications for the attitudes brought into the Oval Office. Political parties consistently have sought candidates with a "reliable social philosophy," which is likely to be found among those "who have thrived under American society's prevailing arrangements." [18] Pessen concludes that "the common characteristic [of presidents] ... for all their dissimilarities in other respects, has been the essential conservatism of their social, economic, and political beliefs ... all of them were champions of the prevailing order." [19] It seems likely that most presidential aspirants will sustain the status quo. The selection process is not neutral in relation to social class.

Two sociologists, E. Digby Baltzell and Howard G. Schneiderman, have more specifically sought to link class origin with performance in office. They correlate Pessen's analysis of class origins with a ranking of presidential performance based on the Murray-Blessing survey of American historians.[20] Their conclusion challenges some of the myths surrounding the presidency. "There has been ... not only a high corre-lation between high social origins and getting to the presidency, as Pessen clearly has shown, [but] once elected to office, men of privileged origins have performed far better than those of lower social status."[21] Of the eight presidents ranked by historians as great or near great, five were from upper-class families (Washington, Jefferson, T. Roosevelt, Wilson, and F. Roosevelt), two from the upper-middle class (Jackson and Truman), and only one from the middle and lower classes (Lincoln, who is generally ranked number one). In contrast, no presidents drawn from the upper class are found among those regarded by historians as failures (A. Johnson, Buchanan, Nixon, Grant, and Harding). Overall, Baltzell and Schneiderman find that eleven of the fifteen upper-class presidents included in their study (73 percent) were judged to have per-formed above average in office, while only six of the twenty-one pres-idents drawn from below the upper class (29 percent) were comparably rated.[22] Although they do not provide a clear explanation for how back-ground is translated into success, these analysts suggest that an upper-class background does make a difference: "Our best aristocratic tradi-tions have stressed *doing* a better job rather than the prevalent, middle-class ideology which has always stressed *getting* a better job."[23]

Richard Neustadt is probably the foremost advocate of electing an experienced politician to the presidency. As he has argued since the first edition of his influential book, *Presidential Power*, appeared in 1960, "The Presidency is no place for amateurs."[24] This seemed an apt aphorism to capture the difficulties experienced by Dwight Eisenhower in the pres-idency, although evaluations of his performance as president have risen with the passage of time. As articulated in some of Neustadt's later edi-tions, experience enhances presidents' self-confidence, which in turn makes it easier for them to make the choices about power that are crit-ical to success. Yet, "the quality of experience" may count "more than the quantity," an admission that Neustadt had to make after two high-ly experienced presidents, Lyndon Johnson and Richard Nixon, seemed to fail in office. He ultimately concludes that "the variety of experience is such that none of it can be applied predictively with confidence." [25] Bert Rockman reaches a similar conclusion after looking at the length and types of government experience in relation to performance. In comparing the government experience of the top ten and bottom ten presidents as ranked by an expert panel, the bottom ten actually had modestly *greater* government experience than the top ten (16.9 mean years versus 15.1) and more than twice as many years of congressional experience (7.6 mean years versus 3.7).[26] Experience, it appears, offers no guarantee of success.

We are left with fundamental uncertainties about how life experience may have a bearing on performance. In addition to social class and career experience, however, there has also been considerable interest in the psychological traits that presidents bring to the office, the subject of the next section.

Psychological Characteristics of U.S. Presidents

In October 1972, just before voters were to choose between Richard Nixon and George McGovern, the political scientist James David Barber drew attention to the inherent shortcomings of focusing on life experience when deciding how to vote. Barber made a prediction. The person who would win had grown up as part of a Republican family in a small town. He had excelled in school, studied piano, had a younger brother rowdier than himself, and had been elected president of his college class. Following military service during World War II, he had attended graduate school and followed an uncertain career path until gaining election to Congress in a contest marked by anticommunist appeals. After two terms in the House and service in the Senate, he was considered a member of his party's liberal wing and respected for hard work and independent thinking. Although the election outcome was virtually certain, Barber had no need to predict a winner because the description fit both Nixon and McGovern. Despite the similarities in life experiences, few doubted that the two would make very different presidents.[27]

The degree of similarity between the major party candidates in 1972 was uncanny even in light of the broadly similar backgrounds from which presidents are drawn. Yet, no two people, regardless of how similar their life circumstances, will bring identical personalities to the office. They inevitably bring a set of distinctive psychological characteristics, features that may loom large under the intense pressures that concentrate on the presidency. In terms of Figure 4-1, psychological traits are more proximate to presidential behavior than life experiences, but that does not make them easier to study or evaluate. Fred Greenstein points out that psychologists view personality as a complex phenomenon, involving diverse factors such as how people adapt to the world around them by screening reality (cognition), how they express their feelings (affect), and how they relate to others (identification).[28] These structures are likely to be deeply rooted, making it even more necessary to "infer" their existence rather than to observe them directly. Personality, in short, is a construct introduced by the analyst to account for the regularities in a person's behavior. For these reasons, examinations of psychological characteristics are more uncertain and subjective than are examinations of professional experience and social backgrounds.

Despite these problems, political scientists and historians have used psychological concepts to help explain why political figures behave as they do, a field of study that has come to be known as *psychobiography*. Several presidents, including Wilson, Lyndon Johnson, Nixon, and Carter, have been the subjects of such biographies.[29] These studies tend to concentrate on the childhood experiences of the subjects, particularly their relationships with their parents, and how such experiences shaped their perceptions of themselves, their self-confidence or lack of it, and their psychological needs.

Even with the upsurge in interest, analysts remain divided on precisely how to conduct these studies and the theoretical framework within which they should be conducted. Two broad approaches can be adopted: single-subject case studies seek to develop a comprehensive analysis of the full array of behaviors manifested by one person with particular attention to explaining the origins of recurrent patterns; multi-case studies also rely on close examination of biographical materials but seek to draw conclusions from similarities found among several actors' behavior.[30] An example of a single-subject case study is Alexander George and Juliette George's highly acclaimed, comprehensive work on Woodrow Wilson, which attempts to explain his strikingly complex and contradictory behavior. James David Barber's study, *The Presidential Character*, has identified similarities between Wilson's conduct and that of three other presidents, Hoover, Lyndon Johnson, and Nixon, so that they may be treated as examples of a similar personality type.

Practitioners of these two styles of inquiry disagree, sometimes quite strongly, on how analysis should proceed.[31] There are multiple, competing theories of personality and a lack of established rules on how such research should be conducted. Although the research remains controversial, it would be unrealistic to overlook the importance of personality in trying to understand the presidency because this office imposes fewer constraints on the occupant's behavior than any other in American government. In other words, there is enormous opportunity for presidents to be themselves in performing their day-to-day responsibilities.

Barber's Approach to Studying Personality

In addition to the prediction concerning the 1972 election already noted, Barber made a more famous forecast that brought considerable attention to himself and to the study of presidential personality. Barber predicted that Nixon would be susceptible to the same "danger" as Wilson, Hoover, and Johnson, namely, "adhering rigidly to a line of policy long after it had proved itself a failure." [32] Given the right set of circumstances, Nixon was likely to pursue a self-defeating plan of action even in the face of mounting evidence of its likely failure. The causes were rooted in his personality—his emotional needs—no less than they had been for the other three presidents Barber cited. Nixon's conduct during Watergate, the extended investigations conducted by Congress during 1973 and 1974 into questionable campaign practices of the 1972 election, seemed to validate the prediction and the method on which it was based.

How did Barber arrive at such a conclusion? Was his prediction lucky, or had he uncovered the secret of how to predict presidential performance in office based on systematic personality analysis? If so, the next step would be to produce more informed decisions by making such insights available to voters before an election.

Barber attempts to identify broad character patterns that will predict broad patterns of presidential conduct in office. Central to his analysis are three personal characteristics—*character, world view,* and *style*—and two environmental conditions—*power situation* and *climate of expectations.* Together, these elements determine the likelihood of presidential success. Character, the most important of Barber's analytic constructs, develops during childhood and is expressed in two analytic dimensions: energy and affect. Presidents may be active or passive in terms of the effort invested in their job; they also may be positive or negative about their position. Both dimensions influence performance.

The resulting four-cell typology is presented in Figure 4-2, with the principal personality trait identified by Barber for each type. *Active-pos-*

Figure 4-2   Barber's Typology of Character

Affect

		Positive	Negative
Activity Level	Active	**Adaptive**, self-confident, power used as means to achieve beneficial results	**Compulsive**, power as a means to self-realization; "driven"; problem managing aggression
	Passive	**Compliant**, seek to be loved; easily manipulated; low self-esteem	**Withdrawn**, respond to sense of duty; avoid power; low self-esteem

Source: James David Barber, *The Presidential Character: Predicting Performance in the White House,* 4th ed. (Englewood Cliffs, N.J.: Prentice-Hall, 1992).

itives evidence personal growth and adaptability; they enjoy their work and find it a challenge to use power productively as a means to pursue goals beneficial to others. Their success rests on a fundamental sense of self-confidence expressed in goal-oriented behavior. Nonetheless, they are flexible in their pursuit of goals and willing to change or abandon them altogether rather than suffer a costly political defeat. In short, they are pragmatic politicians. Barber's active-positives include Franklin Roosevelt, Truman, Kennedy, Ford, Carter, Bush, and Clinton.[33]

Active-negative presidents also invest a great deal of energy in being president, but unlike their active-positive counterparts, they do not appear to derive enjoyment from serving in the office. Rather than exercising political power for the benefit of the citizenry, active-negative chief executives seem to seek power for its own sake, exhibiting a compulsiveness as if they are driven to pursue a political career rather than doing it because the career gives them pleasure. This behavior arises from a poor self-image and lack of self-confidence, traits caused by painful childhood experiences; they seek power and domination over others as compensation for their own lack of self-esteem. In this pursuit, active-negatives may come to believe that the policies they favor are morally right, vital to the nation's interest, and impossible to compromise. A course of action may be pursued even if it obviously is not working, a pattern of "rigidification" that can ultimately cause their own political failure. Thus, they constitute a great danger to the nation. Barber classifies four twentieth-century presidents as active-negatives: Wilson, Hoover, Johnson, and Nixon.

Passive-positive presidents are not in politics to seek power either for the betterment of the American people or to compensate for their own sense of inadequacy. Rather, they choose politics because they are, in Barber's terms, "political lovers." They genuinely enjoy people and want to help them by doing small favors; in return, they get the feeling that they are wanted and loved. Barber suggests that passive-positive presidents have low self-esteem combined with a superficial optimism about life; they tend to let others set goals for them and find it difficult to make decisions. The danger they pose is one of drift, leaving the affairs of state undirected. Barber uses three presidents to illustrate passive-positive chief executives: Taft, Harding, and Reagan.

Passive-negative presidents combine two characteristics one would *not* expect to find in the person who attains the nation's highest office: an unwillingness to invest much energy in that office and a lack of pleasure in serving. Such persons pursue public service because they believe it is something they *ought to do*. Passive-negative presidents have a fundamental sense of uselessness and compensate for that feeling by dutifully agreeing to work on behalf of their fellow citizens. Two presidents who exemplify passive-negative chief executives are Coolidge and Eisenhower.

Barber also examines two other personal factors that influence presidential behavior but play a smaller role in his analysis than does character. *World view* consists of a president's "politically relevant beliefs, particularly his conceptions of social causality, human nature, and the central moral conflicts of the time." [34] Rather than dealing with specific policy issues, these attitudes are general in nature and are therefore more likely to have wide applicability. Barber sees them as developed primarily during adolescence.

Style is the president's "habitual way of performing three political roles: rhetoric, personal relations, and homework." [35] In other words, style focuses on how presidents typically work with words, people, and substantive problems. These patterns are developed largely during early adulthood, particularly in conjunction with the president's "first independent political success," which usually occurs in college or in a first elective or appointive office. *Character* "colors" both world view and style but does not determine them in any direct way.

Barber has analyzed the life histories of all presidents from Taft through Bush, thereby covering all but three of the twentieth-century presidents (his discussion of Clinton is very tentative). These analyses are summarized in Figure 4-3. Some of his classifications have been highly controversial, but since 1972 his views of each candidate have been sought out by journalists during presidential elections, and he

Figure 4-3   Barber's Characterization of Modern Presidents

	Affect	
	Positive	Negative
Active	Franklin Roosevelt Harry Truman John F. Kennedy Gerald R. Ford George Bush William J. Clinton	Woodrow Wilson Herbert Hoover Lyndon Johnson Richard Nixon
Passive	William H. Taft Warren Harding Ronald Reagan	Calvin Coolidge Dwight Eisenhower

Activity Level (left axis label)

Source: James David Barber, *The Presidential Character: Predicting Performance in the White House*, 4th ed. (Englewood Cliffs, N.J. : Prentice-Hall, 1992). For Barber's views on Clinton, see the *News Observer* (Raleigh, N.C.), January 17, 1993.

offered predictions of how the new president will perform in office on the eve of inauguration day.

Views of Bill Clinton

Unlike the case with other recent presidents, Barber has offered only a tentative analysis of Bill Clinton as an active-positive.[36] Another analyst, Stanley A. Renshon, offers a "preliminary assessment" based on events of the presidential campaign and Clinton's first year in office that illustrates the difficulties of analyzing presidential character more generally.[37] Renshon agrees that "on initial impression," Clinton would appear to be an active-positive. Throughout his academic and political career, Clinton has been a prodigious worker, training himself in college to function on five hours of sleep and repeatedly reacting to setbacks with even higher levels of personal activity. Moreover, Clinton's efforts were dedicated to accomplishing purposes beyond simply advancing his own personal ambition.[38]

Renshon, however, notes that Clinton's frenetic activity is "closer to the driven investments of energy of active-negative Lyndon Johnson" than to other active-positives like Kennedy or Truman.[39] Nor is it uniformly obvious that Clinton enjoys the experience. Although he apparently thrives on long days of interpersonal contact and campaigning, Renshon offers evidence of how intensely Clinton resents the limited appreciation he has received in the press and from the public. This was dramatically manifested by an explosive outburst at the end of an interview conducted by two journalists from *Rolling Stone* near the end of his first year in office. When asked about a young supporter who wanted to know what issues Clinton was "willing to stand up for and die on," the president exploded:

But that's the press's fault, too, damn it. I have fought more damn battles here for more things than any president has in 20 years, with the possible exception of Reagan's first budget, and not gotten one damn bit of credit from the knee-jerk liberal press, and I am sick and tired of it, and you can put that in the damn article.

I have fought and fought and fought and fought. I get up here every day, and I work till late at night on everything from national service to family leave to the budget to the crime bill and all this stuff, and you guys take it and you say, "Fine, go on to something else, what else can I hit him about?" So if you convince them I don't have any convictions, that's fine, but it's a damn lie. It's a lie.

... I have fought my guts out for that guy, and if he doesn't know it, it's not all my fault. And you get no credit around here for fighting and bleeding.[40]

Linking this outburst to other features of the president's personality, Renshon suggests that Clinton could be a hybrid type within Barber's framework, a borderline active-negative with a "strong need to be validated."[41] Clinton, argues Renshon, has developed an idealized view of himself—his skills, his accomplishments, and his motives. "Most people wish to think well of themselves but Bill Clinton appears to have come to believe the *best* of himself and to have discounted evidence from his own behavior that all is not as he believes it to be."[42] In this view, when Clinton's self-idealized image collides with criticism and refusal to acknowledge his accomplishments, anger and hurt emerge. Unlike active-negatives who use power to overcome low estimates of themselves, Renshon suggests that "it is also possible that political leaders might well use power to validate high estimates of themselves," something Barber had not anticipated and that Clinton might embody.[43]

Fred Greenstein, another student of presidential personality, points to at least one quality of Clinton's that makes him very much unlike active-negatives: the "capacity (in spite of his thin-skinned tendencies) to admit his own failings" and make self-correcting adjustments. Thus, unlike the compulsive tendency of Woodrow Wilson, Herbert Hoover, Lyndon Johnson, and Richard Nixon to pursue even self-destructive policies, Clinton appears "incapable of sustained error."[44] Yet, Greenstein acknowledges that "much of what is puzzling about him [Clinton] stems from inner complexities that do not figure in Barber's (and per-

haps any other) classification." [45] Indeed, Barber's effort to study presidential personality has attracted extensive commentary, examined in
the next section.

Reactions to Barber

Because Barber's work has been widely popularized in the press, it is
important to assess its analytic quality. Academics have been especially
critical, suggesting it suffers from the fundamental problem common to
all studies in the field—reductionism, paying "insufficient attention to
the full range of possible psychological and non-psychological determinants of behavior." [46] Insufficient attention is given to the impact of the
environment on presidents, including the nature of the problems they
confront, the political support they enjoy, and the constraints within
which they operate.

Barber's classification of presidents also has been questioned. The
behavior patterns associated with his character types fit some presidents
grouped into the same cell better than others. For example, evidence on
Eisenhower published after Barber completed his analysis suggests that
Ike was really a more active president than was generally recognized
when he was in office. [47] Hoover's reluctance to employ extensive federal aid to restore the economy might better be understood as arising
from his world view rather than from his unresolved emotional needs. [48]
Another study, using markedly different methods, finds Ronald Reagan's personality to be most similar to those of Franklin Roosevelt and
Kennedy, although Barber considered Reagan a passive-positive and
the other two active-positives. [49] In fact, Barber acknowledges that no
president fits any of the types perfectly and that each is a mixture of all
four types. [50] Nonetheless, he argues that it is possible to identify a dominant pattern.

Is Barber guilty of positing an ideal personality type that may also
conceal a partisan bias? When Barber's study first appeared, all the
active-positives were liberal Democrats. Republicans Ford and Bush
were subsequently added. The approach may, however, favor the heroic model of presidential leadership that assigns principal responsibility
for solving national problems to the White House. Barber recognizes
that not all active-positives will be successful in office, and may pose
risks for the political system; their "hunger for and attention to results"
may lead them to challenge structures and norms that the public
believes are better preserved than overturned. [51] Franklin Roosevelt's
effort in 1937 to alter the structure of the Supreme Court by increasing

its membership to as many as fifteen posed a challenge to the tradition of checks and balances and illustrates this possible danger.[52]

Can types other than active-positives achieve substantial success in office? Jeffrey Tulis argues that in Barber's terms Abraham Lincoln should be considered an active-negative, but few would argue that Lincoln's stewardship of the nation during the Civil War was not successful.[53]

In sum, Barber's work does not represent a panacea to a nation searching for effective leaders. Like most of social science, Barber's work is best thought of in terms of probabilities rather than certainties. In the long run, Barber aspires to present voters with the kind of information on candidate backgrounds and records that would improve the likelihood of informed electoral choices, but the kind of research necessary for personality analysis is difficult to undertake at any time and perhaps most difficult in the heat of an electoral contest. Journalists may be able to improve their coverage of candidates' records and identify behavior patterns of concern, but the chance of conducting a complete study of candidates' personalities in the midst of a campaign is negligible. Nor is it clear who in our society should be given such inordinate influence as to declare some personalities "fit" and others "unfit" for office. Therefore, the practical value of Barber's work remains a controversial and open question.

Management Styles of Modern Presidents

Presidents do not govern alone. Traditional presidents—those serving prior to Franklin Roosevelt—drew heavily on the assistance of cabinet secretaries and the bureaucracies they headed. Since the Roosevelt administration, another source of advice and assistance has emerged to supplement more traditional sources of help. The modern presidency has become a collectivity of political and policy specialists whose expertise is placed at the president's disposal. To what extent do presidents avail themselves of these institutional sources of assistance? How do they structure their advisory systems and make decisions? This section is a brief discussion of the development of presidential staffing and the management styles presidents use with these assistants.

Just as important as attitudes drawn from life experiences, and skills developed in earlier careers, is a president's aptitude for management. Aides have the potential to magnify whatever skills presidents bring to the office and to compensate for their shortcomings. Moreover, it is pos-

sible that having a layer of advisers between the president and his performance will reduce the impact of undesirable personality traits on the
operation of the office.

The Development of Presidential Staffing

The presidential staff has grown substantially since its modern structure was authorized by Congress in 1939. Today, the Executive Office of
the President houses a wide range of expert staff units, including the
well-known Office of Management and Budget, Council of Economic
Advisers, and National Security Council (all discussed more fully in later
chapters), as well as the lesser-known Office of U.S. Trade Representative and Office of Science and Technology Policy. Perhaps best known,
and certainly most notorious in Washington circles, is the White House
Office, a unit that has traditionally emphasized the president's personal
and political concerns.

Like other presidents before him, Franklin Roosevelt had a limited
number of aides working on his behalf, many in clerical positions who
were borrowed from other parts of the federal bureaucracy. Looking for
a justification to expand these resources, in 1936 he appointed a blue-
ribbon group of public administration professors, headed by Louis
Brownlow, to study the management needs of the modern president.
The resulting structure, based on recommendations from that group but
reorganized many times since, has always been viewed as a response to
the Brownlow Commission's defining sentence: "The President needs
help." As Roosevelt and others recognized, the president required additional "eyes and ears" as well as brains to help him discharge the ever-
growing list of responsibilities placed at the White House door. Presidential staffing, therefore, is an attempt to help presidents avoid the
danger of "overload," the possibility that demands of the job will exceed
the capacity of any individual whose time and ability are finite. While
the staff is a way to *amplify* the capabilities brought by one person to the
presidency, it also may be seen as a structure that can *buffer* the direct
impact of a president's personality on performance. Presidents have
been given great latitude in their use of staff resources, a flexibility that
ensures responsiveness to new problems and perceived needs.

Staff size, although a recurrent political issue, is difficult to monitor
with precision. Best estimates place the size of today's Executive Office
at approximately 1,600 employees.[54] Moreover, the percentage of positions at higher levels of policy-making responsibility appears to have
increased substantially over the years.[55] Staff growth has been accom-

panied by a shift in influence, as well, with one analyst going so far as to suggest that the new structure constitutes a "presidential branch" of government distinct from the larger executive branch.[56] Clearly, presidents can draw upon a wide range of assistance located both outside and within the presidency.

Presidential Management Styles

Style is no doubt an overused term in describing characteristic patterns of presidential behavior, but a number of analysts have focused more narrowly on how presidents structure and use their advisory systems in making decisions. We term this a president's *management style*. Alexander George identifies three personality factors that determine a president's management style: the executive's habitual ways of dealing with information (acquiring, storing, retrieving, evaluating, and using it); the president's sense of competence in dealing personally with problems, which in turn determines the tasks delegated to others; and the president's orientation toward conflict, particularly the tolerance for competition and dissent among advisers.[57]

Because it is based on personality characteristics, each president's management style is unique. However, most analysts agree that recent presidents have chosen to operate within one of three advisory structures consistent with their management style.[58] The *formalistic* pattern emphasizes clear division of labor among staff assistants, well-defined procedures, and a carefully controlled flow of information to the president, usually through a chief of staff, who tries to deflect problems not worthy of presidential attention. Truman, Eisenhower, and Nixon constructed and operated such systems, although differences in operation reflected the unique combination of needs and contributions each of these men brought to the presidency. The *competitive* pattern, typified by Franklin Roosevelt, encouraged conflict among advisers and thrived on diversity of opinion with the president reserving ultimate judgment to himself. Conflict is endemic to decision making within the American government, but Roosevelt encouraged even more of it. Under a *collegial* system, emphasis is on group problem-solving, teamwork, and shared responsibility for outcomes, with the president participating in the process and choosing among identified options. Kennedy, particularly in his decision making during the Cuban missile crisis, typified this style.

Presidents may follow more than one pattern or construct a hybrid. Ford followed a collegial pattern in domestic policy, but was more formalistic in foreign policy.[59] Carter's system has been described as a mixture of collegial and formalistic elements.[60] Reagan constructed a variant of the formalistic and collegial models during his first term that drew considerable praise from many observers, particularly when its successor in the second term proved notably less successful.[61] Clinton's style, discussed below, has evolved from a highly undisciplined, sometimes collegial style to a somewhat more disciplined collegial pattern.

In general, formalistic structures seem to place more modest demands on presidential time and knowledge. Time is conserved by delegating a larger range of tasks to others, which also may increase the probability that experts will deal with the problem. Because much of the work in a formal system is processed in written form, it is less appropriate for presidents who prefer to rely upon group interaction, discussion, and even argument as part of the decision-making process. Competitive and collegial structures both place heavier demands on the president, who not only must rely more heavily on his own substantive knowledge in making choices among competing alternatives but also must be able to monitor a policy-making process that is inherently political in nature. Advisers and the policy areas they represent push hard for the president to adopt their solution to a problem, and the maneuvers used to gain an advantage during such policy struggles are believed to be the keys to success. Unfortunately, winning such battles may come at the expense of good decisions.

In the modern era, Democratic presidents, using Franklin Roosevelt as a model, often have adopted a more interactive advisory system, sometimes described as a "spokes-in-a-wheel" system with the president at the center of several principal aides in and out of the White House. Such a system encourages dispute and argumentation. Republican presidents, with some exceptions, generally have operated within a more highly structured system, in which the chief executive interacts with a narrower range of advisers and relies more heavily on systematic review processes. This approach is thought to be less susceptible to political maneuvering.

Is one pattern more conducive to success than the others? Each has strengths and weaknesses, but unfortunately analysts disagree on the criteria to be used in evaluating the styles, and they even disagree on how the systems perform. There are no reliable measures of which systems produce decisions of higher quality or greater political responsiveness, within reasonable spans of time.[62] Moreover, if the advisory systems ultimately reflect the kind of personality variables identified by Alexander George, it would be impossible to identify one as preferable because it might be inappropriate for the particular president asked to use it.

Multiple Advocacy: Learning a Management Style

The best-known effort to prescribe a specific decision process for presidents to follow is Alexander George's system of *multiple advocacy*.[63] In essence, George has suggested that presidents should be able to learn a set of techniques to follow in managing advisers and making decisions. Although recognizing that a given president may find this style "uncongenial to his cognitive style and work habits," George nonetheless believes that the advantages would make it worthwhile for a president to consider.[64] For example, Richard Nixon found it painful to be the object of direct, face-to-face argument among his advisers, but he might have modified the system to derive its benefits.[65]

George defines multiple advocacy as a *mixed* system that tries to ensure that presidents benefit from a wide review of policy options and hear a variety of viewpoints before making a final policy decision. It tries to build upon the inevitable conflict that arises among individual advisers and bureaucratic agencies by channeling that conflict in productive ways. The overall process must be structured so that every relevant viewpoint receives a fair hearing. One of the major tasks, then, in operating such a system is to monitor the breadth of options being considered and the opportunities that advocates of such views have to be heard. To operate such a system, the president requires a full-time assistant, a "custodian-manager" who acts as an "honest broker" among the advisers pushing their positions on the president.

George's hope is that systematic review of options, one of the claimed benefits of a formalistic system, also can be achieved under multiple advocacy, with the added benefit of the open debate and discussion that are encouraged by competitive and collegial systems. The president should act as a magistrate—"one who listens to the arguments made, evaluates them, poses issues and asks questions, and finally judges which action to take either from among those articulated by advocates or as formulated independently by himself after hearing them."[66] Consistent with this role, presidents need to suppress the urge to announce their own preferences early in the process and ensure that they remain faithful to the premise on which the system rests, the guarantee of giving an equal hearing to all views.

Such a process can be time-consuming, and George recognizes that presidents would have to decide when it should be used. There may be times when presidents feel that they already know the policy they wish to pursue. Nothing will prohibit them from exercising such discretion. As George recognizes, even though advisers may have become indispensable to modern presidents, constitutional responsibility in the American executive remains unitary, not collective. Only two names appear on the election ballot—the president's and the vice president's— and because vice presidents have virtually no independent powers, presidents are singularly responsible for the discharge of executive responsibilities.

Even George does not believe that use of a multiple advocacy system and the magistrate presidential style that accompanies it can ensure good decisions. Rather, he urges its adoption as a way to prevent the bad decisions that result from faulty procedures and to improve the quality of information made available to presidents.[67] There are no guarantees of success.

Understanding Presidents: The Case of Bill Clinton

Explaining presidential behavior and linking its determinants to performance is much like putting together the pieces of a puzzle, but a puzzle whose final shape is uncertain. One way to illustrate how background, experience, personality, and management style shape behavior and performance is to take an in-depth look at an individual case. It is still far too soon to evaluate Bill Clinton's full effectiveness in office, but we can at least trace major features of his life and explore ways in which these may affect his performance as president.

Clinton's life presents an intriguing set of contradictions. He was elected to office as a "new Democrat" seeking to move his party toward more moderate positions, but he encountered scathing criticism during his first year for being a vintage liberal. Although a product of the 1960s, an era known for its revolt against established power structures and social norms, the first "baby boomer" president has been consistently criticized for compromising with power centers, first in Arkansas and later in Washington. A booster of family values and a devout Baptist, Clinton has confronted repeated charges of marital infidelity. Filled with nostalgic pride for his small-town roots, he burned with ambition to succeed on larger stages—Georgetown University, Oxford University, Yale University Law School, Arkansas politics, and the presidency. Making sense of Clinton's life will be a task that many will pursue in the future. We can present only a modest snapshot.

Clinton's Early Life

Bill Clinton entered life in the wake of tragedy. Shortly before the birth of William Jefferson Blythe III, his original name, Clinton's natural father drowned in a roadside ditch following a car accident while driving from Chicago to Hope, Arkansas. The newly widowed Virginia Blythe was a wartime bride whose husband had been shipped off to fight in Europe shortly after their wedding and had spent less than six months with her before his death. After Bill's birth, she traveled to New Orleans to complete her training as a nurse anesthetist, leaving her young son behind for his first two years with her parents, Edith and Eldridge Cassidy, a nurse and the town iceman, respectively. Although his grandmother doted on Bill, her hot temper offset his grandfather's universal friendliness, traits later displayed by the adult Bill Clinton.

When Bill was four, his mother married Roger Clinton, a car dealer also known to deal in bootleg liquor who had been divorced by his first wife for abuse. The new family left Hope two years later for Hot Springs, Arkansas, a resort town where gambling and prostitution were openly pursued. For the next twelve years, the future president lived in two very different worlds: a public world centered on school and church, where he earned plaudits as a model citizen, and a private, turbulent world in which his stepfather had become an abusive alcoholic. It was not until shortly before his stepfather's death during Bill's senior year in college that the two achieved a measure of reconciliation. The situation was stormy: after repeated episodes of abuse, Virginia divorced her second husband in 1962, only to remarry him three months later. During the interlude, Bill Blythe took it upon himself to change his last name to Clinton so that it would be the same as that of his younger brother, Roger Clinton.

Inevitably, Bill Clinton's personality was heavily influenced by this unhappy family life. As the most authoritative biography argues, Clinton assumed the role of "family hero," one of the characteristic roles found among children of alcoholics. Not only does this child assume responsibility for protecting the family, but he may also serve as its redeemer to the outside world by winning awards and praise.[68] Clinton did both. He intervened in one instance to stop his stepfather from abusing his mother, and he tried to protect his halfbrother. Through his high school successes, he brought glory on the family: he was fourth in his graduating class, junior class president, band major and all-state band member, and a delegate to Boys' State and Boys' Nation; as a Boys' Nation delegate, in a memorable moment captured on film, the sixteen-year-old shook the hand of John F. Kennedy. Other accounts note that children of alcoholics have an "exaggerated need to be agreeable" [69] and share the alcoholic's concern that they are not worthy of being liked although accomplishments will make people like them.[70]

After high school, in the fall of 1964, Clinton went off to Georgetown University's School of Foreign Service, the only school to which he applied. He set out to become a leading figure on campus. Chosen freshman and sophomore class president, he was defeated for student council president in his senior year, a bitter rebuke for someone who had worked diligently for the position. "His political skills, his ability to think on his feet, to build coalitions and networks, were unrivaled on campus; but perhaps they were a bit too much, and he was too smooth." [71] Clinton's lesson from the experience: work harder next time, talk to every possible voter, listen more carefully.

Clinton assiduously built networks of acquaintances and potentially helpful contacts even at this early stage of his life. Capitol Hill offered one opportunity to develop an off-campus network through a two-year clerkship with the Senate Foreign Relations Committee, then chaired by Sen. J. William Fulbright (D-Ark.). Back home during the summer, he worked in the unsuccessful Arkansas gubernatorial campaign of Frank Holt, a campaign in which Clinton drove the candidate's family around the state and gained useful experience in organizing and public speaking. His selection as a Rhodes scholar in 1968 delayed the onset of his own political career but enabled him to develop yet another set of friendships that would prove politically beneficial. The two years in England exposed Clinton to a much wider world and must have boosted his self-confidence even further, confirming that he measured up well against the "best and the brightest" of his generation.

Like other male college students of the Vietnam era, Clinton wrestled with the immediate threat of being drafted for military service. Student deferments typically covered undergraduate study but not graduate school, and Rhodes scholars were only slightly less vulnerable than their classmates back home because draft boards sometimes, but not always, made allowances for this unique honor. During his work with the Senate Foreign Relations Committee, Clinton had become more critical of the war, an almost inevitable result, since Fulbright was the most outspoken critic of the Johnson administration's policy in Southeast Asia. Like many other opponents of the war, Clinton developed a strategy to avoid military service: upon returning from one year in Oxford, he arranged to enter the Reserve Officers Training Corps (ROTC) unit at the University of Arkansas, where he promised to enroll in the law school in the fall of 1969. This arrangement persuaded his draft board to cancel his induction, which had been scheduled for late July. Instead of entering law school, however, Clinton returned to England, requested sometime in late September that he be returned to the draft pool, and then benefited from a series of changes in how the draft was administered: graduate students were allowed to complete the year in which they were currently enrolled; the number of inductees was reduced; and a lottery system went into operation on December 1, which established that Clinton's draft number would be 311, well beyond likely induction. Shortly thereafter, Clinton wrote a letter to the University of Arkansas ROTC commander in which he sought to explain his actions, a letter that later formed the basis for charges that he dodged the draft. About the same time, during Christmas vacation, Clinton traveled through Europe, stopping in Prague and Moscow among other places; in 1992, Republican opponents sought to use this itinerary against him. Through these maneuvers, Clinton was able to spend a second year at Oxford, although he did not complete the work necessary for his degree.

Rather than enrolling in his home state's law school when he returned to the United States in 1970, Clinton chose to enter the prestigious Yale University Law School. The school's lax attendance policies enabled him to gain valuable campaign experience in Connecticut as an organizer for Joseph Duffey's Senate campaign in 1970 and in Texas as state coordinator for the presidential candidate George McGovern in 1972. Both experiences extended his network of contacts to a new generation of political activists, heavily motivated by antiwar sentiments and the desire to reform the American political and economic system. Both campaigns further developed his instincts as a mediator and exposed him to the ongoing political problem he would confront during his career: "how to hold together the competing forces within the Democratic party and ... how to champion social change without alienating the vast American middle class." [72]

There was one other lasting effect from his time at Yale: a romance with Hillary Rodham, a no less brilliant and far more focused law school classmate. Clinton returned to Arkansas in the fall of 1973, after a decade of preparation, to an untenured faculty appointment at the state university law school.

Clinton's Pre-presidential Political Career

Throughout college, Clinton had confided to many of his friends his intention to pursue a political career in his home state. After serving for less than a year on the faculty of the University of Arkansas Law School, which he had earlier spurned, Clinton challenged the incumbent U.S. representative John Paul Hammerschmidt in what appeared to be a hopelessly one-sided contest. Instead, Clinton surprised the state's political establishment by running an aggressive, imaginative campaign, even though he lost by 4,000 votes. As the campaign was coming to a close, Hillary Rodham left the House Judiciary Committee's Watergate investigation team, also joined the law school faculty, and became a major figure in Clinton's campaign. They married soon after. His unexpected competitiveness made another election contest inevitable, and in 1976 he won election as Arkansas's attorney general, finally reversing his bad luck of working for a string of losing causes. The contest proved so easy that he was able to serve as Jimmy Carter's state campaign chairman at the same time that he was winning his own election.

Clinton's meteoric rise now assumed an air of inevitability, and he won the governorship in 1978 with 63 percent of the vote, making him the youngest governor in the United States in four decades.[73] Just before the election, however, the Clintons joined another young politico, James McDougal, in an unsuccessful real estate venture later to become famous as Whitewater. But not all their investments were unsuccessful; Hillary, who had joined Arkansas's oldest legal firm as a way to pay the family's bills, parlayed a modest investment into substantial profits in livestock commodity trading. Both business arrangements later came back to haunt them.

Clinton's first two-year term as governor was not unlike his first two years as president. He pursued an overly ambitious, highly idealistic agenda of initiatives intended to reform Arkansas's education system and protect the environment from the timber industry. His young staff ruffled feathers in the Arkansas establishment and was unable to discipline Clinton's "loose, free-ranging management style," which included off-the-cuff comments to the press, an inability to adhere to a schedule, and excessive accessibility to any and all comers.[74] Successes were scarce, and the governor's ratings slipped; he narrowly won the 1980 primary against a weak opponent (Arkansas governors then served two-year terms) as voters protested newly raised automobile license fees and public safety crises that were triggered by protests of the Cuban refugees housed at Fort Chafee.

Clinton lost badly in the general election, making him the youngest defeated governor in American history. The experience was reportedly devastating, triggering months of soul-searching about what had gone wrong as Clinton unenthusiastically entered private law practice. It was apparently a period of intense stress for his marriage, as well. By 1982, however, Clinton's resilience was evident and he was ready for a rematch. In preparation, he apologized to the public for mistakes made as a young governor, essentially admitting that he had become "too big for his britches." The campaign was characterized by extensive use of negative ads on both sides, although the incumbent's seemed unfair given the youthful former governor's admission of errors. Clinton's return to the governor's mansion began a decade of service as chief executive, secured through successful reelection campaigns in 1984, 1986, and 1990, after the term was lengthened to four years.

Clinton's second coming was far different from the first. His youthful aides were replaced by seasoned veterans; the idealistic program of reforms was replaced with a more modest agenda of achievable reforms; compromises were struck with the state's most powerful economic interests.[75] Clinton pursued his most ambitious goal of restructuring public education by providing a major increase in funding while requiring that teachers pass a competency exam, something the education union, a one-time supporter of the governor, vigorously opposed.

As the decade progressed, Arkansas increasingly became a launching pad for Clinton's next career step. He became chairman of the National Governors' Association in 1986, where he developed a new set of issue positions on job creation, welfare reform, and education for an expanded audience; this offered new opportunities for networking with yet another group of potential supporters. He addressed the 1980, 1984, and 1988 Democratic National Conventions. In the last appearance he gave a thirty-two-minute speech nominating Michael Dukakis as the presidential candidate; it was memorable only because of the audience's increasing restiveness and its negative impact on Clinton's own presidential aspirations. In fact, Clinton had come within minutes of running for the 1988 nomination himself, agonizing for weeks whether to run and then disappointing a gathering of friends who had come to Little Rock anticipating an announcement which was not made for another four years.

During his 1990 campaign for a fifth term as governor, Clinton unwisely promised to serve out his full term in office, a commitment that would exclude him from a 1992 presidential bid. Recognizing his error, he later traveled across the state laying the groundwork for a campaign by speaking with citizens about whether he should break that promise and run for president. A speech given by him in May 1991 to the Democratic Leadership Council, a group of moderate to conservative Democrats seeking to redirect the party's principal positions and appeals, excited national press attention and made his candidacy a real possibility. After activating the many networks he had labored so long to cultivate, he announced his candidacy in the fall of 1991, a decision that surprised few of his closest friends. As David Maraniss observes, Clinton had always performed well against the toughest competition: "In settings where he found himself among high-powered peers, whether with the Rhodes Scholars at Oxford or, much later, with the governors of other states, Clinton rose quickly to prominence, outpacing others with his ambition, affability, appetite for ideas and dealmaking." [76] Clinton has always exuded supreme self-confidence in his own skills and capacities, and throughout his life, others had assured him of his presidential potential—his mother, his classmates, his fellow Rhodes scholars, and his wife. The election, reviewed more extensively in Chapter 2, demonstrated his effectiveness as a campaigner and a political strategist.

What Kind of President?

In what ways has Bill Clinton's conduct of the presidency been shaped by his background? Are there recurring patterns that would indicate basic personality orientations, enduring attitudes, or behavioral styles? As in the case of every president, there is no dearth of speculation about these linkages, but the connections discussed below are speculative, at best.

Maraniss, Clinton's principal biographer, portrays him as a man of contradictions: "considerate and calculating, easygoing and ambitious, mediator and predator"; "sincere and deceptive at the same time"; "indecisive, too eager to please and prone to deception" but also "indefatigable, intelligent, empathetic, and self-deprecating." [77] While some might respond to this portrait by asking, "Who is the real Bill Clinton?" it is more realistic to recognize that most people are bundles of contradictions, exhibiting both strengths and weaknesses, combining both admirable and deplorable traits. Presidential characteristics, however, are magnified under the scrutiny of media cynics and political critics.

Most observers are impressed by Clinton's native intelligence and natural abilities, frequently becoming no less enthusiastic than those close friends and associates in his pre-presidential years who encouraged his political ambition. In the same *Rolling Stone* interview cited earlier that revealed his explosive temper and frustration, the two journalists concluded that the "range of his intellect and energy was awesome," an especially impressive conclusion given their familiarity with Washington and its cast of highly successful characters.[78] A seasoned academic observer of presidents declared that Clinton is that "rare combination of a complex policy thinker and a sophisticated thinker about politics."[79] Even some of his harshest critics acknowledge his skills, one of them emphasizing his "talent for language that is rare in politicians" and his "extraordinary gift for intimacy" revealed in his capacity to relate to people, to listen to their concerns, and empathize with their problems.[80]

Perhaps it is precisely because of Clinton's prodigious talents that disappointment was initially widespread about his performance in office. Some of his failings can be traced to basic personality traits and others to unproductive work habits.

Some of Clinton's greatest problems seem to flow from his most notable skills. A major example is his ability to relate to others. Despite recognizing that this is a tremendous asset for someone who must win support through inside bargaining and public persuasion, there have been widespread doubts about his sincerity. He has been described as displaying a "chameleonlike quality," a "plastic political identity" that reflects the president's "habit of adapting to the people around him and trying to present to them the version of himself he thought each would most admire."[81] Maraniss praises Clinton as a "natural politician," but goes on to suggest the problems flowing from such instinctive behavior: "[N]atural politicians are skilled actors, recreating reality, adjusting and ad-libbing, synthesizing the words, ideas, and feelings of others, slipping into different roles in different scenes, saying the same thing over and over again and making it seem like they are saying it for the first time."[82]

Because of these virtuoso skills, people have come to distrust his honesty and to question whether he holds any strong beliefs. Clinton seems to adjust too readily to each new audience he addresses. Throughout his political apprenticeship, Clinton displayed a knack for "speaking the idiom, wherever he was," whether Capitol Hill, the halls of Oxford, an Arkansas roadhouse, or a country store.[83] To one observer, such verbal facility causes him to suffer from an "almost pathological inability to tell the whole truth." [84] His tendency to play word games heightens this impression; instead of admitting to reporters during the 1992 presidential election campaign that he had smoked marijuana, for example, he denied having inhaled.

Even when his honesty was not in question, Clinton's verbal skills were sometimes out of control. Although an unusually gifted extemporaneous speaker, Clinton has made numerous mistakes. During his first two years as president, "Clinton too often thought out loud, too frequently seemed to promise things he either could not or chose not to deliver, and thus too frequently could not be taken at his word." [85] Instead of talking his way through problems, he needs "to engage his considerable brainpower before, rather than during, the engagement of his always loquacious mouth. Rarely does Clinton seem to have an unsaid thought." [86] Nor have Clinton's speaking skills been used strategically. As many commentators have noted since Ronald Reagan's service in the office, modern presidents must rely heavily on direct appeals to the public as a way to gain passage of programs. But Clinton "finds it all too easy to deluge the public with details, and it appears to be difficult for him to transcend policy mechanics and convey the broad principles and values behind his programs ... the antithesis of Ronald Reagan, who was notoriously innocent of policy specifics, but gifted at evoking larger themes." [87]

Confusion over Clinton's larger goals raises another issue: the public, the press, and politicians have wondered what Clinton believes. His harshest critics question whether he has any lasting principles that direct his activity: "Clinton means what he says when he says it, but tomorrow he will mean what he says when he says the opposite. He is the existential President, living with absolute sincerity in the passing moment." [88] A careful reading of his political history suggests that Clinton believes in an activist government and, more than any other policy area, has supported intervention in civil rights. Yet, even that lifelong commitment was sorely tested in 1995 when he ordered a review of government-sponsored affirmative action programs, apparently in response to growing concerns that this could be a major political issue in the 1996 election. Ultimately, he ordered few changes in existing programs, but the seeds of doubt had been sown in the minds of an important constituency.

By no means was the review of affirmative action programs the first time that Clinton seemed to reverse himself on a policy stand. In fact, the president's reversals on policy, several dramatically visible, have become legendary in Washington and among the press corps. For example, Clinton managed to antagonize major segments of his party in October 1995 with a toss-away line offered during a speech to a group of campaign donors in Houston, Texas. Noting that the group of wealthy Democrats might think he had raised their taxes too much in 1993, he suggested they would be surprised to learn that he agreed. Sen. Robert Kerrey (D-Neb.), an opponent for the presidential nomination in 1992, drafted a blistering speech that, while not delivered on the Senate floor, was leaked to the *New York Times*, which published excerpts:

What troubles me is that after three years as President, he doesn't appear to know where he wants to lead America. He is developing some interesting theories about where we have been and where we are, but he doesn't talk consistently about where we should be going. He has a handful of programs for which he is prepared to fight, like national service and Head Start, but even they don't seem to be connected to a clear vision of where he believes America could and should be going. He is very clear about where he wants to go— back to the White House for four more years. But as to the country? Well, that is much less clear.[89]

The reversals and waffling have been explained as a personal fault as well as a political reflex: "President Clinton vacillates ... partly because he cannot make up his own mind and partly because he wants to please the last group to have spoken to him."[90] Others suggest the problem lies in the sophistication of his mind, making him "an indecisive person partly because he has the capacity to look at matters from a variety of angles and partly because he cannot, in the end, decide exactly what his political identity is and what he is willing to fight for."[91] Still others suggest it flows from his frequent efforts to reconcile contradictory positions.[92]

It is clear that ideological consistency has never been a hallmark of Clinton's political career. Over the years, he has frustrated numerous allies by reversing his position on what others had thought were commitments. This was true with organized labor, environmentalists, and teachers while he was governor; congressional Democrats felt betrayed on several occasions by his shifts in strategy. Nor has he ever pursued radical reform. Maraniss points out that he was a "cautious defender of the establishment" as a student leader at Georgetown, a member of the "moderate wing of the antiwar movement," and a partner with corporate interests when necessary.[93] Yet, one of the political consultants who knew him intimately during his gubernatorial years and reemerged in

1995 as a presidential adviser, Richard Morris, has described Clinton's personality as requiring a purpose. "He had to be engaged in some important, valiant fight for the good of the world to lend coherence and structure to his life, and when he didn't have those fights he would turn on himself, he would eat away at himself, he would become depressed, paranoid, surly and, one suspects, escapist." [94] Thus, Clinton may have had difficulty articulating a clear vision of his current goals and have frustrated many in his zigzag course on some policy issues, but there could be a deeper need for coherence that suggests clearer direction might emerge in the future.

Although coherence may have been minimal, there has been no dearth of action. Like Jimmy Carter, Clinton has been accused of failing to set priorities among his many initiatives, resulting in a serious overload of the congressional and public agenda, particularly during his first year. Looking back to his record, one can see a repeat of the problems encountered during his initial year as governor. Clinton acknowledged the problem during an interview late in his first year. "I'm the most impatient person on earth. If there is a legitimate criticism about me, it is that I have thrown myself against the wall this year. I've tried to do so many things that sometimes when I do things, no one notices." [95] That self-description, of course, puts the problem in its best light, the product of trying too hard. A review of Clinton's life makes it clear that the tendency is deep-seated. As noted earlier, Clinton trained himself to function on fewer hours of sleep while a student at Georgetown so that he could accomplish more; as a professor, he "always seemed to be juggling too many things at the same time"; and he has admitted to feeling "an urgent sense to do everything he could in life as quickly as possible" because of his father's death at the early age of twenty-eight.[96]

Fortunately, Clinton has displayed another personality trait, the capacity to bounce back from adversity. This became part of his presidential campaign following the 1992 New Hampshire primary, when Clinton labeled himself the "Comeback Kid," a candidate who overcame damaging stories about marital infidelity, draft dodging, and marijuana use to finish a surprising second in the nation's most-watched primary. He has demonstrated the same resilience throughout his life. Maraniss suggests that Clinton engaged in extended periods of introspection following three major crises: the suicide of fellow Rhodes scholar Frank Aller, which came on the heels of Clinton's own personal torment over the Vietnam draft; his crushing defeat when he sought reelection after his first term as governor; and the arrest of Roger Clinton, his brother, for cocaine dealing. The latter episode produced an extensive round of counseling and the family's first open discussion of how they had been affected by his stepfather's alcoholism, a period when Clinton reportedly linked his own dislike of personal conflict and his desire to please with his family experience.[97] All three were difficult periods for the young adult, the promising politician, and the older brother, yet Clinton navigated each successfully.

This capacity for introspection and self-correction is likely to help him as president. Even when he is wrong he has the laudable ability "to admit his own failings" and make pragmatic adjustments.[98] Clinton seems to have learned about the job while serving as president, a trait most visible in discussions of how he sought to make adjustments.

Clinton's Management Style

It should come as no surprise that after twelve years as governor of Arkansas, Clinton entered the White House with a set of practices and preferences about how to manage his new executive position. And, like most modern presidents, Clinton brought with him a group of acquaintances—from Arkansas legal circles, the 1994 presidential campaign, and his many networks—to whom he turned for advice and assistance. But despite his many years as a chief executive, the transfer of his ways of working received scant applause. In fact, Clinton left the impression of being an enormously skilled but severely undisciplined leader. As one academic pointed out, Clinton seeks to rely "on sheer intellectual acuity and a knack for ringmastering myriad issues in direct dialogue with his advisers and cabinet secretaries," an approach that places such great pressure on his individual skills that it is unlikely to succeed.[99]

Paul Quirk has described such an approach as the "self-reliant" model of presidential leadership based on being "thoroughly involved, completely informed" and associated with Jimmy Carter's earlier style. In marked contrast was the approach of Ronald Reagan, whose "minimalist" style relied on delegating most details of policy substance to others and remaining distant from the day-to-day operations of his staff and the government.[100] Reagan would set the administration's general goals and become deeply involved in selling programs to the public, but he depended heavily on the people around him to develop proposals and implement the programs. Clinton offers a sharp contrast. He has a "predilection to take on large numbers of personal responsibilities and to do little to establish structures of delegation."[101] In fact, Clinton's "aversion to organizational process thinking" has been identified as one of his greatest weaknesses.[102] If Reagan was guilty of delegating too much of his authority to others, Clinton seemed guilty of hoarding too many responsibilities for himself.

Both presidents discovered that the quality of their aides and an effective organization have much to say about the likelihood of success. For Reagan, this did not become clear until the Iran-contra crisis became public in 1986. Subsequent inquiries by a blue-ribbon commission concluded that Reagan had been lax in his oversight of foreign policy; moreover, the team of aides who assisted him during the second term was far less effective than that of his first term. Clinton, consistent with his willingness to entertain self-criticism and introduce corrective action, has shaken up his staff on several occasions in pursuit of a more effective combination of personalities and arrangements, but some have wondered whether he "is so pathologically a-institutional that no manner of reorganization of his team would have any lasting effects." [103]

Clinton has been widely described as a "policy wonk," someone who revels in the details of government programs and policy options. During his first year in office, however, this fascination extended largely to domestic and economic policy, and he seemed largely uninterested and unengaged in foreign policy matters. Problems in Bosnia, Somalia, and Haiti all seemed to explode without eliciting an effective response from the White House. Secretary of Defense Les Aspin was replaced, but the president's two principal advisers, Secretary of State Warren Christopher and National Security Adviser Anthony Lake, remained in place. The president's inattention may have been the principal problem.[104] Later administration successes in returning President Jean-Claude Aristide to power in Haiti through a peaceful American military intervention and advancing the Arab-Israeli as well as the Bosnian peace negotiations mitigated the criticism somewhat, but the impression of selective policy attention persisted. (See Chapter 10.)

It did not take long after his election for problems with Clinton's White House operations to surface. By the end of his first 100 days in office, he began to shuffle staff members and make modest procedural adjustments. Thomas "Mac" McLarty came to Washington with Clinton to serve as his White House chief of staff; friends since kindergarten, McLarty's loyalty and access to Clinton were unquestioned, but McLarty, no less than the president, was a newcomer to Washington and its distinctive ways. In May 1993, McLarty's problems in overseeing White House operations and Clinton's political relations were acknowledged when he was given a second White House deputy. This step followed the defeat of a high-profile economic stimulus plan in the Senate, withdrawal of a controversial administration proposal to provide childhood vaccinations, and slow progress on developing a health care reform plan. Better coordination and greater focus were the announced goals.[105]

But the administration continued to falter; approval ratings declined, the president's economic plan squeaked through a Democrat-controlled House, and a round of media accounts enhanced the sense of crisis by asking "Can Clinton Recover?" and "What's Wrong?"[106] "Disorganization, inexperience and internal rivalries" were blamed for White House drift, presidential indecision, and repeated blunders (firing of staff in the White House travel office, the botched nomination of Lani Guinier, and Clinton's $200 haircut at the Los Angeles airport).[107] David Gergen, a veteran of three Republican administrations, was brought in to help focus the president's communication efforts and provide an experienced hand in setting overall strategy. The administration seemed to oscillate between two distinctive styles: undisciplined, vigorous action on many fronts simultaneously and a more focused, calculating style of political pragmatism.[108]

Despite the initial staff shifts, the president did not change his own undisciplined, overcommitted style. More than a dozen aides reportedly had direct access to him; a group of nonaides (FOBs, or Friends of Bill, and, one must add, Hillary) exercised considerable influence as personal advisers without official standing; and high-level meetings seldom had a clear agenda and functioned more as floating policy seminars than as coherent policy discussions designed to reach a decision. A time and motion study conducted in late 1994 discovered that Clinton was spending 22 percent of his time in staff meetings and enjoyed very little "thinking time," since every lull in his schedule was treated as an invitation for aides to interrupt him.[109]

Imposing order became the principal charge of Leon Panetta, Clinton's original director of the Office of Management and Budget who became White House chief of staff in late June 1994. This second major shakeup was occasioned by an avalanche of problems: responding to investigations into Whitewater; pushing the administration's ambitious legislative agenda of health care and campaign reform, the crime bill, and an international trade agreement; and preparing for the fall midterm elections. Panetta replaced some staff members, redefined others' responsibilities, reallocated the president's time so that only 10 percent was devoted to staff meetings, and doubled his "thinking time" to

35 percent of a typical week. Access to the president was channeled through Panetta's office and restricted to a much smaller number of aides, which reduced, as well, the influence of the infamous FOBs; all payroll and personnel decisions were routed through his office; attendance at staff meetings was restricted to two dozen rather than three dozen aides; policy discussions were focused by using agendas and decision memoranda that included options thoroughly prepared beforehand; and the number of policy themes advanced by the administration was reduced to a manageable number.[110]

The organizational changes, of course, did not ensure success; much of Clinton's legislative program failed to win passage, and the Democrats lost control of Congress. Nonetheless, there was a perception that the new arrangements made presidential success possible whereas the previous disorder made it highly improbable. The changes seemed to help during 1995 and 1996. As Fred Greenstein noted, "Clinton's exceptional talents are in great need of management lest he fly off in all directions, but he is not easily managed."[111] That task falls to Erskine Bowles, Panetta's successor at the outset of Clinton's second term.

Conclusions About Clinton

In truth, it is difficult to draw many conclusions about Bill Clinton's performance and its relationship to his personality and background, but some tendencies seem fairly clear. Like virtually all other presidents, Clinton is a champion of the prevailing order, not someone intent on radical social and economic change. Still, after running a campaign that promised change, Clinton has sought to be a president of achievement, offering the nation a set of ambitious—quite possibly *overambitious*—domestic programs that probably exceeded the potential of his modest electoral mandate. As an executive, Clinton has had many failings, most traced to his highly individualistic, sometimes collegial, and almost never formalized style of management. His administration has struggled to establish the degree of orderly routine needed to take full advantage of the president's prodigious talents. As in his years as governor, Hillary Clinton has figured prominently as both a behind-the-scenes strategist and a public advocate. Moreover, as president, Clinton has employed some of the same tactics to sell policies that he employed in Arkansas.[112]

The result has been a roller coaster ride for the nation, dramatic twists and turns that have contributed to both success and failure. It is still difficult to evaluate Clinton's overall performance in office; at this early point, however, he seems to meet some but fall well short of other criteria commonly used to evaluate presidential greatness as discussed earlier in this chapter. If decisiveness is a trait of great presidents, press and public perceptions of indecision and waffling would seem to rate Clinton poorly. Clinton fares far better on intelligence and the capacity to grow in office, characteristics that ranked close behind decisiveness in importance. Has he provided moral, inspirational leadership? Doubts about the president's personal integrity and questions about his honesty certainly make this dimension problematic and perhaps explain why the White House hoped to make his conduct of the office appear more principled as he wrestled over major policy differences with the Republican Congress at the close of 1995.

Like every president before him, Clinton brought a mix of orientations and experiences to the presidency that were sometimes detrimental and sometimes beneficial to his performance in office. The final balance will differ from analyst to analyst and probably change with the passage of time.

Seeking Presidential Success

Paul Quirk has posed a deceptively simple question: "What does a president need to know?" Quirk identifies a list of presidential competencies that could serve as the basis for making decisions about how best to allocate the president's time, energy, and talent as well as that of the White House staff and the innermost group of presidential advisers.[113] In Quirk's view, presidents require a minimal level of *substantive familiarity* so that intelligent choices can be made among policy options. Moreover, presidents need to have a degree of *process sensibility* that reflects familiarity with how government decisions are made and carried out as well as how such systems might best be designed. Finally, presidents need the capacity for *policy promotion*, the means that make it possible to achieve their goals through bargaining with other Washington elites and through appeals for broad public support. Every president brings a different mix of personal competencies to the job and needs to compensate for personal weaknesses or to complement strengths with the help of others. In Quirk's view, it is critical that each president have a well-designed strategy for how to succeed, what he terms *strategic competence*. This strategy will involve decisions on how to allocate time, energy, and talent in relation to mastering substantive issues, delegating tasks, and establishing the prerequisites for successful delegation, for example, selecting personnel.[114]

How are these competencies developed? Implicitly, Quirk seems to suggest that experience in government at the federal level is a critical qualification for presidents to bring to the position. Without it, adequate levels of process and substantive familiarity would be difficult to develop. But Quirk's advice is directed more to presidents than to voters. Above all else, Quirk urges presidents to approach the office self-consciously with an eye to developing a management strategy—know yourself and take the steps necessary for effectiveness. Only in this way can presidents hope to achieve some measure of success. It is not clear how readily presidents will accept such advice. Are they likely to be sufficiently self-critical to recognize their own shortcomings? One might expect that anyone imbued with ambition and flush with success will proceed to the task of governing filled with self-confidence. Moreover, one might expect that those presidents whose personalities drive them to pursue achievement will be least likely to undertake self-analysis.

In many respects, this chapter has explored a question similar to the one posed by Quirk. *What personal qualities make a successful president?* As we have seen, there are no simple answers to that question. Competencies may be part of the solution, but so are temperament and attitudes. As this chapter demonstrates, we have little sense of how the qualities necessary for success are derived from family background, career experience, personality, and beliefs. This is true in no small measure because success is the product of these personal qualities interacting with the constraints and opportunities of situations. Despite this fundamental uncertainty, there remains a pervasive confidence that the president's personal qualities have the utmost effect on performance in office, and, therefore, the American people are likely to continue their search for men and, perhaps one day, women with heroic qualities.

NOTES

1. Fred I. Greenstein, "Can Personality and Politics Be Studied Systematically?" *Political Psychology* 13, no. 1 (1992): 109. For a general discussion of studying personality and politics with special attention to the presidency, see Fred I. Greenstein, *Personality and Politics: Problems of Evidence, Inference, and Conceptualization*, 2d ed (New York: Norton, 1975); and Bert Rockman, *The Leadership Question: The Presidency and the American System* (New York: Praeger, 1984).

2. Bruce Buchanan, *The Citizen's Presidency* (Washington, D.C.: CQ Press, 1987), 102–104. Buchanan proposes a set of "competent process standards" that are more susceptible to empirical verification. See *The Citizen's Presidency,* 108–134.

3. Bert Rockman, "Conclusions: An Imprint but Not a Revolution," in *The Reagan Revolution?* ed. B. B. Kymlicka and Jean V. Matthews (Chicago: Dorsey, 1988), 205. Other works in this vein include the following: Larry Berman, ed., *Looking Back*

on the Reagan Presidency (Baltimore: Johns Hopkins University Press, 1990); Sidney Blumenthal and Thomas Byrne Edsall, eds., *The Reagan Legacy* (New York: Pantheon Books, 1988); Charles O. Jones, ed., *The Reagan Legacy: Promise and Performance* (Chatham, N.J.: Chatham House, 1988); and John L. Palmer, ed., *Perspectives on the Reagan Years* (Washington, D.C.: Urban Institute, 1986).

4. Schlesinger's initial effort polled fifty-five scholars, and his second included seventy-five, with historians comprising the greater part of each group. Maranell and Dodder included results from 571 historians, and the *Chicago Tribune* poll focused on forty-nine scholars who had studied individual presidents. Finally, the Murray-Blessing poll was based on 846 responses to a nineteen-page, 180-question survey that was sent to 1,997 Ph.D.-holding American historians with assistant professor rank (an additional 107 responses were returned late). For information on poll samples, see Henry J. Abraham, *Justices and Presidents* (New York: Oxford University Press, 1985), appendix B. For discussion of these efforts as well as their own, see Robert K. Murray and Tim H. Blessing, *Greatness in the White House: Rating the Presidents, Washington Through Ronald Reagan,* 2d updated ed. (University Park: Pennsylvania State University Press, 1994), chaps. 1 and 2. The ranking of Ronald Reagan was completed in 1988–90 and is reported in Murray and Blessing's updated edition.

5. Murray and Blessing, *Greatness in the White House,* 24.

6. Ibid., 41–43, and appendix 8, 139. The personal traits conducive to success also were examined in terms of how they changed for different times. For the modern era, 1945 to the present, respondents ranked intelligence first and integrity second, with other qualities in declining order: sensitivity to popular demands, charisma, previous political experience, pleasing physical appearance, intense patriotism, and an aristocratic bearing.

7. Ibid., 63.

8. James MacGregor Burns, *Leadership* (New York: Harper & Row, 1977).

9. Donald Matthews, *The Social Background of Political Decision Makers* (New York: Random House, 1954), 23.

10. Edward Pessen, *The Log Cabin Myth: The Social Backgrounds of the Presidents* (New Haven, Conn.: Yale University Press, 1984), 56–57.

11. Ibid., 171.

12. Ibid., 56–63. Pessen views a family's class as a combination of wealth and possessions, income and occupational prestige, lifestyle, status, influence, and power. He recognizes, moreover, that analysts' characterizations are subjective.

13. Truman attended night classes at the Kansas City Law School, but it was a proprietary institution not then affiliated with a university. It is now part of the Law School of the University of Missouri—Kansas City.

14. Max Weber, "Politics as a Vocation," in *Max Weber: Essays in Sociology,* ed. H. H. Gerth and C. W. Mills (New York: Oxford University Press, 1946), 85.

15. Hugh Montgomery-Massingberd, ed., *Burke's Presidential Families of the U.S.A.* (London: Burke's Peerage, 1975), 250.

16. Ibid., 320.

17. Robert Donovan, *Conflict and Crisis: The Presidency of Harry S Truman, 1945–48* (New York: Praeger, 1977), chap. 40. It should also be noted that military officers have demonstrated leadership skills and may be called upon to develop substantial political skill while building careers or in dealing with foreign leaders. Eisenhower, for example, did both.

18. Pessen, *The Log Cabin Myth,* 172.

19. Ibid., 171.

20. E. Digby Baltzell and Howard G. Schneiderman, "Social Class in the Oval Office," *Society* 26 (September/October 1988): 42–49. The ranking of presidential performance used in this study was conducted by Robert K. Murray and Tim H. Blessing and was first published in the *Journal of American History* 70 (December 1983): 535–555.

21. Ibid., 47.

22. W. H. Harrison and Garfield were not rated because of the brief time they served in office.

23. Baltzell and Schneiderman, "Social Class in the Oval Office," 49.

24. Richard Neustadt, *Presidential Power and the Modern Presidents* (New York: Free Press, 1991), 151.

25. Ibid., 205.

26. Rockman, *Leadership Question,* 212. Rockman uses a performance ranking compiled by the *Chicago Tribune* in 1982.

27. We are indebted to Leonard P. Stark for this account and continuing stimulation on the subject of presidential personality. See his senior honors thesis, "Personality and Presidential Selection: Evaluating Character and Experience in the 1988 Election," University of Delaware, June 1991, 47–48. Barber's article was "The Question of Presidential Character," *Saturday Review,* Sept. 23, 1972, 62–66.

28. Fred I. Greenstein, *Personality and Politics: Problems of Evidence, Inference, and Conceptualization,* 2d ed. (New York: Norton, 1975), 3.

29. Alexander George and Juliette George, *Woodrow Wilson and Colonel House: A Personality Study* (New York: John Day, 1956); Bruce Mazlish, *In Search of Nixon: A Psychohistorical Inquiry* (Baltimore: Pelican, 1973); Doris Kearns, *Lyndon Johnson and the American Dream* (New York: Harper & Row, 1976); Betty Glad, *Jimmy Carter: In Search of the Great White House* (New York: Norton, 1980).

30. For an extended discussion, see Greenstein's treatment of these issues in *Personality and Politics,* chaps. 3 and 4, as well as the introduction.

31. See, for example, Alexander George's discussion of Barber's book, *The Presidential Character: Predicting Performance in the White House.* George, "Assessing Presidential Character," *World Politics* 26 (January 1974): 234–282.

32. James David Barber, *The Presidential Character: Predicting Performance in the White House,* 4th ed. (Englewood Cliffs, N.J.: Prentice-Hall, 1992), 34.

33. James David Barber, "Predicting Hope with Clinton at Helm," *Raleigh* [N.C.] *News Observer,* Jan. 17, 1993.

34. Barber, *Presidential Character,* 5.

35. Ibid.

36. Barber, "Predicting Hope with Clinton at Helm."

37. Stanley A. Renshon, "A Preliminary Assessment of the Clinton Presidency: Character, Leadership and Performance," *Political Psychology* 15, no. 2 (1994). Also see a slightly revised version of the paper in *The Clinton Presidency: Campaigning, Governing, and the Psychology of Leadership,* ed. Stanley A. Renshon (Boulder, Colo.: Westview Press, 1995), 57–87.

38. David Maraniss, *First in His Class: A Biography of Bill Clinton* (New York: Simon & Schuster, 1995).

39. Renshon, "A Preliminary Assessment of the Clinton Presidency," 382.

40. Jann S. Wenner and William Greider, "The Rolling Stone Interview: President Clinton," *Rolling Stone,* Dec. 9, 1993, 81.

41. Renshon, "A Preliminary Assessment of the Clinton Presidency," 381.

42. Ibid., 380.

43. Ibid., 382.

44. Fred I. Greenstein, "The Two Leadership Styles of William Jefferson Clinton," *Political Psychology* 15, no. 2 (1994): 357. Also see Greenstein's essay "Political Style and Political Leadership: The Case of Bill Clinton," in *The Clinton Presidency: Campaigning, Governing, and the Psychology of Leadership*, 137–147.

45. Greenstein, "The Two Leadership Styles of William Jefferson Clinton," 358.

46. Greenstein, *Personality and Politics*, 19.

47. Fred I. Greenstein, *The Hidden-Hand Presidency* (New York: Basic Books, 1982). Barber, however, has responded that the new evidence confirms his original analysis even more fully. Barber, *Presidential Character*, 522–515.

48. See George, "Assessing Presidential Character"; and Michael Nelson, "The Psychological Presidency," in *The Presidency and the Political System*, 4th ed., ed. Michael Nelson (Washington, D.C.: CQ Press, 1995).

49. Dean Keith Simonton, *Why Presidents Succeed: A Political Psychology of Leadership* (New Haven, Conn.: Yale University Press, 1987), 151–152.

50. Barber, *Presidential Character*, 4th ed., 487.

51. Ibid., 298.

52. Ibid., 296–299.

53. Jeffrey Tulis, "On Presidential Character," in *The Presidency in the Constitutional Order*, ed. Jeffrey Tulis and Joseph M. Bessette (Baton Rouge: Louisiana State University Press, 1981), 283–313.

54. Stanley and Niemi, *Vital Statistics on American Politics*, 5th ed., 247–249.

55. Joseph A. Pika, "Management Style and the Organizational Matrix: Studying White House Operations," *Administration and Society* 20, no. 1 (May 1988): 11.

56. John Hart, *The Presidential Branch: From Washington to Clinton* (Chatham, N.J.: Chatham House, 1995).

57. Alexander George, *Presidential Decisionmaking in Foreign Policy* (Boulder, Colo.: Westview, 1980), 139–168.

58. The three basic structures were identified in the early 1970s by R. T. Johnson and have been the object of much discussion. Richard Tanner Johnson, *Managing the White House* (New York: Harper & Row, 1974). Also see Johnson, "Presidential Style," in *Perspectives on the Presidency*, ed. Aaron Wildavsky (Boston: Little, Brown, 1975).

59. Roger Porter, "A Healing Presidency," in *Leadership in the Modern Presidency*, ed. Fred I. Greenstein (Cambridge, Mass.: Harvard University Press, 1988), 218.

60. George, *Presidential Decisionmaking*, 159.

61. Colin Campbell, *Managing the Presidency: Carter, Reagan, and the Search for Executive Harmony* (Pittsburgh: University of Pittsburgh Press, 1986), 93–111; James Pfiffner, *The Strategic Presidency: Hitting the Ground Running* (Chicago: Dorsey, 1988), 30–37; Buchanan, *The Citizen's Presidency*, 124–133.

62. Pika, "Management Style and the Organizational Matrix," 9.

63. Alexander George, "The Case for Multiple Advocacy in Making Foreign Policy," *American Political Science Review* 66 (September 1972): 751–785. Also see George, *Presidential Decisionmaking*, chap. 11.

64. George, *Presidential Decisionmaking*, 203.

65. Ibid., 203–204.

66. Ibid., 201.

67. Ibid., 204.

68. Maraniss, *First in His Class*, 38.

69. Greenstein, "The Two Leadership Styles of William Jefferson Clinton," 358.

70. Michael J. Kelly, "A Man Who Wants to Be Liked, and Is: William Jefferson Blythe Clinton," *New York Times*, Nov. 4, 1992, A1.

71. Maraniss, *First in His Class*, 88.

72. Ibid., 230.

73. Ibid., 357.

74. Ibid., 362.

75. Michael J. Kelly is highly critical of the last pattern, arguing that Clinton betrayed his populist roots and cozied up to the traditional centers of Arkansas power. Michael J. Kelly, "The President's Past," *New York Times Magazine,* July 31, 1994.

76. Maraniss, *First in His Class,* 340.

77. Ibid., 124, 199, 355.

78. Wenner and Greider, "The Rolling Stone Interview," 40.

79. Bert A. Rockman, "Leadership Style and the Clinton Presidency," in *The Clinton Presidency: First Appraisals,* ed. Colin Campbell and Bert A. Rockman (Chatham, N.J.: Chatham House, 1996), 347.

80. Kelly, "A Man Who Wants to Be Liked," A1, and "The President's Past," 25.

81. Kelly, "The President's Past," 25; Colin Campbell and Bert A. Rockman, introduction to *The Clinton Presidency: First Appraisals,* 9; Maraniss, *First in His Class,* 169.

82. Maraniss, *First in His Class,* 323.

83. Ibid., 98.

84. Kelly, "The President's Past," 40.

85. Rockman, "Leadership Style and the Clinton Presidency," 342.

86. Ibid., 343.

87. Greenstein, "The Two Leadership Styles of William Jefferson Clinton," 356–357.

88. Kelly, "The President's Past," 45.

89. David E. Rosenbaum, "Both Sides of the Aisle Sense Capital's Unrest," *New York Times,* Oct. 21, 1995, 8.

90. Graham K. Wilson, "The Clinton Administration and Interest Groups," in *The Clinton Presidency: First Appraisals,* 220.

91. Rockman, "Leadership Style and the Clinton Presidency," 355.

92. Maraniss, *First in His Class,* 72, 74, 367; Stanley A. Renshon, "A Preliminary Assessment of the Clinton Presidency," 386.

93. Maraniss, *First in His Class,* 453.

94. Ibid., 452.

95. Wenner and Greider, "The Rolling Stone Interview," 80.

96. Maraniss, *First in His Class,* 293, 349.

97. Ibid., 422.

98. Greenstein, "The Two Leadership Styles of William Jefferson Clinton," 357.

99. Colin Campbell, "Management in a Sandbox: Why the Clinton White House Failed to Cope with Gridlock," in *The Clinton Presidency: First Appraisals,* 79.

100. Bert A. Rockman, "The Style and Organization of the Reagan Presidency," in *The Reagan Legacy: Promise and Performance;* Paul J. Quirk, "Presidential Competence," in *The Presidency and the Political System,* 174.

101. Greenstein, "The Two Leadership Styles of William Jefferson Clinton," 356.

102. Rockman, "The Style and Organization of the Reagan Presidency," 352.

103. Campbell and Rockman, introduction to *The Clinton Presidency: First Appraisals,* 5.

104. Reportedly, Secretary of State Christopher told Clinton that he needed "to become more engaged in foreign policy by spending at least an hour a week with his national security advisers." Elaine Sciolino, "3 Players Seek a Director for Foreign Policy Story," *New York Times,* Nov. 8, 1993, A1.

105. Gwen Ifill, "Clinton Sees Need to Focus His Goals and Sharpen Staff," *New York Times,* May 5, 1993, A1.

106. Matthew Cooper, Kenneth T. Walsh, and Gloria Borger, *U.S. News and World Report*, June 7, 1993, 24–29; Joe Klein, *Newsweek*, June 7, 1993, 16–19.

107. Bill Turque, "The Staff Shuffle," *Newsweek*, June 7, 1993, 20–21. Also see R. W. Apple, Jr., "An Offering to the Wolves," *New York Times*, May 31, 1993, A1.

108. Greenstein, "The Two Leadership Styles of William Jefferson Clinton."

109. Rick Wartzman, "Why President Clinton Spends Exactly 62.5% More Time on Policy," *Wall Street Journal*, Mar. 14, 1995, A1.

110. Ibid.; Burt Solomon, "Clinton's New Taskmaster Takes Charge," *National Journal*, Aug. 6, 1994, 1872; James Carney, "Drilling Bill's Troops," *Time*, Aug. 29, 1994, 34–35.

111. Greenstein, "The Two Leadership Styles of William Jefferson Clinton," 356.

112. David Maraniss termed these tactics "the permanent campaign," which relied heavily on using polls to "shape the substance and rhetoric of policy debates," controlling the administration's own public message by flanking the press corps and shifting between idealism and pragmatism as necessary. Maraniss, *First in His Class*, 407–408. For discussions of the presidential years, see Charles O. Jones, "Campaigning to Govern: The Clinton Style," in *The Clinton Presidency: First Appraisals*, 15–50; and James A. Barnes, "The Endless Campaign," *National Journal*, Feb. 20, 1993, 460–462.

113. Quirk, "Presidential Competence"; and Paul Quirk, "What Must a President Know?" *Transactional Society* 23 (January/February 1983).

114. Quirk, "Presidential Competence," 170.

READINGS

Barber, James David. *The Presidential Character*. 4th ed. Englewood Cliffs, N.J.: Prentice-Hall, 1992.

George, Alexander, and Juliette George. *Woodrow Wilson and Colonel House: A Personality Study*. New York: John Day, 1956.

Greenstein, Fred I. *Personality and Politics: Problems of Evidence, Inference, and Conceptualization*. New York: Norton, 1975.

Hargrove, Erwin. *Jimmy Carter as President: Leadership and the Politics of the Public Good*. Baton Rouge: Louisiana State University Press, 1988.

___. *Presidential Leadership: Personality and Political Style*. New York: Macmillan, 1966.

Kearns, Doris. *Lyndon Johnson and the American Dream*. New York: Harper & Row, 1976.

Mazlish, Bruce. *In Search of Nixon: A Psychohistorical Inquiry*. Baltimore: Pelican, 1973.

Pessen, Edward. *The Log Cabin Myth: The Social Backgrounds of the Presidents*. New Haven, Conn.: Yale University Press, 1984.

Rockman, Bert A. *The Leadership Question: The Presidency and the American System*. New York: Praeger, 1984.

PART II

THE PRESIDENT AND
THE GOVERNMENT

LEGISLATIVE POLITICS

The basic goal of the GOP's "Contract with America" was to reduce the role and reach of the national government in the economy and American society.

ON NOVEMBER 17, 1995 THE Republican-controlled 104th Congress enacted a comprehensive reconciliation bill *(see Chapter 9)* designed to produce a balanced budget in 2002. It would accomplish this through major reductions in the growth of mandatory spending for Medicare, Medicaid, welfare, and agriculture subsidies and discretionary spending in areas such as education, job training, and environmental protection. The bill also cut taxes by $245 billion during the same period, and it transferred responsibility for caring for the poor to the states. In narrow, party-line votes, the legislation passed the House 237–189 and the Senate 52–47.[1] President Bill Clinton, while supporting the goal of a balanced budget, attacked the bill as unfair to the poor and the elderly. After he vetoed it, he and Republican leaders of Congress engaged in a series of negotiations for several weeks that failed to produce a comprehensive agreement on how to balance the budget by 2002. Nor were they able to complete work on six of the thirteen major appropriations bills that would fund the government in fiscal year 1996, which began on October 1, 1995. A final unresolved bone of financial contention between Clinton and the congressional Republicans was a bill to raise and extend the limit on the national debt. The previous limit had been reached on November 15 and with it the government's authority to borrow funds needed to meet its financial obligations expired.

Although there were substantial differences over money, the fundamental disagreement between the warring parties was a philosophical one over the future role of the federal government. Both sides agreed that the time had come to balance the budget. Initially, Clinton proposed a ten-year plan based on economic assumptions and data provided by the Office of Management and Budget. After weeks of pressure, he proposed a seven-year plan based on Congressional Budget Office information, as the Republicans had insisted. The areas where they differed over money were the size of the tax cut that the plan would include, the amount of reductions that would have to be made in the growth of spending on Medicare and Medicaid, health care entitlement programs for retirees and the poor, and the level of spending for education, environmental protection, and job training.

By mid-January 1996 both Clinton and the Republicans had moved toward each other and appeared to be in a position to split the monetary differences between them. They could not, however, resolve the philosophical conflict. The Republicans wanted to turn control of Medicaid, a federal program administered by the states who put up 40 percent of the cost, over to the states. This would entail removing its status as an entitlement whereby all persons who met the qualifications specified by law were entitled to receive benefits. Federal funds would be provided in a block grant, or lump sum, and not be subject to conditions as to how they would be spent. Nor would they necessarily be increased in the future. The Republicans also passed, and Clinton vetoed in December 1995, a welfare reform bill that would have disestablished Aid to Families with Dependent Children (AFDC) as a federal entitlement.

The negotiations were highlighted by two shutdowns, November 14–20 and December 16–January 5, of all federal departments and agencies whose appropriations for 1996 had not been approved. Essential employees, such as air traffic controllers, continued to work without pay. Although Congress had passed continuing resolutions temporarily extending funding, Clinton vetoed them because they contained unacceptable conditions. In their struggle with Clinton, congressional Republicans had used continuing resolutions and the debt limit extension bill as leverage to try to force his hand. They reasoned that he would rather accept their terms than allow the government to shut down or default on its obligations. He proved to be more resolute than they had anticipated. Moreover, the public placed more of the blame for the shutdowns on Congress than on the president, and the secretary of the Treasury was able to use certain trust funds under his control to prevent default.

This high-stakes game of fiscal "chicken" was a major bump on the rocky road of Clinton's relations with Congress. Two distinct patterns characterize those relations. During his first two years the Democratic 103d Congress passed most of his legislative program, with little support from the Republicans and some opposition from conservative Democrats. He depended on Republican support only to pass two international trade bills. Of the major bills he proposed, just health care reform and welfare reform failed to be enacted. The pattern of Clinton's legislative relations following the Republican takeover of Congress in 1994 is comparable with the experience of Presidents Richard Nixon, Gerald Ford, Ronald Reagan in his last two years in office, and George Bush. Like his predecessors who confronted a Congress controlled by the opposition party, Clinton was engaged in protracted conflict about the direction of public policy and institutional prerogatives. To understand how recent presidents have become locked in no-win struggles with Congress, one must examine the politics of presidential-congressional relations and the ways modern presidents have managed them.

Presidents usually discover, upon taking office, that the skills and techniques of leadership that enabled them to capture their party's nomination and win the election are not identical with those needed to sustain their popularity. Nomination and electoral politics require the ability to raise money, to build an organization composed of election professionals, to project an attractive and engaging image, and to sense the concerns of the public, but the politics of governing—that is, legislating and administering—requires talents that can move a complex, cumbersome government to "get things done." These talents include persuasion, personal and organizational leadership, and managerial skill.

Americans tend to judge presidents primarily by their performance in office. A principal criterion of evaluation is the president's ability to persuade Congress to pass his legislative program. National political leaders expect the president to develop legislative proposals that will achieve the administration's goals; the public and members of the news media expect the president to steer those proposals through Congress. Unwillingness or inability to meet these expectations usually results in loss of presidential popularity and assessments of ineffectiveness or failure. Even presidents philosophically opposed to an active federal government, such as Dwight D. Eisenhower, have found themselves unable to resist the pressures to provide legislative leadership. The public expects presidents to address and solve national problems, but most solutions require congressional approval, which is not always forthcoming. This chapter examines the president's relations with Congress. It begins by tracing the development of the chief executive's legislative role in the twentieth century and then presents an analysis of the constitutional relationship between the president and Congress. A discussion of the president's formal legislative powers and a description of presidential strategies follow. The chapter then analyzes the basis of the president's support in Congress. Finally, it explores how the president's influence on Congress can be evaluated.

Development of the President's Legislative Role

The Constitution, in Article 1, Section 8, grants Congress seventeen powers that cover a wide range of subjects—for example, levying and collecting taxes, borrowing money, and regulating foreign and interstate commerce—and the power to choose the means to execute the specifically enumerated powers. Quite clearly, the Framers expected that Congress would have primary responsibility for formulating national policy and that the president's legislative role would be minor. Until the twentieth century most presidents did limit their involvement in the congressional process. Even Thomas Jefferson and Abraham Lincoln, who were most inclined to try to lead Congress, encountered strong opposition, and their activism did not alter the pattern of congressional supremacy.[2]

Early in the twentieth century, under the leadership of Theodore Roosevelt and Woodrow Wilson, the presidency acquired a greatly expanded legislative role as the national government responded to the problems of industrialization and urbanization. Roosevelt worked closely with congressional leaders and sent several messages to Congress that defined a legislative program. He saw it as the duty of the president to "take a very active interest in getting the right kind of legislation." [3] Wilson, who, as a political science professor, had argued that strong presidential leadership of Congress was needed if the nation was to cope with its growing problems, actively participated in the legislative process.[4] He took the lead in defining the goals of his program, helped formulate bills, reinstated the practice abandoned by Thomas Jefferson of personally delivering the State of the Union message to Congress, used members of his cabinet to build congressional support for bills, and personally lobbied for some of his most important measures, such as the Federal Reserve Act and the Clayton Antitrust Act.

The next major expansion of the president's legislative role occurred under Franklin D. Roosevelt. Taking office in 1933, when the economy was mired in the depths of the Great Depression, FDR called Congress into a special session that lasted for 100 days. During that period the new president proposed, and Congress passed, legislation designed to meet the economic crisis. Together they overhauled the banking system, authorized a program of industrial self-government under the National Recovery Administration, buttressed farm income through passage of the Agricultural Adjustment Act, regulated financial markets under the Truth in Securities Act, and created the Tennessee Valley Authority, a program of comprehensive development of one of the nation's most depressed areas.

During the remainder of his first term FDR continued to submit, and Congress to pass, a series of measures designed to help farmers, industrial workers, and individual citizens. The legislation promoted soil conservation and restricted excess agricultural production; it guaranteed labor the right to organize and bargain collectively; and it established a system of social insurance to protect people against the loss of work due to economic slowdowns, physical disability, or old age. Additional legislation established administrative agencies to implement the New Deal statutes.

FDR's principal mode of operation was to send to Congress messages that analyzed a problem and outlined his proposed solution. Often a draft bill accompanied or followed the messages. He then assigned aides to monitor the bills and lobby for their passage. Beginning in 1935 coordination of his legislative program was accomplished through a clearance process administered by the Bureau of the Budget.[5] FDR also made extensive use of the veto as a means of bending Congress to his will; he threatened to veto legislation that failed to meet his demands or that he regarded as unwise or contrary to his purposes. His major contribution was to establish the expectation that the president would be actively involved at all stages of the legislative process by submitting a legislative program to Congress, working for its passage, and coordinating its implementation.

FDR's two immediate successors, Harry S. Truman and Dwight Eisenhower, institutionalized the president's legislative role by creating structures and processes to assist in carrying it out on a regular, systematic basis.[6] The Bureau of the Budget and members of the White House staff acted for the president. By the mid-1960s it appeared to some observers that the presidency had come to dominate the legislative process. Writing in 1965, Samuel P. Huntington remarked that "the congressional role in legislation has largely been reduced to delay and amendment." Such tasks as initiative in formulating legislation, assignment of legislative priorities, generation of support for legislation, and determination of the final content of legislation had "shifted to the executive branch," which, in Huntington's view, had gained "at the expense of Congress."[7] Others argued, however, that although congressional and presidential roles in the legislative process had changed substantially, Congress remained a vitally important participant. The president's program is critical in determining the congressional agenda, but Congress is constantly modifying and altering policy through appropriations, amendments, and renewals of statutory authorizations.[8]

Moreover, Congress and the president are not engaged in a zero-sum game in which the power of one necessarily decreases as the power of the other increases. In an absolute sense, since 1933 Congress has increased its power as an instrument of government by vastly expanding the subjects on which it has legislated. During that time, however, the power of Congress as an innovator of public policy has declined in relation to that of the president. In three brief periods of legislative activity—1933–1937, 1964–1965, and 1981—activist presidents (FDR, Lyndon Johnson, and Reagan) led responsive Congresses in the adoption of major changes in domestic policy. Congress also responded to presidential leadership in establishing the role of the United States in world affairs during and immediately following World War II.

Nevertheless, there have also been periods in which Congress substantially increased its authority vis-à-vis the president. During the

1970s, for example, Congress expanded its control over the executive branch through increased use of the legislative veto *(see Chapter 6)*, curbed presidential use of military force abroad through passage of the War Powers Resolution of 1973 *(see Chapter 10)*, and strengthened its ability to determine the amount of federal spending through the creation of the congressional budget process *(see Chapter 9)*.

The always-present potential for presidential leadership of Congress became dramatically evident in 1981 when Ronald Reagan took office following his landslide victory. Reagan quickly took command of bipartisan conservative congressional majorities, which passed his taxing and spending proposals and sharply altered the course that domestic social and economic policy had been following since the 1930s.[9] But Reagan's period of dominance was short-lived; congressional critics of his policies regrouped in 1982, support among Republican legislators sagged, and concerns shifted to deficits in the range of $100–200 billion in his 1983–1989 budgets. Reagan discovered, as had Roosevelt in 1937 and Johnson in 1966, that congressional approval of a president's program is not automatic. Congressional support must be cultivated and maintained, and when the conditions that created it change, it can rapidly disappear. Without such support, presidents face frustration and ineffectuality. Rather than emulate his predecessor by presenting an aggressive legislative program, President Bush offered very modest initiatives. Even so, he was unable to develop sustained congressional support. In contrast, President Clinton's ambitious initial legislative agenda received substantial support from congressional Democrats, who enacted much of it—except for major proposals involving health care and welfare reform—with only limited help from Republicans.[10]

The Presidential-Congressional Relationship

There is inherent tension between Congress and the presidency, yet cooperation between the two institutions is necessary if the government is to act in a significant way. The Constitution creates institutional competition through the separation of powers, but it also mandates a sharing of powers among the branches of government. Joint action by the president and Congress is required to authorize programs, appropriate money to pay for them, and levy taxes to provide the funds. Neither branch can achieve its goals or operate the government without the participation of the other. However, since 1970, presidential-congressional relations have become competitive because of the distrust between the branches and intensified party differences between Republican presidents and congressional Democrats.[11] Charles O. Jones describes the relationship as one in which "these separated institutions often *compete* for shared powers." [12]

The Separation of Powers

James Madison's *Federalist* 51 makes it clear that the Framers had contemplated presidential-congressional conflict:

To what expedient ... shall we finally resort, for maintaining in practice the necessary partition of power among the several departments, as laid down in the constitution? The only answer that can be given is ... by so contriving the interior structure of the government as its several constituent parts may, by their mutual relations, be the means of keeping each other in their proper places....

In order to lay a due foundation for that separate and distinct exercise of the different powers of the government, which to a certain extent is admitted on all hands to be essential to the preservation of liberty, it is evident that each department should have a will of its own....

But the great security against a gradual concentration of the several powers in the same department consists in giving to those who administer each department the necessary constitutional means and personal motives to resist the encroachments of the others.... Ambition must be made to counteract ambition. The interests of the man must be connected with the constitutional rights of the place.[13]

Since 1789 the task of governing the United States has been to overcome the constitutional dispersion, and simultaneous sharing, of power among competing institutions. The most important division of power, from the standpoint of making and implementing national policies, is that between the president and Congress.

The pattern of the presidential-congressional relationship has not been static. A cyclical pattern of power aggrandizement by Congress or the presidency and resurgence by the other institution has operated from the beginning of government under the Constitution.[14] In the nineteenth century the institutional surges and declines oscillated evenly within well-defined boundaries and returned at the end of each cycle to the balance envisioned in the Constitution. However, the economic, social, and technological transformations and the emergence from political isolation that occurred during the twentieth century created problems and conditions that called increasingly for executive rather than legislative decision making. The president could act more quickly, more decisively, and more consistently than Congress, which has had difficulty ascertaining its institutional will and coherently pursuing its goals. It is too soon to determine whether the Republican capture of both the House of Representatives and the Senate in 1994 ushered in a new period of congressional ascendancy. The aggressive, ideologically oriented leadership and disciplined response of House Republicans in 1995 succeeded in forcing the Clinton administration into a defensive posture.[15] However, the more individualistic Senate manifested more moderate legislative priorities and proceeded at a slower pace than the House.[16]

Presidential surges have resulted in permanent expansions of executive power and presidential aggrandizements, such as Johnson's use of the war powers to involve the United States in the Vietnam War *(see Chapter 10)* and Richard Nixon's sweeping claims of executive privilege and his extensive impoundments of appropriated funds *(see Chapter 6)*. Although Congress managed to reassert its constitutional authority during the 1970s,[17] the cycle turned again in the 1980s toward increased reliance on presidential power. The nation found that it needed presidential leadership to deal with difficult problems such as severe inflation, economic interdependence, and international terrorism.

Sources of Presidential-Congressional Conflict

Forces promoting conflict are always present in the presidential-congressional relationship. In addition to institutional competition born of the separation of powers, conflict stems from the difference in the constituencies of the members of Congress and the president and from the fragmentation of power within Congress. The 535 members of Congress represent constituencies that vary in geographical area, population, economic structure, and social composition. Each congressional constituency is but a part of the nation. Every member of Congress depends for reelection on constituency-based political forces. Therefore, different members speak for different economic, social, and geographical interests, and all members are necessarily somewhat parochial at times in their policy orientations. Consequently, claims by certain members to be acting in behalf of the national interest must be judged in the context of their constituency interests.

Because congressional parties lack the power to command the votes of their members, there is no institutional basis for any of the elected party leaders of either house to speak on its behalf. The only way the national interest emerges in Congress is through bargaining between members and blocs of members responsive to particular interests. This practice results in the formation of temporary majority coalitions to pass specific measures. Congressional policy making is thus deliberate, incremental or piecemeal, and reactive. Congress often is unable to maintain consistency in its actions in different policy areas or cohesiveness within areas. Speed, efficiency, consistency, and cohesiveness usually are lacking, except in a crisis.

In contrast, the president's constituency is the entire nation. Only the president can claim to speak authoritatively in behalf of the national interest or to act for various inarticulate and unorganized interests who are not adequately represented in Congress. He can resist the demands of well-organized particular interests by posing as the champion of the national interest (even though there may be times when *he* too responds to such pressures). The difficulty that Congress encounters in determining and speaking for the national interest, and the ease with which the president may do so, stem from their differing constituencies and are a continuing source of tension between them.

Changes in electoral politics also have widened the gap between presidents and Congress in the process of governing the nation. Members of Congress have become political entrepreneurs who routinely seek reelection on the basis of constituency-based electoral coalitions that are largely independent of party membership.[18] (Since 1946 more than 90 percent of House and 75 percent of Senate incumbents who have sought reelection have been successful.[19]) They are nominated in direct primaries, their campaigns are financed heavily from nonparty sources, and they sustain electoral support through activities unrelated to their party, such as providing service to constituents. Presidents can exert little leverage on them through appeals to party loyalty or the exercise of party discipline. Moreover, there has been a decline in the strength of presidential coattails and an increase in the number of constituencies supporting a presidential candidate of one party and electing members of Congress from the opposition.

This separation of presidential and congressional electoral coalitions has resulted in a divided government that has reduced pressures on members to support their party's president. It is clear that a president whose party controls both houses of Congress enjoys certain advantages by virtue of party loyalty that are not available to a president faced with a Congress controlled by the opposition party. Since 1933, Democratic

Table 5-1   Partisan Control of the Presidency and
Congress, 1933–1998

Dates	Presidency	Congress
1933–1946	Democratic	Democratic
1947–1948	Democratic	*Republican*
1947–1948	Democratic	Democratic
1949–1952	Democratic	Democratic
1953–1954	*Republican*	*Republican*
1955–1960	*Republican*	Democratic
1961–1968	Democratic	Democratic
1969–1976	*Republican*	Democratic
1977–1980	Democratic	Democratic
1981–1986	*Republican*	Senate-*Rep.* House-Dem.
1987–1992	*Republican*	Democratic
1993–1994	Democratic	Democratic
1995–1998	Democratic	*Republican*

presidents have had to deal with an opposition Congress in 1947–1948 and 1995–1998, while Republican occupants of the White House have confronted full opposition control in all years except 1953–1954 and 1981–1988 *(see Table 5-1).*

Analysts are sharply divided in their assessments of the consequences of divided partisan control of the government. The critics of divided government argue that it renders unworkable the already cumbersome and inefficient separation-of-powers structure established in the Constitution.[20] The critics blame the large federal budget deficits of the 1980s and 1990s on divided government, arguing that under it major policy decisions have become "the result of an institutionally structured bargaining process, with each party possessing a veto," in which the parties engage in a game of fiscal "chicken" waiting to see who will be first to back down.[21] Each branch of government, it is argued, has a stake in the failure of the other. Finally, these critics charge that divided government undermines electoral a]ccountability because it is impossible for voters to hold either party responsible for the policies adopted and the results achieved since the last election.

In contrast, David Mayhew concluded, after a systematic empirical analysis of legislation and congressional investigations since World War II, that it does not make "much difference whether party control of the American government happens to be unified or divided."[22] Morris Fiorina also challenges the conventional wisdom with respect to divided government. Although acknowledging that it results in more "conflictual" congressional-presidential relations, he points out that it is an option available to the electorate under the Constitution and asks whether its consequences are "necessarily bad." [23] He argues that although divided government may limit the potential for social gain through public policy, it also limits potential loss through government action.[24] Finally, Fiorina suggests that divided government is the American electorate's way of establishing the coalition governments that are common in multiparty systems.[25] Whether the effects of divided government are benign or not is, as the saying goes, in the eye of the beholder. Without question, it has dominated presidential-congressional relations for most of the past quarter century.

The frequent inability of Congress to match the decisiveness, cohesion, and consistency of the presidency as a national policy-making institution is also a product of the fragmented structure of its internal authority. Widely recognized are the weakness of congressional parties, the limited power of party leaders, the absence of party discipline in congressional voting, the presence of strong committees and subcommittees, and the ambitions of individual members to enhance their reelection chances and to advance to higher office.[26] (The 1995 emergence under Speaker Newt Gingrich and the Republicans of party government in the House may have been temporary as many party members who were worried about reelection moved to the center in 1996.)

Even an internally fragmented Congress is not without power, but it tends to be a negative and restraining rather than a directive force on the presidency. Also, Congress usually is more comfortable with distributive policies and programs, which provide benefits on a widespread basis, than with redistributive policies, which change the allocation of wealth and power in society.

As presently constituted, Congress values the function of "representation" over that of "lawmaking." [27] This means that Congress is responsive primarily to constituency interests and to well-organized interest groups. Ironically, the presidency might be said to stress the law-making function whereby electoral mandates are translated into policies that are adopted by congressional coalitions.

Patterns of Presidential-Congressional Policy Making

The Constitution mandates cooperation between Congress and the president. Congress has the legislative powers of the government, and its approval is necessary for any kind of executive action. The president can veto measures passed by Congress. Within the boundaries set by the Constitution and by political conditions, most relationships between the presidency and Congress in making national policy involve potential conflict. The patterns in the relationship vary according to issues, presidential leadership styles, and political context. Presidential domination tends to prevail in foreign and military policy and those issues to which presidents attach high priority, such as Lyndon Johnson's Great Society program in 1964 and 1965.[28] Congressional domination was the prevailing pattern in the 1970s, when Congress passed major legislation on the environment, consumer protection, and occupational safety; and Congress always has prevailed on public works. Stalemate characterized much of the energy legislation proposed by presidents in the 1970s, as well as proposals for reducing the federal budget deficit in the 1980s and 1990s. Occasionally, a proposal may be stalemated for years and then move rapidly to passage as conditions change or a new president takes office. Medicare provides a good example. Proposals for national health insurance had languished in Congress since first advanced by President Truman in 1946. The political climate turned favorable for liberal social legislation in 1964 and 1965, following the assassination of John F. Kennedy. Responding to Johnson's forceful leadership, Congress enacted legislation authorizing national health insurance for the elderly (Medicare) in 1965.

Presidential leadership style is related to the pattern of congressional relations with the presidency. An activist president who is committed to an extensive legislative program, such as FDR or Johnson, normally tries to dominate Congress, whereas a president who is more restrained and less active, such as Dwight Eisenhower or Gerald R. Ford, may be more inclined to cooperate with Congress or accept considerable congressional initiative in program development. Ronald Reagan, an activist with a conservative agenda that did not require extensive new legislation, adopted various patterns in his relations with Congress. To achieve his primary goals of reducing the role of the federal government and strengthening the armed forces, he attempted to establish presidential domination. On issues of less importance to him, such as farm policy and Social Security financing, he was willing to share responsibility with Congress. When he disagreed with Congress, as he did over reducing the federal budget deficit, he was willing to settle for a stalemate, but on no matters of consequence did he accept congressional domination. George Bush, a conservative with a limited agenda, sought congenial relations with Congress, but many crucial issues—the deficit, taxes, and civil rights—remained stalemated because of irreconcilable differences on which neither was willing to compromise.

Bill Clinton, a moderate with an ambitious reform agenda, attempted to dominate Congress through the Democratic majority and its leaders.[29] This proved difficult because that majority was divided ideologically. Most of its members, including the leadership, were more liberal than Clinton, who adjusted his agenda to accommodate them. However, this shift alienated moderate and conservative Democrats, some of whom deserted Clinton on important measures such as the economic plan and health care reform. A bipartisan strategy was not viable with respect to economic and domestic legislation. Most Republicans and their leaders, far more conservative than Clinton, were unwilling to compromise with him, and there were only a few moderates who might have been receptive to it. Republican support was essential to the passage of only two major bills—the North American Free Trade Agreement (NAFTA) in 1993 and the renewal of the General Agreement on Tariffs and Trade (GATT) in 1994. On both of those issues a majority of Democrats opposed the president, whose views on international trade were similar to those of most Republicans.

No president in the modern era, which began with FDR, has sought stalemate with Congress, although such a condition has developed on occasion. Stalemates occur more often during periods of divided government than when one party is in power in both branches. A necessary condition for stalemate is a sharp division of opinion between the president and the congressional majority. During the Nixon and Ford administrations presidential-congressional relations were stalemated over several major bills, as two conservative Republican presidents quarreled with liberal Democratic Congresses about presidential prerogatives and spending priorities. From 1982 through 1992, Presidents Reagan and Bush were stalemated with Congress for several months each year over proposed budgets for the ensuing fiscal year. Their disagreements focused on how to reduce deficits that were projected to be from $100 billion to $300 billion. Democratic congressional leaders were joined by some of their Republican counterparts in pressing the two presidents to ease their opposition to cuts in defense spending and to selective tax increases. The presidents insisted that the only means of reducing the deficits was through deep cuts in spending for domestic programs, which most members of Congress were reluctant to make. The results were generally unsatisfactory to both sides: large deficits with small reductions in spending and no major tax increases. During

Clinton's first two years, he and a Democratically controlled Congress were stalemated over two of the centerpieces in his domestic agenda, health care reform and welfare reform. In the next two years Clinton and Congress were stalemated over a Republican agenda that proposed drastic reductions in the activities of the federal government.

The President's Legislative Powers

The president has two sets of tools at his disposal for the accomplishment of his legislative goals: (1) the formal powers vested in him by the Constitution and by statute and (2) the informal resources inherent in the office. The chief executive uses both sets of tools simultaneously and in conjunction with each other. In the interest of analytical clarity, however, this chapter will examine them separately.

The Constitution sets out the president's legislative role. Article II, Section 3, authorizes him to call Congress into special session and requires that he "from time to time give to the Congress information of the state of the Union, and recommend to their consideration such measures as he shall judge necessary and expedient." Article I, Section 7, makes the president a direct participant in the legislative process by providing for his approval or disapproval of "every bill" and "every order, resolution, or vote to which the concurrence of the Senate and House may be necessary." These formal legislative powers are augmented by statutory delegations of authority to the president and to administrative agencies and by implied powers derived from the general grant of executive power in Article II. These delegated and implied powers serve as the basis for presidential legislation through the issuance of executive orders *(see Chapter 6)*.

Special Sessions

The president's power to call Congress into special session is less important today than it was in the past, primarily because Congress, since the 1930s, has remained in session for much of the year, taking periodic short recesses. The expansion in government activity, the complexity of the budgetary process, and the change from indefinite to specific term authorizations of federal programs have so increased the congressional workload that early adjournments have all but disappeared. When Congress was not in almost continuous session, the president could call it back to Washington to consider specific proposals. Calling a special session placed responsibility for action on Congress.

Perhaps the most effective modern use of this power was made by FDR in March 1933, shortly after his inauguration. The special session met for 100 days and enacted the first stage of the New Deal program of economic recovery and social reform statutes. A dramatic exercise of the special session power occurred in July 1948, when President Truman called the Republican-controlled Congress back to Washington from its summer recess to give it the opportunity to enact several major planks in the party's 1948 platform. When Congress failed to act, as Truman had anticipated, he made that inaction the theme in his successful reelection campaign.

Messages

Although contemporary presidents have not gained much leverage over Congress by controlling its sessions, they derive substantial power by virtue of their constitutional duty to report to Congress on the state of the nation and to recommend legislation they deem necessary. Since the Budget and Accounting Act of 1921 and the Employment Act of 1946, Congress has required that the president annually submit messages to it that explain and justify his budget and that report on the condition of the economy. The State of the Union message, the budget message, and the economic report have enabled presidents to set the congressional agenda by laying before Congress a comprehensive legislative program. These mandatory messages announce the president's goals and priorities along with his assessment of the nation's problems, and they are also an attempt to bring the force of public opinion to bear upon Congress. Special messages emphasizing specific problems and proposing bills to deal with them complete the definition of the president's program. (Chapter 8 examines the development of that program.)

Although individual members of Congress introduce a multitude of bills independently of the president, the chief executive is in a position to dominate the congressional agenda. In the twentieth century, members of Congress have come "almost routinely to demand that the president—not their own leaders—develop new policies and programs" to deal with the complex problems the nation faces.[30] The expectation that the president would take the initiative in the legislative process generally held until the Bush administration, when the Democratic majority in Congress advanced proposals in areas that the president did not address, such as civil rights and immigration. In 1993 President Clinton presented Congress with an ambitious agenda based on the themes of his campaign. Following the startling Republican triumph in the 1994 elections, however, Clinton lost control of the agenda to House Speaker Newt Gingrich (R-Ga.).

Clinton's 1995 State of the Union address was notable for "its paucity of specific legislative proposals" and a defensive posture toward a comprehensive conservative agenda based on the "Contract with America" that highlighted the Republicans' successful election campaign.[31] Clinton reemerged as a legislative force in 1996 by taking advantage of the unpopularity of Republican tactics, such as closing the government, and much of their agenda.[32] In 1997 Republican congressional leaders announced that they would wait for the reelected president to present his agenda.

The Veto Power

The Constitution establishes a major legislative role for the president by requiring his approval of measures passed by Congress (Article 1, Section 7, paragraph 2). Within ten days (Sundays excepted) after a bill or joint resolution is presented to the president, he must either (1) sign it into law; (2) disapprove or veto it and return it to the house of Congress in which it originated along with a message explaining his action; or (3) take no action on it, in which case it becomes law without his signature at the end of ten days. If Congress adjourns within that ten-day period and the president does not sign a measure awaiting his action, then it does not become law. In this instance the president exercises a "pocket veto." The president's action is final because adjournment prevents a measure from being returned to Congress for reconsideration and a possible override.

The veto is the president's ultimate legislative weapon; it carries the weight of two-thirds of the members of each house of Congress. In his classic treatise *Congressional Government,* Woodrow Wilson noted the importance of the veto even at a time when Congress dominated the national government: "For in the exercise of his power of veto, which is, of course, beyond all comparison, his most formidable prerogative, the President acts not as the executive but as a third branch of the legislature." [33]

Andrew Jackson adopted a broad interpretation of the veto power as giving him the right to reject legislation on the basis of its wisdom, merit, or equity as well as on constitutional grounds.[34] This "tribunative" view of the veto has been espoused by modern presidents (since 1933), some of whom have used it frequently.

Table 5-2   Presidential Vetoes of Bills, 1933–1996

President	Regular vetoes	Pocket vetoes	Total	Number of vetoes overridden	Percentage of vetoes overridden
FDR (1933–1945)	372	263	635	9	1.4
Truman (1945–1953)	180	70	250	12	4.7
Eisenhower (1953–1961)	73	108	181	2	1.1
Kennedy (1961–1963)	12	9	21	0	0.0
Johnson (1963–1969)	16	14	30	0	0.0
Nixon (1969–1974)	26	17	43	7	16.3
Ford (1974–1977)	48	18	66	12	17.6
Carter (1977–1981)	13	18	31	2	6.5
Reagan (1981–1989)	39	39	78	9	11.5
Bush (1989–1993)	29	17	46	1	2.2
Clinton (1993–1996)	17	0	17	1	5.9

Sources: U.S. Senate Library, *Presidential Vetoes, 1789–1976* (Washington, D.C.: Government Printing Office, 1977) and *Presidential Vetoes, 1977–1984* (Washington, D.C.: Government Printing Office, 1985); *1985 Congressional Quarterly Almanac*, "Vetoes Cast by President Reagan," 6; *1988 Congressional Quarterly Almanac*, "Vetoes Cast by President Reagan," 6; *Congressional Quarterly Weekly Report*, Dec. 19, 1992, "President Bush's Vetoes," 3925–3926; "Six Bills Vetoed," *Congressional Quarterly Weekly Report*, Dec. 14, 1996, 3386.

The data in Table 5-2 demonstrate a much more extensive use of the veto by Presidents Roosevelt, Truman, and Eisenhower than by presidents who have served since 1961. They also show that from 1961 through 1995, Democratic presidents, whose party controlled the Senate from 1961 through 1980 and 1987 through 1994 and the House through 1994, vetoed fewer bills than the Republicans, who faced opposition majorities most of the time. All of President Clinton's seventeen vetoes occurred during the Republican-controlled 104th Congress.

The effect of the veto power on policy is both negative and positive. It is negative by nature; once used, it signifies an impasse between the president and Congress, and policy is unchanged. Sometimes a president finds that the veto is the most effective means of communicating his intentions to Congress. Ford's sixty-six vetoes, for example, were his way of conveying his social and economic policy preferences to a liberal Democratic Congress. The positive aspect of the veto lies in its use as a bargaining tool to "shape, alter, or deter legislation." [35] By threatening to exercise the veto—a threat made credible only by actual use—the president can define the limits of his willingness to compromise with Congress. He can state in advance what he will and will not accept, thereby reducing the likelihood of a showdown over a bill. Selective and sensitive use of the threat to veto can be a means of avoiding or of reconciling conflict with Congress. For example, in his first two years President Bush frequently threatened to veto bills as a way to "stimulate serious bargaining."[36] By not making empty threats and picking them carefully, Bush managed to avoid overrides. Clinton pointed to the absence of vetoes in 1994–1995 as evidence that he and the Democratic Congress could work together. Even in the conflicts with the Republican 104th Congress, he vetoed only seventeen bills and used the veto threat sparingly but effectively to force the Republicans to compromise.

When presidents veto bills they do so most often because they regard the legislation as unwise public policy. In a study of presidential veto messages of 169 public bills "of national consequence" from 1933 to 1981, Richard A. Watson found that presidents gave five general reasons for vetoing legislation: (1) unwise on policy grounds (111 bills); (2) lack of fiscal soundness (33 bills); (3) unconstitutionality (10 bills); (4) administrative unworkability (9 bills); and (5) to protect the executive against legislative encroachment (6 bills).[37] In a related study, Albert Ringelstein reported that "the categories of and reasons for presidential vetoes are remarkably similar from president to president," largely because they are protecting the prerogatives of their office from Congress.[38]

In a systematic analysis of vetoes and congressional responses between 1945 and 1980, David Rohde and Dennis Simon found that the decision to veto, the override attempt, and the success of those attempts depended on the "political environment (e.g., stage of the electoral cycle) and the political resources of the president."[39] They determined that public support was critical for the success of vetoes and for congressional overrides. However, dependence on public support places the president in a "catch 22" situation. As support declines, use of the veto increases, but so does the likelihood of an override.[40] The strategic incentive for the president is to act decisively so as to form partisan or ideological factions on initial passage of the legislation. Timing also enters strategic calculations—the use or threat of a veto is more effective early in the administration. Another strategic consideration is the choice of issues—a social welfare bill imposes more demands on resources than, say, a government management measure.[41] Presidents do not veto bills on the basis of purely subjective judgments or random advice. Rather, they rely on a systematic procedure, begun during Franklin Roosevelt's administration, for the analysis of enrolled bills (those that have passed both houses of Congress) once they are "received" (that is, once they have arrived at the White House).[42]

Table 5-3   OMB and Lead Agency Recommendations and Presidential Action on
Enrolled Bills, January 1969–June 1976

Pattern of advice	Approval by president (percent)
OMB approval/lead agency approval	96
OMB approval/lead agency disapproval	95
OMB disapproval/lead agency approval	65
OMB disapproval/lead agency disapproval	35

Source: Stephen J. Wayne, Richard L. Cole, and James F. C. Hyde, Jr., "Advising the President on Enrolled Legislation," *Political Science Quarterly* 94 (Summer 1979): 310.

The Legislative Reference Division of the Office of Management and Budget (OMB) immediately solicits reactions to a measure from the pertinent departments and agencies and from the budget examiners in the OMB program divisions that have jurisdiction over the bill. Recommendations and supportive rationales for presidential action on the legislation are due from the agencies and examiners within forty-eight hours. Legislative Reference collates the materials and prepares for the president a memorandum that summarizes the features of the legislation, reviews agency reactions, and states OMB's recommendations. One study of presidential disposition of enrolled bill recommendations during the Nixon-Ford administration found that a presumptive bias exists in favor of enrolled bills. A favorable OMB recommendation almost ensures that the president will sign a bill. A negative recommendation, however, is more of a danger signal, and the president and his staff will examine closely the recommendation of the "lead" agency in the federal bureaucracy. When OMB and the lead agency disagree, the president is likely to sign the bill. OMB disapproval carries more weight, however, than disapproval by the lead agency *(see Table 5-3).*

The White House staff does not act independently on enrolled bills; rather, it bases its advice on the positions of OMB and the lead agency. The goals of Nixon and Ford, two Republican presidents facing an opposition Congress, were "to rule and win." [43] That they withstood more than three-fourths of the efforts of Congress to override their vetoes indicates that they were quite successful. The enrolled bill process was an important advisory mechanism in their exercise of the veto power.

The President's Legislative Influence

In 1960 Richard Neustadt startled students of the presidency when, in his now celebrated treatise *Presidential Power,* he asserted that the formal powers of the president amounted to little more than a clerkship. The Constitution, Neustadt argued, placed the president in a position of mostly providing services to other participants in national politics. "Presidential power," Neustadt declared, "is the power to persuade." [44] As the preceding examination of the president's formal legislative powers suggests, this is frequently the case in his relations with Congress. It is not enough for the president to present a legislative program to Congress; he also must persuade congressional majorities to enact each statutory component of that program. To do so, the president employs mostly informal rather than formal methods of influence. These informal legislative tools can be used to exert both indirect and direct pressure on Congress.

Indirect Influence

The principal way a president attempts to influence Congress indirectly is through appeals to the public and by enlisting the support of interest groups. Popular appeals are likely to be most effective when there is evidence of substantial public support for the president's position and when Congress is reluctant to follow his lead. In such circumstances, a careful presidential appeal can generate pressure that causes Congress to act. The tactic is less likely to succeed when public opinion is divided and when there is substantial opposition to the president's position. Presidents also are more likely to use popular appeals successfully in a crisis that appears to require congressional action.

There is at least one major limitation to presidential appeals for popular support. The president can antagonize Congress by too frequently "going over its head" to the people. In doing so he attacks, directly or by implication, the wisdom and the motives of Congress and its members. Presidents have found that selective use of popular appeals can be effective, but indiscriminate use of the device is likely to be counterproductive over time.

Obtaining and marshaling the support of interest groups have become increasingly important to presidents in their efforts to apply leverage on Congress. Since the mid-1960s interest groups have grown in number and in the scope of their efforts to shape national policy. The proliferation of interest groups and the intensification of their activities stem in part from the declining role of parties as mechanisms for linking public opinion with public policy and in part from the increased participation of citizens in national policy politics.

Interest groups, which have become the major vehicle for such participation, take an active part in policy making through informal alliances with congressional committees and administrative agencies.[45] Presidents find it helpful, if not necessary, to obtain the backing of interest groups before moving on major legislation, and the national officers and federal relations directors of important groups often are consulted in the process of formulating such legislation. Interest group representatives are regularly appointed to presidential advisory bodies such as commissions and task forces, and they serve on advisory councils to administrative agencies. (Presidential liaison with interest groups is examined in Chapter 8.)

Direct Influence

Presidents use two informal tools in their direct efforts to persuade members of Congress. They may grant or withhold services and amenities they have at their disposal as rewards for support or sanctions for lack of it; and they may involve themselves in the legislative process. Presidents vary greatly in their skills at exploiting these resources.

Favors. Presidents often gain leverage with members of Congress by bestowing or denying favors. Such favors may be given directly to an individual member or to important people in his or her constituency, or the favor may be of benefit to the constituency itself.[46] Favors given as rewards to individual members include appointments with the president and other high-ranking officials; letters or telephone calls from the president expressing thanks for support on important bills; campaign assistance in the form of cash contributions from the party's national committee, a presidential visit to the constituency, or a presidential endorsement; the opportunity to announce the award of federal grants to recipients in the constituency; invitations to be present at bill-signing ceremonies, to attend White House social functions, and to accompany the president on trips; and White House memorabilia such as pens, cuff links, and photographs. Favors for influential congressional constituents include appointments, appearances by administration officials at organization meetings, invitations to social functions, mailings on important occasions such as anniversaries, memorabilia, and VIP treatment such as White House mess privileges. To some extent all members of Congress share in such benefits, but the president's supporters have more ready access to them and feel more comfortable asking for them.

The most important constituency-related rewards are jobs and projects. There are jobs at all levels of the federal government that are exempt from the Civil Service and are filled by appointment. Congressional recommendations by members of the president's party greatly influence the selection of U.S. district court judges, U.S. attorneys, U.S. marshals, customs collectors for ports of entry, and a variety of lesser positions. Patronage is not an unalloyed advantage to the president, however, because disappointed job-seekers inevitably are resentful. Projects include military installations; research and administrative facilities; public works such as buildings, dams, and navigational improvements to rivers and harbors; government contracts with local firms; grants to local governments and educational institutions; and the deposit of federal funds in banks. Presidential control over projects is exercised through the bureaucracy, and it is limited by previous decisions that have produced the current pattern of government activities. In other words, some benefits will necessarily go to constituencies of the president's congressional opponents. The importance of projects as a source of presidential influence will necessarily decline as some federal activities are reduced in size, eliminated, or turned over to state governments.

Involvement in the Legislative Process. The president can use his involvement in the legislative process, but to do so well requires knowledge and skill, which are the products of his political background, experience, and leadership style. To turn his participation in the legislative process to his advantage, the president should have knowledge of Congress and the Washington community, a sense of timing, a willingness to consult with congressional leaders and to give them notice in advance of major actions, sensitivity to the institutional prerogatives of Congress and to the personal and political needs of its members, and a balance between firmness and flexibility in resolving differences with Congress.

No president has ever possessed all of these skills, nor is one likely to do so. By most accounts, however, Lyndon Johnson exhibited more of them than any other modern president and made the most effective use of his involvement in the legislative process. Johnson believed that constant, intense attention by the president and his administration was necessary to move his legislative program through Congress.[47] His success in persuading Congress to enact the unfinished agenda of President Kennedy's New Frontier program and his own

Great Society bills in 1964 and 1965 makes his approach to Congress a good example for study. To avoid misleading the reader, however, it should be noted that Johnson's legislative triumphs were aided in no small measure by contextual factors for which he could not claim full credit, including public support for the New Frontier measures in the aftermath of the Kennedy assassination, sizable partisan and ideological support in Congress, and popular support for him and his legislative program.

Johnson grounded his legislative strategy in intimate knowledge of Congress as an institution and of its most influential members.[48] He knew whom to approach on various issues and how to approach them. Johnson also placed considerable emphasis on proper timing. He waited to send bills to Congress until the moment seemed right for the maximum support and least opposition. He sent bills singly rather than in a package so that opposition would not develop automatically around several measures at once. In addition, Johnson took care to consult with important senators and representatives in formulating legislation. Just before sending a bill to Congress, Johnson and his top aides would hold a briefing for congressional leaders in which they explained its features. He also gave influential senators notice of major appointments that required confirmation. Another feature of Johnson's congressional strategy was to make cabinet members responsible for the success of legislation in their areas and to use the cabinet to help coordinate administration liaison with Congress. Finally, when crucial votes were approaching on Capitol Hill, Johnson made intense personal appeals to the members whose votes served as cues for others and to members who were identified as uncommitted or wavering.

Johnson was effective in building congressional coalitions in support of his program. Through an analysis of head counts, used by Johnson's congressional liaison office to track House members' positions on bills over time, Terry Sullivan found that the Johnson administration built coalitions by "converting hard core opponents."[49] Sullivan cautions, however, that the influence gained through conversions was not dramatic because it was obtained within the confines of "representative and institutional forces."[50]

Johnson's approach to congressional relations worked well until the political context changed as a consequence of the Vietnam War. The president lost much of his touch with Congress as he became increasingly involved in foreign policy matters and as the momentum of the Great Society gave way to the unpopularity of the war. The loss of forty-eight Democratic seats in the House of Representatives in the 1966 congressional elections also adversely affected Johnson's ability to push bills through Congress.

Like Johnson, President Ford had intimate knowledge of Congress, and he worked diligently to maintain good relations with its leaders, but his success was limited. In contrast, Richard Nixon disdained personal efforts to court Congress, yet he enjoyed modest legislative success early in his administration. His relations with Congress turned sour when he challenged the Democratic majority directly by impounding appropriated funds and by asserting a sweeping doctrine of executive privilege under which administration officials refused to provide information to congressional committees.

Still, it seems clear that the Johnson approach, entailing detailed knowledge of Congress, respect for its constitutional prerogatives, sensitivity to the personal and constituency needs of its members, and the organizational and political capacity to build coalitions, can only increase a president's influence. If the president is able to create a friendly climate on Capitol Hill, one that is not hostile to him personally and in which his proposals are received with an open mind, then his prospects for success are greatly enhanced. President Carter's inability to create such a climate is often cited as a reason for the limited success of some of his major legislative goals, such as welfare reform and a comprehensive energy conservation program. In contrast, President Reagan's congenial manner and relaxed style helped establish within Congress an attitude toward his legislative program that was generally positive and not openly hostile. Reagan's ability to create a friendly climate in his congressional relations appears to have been an important factor in the passage of tax reform legislation in 1986. At critical points during the Ninety-ninth Congress the tax bill seemed doomed, only to be resurrected as members responded to presidential appeals for an equitable tax system.[51]

President Bush's relations with Congress demonstrate that a congenial climate may be unrelated to presidential success. A former member of the House, Bush knew many members of Congress well and maintained close contact with them. Through the end of his third year, however, Bush had prevailed on fewer congressional roll calls than his predecessors at similar points in their first terms.[52]

Although President Clinton lacked Washington experience and most Democrats in Congress had not served with a president of their own party, he had a close and cooperative relationship with the Democratic leadership during the 103d Congress (1993–1994).[53] His legislative achievements were substantial. In both 1993 and 1994, he won on 86.4 percent of the floor votes in Congress on which he took a position.[54] The list of major legislation enacted was impressive: his economic program, which included a major deficit reduction; family and medical leave legislation; reauthorization and revision of the Elementary and Secondary Education Act; expansion of Head Start; motor-voter legislation; national service legislation; the Brady gun control bill; a comprehensive anti-crime bill; the North American Free Trade Agreement; and legislation extending and expanding the General Agreement on Tariffs and Trade. He failed, however, to secure passage of bills to reform health care and welfare. Even though he was productive legislatively and attempted to address seriously the problems of declining middle-class incomes and economic dislocation that stem from changes in the U.S. economy and the globalization of markets, he received no political benefit from the voters in 1994.[55] Congenial relations with Congress may contribute to the enactment of the president's agenda, but they cannot overcome a negative political context characterized by a "sour public mood" and few electoral incentives for politicians to act responsibly rather than pandering to popular sentiments.[56] Clinton's relationship with congressional leaders of both parties was less cordial and more distant during the 104th Congress, but as we have noted, he did not set its agenda.

Modes of Presidential-Congressional Relations

In their relations with Congress, presidents can follow certain modes or patterns of behavior: bargaining, arm-twisting, and confrontation. As befits a relationship among professional politicians, bargaining is the predominant mode of presidential-congressional relations. Occasionally, the president bargains directly with members of Congress whose support is regarded as essential to the passage of a bill. In May 1981, for example, the Reagan administration agreed to revive a costly program to support the price of sugar in exchange for the votes of four Democratic representatives from Louisiana on a comprehensive budget reduction bill.[57]

Presidents usually try to avoid such explicit bargains because they have limited resources available to trade, and the desire among members for these resources is keen. Moreover, Congress is so large and congressional power so decentralized that it is not possible for presidents to bargain extensively over most bills. In some instances the president may be unable or unwilling to bargain. Fortunately, much presidential-congressional bargaining is implicit. Rather than a quid pro quo exchange of favors for votes, implicit bargaining involves generalized trading in which tacit exchanges of support and favors occur.

If bargaining does not result in the approval of his legislative proposals, the president may resort to stronger methods such as arm-twisting, which involves intense, even extraordinary, pressure and threats. In one sense, arm-twisting is an intensified extension of bargaining, but it entails something more, a direct threat of punishment or retaliation if the member's opposition continues.

The most frequent practitioner of arm-twisting among modern presidents was Lyndon Johnson. When more gentle efforts at persuasion failed or when a previously supportive member opposed him on an important issue, Johnson resorted to tactics such as deliberate embarrassment, threats, and reprisals. In contrast, President Eisenhower was most reluctant to pressure Congress. Arm-twisting is understandably an unpopular presidential tactic and, if used frequently, creates resentment and hostility. Still, judicious demonstration that there are costs associated with sustained opposition or desertion by normal supporters strengthens a president's bargaining position.

Presidents who are unable to gain support for their proposals through bargaining and arm-twisting may adopt a confrontational strategy in dealing with Congress. Confrontation might consist of appeals to the public, direct challenges to congressional authority, assertion of presidential prerogative, or similar tactics. President Nixon confronted Congress often and more sharply than any modern president. Disdaining the role of legislative coalition builder, Nixon saw himself instead as deserving of congressional support by virtue of his election mandate and his constitutional position as chief executive. Between 1971 and 1973, for example, he challenged congressional spending decisions that were at variance with his budget proposals by impounding, or refusing to spend, more than $30 billion that Congress had appropriated. Nixon also asserted a sweeping doctrine of executive privilege that denied Congress the authority to question thousands of executive branch officials and to obtain access to routine documentary information.

There are occasions when easing presidential pressures on Congress may be productive. President Carter's energy legislation, which passed in modified form as separate bills in 1978, 1979, and 1980, demonstrates that a willingness to compromise after an intense effort can result in partial success. Also, ending the attempt to pass legislation that has little or no chance, such as Clinton's health care reform bill in 1994, enables an administration to concentrate its energies on other bills with greater chance of success.

A strategy of confrontation is unlikely to result in sustained congressional responsiveness to presidential initiatives. Congress has constitutional prerogatives and constituency bases of support that enable it to resist presidential domination. The imperatives for cooperation between the two branches are so great that most presidents try to avoid confrontations with Congress and enter them only when the constitutional integrity of the presidency is at issue.

Organizing Congressional Liaison

The Eisenhower administration formalized presidential relations with Congress. Under the direction of presidential assistant Bryce Harlow, the liaison office provided information to members of Congress, helped Republicans with constituency-related matters, and lobbied for presidential proposals through explanation and low-key persuasion. During the Kennedy and Johnson administrations, the congressional liaison staff, under presidential assistant Lawrence F. O'Brien, actively asserted itself in behalf of presidential proposals. The staff was deeply involved in the formulation of the president's legislative program, and it furnished a congressional perspective to the process. It also worked closely with department and agency legislative personnel in the preparation of legislative proposals, and it coordinated bureaucratic lobbying with its own efforts.

By the end of the Johnson administration the congressional liaison operation had expanded from the rudimentary efforts under Eisenhower to establish a friendly climate on Capitol Hill to a complex set of activities that now includes intensive lobbying, intelligence gathering, representation, and coordination of executive branch legislative activity. Lobbying involves efforts, through persuasion and use of formal powers, to form congressional coalitions to enact the president's program. Intelligence gathering is the acquisition and evaluation of information about Congress, especially the policy preferences and constituency concerns of individual members. It is of special importance in determining the prospects for passing specific bills. Centralized head counts—the voting intentions of members on a particular bill—are another way presidents gather information. They use that information to enhance their bargaining position with members of Congress.[58] Representation entails acting as spokesperson for the president's position to members of Congress as well as presenting congressional views within the White House. Coordination of executive branch relations with Congress ranges from monitoring and tracking bills, to collaborating with departments' liaison offices, to controlling departments' staff appointments.

Presidential liaison with Congress is now thoroughly institutionalized. The organizational structure of the staff is fairly well fixed (assignments on the basis of the two houses of Congress with geographical subdivision within each house), its activities and tactics are accepted by Congress, and the services it provides to Congress and the president have become routine. The liaison operation is expected to dispense favors and conduct presidential bargaining with Congress. Congressional leaders expect to share in presidential legislative policy making, and members of Congress know that the president will use the liaison office to push his legislative program.

The institutionalization of congressional liaison does not, however, guarantee its effectiveness. Although, for example, President Clinton's first liaison director, Howard Paster, had extensive congressional experience, the administration's liaison operation during the crucial first year was disorganized and lacked coordination.[59] In negotiations over critical legislation, the administration often did not speak with one voice. In May 1993, for example, Secretary of the Treasury Lloyd Bentsen was taking a tougher position on a proposed tax on energy than Paster. Recognizing this, congressional leaders circumvented Bentsen by dealing directly with Paster.[60] At the end of the year, Paster resigned in frustration because the White House chief of staff, Thomas McLarty, could not control uncoordinated and sometimes contradictory statements, or "freelancing," by the staff members, administration officials, and outside consultants.[61]

The President and Legislation

If all presidents approach Congress with the same formal powers and informal tools of influence and operate through well-established institutional arrangements, what accounts for the success or failure of their legislative efforts? Studies have identified at least six factors that affect the president's ability to achieve his legislative goals: his partisan and ideological support in Congress, his popular support, his style in dealing with Congress, the contexts in which the president must operate, cyclical trends in presidential-congressional relations, and the content of his

program. It is not possible to assess the relative importance of each factor, but all of them have come into play since 1933, when FDR inaugurated the modern legislative presidency. The first five factors will be
examined here; the sixth, in Chapter 8.

Congressional Support

The president's support in Congress depends heavily on the size and
cohesiveness of his party's strength there. George Edwards has shown
that from 1961 to 1986, three Democratic and three Republican presidents consistently received strong support on roll-call votes from the
congressional members of their parties.[62] This was the case on four measures of presidential support among members of Congress.[63] Edwards
and Jon Bond and Richard Fleisher have found, however, that Republican presidents receive stronger support on foreign policy legislation
than on domestic policy issues, primarily because of increased backing
from liberal Democrats.[64]

It is interesting to note that partisan support for presidents in Congress apparently owes little to the storied effect of presidential coattails.
The ability of presidents to transfer their electoral appeal to congressional candidates of their parties declined steadily from 1948 to 1988.[65]
Even in 1984, when President Reagan won a landslide victory over the
Democratic candidate, Walter Mondale, the measurable coattail effect
was weak, but it was stronger than in 1980 and 1988.[66] Edwards attributes the decline in the power of coattails to increased split-ticket voting,
the reduced competitiveness of House seats, and the electoral success of
incumbents since 1952. The consequences of the reduced coattail effect
are the loss of presidential leverage with Congress and greater difficulty for presidents in winning congressional approval of their major legislative proposals.

Because the president cannot rely on full support from the members
of his party, he must build coalitions by obtaining support from some
members of the opposition.[67] Coalition building is especially important
when the opposition controls one or both houses of Congress, a condition that has occurred in twenty of the last twenty-six years. Several
factors other than party membership influence congressional voting
decisions: these include constituency pressures, state and regional loyalty, ideological orientations, and the influence of interest groups.[68] On
many occasions, presidents have received crucial support from the
opposition. President Eisenhower, for example, successfully sought
Democratic votes on foreign policy matters; Republicans contributed

sizable pluralities to the enactment of civil rights legislation in the 1960s; conservative Democrats, mainly from the South, often support-ed the domestic policy proposals of Presidents Nixon and Ford; conser-vative Democrats in the House were essential to President Reagan's 1981 legislative victories; and President Clinton depended heavily on Republican support for the passage of NAFTA and GATT.

Congressional support for the president is built, then, primarily on fellow partisans and stems from the policy objectives they share and from their sense of party loyalty. Party affiliation is not by itself, how-ever, a sufficient basis for the enactment of the president's legislative program. Constituency, regional, and ideological pressures reduce the number of partisan backers, and the president must try to attract sup-port from members of the opposition party on the basis of their ideo-logical orientations and their constituency and regional interests. A president's legislative success "is mainly a function of the partisan and ideological makeup of Congress." [69]

Popular Support

The president's prestige, or popular support, also affects congression-al response to his policies. It has been widely observed that a popular president enjoys substantial leeway in dealing with Congress, and a president whose popularity is low or falling is likely to encounter con-siderable resistance. Bond and Fleisher argue, however, that popular support is only marginally related to presidential success on congres-sional floor votes.[70] Similarly, Edwards finds that public approval is a background resource that provides presidents with leverage but not control over Congress.[71]

Although presidential popularity is clearly, if marginally, related to congressional support for the president's legislative program and can be used as a tool of influence, it cannot be easily manipulated. There are factors, such as the erosion of popular support over time and the con-dition of the economy, over which the president has no control.[72] What the president can do is to take advantage of his popularity when it is high to influence congressional opinion, as Lyndon Johnson did in 1964 and 1965 and Ronald Reagan did in 1981 and, to a lesser extent, in 1985 and 1986 until it plummeted because of the Iran-contra affair. The president can also appeal to the public beyond party lines for support.[73] To the extent that he succeeds in building popular support, he can strengthen his support in Congress, if his style in dealing with Congress enables him to exploit it.

Presidential Style and Legislative Skills

The president's style in dealing with Congress has long been considered an important determinant of his legislative success. Presidential style in congressional relations encompasses the degree to which the president is accessible to members of Congress, his interactions with and sensitivity to the members, and the extent of his involvement in the legislative process.[74]

Modern presidents have varied greatly in their accessibility to members of Congress. Johnson and Ford, for example, were usually available to members and leaders alike without great difficulty, whereas Nixon was remote and inaccessible most of the time. Kennedy and Reagan frequently sought contact through telephone calls. Bush maintained a wide range of congressional friends and acquaintances but was criticized for not consulting enough with influential party and committee leaders. During his first two years, Clinton's accessibility and his efforts to cultivate personal relationships with members of Congress was so great that it may have impaired his effectiveness.[75] That accessibility diminished in the 104th Congress, which had an assertive Republican majority and included many Democrats who distanced themselves from a president whom they regarded as a political liability.[76] Although accessibility on demand is not feasible because of the pressures on the president's time, it enhances the president's congressional support if members know they can reach him on matters of great importance to them. Accessibility to congressional leaders of both parties is particularly important if the president is to work effectively with Congress.

The president's interactions with and sensitivity to members of Congress are related to his accessibility. It is not clear how much a president's interpersonal relations influence his congressional support, but they are a distinctive part of his style and affect the disposition of leaders and members toward him. If nothing else, presidential popularity with members of Congress can improve relations even when there are sharp differences over issues. If the president has strained personal relations with many representatives and senators, sustained congressional support will be difficult to achieve even when the president's party has a majority and many members share his goals.

The extent of presidential involvement in the legislative process is an important element of his style in congressional relations. Johnson, Ford, Kennedy, and Reagan all maintained a close interest in the course of legislation, and Johnson even actively directed its progress on occasion. In contrast, Nixon, Eisenhower, and Carter were more detached and had less interest in the building of congressional coalitions. Bush displayed a varied pattern of interest in the progress of legislation, ranging from detachment to active engagement, as in the negotiations over the 1991 budget. Initially, Clinton involved himself so deeply with the details of legislation and made concessions so early that he drew criticism for making it "too easy" for his opponents.[77] Although he adopted the open, highly engaged approach to Congress that had worked well in the past, Clinton's lack of skill as a legislative tactician limited the effectiveness of the approach.

Conventional wisdom holds that a president's legislative skills are a major determinant of congressional support for his program. However, recent empirical analyses have provided little support for that argument. According to Edwards and other scholars, presidential legislative skills are effective at the margins of congressional coalition building and not at the core.[78] Presenting a somewhat different argument, Mark Peterson states that presidents have some, but not unlimited, control over the timing, priorities, and size of their legislative programs. By clearly establishing their priorities and carefully adjusting their "ambitions to fit the opportunities of the day," he concludes, presidents can be perceived as successful leaders of Congress.[79] The conclusion that the president is weakly positioned to lead Congress is supported by careful analysis, but it runs counter to much of the conventional wisdom of scholars and journalists. If nothing else, these analyses should caution observers of the presidency against uncritical acceptance of personalized explanations of presidential success in Congress and encourage the search for other influences.

Contextual Factors

Most students of presidential-congressional relations agree that contextual factors over which the president has limited control—such as the structure of American political institutions and processes, public opinion, the alignment of political and social forces, economic and social conditions, and long-term trends in the political system—are more important than legislative skills as determinants of congressional decisions. For example, the cultural context of American politics is a source of frustration for presidents attempting to influence Congress. Phenomena such as extremely high and often contradictory public expectations of presidential performance, individualism, and skepticism of authority are powerful constraints on presidential leadership.[80] Bond and Fleisher argue that Congress-centered variables, such as the partisan and ideological predispositions of members and leaders, which are determined by the outcome of the last election, are of greater importance than presidency-centered variables in explaining presidential influence in Congress.[81]

Taking a middle position between Edwards's presidency-centered analysis and the Congress-centered perspective of Bond and Fleisher, Peterson provides the most comprehensive and extensive analysis of contextual factors affecting presidential success in Congress. He identifies four contexts that shape congressional action on presidential programs: (1) the "pure context," which includes the "institutional properties" of Congress, political parties, and interest groups and over which the president has little influence and no control; (2) the "malleable context," which consists of "dynamic" political conditions resulting from electoral cycles and economic conditions and over which the president has "greater but unpredictable influence" but no control; (3) the "policy context," which the president can influence and to some extent control by making "strategic choices" in developing an agenda, including the consequence of various proposals for the political system, the relative importance of proposals for presidential policy goals, and the controversiality of proposals; and (4) the "individual context," which includes personal attributes, such as style and skills, and the choices the president makes concerning the organization of the presidency for the exercise of influence that distinguish the president and the administration.[82]

However one defines and classifies the contexts that affect the president's influence or success in Congress, it is important to recognize that they function to provide both constraints upon and opportunities for the exercise of presidential leadership. To a considerable extent, the president can do little to alter most of these contexts. What a president can do is take maximum advantage of the opportunities they present. In doing so the chief executive can act as a facilitator, but not a director who focuses change.

Cyclical Trends

Long-term cyclical fluctuations in presidential and congressional power also appear to affect the fate of specific presidential programs. The inauguration of FDR in 1933 marked the beginning of a period of presidential ascendancy that lasted until Richard Nixon became enmeshed in the Watergate scandal. During that time Congress made extensive delegations of power to the president and to executive branch agencies; presidents assumed responsibility for legislative leadership; Congress acquiesced in presidential domination of foreign and military policy; and the public looked to the presidency more than to Congress to solve the nation's problems.[83] The president and Congress clashed often during that period, but the dominant trend was one of presidential aggrandizement. When conflict occurred, Congress usually took defensive stands against presidential assertiveness.

In 1973 a Congress jealous of what it perceived to be its constitutional prerogatives, angry over the protracted "presidential war" in Vietnam, and fed up with battling President Nixon over impoundment and executive privilege, moved to reassert itself. Seizing the opportunity afforded by Nixon's preoccupation with Watergate, Congress enacted the War Powers Resolution of 1973, the Budget and Impoundment Control Act of 1974, and the National Emergencies Act of 1976.[84] These statutes were the major elements in a congressional resurgence that restrained presidential power. In 1974 the House Judiciary Committee approved three impeachment charges against President Nixon, who resigned on August 9, before the House could act on them. Nixon's two immediate successors, Gerald Ford and Jimmy Carter, had to deal with a resurgent Congress intent on curbing the uses of presidential power and retaining the constitutional parity with the president that it regained, at least partially, in the 1970s. Increased skepticism of claims for presidential prerogative, careful scrutiny of presidential proposals, demands for more extensive consultation of congressional leaders by the White House, and more exacting senatorial confirmation hearings on presidential appointments were the hallmarks of this period of congressional resurgence.

During the Reagan presidency Congress was more willing to accept presidential policy leadership and less assertive in insisting on its institutional prerogatives. The presidential-congressional relationship did not, however, return to the conditions that prevailed under the "imperial presidency."[85] President Reagan had generally friendly relations with Congress despite sharp differences over policy, such as the budget deficit, and over presidential powers, such as impoundments and deferrals of appropriated funds. Reagan's relationship with Congress bent, but did not break, in 1987 following Democratic successes in the 1986 congressional elections and as a consequence of public disenchantment with his detached leadership, which was revealed by the Iran-contra affair.

President Bush enjoyed good relations with Congress until the fall of 1990, when he became embroiled in a protracted battle with leaders and members from both parties over the deficit in the 1991 budget. In October a coalition of Democratic and Republican House members defeated an agreement on a deficit reduction plan that the administration had negotiated with a bipartisan leadership group. After several weeks of bitter wrangling, including charges and countercharges of bad faith, the administration and Congress agreed to a compromise. As the budget battle came to its unsatisfactory close, most congressional Democrats and some Republicans sharply questioned Bush's handling of the Persian Gulf crisis and pressed him to obtain the approval of Congress before initiating military action against Iraq. The administration insisted that it had authority to initiate such action on its own. Both sides cited the Constitution—Congress its power to declare war and the president his power as commander in chief—in defense of their positions. In early January 1991 Congress passed a resolution authorizing the use of U.S. forces to implement UN resolutions calling on Iraq to leave Kuwait or face economic sanctions and, if necessary, military action. The striking success of Operation Desert Storm boosted Bush's popular approval ratings and improved his relations with Congress. However, that relationship lacked durability. By the beginning of 1992 Bush's popular support had fallen to the lowest point of his presidency as the public blamed him for a protracted economic recession.

Two distinct patterns characterized presidential-congressional relations in the Clinton administration. As noted previously, the president initially enjoyed congenial relations with Congress, although it was widely recognized that he could easily be convinced to change his position, or "rolled." The 103d Congress (1993–1994) enacted most of an ambitious presidential agenda, except for health care and welfare reform legislation. Except for trade legislation, and despite the opposition of conservative Democrats in both chambers and the continuation of the congressional assertiveness that began in the 1970s, the items on the agenda were enacted without bipartisan support.

But Clinton's legislative success did not result in political rewards. In the 1994 elections the voters handed control of Congress over to the Republicans for the first time in forty years. The primary reasons for the Democratic reversal included a sense of economic insecurity and negative judgments on President Clinton, the Democratic Party, and liberalism.[86] Republican strategists nationalized the election by directing "mass discontent with government" against the "Democratic congressional establishment." Newt Gingrich's "Contract with America" provided "a clear, focused integrated message that ... energize[d] and mobilize[d] the Republican base." [87]

Although still cordial, presidential-congressional relations changed substantially in the 104th Congress. In 1995 the Republicans seized control of the domestic and economic agenda. Clinton initially withdrew from active involvement in the legislative process. Later, capitalizing on negative public responses to Republican initiatives, he gained the upper hand.

The President's Effect on Congress

What overall impact does the president have on Congress? How can one judge presidential effectiveness with Congress? Analysts have sought answers to these questions through examination of congressional roll-call votes and of aggregate measures based on roll calls such as presidential support scores, discussed previously in this chapter, and presidential box scores, based on the number and percentage of presidential legislative requests that are enacted into law. (Both measures are calculated by Congressional Quarterly, but the box scores were discontinued in 1975.) To further refine the support scores, one can separate members by party and subdivide each group of partisans by region and faction. Analysts also have refined the scores by classifying bills by domestic and foreign policy proposals, which has led to a protracted debate over whether there are "two presidencies," one for domestic policy, in which presidents have less success with Congress, and the other for foreign policy, in which they have more.[88] Such aggregate measures provide an overall picture of presidential effectiveness, but they leave a great many questions unanswered. For example, how controversial were a president's proposals? What potential effect did the proposals have on the economy and society? Did the president risk much or little by making them? Did the successful bills require a major effort at coalition building, and, if so, what was the partisan and regional composition of the coalitions?[89]

A comparison of congressional support for Presidents Johnson, Carter, and Reagan suggests the limitations of aggregate measures (see Table 5-4). According to most assessments, Johnson's legislative accomplishments—mainly the social programs of the Great Society—outstripped those of all modern presidents since FDR in their significance. Carter's legislative record, in sharp contrast, is marked by frustration

Table 5-4   Congressional Support on Key Votes for Presidents Johnson, Carter, and Reagan (Percent)

	Johnson	Carter	Reagan
House of Representatives			
Democrats	68%	59%	29%
Northern	81	64	21
Southern	40	45	50
Republicans	29	29	74
Senate			
Democrats	65	64	32
Northern	75	70	27
Southern	41	50	50
Republicans	49	33	75

Source: George C. Edwards III, *At the Margins: Presidential Leadership of Congress* (New Haven, Conn.: Yale University Press, 1989),177,178,183,184. Data for Reagan are for 1981–1986.

and limited achievement of major goals. Reagan, after a highly successful first year and difficulty thereafter, generally is regarded as standing close to Johnson in his ability to lead Congress. Yet, data based on key votes on congressional roll calls indicate that differences among the three performances are not substantial.

The data also show that Carter enjoyed nearly the same level of support in the House as Johnson. They show that Carter actually did better among southern Democratic representatives and senators than Johnson and that Reagan enjoyed more support from senators of his own party than either Carter or Johnson.

The data also suggest that measurement of presidential impact on Congress requires qualitative as well as quantitative assessments. Even though Congress passed several of Carter's principal requests, such as the Panama Canal Treaty and the establishment of the Departments of Energy and Education, and he compared favorably with Johnson and Reagan using quantitative measures, the prevailing assessments of his legislative accomplishments are quite negative.[90] Clinton's case in 1993 and 1994 resembles Carter's in that, although he scored well quantitatively and Congress enacted many of his major proposals, public and media evaluations of his performance were negative. The explanation of these seemingly counterintuitive evaluations is that presidential legislative records are usually evaluated on the basis of subjective assessments of the substance of the measures that are enacted and the president's management of congressional relations. If the enacted statutes are thought to be of limited importance, if they fall short of the president's announced goals, or if they fail to provide satisfactory solutions to the problems they were designed to address, then the president is likely to be judged harshly. Procedurally, if the president appears to be inept or disinterested in handling congressional relations, critics will probably find fault with his legislative performance.

The experiences of recent presidents in their relations with Congress provide a few lessons. They have found, or at least should have found, that success is not automatic. It requires consultation before and during legislative consideration and a willingness to negotiate and bargain with Congress. Coordination of legislative proposals between the White House and the departments and agencies is most helpful. More important, cooperation between the president and congressional leaders and between the institutional presidency and Congress is essential. The constitutional separation of powers does not allow the two branches to operate independently of each other; rather, it requires that they exercise their shared powers jointly.[91]

Conclusion

The president's relationship with Congress takes place within the framework of the constitutional separation of powers. That framework requires cooperation but ensures conflict. This has been true during the more than 200 years that the Republic has operated under the Constitution. The Framers of the Constitution sought to prevent tyranny by establishing a balance between executive and legislative power. However, the concept of balance entails a static relationship, whereas the relationship that has existed between the president and Congress has been continually in flux. First one branch has expanded its authority; then the second branch has reasserted its prerogatives, recaptured lost powers, and acquired new ones. The cycle of institutional aggrandizement, decline, and resurgence reflects certain strengths and weaknesses in the presidency and Congress and their respective abilities to respond to social forces, economic conditions, and political change.

The need for presidential-congressional cooperation is clear, but there are few ways of obtaining it other than through consultation involving persuasion and bargaining. Presidents cannot command congressional approval of their proposals any more than Congress can direct them in the exercise of their constitutional powers. The threat of government stalemate is always present, and more often than not policy is an unsatisfactory compromise of presidential and various congressional viewpoints.

Clearly, the presidential-congressional relationship is a dynamic one. It varies according to contextual factors, cycles of presidential and congressional assertiveness, and the leadership skills and styles of individual presidents. Changes occur in the relationship, sometimes quickly and dramatically, as between the 1980s and 1990s and the presidencies of Ronald Reagan and Bill Clinton. As the United States moves through its third century, the relationship between the president and Congress will be characterized—as it is today—by the stability provided by the Constitution as well as by adaptations to social, economic, and political change.

NOTES

1. Alissa J. Rubin, "Congress Readies Budget Bill for President's Veto Pen," *Congressional Quarterly Weekly Report,* November 18, 1995, 3512.

2. Stephen J. Wayne, *The Legislative Presidency* (New York: Harper & Row, 1978) 8–12.

3. Theodore Roosevelt, *Autobiography* (New York: Macmillan, 1913), 292.

4. Woodrow Wilson, *Constitutional Government in the United States* (1908; reprint, New York: Columbia University Press, 1961).

5. Richard E. Neustadt, "The Presidency and Legislation: The Growth of Central Clearance," *American Political Science Review* (September 1954): 641–670.

6. Richard E. Neustadt, "The Presidency and Legislation: Planning the President's Program," *American Political Science Review* (December 1955): 980–1018; Wayne, *The Legislative Presidency;* Larry Berman, *The Office of Management and Budget and the Presidency*(Princeton, N.J.: Princeton University Press, 1979); Paul C. Light, *The President's Agenda: Domestic Policy Choice from Kennedy to Reagan,* rev. ed. (Baltimore: Johns Hopkins University Press, 1991).

7. Samuel P. Huntington, "Congressional Responses to the Twentieth Century," in *The Congress and America's Future,* ed. David B. Truman (Englewood Cliffs, N.J.: Prentice-Hall, 1965), 23.

8. Ronald C. Moe and Steven C. Teel,. "Congress as Policy-Maker: A Necessary Reappraisal," *Political Science Quarterly* (Fall 1970): 443–470; John R. Johannes, *Policy Innovation in Congress* (Morristown, N.J.: General Learning Press, 1972); Gary Orfield, *Congressional Power: Congress and Social Change* (New York: Harcourt Brace Jovanovich, 1975).

9. In the Senate the Republicans had a 53–47 majority. In the House, the 192 Republicans, who voted together on the major elements of President Reagan's economic legislation in a remarkable display of cohesion, were joined by a sizable bloc of conservative southern Democrats called the "Boll Weevils." In both chambers, Republicans and conservative Democrats maintained voting cohesion that provided the majorities to enact the Reagan program.

10. Barbara Sinclair, "Trying to Govern Positively in a Negative Era," in *The Clinton Presidency: First Appraisals,* ed. Colin Campbell and Bert A. Rockman (Chatham, N.J.: Chatham House, 1995), 121.

11. Bert A. Rockman, "Entrepreneur in the Political Marketplace: The Constitution and the Development of the Presidency" (Paper presented at the annual meeting of the American Political Science Association, San Francisco, Aug. 30–Sept. 2, 1990), 26–27.

12. Charles O. Jones, *The Presidency in a Separated System* (Washington, D.C.: Brookings, 1994), 16.

13. Alexander Hamilton, John Jay, and James Madison, *The Federalist Papers* (New York: Modern Library, 1938), 335–337.

14. Lawrence C. Dodd, "Congress and the Quest for Power," in *Congress Reconsidered,* ed. Lawrence C. Dodd and Bruce I. Oppenheimer (New York: Praeger, 1977), 298–302.

15. David S. Cloud, "Republicans Pushing the Envelope with Confrontational Approach," *Congressional Quarterly Weekly Report,* Aug. 5, 1995, 2331–2334.

16. Ibid., 2333.

17. James L. Sundquist, *The Decline and Resurgence of Congress* (Washington, D.C.: Brookings, 1981).

18. Thomas E. Mann, "Elections and Change in Congress," in *The New Congress,* ed. T. E. Mann (Washington, D.C.: American Enterprise Institute, 1981).

19. Roger H. Davidson and Walter J. Oleszek, *Congress and Its Members,* 4th ed. (Washington, D.C.: CQ Press, 1994), 63.

20. Among the leading critics of divided government are James L. Sundquist, "Needed: A Political Theory for the New Era of Coalition Government in the United States," *Political Science Quarterly* (Winter 1988–1989): 613–635; Lloyd N. Cutler, "To Form a Government," Foreign Affairs 59 (Fall 1980): 126–143; Cutler, "Now Is the Time for All Good Men," *William and Mary Law Review* 30 (Fall 1989): 387–402; and Michael L. Mezey, *Congress, the President, and Public Policy* (Boulder, Colo.: Westview, 1989).

21. Gary W. Cox and Samuel Kernell, "Conclusion," in *The Politics of Divided Government,* ed. Gary W. Cox and Samuel Kernell (Boulder, Colo.: Westview, 1991), 242–243. Also see Matthew D. McCubbins, "Government on Lay-Away: Federal Spending and Deficits Under Divided Party Control," in ibid., 113–153.

22. David R. Mayhew, *Divided We Govern: Party Control, Lawmaking, and Investigations, 1946–1990* (New Haven, Conn.: Yale University Press, 1991), 198.

23. Morris Fiorina, *Divided Government* (New York: Macmillan, 1992), 107, 108.

24. Ibid., 111.

25. Ibid., chap. 6.

26. Davidson and Oleszek, *Congress and Its Members,* chaps. 3–5; David R. Mayhew, *Congress: The Electoral Connection* (New Haven, Conn.: Yale University Press, 1974).

27. Davidson and Oleszek, *Congress and Its Members,* chap. 1.

28. The main components of the Great Society were the Economic Opportunity Act of 1964, which launched a "war on poverty"; the Civil Rights Act of 1964; the Voting Rights Act of 1965; the Elementary and Secondary Education Act of 1965; and the Medicare Act of 1965.

29. This discussion follows Sinclair, "Trying to Govern Positively," 91–119.

30. Sundquist, *The Decline and Resurgence of Congress,* 143.

31. David S. Cloud, "Lack of New Proposals Reflects New Dynamic on the Hill," *Congressional Quarterly Weekly Report,* Jan. 28, 1995, 259–260; Donna Cassata, "Swift Progress of 'Contract' Inspires Awe and Concern," *Congressional Quarterly Weekly Report,* Apr. 1, 1995, 909–912.

32. Carroll J. Doherty, "Clinton's Big Comeback Shown in Vote Score," *Congressional Quarterly Weekly Report,* Dec. 21, 1996, 3427–3428.

33. Woodrow Wilson, *Congressional Government* (1885; reprint, New York: Meridian, 1956), 53.

34. Joseph E. Kallenbach, *The American Chief Executive* (New York: Harper & Row, 1966), 354.

35. Robert J. Spitzer, *The Presidential Veto: Touchstone of the American Presidency* (Albany: State University of New York Press, 1988), 100–103.

36. Janet Hook, "Avalanche of Veto Threats Divides Bush, Congress," *Congressional Quarterly Weekly Report,* Sept. 22, 1990, 2991. Hook cites an OMB spokeswoman as stating that the Bush administration had issued 120 veto threats since January 1989.

37. Richard A. Watson, "Reasons Presidents Veto Legislation" (Paper presented at the annual meeting of the American Political Science Association, Chicago, Sept. 3–6, 1987), 6, 7.

38. Albert C. Ringelstein, "Presidential Vetoes: Motivations and Classifications," *Congress and the Presidency* (Spring 1985): 52–53.

39. David W. Rhode and Dennis M. Simon, "Presidential Vetoes and Congressional Response: A Study of Institutional Conflict," *American Journal of Political Science* (August 1985): 307.

40. Ibid., 425.

41. Ibid.

42. Stephen J. Wayne, Richard L. Cole, and James F. C. Hyde, Jr., "Advising the President on Enrolled Legislation," *Political Science Quarterly* 94 (Summer 1979): 303–318.

43. Ibid., 316.

44. Richard E. Neustadt, *Presidential Power: The Politics of Leadership* (New York:Wiley, 1960), 10.

45. Theodore J. Lowi, *The End of Liberalism,* 2d ed. (New York: St. Martin's Press, 1979); Randall B. Ripley and Grace A. Franklin, *Congress, the Bureaucracy, and Public Policy,* 5th ed. (Pacific Grove, Calif: Brooks/Cole, 1991).

46. Joseph A. Pika, "White House Office of Congressional Relations: A Longitudinal Analysis" (Paper presented at the annual meeting of the Midwest Political Science Association, Chicago, Apr. 20–22, 1978).

47. Lyndon B. Johnson, *Vantage Point* (New York: Holt, Rinehart & Winston, 1971), 448; Doris Kearns, *Lyndon Johnson and the American Dream* (New York: Harper & Row, 1976), 226.

48. George C. Edwards III, *Presidential Influence in Congress* (San Francisco: Freeman, 1980), 117–120.

49. Terry Sullivan, "Headcounts, Expectations, and Presidential Coalitions in Congress," *American Journal of Political Science* (August 1988): 567. Elsewhere, Sullivan demonstrates that head counts are a valuable presidential tool for signaling congressional supporters and for obtaining information from them. "Explaining Why Presidents Count: Signaling and Information," *Journal of Politics* (August 1990): 939–962.

50. Ibid., 582.

51. Jeffrey H. Birnbaum and Alan S. Murray, *Showdown at Gucci Gulch* (New York: Random House, 1987), 40–41, 94–95, 118, 169–171.

52. Chuck Alston, "Bush's High Public Standing Held Little Sway on Hill," *Congressional Quarterly Weekly Report,* Dec. 28, 1991, 3751.

53. Barbara Sinclair, "Trying to Govern Positively," in *The Clinton Presidency: First Appraisals,* ed. Colin Campbell and Bert A. Rockman (Chatham, N.J.: Chatham House, 1995), 96–100.

54. Steve Langdon, "Clinton's High Victory Rate Conceals Disappointments," *Congressional Quarterly Weekly Report,* Dec. 31, 1994, 3619.

55. Sinclair, "Trying to Govern Positively" 121.

56. Ibid., 121, 122.

57. Laurence L. Barrett, *Gambling with History* (Garden City, N.Y.: Doubleday, 1983), 334.

58. Terry Sullivan, "Bargaining with the President: A Simple Game and New Evidence," *American Political Science Review* (December 1990): 1167–1196.

59. M. Stephen Weatherford and Lorraine M. McDonnell, "Clinton and the Economy: The Paradox of Policy Success and Political Mishap" (Paper presented at the annual meeting of the American Political Science Association, Chicago, Aug. 31–Sept. 3, 1995), 40.

60. Bob Woodward, *The Agenda* (New York: Simon & Schuster, 1994), 217.

61. Ibid., 319. Although Leon Panetta moved to curtail the freelancing upon taking over as chief of staff in July 1994, it continued to plague the administration; Solomon, "Bill Who?" 912.

62. George C. Edwards III, *At the Margins: Presidential Leadership of Congress* (New Haven, Conn.: Yale University Press, 1989), chap. 3.

63. Edwards developed four indexes, which are percentages of support for roll-call votes on which the president has taken a stand: (1) overall support on all votes on which the president has taken a stand; (2) support that was not unanimous on votes on which the winning side fell below 80 percent; (3) support on the single most important vote on each bill; and (4) key votes selected by Congressional Quarterly as being highly significant. He found that the non-unanimous support index was the most broadly representative and that the key votes index revealed relationships hidden by the broader indexes. Ibid., chap. 2.

It should be noted that use of Congressional Quarterly's presidential support scores is controversial. See Anita Pritchard, "An Evaluation of CQ Presidential Support Scores: The Relationship between Presidential Election Results and Congressional Voting Decisions," *American Journal of Political Science* (May 1985): 493–494; Jon R. Bond and Richard Fleisher, *The President in the Legislative Arena* (Chicago: University of Chicago Press, 1990), 62–66; Mark A. Peterson, *Legislating Together: The White House and Capitol Hillfrom Eisenhower to Reagan* (Cambridge, Mass.: Harvard University Press, 1990), 303–305.

64. Edwards, *At the Margins,* 68–69; Bond and Fleisher, *The President in the Legislative Arena,* 171–175.

65. Gary C. Jacobson, *The Electoral Origins of Divided Government* (Boulder, Colo.: Westview, 1990), 80–81.

66. Gary C. Jacobson, *The Politics of Congressional Elections,* 3d ed. (New York: HarperCollins, 1992), 161–162.

67. Sullivan, "Headcounts, Expectations, and Presidential Coalitions in Congress," 573–582.

68. John W. Kingdon, *Congressmen's Voting Decisions* (New York: Harper & Row, 1981); Aage R. Clausen, *How Congressmen Decide* (New York: St. Martin's Press, 1973).

69. Bond and Fleisher, *The President in the Legislative Arena,* 221.

70. Ibid., 182.

71. Edwards, *At the Margins,* 124–125.

72. John E. Mueller, *War, Presidents and Public Opinion* (New York: Wiley, 1973).

73. Samuel Kernell, *Going Public: New Strategies of Presidential Leadership,* 2d ed. (Washington, D.C.: CQ Press, 1993), chap. 1.

74. Wayne, *The Legislative Presidency,* 166.

75. Elizabeth Drew, *On the Edge* (New York: Simon & Schuster, 1994), 54, 266.

76. Solomon, "Bill Who?" 910–914.

77. Drew, *On the Edge,* 266.

78. Edwards, *At the Margins,* 211. Also see Bond and Fleisher, *The President in the Legislative Arena,* 219; Bert A. Rockman, *The Leadership Question: The Presidency and the American Political System* (New York: Praeger, 1984), 214.

79. Peterson, *Legislating Together,* 267.

80. Edwards, *At the Margins*, 8–15.

81. Bond and Fleisher, *The President in the Legislative Arena*, 220–234.

82. Peterson, *Legislating Together*, 92–94; chaps. 4 and 5.

83. Arthur M. Schlesinger, Jr., *The Imperial Presidency* (Boston: Houghton Mifflin, 1973).

84. Sundquist, *The Decline and Resurgence of Congress*.

85. In the second edition of *The Imperial Presidency* (Boston: Houghton Mifflin, 1989), Schlesinger maintains that Reagan moved two-thirds of the way toward restoring the imperial presidency. He met two of Schlesinger's "tests"—extensive presidential war making and heavy reliance on secrecy—but Reagan did not direct his powers against administration critics, 451, 457.

86. Alfred J. Tuchfarber, Stephen E. Bennett, Andrew E. Smith, and Eric W. Rademacher, "The Republican Tidal Wave of 1994: Testing Hypotheses About Realignment, Restructuring, and Rebellion" (Paper presented at the annual meeting of the American Political Science Association, Chicago, Aug. 31–Sept. 3, 1995), 29.

87. Walter Dean Burnham, "Realignment Lives: The 1994 Earthquake and Its Implications," in *The Clinton Presidency*, 370.

88. Aaron Wildavsky, "The Two Presidencies," *Transaction* 4 (December 1966): 7–14; Lance T. LeLoup and Steven A. Shull, "Congress versus the Executive," *Social Science Quarterly* (March 1979): 704–719; Steven A. Shull, ed., *The Two Presidencies: A Quarter-Century Assessment* (Chicago: Nelson-Hall, 1991); Edwards, *At the Margins*, chap. 4; and Bond and Fleisher, *The President in the Legislative Arena*, chap. 6.

89. Peterson provides an excellent discussion of the problems with aggregate measures, and he offers useful suggestions for overcoming them. See *Legislating Together*, 309–315.

90. Randall B. Ripley, "Carter and Congress," in *The Presidency: Studies in Policy Making*, ed. Steven A. Shull and Lance T. LeLoup (Brunswick, Ohio: King's Court Communications, 1979), 65–82.

91. This is the central theme of Peterson's *Legislating Together*, in which he advocates a "tandem institutions" perspective on presidential-congressional relations.

READINGS

Bond, Jon R., and Richard Fleisher. *The President in the Legislative Arena*. Chicago: University of Chicago Press, 1990.

Cox, Gary W., and Samuel Kernell, eds. *The Politics of Divided Government*. Boulder, Colo.: Westview, 1991.

Edwards, George C., III. *At the Margins: Presidential Leadership of Congress*. New Haven, Conn.: Yale University Press, 1989

Fiorina, Morris. *Divided Government*. New York: Macmillan. 1992.

Fisher, Louis. *Constitutional Conflicts Between Congress and the President*. 3d ed. Lawrence: University Press of Kansas, 1991.

Mayhew, David R. *Divided We Govern: Party Control, Lawmaking, and Investigations, 1946–1990*. New Haven, Conn.: Yale University Press, 1991. Peterson, Mark A. *Legislating Together: The White House and Capitol Hill from Eisenhower to Reagan*. Cambridge, Mass.: Harvard University Press, 1990.

Shull, Steven A., ed. *The Two Presidencies: A Quarter-Century Assessment*. Chicago: Nelson-Hall, 1991.

Spitzer, Robert J. *President and Congress: Executive Harmony at the Crossroads of American Government*. New York: McGraw-Hill, 1993.

___. *The Presidential Veto: Touchstone of the American Presidency.* Albany: State University of New York Press, 1988.

Sundquist, James L. *The Decline and Resurgence of Congress.* Washington, D.C.: Brookings, 1981.

Thurber, James A., ed. *Divided Democracy: Cooperation and Conflict Between the President and Congress.* Washington, D.C.: CQ Press, 1991.

Thurber, James A., ed. *Rivals for Power: Presidential-Congressional Relations.* Washington, D.C.: CQ Press, 1996.

Wayne, Stephen J. *The Legislative Presidency.* New York: Harper & Row, 1978.

ONE OF THE COMMONEST SYN-onyms for president is "chief executive." In U.S. political life the president is held responsible for the operation of the government, and, if government fails to meet popular expectations, the president takes the blame. Indeed, when President Jimmy Carter explained his administration's failure to fill some of its major campaign promises by saying that he had learned there were certain things that government could not do, his critics suggested that it was time to replace him with someone who could make government work. But most modern presidents have encountered difficulties in their efforts to direct the executive branch. John F. Kennedy lamented the inertia of the State Department and Ronald Reagan made his campaign attack on an overgrown federal bureaucracy one of the enduring themes of his presidency. Richard Rose, who has

In 1993 Vice President Gore (depicted in the above cartoon) presented a report commissioned by the president to "reinvent government." In endorsing that report, President Clinton pledged the elimination of over 250,000 federal jobs.

studied the president as a manager, has remarked that the "president's title of chief executive is a misnomer; he can more accurately be described as a nonexecutive chief." [1] The essence of Rose's argument is that even within the executive branch the president's powers of command are limited and that his success as an administrator depends to a great extent on his ability to win the trust of others.

This chapter examines the president's responsibilities as chief executive and the factors that affect his administrative performance. It opens with a discussion of the president's executive role and an examination of that role's constitutional, legal, and administrative foundations. Then it explores the president's relationships with the executive branch and the cabinet. Having established that the president's powers of command over the units of the executive branch are limited, the chapter analyzes the formal powers and managerial tools that modern presidents have available to them in discharging their administrative duties.

The President as Executive

The president's executive role is grounded in Article II of the Constitution. In ambiguous language the Constitution vests "the executive power" in the president and directs him to "take care that the laws be faithfully executed." He may also "require the opinion, in writing, of the principal officer in each of the executive departments" and "grant reprieves and pardons." He derives substantial power from his designation as "commander-in-chief of the army and navy." Modern presidents have tended to interpret these constitutional provisions broadly and have derived from them substantial additional powers. In addition to their constitutionally based powers, presidents have received extensive delegations of statutory authority from Congress.

There is an apparent paradox in, on the one hand, the president's considerable formal legal powers and his position as head of a vast, complex military and civilian bureaucracy and, on the other hand, his limited ability to direct that bureaucracy toward the achievement of his policy objectives and program goals. One may better understand that paradox by considering the constitutional relationship of the presidency to the legislative and judicial branches of government and the nature of the federal bureaucracy and the president's relationship to it.

The president is dependent on congressional cooperation to carry out the executive responsibilities of the office. Only Congress can authorize government programs, establish administrative agencies to implement the programs, and appropriate funds to finance them. However, presidents find that congressional cooperation may be difficult to obtain because presidents and members of Congress have different constituency and institutional perspectives.

There are also occasions when the exercise of presidential power must be approved by the judiciary. A notable instance of judicial disapproval of executive action involved President Harry S. Truman's seizure of U.S. steel mills in 1952 to forestall a strike during the Korean War.[2] The points to be made here are that presidential power is not self-executing and that it is subject to restraint. Presidents require the cooperation of Congress and the judiciary but frequently find themselves in conflict with these other branches of government.

Although the federal bureaucracy is the bulk of the executive branch, and the accomplishment of government objectives depends largely on its performance, it must be recognized legally as the creation of the legislative branch. In establishing federal departments and agencies, Congress is responding not only to presidential requests, but also to demands and pressures from constituency forces, interest groups, and the general public. The result is that the structure of the federal bureaucracy is not hierarchical; rather, it tends to reflect the political fragmentation and committee jurisdiction of Congress. The president does not look down upon subordinate administrative units from a position at the apex of a pyramid of authority. Instead, he confronts a complex and confusing array of departments and agencies with varying degrees of independence from him.

In addition, bureaucratic units are staffed principally by career civil servants who constitute a permanent government. They respond to demands from interest groups and to direction from congressional committees as well as to presidential leadership. Most modern presidents have entered office believing, or soon becoming convinced, that they cannot take the support and loyalty of the bureaucracy for granted but must constantly strive to acquire them.[3]

Moreover, the vastness and scope of the federal bureaucracy, as measured by expenditures or numbers of employees, further contribute to the difficulty of the president's executive role. From 1933 through 1980, as the functions of the federal government expanded, the task of defining objectives and coordinating their achievement grew increasingly difficult for presidents.

The president's task as the nation's chief executive is much more, therefore, than issuing commands. Nor is the job mainly that of finding ways to bring a large complex bureaucracy under operational control. Rather, he must secure congressional cooperation while suppressing the executive branch's natural tendencies toward conflict with the legislative branch, and he must give direction to the bureaucracy so that it will work with him in accomplishing his administration's goals.

The President and the Executive Branch

Ideally, presidents should use the White House staff and other units of the Executive Office of the President to help them define their objectives, convert them into operating programs, allocate resources to the agencies that administer the programs, and coordinate the implementation of programs within the federal government and among federal, state, and local governments. Department managers should direct the work of the career civil servants, coordinate the operations of their component bureaus, and develop and maintain links with other federal departments and agencies and with state and local governments. Presidents quickly discover, however, that the reality of their relations with the federal bureaucracy bears little resemblance to the idealized vision just described. For example, Joseph Califano, a former presidential aide and cabinet officer, has observed that "smaller federal agencies and numerous bureaus within large departments respond to presidential leadership only in the minds of the most naive students of government administration." [4]

Tension between the White House and the bureaucracy has been present in every modern administration. It exists, at least in part, because of what Hugh Heclo has identified as the distinction between "political leadership in the bureaucracy" and "bureaucratic power." [5] The direction and effectiveness of the political leadership the president provides depend on the personality, leadership style, and values of the president as well as on external events and conditions. In contrast, bureaucratic power is relatively permanent and does not depend on personalities and transitory political and environmental factors. It is a power that belongs to the career civil servants who compose the permanent government. How the government performs, Heclo suggests, "can be thought of as the product of political leadership times bureaucratic power." [6]

At least five general factors contribute to bureaucratic power and shape the pattern of presidential-bureaucratic relations: the size, complexity, and dispersion of the executive branch; bureaucratic inertia and momentum; the personnel of the executive branch; the legal position of the executive branch; and the susceptibility of executive branch units to external political influence. Major consequences of the interaction of these factors are presidential frustration and a pattern of policy making that often is sharply at odds with the norm of democratic accountability.

Size, Complexity, and Dispersion of the Executive Branch

The enormous expansion in the scope of federal government activities since 1933 has tremendously increased the number of agencies and the programs the agencies administer. The size of the budget and the number of federal employees indicate the magnitude of their operations. By early 1995 the proposed 1996 budget had grown to $1.6 trillion, and there were more than 2.0 million civilian and 1.5 million active duty military employees. The domestic activities of the federal government reach into every community in the nation and touch the lives of individuals from birth to death. Considerations of national security extend U.S. military and foreign policy activities around the world. It is hardly surprising that providing leadership and direction to the federal bureaucracy is a difficult task. It would be so even if the president could command prompt and unquestioning obedience from subservient departments and agencies.

The multiplicity of agencies and programs creates an additional obstacle to effective political leadership in the executive branch. The complexity that results from overlapping jurisdictions leads to duplication of efforts and complicates the president's job. It places a premium on coordination by the presidency. When he defines his goals for a policy area, the president usually does not deal with individual administrative units but with many. In outdoor recreation, for example, the Forest Service (a unit of the Agriculture Department), the National Park Service (a unit of the Interior Department), and the Army Corps of Engineers all maintain facilities for public use. Or consider the use of land owned by the federal government. Policies of the Forest Service and the Interior Department's Bureau of Land Management are sometimes in sharp conflict.

Bureaucratic complexity also stems from the interdependence of many federal activities. It is apparent that policy goals in one area are affected by objectives in other areas. The difficult trade-off between energy and environmental policies, which was acutely experienced in the 1970s, illustrates policy interdependence. Efforts to conserve energy and reduce foreign oil imports often were at variance with attempts to reduce air and water pollution. At times the Department of Energy and the Environmental Protection Agency appeared to be working at cross purposes—for example, substituting coal for oil reduced dependence on imported oil but increased problems of maintaining air quality. Housing policy decisions also illustrate interdependence. Programs that may help to increase the stock of lower middle-income housing may have undesirable consequences elsewhere. The impact of these decisions on inflation, unemployment, the environment, and racial segregation needs to be considered.

The great size of the federal bureaucracy further frustrates presidential efforts at direction and control because its activities are so widely dispersed. Presidents, their aides, and their principal political appointees are at the center of government. The people who operate programs, deliver services to individuals, and regulate the conduct of businesses and other organizations are at the periphery. These people, almost all of whom are civil servants, were there when the president and his staff took office, and they will be there after the political executives have departed. They know their programs and the pitfalls involved in administering them. They control the resources, human and material, that are needed to implement programs successfully. Their position, at the point of delivery "where programs meet people," is the source of much of their power. [7]

Another aspect of bureaucratic size and complexity that impedes presidential management is what the political scientist Paul Light labels "thickening." The addition over time of layers of management and growth in the number of presidential appointees and other senior executives at each layer have increased the height and width of the hierarchy. Consequently, "presidents have grown increasingly distant from the front lines of government, and the front lines from them." When President Clinton took office, he "faced a more complicated hierarchy than any president in history." [8]

Bureaucratic Inertia and Momentum

The executive branch, composed of multiple bureaucracies, is difficult to manage because of bureaucratic inertia. It is hard to get a new government activity started, and, once it is under way, it is even more difficult to stop or significantly change the activity. Francis Rourke cites a "celebrated law of bureaucratic inertia," which holds that "bureaucracies at rest tend to stay at rest and bureaucracies in motion tend to stay in motion." [9] Rourke attributes bureaucratic inertia to organizational routines—prescribed operating procedures that have worked successfully in the past. Another important factor contributing to bureaucratic inertia is the support of interest groups for programs that benefit them and in which they have material stake.

The aspect of bureaucratic inertia primarily responsible for presidential frustration is the momentum of ongoing programs. The degree of that momentum is revealed in the number of activities to which the government is committed by public laws, the amount of money allocated for those activities in annual appropriations, and the number of civil service and military employees who carry out the activities.[10] Mandatory expenditures that the government was obligated to make constituted about 67 percent of President Bill Clinton's proposed 1996 budget. The principal mandatory items included interest on the national debt; entitlement programs such as Social Security, Medicare, and Medicaid; federal retirement and veterans' benefits; food stamps; and unemployment compensation. Even the discretionary portion of the budget is highly resistant to cuts because of support from groups that benefit from those expenditures. Presidents can influence the shape of the federal budget, but major changes usually require several years to be implemented. From one year to the next, presidents tend to be limited to incremental changes.

Presidents, however, are often impatient to make changes. They have a fixed term of office in which to accomplish their objectives. The incremental adjustments that are possible through annual budgeting hardly seem adequate given the scope of their objectives and the time available to them. The time perspective of the bureaucracy is much different. Members of the permanent government can afford to be patient. In the budget process they fight to maintain their "base," which is their current appropriation, and to add as large an increment to it as possible.[11] Over time, successful pursuit of such a strategy results in sizable growth, as small annual increases are transformed into large permanent gains. Bureaucratic momentum thus works to the advantage of the permanent government and acts as a constraint on presidents who try to counter it. President Reagan and his successors have tried to overcome the effects of incremental budgeting by means of a top-down process that restricts total government spending and forces agencies and their congressional and interest group supporters to accept cuts or limited growth. These efforts had only limited success.[12] (The reasons are discussed in Chapter 9.)

The large number of career federal employees also commits the president to maintain ongoing programs. Major reductions in personnel or redirection of their activities are economically and politically costly. People will oppose actions that threaten to deprive them of their jobs or that require them to move, undergo additional training, or reduce their sense of security and importance. Most presidents can make only modest adjustments in the size and mission of the federal work force. President Clinton has been somewhat more successful in this regard than other modern presients. In September 1993 Vice President Al Gore presented to Clinton the final report of the National Performance Review, a task force commissioned to "reinvent government." In endorsing that report, Clinton pledged the elimination of 252,000 federal jobs over a five-year period. (Congress later increased the figure to 272,900.)[13] The 1995 budget estimated that the net reduction in full-time positions would amount to 118,300 by the end of that fiscal year.[14]

Bureaucratic Personnel

Presidents depend on political and career officials to operate the federal bureaucracy. The characteristics and roles of these political and career executives differ sharply, and the relationships between them have tended to hinder presidential direction of the implementation of policies. The political executives constitute what Hugh Heclo has called a "government of strangers." [15] Aside from cabinet officers, a few important subcabinet appointees, and the heads of major independent agencies, they are unknown to the president and to one another.

Selection of the cabinet, especially at the beginning of an administration, involves the president directly and traditionally is an attempt to build support for the administration by including representatives of various constituencies in the party and the country.[16] Cronin maintains that presidents sometimes appoint personal friends to inner cabinet departments because of the close counseling relationship involved.[17] In his study of cabinet appointments since 1861, Jeffrey Cohen found modest support for Cronin's thesis about pretenure ties between presidents and cabinet members.[18] Selection of other political executives is also affected by multiple and often conflicting pressures, such as loyalty to the president, party membership, technical competence, the wishes of the cabinet member under whom the appointee will serve, and the demands of congressional members, interest groups, and state and local party leaders.

The process through which presidents recruit people to serve in their administrations is significant as an instrument of control over policy, as a tool of administrative management, and as a major component of presidential relations with Congress, interest groups, and political parties. Consequently, it is a highly political process. Presidents since Eisenhower have used personnel staffs located in the White House to run the appointment process for them. The process has tended to be rather chaotic at the start of a new administration, because of the large number of positions to be filled, pressures for jobs from campaign workers and party members, and uncertainty about how to proceed, but it eventually becomes fairly systematic. Calvin Mackenzie, in a 1981 study of the process, concluded that presidential personnel staffs have served modern presidents well.[19]

More recent research by Thomas Weko substantiates Mackenzie's finding that centralization of appointment decisions in the Presidential Personnel Office has increased presidential control and bureaucratic responsiveness. Weko also finds, however, that there have been unintended and costly consequences of the process. It has permitted job seekers, interest groups, members of Congress, and campaign contributors to press their claims directly on the White House staff, moved into the White House conflicts that once were waged outside of it, and provoked conflict between the appointments staff and administrative units. These developments have crowded out of the appointment process the "programmatic perspectives of the departments," thus diminishing the capabilities and disrupting the "continuity and integrity of the administrative establishment."[20]

Both Weko and Mackenzie agree that the essential ingredient for effective recruitment and selection of appointees is active presidential involvement in the process and sustained presidential support for the personnel staff. Ronald Reagan excelled in this regard, whereas Richard Nixon's lack of interest contributed to his inability to establish effective control over the executive branch. The Reagan administration succeeded in filling sensitive positions with individuals loyal to the president and committed to his ideology. Its White House personnel staff exercised tight control over the recruitment of political executives.[21] Cabinet members were not permitted to conduct independent searches for sub-cabinet officials, and final approval of subordinate appointments was retained by the White House. Beginning work during the transition period, the personnel staff made ideological affinity the primary criterion for appointment. Prospective appointees were screened for policy views, political and personal backgrounds, and, if considered necessary, expertise. Although it took the Reagan administration a long time to get its political executives in place (it took the Bush and Clinton administrations even longer), the result was tighter control over the executive branch and greater cohesion within it than other modern presidents have been able to achieve.[22]

Bill Clinton's experience illustrates the difficulty that presidents encounter when they use political appointments as instruments of policy control and political leadership. To Reagan's rationale for centralization of appointments that "personnel is policy," Clinton added that it also was "in large part politics." The Clinton personnel operation had almost 300 employees during the transition and over 100 in the Presidential Personnel Office in March 1993. Its objective was to create a competent staff for the new administration that responded to the claims and demands of campaign workers and contributors and represented the diverse blocs, movements, and constituencies that had brought electoral victory. Its political success was reflected in the diversity of the appointees. That achievement, however, "strained its capacities and reputation as an instrument of policy leadership." Its preoccupation with diversity, ethical concerns, and a series of botched nominations resulted in a slowed pace of appointments that brought sharp criticism from Congress, constituency groups within the Democratic Party, and the media. Clinton's personnel staff "found it extraordinarily difficult to meet the demands from contemporary electoral politics, *and* to ensure that ... political appointments were used to achieve presidential control of the bureaucracy."[23]

The political executives chosen by the presidential appointment process often are amateurs in the precarious world of Washington politics. They lack the political knowledge and substantive skills needed to provide effective leadership in their jobs. They quickly discover their dependence on career executives and other lower-ranking civil servants for the information and advice they need to serve the president effectively. That support is not obtained without a price, however—loyalty to the agency and support for its programs within the administration, before Congress, and with the public.

By the time most political executives learn their jobs and strike a balance between the often conflicting claims of the White House and the permanent government, they will have left their positions. It is generally conceded that it takes from twelve to eighteen months for political executives to master their jobs, but their average tenure is only two years. The high rate of turnover makes it difficult to develop teamwork within departments and agencies. Cabinet secretaries are continually adapting to new subordinates, and people on the same administrative level barely get to know one another. One result is that expectations and roles are in flux, and there are problems of coordination and control.

Political executives in the bureaucracy are in a kind of twilight zone where they look upward to the president for support and direction and downward to the permanent government for support and services. In such a position they are imperfect instruments for presidential control of the bureaucracy. They can best serve the president by winning the trust of the careerists who make up the permanent government, but to do so they find it expedient to maintain a considerable degree of independence from the White House.

Career executives and other civil servants provide the institutional resources, such as political experience, substantive knowledge, and technical competence, required to accomplish an agency's mission. They are aware of political problems the agency faces and of its political resources. They have established links with its clientele and with the congressional committees that oversee it through legislative and appropriations powers. They also have a vested interest in their agencies and their programs. Their loyalties are based on norms of bureaucratic and occupational professionalism. They recognize the legitimacy of the president's position and of the claims of political executives for their support, but they will not hesitate to use their substantial capacity to resist the directives of their political superiors.

In most recent administrations, conflict has arisen between the White House and career executives. The reasons for this adversity lie in behavior patterns and perspectives that are fairly common among career executives. The relatively secure tenure of higher civil servants (as contrasted with the expendability and shorter tenure of political executives) allows them to take a more gradual approach to avoid direct confrontation and to pursue their objectives obliquely and by indirection, because such an approach is less likely to generate political opposition. In contrast, political executives tend to pursue their goals quite directly and to see virtue in conflict.

Careerists also try to avoid becoming identified with a political party or a political appointee. The civil servant must remain politically neutral to remain a civil servant; hence, he or she is cautious about political involvement. Political executives, many of whom are unfamiliar with the ways of the bureaucracy, often mistake such caution for opposition or disloyalty. This point of view is reinforced by the high value that career executives place on maintaining their relationships with clientele group representatives, congressional members and staff, and individuals outside the Washington community who are involved in or knowledgeable about their agency's programs.

Such relationships, or networks, provide information and support that help the bureaucrats be of service to their political superiors. Involvement in the networks, however, can place a strain on the career executives' relations with their superiors, who often regard civil servants' informal contacts outside the agency as evidence of disloyalty. This perspective, which is especially pronounced among members of the White House staff, is understandable, but it overlooks the importance of such relationships to the services that career executives provide.

To correct perceived deficiencies in the career service and to increase presidential control over the higher civil service, the Carter administration engineered the passage of the Civil Service Reform Act (CSRA) of 1978. The CSRA established the Senior Executive Service (SES), a professional managerial corps of career civil servants, whose members are eligible for financial bonuses. It also increased the ability of political executives to transfer career officials within and between agencies and to raise the number of noncareerists in the SES and lower positions.[24] Another provision of the CSRA replaced the three-person bipartisan Civil Service Commission with the single-headed Office of Personnel Management (OPM), which gave the president more control of the career service. Reagan's first director of the OPM, Donald J. Devine, aggressively implemented a partisan style of leadership.[25] Neither Bush nor Clinton used politicization of the career service as extensively as Reagan did to direct the executive branch.

Legal Arrangements

The ambiguous legal position of the executive branch is the fourth factor that affects a president's control over the bureaucracy. All departments and agencies are established by Congress and derive their authority to operate from statutes. Presidents do not enter into contracts, initiate projects, or make grants. Their subordinates do so, but not in response to presidential directives. It is true that presidents act through subordinates, but they do so principally through persuasion because of the nature and source of their legal authority and that of their subordinates.

Although the Constitution charges the president with responsibility for executing the laws, his legal position as chief executive is somewhat unclear because Congress has—with presidential approval—delegated authority to and imposed duties directly on various administrative officials. In some cases, such as independent regulatory commissions and the Federal Reserve Board, the president has no formal power to direct agency actions or set agency policy. His influence upon these units is based on his budgetary and appointment powers and on his persuasive abilities. For cabinet members, heads of independent agencies, and other political executives with operating authority to whom Congress has directly delegated power, the situation is ambiguous. As chief executive the president, by virtue of the "take care" clause of the Constitution, can command the decisions of his subordinates. In doing so, however, he risks confrontation with Congress and with the clientele groups and individuals affected by the administrative units involved. Also, the Supreme Court long ago ruled that the president may not interfere with the performance of a "purely ministerial" duty that does not involve the exercise of discretion or judgment.[26] Nor may the president prevent the execution of the law by subordinates.

The growth of the public bureaucracy has been accompanied by broad delegations of discretionary authority to administrative officials. Such delegations have been necessary because Congress cannot legislate in sufficient detail to cover all contingencies that may arise. Congress also has made vague and general grants of power because it finds it politically advantageous to shift difficult and potentially unpopular decisions to the bureaucracy. The Supreme Court has approved the delegation of legislative authority to the executive branch with the proviso that the delegations be accompanied by clear statutory guidelines.[27] However, the Court's insistence on specific statutory standards has seldom been followed by Congress or by the judiciary.[28] The standards the Court uses have tended to be vague and unspecific, such as "just and reasonable rates," "excess profits," and "the public interest, convenience, and necessity." In spite of judicial review of the fairness of administrative procedures and judicial reference to the legislative history of statutes as found in congressional committee hearings and reports and floor debates in Congress, administrative officials retain substantial discretionary authority that complicates the president's task of controlling the bureaucracy.

Susceptibility to External Influence

It is often observed that the federal bureaucracy is susceptible to external influence and pressure. A primary reason for this susceptibility to forces outside of individual departments, agencies, and bureaus is the inability of American political parties to provide administrative units with political support and to link party programs with the pursuit of presidential policy goals.

In contrast to "the government" in parliamentary democracies such as the United Kingdom or Canada, American presidential administrations are not integrated by ties of party loyalty and commitment to a party program. Administrations lack internal policy cohesiveness and depend on the president's personal leadership to hold them together. In the face of external criticism and pressure, executive branch units are unable to find much support within the administration. Demands on the president are extensive, his energy and attention are not unlimited, and he tends to conserve his political resources for high-priority objectives.

If presidential support for an agency is lacking, the agency must look elsewhere for help in maintaining its authority, funding, and personnel. It looks to the public for support, especially among the individuals and groups who are affected by its programs, and it looks to Congress, particularly to the committees or subcommittees with jurisdiction over its legislative authorizations and its appropriations.

The regulations that agencies promulgate and enforce, or the benefits and services they deliver, provide the basis for the development of enduring ties between them and their clientele groups. An agency without a well-organized clientele is in a precarious position. Clientele groups can publicize an agency's accomplishments and defend it against attack. In exchange, the agency administers its programs with a manifest concern for the interests of the clientele. The agency consults with clientele group officials and with individual notables who are attentive to its activities. Such outsiders often are invited to participate in agency decision making. They do so by serving on advisory councils and panels and through informal personal contacts. Agencies seldom perform acts such as drafting guidelines and regulations or awarding grants without extensive external participation and consultation. There is also a two-way flow of personnel between agencies and their clientele organizations. These mutually beneficial relations between agencies and their clientele are characteristic of most domestic policy areas in the federal government.

Washington has countless examples of these relationships. The National Education Association (NEA) and several other education interest groups provide support and protection to the Department of Education in exchange for access and information. The NEA led the congressional effort to elevate the former U.S. Office of Education to departmental status in 1979 and the battle to prevent the abolition of the fledgling department during the Reagan administration. Over the years several Department of Education political executives have found employment with the NEA and other education interest groups after leaving the government. On occasion, those lobbies have helped to recruit or have provided personnel to staff the agency.

Agencies also find it easy and convenient to develop strong ties to the congressional committees or subcommittees with which they deal. Committee members usually receive immediate attention and preferential treatment from agency personnel. Congressional requests for consideration on appointments and grants, suggestions concerning program administration, and inquiries on behalf of constituents are quickly acknowledged. Congressional influence with the agencies strengthens the committee members in their constituencies.[29] Bureaucrats use their connections with congressional committee members to effect changes in their statutory authority and gain favorable treatment during budget negotiations. Agencies may use their committee ties to obtain more funds than the president has recommended for them or to modify their activities in a way that is not fully in accord with presidential preferences.

Agencies are not, however, totally resistant to presidential directives, nor is it in their interest to be so. Agencies frequently need presidential support and attention. Moreover, they often find that their interests coincide with those of the president. Agencies and the president need each other to accomplish their goals. If the true test of a president's power is his power to persuade, one of the best measures of an agency's strength is the degree to which a president must "bargain with it in order to secure its cooperation."[30]

The President and the Cabinet

Most modern presidents have come to office determined to make more extensive use of the cabinet as a collective decision-making body than the previous incumbent did. The public has tended to applaud candidates' pledges that the cabinet will play a major role in their administrations. Yet, with the exception of Dwight Eisenhower, presidents have not used their cabinets as vehicles of collective leadership. Moreover, they have experienced strained relationships with many individual cabinet members.

This gap between expectation and experience suggests that there is a widespread lack of understanding of the cabinet on the part of the public and most political leaders. In point of fact, the Constitution places executive authority, ultimately, in the president alone. The notion of collective or collegial leadership is incompatible with constitutional reality and inconsistent with American practice. The president is not first among equals; he is explicitly "number one," the person in charge. Cabinet members are the president's appointees, and they serve at his pleasure. He has no obligation to consult them as a group or, when he does so, to act according to their wishes. The cabinet has no formal constitutional or legal standing. It exists by custom, and presidents are free to use it as little or as much as they see fit.

The fact that the cabinet has seldom been a high-level decision-making body does not mean that it lacks political significance. It has great symbolic value as a means of representing major social, economic, and political constituencies in the highest councils of the administration.[31] Newly elected presidents try to select cabinet members whose presence will unify those constituencies behind him and his administration.

As noted previously, in selecting cabinet members, presidents have used criteria such as prior political experience, identification with politically significant groups, and technical expertise. There is no dominant criterion, but Nelson Polsby found in a study of the Nixon and Carter cabinets that presidents tend initially to select cabinets that are broadly representative and whose members can speak for clientele groups and party constituencies.[32] This observation characterized Bill Clinton's initial cabinet appointments *(see Table 6-1)*. Clinton's cabinet at the start of his second term reflected a much greater emphasis on experience than representation.

Presidents face constraints in selecting cabinet members. Appointees to head some departments, such as Agriculture, generally must be acceptable to clientele groups. In choosing the secretaries of Defense and Treasury, presidents may give weight to their expertise and experience. Generalist administrators, however, often are named to head the departments of Commerce, Health and Human Services, Housing and Urban Development, and Transportation.

Presidents often try to use the cabinet as a decision-making body early in their administrations, but most of them eventually abandon the effort.[33] They find that most cabinet members are concerned primarily with issues that affect their departments and with their personal relationships with the president. There is often competition between cabinet members for the president's attention, and personality clashes within the cabinet are not infrequent. Under these circumstances, cabinet

Table 6-1   Initial Clinton Cabinet Appointments by Criteria of Appointment

	Political experience	Clientele or ethnic group identification	Technical expertise	Pre-tenure friendship
INNER CABINET				
Defense				
Les Aspin	✓		✓	
Justice				
Janet Reno		✓	✓	
State				
Warren M. Christopher	✓		✓	
Treasury				
Lloyd Bentsen	✓		✓	
OUTER CABINET				
Agriculture				
Mike Espy	✓	✓		
Commerce				
Ronald H. Brown	✓	✓		
Education				
Richard W. Riley	✓			✓
Energy				
Hazel O'Leary		✓	✓	
Health and Human Services				
Donna E. Shalala		✓		✓
Housing and Urban Development				
Henry G. Cisneros	✓	✓		
Interior				
Bruce Babbitt	✓			
Labor				
Robert B. Reich			✓	✓
Transportation				
Federico Peña	✓	✓		
Veterans Affairs				
Jesse Brown		✓		
CABINET-LEVEL POSITIONS				
EPA Administrator				
Carol M. Browner	✓	✓	✓	
OMB Director				
Leon E. Panetta	✓		✓	
United Nations Ambassador				
Madeleine K. Albright		✓	✓	
U.S. Trade Representative				
Michael Kantor		✓		

meetings are unsatisfactory devices for focused, analytical discussion of major issues. At best they can serve as forums for informal discussion of issues and problems and for the exchange of information. The crucial factor limiting the role of the cabinet is the absence of any integrating force within the administration other than the president. The weakness of political parties in the governing process and the president's preeminent constitutional and political position combine to make him the only source of cohesion and policy coordination. Individual cabinet members feel loyal to the president *and* to the permanent governments within their departments. These conflicting loyalties inhibit the development of an informal sense of unity and purpose without which the cabinet cannot realize its potential as a formal advisory body and policy-making mechanism.[34]

Although it may be an overstatement to assert, as did Charles G. Dawes, the first director of the Bureau of the Budget, that departmental and clientele pressures make cabinet members "natural enemies" of the president, there is an unavoidable tension in their relationship that constitutes a great dilemma for him.[35] No president can function effectively if cabinet members regularly choose departmental over presidential interests. However, cabinet members who display unquestioning responsiveness to the president's desires and are insensitive to the needs and concerns of their departments jeopardize their capacity to implement his policies effectively. Furthermore, cabinet members are not fully in command of their departments. The strongest clientele pressures are applied to the bureaus that administer programs, not to the department heads. Cabinet members deal with their bureaus mainly through persuasion, and the source of their strength is access to the president and presidential support. Presidents and presidential aides who fail to give cabinet members support and who expect quick and complete obedience to White House directives almost ensure the ineffectiveness of the cabinet members, as well as their own frustration.

Presidents frequently have developed strong, positive relationships with individual cabinet members and, through them, with their departments, but there is no guarantee that this will happen. A personality conflict between the president and a cabinet member or antipathy on the part of the White House staff can prevent such a development. There is a tendency in most administrations for one or two cabinet members to stand out and to develop close ties with the president. During Reagan's second term, Attorney General Edwin Meese III and Secretary of the Treasury James A. Baker III enjoyed considerable leeway to pursue their own agendas without aggressive interference from the White House staff, provided they did not conflict with the president's ideological precepts.[36] In the Bush administration James Baker (State), Robert A. Mosbacher (Commerce), and Nicholas F. Brady (Treasury), all old friends of the president, enjoyed high standing with him.[37] During the Persian Gulf crisis of 1990–1991, Secretary of Defense Richard Cheney also emerged as a major figure. In contrast to the general pattern, no single member dominated the Clinton cabinet. But Treasury Secretary Lloyd Bentsen, who had been a powerful Democratic senator and who served until late 1994, enjoyed independent political stature. Clinton's cabinet did not work effectively as a unit, but its members acted individually, in Washington and throughout the country, as advocates for the administration's policy goals.[38]

Whatever the variations in relations between individual presidents and their cabinet members, there has been a tendency for modern presidents to develop close ties with the heads of the departments of State, Defense, Treasury, and Justice. Cronin refers to these as the "inner cabinet" departments because their activities and responsibilities are of the highest priority—national security, the condition of the economy, civil rights, and the administration of justice—and because they cut across the concerns of the public and all members of Congress. These matters tend to dominate the president's time and attention.[39] Inner cabinet members, therefore, almost always have direct, frequent, and continuing contact with the president.

The heads of the other departments—Agriculture, Commerce, Education, Energy, Health and Human Services, Housing and Urban Development, Interior, Labor, Transportation, and Veterans Affairs—constitute the "outer cabinet."[40] Their departments have more sharply focused activities. Outer cabinet members, subjected to strong clientele and congressional pressures, find themselves acting as advocates for those interests within the administration.[41] Frequently, those pressures conflict with the president's broader priorities.

Because of the diversity and scope of department activities and the particular orientations of some cabinet members, presidents generally have looked to sources other than the cabinet for policy advice. The inner cabinet reflects top policy priorities. Presidents have additional sources of advice in these areas in the Executive Office of the President. Since its creation in 1947, the National Security Council (NSC) and its staff have been used extensively by presidents to coordinate the making and execution of foreign and military policy *(see Chapter 10)*. In the important areas of economic policy, presidents work closely with the chair of the Council of Economic Advisers, the director of the Office of Management and Budget (OMB), the secretary of the Treasury, and the chair of the Federal Reserve Board *(Chapter 9)*. In the domestic policy areas, which involve primarily the outer cabinet departments, domestic policy staffs and OMB have provided assistance to the president in policy formulation *(Chapter 8)*, and cabinet committees, interagency committees, and policy councils have been employed to coordinate policy making and implementation.

Cabinet committees, which are usually appointed on an ad hoc basis to handle specific problems, can focus quickly on them and attempt to develop solutions. Their usefulness for long-term monitoring of policy implementation is limited, however, by other demands on their members and by the tendency of their operations to become routine and to lose flexibility. Interagency committees, which operate mostly at the agency and subcabinet levels, may achieve a measure of coordination, but their work is often hampered by competition between agencies and by their lack of status and visibility.

Presidents also have used policy councils to highlight particular problems. Before the Reagan administration, most policy councils, other than the NSC, had more symbolic value than operational utility to presidents in their management of the executive branch. In his first term Reagan invested heavily in the cabinet council approach. He established seven councils in addition to the NSC: commerce and trade, economic affairs, energy and natural resources, food and agriculture, human resources, legal policy, and management and administration. The theory behind the cabinet council system was that issues would move upward through the full cabinet to the president for decision. Over time, it became apparent that the system was unduly cumbersome, and for his second term Reagan reduced the number of cabinet councils to two. The remaining councils—the Economic Policy Council and the Domestic Policy Council—had more clearly defined jurisdictions and lines of authority.

President Bush continued to utilize the Economic Policy Council and the Domestic Policy Council, but with apparently limited effectiveness. Early in 1992, amid reports of "squabbling over domestic policy and rivalries among policy makers," Secretary of Transportation Samuel Skinner replaced John Sununu as White House chief of staff and Secretary of Agriculture Clayton Yeutter was named to the new post of counselor for domestic policy and charged with "centralizing what had been a diffuse policy-making apparatus." [42] Yeutter was not effective in managing domestic policy and left the White House in August 1992.

Clinton began his presidency with three policy staff units in the White House: the National Economic Council, the Domestic Policy Council, and the Office of Environmental Policy, headed by a presidential assistant or deputy assistant.[43] In addition, there were three high-level individuals with access to the president: the senior adviser for policy development, Ira Magaziner; the senior adviser for policy and strategy, George Stephanopoulos; and the First Lady, who chaired the task force that developed the administration's health care reform proposal. The fragmentation of advice that this structure produced reflected Clinton's desire to be at the center of an informal, collegial policy-making process, which he ran like a continuous seminar.[44] With respect to selling and implementing his policy choices, however, Clinton preferred a more formal structure.[45]

Presidential Control of the Bureaucracy

The preceding analysis of presidential relations with the cabinet and the bureaucracy has revealed that presidents encounter obstacles to control of policy making and implementation. Presidents are not, however, without resources for this effort. They have substantial powers granted by the Constitution, delegated by Congress, and derived from the nature of their office. The most important are the powers to appoint and remove subordinates, to issue executive orders, and to prepare the annual federal budget and regulate expenditures.

Appointment and Removal

The essential powers for presidential control of the bureaucracy are the powers to appoint and remove subordinate officials. As critical as these powers are to the president's executive responsibilities, however, they are subject to limitation by Congress.[46] The Constitution gives the president broad powers of appointment (Article II, Section 2, paragraph 2), but it makes high-ranking officials subject to senatorial confirmation, and it authorizes Congress to vest the appointment of lower officials in the president, in department heads, or in the courts. Congress determines whether an appointment to a position must be confirmed by the Senate. In addition, it can narrow the president's discretion in making appointments by establishing detailed qualifications for various offices. Congress cannot, however, give itself the power to appoint executive officials.[47] Neither can it force the president to make an appointment to a vacant position.[48] The president's appointive powers also are constrained by political considerations and practices such as senatorial courtesy, whereby the president gives the senators of his own party a veto over certain administrative and judicial appointments in the states.

The Senate generally has given presidents considerable leeway in the appointment of top-level political executives, but confirmation is not automatic, and the Senate has used rejections to express disapproval of specific individuals or of particular practices.[49] Since the Watergate scandal of 1972–1974, the Senate has tended to be more careful and procedurally consistent in examining the backgrounds, qualifications, and relevant policy views of presidential nominees. However, the confirmation process has "become more tedious, time-consuming, and intrusive for the nominees." [50]

The Constitution also empowers the president to make appointments when the Senate is in recess. Such appointments must be confirmed by the end of the Senate's next session, but in the interim the appointee continues to serve. Senators often object to recess appointments to high-level positions because they feel inhibited from thoroughly examining people who have already begun their duties. Because Congress now remains in session most of the year, however, presidents have fewer opportunities to make recess appointments.

The removal power is the logical complement of the appointment power. The ability to remove subordinate officials on performance or policy grounds is fundamental to presidential control of the executive branch. Without the removal power, the president cannot be held fully responsible for the actions of his subordinates or for failure of departments and agencies to achieve his objectives. The Constitution is silent, however, concerning the removal of executive officials other than through impeachment, a cumbersome process that is limited to instances of "bribery, treason, and other high crimes and misdemeanors."

Presidents have clashed with Congress over the removal power. The post–Civil War conflict between President Andrew Johnson and Congress over reconstruction policy involved the removal power. In 1867 Congress brought impeachment proceedings against Johnson for violating the Tenure of Office Act, which it had passed over his veto. That statute authorized all persons appointed with the advice and consent of the Senate to continue to hold office until the president appointed and the Senate confirmed a successor. Although Johnson survived the impeachment trial by one vote, the issue of the removal power remained unresolved. (Congress repealed the Tenure of Office Act in 1887.)

The Supreme Court dealt directly with the removal power in a decision involving a challenge to President Woodrow Wilson's summary removal of a postmaster.[51] The Court invalidated an 1876 law that required senatorial consent for the removal of postmasters. It held that the Constitution gave the president the removal power and that Congress could not place restrictions on its exercise. Nine years later, however, the Court upheld the provisions of the Federal Trade Commission Act, which limited the grounds for removal of its members.[52] The Court ruled that the president's unqualified power of removal is limited to "purely executive offices" and that Congress may prescribe conditions for the removal of officials performing "quasi-legislative" and "quasi-judicial" functions. However, the Court has not clarified fully the meaning of these terms. One of the most dramatic instances of the removal power occurred in August 1981 when President Reagan fired 11,400 striking members of the Professional Air Traffic Controllers Organization. A U.S. court of appeals upheld the action, interpreting it as a discharge of the president's obligation to enforce a statute prohibiting strikes by federal employees.[53]

Although there are some statutory and judicial restrictions on the removal power, its precise limits remain somewhat undefined. Moreover, the president may be able through informal means to force officials from office for reasons other than statutory cause. The president can call publicly for an official's resignation, or he may revoke authority he has delegated to an official as a means of indicating displeasure and lack of confidence. Secretary of Defense Les Aspin resigned under pressure from the White House staff in November 1993. Aspin had come under sharp criticism in Congress and the media following the deaths in August 1993 of eighteen U.S. servicemen who were part of the United Nations peacekeeping force in Somalia. Prior to that incident he had rejected a request from the military for additional equipment for the peacekeepers.[54] Clinton fired Surgeon General Jocelyn Elders in December 1994 after she suggested publicly that sex education should include instruction in masturbation.

Executive Orders

Under a strict interpretation of separation of powers, the president has no direct legislative authority. From the beginnings of the Republic, however, presidents have issued orders and directives on the basis of Article II. Most modern presidents have followed Theodore Roosevelt's "stewardship" theory of executive power, which holds that Article II confers on them inherent power to take whatever actions they deem necessary in the national interest unless prohibited from doing so by the Constitution or by law. Executive orders have been a primary means of exercising this broad presidential prerogative power.

It is generally recognized that to have the force of law, executive orders must find their authority in the Constitution or in an act of Congress. As noted, the Supreme Court has upheld delegations of legislative power to the executive branch provided Congress establishes "intelligible" standards to guide administrative officials in the exercise of their authority.[55] In reviewing challenges to statutory delegations, however, the Court has consistently adopted a presumption in favor of statutes authorizing executive action by order or rule.

Executive orders have played a major role in presidential policy making. Presidents have used them in crucial areas such as civil rights, economic stabilization, and national security. In the realm of civil rights Franklin Roosevelt established a Fair Employment Practices Commission in 1943 to prevent discriminatory hiring by government agencies and military suppliers. In 1948 Truman ended segregation in the armed forces by executive order. Shortly after taking office, John Kennedy in March 1961 issued a sweeping order creating the Equal Employment Opportunity Commission and giving it broad enforcement powers. Lyndon Johnson went even further, requiring by executive order preferential hiring of minorities by government contractors. Following passage of the Civil Rights Act of 1964, presidential orders involving civil rights declined, but before that landmark statute, presidents used executive orders to make policy in a sensitive area in which Congress was unable or unwilling to act.

Roosevelt established broad precedents for the use of executive orders to achieve economic stability. During World War II he issued executive orders to establish the Office of Price Administration (OPA) and the Office of Economic Stabilization and to give them extensive powers over prices, wages, and profits. The OPA also rationed scarce consumer goods such as meat, butter, sugar, shoes, automobile tires, and gasoline. As a basis for his actions Roosevelt cited his responsibility as president to respond to the "unlimited emergency" created by the war. The Emergency Price Control Act of 1942 provided retroactive statutory endorsement for the establishment of the emergency agencies and the measures implemented by them.

In 1970, in the face of persistent inflation, Congress passed the Economic Stabilization Act, which authorized the president to issue orders that would control wages and prices, but with few criteria to guide these actions. On August 15, 1971, President Nixon issued an executive order imposing a ninety-day freeze on nonagricultural wages and prices and establishing the Cost of Living Council to administer the controls. A subsequent order, issued October 15, extended the controls and established additional machinery to aid in administering them. A legal challenge to the statute, as an unconstitutional delegation of unbridled authority, failed before a U.S. district court.[56] The court found that Congress had considered the statute carefully and concluded that the president needed extensive discretion to deal with inflation. The court decided that the delegation was therefore reasonable, and it stated that experience in administering previous price control statutes, passed in 1942 and 1950, furnished implicit standards for guidance in implementing the 1970 law.

President Reagan used an executive order early in his first term to establish a comprehensive program to oversee the issuance of regulations by departments, agencies, and independent regulatory commissions. The order, which formally implemented Reagan's commitment to administrative deregulation, created the President's Task Force on Regulatory Relief, set up the Office of Information and Regulatory Affairs in OMB, and required that all regulations meet a uniform cost-benefit standard "to the extent permitted by law."[57]

President Clinton issued an executive order shortly after taking office to reverse a Bush administration policy that he had criticized in the campaign. He ended the prohibition against doctors at federally funded clinics providing advice and information about abortions.[58]

Presidents also have used executive orders in pursuit of national security. In 1942, for example, Roosevelt ordered the internment of all persons of Japanese ancestry living in the Pacific coastal states, 70,000 of whom were U.S. citizens. The Supreme Court upheld this massive deprivation of basic civil liberties on the basis of the commander-in-chief clause.[59] During the Korean War, however, the Supreme Court invalidated Truman's seizure of the steel industry on the grounds that he had not used the machinery established in the Taft-Hartley Act of 1947 to avert a strike.[60]

From 1932 until 1983 Congress exerted a measure of control over executive lawmaking through use of the legislative veto. Provisions added to certain statutes gave Congress the power to review and reject executive orders or administrative regulations authorized by the legislation. The legislative veto took various forms. It allowed disapproval of regulations by concurrent resolution, or by simple resolution of either house, or by action of a committee of either house. In its most common form, the legislative veto required that the proposed action lie before Congress for a specified period—usually sixty or ninety days—during which either chamber could disapprove it. The president's reorganization authority, which Congress first authorized in 1939, carried such a procedure. Other major statutes that contained a form of legislative veto include the War Powers Resolution of 1973, the Budget and Impoundment Control Act of 1974, the Federal Elections Campaign Act of 1974, and the National Emergencies Act of 1976. In all, more than 250 statutes provided for some type of legislative veto before the Supreme Court invalidated it in 1983.

The Court held, in *Immigration and Naturalization Service v. Chadha,* the one-house legislative veto provision of the Immigration and Nationality Act to be unconstitutional.[61] The Court reasoned that the veto involved "the exercise of legislative power" without "bicameral passage followed by presentment to the President." Initial reaction to *Chadha* was that it was not a definitive ruling and that somehow Congress would find a way statutorily to control executive branch lawmaking.[62] The Court's ruling in *Chadha* appears to have invalidated the use of resolutions by one or both houses of Congress to disapprove an executive action on the basis of delegated power. Committee vetoes also are invalid, but since *Chadha,* Congress has enacted more than 200 new legislative veto provisions, most of which require agencies to obtain approval from the appropriations committees. In addition, it has made extensive use of informal nonstatutory agreements with agencies.[63] Arrangements between committees and agencies are not binding, but executive branch officials observe them because Congress can revoke the discretionary authority that it has delegated.

In addition to the persistence of de facto committee vetoes, Congress has employed a device, the joint resolution of approval, that accomplishes the purpose of the legislative veto and is compatible with the *Chadha* ruling. Instead of providing that an executive action will become effective unless Congress acts to disapprove it by joint resolution—in which case the president may exercise his veto—the resolution of approval requires passage of a joint resolution before an action can be taken.[64] For example, the Reorganization Act Amendments of 1984 provide that a presidentially prepared reorganization plan submitted to Congress cannot take effect unless approved by a joint resolution within ninety days. This provision places the burden on the president rather than on Congress, and the president has only a specific number of days in which to act. In effect, the joint resolution of approval works like a one-house legislative veto: if either house refuses to approve an action, it cannot be taken. The major disadvantage of the device for Congress is that it requires much time, and extensive use of it would threaten the congressional agenda with legislative gridlock.

Presidents and Money

Presidents have substantial financial powers, delegated by Congress, which they use in their efforts to control the bureaucracy. The most important of these is the power to formulate the budget, which controls the amount of spending by federal departments and agencies. It also establishes the president's spending priorities, sets the timing of program initiatives, and distributes rewards to and imposes sanctions on executive branch units.[65] By controlling the total amount of the budget, the president can attempt to influence the performance of the economy *(see Chapter 9)*.

Presidential use of the executive budget is a twentieth-century development. The enormous increase in expenditures during World War I, and the task of managing the sizable national debt that resulted, convinced Congress of the need for an executive budget. The Budget and Accounting Act of 1921 made the president responsible for compiling department and agency estimates and for submitting them annually to Congress in the form of a budget. The statute established the Bureau of the Budget (BOB), located in the Treasury Department, to assist the president in assembling and revising these estimates. The departments and agencies were prohibited from submitting their requests directly to Congress as they had done previously.

The initial emphasis in the development of the federal budget process was on the control of expenditures and the prevention of administrative abuses.[66] The focus of the budget was on objects of expenditure, that is, the personnel, supplies, and equipment needed to operate each agency. During the New Deal period, in the 1930s, the emphasis shifted from control to management. The budget was seen as a means of evaluating and improving administrative performance. The focus of the budget also shifted from objects of expenditure to the work and activities of departments and agencies. The transfer of BOB in 1939 from the Treasury Department to the new Executive Office of the President symbolized the management orientation. BOB was to become the president's management arm. A decade later, upon recommendation of the Hoover Commission, the government adopted a performance budget organized by functions and activities rather than by line items representing objects of expenditure.

The third and current stage in the development of budgeting is its orientation toward planning. This emphasis attempts to link annual budgeting, geared to the appropriations process in Congress, to long-range planning of government objectives. The focus is on the relationship of long-term policy goals to current and future spending decisions. The limited success of the planning orientation is reflected in the rapid arrival and departure of budgeting systems, such as the program planning budgeting system (PPBS) and zero-base budgeting (ZBB).[67] The traditional budgeting process, as it had developed by the early 1970s, embodied all three orientations, but it was least effective as a planning device.

The limitations of the executive budget as an aid to presidential decision making stem from the incremental nature of the traditional budget process and from restrictions and conditions imposed by Congress. Budgeting is inherently incremental because it is done annually. The budget cycle forces the president and Congress to act according to a timetable that stretches from twenty-two months before the start of the fiscal year (October 1) through the ensuing year. Decision makers in Congress and the bureaucracy are concerned primarily with how large an increase or decrease will be made in a department's or agency's budget. Since the mid-1980s, the advent of huge federal deficits accompanied by strong public resistance to tax increases have caused presidential and congressional budget decisions to be focused primarily on reducing spending.

Congress makes its own budget decisions and is not bound by the president's requests. It limits total spending through resolutions proposed by the budget committees in each house. Although the congressional budget total is usually fairly close to the president's, the priorities in the two budgets often differ sharply. In the 1970s Congress quarreled bitterly with Nixon and Ford over spending for domestic programs and, as already noted, in the 1980s it squared off with Reagan over the size of the deficits in his proposed budgets and the role of spending cuts and tax increases in reducing them. In the early 1990s it continued these battles with Bush.

Bill Clinton encountered the constraints imposed by deficit politics when he attempted to use his first budget as a vehicle for policy change.[68] Although Congress narrowly (with no Republican support) accepted most of his five-year plan (1994–1998) to reduce the deficit by almost $500 billion—one-third through tax increases and two-thirds through spending cuts—it embarrassed Clinton by rejecting a $16 billion package to stimulate the economy.[69] In 1995 the first Republican-controlled Congress in forty years ignored the administration's budget, which did not contain proposals for eventually eliminating the deficit, and adopted a budget resolution that projected a balanced budget in fiscal year 2002.

The fiscal stress that the government experienced beginning in the mid-1970s has led to adjustments in the budget process designed to reduce pressures for increased spending and to enhance restraint. Among the major adjustments are norms or targets imposed from the top down, baseline budgeting, and multi-year budgeting. The baseline assumes no changes in budget policy and extrapolates revenue and expenditure trends. Underlying the projections is the message that unless cutbacks are made, future spending deficits will be excessive.[70] Baseline budgeting reorients the process from increments to cutbacks. Multi-year budgets also have been redirected from plans for growth of programs and expenditures to devices for averting them.[71] These adaptations have not been overly successful, however, and pressures to protect and increase spending remain strong.

In addition to budgeting, presidents have certain discretionary spending powers that increase their leverage over the bureaucracy. They have substantial nonstatutory authority, based on understandings with congressional appropriations committees, to transfer funds within an appropriation and from one program to another. The committees expect to be kept informed of such "reprogramming" actions.[72] Fund transfer authority is essential to sound financial management, but it can be abused to circumvent congressional decisions. In 1970, for example, Nixon transferred funds to support an extensive unauthorized covert military operation in Cambodia. Nevertheless, Congress has given presidents and certain agencies the authority to spend substantial amounts of money on a confidential basis, the largest and most controversial of which are for intelligence activities.

Presidents also have exercised some measure of expenditure control through the practice of impounding or returning appropriated funds to the Treasury. Since George Washington, presidents have routinely impounded funds as a means of achieving savings when expenditures fall short of appropriations.[73] They also have withheld funds when authorized or directed to do so by Congress for purposes such as establishing contingency reserves or imposing a ceiling on total expenditures. Presidents from FDR through Lyndon Johnson also impounded some of the funds that Congress had added, over their objections, for various programs. Although such actions often drew congressional criticism, they did not lead to confrontation because they occurred infrequently and were generally focused on expenditures for specific programs or projects. Congress recognized that circumspect use of impoundments helped its members to resist strong pressures for increased spending.[74]

Impoundment became a major constitutional issue during the Nixon administration. Sweeping impoundments in domestic program areas, especially agriculture, housing, and water pollution control, led to charges that the president arbitrarily and illegally had substituted his spending priorities for those of Congress. What distinguished the Nixon impoundments from those of earlier administrations was their "magnitude, severity, and belligerence." [75] Specifically, Nixon's impoundments differed from those of other presidents in several ways: they involved larger amounts; some were made in direct violation of explicit congressional instructions to spend the funds; some were designed to terminate entire programs rather than individual projects; and some were directed at appropriated funds that had not been included in the president's budget proposals. Moreover, Nixon claimed constitutional rather than statutory authority for impoundment.[76] He used impoundments as the primary weapon in a battle with Congress over domestic spending priorities. He did not bargain or negotiate over them but imposed his priorities by fiat.

Nixon's actions resulted in lawsuits to compel release of the funds, most of which were decided against the president on statutory grounds. Congress also passed the Budget and Impoundment Control Act of 1974. The Antideficiency Act of 1950 had limited the purposes of impoundments to establishing contingency reserves and the saving of money that otherwise would be wasted. The 1974 statute established procedures for congressional review by requiring that the president report all impoundments to Congress. Proposals to rescind appropriated funds, that is, to return them to the Treasury, must be approved by both houses within forty-five days. Proposals to defer spending to the next fiscal year could be disapproved by either house.

The Supreme Court's ruling invalidating the legislative veto affected congressional power to control deferrals. (Since the 1974 legislation called for approval of recisions by both houses, *Chadha* did not invalidate that procedure.) But the only way left for Congress to overturn a deferral is to pass a bill or joint resolution. Because such a measure is subject to presidential veto, the president's deferral power is strengthened. Congress's most effective way to circumvent a possible veto is to attach a rider canceling the deferral to an appropriation bill that the president feels compelled to sign in order to keep the involved agencies operating. But riders are a cumbersome device. When Reagan began to defer sizable amounts ($5.4 billion for fiscal 1986) in his second term as a means of reducing spending on programs he opposed, Congress found itself without a viable means of controlling the deferrals.[77]

Presidential Management of the Bureaucracy

In addition to their formal powers, modern presidents have relied on managerial tools in their ongoing efforts to coordinate and direct executive branch operations. Three major tools—staffing, reorganization, and planning—have been employed with mixed results. The limited success of presidential efforts to manage the federal bureaucracy more effectively stems primarily from the political character of the administration of the executive branch. This branch is not a tightly structured hierarchy in which the president is supreme and officials at all levels act in response to directives from above. As noted previously, the president must rely more on persuasion than command to achieve his objectives, and departments and agencies have substantial autonomy. This is not to argue that the public sector is inhospitable to modern management techniques, but to suggest that their use is significantly affected by political forces.[78]

Staffing

Unquestionably, staffing is crucial to presidential management of the bureaucracy. As discussed in Chapter 4, the institutionalized presidency has grown steadily as presidents have turned to staff support as a means of discharging their many roles and of directing the executive branch. The roles of presidential staff in program implementation and of the cabinet in advising the president have varied in recent administrations, but the tendency has been toward reliance on a strong, sizable, and centralized White House staff to protect the political interests of the president, to act as his principal policy advisers, and to direct (as opposed to monitor and coordinate) the implementation of his priorities by the bureaucracy.

Critics of this structure argue that it has undercut the advisory potential of the cabinet, narrowed the president's perspective on policy choices, and inhibited effective and responsive bureaucratic performance. Stephen Hess cautions that reliance on a centralized White House staff has been "self-defeating."[79] Experience under Nixon and Reagan supports this view. Yet, Ford and Carter both tried a decentralized model of White House staffing and abandoned it in favor of hierarchical arrangements.

President Bush adopted the hierarchical model of White House organization at the start of his administration. His chief of staff, former New Hampshire governor John Sununu, maintained tight control over

White House operations, at times with a heavy hand. He functioned as the guardian of the president's political interests, serving as Bush's link to conservatives, and he often appeared to have set the administration's course on domestic social policy issues. In these roles, he was the target of considerable congressional and media criticism.[80] As that criticism extended to Sununu's ostentatious use of White House "perks," such as taking a White House car and chauffeur to attend a New York stamp auction, he became a political liability to the president. Bush replaced Sununu in late 1991. Samuel Skinner, the new chief of staff, brought in several new people and ran the office less despotically than his predecessor, but experienced difficulty in asserting and maintaining control.[81]

The Clinton White House reflected the leadership style of a highly intelligent, energetic, enthusiastic, and enormously self-confident president who lacked self-discipline, assumed large numbers of personal responsibilities, had difficulty focusing his goals and managing his efforts, and was reluctant to delegate tasks to others.[82] Clinton entered office with no plan for organizing the White House and proceeded to staff it largely with consultants who had worked on his campaign and friends and political associates from Arkansas.[83] The chief of staff, Thomas F. McLarty III, was a public utility executive whom Clinton had known since childhood.

The initial White House staff lacked the Washington experience and political stature that might have prevented damaging early missteps such as the botched nominations of Zoe Baird and Kimba Wood to be attorney general, the conflict with Congress over ending discrimination against gays in the military, and the defeat of the economic stimulus bill. Even the appointment of David Gergen (a veteran of the Reagan and Bush White Houses), in May 1993, failed to prevent further political damage or lead to a more effective organization. In January 1994, the journalist Burt Solomon described an "amorphously organized" Clinton White House in which a "muddled management structure" did business through a "snarl of networks" that included the consultants, the Arkansans, a group centered on Vice President Gore, and one that included Gergen and several aides whom the Clintons had met at Renaissance Weekend (annual meritocratic retreats held at Hilton Head, South Carolina).[84]

The replacement of McLarty with Leon Panetta, the director of OMB, on June 27, 1994, brought some much-needed order to the Clinton White House. Panetta established control over the flow of communications and personal access to the president.[85] A greater degree of centralization and formal organization proved to be an operational necessity to counteract Clinton's lack of discipline. Clinton also demonstrated the ability to recognize his failings and take corrective action.

White House staff personnel at the start of Clinton's second term were more pragmatic and less ideological and had more Washington experience than their first term counterparts.[86] This reflected the modest centrist agenda on which he had successfully campaigned.

Since the Reagan administration, the presidency has become increasingly centralized and politicized. Terry Moe defends these developments as an inescapable consequence of the extensive expectations that impinge upon the presidency.[87] A similar conclusion emerged from a 1986 symposium featuring eight former White House chiefs of staff (or their functional equivalents) who served presidents from Eisenhower through Carter. In their view, "the demands for activism and the requirements of self-reliance encourage presidents to look favorably upon the kinds of services provided by a rationalized White House run by a strong chief." [88]

Reorganization

[It has been almost an article of faith among political leaders and public administration theorists that executive reorganization can increase presidential power over the bureaucracy.]Johnson, Nixon, and especially Carter had strong convictions that the performance of the executive branch could be improved and the bureaucracy brought to heel through changes in administrative structure.(Yet by most accounts, the results of Carter's reorganization efforts were modest.[89]

Organizational structure and administrative arrangements are significant because they reflect values and priorities and because they affect access to decision makers. The location and status of an administrative unit—as a department, an independent agency, or a component of a department—symbolize the importance of its goals and the interests it serves. Administrative arrangements also can contribute to or frustrate the achievement of accountability to Congress and the public. Reorganizing, however, does not necessarily result in increased efficiency of operation, greater program effectiveness, or enhanced public accountability. This is true because there is no ideal form for a government agency or a consistent set of prescriptions for organizing the executive branch. One set of standard prescriptions tends to centralize authority and another tends to disperse it. More important, the most profound consequences of organizational change are not in the "engineered realm of efficiency, simplicity, size, and cost of government"; rather, they lie in the areas of "political influence, policy emphasis, and communication of governmental intentions." [90] For example, the placement of the Occupational Safety and Health Administration in the Department of Labor rather than in the Department of Health, Education and Welfare led to an initial focus of regulations on mechanical rather than on biological hazards in the workplace. Experience has shown that although the rationale for reorganization is couched in the rhetoric of economy and efficiency, the crucial factors in decisions to reorganize are power, policy, and symbolic significance.

In 1939 Congress authorized presidents to propose executive reorganization plans that take effect after sixty days unless disapproved by both houses. When extending that authority in 1949, Congress allowed either house to disapprove such plans. Congress continued to renew the reorganization authority with little change until 1973, when it was allowed to lapse in the conflict with Nixon over his efforts to centralize control of the executive branch. In 1977 Carter requested and received renewal of the authority with provision for veto by either house. Neither Reagan, Bush, nor Clinton displayed any interest in using the reorganization power to enhance presidential control of the executive branch.

Carter's reorganization achievements exceeded those of his immediate predecessors and of his successors but fell far short of the thorough restructuring of the executive branch and reduction in the number of agencies he had promised. Congress passed legislation that established new cabinet departments of Energy and of Education and allowed five reorganization plans to take effect.

There are both operational and conceptual explanations of the limited success of Carter's reorganization efforts. Operationally, observers assert, the president and his reorganization staff failed to comprehend the highly political nature of the task.[91] They were unprepared for the jurisdictional conflicts that accompanied congressional consideration of the proposals. Conceptually, the president lacked a well-conceived, comprehensive strategy that could be defended on political grounds. For Carter the principal goal of reorganization was the fulfillment of campaign commitments. What was lacking was an understanding of reorganization as a means of redistributing influence and redirecting policy. The Carter experience indicates that reorganization has its uses, but they are more in the realm of policy and politics than of management improvement.

The Clinton administration ignored reorganization in favor of the personnel reductions called for in Vice President Gore's *National Performance Review Report* along with the report's recommendations to cut red tape, enhance customer satisfaction, empower employees, and eliminate unneeded functions. The Gore report represented a sharp break with the administrative management paradigm that had dominated presidential efforts to manage the bureaucracy since the Brownlow Committee report of 1937. That philosophy, which the reports of the Hoover Commission (1949) and the Ash Council (1971) also embodied, "emphasized the need for democratic accountability of departmental and agency officers to the President and his central management agencies and through these institutions to the Congress." [92] In its stead, the Gore report embraced the entrepreneurial management paradigm made popular by Osborne and Gaebler in their book, *Reinventing Government*.[93] They call for a "cultural and behavioral shift in the management of government" from a bureaucratic to an entrepreneurial government. In their view public agencies are entrepreneurial organizations competing in a market environment in which success is determined by the degree of customer satisfaction.

This paradigm, Ronald Moe argues, substitutes results for processes and amounts to abandonment of public law as the basis of political accountability. The political scientist James Q. Wilson doubts whether in the era of big government "political accountability can any longer be equated with presidential power." [94] Although expressing support for the spirit of the Gore report, Wilson chided it for not asking what government ought to do and what it can do. Similarly, the famed management consultant Peter Drucker called for a new theory that "asks what the proper functions of government might be and could be ... [and] what results government should be held accountable for." [95]

Planning

Wildavsky defined planning as "current action to secure future consequences." [96] Foresight in anticipating problems and developing solutions to them is the essence of effective planning. One of the hallmarks of successful corporate management has been long-range planning, but the federal government has not had a high degree of success in this area. Planning is applicable to all major activities of the government—national security, economic affairs, human resources, and natural resources—and the nation has "paid a heavy price" for the government's failure "to take adequate account of the future." [97] In the early

1950s, for example, experts were warning of the eventual depletion of domestic oil sources, yet only after the oil embargo of 1973–1974 did the government begin to develop an energy policy that looked to the future. When oil again became plentiful in the 1980s, the United States abandoned that policy because it was politically unpopular.

The reasons for the limited success of planning by the federal government lie in the nature of the planning process and its relationship to politics. Planning is a rational process. It operates on the assumption that objectives are known and accepted. The task is to select the best means appropriate to the achievement of the desired ends. Planning decisions are made comprehensively, that is, "as if a single mind were supporting a single set of preferences." [98] Conflict and disagreement do not interfere because the planners know what is desired. However, public planning, like all other planning, takes place in an uncertain world. Planners do not have adequate knowledge of the future, and their predictions often are fallible.

In addition to the intellectual limitations of all planning, public planning is limited by politics. Public planners do not have the power to command acceptance of their choices. Public choices are made on the basis of the preferences of individuals and groups through a process of bargaining and compromise. The agreements reached in the process of political decision making determine the objectives of public planners. There is no correct result because political preferences are continually changing. As a consequence, political planners make accommodations to social forces. They shorten their time frames (usually extending them no further into the future than the next election), thus reducing the need for prediction, and offer their plans as proposals or suggestions rather than as directives. The result is that political factors tend to dominate planning, and planning tends to blend with regular political decision making.

Presidents have engaged in long-range planning with only limited success. As noted, attempts to combine annual budgeting with comprehensive planning through the program planning budgeting system and zero-base budgeting have not succeeded. Introduced throughout the government by President Johnson in 1965, PPBS used cost-benefit calculations to choose between alternative programs and formulate long-range objectives. ZBB, a project of President Carter, compared the effects of alternative funding levels on long-term objectives within a single program. Both approaches entailed comprehensive attempts to relate spending decisions to long-range consequences. Each required extensive amounts of information and analyses that were never integrated with budget decisions. Thus, bureau and agency officials did not find it worthwhile to take either process seriously. A fatal defect of both PPBS and ZBB was neglect of the hard political choices involved in the budget process. Nor was Congress supportive of either device.

President Nixon introduced a similar technique that focused on goals, management by objectives (MBO), to strengthen his oversight of the executive branch. He directed twenty-one departments and agencies to prepare rank-order lists of their principal objectives. After the Office of Management and Budget reviewed the lists, the president approved objectives for each reporting unit. These presidential objectives then became the standard for monitoring the performance of the units. MBO differed from the planning process of PPBS and ZBB in that it focused first on immediate objectives, then on intermediate objectives that could be achieved in a fiscal year, and finally on long-term goals.[99] MBO was primarily useful within departments and agencies for routine oversight of agreed-on actions. It helped to spot problems and it facilitated communications between the departments and OMB. What it could not do was aid in the choice between objectives. In this respect it was outside the political process and the concerns of the president.

MBO lapsed into desuetude under Carter. Aside from ZBB, Carter's major planning effort was to require agencies to use a multiyear framework in planning their budget requests. The objective was to integrate planning with the budget cycle. Other than to continue multiyear budgeting, Reagan demonstrated little interest in planning. He appeared to believe that domestic policy planning was socialistic and incompatible with a free-market economy. Bush, although neglecting domestic policy planning, was committed to and actively involved in foreign and defense policy planning. Generally, these areas have been more successful than domestic policy planning, and future presidents will always need to engage in national security planning. Clinton had an intense interest in domestic and economic policy and an understanding of planning. His proposals for reforming health care and the welfare system included planning that linked them to the five-year deficit reduction that was integral to the 1994 budget. He exhibited little by way of planning, however, after the Republicans assumed control of Congress in 1995.

Conclusion

Can the president lead the executive branch? Many of the studies discussed in this chapter raise doubts that he can.[100] It is apparent that although the president has substantial formal powers and managerial resources, he is by no means fully in control of his own branch of government. His capacity to direct its many departments and agencies in the implementation of his policies is limited by bureaucratic complexity and fragmentation, conflict between the presidency and the bureaucracy, external pressure and influence on the bureaucracy, and the extreme difficulty of establishing an effective management system within the government.

The continuing attempts of modern presidents to overcome such obstacles and to strengthen presidential leadership and management of the executive branch have involved three major areas: personnel administration, advice and assistance, and management. The most noteworthy examples include Roosevelt's creation of the Executive Office of the President in 1939, Johnson's enthusiastic endorsement of the program planning budgeting system in 1966, Nixon's centralization of executive authority in an administrative presidency, Carter's reorganization program and endorsement of the Civil Service Reform Act of 1978, and Clinton's endorsement of the *National Performance Review Report*.

Reagan devised a strategy to accomplish policy change through administrative action.[101] His experience indicates that although presidents cannot achieve complete control of the executive branch, they can establish to a substantial degree the direction of executive branch policy making. In establishing that control, Reagan used to great advantage careful, centralized control of appointments, making ideological compatibility with his goals the principal criterion.

The second element of Reagan's administrative strategy involved staffing and decision making. By initially selecting a model of White House organization that was compatible with his personal administrative style and his policy objectives—a modified spokes-in-a-wheel model—and using cabinet councils to coordinate policy, Reagan achieved a higher degree of policy consistency than other recent administrations. He also adapted staffing and decision-making arrangements to changes in personnel and in political and other conditions. However, his adoption of the chief-of-staff model in his second term failed to prevent the politically damaging Iranian arms scandal.

The major managerial feature of Reagan's administrative strategy was to use the budget to enforce presidential spending priorities on departments and agencies. In the face of strong pressures to reduce spending, Reagan reversed the traditional pattern of budget preparation from the bottom up, in which agencies attempt to protect their bases, and instituted top-down budgeting with presidential and OMB decisions being determinative.[102]

The final element in Reagan's administrative strategy was the attempt to accomplish policy change administratively wherever possible. This involved establishing procedures for review of regulations by OMB, diminishing the intensity of regulatory enforcement, and reinterpreting agency functions and relations with clientele in accordance with the administration's ideology.[103]

The relatively successful administrative presidency of Ronald Reagan should not blind one to the substantial difficulties that the president faces in his role as chief executive. Even a federal government that is no longer expanding its activities is still vast and complex. Interest groups and Congress present major external obstacles to presidential control and direction. Reagan overcame these to some extent by virtue of his temperament, leadership style, and perhaps most important, his limited, well-defined agenda, which tried to curtail rather than expand the role of government. Yet, his detached, "laid back" administrative style was a major factor leading to the most difficult event of his presidency, the Iran-contra scandal. Reagan's approach to his executive responsibilities should indicate to future presidents that leadership of the president's own branch is a difficult task at best and that there is no way to accomplish it that will ensure effectiveness and please everyone involved.

President Bush's experience indicates that a "hands on," engaged administrative style is no guarantee of success. Although the Bush administration was free of major scandals, it encountered difficulty dealing with problems such as controlling federal spending, managing the bailout of failed federal savings and loan institutions, and developing consistent domestic policies. While Bush's problems with the executive branch were less severe than Reagan's, his triumphs were less notable. He did not adopt Reagan's administrative presidency strategy, and he consciously sought to create a positive relationship with the career bureaucracy. He was skeptical of expanding the role of the state, but he clearly cared about its institutions, "including the bureaucracy." [104]

President Clinton's administrative style can best be described as eclectic. He involved himself deeply in policy formulation in an informal and often haphazard manner while adopting a formal approach to policy implementation that employed delegation of responsibility to others. His commitment to diversity in the composition of his administration resulted in delays in appointments that frustrated his cabinet officers and some

EXECUTIVE POLITICS 283

members of Congress. Charges of improper conduct led to the resignation of his first secretary of agriculture, Mike Espy, and threatened the tenure of Commerce Secretary Ron Brown, while the Whitewater scandal plagued the Clinton administration from its first days.

NOTES

1. Richard Rose, "Government Against Subgovernments: A European Perspective on Washington," in *Presidents and Prime Ministers,* ed. Richard Rose and Ezra N. Suleiman (Washington, D.C.: American Enterprise Institute, 1980), 339.
2. *Youngstown Sheet and Tube Co. v. Sawyer,* 343 U.S. 579 (1952).
3. James P. Pfiffner challenges this viewpoint and maintains that presidents tend to overestimate the opposition they will get from the bureaucracy. See Pfiffner, "Political Appointees and Career Executives: The Democracy-Bureaucracy Nexus in the Third Century," *Public Administration Review* (January/February 1987): 57–65.
4. Joseph A. Califano, Jr., *A Presidential Nation* (New York: Norton, 1975), 23.
5. Hugh Heclo, *A Government of Strangers* (Washington, D.C.: Brookings, 1977), 7.
6. Ibid.
7. Richard Rose, *Managing Presidential Objectives* (New York: Free Press, 1976), 160.
8. Paul C. Light, *Thickening Government: Federal Hierarchy and the Diffusion of Accountability* (Washington, D.C.: Brookings, 1995), 8–9. Light found that between 1960 and 1992 the number of layers at executive levels I-V had increased from 17 to 32 and the number of positions in those levels had grown from 451 to 2,393.
9. Francis E. Rourke, *Bureaucracy, Politics, and Public Policy,* 3d ed. (Boston: Little, Brown, 1984), 32.
10. Rose, *Managing Presidential Objectives,* 13–20.
11. Aaron Wildavsky, *The New Politics of the Budgetary Process,* 2d ed. (New York: HarperCollins, 1992), 87–88.
12. David A. Stockman, *The Triumph of Politics: Why the Reagan Revolution Failed* (New York: Harper & Row, 1986).
13. Light, *Thickening Government,* 32–33.
14. Office of Management and Budget, *Budget of the United States Government, Fiscal Year 1995* (Washington, D.C.: U.S. Government Printing Office, 1994), 248.
15. Heclo, *Government of Strangers.*
16. Jeffrey C. Cohen, *The Politics of the U.S. Cabinet: Representation in the Executive Branch, 1789–1984* (Pittsburgh: University of Pittsburgh Press, 1988), chaps. 3, 4.
17. Thomas E. Cronin, *The State of the Presidency,* 2d ed. (Boston: Little, Brown, 1980), 282.
18. Cohen, *The Politics of the U.S. Cabinet,* 136–139.
19. G. Calvin Mackenzie, *The Politics of Presidential Appointments* (New York: Free Press, 1981).
20. Thomas J. Weko, *The Politicizing Presidency: The White House Personnel Office, 1948–1994* (Lawrence: University Press of Kansas, 1995), 149–151, 157.
21. James P. Pfiffner, *The Strategic Presidency* (Chicago: Dorsey, 1988), 74–76.
22. Richard P. Nathan, *The Administrative Presidency* (New York: Wiley, 1983), 74–76.
23. Weko, *The Politicizing Presidency,* 100, 101–102, 102–103.
24. Edie N. Goldenberg, "The Permanent Government in an Era of Retrenchment and Redirection," in *The Reagan Presidency and the Governing of America,* ed.

Lester M. Salamon and Michael S. Lund (Washington, D.C.: Urban Institute Press, 1984), 381–404.

25. Chester A. Newland, "A Midterm Appraisal—The Reagan Presidency, Limited Government and Political Administration," *Public Administration Review* (January/ February 1983): 15–16.

26. *Kendall v. United States*, 37 U.S. (12 Pet.) 524 (1838).

27. *Panama Refining Co. v. Ryan*, 293 U.S. 338 (1934); *Schechter Poultry Co. v. United States*, 295 U.S. 495 (1935).

28. Louis Fisher, *Constitutional Conflicts Between Congress and the President*, 3d ed. (Lawrence: University Press of Kansas, 1991), 98; Theodore J. Lowi, *The End of Liberalism*, 2d ed. (New York: Norton, 1979), chap. 5.

29. Morris P. Fiorina, *Congress: Keystone of the Washington Establishment*, 2d ed. (New Haven, Conn.: Yale University Press, 1989).

30. Rourke, *Bureaucracy, Politics, and Public Policy*, 74.

31. Cohen, *The Politics of the U.S. Cabinet*, 173–176.

32. Nelson W. Polsby, "Presidential Cabinet-Making Lessons for the Political System," *Political Science Quarterly* (Spring 1978): 15–25.

33. Pfiffner, *The Strategic Presidency*, 41–42, 65–66; Stephen Hess, *Organizing the Presidency*, 2d ed. (Washington, D.C.: Brookings, 1988), 200.

34. Richard F. Fenno, Jr., *The President's Cabinet* (New York: Vintage Books, 1959), 132.

35. Cohen, *The Politics of the U.S. Cabinet*, 33.

36. Ronald Brownstein and Dick Kirschten, "Cabinet Power," *National Journal*, June 28, 1986, 1582–1589.

37. Burt Solomon, "A Cabinet Member Gets the Boot ... And More Turnover Seems Likely," *National Journal*, Dec. 22, 1990, 3098–3099.

38. James A. Barnes, "Like His Home-State Razorbacks ... Clinton's Cabinet Plays to Win," *National Journal*, Apr. 9, 1994, 852–853.

39. Cronin, *The State of the Presidency*, 270–272.

40. Ibid., 282–285.

41. Cohen, in *The Politics of the U.S. Cabinet*, finds a distinction between the older and newer outer departments based on "the importance of interests in creating the department and on the complexity of its interest group environment," 144. The older departments—Agriculture, Commerce, Labor, and Interior—were created in response to demands from single interests that continue to provide them with some protection from presidential control. The newer departments tend to operate in "more complex interest group environments" that may result in "intradepartmental conflict among advocates of the competing interests," 138, 139.

42. Andrew Rosenthal, "Sununu's Out and Skinner Is In, But White House Troubles Persist," *New York Times*, Feb. 11, 1992, A1, A13. Also see Burt Solomon, "Bush's Renovated Inner Circle Has a Bit of a Reaganesque Look," *National Journal*, Feb. 8, 1992, 346–347.

43. John Hart, *The Presidential Branch: From Washington to Clinton*, 2d ed. (Chatham, N.J.: Chatham House, 1995), 91.

44. Margaret C. Hermann, "Advice and Advisers in the Clinton Presidency: The Impact of Leadership Style," in *The Clinton Presidency: Campaigning, Governing, and the Psychology of Leadership*, ed. Stanley A. Renshon (Boulder, Colo.: Westview, 1995), 157.

45. Ibid., 159.

46. Fisher, *Constitutional Conflicts*, chaps. 2, 3.

47. *Buckley v. Valeo*, 421 U.S. 1 (1976).

48. In 1973 President Nixon named Howard J. Phillips acting director of the Office of Economic Opportunity (OEO), an agency that Nixon planned to dismantle.

Phillips began to phase out its programs and withhold funds from it. Sen. Harrison A. Williams, D-N.J., took legal action to force Nixon either to submit Phillips's name to the Senate for confirmation or to stop dismantling the OEO. A U.S. court of appeals ruled that Phillips was illegally holding office and enjoined him from further actions. See James P. Pfiffner, *The President, the Budget, and Congress: Impoundment and the 1974 Budget Act* (Boulder, Colo.: Westview, 1974), 116–117.

49. Perhaps the most notable examples are the Senate's rejection of former Senator John Tower, R-Texas, to be secretary of defense in 1989, and its long delay in acting on the nomination of Dr. Henry Foster, Jr., to be Surgeon General of the United States. Tower had antagonized several of his former colleagues during his service in the chamber and was objectionable to many Democratic senators because of his hawkish views. Foster, a distinguished obstetrician and gynecologist, became a political football in the debate over abortion. The White House Personnel Office, in an inexplicable blunder, neglected to ask Foster if he had ever performed abortions until after the president announced his nomination on February 2, 1995. When Foster gave three different answers and explained them as due to a faulty memory, abortion opponents made the nomination a *cause célèbre* and Senators Robert Dole and Phil Gramm, both Republican presidential hopefuls, tried to outdo each other in their opposition to the nomination by threatening to keep it from coming to a vote in the Senate. The abortion issue then became entwined with Foster's credibility. Following confirmation hearings at which Foster performed very credibly, the Senate Labor and Human Resources Committee on May 24, 1995, approved the nomination by a 10–8 vote. A successful Republican filibuster prevented the nomination from coming to an up or down vote.

50. Christopher J. Deering, "Damned If You Do and Damned If You Don't: The Senate's Role in the Appointment Process," in *The In-and-Outers*, 119.

51. *Myers v. United States*, 272 U.S. 52 (1926).

52. *Humphrey's Executor v. United States*, 295 U.S. 602 (1935).

53. Fisher, *Constitutional Conflicts*, 79.

54. Elizabeth Drew, *On the Edge: The Clinton Presidency* (New York: Simon & Schuster, 1994).

55. *J. W. Hampton and Co. v. United States*, 276 U.S. 394 (1928).

56. *Amalgamated Meat Cutters v. Connally*, 337 F. Supp. 737 (1971).

57. George C. Eads and Michael Fix, *Relief or Reform: Reagan's Regulatory Dilemma* (Washington, D.C.: Urban Institute Press, 1984).

58. Lawrence R. Jacobs and Robert Y. Shapiro, "Public Opinion in Clinton's First Year: Leadership and Responsiveness," in *The Clinton Presidency*, 201.

59. *Hirabayashi v. United States*, 320 U.S. 581 (1943); *Korematsu v. United States*, 323 U.S. 214 (1944).

60. *Youngstown Sheet and Tube Co. v. Sawyer*, 343 U.S. 579 (1952).

61. *Immigration and Naturalization Service v. Chadha*, 462 U.S. 919 (1983).

62. Joseph Cooper, "Postscript on the Congressional Veto," *Political Science Quarterly* (Fall 1983): 427–430; Barbara Hinkson Craig, *The Legislative Veto: Congressional Control of Regulation* (Boulder, Colo.: Westview, 1983), 139–150; Fisher, *Constitutional Conflicts*, 152.

63. Fisher, *Constitutional Conflicts*, 150–152.

64. Louis Fisher, "Judicial Misjudgments about the Lawmaking Process: The Legislative Veto Case," *Public Administration Review* (November/December 1985): 709–710.

65. Richard M. Pious, *The American Presidency* (New York: Basic Books, 1979), 256–257.

66. Allen Schick, "The Road to PPB: The States of Budget Reform," *Public Administration Review* (December 1966): 243–258.

67. Wildavsky, *The New Politics of the Budgetary Process*, 436–440.

68. Allen Schick, *The Federal Budget: Politics, Policy, Process* (Washington, D.C.: Brookings, 1995), 2–4.

69. Bob Woodward, *The Agenda: Inside the Clinton White House* (New York: Simon & Schuster, 1994).

70. Allen Schick, "Macro-Budgetary Adaptations to Fiscal Stress in Industrialized Democracies," *Public Administration Review* (March/April 1986): 129.

71. Ibid., 130.

72. Louis Fisher, *Presidential Spending Power* (Princeton, N.J.: Princeton University Press, 1979), chap. 4.

73. Ibid., 148.

74. Vivian Vale, "The Obligation to Spend: Presidential Impoundment of Congressional Appropriations," *Political Studies* (1977): 508–532.

75. Fisher, *Constitutional Conflicts*, 196.

76. Pfiffner, *President, Budget, and Congress*, 40–44.

77. Jonathan Rauch, "Power of the Purse," *National Journal*, May 24, 1986, 1261.

78. Peri Arnold concludes his authoritative study of "the managerial presidency" by observing that "no modern president has fully managed the executive branch." He further argues that the "managerial conception of the presidency is untenable" because it "places impossible obligations on presidents" and creates unrealistic "public expectations of presidential performance." Peri E. Arnold, *Making the Managerial Presidency: Comprehensive Reorganization Planning 1905-1980* (Princeton, N.J.: Princeton University Press, 1986), 361–362.

79. Steven Hess, *Organizing the Presidency*, 2d ed. (Washington D.C.: Brookings, 1988), 230–231.

80. Jack W. Germond and Jules Witcover, "Bush Left with Little Room for Error," *National Journal*, Dec. 22, 1990, 3104.

81. Rosenthal, "Sununu's Out and Skinner Is In."

82. Fred I. Greenstein, "Political Style and Political Leadership: The Case of Bill Clinton," in *The Clinton Presidency*, 141.

83. Ibid., 142.

84. Burt Solomon, "Drawn and Redrawn ... The Lines in the West Wing Get Blurrier," *National Journal*, January 15, 1994, 134; and "Crisscrossed with Connections ... West Wing Is a Networker's Dream," *National Journal*, January 29, 1994, 256–257.

85. Burt Solomon, "Clinton's New Taskmaster Takes Charge," *National Journal*, August 6, 1994, 1872.

86. Todd S. Purdum, "The Ungreening of the White House Staff," *New York Times*, Dec. 22, 1996, E10.

87. Terry M. Moe, "The Politicized Presidency," in *The New Direction in American Politics*, ed. John E. Chubb and Paul E. Peterson (Washington, D.C.: Brookings, 1985), 235–271.

88. Samuel Kernell, "The Creed and Reality of Modern White House Management," in *Chief of Staff: Twenty-Five Years of Managing the Presidency*, ed. Samuel Kernell and Samuel L. Popkin (Berkeley: University of California Press, 1986), 228.

89. John R. Dempsey, "Carter Reorganization: A Midterm Appraisal," *Public Administration Review* (January/February 1979): 74–78; Arnold, *Making the Managerial Presidency*, chap. 10.

90. Herbert Kaufman, "Reflections on Administrative Reorganization," in *Setting National Priorities: The 1978 Budget*, ed. Joseph A. Pechman (Washington, D.C.: Brookings, 1977), 403.

91. Dempsey, "Carter Reorganization," 75.

92. Ronald C. Moe, "The 'Reinventing Government' Exercise: Misinterpreting the Problem, Misjudging the Consequences," *Public Administration Review* (March/April 1994): 112.

93. David Osborne and Ted Gaebler, *Reinventing Government: How the Entrepreneurial Spirit Is Transforming the Public Sector from Schoolhouse to State House, City Hall to Pentagon* (Reading, Mass.: Addison-Wesley, 1992), 111.

94. James Q. Wilson, "Reinventing Public Administration," *P. S.: Political Science and Politics,* December 1994, 671.

95. Peter Drucker, "Really Reinventing Government," *Atlantic Monthly,* February 1995, 61.

96. Aaron Wildavsky, *Speaking Truth to Power* (Boston: Little, Brown, 1979), 120.

97. Fred V. Malek, *Washington's Hidden Tragedy* (New York: Free Press, 1978), 129.

98. Wildavsky, *Speaking Truth to Power,* 129.

99. Rose, *Managing Presidential Objectives,* chap. 6.

100. See, for example, Arnold, *Making the Managerial Presidency;* Colin Campbell, *Managing the Presidency: Carter, Reagan, and the Search for Executive Harmony* (Pittsburgh: University of Pittsburgh Press, 1986); Hess, *Staffing the Presidency;* and Rose, *Managing Presidential Objectives.* Also see Walter Williams, *Mismanaging America: The Rise of the Anti-Analytic Presidency* (Lawrence: University Press of Kansas, 1990).

101. Richard P. Nathan, *The Administrative Presidency* (New York: Wiley, 1983).

102. Allen Schick, "The Budget as an Instrument of Presidential Policy," in *The Reagan Presidency and the Governing of America,* 113.

103. Lester M. Salamon and Alan J. Abramson, "Governance: The Politics of Retrenchment," in *The Reagan Record,* ed. John L. Palmer and Isabell V. Sawhill (Cambridge, Mass.: Ballinger, 1984), 97; Joseph A. Pika and Norman C. Thomas, "The President as Institution Builder: The Reagan Case," *Governance* (October 1990): 444–447.

104. Joel D. Aberbach, "The President and the Executive Branch," in *The Bush Presidency: First Appraisals,* ed. Colin Campbell and Bert A. Rockman (Chatham, N.J.: Chatham House, 1991), 243.

READINGS

Arnold, Peri E. *Making the Managerial Presidency.* Princeton: Princeton Univ. Press, 1986.

Campbell, Colin. *Managing the Presidency: Carter, Reagan, and the Search for Executive Harmony.* Pittsburgh: University of Pittsburgh Press, 1986.

Cohen, Jeffrey E. *The Politics of the U. S. Cabinet: Representation in the Executive Branch, 1789–1984.* Pittsburgh: University of Pittsburgh Press, 1988.

Cronin, Thomas E. *The State of the Presidency.* 2d ed. Boston: Little, Brown, 1980.

Fisher, Louis. *Constitutional Conflicts Between Congress and the President,* 3d ed., rev. Lawrence: University Press of Kansas, 1991.

Hart, John. *The Presidential Branch.* 2d ed. Chatham, N.J.: Chatham House, 1995.

Hess, Stephen. *Organizing the Presidency.* 2d ed. Washington, D.C.: Brookings, 1988.

Light, Paul C. *Thickening Government: Federal Hierarchy and the Diffusion of Accountability.* Washington, D.C.: Brookings, 1995.

Nathan, Richard P. *The Administrative Presidency.* New York: Wiley, 1983.

Pfiffner, James P. *The Strategic Presidency.* Chicago: Dorsey, 1988.

Warshaw, Shirley Anne, *Powersharing: White House-Cabinet Relations in the Modern Presidency.* Albany: State University of New York Press, 1996.

Weko, Thomas J. *The Politicizing Presidency: The White House Personnel Office, 1948–1994.* Lawrence: University Press of Kansas, 1995.

7 JUDICIAL POLITICS

IN OCTOBER 1991 HIGH DRA-ma gripped the nation as the Senate Judiciary Committee considered President George Bush's nomination of Clarence Thomas of Georgia to be an associate justice of the United States Supreme Court. If confirmed, the conservative Thomas would become the second African American to serve on the Court. He would replace the liberal Thurgood Marshall, the first African American justice.

During the hearings before the Judiciary Committee in September, Democratic senators had questioned Thomas about his views regarding a wide range of sensitive issues such as abortion and affirmative action. They also tried to ascertain his judicial philosophy, that is, how he believed the Supreme Court should interpret the Constitution and exercise its power of judicial review. Thomas resisted efforts to draw him out, saying that it would be inappropriate for him to

Supreme Court Justice Ruth Bader Ginsburg was one of a majority of "nontraditional" candidates Clinton appointed to judgeships.

respond as it would damage his ability to be impartial if such matters should come before the Court.[1] His critics questioned his qualifications for serving on the Court, pointing out that he had been a federal appeals court judge for only eighteen months, he had no other judicial experience, nor had he distinguished himself as a legal scholar. In addition, the hearings included appearances by representatives of interest groups supporting and opposing the nomination.

On September 27 the Judiciary Committee divided, 7–7, on recommending the nomination to the full Senate, then voted 13–1 to send it to the floor without a recommendation.[2] In spite of the protracted and stormy hearings, Thomas's confirmation appeared likely as thirteen Democratic senators announced their support. However, on October 5, two days before the Senate was scheduled to vote, news broke that Professor Anita Hill of the University of Oklahoma Law School had accused Thomas of sexually harassing her when she worked for him at the Equal Employment Opportunity Commission. It is thought that a Judiciary Committee staff person leaked the information, which was known to the committee for a month, to the press. When it became clear that the committee intended for the full Senate to vote on the confirmation without knowledge of the allegation, a firestorm of protest erupted. Women members of Congress, leaders of women's organizations, and women from across the nation complained that the all-male committee failed to understand the seriousness of the charge.

In response to angry bipartisan protests, the Senate's leaders postponed the vote and instructed the committee to reopen the hearings so that the charge could be investigated. The reopened hearings "marked one of the wildest spectacles in modern congressional history."[3] Televised nationwide during prime viewing hours over a weekend, the hearings produced poised and detailed testimony by Hill, who graphically described the alleged harassment, and Thomas's angry, categorical denial in which he accused the committee of a "high-tech lynching."[4] Their effect on the outcome was limited. Only three senators who had previously announced their position changed it. On October 19 the Senate confirmed Thomas, 52–48, with eleven Democrats supporting him and two Republicans opposing. It was the closest margin of approval for a Supreme Court justice in U.S. history.

The relationship between the president and the judiciary is highly visible when the Senate considers the confirmation of a Supreme Court justice. It is also apparent when the Court has had before it challenges to the constitutionality of a president's program, such as Franklin Roosevelt's New Deal, or actions, such as Harry Truman's seizure of the steel industry during the Korean War.

The Founders clearly expected the executive and legislative branches to be in perennial conflict with each other, and they deliberately constructed the U.S. constitutional system to accomplish that result. As James Madison explained in *Federalist* 51, "Ambition must be made to counteract ambition." [5] Their intentions toward the relationship between the executive and judicial arms of the government were, however, quite different. Neither John Locke nor Montesquieu, the two political philosophers from whom the Founders drew their ideas on the separation of powers, provided for a separate judicial branch of government. Rather, both considered the power to decide disputes and to enforce the law to be a function of the executive arm of the government. Although the Founders created a distinct judicial branch, they considered its principal function to be similar to that of the executive: both would expound and enforce the law once the legislature enacted it. In *Federalist* 78 Alexander Hamilton wrote that the major differences between judicial and executive powers were how they would be exercised: the former would depend on "judgment," the latter on "force" or "will." [6]

The Founders also based their expectations about the affinity of the executive and judicial branches on considerations other than the similarity of functions they were to perform. They deliberately increased the powers of both branches at the expense of Congress because they feared the legislature would dominate the political system as it had done under the Articles of Confederation. [7] Therefore, they granted broad authority to both the executive and the judiciary. Article II of the Constitution states, "The executive Power shall be vested in a President of the United States"; Article III says, "The judicial power of the United States shall be vested in one supreme Court, and in such inferior Courts as the Congress may from time to time ordain and establish." In contrast, Article I begins, "All legislative powers *herein granted* shall be vested in a Congress of the United States" (italics added). As a result, to undertake a particular activity, the first two branches need only claim that it is executive or judicial in nature and that it is not forbidden by the Constitution; however, to justify its passing a law, Congress must point to a specific power listed in Article I, Section 8, or show that such a law is, broadly speaking, "necessary and proper" for executing one or more of those specific powers.

However, the Founders left open a question that created a major source of potential conflict between the president and the Supreme Court: Who has the final power to interpret the Constitution? If, as Hamilton asserted in *Federalist* 78, the Supreme Court does, then it is in a position to nullify actions of the president that the judges consider to be unconstitutional. If each branch, however, is empowered to interpret the Constitution as far as its own duties are concerned—a position taken by Thomas Jefferson—then the president is the judge of the constitutionality of executive actions and will not be subject to judicial control in that respect.

This chapter examines the basic relationship between the president and the federal courts. The first section analyzes the most important influence the president exerts over these courts: the power, with the consent of the Senate, to appoint their members. The chapter next explores other means by which the chief executive affects the business of the courts, and, finally, it examines the reverse situation: how the federal courts, and the Supreme Court in particular, influence the actions of the president.

Presidential Appointment of Federal Judges

Perhaps the greatest impact the president can have on the courts is the selection of federal judges who share his policy goals. Certainly this impact has been apparent since 1981, as the conservatives appointed by Presidents Reagan and Bush have come to dominate all levels of the federal judiciary. Among major presidents, only Franklin Roosevelt so fully realized this potential to control the courts.

Following its constitutional mandate, Congress has ordained and established two types of "inferior" federal courts: the district courts, the trial bodies in which federal cases are first heard, and the U.S. courts of appeals.[8] The appeals courts are sometimes referred to as "circuit courts," which serve as major appellate tribunals, reviewing principally the civil and criminal decisions in cases initially heard in federal district courts, as well as the orders and decisions of federal administrative units, particularly the independent regulatory agencies.[9] As for the Supreme Court, the Constitution mentions only the method of appointment of its judges: they are to be chosen by the president with the advice and consent of the Senate. Congress has provided, however, for the same process to be used for staffing the lower federal courts, so the president and the Senate are partners in the appointment process for all federal judges.

Although the formal process for selecting all federal judges is the same—presidential nomination and ultimate appointment with the consent of the Senate—the president's role in federal judicial appointments varies considerably, depending upon the court involved. The following discussion analyzes first the appointments to the two lower federal courts and then the selection of justices to the nation's highest tribunal, the Supreme Court.

Selection of Lower Court Judges

Although the president makes the formal nomination of judges to the lower federal courts, in fact the responsibility usually is delegated to others.[10] The president typically assigns this task to the attorney general, who, in turn, often delegates it to the deputy attorney general with advice on how to proceed. In the Bush administration, however, Attorney General Richard Thornburgh "decided that judicial selection should remain centered in his office," and Clinton assigned it to an office in the Justice Department.[11]

The executive branch recruitment and screening process for judicial candidates entails several considerations. Justice Department officials frequently turn to members of their department who may have special knowledge about lawyers in their own states. They also have the Federal Bureau of Investigation check into the professional standing and integrity of prospective candidates. As discussed later in this section, sitting federal judges often are asked for their opinion about candidates, and members of the Standing Committee on Federal Judiciary of the American Bar Association (ABA) usually are requested to investigate the qualifications of prospective nominees and to make recommendations regarding them.

Just as the attorney general plays a major role in choosing lower federal judges, so do senators of the president's party from the state in which the nominee is to serve (all states have at least one federal district court), or, for courts of appeals judges, the state of his or her residence.

Since the early days of George Washington's administration, an informal rule of "senatorial courtesy" has applied whereby members of the Senate generally refuse to confirm people to federal positions who do not have the support of the senator or senators of the president's party from the state in which the vacancy exists.[12] If there are no senators from the president's party in the state in which the vacancy occurs, the president usually consults the opposition senators.[13] This informal practice places the senators from the state in which a judge is to serve in a powerful position to influence judicial appointments.

Therefore, the attorney general and a particular senator determine who will be chosen. If these individuals differ, a stalemate may occur. The senator usually can block the president's nominee by invoking senatorial courtesy. The attorney general can advise the president not to fill the vacancy, thereby putting pressure on the senator to do something about the situation or face the problem of a backlog of federal cases in his or her home state. Or the president can wait until the end of the session and make a recess appointment, which does not require immediate Senate confirmation. Although Senate approval for the temporarily appointed judge is required in the next session of Congress, the president may benefit from the fact that in the meantime this person has been a sitting judge, and a good performance may deter the Senate from refusing the confirmation.

What typically occurs with lower federal court appointments is that one party is given the major role in initially recruiting candidates for the bench, but the other retains a veto power over those it finds unacceptable. On federal district court appointments, the attorney general (and thus the president) usually defers to the wishes of the senator from the state concerned. Few chief executives are willing to risk the loss of a senator's political support over a district court judgeship, since the work of such a tribunal is seldom crucial to the executive's political goals or programs.

The president is generally more interested and influential in the selection of judges to the U.S. courts of appeals, and there are two reasons why. First, the courts of appeals handle matters more important to the chief executive. Their review of actions of the independent regulatory commissions, for example, can affect his overall economic program. Second, courts of appeals judgeships are less numerous and more prestigious and therefore invite the interest of his major political supporters. Furthermore, senators are in a weaker bargaining position on appointments to the courts of appeals. Because these courts encompass several states, the Senate does not accord any senator the privilege to name an appointee. By political custom these judgeships are apportioned among the various states involved, but the president and his advisers determine how and in what sequence to do so. As a result, the president's advisers take the initiative in recruiting judges to the U.S. courts of appeals, and the senator from the state in which a candidate resides retains the right to veto the nomination, providing the lawmaker can persuade the rest of the Senate that the person truly is objectionable.

Although the attorney general and individual senators are chiefly responsible for appointments to the lower federal courts, many other people and groups are involved in the selection process. Ideally, the "post should seek the person," but in reality candidates who aspire to a federal judgeship must take actions to advance their own cause.[14] Candidates must make it clear to those involved in the appointment process that they desire the position, either by actively seeking it or by having others campaign on their behalf. Candidates help their cause if they have been active in past political campaigns, especially those of the president or of the appropriate senator.

Party leaders also influence appointments to the lower federal courts. For example, a Justice Department official in a Democratic administration was emphatic that in the making of judicial appointments to the district courts in Illinois the late mayor Richard J. Daley of Chicago "had to have a seat at the conference table." [15] Sitting federal judges can become involved in federal judicial appointments if they are asked their opinion about a prospective candidate by the attorney general or the ABA committee. At times, however, judges take the initiative either to advance a candidate of their own or to try to prevent the appointment of someone they feel will not make a good judge. Most often the judges involved are those who sit on a federal district court or court of appeals. Supreme Court justices also may interpose themselves into the process for choosing lower federal court judges. Most notorious in that respect was William Howard Taft, who took a keen interest in appointments to those courts while he served as chief justice.[16]

Another participant in the selection process for judges of lower federal courts is the Standing Committee on Federal Judiciary of the ABA. First established in 1946 with the goal of promoting professionally qualified people for the federal bench, the group had little success in influencing judicial appointments during the Truman administration. When Dwight D. Eisenhower came into office in 1953, however, his administration agreed to an arrangement whereby the Justice Department would ask the committee to evaluate nominees to the federal bench in return for the committee's agreement to stop recommending its own candidates for the federal courts. The committee was most influential during the last two years of the Eisenhower administration, when no one was nominated for a federal judgeship without committee approval. Grossman states, "It was during this period that the committee's right to be consulted on each prospective nomination grew into a virtual veto power."[17]

The committee has continued to be important in federal judicial selection, but it has never regained the virtual veto power it had from 1958 to 1961. Neither the administration of John F. Kennedy nor of Lyndon B. Johnson was as deferential to the committee as Eisenhower's had been. Initially, it was thought that Richard Nixon's Justice Department would restore the committee's veto power over nominations to the federal courts, but, as discussed in the following section, serious disagreements between the committee and the Nixon administration over the qualifications of some of his Supreme Court nominees damaged the relationship. The influence of the committee at the end of the Carter administration was "somewhere below the level it reached during the later Eisenhower years and above that of the Nixon years."[18] The Reagan administration did not consult the ABA committee in the prenomination stage of judicial selection. However, the Bush and Clinton administrations provided it with the names of prospective nominees for rating purposes.[19]

President Carter introduced changes in the selection of lower federal court judges that placed greater emphasis on professional competence and less on party loyalty. The effect of the changes was that individual senators became less influential while the president's role increased. However, most of the changes, including a new entity, the Circuit Judge Nominating Commission, did not survive his administration.

Major changes in the nomination of lower federal court judges also occurred during the Reagan administration. In Reagan's first term, responsibility in the Justice Department for suggesting prospective judges included not only the attorney general and deputy attorney general but also the assistant attorney general for legal policy and the special counsel for judicial selection.[20] A new Office of Legal Policy (OLP) in the Justice Department screened candidates. Serious contenders came to Washington—at their own expense—for interviews by OLP staff. The President's Committee on Federal Judicial Selection, which was chaired by the counsel to the president and included the attorney general and the White House chief of staff, then evaluated the surviving candidates, paying close attention to ideology, judicial philosophy, and political factors. The committee also proposed candidates. The Reagan selection process subordinated traditional patronage and professional considerations to presidential policy priorities. When Edwin

Meese III eventually became attorney general, "the cooptation of judicial selection by the Reagan White House" was "completed." [21]

In addition, the Reagan administration introduced still other changes in the nomination of lower federal court judges. His was the first Republican administration in thirty years in which the ABA's Standing Committee on Federal Judiciary was not actively used and consulted before judges were nominated. Reagan also abolished Carter's selection commission for appellate judges, and in the process abandoned "the most potentially effective mechanism for expanding the net of possible candidates to include women and racial minorities." [22] The Carter administration also sought to appoint liberals to the lower courts, but in the Reagan administration conservatism on issues such as abortion was an important criterion. [23]

According to one student of the courts, Reagan so extensively transformed the process of judicial selection "that future administrations, whether Democratic or Republican, are sure to follow Reagan's lead in vigorously pursuing their legal policy goals when picking judges." [24] The Bush administration appears to have validated this prediction. It continued the "systematic screening process emphasizing judicial philosophy and including extensive personal interview of the major candidates" and the President's Committee on Federal Judicial Selection. [25] However, it abolished the Office of Legal Policy, which played the central role in the Justice Department's judicial selection activities.

The Clinton administration assigned responsibility for judicial selection to the Office of Policy Development in the Justice Department, which worked closely with the Office of Counsel to the President. [26] The Justice Department handled the selection of nominees to the district court judgeships, and the counsel to the president took the initiative on nominations to the Supreme Court and courts of appeals. The president participated by suggesting names and was frequently consulted. The Justice Department conducted the initial screening and interviewing of all prospective nominees. Unlike the ideological focus of the Reagan-Bush process, Clinton's concentrated on obtaining "a sense of the person, the individual's temperament, intellect, ability to articulate legal concepts, and the individual's commitment to fairness." [27]

Despite the differences among Carter, Reagan, Bush, and Clinton in their appointments of lower federal court judges, all four presidents shared one great advantage: the opportunity to make a large number of appointments to the lower courts. In his four years in office, Carter named 202 district and 56 appeals court judges. During his two terms,

Reagan appointed 290 district and 78 appeals court judges. In addition, he appointed 3 associate justices of the Supreme Court—Sandra Day O'Connor, Antonin Scalia, and Anthony Kennedy—and raised Associate Justice William Rehnquist to chief justice. In his one term of office, Bush appointed 148 district and 37 appeals court judges and 2 Supreme Court justices—David Souter and Clarence Thomas. By the end of his first term in office, Clinton had appointed 202 lower court judges and 2 justices of the Supreme Court—Ruth Bader Ginsburg and Stephen Breyer.

Characteristics of Lower Court Judges

All presidents tend to appoint to the lower federal courts people who have certain qualities in common. One is membership in the legal profession. Although this is not a legal requirement, it is an informal qualification: only lawyers have been appointed to federal judgeships. Moreover, in keeping with the contemporary preparation of lawyers, virtually every judge appointed to the federal bench since the end of World War II has been a graduate of a law school; in the past the typical method of studying law was to serve an apprenticeship in a law office. A second characteristic is that most have been active in political party affairs, which is how they get the attention of senators and attorneys general, and have held public office, most often an office associated with the courts, such as city, county, or state prosecutor, district attorney, or U.S. attorney. Another common trait is that many have held judicial positions: federal district judges quite often have been state judges, and those who sit on the courts of appeals frequently come to that bench from a federal district court.

The president, however, does make a difference in the types of lawyers who are appointed to the lower federal courts. The most striking difference between Clinton's appointees and those of his three immediate predecessors is in the appointment of "nontraditional" judges, that is, those who were *not* white males.[28] Although Carter pioneered in the appointment of women and minorities, Reagan was the first Republican to move beyond tokenism, and Bush appointed more women than Carter. Clinton was the first president to appoint nontraditional candidates to a majority of all judgeships[29] (sixty-one percent of his appointees were other than white males).[30] Moreover, he achieved greater diversity without sacrificing quality. The Clinton appointees had educational and professional backgrounds comparable to those of the Bush, Reagan, and Carter appointees, and there are but marginal differences in the occupations from which they came to the bench.[31] Indeed, when measured by the proportion securing the highest American Bar Association rating, the Clinton appointees are better qualified than those of the three previous presidents.

Effects of Lower Court Appointments

The appointment process and background characteristics of lower federal court judges reflect important political considerations. Presidents are in a position to reward people who have been active in their political campaigns or in those of important senators. Federal judgeships also give the president the opportunity to make appointments that have symbolic value for certain groups. These considerations may, in turn, help to win the loyalty of such groups to the president and his political party. Thus, judicial appointments, like those to executive posts, are an important form of political patronage.

The question remains, however, whether appointments to lower federal courts affect public issues that come before those courts, that is, whether there are consequences for *policy* as well as personnel in such appointments. A study of the voting behavior of courts of appeals judges from July 1, 1983, to December 31, 1984, determined that judges appointed by the Democratic presidents Carter, Johnson, and Kennedy were much more likely to vote on the liberal side of issues than were those chosen by the Republican presidents Reagan, Ford, and Nixon.[32] Also, a study of decisions by Reagan's 1981–1986 appointees to the courts of appeals found "a vast ideological gulf separating Republican from Democratic judges." [33]

It seems clear that presidential appointments to the lower federal courts do affect policy. Democratic presidents tend to take liberal positions on issues; Republican presidents, conservative positions. When presidents appoint judges from their own political party, the rulings of such judges usually are consistent with the president's philosophy.

As the next section indicates, the politics of the appointment and confirmation of Supreme Court justices is quite different from that of lower federal court judges. Although the individuals and groups involved in choosing both kinds of judges are essentially the same, their relative influence in the two selection processes is not the same.

Selection of Supreme Court Justices

The president clearly dominates the process of selecting members of the Supreme Court. The decisions reached by the Court are of vital interest to the president because they affect his programs, the operation of the entire political system, and the functioning of U.S. society in general. Besides a keen interest in who sits on the Court, the chief executive has a relatively free hand in choosing its members.

As with lower federal court judges, the attorney general assists the president in identifying and screening potential candidates for the nation's highest court. Because vacancies for the Supreme Court occur so infrequently (one every two years, on average), the president can concentrate his efforts on the appointment in a way that simply is not possible for the numerous appointments made to the federal district and appeals courts. Robert Scigliano estimates that as of mid-1970, presidents had known personally 60 percent of the 134 nominees for the High Court.[34] In some instances, presidents have had close personal relationships with their appointees. Frederick M. Vinson, an old friend of President Truman's, was serving as secretary of the Treasury Department at the time of his appointment as chief justice. Byron R. White had chaired a national citizens' committee for the election of John F. Kennedy in 1960. Thurgood Marshall had served as solicitor general for Lyndon Johnson before Johnson appointed him to the Court.

Since the Johnson administration, none of the twelve justices who have joined the Court have had a close relationship with the president who appointed them. Modern presidents tend to rely on their attorneys general and close White House advisers to identify prospective nominees. For example, Attorney General William French Smith took the lead in recruiting Justice Sandra Day O'Connor, Reagan's first appointee to the Court, while the White House chief of staff John Sununu played an important role in President Bush's appointment of David Souter, a federal appeals court judge from Sununu's home state of New Hampshire. Appointments to the Court "have become less a personal presidential decision than a hard choice from among candidates promoted by various vested-interest groups."[35] Consequently, the nomination and confirmation process involves compromises and bargaining.

Individual senators do not play as important a role in the selection of Supreme Court justices as they do for judges appointed to the lower federal courts (especially the district courts). The principal reason for the distinction is that the High Court's geographical jurisdiction encompasses the entire nation, so no senator or group of senators can claim that the appointment is within his or her special province. Presidents usually obtain the blessing of the senators of their own party from the state of residence of the nominee, as Reagan did from Barry Goldwater,

R-Ariz., for the appointment of O'Connor, but senators generally are presented with a fait accompli rather than being involved in the recruitment process. A lawmaker would think long and hard about trying to prevent a constituent from having the honor of sitting on the nation's highest tribunal, especially knowing that in the face of opposition the president could then turn to a citizen of another state for the appointment. Both Democratic senators from Georgia, for example, voted to confirm Clarence Thomas in 1991.

Two other groups that play a much smaller role in the selection of Supreme Court justices than in the selection of members of the lower federal courts are the likely candidates and party leaders. The adage "the post should seek the person" is more applicable for positions on the nation's highest tribunal, so even those on the proverbial short list usually do not actively promote their own candidacy. Also, because appointments to the Supreme Court are considered to be above partisan politics, even the national party chairs do not influence appointments to the same extent as state party leaders influence appointments to the lower federal courts, especially at the district level.

Supreme Court justices themselves are more influential in selecting their colleagues than are their counterparts in lower federal courts. No fewer than 48 of the 101 persons who had sat on the High Court as of 1976 attempted to exert influence in behalf of a candidate or a philosophy of judicial selection.[36] Leading the way were William H. Taft with eighteen attempts (fourteen were successful) and Harlan F. Stone with nine (five were successful). This influence has been exerted both in behalf of proposed candidates (Chief Justice Warren E. Burger suggested the name of Harry A. Blackmun in 1970 and recommended O'Connor in 1981) and against them.[37]

One group that is often consulted on lower federal court appointments, but rarely on those for the Supreme Court, is the ABA's Standing Committee on Federal Judiciary. Beginning with the appointment of Justice William J. Brennan, Jr., by President Eisenhower in 1956 and continuing until 1970, the committee was asked to evaluate candidates for the Supreme Court but only *after* the appointment had been publicly announced and transmitted to the Senate Judiciary Committee for action. After the difficulties that led to the rejection of nominees Clement Haynsworth, Jr., and G. Harrold Carswell, the Nixon administration decided to allow the ABA committee to screen candidates before their names were submitted to the Senate Judiciary Committee. The arrangement was short-lived, however; one of the first actions of the

ABA committee when two vacancies occurred in 1971 was to express serious doubts about the capabilities of President Nixon's two top choices, Mildred Lillie, a California appeals court judge, and Herschel Friday, an Arkansas lawyer. This led Attorney General John Mitchell to withdraw the screening privilege of the committee. Ford restored it, and the committee responded by giving his only nominee to the Court, John Paul Stevens, a high rating. The committee was not consulted, however, by Reagan, Bush, or Clinton prior to their nominations to the Court.

Thus, the process of recruiting justices to the Supreme Court is controlled by the president with the assistance of the attorney general, the president's high-level advisers, and sitting Supreme Court justices. The president faces one other obstacle, however, that is far more formidable than obstacles to lower court appointments: the nominee must be confirmed by the *entire Senate*. Operating through the Judiciary Committee, which since 1955 has held hearings in which it questions nominees and receives testimony from interested groups, the Senate takes seriously its role of consenting to the appointment of a person to the nation's highest court. An indication of just how seriously the Senate takes this responsibility is that about 30 percent of the nominees to the Court have not been confirmed by the Senate.[38]

Certain factors tend to be linked with the Senate's failure to confirm Supreme Court nominees. Rejections are most likely to occur when the Senate is controlled by the political party in opposition to the president.[39] Moreover, rejections are particularly evident in the last year of a president's term because opposition leaders in the Senate want to hold the position vacant in hopes that the new president will be from their party. The Senate refused to confirm Lyndon Johnson's nomination of Abe Fortas as chief justice when Earl Warren announced his retirement in 1968 in part to save the seat for the next president. When Richard Nixon became president in 1969 he appointed Warren Burger, a Republican, as chief justice, and the Senate approved the choice.

Certain characteristics of the nominees also are associated with the Senate's failure to confirm.[40] One is involvement with controversial issues of public policy, a situation that often stimulates concerned interest groups to oppose the nomination. All five nominees who were rejected by the Senate in this century were opposed by interest groups. John P. Parker, a southern court of appeals judge nominated by Herbert Hoover in 1930, fell victim to the combined opposition of the American Federation of Labor and the National Association for the Advancement of Colored People, which considered his rulings as an appeals judge to be antilabor and racist. Two Nixon nominees, Haynsworth, a federal court of appeals judge from South Carolina, and Carswell, a federal court of appeals judge from Florida, were rejected within a few months of each other in late 1969 and early 1970. Both were opposed by African American and liberal interest groups for their rulings on civil rights cases. (Haynsworth was opposed by labor as well.) Fortas's nomination for chief justice was bitterly attacked by conservative groups because of his liberal decisions in obscenity cases and suits concerning the rights of the accused in criminal proceedings.[41] A major effort by civil rights, women's, and other liberal groups contributed to the defeat in 1987 of Reagan's nomination of Robert Bork, a controversial conservative federal appeals court judge.

Sometimes other problems are involved. Some considered Fortas's acceptance of a legal fee from a family foundation and his advising President Johnson on political matters to be unethical activities for a justice of the Supreme Court. Haynsworth was criticized for ruling on cases in which he had a personal financial interest. Much of the opposition to Carswell from members of the bar, particularly law professors, stemmed from his lack of professional qualifications, indicated by the mediocrity of his decisions.[42] The only presidential nominee to the Supreme Court since Carswell to be attacked on grounds of a lack of professional competence was Clarence Thomas. His critics also objected to his conservative ideology and his judicial philosophy. In the latter respect, the controversy over Thomas followed the pattern set in the Senate's challenges to Reagan's nominations of O'Connor, Rehnquist, Scalia, Bork, and Kennedy and Bush's nomination of Souter.[43]

Characteristics of Supreme Court Justices

The characteristics of Supreme Court justices reflect the informal qualifications that presidents take into account when appointing them. Scigliano places these qualifications into three categories: professional, representational, and doctrinal.[44]

The *professional* qualifications are similar to those described for lower court judges. Although not required to be lawyers, all of the justices who have served on the Supreme Court have been attorneys. Not only have they been trained as lawyers, their professional lives have been devoted primarily to the practice or teaching of law. Moreover, all but one justice previously held public office; many of these offices were associated with the courts, such as those of prosecutor and district attorney. An analysis of the occupations of Supreme Court justices at the time of their appointment reveals that they have come principally from four types of positions: twenty-two held federal office in the executive branch; twenty-seven were judges of a lower federal court; twenty-two were judges of a state court; and eighteen were attorneys in private practice. Elected officials also have served on the nation's highest bench, including one president, eight U.S. senators, four members of the House of Representatives, and three state governors.

Representational qualifications are the aspects of a nominee's background that are thought to make various groups feel that they have a representative on the Supreme Court. The representational qualification most often considered is the partisan affiliation of the justices, most of whom have been from the same political party as the president who appointed them.

Presidents are interested in other representational qualifications as well. Early in the nation's history, geography was a major consideration because various states, for example, Pennsylvania, New York, and Virginia, and sections of the country were thought to be entitled to representation on the Court. This factor has not been of consequence in this century, however, except when Nixon made clear early in his administration his intention to appoint a Southerner. (His unsuccessful nominations of Haynsworth and Carswell failed to achieve that result, but he eventually appointed Lewis Powell, a Democrat from Virginia.) More salient in recent years are qualifications based on religion, race, and sex. At various times justices have been appointed to a "Catholic seat" (Justice Brennan) or a "Jewish seat" (Justice Fortas). In 1967 Johnson appointed Thurgood Marshall, an African American, and in 1991 Bush appointed Clarence Thomas to Marshall's seat. Ronald Reagan pledged in his 1980 presidential campaign that, if elected, he would appoint a woman to one of his first vacancies on the Court, a promise he fulfilled by making Justice O'Connor his first appointee. Both of Clinton's appointees were Jewish, and one, Ginsburg, was the second woman to serve on the Court.[45]

Doctrinal qualifications refer to the perception by the president that a nominee shares his political philosophy and approach to public policy issues. For this reason, Reagan's choice of O'Connor had both representational and doctrinal qualifications. Meeting with her as a prospective nominee, Reagan discussed social and family issues and was reported to be pleased to hear that she regarded abortion as personally abhorrent; moreover, he found that her political views were generally conservative, like his own. As a state judge, O'Connor had been inclined to defer to the actions of legislative and executive officials and to favor shifting more responsibilities from the federal to the state courts, positions consistent with Reagan's judicial philosophy and advocacy of states' rights.

Reagan's choices of Rehnquist for chief justice, of Scalia and Kennedy as associate justices, and the unsuccessful nomination of Robert Bork appear to have been motivated primarily by doctrinal considerations.[46] Rehnquist's fifteen-year record as an associate justice demonstrated that of all the justices, he came closest to Reagan's views in opposing abortion, busing, and affirmative action and in being generally disposed to defer to state and congressional legislation and to executive authority. Scalia's legal writings (he had served on the law school faculties of the University of Chicago and the University of Virginia) and his opinions written while he was a judge on the U.S. court of appeals in Washington reveal essentially the same conservative legal philosophy. Bork's extensive writings—he was also a former law professor at Yale and a sitting federal judge—gave clear indication of his conservative views. Senate and interest group opponents of his nomination focused on that written record, but it was Bork's coolly articulate performance in his confirmation hearings, which portrayed him as having an unacceptably narrow interpretation of the Constitution and of the Court's role in protecting constitutional rights, that led to his defeat. The 58–42 vote in the Senate ended one of "the most contentious [Supreme Court] confirmation battle[s] in American history."[47]

Bush's nomination of David Souter appears to have been based on doctrinal and professional qualifications. In contrast to Bork, Souter's views were not well known, and the opinions he had written as a state judge and a federal appeals court judge were not very revealing. This paucity of material frustrated liberal groups, who assumed that he was a conservative. They were unable to mount a successful campaign against his confirmation because he was professionally qualified and he had not left a "paper trail" that could be attacked.

The choice of Clarence Thomas reflected representational and doctrinal concerns. In naming an African American, Bush hoped to prevent the coalition that had defeated Bork from prevailing again. If the Senate rejected Thomas, there would be no African American on the Court. Although he had few published writings, Thomas's conservative views were widely known as a result of his service as head of the Equal Employment Opportunity Commission during the Reagan administration.

Clinton's selections of Ginsburg and Breyer, although applauded for their representational impact, drew doctrinal criticism, but from an unusual source. Liberal Democrats were distressed that the first Democratic president since Lyndon Johnson with the opportunity to fill vacancies on the Court (Carter made no appointments) picked candidates with moderate, mainstream rather than activist, liberal constitutional views. In the interest of avoiding a confirmation battle in the Senate, Clinton initially wanted to name a prominent Democrat, such as Gov. Mario Cuomo of New York for the first nomination or Sen. George Mitchell of Maine for the second.[48] When both of them removed themselves from consideration, he moved to experienced and moderate federal appeals court judges, first Ginsburg and then Breyer. Both nominees were ideologically safe and had strong support from liberals and conservatives on the Senate Judiciary Committee.

The Clinton appointments indicate that doctrinal considerations can have different implications for presidents. Their concern may not be to pack the court with justices who will pursue particular policies, but rather to appoint persons whose general philosophy is similar to their own and reflects the mood of the country. Moreover, as the following section indicates, even when presidents try to choose justices who will rule the way they want, they are not always successful.

Effects of Supreme Court Appointments

Do Supreme Court appointments have *policy* consequences? Are the actions presidents take while in office more likely to be supported by their appointees or by justices from their political party than by other members of the Court? An even broader question: Are presidents' values more likely to be protected in judicial rulings made by their appointees or by members of their party than by the other justices of the Court?

Stuart Nagel sought to answer the first question by examining the decisions in 100 Supreme Court cases involving the use of presidential power.[49] He found that when justices appointed by the president and those not appointed by him differed in their opinions (68 percent of the time), the president's appointees were more supportive of his actions. He also found that in 64 percent of comparable cases a greater proportion of justices from the president's own party upheld his use of power than did those from the opposing political party.

Scigliano examined the broader question of whether presidents get what they want and expect from the justices they appoint to the Court, that is, whether their appointees do in fact make decisions that reflect their values.[50] Taking into account presidents' direct and indirect statements about their appointees, as well as assumptions about whether decisions reached by such appointees reflected the views of the president, his study concludes that approximately three-fourths of the justices conformed to the expectations of the chief executive who appointed them. The remaining one-fourth did not.

The Reagan, Bush, and Clinton appointments provide support for Scigliano's findings. During the 1994–1995 term of the Supreme Court, Chief Justice Rehnquist (who had been promoted by Reagan), Reagan appointee Scalia, and Bush appointee Thomas were joined by the two Reagan appointees who had previously appeared to be centrists— O'Connor and Kennedy—to form a solid conservative majority. This activist bloc reexamined long-held constitutional principles regarding the authority of the national government, the federal-state relationship, and the role of race in making public policy.[51] In opposition were a liberal bloc composed of Souter (a Bush appointee), Ginsburg and Breyer (who had been appointed by Clinton), and Stevens (who had been named by Ford). Souter's emergence as a liberal on the court's new ideological continuum was quite surprising.

Scigliano suggests various reasons why one in four justices do not meet the expectations of the presidents who appoint them. One is that they simply do not have the values the president thinks they do, possibly because the president does not probe them sufficiently or thinks that because a prospective justice has a certain position on one issue, he or she will hold a comparable view on another. Also, people can and do change their views over time, and justices may do so after they go on the Court, especially if they are influenced by their peers.[52] Finally, justices have a sense of judicial obligation and may rule according to judicial precedents or their understanding of the Constitution rather than on the basis of their own value preferences. Whatever the reason for their actions, justices of the Supreme Court are virtually immune from pressures from the chief executive. There is no more prestigious office to which they can be appointed as a reward for pleasing the president; moreover, because they hold office for life (no Supreme Court justice has ever been removed from office), there is little chance to punish them.

Despite these limitations, if a president makes the effort to learn the values of prospective nominees, then appoints a person with values like his own, he usually is rewarded with decisions that reflect his views. A study of Supreme Court cases decided from 1958 through 1973 reveals that the Court had a definite liberal cast when most of its members were appointees of Democratic presidents. However, with Nixon's appointment of Chief Justice Burger in 1969, the tide began to turn in a conservative direction.[53] That turn to conservatism accelerated with the Reagan and Bush appointments to the Court.[54]

Other Presidential Influences on the Federal Courts

Although the appointment of federal judges is the most important method by which the president affects the courts, there are other ways to influence their activities. The first is his relationship with the solicitor general, an official Scigliano calls "the lawyer for the executive branch." [55] The second is the president's role in legislation that affects the operation of the Supreme Court. The third is the role the president plays in the enforcement of court decisions.

Role of the Solicitor General in the Appellate Courts

The solicitor general, an official appointed by the president with the consent of the Senate, is the most important individual in setting the agenda of the federal appellate courts. First, the solicitor general determines which cases of those the government loses in the federal district courts will be taken to the courts of appeals. Second, of the cases the government loses in the courts of appeals (or, in some instances, district court cases that are directly appealable to the Supreme Court), the solicitor general decides which to recommend that the High Court hear. Unlike the courts of appeals, which *must* take cases properly appealed to them, the Supreme Court chooses the cases it hears, and it is more likely to take those proposed by the solicitor general than by other parties, including those who lost to the federal government in the lower courts.

The solicitor general's influence in determining the Supreme Court's agenda is not restricted, however, to cases in which the federal government itself is a party. He or she also decides whether the government will file an amicus curiae (friend of the court) brief supporting or opposing appeals by other parties to have their cases heard before the Court. In addition, he or she supervises the writing of briefs that present reasons why the Court should either accept or reject certain cases. Moreover, once the Court decides to accept a case involving the federal government, the "lawyer for the executive branch" decides the position the government should take and the arguments that should be made to support that position. The same applies when the government is not a direct party to the suit but an amicus supporting the position of one of the two immediate parties. Thus, "the Solicitor General not only determines whether the executive branch goes to the Supreme Court but what it will say there." [56]

The federal government's amicus role has expanded greatly. Steven Puro, who analyzed the briefs filed from 1920 through 1973, found that 71 percent occurred in the last twenty years of that period.[57] He concluded that whether by its own initiative or as a result of an invitation from the Supreme Court, the federal government participated as amicus in almost every major domestic question presented before the Court since World War II. Particularly prominent is the government entrance into the controversial issues of civil liberties, civil rights, and the jurisdiction and procedures of the courts.

When the federal government becomes involved in a case before the Supreme Court, it is usually successful. Scigliano's analysis of Court opinions chosen at ten-year intervals beginning in 1800 shows that the United States won 62 percent of its litigation there during the nineteenth century and 64 percent during this century. Its record as amicus is even more impressive. Puro found that in the political cases he examined, the federal government supported the winning side in almost 74 percent of its appearances. An analysis of race discrimination employment cases from 1970 to 1981 showed that the government won 70 percent of the cases in which it was a direct party and 81.6 percent of those in which it filed amicus briefs.[58]

There are several reasons why the federal government is so successful in its appearances before the Supreme Court. One is that solicitor generals develop a great deal of expertise in dealing with the Court, since they or members of their staff argue far more cases there than any other party, including any law firm in the country.[59] Also, solicitor generals tend to build up credit with the Court because they help its members manage their caseload by holding down the number of government appeals and provide the Court with high-quality briefs. Moreover, the executive and judicial branches share a common perspective based upon a similar concern with the execution or enforcement of the law. Finally, the justices tend to share the doctrinal attitudes of the presidents who appoint them. Amicus briefs filed by solicitor generals in the 1960s tended to take the liberal side in civil liberties cases; they defended the individual against state and local governments and corporations.

That situation changed during the Nixon administration, however, when the federal government's amicus briefs took the conservative position on such issues, siding with state and local governments and corporations against the individual; and the Court began to adopt a more conservative position in its rulings.

With the Reagan administration came a concerted effort to use the solicitor general's office to help implement the president's conservative political agenda.[60] Described as Reagan's "other campaign" (separate from appointing conservatives to the federal bench), the campaign led by Solicitor General Rex Lee entailed efforts to persuade the Supreme Court to change previous "liberal" rulings on matters such as abortion, prayer in the public schools, busing, affirmative action, the rights of the accused in criminal cases, and federal-state relations.[61] Lee's successor, Charles Fried, continued that campaign.

Under Reagan, then, the solicitor general's function changed from a traditional posture of restraint to one of aggressively pushing the Court to take cases that advanced the administration's social policy agenda.[62] The result of this transformation was a loss of the Supreme Court's trust in the solicitor general's presentation of facts and interpretation of the law.[63] There is, however, no evidence that Presidents Bush and Clinton continued Reagan's aggressive use of the solicitor general's office for policy purposes.

Although independent, solicitor generals are not immune from presidential influence. The appointment process parallels that for federal judges.[64] Sometimes the president makes the selection, as when Truman chose his friend J. Howard McGrath. In other instances, state political figures may influence the choice, as was true of McGrath's successor, Philip Pearlman, who owed his appointment to the support of Maryland political leaders.

There is, however, a major distinction between the solicitor general and a federal judge: the solicitor general is an employee of the executive, not the judicial, branch and therefore is subject to direction from the attorney general and, on occasion, the president. Also, the solicitor general is considerably less politically insulated than a federal judge. The post does not entail life tenure. Solicitor generals serve for an average length of two years. Not only can they be removed from office by the president but they can also be rewarded with a more prestigious position. For example, Stanley Reed and Robert Jackson, who served under Franklin Roosevelt, and Thurgood Marshall, who was solicitor general under Lyndon Johnson, all were appointed justices of the

Supreme Court by the chief executive who had previously chosen them as solicitor general.

The President's Role in Legislation Affecting the Supreme Court

The president also can affect the actions of the Supreme Court through legislation. The president's authority to propose bills to Congress and to work for their adoption, as well as his power to oppose measures favored by members of Congress and, if necessary, to veto them, means that the president can influence legislation affecting the Court.

Over the years presidents have become involved in the power of Congress to establish the size of the Supreme Court. In the latter days of the John Adams administration, the lame-duck Congress, still controlled by the Federalists, passed the Judiciary Act of 1801, which reduced the number of justices from six to five, to prevent the incoming president, Democratic-Republican Thomas Jefferson, from appointing a replacement for an ailing justice, William Cushing. The following year, however, Congress—by then under control of the Democratic-Republicans—repealed the 1801 law and restored the number of justices to six. In 1807 the number of justices was increased to seven to accommodate population growth in Kentucky, Tennessee, and Ohio. This first attempt to thwart a president from making appointments to the Supreme Court, therefore, ended in failure: Jefferson went on to name three justices, including Thomas Todd to occupy the new seat. (Cushing recovered and lived until 1810; his successor was named by James Madison, not Jefferson.)

Manipulation of the size of the Court so as to affect presidential appointments also occurred in the 1860s. The 1863 Judiciary Act expanding the Court from nine to ten members enabled Abraham Lincoln to appoint Stephen J. Field, who subsequently supported the president on war issues. Shortly thereafter, the Radical Republicans, who controlled Congress, passed legislation reducing the number of justices to prevent Lincoln's successor, Andrew Johnson, from naming justices they feared would rule against the Reconstruction program. Soon after Ulysses S. Grant was inaugurated in March 1869, the size of the Court was again expanded; this expansion, plus a retirement, enabled Grant to appoint Justices William Strong and Joseph P. Bradley. Both voted to reconsider a previous Supreme Court decision, *Hepburn v. Griswold*, that had declared unconstitutional the substitution of paper money for gold as legal tender for the payment of contracts.[65] The new decision validated the use of "greenbacks" as legal tender.[66] The three successive changes in the size of the Court within a six-year period brought the desired results.

In 1937 President Franklin Roosevelt attempted to increase the size of the Court once more. Frustrated by the invalidation of much of the early New Deal (between January 1935 and June 1936 the Court struck down eight separate statutes), Roosevelt asked Congress in early 1937, shortly after his landslide electoral victory in 1936, to pass legislation permitting him to appoint one justice, up to six in number, for each sitting member of the Court who failed to retire voluntarily at age seventy. The president contended that the additions were necessary to handle the Court's caseload, but his real purpose was to liberalize the Court. No one was deceived by the ploy, however, and the proposal stimulated violent opposition from members of the bar, the press, and many of Roosevelt's political supporters in Congress. At this point, Justice Owen J. Roberts, who had been aligned with four conservative colleagues in striking down New Deal legislation, began to vote with the other four justices to uphold the legislation. The unpopularity of Roosevelt's proposal, Justice Roberts's mitigating action—some observers dubbed this development "the switch in time that saved nine"—and the sudden death of Majority Leader Joseph Robinson of Arkansas, who was leading the president's effort in the Senate, resulted in Congress's failure to adopt the "court-packing plan." The incident had mixed results. Although Roosevelt lost the political battle in Congress to pack the Court with new liberal appointees, he won the legal war with the Court over the constitutionality of the New Deal.

Presidents also can conceivably affect the operation of the Supreme Court by becoming involved in legislative actions of Congress that remove certain categories of cases from the appellate jurisdiction of the Supreme Court. The most notorious use of that congressional power occurred just after the Civil War. William McCardle, an editor of a Mississippi newspaper, was arrested and held for trial by a military tribunal for criticizing in his editorials the Reconstruction program imposed on the South by military government. He sought a writ of habeas corpus in the federal court of appeals, arguing that the Reconstruction Acts, which allowed his arrest and trial by a military tribunal, were unconstitutional. When the court denied the writ, he took advantage of an 1867 law expanding the appellate jurisdiction of the Supreme Court to review denials of such writs and brought his case to the High Court.[67] Concerned that the Supreme Court might use the *McCardle* case to declare the Reconstruction Acts unconstitutional, Congress passed a law repealing the 1867 statute and prohibiting the Court from acting on any appeals then pending. President Johnson, who opposed the Recon-struction program of the Radical Republicans, vetoed the law, but Con-gress overrode his veto. The Court then dismissed the *McCardle* case, on which it had heard arguments but not yet ruled. Although Congress prevailed over President Johnson in that particular instance by overrid-ing his veto, the incident nonetheless illustrates the power of the pres-ident to affect the appellate jurisdiction of the Supreme Court through his sharing of the legislative power with Congress.

Presidents also have been involved in instances in which Congress has enacted legislation that had the effect of reversing specific rulings of the Supreme Court. The difference that individual presidents can make in such matters is illustrated by the tidelands oil dispute. In 1951, after the Supreme Court ruled first in 1947 and again in 1950 that the federal government, not the states, owned the three-mile strip of oil-rich, submerged lands off the ocean shores, Congress passed legislation granting ownership of these tidelands to the states. Democratic president Truman successfully vetoed the legislation, however, and the matter became an issue in the 1952 presidential campaign, in which the Republicans promised to restore the lands to the states. They kept their promise when Eisenhower won the elec-tion and subsequently approved new legislation passed in 1953 ced-ing the federal mineral rights in offshore lands to the states. More recently, Republican presidents Reagan and Bush sought to overturn the Supreme Court's 1973 abortion decision by pressuring Congress to propose a constitutional amendment outlawing abortion.[68] Although unsuccessful in this effort, both presidents signed legislation that lim-ited use of federal funds for abortions and made access to abortions more difficult.

These then are the major ways in which presidents can become involved with Congress in legislation affecting the Supreme Court. The next section analyzes the influence the president exercises through an important executive function—the enforcement of court decisions.

Enforcement of Court Decisions

Although the federal courts have the authority to hand down deci-sions on cases within their jurisdiction, in some instances they depend upon the president to enforce them. President Lincoln once ignored a court order against a military officer under his direct command.[69] Lincoln's decision was, however, an exception to the rule, for chief executives usually have enforced court decisions, even when they would have preferred not to.[70] Immediately after the Supreme Court held in 1952 that Truman's seizure of the steel mills was unconstitutional, he ordered them restored to private operation.[71] Nixon complied with the Court's 1974 ruling in *United States v. Nixon* that he turn over to a federal district court tapes of his conversations with executive aides.[72] That action produced evidence of the president's involvement in the Watergate affair and led to the House Judiciary Committee's impeachment charges against him.

Thus presidents, through their appointment of federal judges and solicitors general, their involvement in congressional legislation affecting the Supreme Court, and their authority to determine whether judicial decisions will be enforced, influence the operation of the federal courts. The following section analyzes the reverse situation: the extent to which federal courts affect the way presidents conduct the responsibilities of their office.

Judicial Checks of Presidential Action

The Founders left open the question of who had the final power to interpret the Constitution. If, as Jefferson contended, each branch has the authority to interpret the Constitution as far as its own duties are concerned, then the president, like Congress, is the judge of the constitutionality of executive actions. If, however, the Supreme Court has the right to make the final judgment on such matters through the power of judicial review, then the Court is in a position to check the actions of the president as well as those of Congress. Although the Court established its power of judicial review with respect to acts of Congress in 1803 in *Marbury v. Madison*,[73] it did not declare a presidential action unconstitutional until after the Civil War.

Major Cases Invalidating Presidential Actions

Of the forty-two people who have served as president over the course of the nation's history, only four have been objects of major court decisions invalidating their actions. The first, Abraham Lincoln, was a nineteenth-century chief executive; the other three, Franklin Roosevelt, Harry Truman, and Richard Nixon, are products of the modern presidency.

Abraham Lincoln. Lincoln's battle with the judiciary stemmed from the conditions surrounding the Civil War. Early in that conflict Lincoln concluded that existing laws and judicial procedures were inadequate for dealing with spying, sabotage, and other acts of disloyalty, and he suspended the traditional writ of habeas corpus when he felt that the public safety required it. It is better, Lincoln argued, for the president to violate a single law to a limited extent than to have "the government itself go to pieces" because of a failure to suppress the rebellion. During the war many people, including civilians, who were engaged in activities thought to be dangerous to the public safety were arrested and tried by military commissions.

In 1866, a year after Lincoln's death and the end of the war, the Supreme Court heard the case of L. P. Milligan, a civilian sentenced to death by a military commission for releasing and arming rebel prisoners for the purpose of invading Indiana. The Court held that the trial of a civilian by a military commission in an area remote from the theater of war violated the Constitution. In so ruling, the Court used language that seemed to reject the power claimed by Lincoln: "No doctrine, involving more pernicious consequences, was ever invented by the wit of man than that any of its [the Constitution's] provisions can be suspended during any of the great exigencies of government." [74] The majority opinion went on to state that martial law cannot arise from a *threatened* invasion but only an actual one that effectually closes the courts.

Franklin Roosevelt. President Roosevelt ran into major difficulties with the Supreme Court, which invalidated much of his early New Deal legislation for exceeding the powers of Congress. The Court also struck down an action entailing his administrative power. The case involved FDR's removal of Federal Trade Commissioner William Humphrey on policy grounds rather than statutory criteria for such removal.

Harry Truman. President Truman was the subject of a landmark case, *Youngstown Sheet and Tube Co. v. Sawyer,* invalidating one of his actions. What became known as the "steel seizure case" grew out of an impending industry-wide strike during the Korean War by the United Steel Workers of America when the Wage Stabilization Board failed to settle a dispute between the union and the owners. Truman ignored the provisions of the Taft-Hartley Act that permitted the president to obtain an injunction postponing for eighty days a strike that threatened the national safety and welfare. Instead, he issued an executive order seizing the steel mills, based on his authority under the Constitution and U.S. law and as commander in chief. The steel companies protested the seizure as unconstitutional, and the case went to the Supreme Court.

By a 6–3 vote the Court invalidated the president's action. Justice Hugo L. Black, who wrote the majority opinion (five other justices provided lengthy concurring opinions), summarily rejected Truman's claims of executive prerogative and based his decision on the fact that, in its deliberations over the Taft-Hartley law, Congress had decided against authorizing the president to seize industrial property. Therefore, the chief executive had acted against the will of Congress, which amounted to an unconstitutional usurpation of legislative power. In a notable concurring opinion, Justice Jackson defined three categories of separation-of-powers cases: when the president acts pursuant to an express or implied grant of authority by Congress; when the president acts contrary to the express or implied will of Congress; and, a twilight zone in which the president acts in the absence of either a congressional grant or denial of authority.[75] In this instance, the steel mill seizure was contrary to the intent of Congress, which had not left the area to the president's control. The dissenting opinion, written by Chief Justice Vinson, took the position that in times of a national crisis the president must exercise discretionary prerogative power.

Richard Nixon. When Nixon assumed the presidency, he vowed to appoint to the Supreme Court "strict constructionists" who would not read their own values into the Constitution so as to interfere with the right of public officials (especially police officers) to carry out their duties. During his first term the president appointed four new members to the Court: Chief Justice Burger and Associate Justices Blackmun, Powell, and Rehnquist. Ironically, Nixon himself became the object of no fewer than five adverse decisions of the Supreme Court, and in some of those decisions his own appointees voted against him.

The first case, *New York Times v. United States,* arose out of the publication by the *New York Times* and the *Washington Post* of the *Pentagon Papers,* an inside analysis of U.S. involvement in the war in Southeast Asia, prepared by the Department of Defense.[76] Acting under the president's direction, Attorney General John Mitchell sought a court injunction to prevent publication on the grounds that it would cause grave and irreparable damage to national security and that it violated a provision of the Espionage Act of 1917 forbidding the communication of defense information harmful to the nation's security. Six of the justices decided that such "prior restraint" was unconstitutional. Black and Douglas held that such restraint violates the First Amendment no matter how great the threat to national security; Brennan could find no threat to national security in this particular instance; and White, Marshall, and Stewart based their decision on the absence of statutory authority for federal courts' issuing prior restraint injunctions in national security cases. The three dissenters—Burger, Blackmun, and Harlan—felt that the courts should be more flexible in handling conflicts between First Amendment freedoms and issues of national security.

The most damaging decision for the president, *United States v. Nixon*, was handed down in July 1974 and led ultimately to his resignation.[77] The case grew out of the Watergate affair and involved Special Prosecutor Leon Jaworski's attempt to subpoena tapes of sixty-four conversations between the president and his assistants that Jaworski needed in criminal litigation against some of the leading figures in the Nixon administration. The president refused to surrender the tapes, claiming the existence of an executive privilege relating to private conversations between the chief executive and his advisers. In a unanimous opinion written by Chief Justice Burger, Nixon's first appointee to the Court, the Court recognized for the first time the principle of executive privilege as having "constitutional underpinnings." The opinion went on to say, however, that the Court, not the president, is the final judge of the proper use of executive privilege. Moreover, in this instance, the general claim of the privilege, when unrelated to military, diplomatic, or national security issues, must give way to the more immediate need for evidence in a criminal case and to the fundamental principles of due process of law and the fair administration of justice.

After Nixon left office, he suffered two more judicial defeats. In *Train v. City of New York*, the Court held that the president's impoundment (refusal to make expenditures) of moneys appropriated by Congress under the Water Pollution Control Act of 1972 was unconstitutional because the statute gave him no authority to do so.[78] In so ruling, the Court rejected the president's argument that as chief executive he could impound funds when spending would result in either increased prices or taxes for the American people. In *Nixon v. Administrator, General Services Administration*, the Court upheld the Presidential Recordings and Materials Preservation Act of 1974, placing in federal custody tapes and papers of the Nixon administration.[79] In reaching its decision, the justices weighed the harm done to the individual rights of the former president against the public interest in preserving the Nixon materials and concluded that the latter interest should prevail.

Thus, the federal courts have been willing on some occasions to invalidate presidential actions that exceed constitutional authority. There are also, however, limitations on the willingness of justices to rule against the chief executive.

Limitations on Judicial Checks of Presidential Action

The fact that courts have struck down actions of the president as unconstitutional in only eleven major cases in more than 200 years indicates their reluctance to do so, especially in times of foreign and military crises. None of the major wartime presidents—Lincoln, Wilson, or Franklin Roosevelt—was seriously impeded by the courts in the prosecution of hostilities. During the Civil War the Court in the *Prize Cases* upheld the Union blockade of Southern ports on the grounds that Lincoln's action was necessary to deal with the rebellion.[80] As previously noted, it waited until after the war to decide the *Milligan* case.

During World War I the "hands-off" policy of the courts continued: convictions under the Espionage and Sedition Acts of persons charged with interfering with the war effort were upheld in cases decided after the war was over.[81] During World War II the Supreme Court upheld the government program relocating people of Japanese ancestry, including those who were American citizens, living on the West Coast to camps in the interior, as well as the trial of German saboteurs by a military commission.[82] Only after the relocation centers were being disbanded did the Supreme Court decide that it was unlawful to detain a loyal U.S. citizen of Japanese background.[83] Moreover, in a decision similar to that in the *Milligan* case, the Court ruled that it was unconstitutional for a civilian to be tried by a military commission in Hawaii, but that decision was handed down six months after the hostilities were over.[84] When the Court must rule on presidential actions, particularly in times of crisis, it tends to support the chief executive, or it delays making an adverse decision until the crisis is over.

The federal courts have devised another means of avoiding adverse decisions against the president: they simply declare that a particular issue is a "political question" and refuse to rule on the matter. In doing so the courts rely "on the separation of powers theory—that the Supreme Court exercises the judicial power and leaves political, or policy, questions to Congress and the president." [85] Differentiating between a judicial issue and a political or policy issue is not an easy matter, but the fact that the courts themselves make the distinction allows them to invoke the doctrine when for one reason or another they choose not to invalidate presidential or congressional action. The doctrine is invoked most often in the area of foreign policy. A federal court of appeals used it in 1973 to avoid ruling on the constitutionality of U.S. involvement in the civil war in Cambodia.[86] Finally, some presidential actions simply cannot be dealt with by the courts at all. The qualities Hamilton identified with the executive—"decision, activity, secrecy and dispatch"—are such that the president can present the courts with a fait accompli, about which they can do little or nothing. The most momentous decisions that presidents make, such as those of President Truman to drop the atomic bomb and to send U.S. troops into Korea, do not lend themselves to adjudication and must be dealt with in the political, not the judicial, arena.

Presidential Immunity from Lawsuits

The issue of the president's personal liability for official actions arose in a suit for damages against President Richard Nixon and other high-level officials filed by an air force civil servant who charged that he had been fired at the request of the president for whistle-blowing. In a 5–4 decision, the Supreme Court ruled that presidents have "absolute immunity" from damages resulting from their "official acts."[87] The Court majority reasoned that such lawsuits would likely be numerous and that they would be disruptive and distractive. It maintained that the president should be free to make difficult decisions without fear of personal financial loss.

The issue took on an additional dimension in 1994 when Paula Jones, a former Arkansas state employee, filed suit against President Bill Clinton for an act of sexual harassment allegedly committed in 1991 when he was governor of Arkansas.[88] His attorney argued that the president should have immunity from all civil lawsuits, including those for acts committed before taking office, because they, too, "would distract him from his official duties and throw the Government into disarray."[89] The Justice Department supported Clinton's claim, and U.S. District Court Judge Susan Wright agreed in part. She ruled that a trial in the case should be delayed until Clinton leaves office, but that ruling was reversed in January 1996 by a federal appeals court decision. The Supreme Court heard arguments on the case in January 1997.

President Clinton's legal troubles stemming from acts prior to becoming president were not limited to the Jones lawsuit. His and Mrs. Clinton's investment in an Arkansas real estate venture, the Whitewater Development Company, prompted questions about the propriety and legality of his conduct and led to the appointment of a special prosecutor to investigate.[90] Because these actions did not involve Clinton's official conduct as president he had to pay the costs of dealing with them himself. A legal defense fund established for this purpose resulted in additional charges of impropriety, even though it was supported by voluntary contributions.

Conclusion

Although presidents do not have the day-to-day relationship with the federal courts that they have with Congress and other members of the executive branch, they possess two powers in particular through which they can significantly influence the activities of the courts. One is the power to appoint the members of all federal courts, especially U.S. district courts, U.S. courts of appeals, and the U.S. Supreme Court. The other is the power to help shape the agenda of the appellate courts through the actions of another appointee, the solicitor general of the United States. Moreover, both of these powers have long-term consequences: federal judges, unlike members of Congress and the political appointees of the executive branch, serve for life; and Supreme Court decisions that the solicitor general helps to determine usually are followed by future justices because of the principle of *stare decisis*.

There appears to be a trend toward greater presidential involvement in the selection of federal judges, even those who serve on the lower federal courts. The Carter, Reagan, and Bush administrations paid particularly close attention to the political philosophy of potential judges. The Carter administration also made a major effort to recruit women and members of minority groups to the lower federal bench, and the Reagan administration placed the first woman on the Supreme Court. Because Congress in the mid-1970s and 1980s created a large number of new lower court judgeships, Carter, Reagan, and Bush were able to choose an unusually large proportion of the members of those courts.

Recent presidents (especially Reagan) also made a greater effort to shape federal court opinions through the actions of the solicitor general. Increasingly, that official is chosen with the expectation that he or she will try to implement the president's political agenda, especially by filing amicus curiae briefs in a broad range of cases.

The Reagan administration was much more ambitious than other modern presidencies in its employment of a judicial strategy that attempted to use the federal courts to implement policy goals that it was unable to accomplish through the regular political process. It sought, for example, to outlaw abortion and to provide for voluntary prayer in the public schools. In addition to ideologically driven appointments, the elements of that strategy included an instrumental view of the law and politicization of the administration of justice. Although the Bush administration continued careful ideological screening of judicial appointees, it did not retain the other elements of Reagan's judicial strategy. Clinton had no apparent judicial strategy beyond making the courts more representative of the population by emphasizing diversity in his appointments.

NOTES

1. Joan Biskupic, "Thomas Hearings Illustrate Politics of the Process," *Congressional Quarterly Weekly Report*, Sept. 21, 1991, 2688–2689.

2. Joan Biskupic, "Thomas Picks Up Support as Senate Nears Vote," *Congressional Quarterly Weekly Report*, Oct. 5, 1991, 2867.

3. Joan Biskupic, "Thomas' Victory Puts Icing on Reagan-Bush Court," *Congressional Quarterly Weekly Report*, Oct. 19, 1991, 3026.

4. Ibid., 3030.

5. Alexander Hamilton, James Madison, and John Jay, *The Federalist Papers*, ed. Clinton Rossiter (New York: New American Library, 1961), 322.

6. Ibid., 465.

7. Robert Scigliano, *The Supreme Court and the Presidency* (New York: Free Press, 1971), chap. 1.

8. There are ninety-four U.S. district courts and 649 district court judgeships. There are from one to four judicial districts per state, depending on population. In addition, there are districts in the District of Columbia, Puerto Rico, Guam, the Virgin Islands, and the Northern Mariana Islands. There are thirteen courts of appeals, including one in the District of Columbia. These courts have 179 judgeships.

9. In addition to the federal courts of general jurisdiction authorized by Article III, special courts handle disputes arising from particular functions of Congress under powers granted by Article I. Included are the U.S. Court of Appeals for the Federal Circuit, the U.S. Court of Military Appeals, the U.S. Court of Veterans Appeals, territorial courts, U.S. Claims Court, the U.S. Tax Court, and the U.S. Court of International Trade.

10. Harold Chase, *Federal Judges: The Appointing Process* (Minneapolis: University of Minnesota Press, 1972), 17.

11. Sheldon Goldman, "The Bush Imprint on the Judiciary: Carrying on a Tradition," *Judicature* (April/May 1991): 294–306; and "Judicial Selection Under Clinton: A Midterm Examination," *Judicature* (May/June 1995): 278.

12. Joseph Harris, *The Advice and Consent of the Senate* (Berkeley: University of California Press, 1953), 40.

13. Harold F. Bass, Jr., "Chief of Party," in *Guide to the Presidency*, ed. Michael Nelson (Washington, D.C.: Congressional Quarterly, 1989), 625.

14. Joel Grossman, *Lawyers and Judges: The ABA and the Politics of Judicial Selection* (New York: Wiley, 1965), 42.

15. Chase, *Federal Judges*, 29.

16. Walter Murphy, "Chief Justice Taft and the Lower Court Bureaucracy: A Study in Judicial Administration," *Journal of Politics* (August 1962): 453–476.

17. Grossman, *Lawyers and Judges*, 73.

18. Alan Neff, *The United States District Judge Nominating Commissions: Their Members, Procedures, and Candidates* (Chicago: American Judicature Society, 1981), 14.

19. Goldman, "The Bush Imprint on the Judiciary," 296; Goldman, "Judicial Selection Under Clinton," 283, 288.

20. Sheldon Goldman, "Reorganizing the Judiciary: The First Term Appointments," *Judicature* (April/May 1985): 315–317.

21. Ibid., 315–316.

22. Ibid., 316.

23. Lawrence Baum, *The Supreme Court*, 5th ed. (Washington, D.C.: CQ Press, 1995), 43–45.

24. David M. O'Brien, "The Reagan Judges: His Most Enduring Legacy?" in *The Reagan Legacy*, ed. Charles O. Jones (Chatham, N.J.: Chatham House, 1988), 63.

25. Goldman, "The Bush Imprint on the Judiciary," 296.

26. Goldman, "Judicial Selection Under Clinton," 278–279.

27. Ibid., 278.

28. Sheldon Goldman and Matthew D. Saronson, "Clinton's Nontraditional Judges: Creating a More Representative Bench," *Judicature* (September/October 1994): 68–73.

29. Ibid., 73.

30. Goldman, "Judicial Selection Under Clinton," 283.

31. Ibid., 280, 286.

32. Jon Gottschall, "Reagan Appointments to the United States Court of Appeals: The Continuation of a Judicial Revolution," *Judicature* (June/July 1986): 48–54.

33. Timothy B. Tomasi and Jess A. Velona, "All the President's Men? A Study of Ronald Reagan's Appointments to the U.S. Courts of Appeals," *Columbia Law Review* 87 (May 1987): 792.

34. Scigliano, *The Supreme Court and the Presidency*, 95.

35. David M. O'Brien, *Storm Center: The Supreme Court in American Politics*, 2d ed. (New York: Norton, 1990), 73.

36. Henry Abraham and Bruce Murphy, "The Influence of Sitting and Retired Justices on Presidential Supreme Court Appointments," *Hastings Law Quarterly* 3 (Winter 1976): 37–63.

37. Baum, *The Supreme Court*, 35.

38. Henry Abraham, *The Judicial Process*, 6th ed. (New York: Oxford University Press, 1993), 75.

39. Scigliano, *The Supreme Court and the Presidency*, chap. 4.

40. Henry Abraham, *Justices and Presidents: A Political History of Appointments to the Supreme Court* (New York: Penguin Books, 1974), chap. 2.

41. It should be noted that Associate Justice William Rehnquist's nomination for chief justice in 1986 was attacked by liberal groups because of his alleged insensitivity to the rights of minorities and women. He was ultimately confirmed, but the thirty-three votes against him were the most ever cast against a confirmed justice up to that point.

42. One of Carswell's supporters, Republican senator Roman Hruska of Nebraska, tried to defend him on the grounds that there are many mediocre judges, lawyers, and other people who are entitled to representation on the Court. As Baum

suggests, his statement seemed to support the charges of incompetence against Carswell (*The Supreme Court*, 57–58). In any event, the nomination was rejected by a 51–45 vote.

43. Walter Murphy notes that the ABA Standing Committee on the Federal Judiciary accorded "O'Connor, Rehnquist, Scalia, Bork, and Kennedy its highest ranking." (However, four members of the committee found Bork "not qualified" and one abstained.) Walter F. Murphy, "Reagan's Judicial Strategy," in *Looking Back on the Reagan Presidency*, ed. Larry Berman (Baltimore: Johns Hopkins University Press, 1990), 217. Another Reagan nominee, federal appeals court judge Douglas Ginsburg, withdrew before he could be rated following revelations that he had used marijuana while a faculty member at the Harvard Law School. The ABA committee also gave Souter its highest rating, but found Thomas only to be "qualified." Both Clinton nominees, Ruth Bader Ginsburg and Stephen Breyer, received the committee's highest ranking.

44. Scigliano, *The Supreme Court and the Presidency*, chap. 4.

45. Despite the recent concern with minority representation on the Supreme Court, as John Schmidhauser has pointed out, "The typical Supreme Court justice has generally been white, Protestant (with a penchant for a high social status), usually of ethnic stock originating in the British Isles, and born in comfortable circumstances in an urban or small-town environment." See *Judges and Justices: The Federal Appellate Judiciary* (Boston: Little, Brown, 1979), 96. That description also fits the presidents who have appointed the justices.

46. Although Scalia is the first Italian American to serve on the High Court, little was made of that fact at the time of his nomination and confirmation.

47. Herman Schwartz, *Packing the Courts: The Conservative Campaign to Rewrite the Constitution* (New York: Scribner's, 1988), 140.

48. Elizabeth Drew, *On the Edge: The Clinton Presidency* (New York: Simon & Schuster, 1994), 212–221.

49. Stuart Nagel, "Comparing Elected and Appointed Judicial Systems," *Sage Professional Papers, No. 64-001* (Beverly Hills, Calif.: Sage Publications, 1973), 25–26.

50. Scigliano, *The Supreme Court and the Presidency*, chap. 3.

51. Linda Greenhouse, "Farewell to the Old Order in the Court: The Right Goes Activist and the Center Is a Void," *New York Times*, July 2, 1995, 1-E.

52. A classic instance of justices changing their views was Thomas Jefferson's appointees to the Court, who came under the influence of his political enemy, Chief Justice John Marshall. See Scigliano, *The Supreme Court and the Presidency*, 127.

53. David Rohde and Harold Spaeth, *Supreme Court Decision Making* (San Francisco: Freeman, 1976), 144.

54. Schwartz, *Packing the Courts*, 174–178; Linda Greenhouse, "Judicious Activism: Justice Thomas Hits the Ground Running," *New York Times*, March 1, 1992, E1.

55. Scigliano, *The Supreme Court and the Presidency*, chap. 6.

56. Ibid., 172.

57. Steven Puro, "The United States as Amicus Curiae," in *Courts, Law, and Judicial Processes*, ed. S. Sidney Ulmer (New York: Free Press, 1981), 220–230.

58. Scigliano, *The Supreme Court and the Presidency*, chap. 6; Puro, "The United States as Amicus Curiae"; Karen O'Connor, "The Amicus Curiae Role of the U.S. Solicitor General in Supreme Court Litigation," *Judicature* (December/January 1983): 261.

59. This situation is to be contrasted with the paucity of experience attorneys general have before the Court: traditionally, they argue only one case before their term is over. For an interesting account of Robert Kennedy's first appearance before

the Court two years after he became attorney general, see Victor Navasky, *Kennedy Justice* (New York: Athenaeum, 1980), chap. 6.

60. Lincoln Caplan, *The Tenth Justice: The Solicitor General and the Rule of Law* (New York: Random House, 1987).

61. Elder Witt, *A Different Justice* (Washington, D.C.: Congressional Quarterly, 1986), chaps. 6, 7.

62. Caplan, *The Tenth Justice*, 79–80.

63. Ibid., 255–256.

64. Steven Puro, "Presidential Relationships with the Solicitor Generals of the United States: Political Science Research at Presidential Libraries" (Paper delivered at the 1978 annual meeting of the Missouri and Kansas Political Science Association).

65. *Hepburn v. Griswold (First Legal Tender Case)*, 8 Wall. 506 (1870).

66. *Knox v. Lee, Parker v. Davis (Second Legal Tender Case)*, 12 Wall. 457 (1871).

67. *Ex parte McCardle*, 7 Wall. 506 (1869).

68. *Roe v. Wade*, 410 U.S. 113 (1973).

69. *Ex parte Merryman*, 17 F. Cases 144 (1861).

70. The president's obligation to obey judicial orders has not been fully clarified (see Scigliano, *The Supreme Court and the Presidency*, chap. 2). One reason is that few conflicts of this nature have arisen. A second is that the area is cloudy because both the president and the judges are sworn to uphold the Constitution, and under the separation of powers doctrine, neither is superior to the other. In the event that a president should flatly disobey a judicial order, the issuing court could hold him in contempt and order him jailed until he carried out the directive. However, the court would have to depend on executive branch officials to arrest the president. A second recourse to presidential disobedience of a judicial order would be for Congress, not the judiciary, to initiate impeachment proceedings. Ultimately, the issue could be decided through the electoral process. Most likely, both the courts and the president would make every effort to avoid precipitating a constitutional crisis.

71. *Youngstown Sheet and Tube Co. v. Sawyer*, 343 U.S. 579 (1952).

72. *United States v. Nixon*, 418 U.S. 683 (1974).

73. *Marbury v. Madison*, 1 Cr. 137 (1803).

74. *Ex parte Milligan*, 4 Wall. 2, 121 (1866).

75. *Youngstown Sheet and Tube Co.*, 343 U.S. at 637.

76. *New York Times v. United States*, 403 U.S. 713 (1971).

77. *United States v. Nixon*, 418 U.S. 683 (1974).

78. *Train v. City of New York*, 420 U.S. 35 (1975).

79. *Nixon v. Administrator, General Services Administration*, 443 U.S. 425 (1977).

80. *Prize Cases*, 2 Black 635 (1863).

81. *Schenck v. United States*, 249 U.S. 47 (1919); *Abrams v. United States*, 250 U.S. 616 (1919); and *Pierce v. United States*, 252 U.S. 239 (1920).

82. *Korematsu v. United States*, 323 U.S. 214 (1944); *Ex parte Quirin*, 317 U.S. 1 (1942).

83. *Ex parte Endo*, 323 U.S. 283 (1944).

84. *Duncan v. Kahanamoku*, 327 U.S. 304 (1946).

85. Elder Witt, ed., *Guide to the U.S. Supreme Court*, 2d ed. (Washington, D.C.: Congressional Quarterly, 1990), 200.

86. *Holtzman v. Schlesinger*, 484 F. 2d 1307 (1973).

87. *Nixon v. Fitzgerald*, 457 U.S. 731 (1982).

88. Neil A. Lewis, "Clinton to Seek Immunity from Lawsuits," *New York Times*, May 20, 1994, A-1.

89. Ibid.

90. "The Prosecutor's Brief," *U.S. News & World Report*, March 21, 1994, 31. Some possible questions were (1) Were taxpayer-insured deposits from Madison Guaranty (a failed federal savings and loan institution) diverted into Whitewater accounts to help the Clintons or the corporation? (2) Was Madison money illegally diverted to pay off Bill Clinton's 1984 gubernatorial campaign debt? (3) Did the Clintons claim tax deductions for Whitewater interest payments they did not make? (4) Was it improper for Mrs. Clinton [an attorney] to represent Madison in 1985 as it was seeking approval for new capital from a state regulator appointed by Bill Clinton?

READINGS

Abraham, Henry. *Justices and Presidents: A Political History of Appointments to the Supreme Court.* 2d ed. New York: Oxford University Press, 1985.

Baum, Lawrence. *The Supreme Court.* 5th ed. Washington, D.C.: CQ Press, 1995.

Biskupic, Joan, and Elder Witt. *The Supreme Court and the Powers of the American Government.* Washington, D.C.: CQ Press, 1996.

Bonner, Ethan. *Battle for Justice: How the Bork Nomination Shook America.* New York: Norton, 1989.

Caplan, Lincoln. *The Tenth Justice: The Solicitor General and the Rule of Law.* New York: Random House, 1987.

Carp, Robert, and Ronald Stidham. *The Federal Courts.* 2d ed. Washington, D.C.: CQ Press, 1991.

Chase, Harold. *Federal Judges: The Appointing Process.* Minneapolis: University of Minnesota Press, 1972.

Grossman, Joel. *Lawyers and Judges: The ABA and the Politics of Judicial Selection.* New York: Wiley, 1965.

Jackson, Robert. *The Struggle for Judicial Supremacy.* New York: Knopf, 1941.

Neff, Alan. *The United States District Judge Nominating Commissions: Their Members, Procedures, and Candidates.* Chicago: American Judicature Society, 1981.

Schwartz, Herman. *Packing the Courts: The Conservative Campaign to Rewrite the Constitution.* New York: Scribner's, 1988.

Scigliano, Robert. *The Supreme Court and the Presidency.* New York: Free Press, 1971.

Witt, Elder. *A Different Justice.* Washington, D.C.: Congressional Quarterly, 1986.

PART III

THE PRESIDENT AND
PUBLIC POLICY

8 THE POLITICS OF DOMESTIC POLICY

The newly sworn-in President Clinton visits a day-care center in 1993. Clinton had entered office committed to being a "domestic policy president."

BILL CLINTON WAS THE FIRST PRESI-dent since FDR to win election with a campaign that focused almost exclusively on domestic problems. In fact, one of Clinton's sharpest criticisms of Bush was that he had neglected serious social and economic conditions in the U.S. while concentrating on foreign policy. Clinton appeared to be undaunted by the conventional wisdom, in vogue since the end of World War II, that has regarded domestic policy as the black hole of presidential politics.

As soon as a president takes office he confronts a vast array of problems, issues, and demands for government action. Already in operation are numerous, complex and costly programs that compete for limited funds. Many of them enjoy the support of powerful interest groups and congressional leaders. Whatever the president does (or fails to do) in response to public demands is likely to cost him political support.

Presidents face a congested public policy agenda that results from interrelatedness, overlapping, and layering of issues.[1] Many political scientists have classified public policy for analytical purposes, but the most widely used classification scheme, or typology, is Theodore Lowi's division of policies into distributive, regulatory, and redistributive categories.[2] He based his categories on whom the policies affect, ranging from individuals to the entire society, and the likelihood that the government will have to exercise coercion to implement the policy.

Distributive policies have the most diffused impact. They affect specific groups of people and provide individualized benefits. They have low visibility, produce little conflict, and are not likely to require the application of coercion. Examples of distributive policies include agricultural price supports, public works projects, and research and development programs. *Regulatory* policies affect large segments of society and involve the application of coercion. Although regulatory issues tend to be highly technical, they often are quite visible and controversial. Examples include pollution control, antitrust, and occupational safety and health. *Redistributive* policies have the broadest impact on society. They involve the transfer of resources (wealth and income) from some groups to others. They require coercion, are highly visible, and usually are accompanied by social or class conflict. Examples of redistributive policies include Social Security and tax reform.

Lowi argued that the type of policy determines the focus and behavior of political actors. Distributive policy politics involve limited presidential and extensive congressional participation and decision making that relies heavily on logrolling—the mutual exchange of support for legislation. Regulatory policy politics produce moderate presidential and substantial congressional interest and involvement, with frequent conflict between the president and Congress. Redistributive policy politics often are fraught with ideological disputes and presidential-congressional conflict. Presidents tend to be most involved with redistributive policy issues. This is the case whether the government is seeking to expand or contract the scope of its activities.

Steven Shull has used Lowi's policy typology to examine presidential and congressional roles in domestic policy formation. He found that there were "some differences in presidential and congressional behavior . . . along lines anticipated by the 'theory,'" and that "modest empirical distinctions" exist among the three policy categories.[3] The principal problem with Lowi's typology is the difficulty in making it operational for purposes of measurement. The problem arises because an issue may change its designation over time, starting out, for example, as a redistributive issue and becoming distributive. This is what happened to Title I of the Elementary and Secondary Education Act of 1965, a program of federal assistance to local school districts for economically disadvantaged children. As a new program, it sparked controversy because of its redistributive effects, but over time it became a routinized distribution of federal funds that was part of the established structure of school finance. In other words, Lowi's categories are not fixed in time. Shull concluded that Lowi's typology is not as useful as substantive classification based on policy content.

John Kessel has broken down domestic policy into areas involving social benefits, civil liberties, agriculture, and natural resources.[4] Each area entails a specific type of politics and its own temporal pattern, both of which have implications for presidential participation. The politics of social benefits, such as housing and Social Security retirement, are allocative: there is a strong similarity here to Lowi's distributive and redistributive categories. Presidents use the distribution of social benefits to build public support; therefore, they tend to pay most attention to social benefits as they approach reelection, after which, if they are successful, they are much less concerned. Civil rights involves a pattern of politics that is regulatory and highly sensitive because of differing conceptions of fairness. Presidents are most likely to act on civil rights issues immediately after their election, both because these issues are highly controversial and because campaign promises must be fulfilled. The politics of natural resources and environmental protection are primarily regulatory, and agriculture mostly involves allocation. The temporal patterns in natural resource and agricultural policy politics are a function of long-range developments and entail limited presidential participation.

Whether one approaches domestic policy using Lowi's analytical typology or Kessel's substantive classifications, it is clear that as a practical matter presidents can become fully involved with only a small number of problems and issues. The Lowi and Kessel approaches suggest that in domestic policy, presidents tend to focus on matters such as maintaining the financial integrity of the Social Security system, reforming welfare, and major civil rights proposals. They do not take up all major redistributive, social benefit, and civil rights issues and may consciously avoid some that may involve enormous financial or political costs. They are unlikely to become bogged down with routine distributive policies or with the technicalities of economic and social regulation. Jimmy Carter harmed himself politically when he tangled with Congress over eighteen water projects he regarded as unnecessary. Other presidents have been content to leave the distribution of "pork barrel" projects to Congress.

The range and complexity of domestic problems and issues produces a policy congestion that makes coordination the essential presidential function in this area. Coordination has been complicated, however, by the interrelatedness of domestic, economic, and national security policy. If, on the one hand, presidents attempt to coordinate policies through simplification—say, by proposals to balance the budget or reorganize the bureaucracy—they encounter the opposition of powerful forces mobilized around policy issues. Ronald Reagan's 1982 proposals to move toward a balanced budget by reducing Social Security cost-of-living allowances provide an excellent example. Opposition from the "gray lobby" and most members of Congress quickly stymied the idea. If, on the other hand, presidents fail to coordinate complex policies effectively, they risk loss of popular and congressional support as well as interest group opposition. This happened in 1993 and 1994 when Bill Clinton was unable to relate his health care and welfare reform proposals to each other and to the budget deficit.

The Domestic Policy Process

The domestic policy process has formal and informal dimensions, both of which affect the presidency. The formal dimension consists of actions that culminate in the development and presentation of legislative proposals to Congress, the issuance of executive orders, and the preparation and submission of annual budgets. There is a cyclical regularity to much of the formal policy process because annual events, such as the State of the Union, budget, and economic messages, define the broad outlines of the president's program.[5] (Although these events occur at approximately the same time each year, the full cycles last longer than a year. The budget for the fiscal year beginning on October 1, 1997, for example, had its origins in the budget review process conducted in the spring of 1995.) The formal policy cycles are preceded by and merge with an informal process that sets the president's agenda.

Policy Streams

The process of setting the president's domestic policy agenda can be understood as the convergence in the White House of three tributary streams: the first identifies problems and issues requiring attention; the second produces proposed solutions to the problems; and the third carries the political factors that establish the context for policy making. According to John Kingdon, the three streams operate largely, but not absolutely, independently of one another. Problems and solutions develop separately and may or may not be joined, and political factors may change regardless of whether policy makers have recognized a problem or whether a potential solution is available. In Paul Light's model, the streams are brought together by two "filters"—resources and opportunities. In reality, he argues, presidents keep the flow of problems and solutions under control by having the White House staff, including the domestic policy apparatus, make the "filtering decisions." Successful policy leadership results from combining appropriate problems and solutions under favorable political circumstances.[6]

Problems and Issues. Problems and issues move onto the president's domestic policy agenda either because their seriousness and high visibility make it impossible to avoid them or because of presidential discretion. Examples of unavoidable problems include the energy shortages of the 1970s, high rates of inflation and unemployment, the emergence of acquired immune deficiency syndrome (AIDS) as a major threat to public health, and the problems resulting from increased drug usage.

Problems and issues stand a good chance of gaining a place on the agenda when enough important people, inside and outside the government, begin to think that something should be done about them.[7] This may happen as a consequence of changes in economic and social indicators, such as rates of inflation, unemployment, infant mortality, and students' scores on various standardized tests. Influential decision makers in the presidency, the bureaucracy, Congress, the private sector, and state and local governments routinely monitor changes in a large array of indicators. Whether these changes add up to a problem is a matter of interpretation. That interpretation takes place in the context of the symbolic significance of the matter, the personal experiences of the president and the other decision makers with it, and the relationship of the subject to other problems and issues.

The president and other decision makers may be moved to recognize a condition as a compelling problem because of a "focusing event," such as a disaster or a crisis. For example, the near meltdown of a reactor at the Three Mile Island power plant in March 1979 thrust the issue of

nuclear safety to the forefront of the domestic agenda after its proponents had struggled for years with little success to gain recognition for
it. Similarly, riots in Los Angeles in May 1992 rekindled interest in
urban policy for the first time since the 1960s.

In addition, the president on occasion has no choice but to deal with
a problem, even though he may prefer not to do so. The situation in Los
Angeles prodded a reluctant President George Bush to propose legislation to aid the damaged city. Similarly, events in Somalia, Haiti, and
Bosnia forced President Bill Clinton to devote more attention than he
wished to foreign policy.

Some problems and issues remain on the agenda through successive
presidential administrations. Feasible solutions may not have been
found, solutions may have been tried unsuccessfully, or the problem
may have been "solved" only to reemerge in a different form. Health
care exemplifies such an issue. President Harry S. Truman proposed a
comprehensive national health insurance program in 1945 as an additional Social Security benefit.[8] The American Medical Association and
major business associations successfully attacked the proposal as
"socialized medicine." Both Presidents John F. Kennedy and Lyndon B.
Johnson advanced proposals for national health insurance and in 1965
Congress responded partially with Medicare, a health insurance plan
for Social Security retirees aged sixty-five and over. Since then, pressures have continued for a plan that would provide universal coverage.
In the 1970s it received support from Presidents Richard M. Nixon and
Jimmy Carter, as opinion polls showed that a majority of the population favored some kind of national health insurance program. During
the recession in the early 1990s, health care reform became a salient
issue as millions of workers either lost or feared losing health insurance
along with their jobs. In 1991 Harris Wofford, an unknown Pennsylvania Democrat, defeated a popular Republican ex-governor and former U.S. attorney general, Richard Thornburg, in a special Senate election by advocating health care reform. Bill Clinton made the need for
health care reform one of the central issues in his 1992 presidential
campaign and it became one of the principal goals of the domestic policy agenda in his first two years.

Not all issues, however, can command a place on the president's
agenda, and presidents have broad discretion to determine which they
emphasize. Presidents choose to deal with certain problems because
they see them as instrumental to the achievement of their goals. Three
goals affect presidents' selection of problems and issues for their agen-

das: reelection (for a first-term president); historical achievement; and a desire to shape public policy in accordance with their beliefs.[9] Presidents vary in the emphasis they place on these goals. Richard Nixon's willingness to propose innovative policies for welfare reform and revenue sharing, even at the expense of alienating some of his conservative supporters, reflected his concern with historical achievement.[10] Reagan consistently defined domestic policy in terms of his conservative ideology, even at the risk of electoral disadvantage. As he approached his reelection campaign, Carter shifted from making agenda decisions on the basis of his beliefs to making them on the basis of politics. Bush drew frequent criticism for his limited, largely reactive domestic agenda that "intrigued some in Washington less for what it contained . . . than for what it ignored."[11] Clinton's initial agenda reflected his desire to implement substantial domestic policy reforms in accordance with his centrist strategy as a New Democrat. After the Republican victory in the 1994 congressional elections, Clinton scaled down and modified his agenda with a view toward his 1996 reelection campaign.

Solutions. Once a problem or an issue has been recognized, the availability of a solution becomes an important determinant of whether it will rise to a high position on the president's agenda.[12] Rarely do presidents attempt to find new solutions because the incentives to do so are few.[13] Solutions take several forms, ranging from direct actions, such as legislative proposals or executive orders, to symbolic actions, such as appointment of a study commission or a task force, to no action at all. Problems can have several solutions, and a solution can be applied to more than one problem. Solutions attach themselves to a problem, or they may be consciously selected from among competing alternatives. Most solutions that are coupled with problems on the president's agenda come from ideas generated outside the presidency, because the presidency is a small institution in relation to its external environment, which contains an enormous number of potential sources of ideas. Also, there is not sufficient time for those assisting the president independently to analyze problems and issues and to evaluate alternative solutions to them. The principal external sources of ideas are Congress, the bureaucracy, interest groups, universities, "think tanks" or research institutes, and state and local governments. Within the presidency, the president's campaign promises are a source of policy proposals and a benchmark for evaluating externally generated ideas.[14] Occasionally, the president's domestic policy staff may develop new ideas.

Many of the ideas that emerge as proposed solutions to problems on the president's agenda have been circulating among members of "issue networks" that develop around clusters of related problems and issues. Individual policy entrepreneurs in Congress, government agencies, research organizations, universities, and state and local governments promote specific ideas and proposals, such as health care reform, welfare reform, and tax reform. These advocates are motivated by a desire to advance their personal and organizational interests and to influence public policy in accordance with their values. They study, analyze, and discuss problems and solutions among themselves, and they attempt to inform and influence the major decision makers in government, the most important of whom is the president.

The process by which ideas develop, advance, and either succeed or fail to gain acceptance in an issue network is often lengthy and generally diffused. John Kingdon describes it as a "policy primeval soup" in which ideas are continually bumping into one another, and either surviving, dying, combining, or emerging into new forms.[15] Those that manage to become incorporated into policy proposals that the president accepts are evaluated according to three criteria: economic, political, and technical feasibility.

The cost of a potential solution is especially important, as demands for federal expenditures far outweigh the government's capacity to supply the necessary funds. Few proposals for major new spending programs are likely to survive in an era of resource constraints. Proposals to restrain or reduce spending are more attractive to a president struggling to control the budget deficit. A proposal's political feasibility is determined initially by its compatibility with the values and interests of other important decision makers, particularly in Congress. Ultimately, a proposal must gain the acquiescence, if not the acceptance, of the public. The technical feasibility of a proposal—the question of its workability—does not receive as much attention as its economic and political costs. Some ideas—such as proposals for welfare reform that maintain reasonably high payments, reduce inequities between recipients in different states and between recipients and the working poor, and do not increase the cost to the government—are economically and politically very attractive but unworkable in practice. Presidents Nixon and Carter made this discovery, much to their dismay, after the failure of their major efforts to achieve welfare reform.[16]

Similar problems plagued the Clinton administration and the Republican leaders of the 104th Congress as they sought to develop a mutually acceptable wefare reform bill in 1995. Both sides wanted legislation that would reduce welfare dependency with no increase in the budget. Not only were such goals incompatible, but Clinton and the Republicans disagreed fundamentally over the means to achieve them.[17] Twice, in December 1995 and January 1996, Clinton vetoed Republican bills that ended welfare as a federal entitlement by turning it over to the states, but in August 1996 he signed a similar compromise bill.[18] Such conflict among the three criteria is always present. Budget costs may rule out a proposal that is politically and technically feasible, such as rapid cleanup of toxic waste sites. Or political costs may prevent acceptance of a workable proposal that is compatible with a tight budget, such as freezing Social Security cost-of-living increases. Eventually, a short list of presidential proposals emerges from a multitude of potential solutions.

Political Factors. The third major component of the presidential policy stream is the tributary that carries political factors.[19] It flows independently of the problems and solutions streams, but it affects the setting and implementation of the president's agenda. The principal political factors are the national mood, the balance of political forces, and events within the government.

The national mood is a somewhat amorphous phenomenon that is difficult to define. It is not identical with public opinion, nor can it be ascertained through survey research. It is perhaps best described as the perception among important decision makers that a consensus exists or is building in the country among various attentive publics and political activists for specific government policies. Politicians sense the national mood in suggestions, requests, and other communications from interest groups, state and local government officials, corporate executives, and politically active citizens; in news media coverage of events; and in editorial commentary. The national mood also reflects the influence of social movements such as civil rights, environmentalism, and family values. Without a favorable national mood, major new policies, such as health care reform during the Clinton administration, are not likely to be adopted. Although initially supportive, the public became increasingly skeptical of the Clinton health plan. The national mood is, then, a reflection of the politically relevant climate or temper of the times.

Considerably more concrete than the national mood is the extent of consensus and conflict among organized political forces. The prospects for adoption of a proposed policy change depend on the balance of organized interests and other forces, but assessing the balance on any issue is largely a matter of informed guesswork. The complex pattern of pluralistic political forces and the fragmentation of government authority combine to provide a strong advantage to the *opponents* of policy change. Often, heavy political costs are associated with even raising an issue for consideration, let alone obtaining adoption of a proposal. This is particularly the case with existing government programs, most of which have powerful clientele groups that stand ready to defend their programs. Clientele interests, in triangular alliances with agencies that administer "their" programs and with congressional subcommittees with jurisdiction over those programs, engage in bargaining and logrolling to maintain and enhance the programs. To overcome the natural inertia of the government, a strong constituency for political change must be mobilized; otherwise, a proposal will encounter much difficulty. For example, the Carter administration's efforts to enact a national energy policy were unsuccessful despite widespread shortages of fuels, until compromises made the proposal acceptable to the oil industry and consumer interests.

Events in government are the third major political factor that shapes the president's policy agenda. Election outcomes can produce fundamental changes in the agenda. The 1980 election, which brought Ronald Reagan to the presidency and gave the Republicans control of the Senate for the first time in a quarter of a century, was such an event. An ideologically defined, conservative agenda replaced the liberal agenda that had been in effect since the New Deal. Similarly, the 1994 election, in which the Republicans captured control of both houses of Congress for the first time in forty years, profoundly reshaped President Clinton's domestic agenda. Much of the revised agenda consisted of defensive reactions to Republican proposals to curtail affirmative action and regulatory policies affecting the environment, occupational health and safety, and business and financial practices, and to achieve major cost savings in Medicare. Moreover, it did not include health care reform, and the welfare reform proposal was conservatively fashioned to compete with Republican plans. Even the appointment of one official, such as Donald Regan as White House chief of staff in February 1985, can have a substantial effect on the formulation and content of the agenda. Under Regan, the domestic issue agenda began to be determined by a few aggressive cabinet members—Attorney General Edwin Meese III and Treasury Secretary James A. Baker III—rather than by several cabinet committees, as in Reagan's first term.[20]

Jurisdictional matters are another intragovernmental development that may affect agenda setting. Disputes over bureaucratic and committee turf often delay or prevent action, although jurisdictional competition occasionally may accelerate consideration of a popular issue. Also, a proposal may be structured so that it will be handled by a committee or agency that is favorably disposed to it.

In sum, the most significant domestic policy action is likely to occur when the national mood and election outcomes combine to overcome the normal inertia produced by the balance of political forces and the fragmentation of government authority among numerous bureaucratic and congressional fiefdoms. Once items begin to rise on the agenda, however, organized political forces attempt to shape policy proposals to their advantage or to defeat them outright.

Resources and Opportunities

The convergence of specific problems and solutions under favorable circumstances creates a strong probability of a place on the president's agenda. Not all problems and solutions, however, can receive the president's attention and consideration. Because agenda space is limited, presidents must establish priorities.[21] This is accomplished through what Light calls a "filtering process" that maintains an orderly flow of problems and solutions to the president and merges them to produce policy proposals. The objectives of the process are to control the flow of items so that important problems, issues, and alternatives receive attention without overloading the president and to ensure that policy proposals have been formulated with due regard to relevant political factors. There are two filters through which problems and solutions pass as they are melded into presidential decisions: resources and opportunities.

Presidents cannot place all policy proposals they receive on their agenda. Some proposals are not compatible with their overall objectives and their ideologies, but many otherwise acceptable proposals never reach the agenda because limitations on their resources impose constraints on the choices open to presidents. When Reagan took office, a lengthy list of conservative policy goals awaited action. He decided to focus on reducing the scope of domestic programs, increasing military preparedness, and reducing taxes. He accomplished most of these goals during his first year in office. He disappointed many of his supporters, however, by not moving forward with equally strong support for proposals that would end abortion, restore prayer in public schools, and provide financial aid to parents of children enrolled in private schools.

Reagan and his staff recognized that his resources, although substantial, were limited and that successful policy leadership requires the careful use of them.

"Political capital" is the reservoir of popular and congressional support with which newly elected presidents begin their terms. As they make controversial decisions, they "spend" some of their capital, which they seldom are able to replenish. They must decide which proposals merit the expenditure of political capital and in what amounts. Reagan, for example, was willing to spend his capital heavily on reducing the role of the federal government, cutting taxes, and reforming the income tax code, but not on antiabortion or school prayer amendments to the Constitution. Material resources determine which proposals for new programs can be advanced and the emphasis to be placed on existing programs.

Bill Clinton's initial political capital was not sufficient to enact his ambitious agenda.[22] Although he won a clear electoral college victory and had a 6 percent vote margin over George Bush, he received only 43 percent of the popular vote. Immediately after the election the Republican Senate leader, Bob Dole, pointedly claimed to speak for the 57 percent of the electorate who had opposed Clinton. Although Clinton's victory ended twelve years of divided government, the potential for ending presidential-congressional stalemate over domestic policy was diminished with the Republican gain of ten seats in the House of Representatives. Congressional Republicans, no longer constrained by loyalty to their own president, were free to oppose Clinton in order to discredit his leadership. Moreover, the centrist New Democrat stance that Clinton adopted to win election was not shared by a majority of congressional Democrats, who were considerably more liberal. Finally, the damage to Clinton's image done in the campaign by allegations of sexual misconduct and his avoidance of military service in the Vietnam War reduced the public's trust and support of him.

Opportunities often are described metaphorically as windows: they open for a while and then close. They may be scheduled or unscheduled. Scheduled opportunities occur in conjunction with the annual cycle of presidential messages to Congress (State of the Union, budget, and economic report), the congressional calendar, and action-forcing deadlines, such as renewals of program authorizations. The president's greatest opportunity to set the agenda occurs during January and February, when Congress begins a new session and he delivers his messages, and in August and September, when Congress returns from recess and earlier proposals can be replaced or modified.[23] Unscheduled opportunities occur as the result of focusing events or changes in political conditions. Both scheduled and unscheduled windows of opportunity eventually close, some sooner than others. An opportunity is more likely to be seized and an issue given a high place on the president's agenda when problems, solutions, and political factors come together.[24] Without a viable solution and in the absence of favorable political conditions, a problem has a limited chance of moving up on the agenda. For instance, popular support for biomedical research is substantial, but the slow pace of development of treatments and cures for cancer limits presidential attention to the issue.

Opportunities also fluctuate as a presidential term progresses. In a president's first year in office, Congress and the public have high expectations of policy change based on campaign promises and the election mandate. Opportunities tend to be at their peak during the so-called honeymoon period. In the second and fourth years of a president's term, concern focuses increasingly on the forthcoming election campaign, and policy opportunities decline. The third year frequently is regarded as crucial, for the administration is by then experienced, mature, removed from immediate electoral pressures, and anxious to make its mark.[25] Opportunities are most likely to be exploited effectively then and in the first year of a president's second term, assuming he is reelected. Because a second-term president will not continue in office, his "lame-duck" status tends to restrict further his policy opportunities. The effects of lame-duck status on presidential initiatives are especially notable following the midterm congressional election in a president's second term.

There are conflicting patterns in the progression of a president's opportunities as he moves through his term. On the one hand, as presidents acquire experience and expertise, they become more effective and thus increase their policy opportunities. On the other hand, as their congressional and popular support declines through the term, they lose opportunities. Light describes these as cycles of increasing effectiveness and declining influence.[26] It is ironic that as presidents become more skilled at finding opportunities, they become less able to exploit them.

The Domestic Policy Environment

The most outstanding characteristic of the domestic policy environment is its complexity. Myriad actors—individuals, groups, and other government institutions and agencies—all pursue a seemingly incalculable range of objectives and protect countless interests. Although the president's power is limited, he is better situated than anyone else to give direction and bring some degree of coordination to the domestic policies of the U.S. government.

The fragmentation of political power and influence that is the hallmark of the U.S. political system is the product of a heterogeneous and pluralistic society and of constitutional arrangements designed to produce deliberate rather than expeditious government decision making. Nowhere is the fragmentation of power more apparent and more profound than in the domestic policy environment.

Outside the government, thousands of interest groups constantly seek to influence policy. They range from organizations that are concerned with the full range of the government's activities, such as Americans for Democratic Action, to those that focus on a single issue, such as the National Rifle Association (NRA), which is dedicated to preventing the adoption of strict gun control legislation. Interest groups are concerned not only with virtually every government program that distributes benefits to individuals and organizations and regulates their conduct but also with possibilities for new programs. Simply stated, the objectives of interest groups are to secure the adoption of policies that are beneficial to their members and to prevent the adoption of policies they view as harmful to them. Interest groups operate in all sectors of domestic policy—agriculture, civil rights, social welfare, and natural resources. They include organizations that represent business, labor, the professions, consumers, state and local governments and their subdivisions, public officials, social groupings based on age, sex, race, religion, shared attitudes and experiences, and groups that present themselves as protectors of the unorganized public interest.

Within the national government, interest groups attempt to exert influence directly on Congress, the bureaucracy, the courts, and the presidency. Beginning with Lyndon Johnson, presidents have responded by assigning individual White House aides the responsibility for maintaining liaison with interest groups in policy areas such as civil rights, education, and health. When a few individual aides were unable to manage the function of interest group liaison, as increasing numbers of groups sought access to the presidency, the White House established the Public Liaison Office as a counterpart to the Congressional Liaison Office. Interest groups have attempted to exert influence indirectly, principally by endorsing and making campaign contributions to presidential and congressional candidates and by urging their members to bring pressure to bear on the White House and on their representatives in Congress.

It is difficult to measure the effectiveness of interest group influence on public policy because there are multiple points of access to government decision makers; numerous groups usually seek to influence a particular policy or set of related policies; and powerful forces other than interest groups also are at work. Nonetheless, there is widespread belief that the growth in interest group activity since 1965 contributed substantially to the rise of federal spending on domestic programs and the expansion of federal regulation into noneconomic areas, such as consumer protection, product safety, and occupational safety and health.[27] Since 1965 previously unorganized groups—for example, consumer groups, public interest groups, and groups representing various minorities and the poor—have successfully demanded federal benefits and regulatory intervention in behalf of their members. These demands, often asserted as a matter of "right" and defended on grounds of fairness or improving the quality of life, strained the fiscal capacity of the federal government and created new conflicts in society.

Mancur Olson, an economist, has argued that societies with large numbers of powerful "distributional coalitions" (his term for interest groups) have experienced unsupportably high public spending and little or no economic growth as a consequence of the political influence of such groups. The groups press for public benefits for their members even though the result may be disadvantageous to the entire community. According to Olson, unless an interest group encompasses most of the population, there is "no constraint on the social cost such an organization will find it expedient to impose on the society in the cause of obtaining a larger share of the social output for itself." [28] To a substantial extent, domestic policy politics have become the pursuit of narrow group interests, even at the expense of the general public interest, which is usually unorganized, unarticulated, and difficult to identify or define. The president is better situated, in terms of political resources, than anyone else to define, enhance, and defend the public interest. That is his principal challenge in the domestic policy area. President Truman was fond of saying that his job was to act as a lobbyist for the American people, most of whom are not represented by lobbyists.

The pattern of interest group activity traditionally has been described as "policy subgovernments," mutually beneficial triangular relationships between interest groups, administrative agencies, and congressional subcommittees. Subgovernments, and the more open and amorphous "issue networks" that cut across and intersect with them, contribute to the fragmentation of power and influence in the domestic policy environment. That fragmentation is enhanced by constitutional arrangements that divide power among the branches of government and between the national and state governments and also by the internal structures of Congress and the federal bureaucracy. The constitutional design was created to prevent the abuse of power through the establishment of a system of "separated institutions sharing power." [29]

The Framers invented federalism as a means of resolving the seemingly insoluble conflict between advocates of a consolidated system of government and the proponents of state sovereignty. Their ingenious compromise, which artfully avoided establishing a precise boundary between national and state powers, has been adapted to the needs of the times by successive generations of political leaders. The current system of federalism still leaves primary responsibility for most basic government services in the hands of the states and their local subdivisions. These services include public education, public and mental health, public safety, and construction and maintenance of streets, roads, and highways. The federal government has programs that help finance state and local activities in these and other areas, and it exerts a substantial degree of influence on them by virtue of its grant and regulatory programs. Still, most of its domestic policy activity does not entail direct federal administration.

The president's leadership role in domestic policy requires that he persuade, bargain, and cooperate with Congress, federal administrators, and state and local officials. In these relationships he has limited power to command. Rather, he must rely on his skills as a political leader—principally persuasion and bargaining—to achieve his goals.

The structure of authority in Congress has varied over time with a prevailing tendency toward fragmentation. The reforms of the early 1970s, while strengthening somewhat the majority party leadership in the House, provided members with extensive opportunities to influence policy. [30] Consequently, Congress often found it difficult to give direction to public policy, and presidents encountered problems in their relations with Congress. Unlike the political environment of the late 1950s and 1960s, presidents could not easily negotiate agreements with top party leaders and one or two influential chairs in each house and be confident that those agreements would prevail in floor voting. Rather, recent presidents have had to deal separately, in each house, with several committee chairs, subcommittee chairs, and party leaders. Agreements reached at one stage in the legislative process have often come undone later on.

The congressional environment changed dramatically following the Republican takeover in 1994. In the House the new majority leadership under Speaker Newt Gingrich (R-Ga.) imposed tight discipline on Republican members and committee chairs, who were eager to implement a conservative policy revolution.[31] Party government not seen since the first decade of the twentieth century seemed to have returned, at least for the time being. Although the new Senate was predictably less disciplined, its Republican majority demonstrated considerable unity given the disruptiveness of the presidential candidacies of majority leader Bob Dole and Phil Gramm of Texas. The durability of the new pattern of greater party unity and increased ideological polarization in Congress and their impact on the president's role in domestic policy making are not yet fully apparent.

The effects of extensive congressional fragmentation on the president's involvement in domestic policy have been mixed. Congress has been unable to counterbalance the presidency by providing alternative policy leadership, but at the same time, presidents have found it increasingly difficult to lead Congress. Congressional influence has been extensive, if only in a negative sense, because of its inertia and its ability to resist presidential direction. Whether this condition will change with increased centralization of authority and purpose on the part of the congressional majority remains to be seen.

Fragmentation of a different sort characterizes the federal bureaucracy. As noted in Chapter 6, an independent power exists in the bureaucracy that is based in career civil servants, who constitute a permanent government. The members of the permanent government have professional and agency loyalties and close ties to the interest groups who constitute their clientele and to the congressional subcommittees with jurisdiction over their appropriations and the legislation that authorizes their programs. Subgovernments and issue networks comprise members of the permanent government and complicate presidential control of policy development and implementation in the bureaucracy. Also, the fragmentation resulting from the size and complexity of the federal bureaucracy creates enormous problems of management and policy coordination for the president.

The Domestic Policy Apparatus

The need for presidential coordination in domestic policy has been recognized for some time. The principal effort to enable presidents to provide the necessary coordination was the development of a domestic policy staff apparatus in the Executive Office of the President. The domestic policy staff evolved slowly, in conjunction with the development of the president's legislative role *(see Chapter 5)*. This was an evolutionary process that relied initially on the Bureau of the Budget (BOB) and later saw the establishment of a separate staff to formulate and implement domestic policy.

BOB: Central Clearance and Legislative Program Planning

From the early nineteenth century until the creation of the Bureau of the Budget in 1921, the president's role in domestic policy formulation was ad hoc and unorganized.[32] In its first year of operation, BOB required that all agency legislative proposals for the expenditure of federal funds be submitted to it before being sent to Congress. Those proposals that BOB determined were not in accord with the president's financial program were not sent forward, and agencies were to inform Congress if pending legislation had been found not in accord. This procedure, known as "central clearance," was expanded during Franklin D. Roosevelt's administration to cover the substantive content of proposed legislation. Its original function was to ensure that legislative proposals of various departments and agencies were compatible with the president's overall program goals.[33] Over time, central clearance acquired additional functions, including supervising and coordinating executive branch legislative initiatives, providing a clear indication to congressional committees of the president's position on proposed legislation, and making various administrative units aware of one another's goals and activities.

Beginning in 1947, BOB's domestic policy role expanded to include participation in developing the president's legislative program.[34] Its Legislative Reference Division worked directly with Truman's White House staff in reviewing agency recommendations and integrating them in a comprehensive legislative program. The addition of responsibilities to formulate policy involved BOB personnel in the pursuit of the president's political goals, a development that may later have resulted in questions about its ability to provide professional staff services to the president. Moreover, in the 1960s, as BOB became deeply involved in program planning, White House staff played a larger role in the clearance process, and the line between clearance and legislative planning became more and more blurred.[35]

When Dwight D. Eisenhower came into office, he was initially unprepared to submit a legislative program to Congress, but quickly recognized that he was expected to do so. The centralized clearance and planning processes lodged in BOB were quite compatible with Eisenhower's penchant for systematic staff operations, and he continued to employ them throughout his administration. The principal distinction between him and his predecessor in this regard was that Eisenhower attached a lower priority to new domestic policy proposals. Central to the process of legislative programming as it had developed by 1960 were annual submissions of legislative proposals by departments and agencies. Items that were not enacted in one year were introduced in the next. The result was a highly routinized process that was nearly impervious to new ideas. This system was quite suitable for Eisenhower's limited domestic policy initiatives.

Task Forces and Study Commissions

The activist Democratic presidents of the 1960s, John Kennedy and Lyndon Johnson, overcame the rigidities and bureaucratic domination of the BOB-based program planning process by obtaining ideas and suggestions from nongovernment sources.[36] The mechanism used for this purpose was the task force. Before his inauguration, Kennedy appointed several study groups, or task forces, of experts from inside and outside the government to advise him on the major issues and problems facing the new administration. The reports of these task forces, and of a number of others appointed after Kennedy took office, provided the basis for much of his New Frontier program.[37]

Although Kennedy remained eager for new ideas and suggestions, he did not rely heavily on outside sources of advice after the initial round of task forces. Instead, he turned primarily to his cabinet for suggestions. Johnson appointed a set of task forces in the spring of 1964 with the specific mission of developing a distinctive program for his administration. Johnson's task forces were made up of outsiders, and they operated in secret. He was so pleased with their reports, which furnished much of the form and substance of his Great Society program, that he made task forces a regular part of his program development process. The White House staff coordinated the task force operations, and BOB integrated the proposals into the annual legislative program.

Johnson favored the task force process because it largely avoided the tortuous task of bargaining with departments and agencies and because it was not adulterated by bureaucratic, congressional, and interest group pressures.[38] He used the task force device so extensively, however—in 1967 alone at least fifty task forces were preparing reports—that it became routinized and lost the informality and flexibility that had made it so valuable for developing new proposals. Moreover, later in his presidency, Johnson's emphasis shifted from domestic to foreign and military policy as the nation became embroiled in the Vietnam War.

The presidents who followed Johnson made little use of task forces. (Nixon appointed fourteen task forces during his campaign, but their suggestions did not figure prominently in his initial legislative proposals.) Instead, they relied on more formal advisory bodies, such as commissions and White House conferences, to study issues and problems and to gather outside recommendations. Presidential commissions are broadly representative bodies that often are appointed to defuse highly sensitive issues. In September 1981, for example, President Reagan appointed the National Commission on Social Security Reform to develop a solution to a crisis in Social Security funding. Although the commission did not solve the crisis, it provided "cover" under which the principals, Reagan and House Speaker Thomas P. O'Neill, worked out a compromise solution.[39] As one of his first official actions, President Clinton appointed a Task Force on National Health Care Reform to develop the administration's proposed legislation within a hundred days.[40] Headed by the first lady, Hillary Rodham Clinton, and the senior adviser for policy development, Ira Magaziner, the task force consisted of 500 experts from inside and outside of government who divided into thirty-four groups and operated secretly. The unprecedented size of the task force, its cumbersome secret process, and Mrs. Clinton's role in it made it a target for criticism well before it finished its work. Five months after the deadline, the unwieldy body produced a 1,350-page proposal for a Health Care Security Act. The delay in developing the proposal postponed congressional consideration of it until 1994, when it became caught up in election year politics. The proposal's "complexity, high cost, and obtrusive bureaucracy made it an easy target for Republicans" and contributed to the failure of Congress to enact it.[41]

Because of the representative character of presidential commissions, their reports often blur critical issues. This occurs in consequence of their efforts to obtain consensus. Or, commissions may make findings and suggestions that embarrass the president, as did the 1970 report of the Scranton Commission, which blamed campus disorders on President Nixon.

White House conferences bring together groups of experts and distinguished citizens for public forums held under presidential auspices. Their principal function is to build support among experts, political leaders, and relevant interests for presidential leadership to deal with the problems at issue. Neither White House conferences nor presidential commissions have served as the basis for major legislative proposals, but they have given legitimacy to certain presidential undertakings.

Domestic Policy Staffs

Since Johnson, presidents have not regularly employed task forces in developing their legislative programs, nor have they relied almost entirely on agency submissions, as did Presidents Truman and Eisenhower. Instead, they have used domestic policy staffs in the Executive Office of the President and a more politicized Office of Management and Budget (OMB).

Nixon established the Domestic Council in 1970 as part of a reorganization of the presidency, in which the Bureau of the Budget was renamed the Office of Management and Budget. The Domestic Council comprised the president, the vice president, the attorney general, and the secretaries of agriculture, commerce, housing and urban development, interior, labor, transportation, Treasury, and health, education and welfare, as well as the director and deputy director of OMB. The Domestic Council was to be a top-level forum for discussion, debate, and determination of policy analogous to the National Security Council (NSC) *(see Chapter 10)*. Like the NSC, the Domestic Council had a staff of professionals and support personnel. Headed by John Ehrlichman, the presidential assistant for domestic policy, the staff dominated Nixon's domestic policy-making process during the last two years of his first term, 1971–1972.[42]

The Domestic Council conducted its activity through work groups headed by one of six assistant directors. These groups prepared working papers for the president, evaluated departmental proposals for legislation, and participated in drafting presidential messages to Congress and preparing supportive materials for specific legislative proposals. In addition to assisting the president in formulating policy proposals, the Domestic Council also advocated, monitored, and evaluated policy.[43] This arrangement, in effect, made Ehrlichman the president's general agent for domestic policy. Under him the Domestic Council centralized control over domestic policy in the White House. The president's interests, as defined and expressed by Ehrlichman, took precedence over the interests of departments and agencies, as conveyed by cabinet members and agency heads.

The council's domination of domestic policy did not survive Ehrlichman's departure from the White House in April 1973.[44] The influence of the staff was clearly a function of Ehrlichman's status with the president. Under Ehrlichman's successor, Kenneth Cole, the Domestic Council became more of a service unit, and OMB resumed many of the functions of planning legislative programs.

In addition to the development of a presidential staff for domestic policy, Nixon also effected a major transformation in OMB by using it for political purposes. The OMB director became indistinguishable from other high-level presidential assistants, and a layer of political appointees, called "program assistant directors," was placed above OMB's career staff. Nixon's politicization of OMB reduced its ability to serve the institutional needs of the presidency as an impartial professional staff agency.[45]

President Ford used OMB to facilitate the unusual transfer of power from Nixon to himself, and he relied on it to help plan and coordinate programs in a more traditional and less partisan manner than Nixon had. Initially, Ford intended to give the Domestic Council a major planning role by making Vice President Nelson Rockefeller its chair. However, Rockefeller never became Ford's general agent for domestic policy. The long delay in congressional confirmation of Rockefeller's appointment and his conflict with White House chief of staff Donald Rumsfeld appear to have prevented such a development.[46] The council's staff director, James Cannon, a Rockefeller appointee, never gained influence with Ford, who sought advice from a wide range of sources, including OMB, several cabinet members, and the Economic Policy Board, which was established in 1974 as a result of Ford's concern with economic policy problems (see Chapter 9). That emphasis partly explains why Ford seldom used the Domestic Council for policy planning. Indeed, by the fall of 1976 the council no longer participated in legislative programming, and the staff was engaged in diverse activities such as answering presidential mail, preparing policy option memoranda, drafting presidential statements on legislation, and helping to explain the president's program to Congress.[47]

President Carter abolished the Domestic Council shortly after taking office, but he retained a domestic policy staff headed by one of his top aides, Stuart Eizenstat. In some respects Eizenstat and his staff acquired a policy-making role that resembled that of Ehrlichman and the Domestic Council in the Nixon administration. However, Eizenstat and the domestic policy staff did not dominate the domestic policy process and they functioned more in the role of "effective administrator and of contributing advisor." [48]

Ronald Reagan, who came to office with a set, ideologically defined policy agenda and a strong commitment to cabinet government, created a new policy apparatus. The principal units were OMB, the Office of Policy Development (OPD), and seven cabinet councils. OMB's domestic policy involvement was especially crucial during Reagan's first year in office (1981), when the prime objective of drastically reducing the role of the federal government was linked to a budget reduction strategy that was implemented through use of the congressional budget process *(see Chapter 9)*. OMB director David Stockman was the principal architect of the first substantial rollback of the government's domestic programs since the New Deal.

The OPD was the Reagan administration's equivalent of Carter's domestic policy staff. Headed by a presidential assistant for policy development, the OPD worked through cabinet councils, which had jurisdiction over economic affairs, commerce and trade, human resources, natural resources and environment, food and agriculture, legal policy, and management and administration.[49] The councils' members included appropriate cabinet and subcabinet officers and personnel from OMB and the White House staff. Each council had a secretariat composed of department and agency representatives and used working groups to provide expertise and to analyze issues.

The OPD/cabinet council system did not, however, become the directing force for domestic policy. Other factors, particularly the president's long-range objectives and budget pressures, determined the agenda from the beginning of the administration. Reagan's domestic policy apparatus worked out "details secondary to the president's fixed view of government." [50] In other words, it performed an administrative rather than an advisory role.

Developments in the first year of Reagan's second term resulted in a further diminution of the OPD/cabinet council system. The newly appointed White House chief of staff, the former secretary of the Treasury Donald Regan, moved quickly to bring the three major policy areas—economics, national security, and domestic policy—under his control. The number of cabinet councils was reduced from seven to two,

Economic Affairs and Domestic Policy. (The National Security Council, a statutory body, remained as it was.) Secretary of the Treasury Baker and Attorney General Meese chaired the economic and domestic policy councils, respectively. OPD was reduced in size, and its director reported to Regan. In addition to simplifying and reducing the size of the OPD/cabinet council system, Regan centralized authority over domestic policy in his office. However, the two remaining cabinet council chairs, Meese and Baker, enjoyed substantial autonomy to pursue policy projects of their own choosing. By early 1986 Regan had gained control of all access to the president with respect to domestic policy not under the purview of the two cabinet councils.

The diminished domestic policy apparatus of Reagan's second term reflected a shift in the administration's orientation from changing policies to defending them. Having accomplished most of his initial domestic agenda, principally curtailment of the growth of federal agencies and a reduction in spending on them, Reagan concentrated his energies on national security and economic policy objectives. The domestic policy apparatus under Reagan was at least partially deinstitutionalized.

The same condition continued under President Bush.[51] The assistant to the president for economic and domestic affairs, the former Harvard professor Roger Porter, directed the Office of Policy Development. The OPD and the White House Office of Cabinet Affairs provided staff support for the Domestic Policy Council and the Economic Policy Council. However, major issues usually bypassed the cabinet council system and were resolved by Chief of Staff John Sununu or the budget director, Richard Darman. Sununu's self-defined role was to protect the conservative integrity of the administration against the incursions of pragmatism, while Darman functioned as a nonideological guardian of the budget and advocate of economic growth. Both intervened frequently on low-level issues. However, some cabinet members, such as Secretary of Housing and Urban Development Jack Kemp and Secretary of Transportation Samuel Skinner, took the lead in developing major domestic legislative proposals and pushing them in Congress.[52]

The domestic policy process during the first two years of the Clinton administration was frequently frenetic and uncoordinated.[53] The Domestic Policy Council did not meet regularly. Development of health care reform, the principal initiative, was the responsibility of the large task force headed by First Lady Hillary Clinton and Ira Magaziner. Cabinet members, such as Health and Human Services Secretary Donna Shalala, did not play a major role in developing initiatives.

Although formally lodged in a Domestic Policy Council chaired by a high-level presidential assistant, the policy process was operationally centered in the president himself. Clinton, with his intense interest in domestic policy, presided over numerous wide-ranging and intensive meetings with his advisers that shifted back and forth between various policy alternatives. There was no single individual, such as the chief of staff, or group comparable to Reagan's Legislative Strategy Group responsible for resolving disputes, imparting coherence and practicality to the many proposals, and moving them forward to Congress in a timely manner. Clinton resisted delegating such authority to others. Despite his intellectual brilliance and energy, however, he was unable to "ringmaster" the domestic policy process effectively on his own.[54]

Modern Presidents and Domestic Policy

Modern presidents have varied greatly in the extent of their interest and involvement in domestic policy. Franklin Roosevelt was preoccupied with domestic policy during his first two terms (1933–1941) as he orchestrated the development, enactment, and implementation of the New Deal, which encompassed the most extensive set of social and economic reforms in U.S. history. Its immediate stimulus was the Great Depression, but it was also a response to the effects of urbanization and industrialization.

Roosevelt's approach to domestic policy was pragmatic. He tried a wide range of policies. Those that did not work were quickly discarded. Those that were successful were incorporated in a greatly expanded role for the federal government, which assumed positive responsibilities for individual, corporate, and general welfare that went far beyond the traditional negative functions of safeguarding public health, safety, and morals. Among the most prominent legacies of the New Deal are the Social Security system; unemployment compensation; support of agricultural prices; insurance of bank deposits; extensive public works projects such as the Grand Coulee Dam and the Tennessee Valley Authority; and federal regulation of securities exchanges, communications, and energy. During his final years in office (1941–1945), FDR devoted himself almost exclusively to national security policy, as "Dr. Win-the-War" took over from "Dr. New Deal."

Roosevelt's successor, Harry Truman, was deeply involved with national security from the start of his presidency, even though his interests and experience lay in the area of domestic policy. In his first term

(1945–1949) Truman offered few domestic policy initiatives, for he was occupied with the transition from war to peace and with difficulties in dealing with America's wartime ally, the Soviet Union. Following his upset reelection victory in 1948, Truman proposed a comprehensive set of domestic policy reforms called the Fair Deal. The Fair Deal agenda included national health insurance, federal aid to education, and expanded agricultural price supports. Little of the Fair Deal was implemented, however, as the cold war intensified and the United States became involved in the Korean War (1950–1953).

Truman's successor, Gen. Dwight Eisenhower, a World War II hero, was a conservative who had no desire to expand the federal government's role in the life of the nation. He did not, however, attempt to repeal any of the New Deal reforms. His administration (1953–1961) was marked by economic expansion, punctuated by recessions in 1954 and 1958, and by stabilization in international affairs. Among Eisenhower's major domestic policy accomplishments were the passage of legislation authorizing construction of the Interstate Highway System; the National Defense Education Act in 1958, a direct response to the Soviet success in launching the first earth satellite; and limited civil rights bills in 1957 and 1960.

Domestic policy innovation and expansion of federal programs were a central objective of John Kennedy (1961–1963) and Lyndon Johnson (1963–1969). Kennedy developed and submitted to Congress an extensive domestic policy agenda labeled the New Frontier. It included most of the unfinished agenda of the Fair Deal plus proposals for expanded civil rights legislation.

At the time of Kennedy's assassination, in November 1963, Congress was considering several pieces of New Frontier legislation. Johnson moved quickly and effectively in 1964 to secure passage of much of the Kennedy agenda, for example, the Vocational Education Act, the Higher Education Act, and the Civil Rights Act of 1964. In addition, Johnson launched the War on Poverty, featuring the Economic Opportunity Act of 1964, which established the Office of Economic Opportunity. In his 1964 election campaign, Johnson proposed additional domestic reforms under the rubric the Great Society. The year 1965 witnessed the largest outpouring of new domestic policy legislation since the New Deal. Congress passed the Elementary and Secondary Education Act, the Voting Rights Act, and legislation authorizing Medicare, Medicaid, and the model cities program. The departments of Housing and Urban Development and Transportation were established. Hundreds of new federal grant-in-aid programs for state and local governments were implemented. Johnson's zealous pursuit of domestic policy goals gave way, however, to international concerns. His attention in his last two years in office (1967 and 1968) was taken up by the Vietnam War. Funds for Great Society programs were restricted before many of them could be fully implemented as the costs of the war consumed an increasing portion of the federal budget. Opposition to the war in the United States and from abroad led Johnson to retire from public life rather than seek reelection.

Although Richard Nixon, who succeeded Johnson in 1969, was primarily interested in national security policy, he offered an innovative proposal to reform the welfare system, which Congress ultimately rejected. He also considered a variety of suggestions for reforming the financing of public education. Perhaps his principal domestic policy accomplishment was the establishment of federal revenue sharing with state and local governments. Nixon's major achievements, however, were in the realm of national security policy.

Nixon's successor, Gerald Ford, was a conservative who confronted a liberal Democratic Congress that precluded domestic policy innovation. Despite his substantial background in domestic policy, Ford was necessarily a passive president in this area.

Jimmy Carter, a moderate in a largely liberal party, presented a wide range of domestic policy proposals during his administration. He struggled with Congress over a national energy policy; the legislation that eventually passed was a watered-down compromise. He was unable to obtain passage of his proposal for welfare reform, and he temporized at length before proposing a national health insurance plan. Carter was an active president in domestic policy, but he achieved few of his major objectives.

Reagan campaigned successfully for the presidency in 1980 with the most radically conservative proposals for domestic policy since the New Deal. Reagan's stated purpose was no less than to institute a "new American Revolution." The essentials of that revolution in domestic policy were defined in terms of Reagan's conservative ideology. Except for the armed forces and support for law enforcement, the role of the federal government would be drastically curtailed. There would be a massive devolution of federal programs to state and local governments. The reduction in federal spending for domestic programs would provide the resources for an overdue military buildup, made necessary by the threat posed by the Soviet Union, and for a substantial cut in income taxes. Reagan further believed that the tax cut would stimulate an economic expansion that would generate enough revenue to bring the federal budget into balance. Finally, he was committed to drastic reductions of federal regulation of the economy, the environment, and the workplace.

The foundation of Reagan's domestic policy goals was an unswerving belief in the viability of a free market as the means of rationally and efficiently allocating resources and maximizing productivity. Allowing the free market to operate would increase material well-being and enhance individual freedom. Reagan's domestic policy objectives were long-range. He was not interested in the details of specific programs. What was done in domestic policy had to be compatible with the long-term goals that flowed from his ideological frame of reference. Pragmatic adjustments and compromises with individuals and interests who did not share his ideology were to be avoided at all costs. In this respect Reagan stood in sharp contrast to his predecessors from FDR to Carter.

George Bush's domestic policy agenda was characterized by its limited scope and the absence of a clear vision of American society.[55] A major theme for domestic policy—"empowerment" of individuals by means such as allowing public housing residents to buy their homes and giving parents greater freedom in choosing schools for their children—did not emerge until late in the second year of his administration.[56] Taking office at a time "ripe for inaction" (the public supported neither further reductions in the size of government nor major new domestic programs), the nonideological Bush devoted most of his energy to national security issues.[57] Moreover, budget constraints created by the massive deficits of the Reagan years permitted very little opportunity for policy initiatives.

In spite of the lack of a comprehensive domestic policy agenda, the Bush administration was not without several major legislative achievements.[58] These included a bailout for the financially devastated savings and loan industry, the first major revision of the Clean Air Act in a decade, a bill establishing rights for the disabled, a sweeping child care bill, and revision and reauthorization of federal housing programs. One close observer remarked that "in many domestic policy fields, Bush has done better than his Administration's phlegmatic reputation suggests."[59]

Bill Clinton entered office committed to be a domestic policy president. His extensive agenda was centrist, or New Democrat, in its ideological orientation. Determined to "hit the ground running" and avoid the early missteps that had plagued the Carter administration, Clinton's first 100 days—a traditional testing period—were notable for some easy early victories, a costly defeat, and indications of difficulties ahead.[60]

The easy wins came with enactment of Clinton's campaign proposal for a National Service program and leftover measures from the Bush years: the Family and Medical Leave Act, the Motor Voter Registration law, and the Brady handgun registration bill. The defeat resulted from Clinton's effort to fulfill a campaign pledge to end discrimination against gays and lesbians in the armed forces. The announcement that this would be accomplished by an executive order—as Truman had ended racial discrimination in the military—met with strong opposition from the chairman of the Joint Chiefs of Staff, Gen. Colin Powell, and other high-ranking military officers and from many members of Congress, including Sen. Sam Nunn (D-Ga.), chairman of the Armed Services Committee. In the face of such opposition and strongly negative media and public reaction, Clinton retreated and negotiated a compromise "don't ask, don't tell" policy that pleased no one. The debate over the issue hurt Clinton politically because it "raised doubts about the strength of his leadership," disappointed one of his important support groups, and identified him with an unpopular and openly liberal cause.[61]

That Clinton would encounter difficulties in securing the enactment of his domestic agenda became apparent early in 1993 when Congress rejected his economic stimulus proposal. His economic program, embodied in the 1994 congressional budget resolution and the subsequent reconciliation bill, passed narrowly with no Republican support in either the House or Senate (see Chapter 9). Although the legislation fulfilled the campaign commitment to reduce the budget deficit substantially, a tax increase (on business and the wealthy) was necessary to do so.

Clinton's major domestic policy achievements in 1993 and 1994 were accomplished with difficulty and did not receive wide popular approval or media recognition. Two important bills designed to enhance competitiveness and expand export markets by liberalizing foreign trade—the North American Free Trade Agreement (NAFTA) in 1993 and the General Agreement on Tariffs and Trade (GATT) in 1994—passed over the opposition of organized labor and a majority of House Democrats. The $30 billion crime prevention bill passed in August 1994 with the support of forty-two House Republicans after nearly being defeated by a coalition of the Black Caucus and conservatives opposed to the ban on assault weapons.

The bipartisan support that was essential to these achievements did not materialize for health care reform, the centerpiece of Clinton's domestic agenda.[62] In addition, powerful interest group opposition arose after the introduction of the legislation, which was detailed, complex, and not easily understood. In Congress, the committee process broke down as three House and two Senate committees were unable to resolve the substantive and political problems with the legislation. None of the House committees and only one Senate committee, Finance, was able to report a bill. The Democratic leadership in each chamber was unable to fashion a compromise that stood a chance of passage, and no floor votes were taken. (Clinton's threat in January 1994 to veto any bill that did not provide for universal coverage was an obstacle to developing a bipartisan compromise.)

Kingdon's policy-streams model provides a framework for analyzing the demise of health care reform.[63] Two problems secured the issue's place on the agenda—rapidly increasing costs and uneven access. On balance, political conditions favored action. However, as is the case with any redistributive policy legislation, there was potential for interest group opposition. Moreover, favorable public opinion could be moved (as it subsequently was), and public opposition to additional taxes to finance reform and the budget deficit constrained the alternatives. The greatest difficulties occurred in the policy stream. None of the three primary alternatives—a single-payer national health insurance system run by the federal government, a system of managed competition, and incremental changes in current insurance arrangements—could muster a majority among the advocates of reform. Consequently the administration and Democratic congressional leaders were unable to build a consensus "among the advocates and specialists around a particular package of policies." [64]

In the second half of Clinton's term, the Republican leadership in Congress seized and dominated the domestic policy agenda. With considerable success, Clinton fought Republican efforts to finance massive tax cuts at the expense of Medicare, end affirmative action, and cripple regulatory programs. In an action that was essential to his reelection strategy to run as a centrist, he kept his 1992 campaign promise to "end welfare as we know it." On August 22, 1996, despite misgivings, he signed a compromise bill that had the support of almost all congressional Republicans and half of the Democrats.

The relationship of the modern presidents to domestic policy can be understood in terms of a cyclical theory of politics and policy.[65] Domestic political change in the twentieth century has taken place in recurring cycles of "electoral politics and governmental response" that focus on the presidency. At the center of each cycle is a "presidency of achievement" marked by legislation that alters "the role of the federal government in American society." [66] Three conditions are required for a presidency of achievement to occur: "an empowering election, leadership skill, and ideas." [67] Each presidency of achievement usually has been preceded by one or more presidencies of "preparation" and followed by one or more presidencies of "consolidation" in which the reforms are rationalized and legitimized. Although the cycle of preparation, achievement, and consolidation is recurring, it is not inevitable. [68]

In terms of this theory, Roosevelt was a president of achievement, even though a presidency of preparation did not precede him because the system-threatening crisis of the Great Depression disrupted the cycle. Truman's was a "presidency of stalemate" in which he sought to "set off a new round of achievement in the face of a strong public disposition for consolidation." [69] Eisenhower was "the quintessential president of consolidation" who brought stability and order to the changes initiated under Roosevelt's New Deal.[70] Kennedy served to prepare the way for Johnson's presidency of achievement—the Great Society—which was consolidated under Nixon. Ford fell outside the cycle with a "presidency of stasis," characterized by confusion regarding policy problems and solutions.[71] Carter's was a presidency of preparation for Reagan's achievements. His rhetoric and some of his actions involving deregulation, scaling back the size and scope of domestic programs, and strengthening the military foreshadowed the achievements of Reagan's conservative "revolution." [72] Bush consolidated the changes implemented under Reagan and thus fits nicely into the cycle.

Clinton took office with an ambitious agenda; the accomplishment of that agenda would have stamped him as a president of achievement. As he began his second term, committed to balancing the federal budget and a centrist agenda,[73] Clinton's presidency appeared to be one of consolidation. Only one of the three conditions Nelson specifies as required for a presidency of achievement—an empowering election, presidential leadership skills, and ideas—was present in the first term. His problematical election mandate, his unfocused and primarily tactical skills, and his desire to please weakened his leadership. Although he had ideas in abundance, political, institutional, and economic factors limited their applicability to the solution of policy problems. The next presidency of achievement must await the development of the necessary conditions.

Conclusion

Presidents approach the task of making domestic policy with varying amounts of resources and differing policy opportunities. Their domestic policy leadership depends to a large extent on their effectiveness in using the available resources to exploit existing opportunities and create new ones. They are most apt to do this effectively when the three components of the policy stream—problems, solutions, and politics—converge. A president's ability to bring these three tributary streams together is one indication of effective policy leadership.

Successful policy leadership requires that presidents spend their resources carefully and exploit opportunities skillfully. To do so presidents must pay particular attention to four strategic factors: goals, priorities, timing, and costs and benefits.

Modest, flexible goals usually are easier to achieve than those that are extensive and ideologically derived. So, too, are goals that enjoy substantial support among the public and policy-making elites. In establishing their goals, presidents take such considerations into account along with their values and beliefs. A primarily pragmatic set of objectives tends to be easier to accomplish than one that is ideologically derived. It is less likely, however, to have an impact on society than a more visionary and comprehensive set of objectives. In some circumstances ideological goals may be highly appropriate. For example, Ronald Reagan initially struck a responsive note in Congress and the public with his unabashedly conservative domestic program. Presidents are free to be as pragmatic or as ideological as they wish in establishing their goals. However they decide, the mix they choose affects their policy leadership.

Closely related to goals, priorities also affect policy leadership. Presidents who clearly define their priorities generally have been more successful than those who have not done so, because the policy process can handle only a few major issues at a time, even though many contend for attention. If a president does not indicate his preferences, other participants will pursue their own objectives, possibly to the detriment of the president's. Nor is it realistic for presidents to expect that all of their goals will receive consideration to the exclusion of those of other participants. In this respect a comparison between Carter and Reagan is instructive. Carter developed a lengthy domestic agenda and insisted that all of his goals were vitally important to the nation and deserving of enactment. Congress responded by taking its time in dealing with

Carter's program and by pursuing many of its own objectives. Some of Carter's goals, such as welfare reform and national health insurance, were never adopted; others, such as a national energy policy, were passed in greatly modified form after extensive delay and bargaining. Many congressional Democrats complained that Carter failed to provide them with direction and guidance for his domestic proposals. In contrast, Reagan made his priorities clear at the beginning of his administration, and he continued to do so. Congress had little doubt about which goals Reagan considered vital and on which he would spend political capital and those that were less important to him. Cutting domestic spending, strengthening national defense, and reducing and reforming taxes took precedence over balancing the federal budget, ending legalized abortion, and restoring school prayer.

Timing, the third strategic consideration in successful policy leadership, is crucial to effective exploitation of opportunities. If opportunities are missed, they may be lost indefinitely. Good timing also involves taking advantage of the regular policy and electoral cycles. Proposals submitted at appropriate times in those cycles have greater likelihood of adoption. Proposals also can be withheld until conditions are ripe for their submission. A proposal that has limited support can be moved to the top of the agenda and pushed successfully as the result of a disaster, crisis, or other focusing event. Presidents who are able to time the presentation of proposals to coincide with favorable events and conditions are more likely to be effective policy leaders than those who lack such a sense of timing. Two presidents whose timing of domestic proposals was effective were Franklin Roosevelt during the first 100 days of the New Deal, when the Great Depression provided the rationale for a comprehensive set of economic recovery and reform laws, and Lyndon Johnson, who in early 1964 used the shock of the Kennedy assassination to secure passage of the Civil Rights Act. In contrast, Bill Clinton's poor timing of his health care reform and welfare reform proposals contributed to their failure.

Finally, successful policy leadership requires that presidents be attentive to the costs and benefits of raising problems for consideration and posing solutions to them. As presidents decide which problems and issues to emphasize, they focus on political benefits. They select agenda items according to the prospective electoral, historical, and programmatic benefits of the times.[74] When presidents select solutions for problems they are addressing, their emphasis is on costs.[75] Political costs, assessed in terms of congressional, electoral, bureaucratic, and interest group support, enter their calculations at each stage of the process. Increasingly, presidents and other actors have tended to view political costs in terms of avoiding blame and claiming credit for the outcomes.[76]

Economic costs have sharply limited the alternatives in recent years as budget pressures have mounted. They force presidents to make hard choices, such as whether to support new programs and which existing programs to emphasize, maintain, or reduce. Technical costs and questions of workability also enter the selection of policy alternatives.

No prescription or formula can guarantee that a president will provide successful domestic policy leadership, in part because some problems, such as the high unemployment rate among African American men, are very difficult to solve, or solutions for them do not exist. Another reason for the absence of a workable formula is that conditions constantly change. Some problems may be solved only to reemerge in a new form; others may decline in importance. Solutions that are viable today may not be so a few years hence, or solutions may have unanticipated consequences or side effects that become problems in their own right. Political conditions, such as the popular mood or control of Congress, are in flux, so strategies may have to be modified frequently. Because many of the requirements of successful policy leadership are not fixed, what worked well for one president may be only partially useful to those who come later.

Even presidents who take office committed to concentrating their energies on domestic policy encounter extensive frustrations. They may enjoy some initial successes, as did Reagan; but the difficulties of accomplishing additional objectives eventually increase, and the sharing of power with Congress, the bureaucracy, and organized interests becomes ever more burdensome. The natural tendency is for presidents to turn their attention to national security or economic policy. In these policy areas, the challenges are more immediately threatening to the general welfare; the constraints on their ability to act, although very real, are not as frustrating; and successful policy leadership appears less elusive.

NOTES

1. The concept of "issue congestion" was developed by Hugh Heclo, "One Executive Branch or Many?" in *Both Ends of the Avenue,* ed. Anthony King (Washington, D.C.: American Enterprise Institute, 1983), 26–58.

2. Theodore J. Lowi, "American Business, Public Policy, Case Studies, and Political Theory," *World Politics* (July 1964): 677–715.

3. Steven A. Shull, *Domestic Policy Formation: Presidential-Congressional Partnership?* (Westport, Conn.: Greenwood Press, 1983), 155; Steven A. Shull, "Change in Presidential Policy Initiatives," *Western Political Quarterly* (September 1983): 497.

4. John H. Kessel, *Presidential Parties* (Homewood, Ill.: Dorsey, 1984), 112–115.

5. Ibid., 68–69.

6. The policy-stream metaphor borrows from Paul Light, "The Presidential Policy Stream," in *The Presidency and the Political System,* ed. Michael Nelson (Washington, D.C.: CQ Press, 1984), 423–448; and John W. Kingdon, *Agendas, Alternatives, and Public Policies,* 2d ed. (New York: HarperCollins, 1995), 85–86.

7. This discussion follows Kingdon, *Agendas,* chap. 5.

8. This discussion of the development of the health care issue follows B. Guy Peters, *American Public Policy: Promise and Performance,* 3d ed. (Chatham, N.J.: Chatham House, 1993), 230–235.

9. Paul Light, *The President's Agenda: Domestic Policy Choice from Kennedy to Reagan,* 2d rev. ed. (Baltimore: Johns Hopkins University Press, 1991), chap. 3; and Light, "Presidential Policy Stream," 427–428.

10. Ironically, Nixon's preoccupation with the judgment of history helped to cut short his presidency. He has consistently explained the installation of the secret taping system in the Oval Office as motivated by his desire to have a complete and accurate record for use by historians. That taped record provided the "smoking gun" that led the House Judiciary Committee to vote the impeachment charges that prompted his resignation in August 1974.

11. Burt Solomon, "Bush Plays Down Domestic Policy in Coasting Toward Reelection," *National Journal,* Mar. 30, 1991, 752–753.

12. Kingdon, *Agendas,* 142–143.

13. Light, *The President's Agenda,* 149.

14. Jeff Fishel, *Presidents and Promises: From Campaign Pledge to Presidential Performance* (Washington, D.C.: CQ Press, 1984).

15. Kingdon, *Agendas,* 131.

16. Vincent J. Burke and Vee Burke, *Nixon's Good Deed: Welfare Reform* (New York: Columbia University Press, 1974); Laurence E. Lynn, Jr., and David deF. Whitman, *The President as Policymaker: Jimmy Carter and Welfare Reform* (Philadelphia: Temple University Press, 1981).

17. Jack W. Germond and Jules Witcover, "On Welfare, It's Politics as Usual," *National Journal,* Aug. 5, 1995, 2021.

18. "Social Policy," *Congressional Quarterly Weekly Report,* Nov. 2, 1996, 3148–3149.

19. This discussion is based on Kingdon, *Agendas,* chap. 7.

20. Ronald Brownstein and Dick Kirschten, "Cabinet Power," *National Journal,* June 28, 1986, 1589.

21. This discussion follows Light, "Presidential Policy Stream," 440–446.

22. Paul J. Quirk and Joseph Hinchcliffe, "Domestic Policy: The Trials of a Centrist Democrat," in *The Clinton Presidency: First Appraisals,* ed. Colin Campbell and Bert A. Rockman (Chatham, N.J.: Chatham House, 1995), 264–267.

23. Light, "Presidential Policy Stream," 444–445.

24. Kingdon, *Agendas,* 194–195.

25. Kessel, *Presidential Parties,* 60.

26. Light, *The President's Agenda,* 36–38.

27. Harold Wolman and Fred Tietlebaum, "Interest Groups and the Reagan Presidency," in *The Reagan Presidency and the Governing of America,* ed. Lester M. Salamon and Michael S. Lund (Washington, D.C.: Urban Institute Press, 1985), 299–301.

28. Mancur Olson, *The Rise and Decline of Nations* (New Haven, Conn.: Yale University Press, 1982), 44.

29. Richard E. Neustadt, *Presidential Power and the Modern Presidents: The Politics of Leadership from Roosevelt to Reagan* (New York: Free Press, 1990), 29.

30. Leroy Rieselbach, *Congressional Reform: The Changing Modern Congress* (Washington, D.C.: CQ Press, 1994); Roger H. Davidson, ed., *The Postreform Congress* (New York: St. Martin's Press, 1992).

31. Donna Cassata, "Republicans Bask in Success of Rousing Performance," *Congressional Quarterly Weekly Report,* Apr. 8, 1995, 986, 988, 990; Jennifer Babson, "Armey Stood Guard over Contract," *Congressional Quarterly Weekly Report,* Apr. 8, 1995, 987; and Adam Clymer, "House Party: With Political Discipline It Works Like Parliament," *New York Times,* Aug. 6, 1995, E6.

32. Lester M. Salamon, "The Presidency and Domestic Policy Formulation," in *The Illusion of Presidential Government,* ed. Hugh Heclo and Lester M. Salamon (Boulder, Colo.: Westview, 1981), 179.

33. Richard E. Neustadt, "The Presidency and Legislation: The Growth of Central Clearance," *American Political Science Review* (September 1954): 641–670; Robert S. Gilmour, "Central Clearance: A Revised Perspective," *Public Administration Review* (March/April 1971): 150–158.

34. Richard E. Neustadt, "The Presidency and Legislation: Planning the President's Program," *American Political Science Review* (December 1955): 980–1018; Larry Berman, *The Office of Management and Budget and the Presidency* (Princeton, N.J.: Princeton University Press, 1979), 42–43; Stephen J. Wayne, *The Legislative Presidency* (New York: Harper & Row, 1978), 103–105.

35. Gilmour, "Central Clearance"; Berman, *The Office of Management and Budget.*

36. Norman C. Thomas and Harold L. Wolman, "The Presidency and Policy Formation: The Task Force Device," *Public Administration Review* (September/October 1969): 459–471.

37. Texts of the reports were published in *New Frontiers of the Kennedy Administration* (Washington, D.C.: Public Affairs Press, 1961).

38. Lyndon B. Johnson, *The Vantage Point* (New York: Holt, Rinehart & Winston, 1971), 326.

39. Paul Light, *Artful Work: The Politics of Social Security Reform* (New York: Random House, 1985), 232.

40. Quirk and Hinchcliffe, "Domestic Policy," 274–275.

41. Ibid., 275.

42. Raymond J. Waldman, "The Domestic Council: Innovation in Presidential Government," *Public Administration Review* (May/June 1976), 260–268.

43. Margaret Jane Wyszomirski, "The Roles of a Presidential Office for Domestic Policy: Three Models and Four Cases," in *The Presidency and Policy Making,* ed. George C. Edwards III, Steven A. Shull, and Norman C. Thomas (Pittsburgh: University of Pittsburgh Press, 1985), 134.

44. John Helmer and Louis Maisel, "Analytical Problems in the Study of Presidential Advice: The Domestic Council Staff in Flux," *Presidential Studies Quarterly* (Winter 1978), 52–53.

45. A sharp debate rages over politicization of OMB and the institutionalized presidency generally. Berman, in *The Office of Management and Budget,* argues that politicization has damaged, if not destroyed, the capacity of OMB to serve the institutional needs of the presidency in a professional manner. In contrast, Terry Moe in a seminal essay, views politicization as a logical (indeed necessary) institutional development resulting from the extensive and steady growth of "expectations surrounding presidential performance." See "The Politicized Presidency," in *The New*

Direction in American Politics, ed. John E. Chubb and Paul E. Peterson (Washington, D.C.: Brookings, 1985), 269.

46. Wyszomirski, "Roles of a Presidential Office," 136–137.

47. Wayne, *The Legislative Presidency,* 123.

48. Wyszomirski, "Roles of a Presidential Office," 140.

49. For an extended description of the OPD/cabinet council system, see Chester A. Newland, "Executive Office Policy Apparatus: Enforcing the Reagan Agenda," in *The Reagan Presidency,* 153–159. Martin Anderson, who was Reagan's first director of the OPD, provides a participant's perspective on the cabinet councils in *Revolution* (New York: Harcourt Brace Jovanovich, 1988), chap. 19.

50. Ibid., 160.

51. This discussion follows Colin Campbell, S.J., "The White House and the Presidency under the 'Let's Deal' President," in *The Bush Presidency: First Appraisals,* ed. Colin Campbell and Bert A. Rockman (Chatham, N.J.: Chatham House, 1991), 210–212.

52. Julie Rovner, "On Policy Front, Home Is Not Where Bush's Heart Is," *Congressional Quarterly Weekly Report,* Feb. 2, 1991, 292.

53. This discussion follows Colin Campbell, "Management in a Sandbox," in *The Clinton Presidency,* 77–80.

54. Ibid., 79.

55. Paul J. Quirk, "Domestic Policy: Divided Government and Cooperative Presidential Leadership," in *The Bush Presidency,* 73–76.

56. Burt Solomon, "'Empowerment,' Whatever It Is, Powers Ahead in Policy Circles," *National Journal,* Dec. 12, 1990, 3046–3047; Solomon, "Power to the People?" *National Journal,* Jan. 26, 1991, 204–209.

57. Quirk, "Domestic Policy," 73; Kenneth T. Walsh, "George Bush's Idea-free Zone," *U.S. News & World Report,* Jan. 14, 1991, 34–35.

58. Rovner, "Home Is Not Where Bush's Heart Is," 292–293; Burt Solomon, "Grading Bush," *National Journal,* June 8, 1991, 1331–1335.

59. Solomon, "Grading Bush," 1331.

60. This discussion follows Quirk and Hinchcliffe, "Domestic Policy," 267–268.

61. Ibid., 268.

62. This discussion follows Alissa J. Rubin, "Overhaul Issue Unlikely to Rest in Peace," *Congressional Quarterly Weekly Report,* Oct. 1, 1994, 2797–2801.

63. This discussion follows Kingdon, *Agendas,* 217–221.

64. Ibid., 221.

65. Erwin C. Hargrove and Michael Nelson, *Presidents, Politics, and Policy* (New York: Knopf, 1984); and Michael Nelson, "The Presidency: Clinton and the Cycle of Politics and Policy," in *The Elections of 1992,* ed. Michael Nelson (Washington, D.C.: CQ Press, 1993), 125–152.

66. Nelson, "The Presidency," 126.

67. Ibid., 145.

68. Ibid., 128.

69. Hargrove and Nelson, *Presidents, Politics, and Policy,* 68.

70. Ibid., 72.

71. Ibid., 68.

72. Ibid., 81–83.

73. William Schneider, "Clinton Aims to Govern from the Center," *National Journal,* Dec. 21, 1996, 2771; James A. Barnes, "Clinton's Tenuous Bridge to the Center," *National Journal,* Jan. 4, 1997, 25.

74. Light, *The President's Agenda,* 71.

75. Ibid., 134–136.

76. R. Kent Weaver, *Automatic Government: The Politics of Indexation* (Washington, D.C.: Brookings, 1988), chap. 2.

READINGS

Anderson, Martin. *Revolution.* New York: Harcourt Brace Jovanovich, 1988.

Baumgartner, Frank R., and Byron D. Jones. *Agendas and Instability in American Politics.* Chicago: University of Chicago Press, 1993.

Boaz, David, ed. *Assessing the Reagan Years.* Washington, D.C.: Cato Institute, 1988.

Fishel, Jeff. *Presidents and Promises: From Campaign Pledge to Presidential Performance.* Washington, D.C.: CQ Press, 1984.

Hargrove, Erwin C., and Michael Nelson. *Presidents, Politics, and Policy.* New York: Knopf, 1984.

Kessel, John H. *Presidential Parties.* Homewood, Ill.: Dorsey, 1984.

Kingdon, John W. *Agendas, Alternatives, and Public Policies.* 2d ed. New York: Harper-Collins, 1995.

Light, Paul C. *Artful Work: The Politics of Social Security Reform.* New York: Random House, 1985.

———. *The President's Agenda: Domestic Policy Choice from Kennedy to Reagan.* 2d rev. ed. Baltimore: Johns Hopkins University Press, 1991.

Lynn, Laurence E., Jr., and David deF. Whitman. *The President as Policymaker: Jimmy Carter and Welfare Reform.* Philadelphia: Temple University Press, 1981.

Palmer, John L., and Isabel V. Sawhill, eds. *The Reagan Record.* Washington, D.C.: Urban Institute Press, 1984.

Shull, Steven A. *Domestic Policy Formation: Presidential-Congressional Partnership.* Westport, Conn.: Greenwood Press, 1983.

———. *The President and Civil Rights Policy: Leadership and Change.* Westport, Conn.: Greenwood Press, 1989.

Sundquist, James L. *Politics and Policy: The Eisenhower, Kennedy, and Johnson Years.* Washington, D.C.: Brookings, 1968.

Weaver, R. Kent. *Automatic Government: The Politics of Indexation.* Washington, D.C.: Brookings, 1988.

9   THE POLITICS OF ECONOMIC POLICY

During the Great Depression, Franklin Roosevelt used radio broadcasts from the White House, known as "fireside chats," to persuade the public to support his unprecedented economic policies.

ECONOMIC ISSUES DOMINATED the 1992 presidential election campaign. Polls indicated that the public blamed President George Bush and his administration for the 1991–1992 recession. Bush insisted that the economy was fundamentally sound and that recovery from the recession had begun. The Democratic candidate, Bill Clinton, charged that Bush had indeed neglected the economy and focused his campaign on economic issues. A sign stating, "It's the Economy, Stupid" hung on the wall of his national campaign headquarters.[1] Clinton promised to end the recession, ensure long-run prosperity through investments in human capital and physical infrastructure, and reduce the substantial federal budget deficit. The Independent candidate, Ross Perot, stressed the importance of ending the deficit and reducing the expanding national debt. The electorate responded by choosing Clinton, while giving Perot 19 percent of the vote. Not surprisingly, the deficit and other economic issues would dominate Clinton's first two years in office.

Presidents have been concerned about the condition of the economy since the early years of the Republic. Some who confronted serious economic adversity, such as Martin Van Buren in 1837, Ulysses S. Grant in 1873, Grover Cleveland in 1893, Theodore Roosevelt in 1907, and Warren G. Harding in 1921, did little more than ride out the storm. The electorate, however, reacted by denying reelection to Van Buren and inflicting sizable losses on the president's party in the midterm congressional elections of 1838, 1874, and 1894. In fact, the existence of a relationship between business cycles and election results was known long before Edward Tufte's precise empirical analysis of the phenomenon.[2] Only since the 1930s, however, have presidents attempted to control business cycles through public policy, and the public has come to expect them to do so.

This chapter examines the president's economic policy responsibilities and activities. It begins by distinguishing between actions designed to manage the entire economy (macroeconomic policy) and to control specific aspects of the economy (microeconomic policy). The primary focus of the chapter is on macroeconomic policy. It reviews presidential efforts to manage the economy from 1933 to 1996 and then describes the politics of macroeconomic policy making. Next, the chapter analyzes how the presidency functions in making economic policy and the ways in which presidents since Dwight D. Eisenhower have handled the problem of coordinating economic policy. The chapter concludes with an assessment of the congressional role in macroeconomic policy making.

Macroeconomic Policy

Management of the entire economy by the government is known as macroeconomic policy, and the government has two principal tools to use: fiscal policy and monetary policy. Fiscal policy refers to the government's efforts to regulate the level of the nation's economic activity by varying taxes and public expenditures. Fiscal policy seeks to expand the economy by increasing spending and reducing taxes or to contract it by decreasing spending and increasing taxes. A budget deficit, therefore, is expansionary whereas a budget surplus is deflationary. The president and Congress jointly make fiscal policy. They determine expenditures through budgeting and appropriations, and they establish taxes through legislation. Monetary policy refers to a government's efforts, through its central bank (in the United States, the Federal Reserve System), to regulate economic activity by controlling the supply of money.

An independent agency, the Board of Governors of the Federal Reserve System, makes monetary policy.

The goals of macroeconomic policy have remained constant since the Great Depression of the 1930s: to hold down the rate of inflation, to establish and maintain full employment, and to achieve a steady rate of economic growth. There are, however, alternative theories that have guided policy makers in their pursuit of these goals: classical conservative economics, Keynesianism, monetarism, and supply-side economics.

Conservative economic theory lost credibility during the Great Depression when the budget-balancing efforts of the administrations of Herbert Hoover and, early on, of Franklin D. Roosevelt failed to restore confidence in the economy and produce the desired upturn. FDR quickly discovered that emergency spending and loan programs provided relief and produced a measure of recovery. The ideas of John Maynard Keynes, a British economist whom Roosevelt met in 1934, offered an explanation of the phenomenon of economic response to fiscal stimulus and eventually provided a rationale for deficit spending. Keynes argued that the cause of an economic decline was a drop in private demand for goods and services. Government could stimulate demand by increasing its expenditures or by reducing taxes. The temporary deficits created by fiscal stimulation would be financed by government borrowing and repaid during periods of hyperactivity in the economy. FDR did not fully accept Keynesian ideas until a sharp recession followed his attempt to return to a balanced budget in 1937. Eventually, the recovery of the economy as a result of mobilization during World War II provided most economists with empirical validation of Keynes's basic theories. Conservative economics, however, retained its hold on many political leaders, such as Eisenhower, who made balanced budgets their goal and regarded fiscal stimulation of lagging demand as an emergency measure.

While Keynesianism was establishing itself as the new orthodoxy, another theory emerged to challenge it. The monetarists, under the leadership of the economist Milton Friedman, held that the key to maintaining economic stability lay not in the stimulation of demand, but in limiting the growth rate of the money supply to no more than the actual growth rate of the economy. Inflation occurs, monetarists claim, when the money supply expands too rapidly. The only remedy for inflation is a painful contraction in the money supply. Fiscal policy and the size of budget deficits are held to be subordinate to the basic means of managing the economy.

Monetarism gained adherents as the limitations of Keynesianism became apparent during the 1970s. A primary defect of Keynesian theory as the basis for macroeconomic policy was its inflationary bias. Decisions on taxing and spending are made by the president and members of Congress—politicians concerned with reelection—and not by professional economists. Consequently, it has proved easier in practice to increase spending and cut taxes, the Keynesian prescription for expansion, than to cut spending and increase taxes, the remedy for inflation. In the 1970s, when inflation became the nation's leading economic problem, the Keynesian solution was ineffective because political decision makers were unwilling to impose it. They feared the electoral consequences of reducing government spending and raising taxes when their constituents were struggling to make ends meet. Although the inflationary bias of Keynesianism is a political defect rather than a weakness in the theory itself, the effect has been its reduced attractiveness as a guide to policy.

Monetarism, whatever its theoretical merits and limitations, offered the prospect of controlling inflation in a politically less painful manner by having the autonomous Federal Reserve Board, known as the Fed, contract the money supply. Political officeholders can blame the consequences of monetary contractions, such as high interest rates and rising unemployment, on the Fed and its amorphous supporters: "Wall Street" and the banks. The attempt to compensate for the lack of fiscal discipline by monetary contraction during the 1970s eventually proved so painful that monetarism also became politically unattractive. By the early 1980s a new theoretical approach, supply-side economics, had emerged and was embraced by President Ronald Reagan.

Essentially, supply-side economics is an amalgam of Keynesianism and monetarism.[3] Supply-siders endorse strict monetary restraint as the means to control inflation, but they reject the monetarist reluctance to use fiscal policy to achieve macroeconomic policy objectives. The supply-siders maintain, however, that the Keynesian focus on stimulating demand is misdirected. Instead, they advocate tax cuts designed to provide incentives that encourage investments and productivity, which in turn increase the supply of goods and services. Increasing the *supply* of goods and services stimulates the demand for them. Supply-siders are not disturbed by budget deficits resulting from tax-cut incentives. They argue that the stimulative effect of the tax cuts will create enough additional savings to finance the added deficits without an inflationary expansion of the money supply, and an expanded economy eventually will generate enough revenues at lower rates of taxation to balance the budget.

Supply-side economics draws sharp criticism, on the one hand, from liberals who charge that it is but another version of the discredited "trickle down" approach to economic policy, under which tax advantages for the affluent are justified on the grounds that they eventually lead to prosperity for all. On the other hand, conservatives fear that supply-side tolerance of budget deficits will lead to excessive rates of inflation and erosion of confidence in the monetary system. Conservatives and Keynesian liberals alike doubt the validity of the assumptions on which supply-side economics rests. Although they would like it to work, they do not believe that it can. Experience since 1981 with a massive cut in federal income taxes, based on supply-side reasoning, supports their pessimism. The economy expanded during the 1980s, but revenues did not rise sufficiently to reduce, let alone balance, the federal budget.

Microeconomic Policy

Microeconomic policy is a term used to describe government regulation of specific economic activities; it also encompasses antitrust policy. Microeconomic policies focus on specific industries or on economic practices in several industries. They are designed to affect directly the infrastructure of the economy and only indirectly its performance. Modern presidents generally have paid less attention to microeconomic than to macroeconomic policy, largely because its impact is so much more narrowly focused. Most presidents, however, have on occasion endorsed specific microeconomic policies or used microeconomic policy tools to achieve macroeconomic or other policy goals. President Reagan, for example, strongly supported deregulation and privatization as a means of reducing the role of government and strengthening the free market. Greater reliance on the market, he believed, would lead to a more productive economy.

Earlier in the nation's history, presidents were involved only with microeconomic policy and did not regard overall management of the economy as a primary policy responsibility. To preserve competition in the market, Theodore Roosevelt and William Howard Taft vigorously enforced the Sherman Anti-Trust Act of 1890–Roosevelt with great fanfare and Taft with quiet effectiveness. Woodrow Wilson persuaded Congress to establish an independent regulatory agency, the Federal Trade

Commission, with extensive authority to regulate anticompetitive and unfair business practices. Roosevelt, Taft, and Wilson believed that the federal government should act to correct imperfections in the operations of the free market economy.

During the New Deal, Franklin Roosevelt endorsed legislation that established or strengthened independent regulatory agencies: the Securities and Exchange Commission (SEC), the Federal Power Commission (FPC), the Federal Communications Commission (FCC), the Civil Aeronautics Board (CAB), and the National Labor Relations Board (NLRB). These agencies received broad grants of authority to regulate the interstate aspects of specific industries, such as trade in stocks and bonds, electric power and natural gas, broadcasting and wire communications, and air transportation, as well as economywide activities such as labor-management relations. In addition, FDR experimented with a form of government-sponsored industrial self-government in the National Industrial Recovery Act as a means of mitigating the effects of destructive competition. In 1937 he ordered an intensified enforcement of the antitrust laws, charging that anticompetitive practices were responsible for the continuation of the Great Depression. FDR's use of microeconomic policy was characterized by a pragmatic search for techniques of government intervention that would improve the operation of certain economic sectors or lead to an improvement in the overall health of the economy. Policies that worked were retained; those that failed were abandoned.

FDR's successors varied in their use of microeconomic policies. Presidents Harry S. Truman, Dwight D. Eisenhower, John F. Kennedy, and Lyndon B. Johnson appeared to accept the legitimacy of the pattern of government regulation of economic activity that had been established by 1940, including antitrust policy. They differed mainly in the intensity of enforcement and their willingness to use certain microeconomic policy tools.

Beginning in the late 1960s and continuing into the 1970s, Congress passed a new set of statutes expanding federal regulation of economic activity as a means of achieving noneconomic goals, such as a cleaner physical environment, safer automobiles and other consumer products, and a higher degree of safety and health in the workplace. Presidents initially approved the new regulatory activities, but as their economic costs became apparent, Richard Nixon and Gerald R. Ford raised questions about the appropriateness of federal regulation in general. A deregulatory movement gained support, endorsed by Ford and Jimmy

Carter. Ford assigned overall responsibility for deregulation to a member of the Council of Economic Advisers (CEA) and issued an order that required agencies to analyze the impact of their actions on inflation. Carter established the Regulatory Analysis Review Group, chaired by a CEA member, with responsibility for reviewing new rules and regulations with potential economic costs of $100 million or more. There is little evidence, however, that these actions reduced the volume of new regulations or the economic impact of regulation on industry.[4] Carter also gave his support to legislation that provided for deregulation of the airline and trucking industries. (The CAB ceased to function at the end of 1984, but the Interstate Commerce Commission continued to regulate railroads.)

Ronald Reagan promised in his 1980 election campaign to reduce substantially the amount of federal regulation; he argued that regulation was a primary cause of the decline of productivity in the economy. Reagan established the Task Force on Regulatory Relief, headed by Vice President George Bush, to analyze the economic effects of existing and proposed regulations. The task force prepared the way for the establishment, in the Office of Management and Budget (OMB), of the Office of Information and Regulatory Affairs to review proposed agency regulations. Reagan also issued two executive orders, numbers 12291 and 12498, that mandated that all major regulations be subjected to cost-benefit analysis, authorized the OMB director to delay the implementation of regulations, and required each agency annually to prepare a regulatory program that specified all regulatory actions in progress and planned for the future. These changes ensured continued presidential influence over the regulatory process. The Reagan administration employed a three-pronged administrative strategy that substantially reduced the effectiveness of regulation.[5] First, OMB review procedures were used to kill or to slow the issuance of regulations. Second, the intensity of regulatory enforcement was reduced. Third, Reagan appointees changed their agencies' orientation from confrontation to cooperation as a means of achieving compliance.

President Bush did not change the regulatory review process that Reagan established with his two executive orders. Like Reagan, he involved his vice president in an antiregulation effort. Dan Quayle chaired the Council on Competitiveness, which had broad authority to intervene in drafting federal regulations. However, Bush's regulatory policy differed markedly from that of his predecessor. Whereas Reagan implemented a regulatory reform agenda based on his conservative ideology, Bush had no holistic vision for regulatory reform. His regulatory strategy was passive and fragmentary. With respect to policy content, Bush did not continue Reagan's opposition to social regulation—especially occupational safety and environmental protection—and he gave stronger support to economic regulatory policy. His appointments of moderates to regulatory positions contrasted sharply with Reagan's, who were primarily ideologues opposed to regulations.[6]

Regulatory policy was not a major concern of the Clinton administration during 1993–1994. Its legislative proposals extended the existing regulatory philosophy. Following their takeover of Congress in 1995, the Republicans introduced legislation designed to provide relief from environmental regulation to businesses and individuals.[7] The bills restricted the authority of federal agencies to issue regulations by requiring justification of proposed rules through cost-benefit analysis and risk analysis. Also, they made it easier for parties likely to be subject to regulations to challenge them before they are issued.[8] President Clinton responded by threatening to veto any legislation that greatly relaxed environmental regulation, and he adopted a strong defensive posture regarding efforts to weaken and relax federal regulation generally.

In all modern presidential administrations, microeconomic policies have been secondary to macroeconomic policy. Microeconomic policies, such as vigorous antitrust enforcement or support for deregulation, can be used to achieve macroeconomic policy goals and to highlight the theoretical rationale for administration policy, but microeconomic policies cannot replace fiscal and monetary policies as the primary means by which presidents discharge their responsibility for the health of the nation's economy.

Presidents and the Economy: 1933–1996

The modern era of macroeconomic policy and the president's role as manager of the economy date from FDR's New Deal. One of the hallmarks of the New Deal was its commitment to make positive use of the federal government's power to bring about recovery from the Great Depression. The most significant theoretical achievement of the New Deal for economic policy was not the adoption of a comprehensive ideology for the development of a welfare state but the discovery of Keynesian economics and its prescription of increased government spending to compensate for inadequate private spending for investment and consumption.

Ultimately, it was not the New Deal reforms and recovery programs that ended the depression but the huge increase in government spending during World War II. All of the nation's unused productive capacity—capital facilities and human resources—were mobilized to achieve victory, and government borrowing financed much of that mobilization.

After the war Congress passed the Employment Act of 1946, a statute that committed the U.S. government to maintain "maximum employment, production, and purchasing power." The act translated into law the widespread expectation that had developed during the Roosevelt administration that the government would guarantee to the fullest extent possible a prosperous economy. It also made the president primarily responsible for providing economic policy leadership, although it furnished him with few new tools for the task. It created a Council of Economic Advisers and an accompanying staff, and it required the president to report annually to Congress on the condition of the economy and to offer proposals for improving or maintaining its health. Ultimate power over the president's economic proposals, however, remains with Congress.

From the end of World War II until the late 1960s, presidents and Congress fought with each other over economic policy. Truman struggled unsuccessfully with Congress over its desire to reduce wartime taxes. He was somewhat more effective in controlling the inflation that resulted from spending for the Korean War. Eisenhower's conservative policies tended to prevail over the plans of a Democratic Congress to increase domestic spending. The Eisenhower administration was marked by two recessions, in 1954 and 1958, with a period of expansion between them. The Kennedy-Johnson administration fully embraced Keynesian theory, and a 1964 income tax cut had the desired effect of expanding the economy and increasing revenues. It was thought that economic forecasting and management of the economy had developed to the point where finetuning of unemployment and the inflation rate was possible.[9]

In 1966, however, economic conditions began to change. Vietnam War expenditures rose rapidly, the deficit increased, and President Johnson shifted his focus from economic expansion to economic restraint. Congress resisted Johnson's requests for higher excise taxes, and for political reasons he refrained from asking for income tax increases. He feared that Congress would refuse the request and that in the course of congressional debate embarrassing questions would be raised about the war and its cost. With a congressional election scheduled in 1966, he was unwilling to risk debate and defeat. By the time Johnson requested additional income taxes and Congress responded by approving a temporary 10 percent income surtax, the economy had begun a prolonged inflationary period in which the conditions that had been relatively stable since 1946 began to change drastically. (An inflation rate of approximately 3 percent a year, an unemployment variance between 4 percent and 8 percent, and sustained growth in the gross national product had characterized the first twenty-five years of the post–World War II period.)

Presidents since Johnson have had to contend with a changing and increasingly less manageable economy. Inflation rates crept upward into double digits in the late 1970s before declining; unemployment has remained high by postwar standards; and the federal budget has run a deficit in every year since 1970 *(see Table 9-1)*. Underlying these developments have been systemic factors beyond the control of the government: the increased dependence of the economy on foreign sources of raw materials, especially oil; the growing interdependence of the U.S. economy with those of other industrial democracies; the declining productivity of the U.S. economy in relation to foreign competition; the growth and maturation of domestic social welfare programs based on statutory entitlements; and a commitment to improve the quality of the physical environment even at substantial cost to economic growth and productivity.

Richard Nixon was the first president to encounter the changing economic environment of the United States. His response was two-pronged. He consistently pursued the classical conservative course of attempting to counter inflation by pushing Congress for reductions in federal spending in order to balance the budget. In addition, Nixon took the extraordinary step, for a conservative Republican, of freezing prices and wages in August 1971. The imposition of wage and price controls is an extreme measure, for through it the president suspends the normal operation of market forces. Although Roosevelt and Truman imposed controls during World War II and the Korean War, Nixon has been the only president to do so in peacetime. He acted under authority that Congress delegated to the president in the Economic Stabilization Act of 1970, which it passed over his strong objections. The wage and price freeze experience during 1971–1973 suggests that peacetime wage and price controls are at best a temporary means of curbing inflation and that they can quickly become a political liability unless their impact is moderated.

Table 9-1   Inflation, Unemployment, and
Federal Budget Deficits, 1970–1996

	Inflation[a]	Unemployment[b]	Deficit[c]
1970	5.7%	4.9%	$ 2.8
1971	4.4	5.9	23.0
1972	3.2	5.6	23.4
1973	6.2	4.9	14.9
1974	11.0	5.6	6.1
1975	9.1	8.5	53.2
1976	5.6	7.7	73.7
1977	6.5	7.0	53.6
1978	7.6	6.6	59.2
1979	11.3	5.8	40.2
1980	13.5	7.1	73.8
1981	10.3	7.5	78.9
1982	6.2	9.5	127.9
1983	3.2	9.6	207.8
1984	4.3	7.5	185.3
1985	3.6	7.2	212.3
1986	1.9	7.0	221.2
1987	3.6	6.2	149.7
1988	4.1	5.5	155.1
1989	4.8	5.3	153.4
1990	5.4	5.5	220.4
1991	4.2	6.7	268.7
1992	3.0	7.4	290.2
1993	3.0	6.7	254.7
1994	2.6	6.1	234.8
1995	3.1	5.8	192.5
1996	3.0	5.3	107.0

[a] Percent increase in the consumer price index.
[b] Percent of the civilian noninstitutional population 16 years of age or over.
[c] In billions of dollars.

Sources: Statistical Abstract of the United States for years through 1992; *Congressional Quarterly Weekly Report,* Feb. 11, 1995, 406, 430, for 1993–1995. *The Economist,* Jan. 18–24, 1997, 104, and *Congressional Quarterly Weekly Report,* Nov. 16, 1996, 3281, for 1996. Data for 1994, 1995, and 1996 are esti-

Upon taking office in August 1974, President Ford assumed that the principal economic problem confronting the United States was inflation, and he pushed to cut federal spending. Almost before his anti-inflation campaign was launched, however, economic conditions changed, and Ford spent his last year as president combating a recession that contributed to his electoral defeat in 1976. Ford's successor, Jimmy Carter, fared little better. Carter initiated an antirecession program of increased federal spending and tax cuts to stimulate business investment. The economy responded almost too quickly, and Carter was confronted with surging inflation rates that reached double digits during his last two years in office.

Perhaps Carter's most important decision affecting the economy was his naming of Paul Volcker as chairman of the Federal Reserve Board in 1979. Volcker's appointment reflected Carter's disenchantment with the ability of Keynesian theory to provide solutions to the problem of stagflation, a combination of a stagnant economy and rising prices. Essentially a monetarist, Volcker moved quickly to curb inflation by restraining the growth of the money supply. Although Carter did not fully abandon Keynesianism, he gave monetarism a prominent role in macroeconomic policy making for the first time.

The rate of inflation did not respond quickly to Volcker's efforts to tighten the money supply, but interest rates rose sharply. These developments undoubtedly contributed to Carter's defeat by Ronald Reagan in the 1980 election. One of Reagan's campaign pledges was to restore vitality to the economy through a revolutionary program of major reductions in taxing and spending. Congress responded positively to Reagan's initiatives in 1981 by enacting the largest income tax cut in U.S. history and by reducing domestic spending in nonentitlement programs. Congress also supported Reagan's proposals for a major defense buildup, projected over five years from 1981 through 1986.

The results of the Reagan administration's macroeconomic policies were mixed. The major accomplishment—credit for which must also be given to the Fed—was the curtailment of inflation, which fluctuated between annual rates of 1.9 to 4.3 percent from 1983 through 1988. Also, in 1983 the economy began a sustained period of growth that lasted through 1990. Before that growth spurt, however, the United States experienced the most severe recession since World War II, with unemployment rising to 10.75 percent in the fourth quarter of 1982. In spite of the prosperity achieved since 1982, unemployment did not drop below 5 percent.

Without question, the major problem resulting from the Reagan administration's macroeconomic policies has been massive federal budget deficits (see Table 9-1). The deficits grew rapidly as a result of the recession of 1982, when revenues fell, automatic countercyclical spending (such as unemployment compensation) rose, and the tax cuts and increased defense spending authorized in 1981 became effective. The latter created a large structural, or permanent, deficit as the increases in federal revenues promised by supply-side advocates failed to materialize, and sizable additional cuts in nondefense spending could not be obtained from Congress.

In addition, the large annual deficits resulted in a rapid growth in the national debt and in interest payments on the debt. From $990 billion in 1980, the debt rose to $3.1 trillion ten years later.[10] Net interest payments have become one of the fastest growing items in the federal budget. Interest has become a major obstacle to reducing the deficit and a constraint on spending for other purposes.

The deficits proved embarrassing to President Reagan because they are contradictory to traditional conservative values of fiscal restraint. But the deficits also brought political advantage to the Reagan administration. They created additional demand that stimulated the economy and served as the basis for the sustained recovery from the 1981–1982 recession. That recovery was crucial to Reagan's 1984 reelection victory, for voters concluded that his economic policies had worked quite well. That Reagan had become a practitioner of Keynesian demand management on a grand scale was immaterial to him and his supporters. The deficits also provided Reagan with an effective rationale for restraining the growth of nondefense spending.

George Bush's victory in the 1988 presidential election was an endorsement of the status quo. The country was prosperous and not at war. The only economic policy mandate Bush received derived from his pledge that there would be "no new taxes." Like Reagan, Bush promised to eliminate the budget deficit by reducing spending. He held to his promise not to raise taxes until October 1990, when his administration negotiated a budget deal with Congress that would balance the budget by 1996. However, the reductions in the deficits for 1991 and 1992 were overcome by unanticipated expenditures for the Persian Gulf War and bailing out failed savings and loan institutions insured by the federal government, shortfalls in revenues arising from "technical re-estimates," and higher projected spending for Medicaid.[11] The deficits for fiscal 1991 ($268.7 billion) and 1992 ($290.2 billion) were the highest ever. In 1991, annual interest on the debt amounted to $214.3 billion and rose to $292.3 billion in 1992.[12] The recession that began in late 1990 and continued into 1992 increased spending pressures and constrained any moves to raise taxes, thus impeding administration and congressional efforts to curb the deficit.

The 1992 election gave a clear indication of voter dissatisfaction with the condition of the economy, but it produced no general agreement on economic policies. This was due in part to Bill Clinton's lack of a clear electoral mandate—he received only 43.3 percent of the vote—and in part to the candidate's failure to provide concrete proposals for deficit reduction out of fear of antagonizing the voters. "While concerned about ending deficits, the voters [were] even more concerned with preventing the spending cuts and tax increases necessary to accomplish that goal." [13]

President Clinton moved quickly to address economic problems. His economic program, unveiled on February 17, 1993, contained three basic parts: deficit reduction; investment in research, education and training, and physical infrastructure; and short-term spending to stimulate the economy. During 1993, Congress narrowly passed legislation (called a reconciliation bill) that reduced the deficit by $496 billion over five years but substantially reduced the investment spending proposals. It rejected the economic stimulus bill, except for extending unemployment compensation.

Economic conditions improved quickly under Clinton. Unemployment dropped from about 7 percent at the time of the 1992 election to 5.8 percent in 1994, inflation was moderate at 2.8 percent, and the economy grew at a healthy annual rate of almost 4 percent in 1994.[14] As a result of the 1993 deficit reduction package and a stronger than anticipated economic performance, the budget deficit fell to $107 billion by 1996.[15] Evaluated in terms of these conventional indicators, Clinton's economic policies had succeeded, but he received no immediate political reward. In the 1994 congressional elections, which have been regarded as a referendum on Clinton's overall performance, the voters handed the Democratic Party a stunning defeat as the Republicans regained control over Congress for the first time in forty years.

The Politics of Macroeconomic Policy Making

Presidents do not make macroeconomic policy in a vacuum solely according to economic theories. Their decisions in this crucial area are intensely political and are affected by consideration of other policy goals (including microeconomic policy), electoral politics, interest group politics, and bureaucratic politics among institutional participants in the policy-making process. In a very real sense the United States has a political economy, and it is an economic polity. The president is the focal point of the relationships involved in both of these entities.

Policy Politics

The achievement of macroeconomic policy goals is affected by, and has an effect on, other policy goals. National security policy objectives, for example, often have a profound impact on economic policy. In the 1980s the widely held consensus that United States military strength had declined compared with that of the Soviet Union resulted in substantial increases in defense spending beginning in fiscal year 1982. These increases, however, were a major obstacle to efforts to balance the budget. The added deficit resulting from increased military expenditures contributed to upward pressure on interest rates, which in turn impeded the ability of tax-cut incentives to stimulate productivity.

Budget-balancing efforts in domestic program areas conflicted with commitments made to Social Security beneficiaries, welfare recipients, retired federal employees, and numerous other groups served by federal programs. In addition, the macroeconomic goals of economic growth, increased productivity, and full employment often are at odds with regulatory policies designed to improve environmental quality, enhance occupational safety and health, increase the safety of automobiles and other consumer products, and protect consumers against a variety of unfair business practices.

Foreign policy also intrudes on macroeconomic policy. For example, foreign military and economic assistance and the stationing of U.S. forces overseas contribute to the nation's balance-of-payments deficit, which in turn undercuts confidence in the dollar and reduces economic stability. The end of the cold war between the United States and the Soviet Union in late 1991 precipitated a budget struggle over the disposition of the "peace dividend" that congressional Democrats believed should result from the reduction of tensions. An October 1990 budget agreement between President Bush and Congress required that for the next three years any reductions in either defense or discretionary domestic spending be devoted to reducing the deficit. Democratic leaders in Congress sought to reopen the agreement so as to use some defense cuts for domestic programs. President Bush opposed their plans to slash defense spending as premature and argued that in any event the agreement should remain in place. In 1995 President Clinton battled over defense spending with the new Republican majority in Congress. The Republicans charged that the level of spending proposed in his 1996 budget sacrificed "necessary modernization and development" of weapons and equipment to fiscal considerations.[16]

These examples illustrate the interrelationship of macroeconomic policy goals with those of other policies.

Electoral Politics

A second dimension of the politics of macroeconomic policy is its relationship to electoral politics. It has long been recognized that presidential administrations and congressional majorities have manipulated economic policy to produce short-term improvements in economic conditions to enhance their party's election prospects. The timing and location of benefits may be adjusted to achieve this end.

Presidents do not, however, attempt to change the underlying structure of the economy for short-term political advantage. Rather, they seek to make marginal adjustments in the rates of inflation and unemployment or in disposable income. Because of electoral politics, however, what is economically optimal is not always done or may be substantially modified as a result of the pressures. Political influence on economic policy can have substantial costs, including "a lurching, stop-and-go economy," a preference for policies that contain "highly visible benefits and deferred hidden costs," and responsiveness of "coalition-building politicians" to special interests.[17] In such a politically sensitive environment, long-range economic planning is most difficult.

Recent presidents, however, have shown a capacity to resist pressures from party and special constituencies to avoid hard political choices.[18] Ronald Reagan remained firm throughout his presidency in his commitment to the 1981 income tax cut based on supply-side theory, even though it meant proposing and defending record peacetime budget deficits (of around $200 billion) that were anathema to his conservative supporters. George Bush adhered to his 1988 campaign pledge not to raise taxes until the budget agreement with Congress in October 1990. He reluctantly agreed to tax increases of $146 billion as part of a five-year $496 billion deficit reduction package. (Opponents attacked him for breaking that pledge in the 1992 election campaign and he expressed regret at having done so.) In response to congressional pressures from Republicans and conservative Democrats and advice from his economic advisers, Bill Clinton abandoned his campaign promise of a tax cut for the middle class and settled for half of the major investments in human resources and infrastructure that were key elements in his proposed 1993 economic program. As finally enacted, the program emphasized cutting the deficit. It provided for a deficit reduction of $486 billion over five years to be achieved through $240 billion in tax increases and $246 billion in spending cuts.[19]

Interest Group Politics

Presidents also are subjected to pressures from several important groupings of interests, including business, labor, agriculture, the financial community, state and local governments, and foreign governments. Their effect on policy varies according to the issues and to current economic conditions in the United States and elsewhere.

Business interests include the full array of private corporations engaged in producing goods and services (except those involved in financial affairs, which will be considered separately). Businesses attempt to exert influence collectively through umbrella organizations, such as the Chamber of Commerce of the United States and the National Association of Manufacturers, and through industry-based trade associations like the Automobile Manufacturers Association and the American Gas Association. Individual companies, especially large corporations, also try to shape policy to their liking. Businesses usually concentrate their lobbying on microeconomic policies that specifically affect their operations. To the extent that business influences macroeconomic policy, it does so by expressing support for balanced budgets, tax-cut incentives, and monetary restraint to control inflation. Presidents know that conservative fiscal and monetary policies normally will receive strong business support.

Labor encompasses the giant AFL-CIO and a host of independent unions. Its position on macroeconomic policy issues is usually in sharp contrast to that of business. Labor supports fiscal stimulation of the economy in periods of recession and opposes the use of monetary restraints to curb inflation. It is not unduly disturbed by budget deficits. As a rule, labor is much more worried by unemployment than by inflation. Labor takes great interest in microeconomic policy, including regulation of labor-management relations and regulations in behalf of occupational safety and health.

Agricultural interest groups are not monolithic. The American Farm Bureau Federation and the National Grange support conservative policies, while the National Farmers Union and the National Farmers Organization take a much more liberal stance. Regardless of their ideology, farm organizations tend to oppose monetary policies that result in high interest rates, because the use of credit is an essential feature of farm management.

The financial community consists of two principal components, the securities exchanges, or Wall Street, and banks and other financial institutions. Wall Street and financial institutions buy and sell "paper," which are government and private financial obligations, and bonds, the longer-term securities. The reaction of Wall Street to monetary and fiscal policies is registered in the price of corporate stocks traded on the major stock exchanges. Movements of stock market indicators, such as the Dow Jones Index of thirty leading industrial stocks, often reflect the degree of investor confidence in administration policies. Bond prices move upward or downward inversely with interest rates and thus reflect monetary policy shifts. The interest paid on short-term government and commercial paper varies directly with monetary policy.

An administration's main interest in the financial community is that its policies be favorably received by Wall Street. It also seeks the approval of major banks and other leading financial institutions. A vote of "no confidence" by the financial community in the government's economic policies makes the administration vulnerable to criticism by political opponents and weakens its popular support. As in the broader business world, members of the financial community tend to support conservative fiscal policies and monetary restraint to control inflation. They fear large deficits, whether due to high spending levels or sizable tax cuts.

With the advent of the Great Society domestic programs in the mid-1960s, state and local governments became vitally interested in macroeconomic policy. The federal government is a source of funding for a wide range of state and local programs in areas such as education, welfare and social services, housing and urban development, transportation, and health care. In addition, states and their local subdivisions received unrestricted federal revenue-sharing funds from 1972 through 1987. Consequently, many state and local governments, both through national associations, such as the U.S. Conference of Mayors, and individually through the efforts of members of Congress, have exerted pressure to maintain the flow of federal funds, even though this could be accomplished only at the expense of larger and potentially inflationary budget deficits.

President Reagan's successful effort in 1981 to reduce federal funding for many state and local activities and his subsequent proposals for further reductions were an essential part of his long-term objective of balancing the budget. Although some state and local officials backed Reagan, the responses of most such officials ranged from cautious skepticism to strong opposition. His objective of a major reordering of federal fiscal functions was not accomplished.[20] Perhaps the most important aspect of Reagan's approach to intergovernmental financial relations was that he seized the initiative. Instead of responding to the requests of state and local officials for ever-increasing support, he sought to direct state and local governments into a posture of reduced dependence on federal funding. This innovative attempt to restructure fiscal federalism in a way that served macroeconomic policy objectives appears to have provided a model for President Bush.

President Clinton struggled with Congress over fiscal federalism. In 1993 and 1994, facing mounting budget deficits and strong congressional opposition from Republicans and conservative Democrats, he obtained passage of only half of the infrastructure spending that was a central component of his economic program. The activities represented by this spending, his opponents argued, were more appropriate for state and local governments. He was able, however, to resist conservative demands to shift financial responsibility for major redistributive programs to the states. In 1995 the Republican majority in Congress proposed ending entitlement status for welfare (Aid to Families with Dependent Children) and Medicaid. The Republicans also sought to cut back further on federal infrastructure spending. These changes were to be accomplished by converting federally funded programs, which were accompanied by extensive federal rules and regulations, to programs giving block grants to states. Under these programs states would be freed from most federal controls, but funding would be fixed and would not increase as demands for services expanded. Initially, Clinton opposed the changes but in 1996 he compromised with the Republicans. Welfare, but not Medicaid, lost its entitlement status and became a block grant program.

The 1995 battle over the budget brought other major interest groups into the picture. The American Association of Retired Persons fought Republican efforts to reduce spending on Medicare and Medicaid. The American Medical Association supported proposed Medicare cuts after receiving assurances from Republican leaders that payments to physicians treating Medicare patients would be increased by charging higher premiums and raising deductibles.

Foreign governments are another important constituency with an interest in macroeconomic policy. Friendly governments—the European Community, Japan, and Saudi Arabia—are especially significant. They favor a dollar that is neither overvalued nor undervalued and a healthy

U.S. economy with full employment and a low inflation rate. If the dollar is weak, the value of much of their international currency reserves declines, and their goods are less competitive in U.S. markets. If the dollar is too strong, their investment capital migrates to the United States, and the high competitiveness of their products in U.S. markets threatens to provoke trade restrictions. If unemployment in the United States rises, the major market for their goods declines. If interest rates are higher in the United States than in Europe or Japan, investment capital moves to the United States. Consequently, foreign governments press U.S. administrations to keep the exchange value of the dollar from fluctuating widely and to hold down interest rates. Foreign governments feel less free to influence fiscal policies designed to stimulate the economy because these entail essentially domestic decisions. Presidents and their administrations are constrained to some degree, however, by the effect of economic policy decisions on the economies of other countries.

Presidents do not respond to all interest group constituencies, and the constituencies whose support they do seek vary in importance to them. In no case, however, do presidents make macroeconomic policy decisions without regard to some of the interest groups, which are a major feature in the politics of economic policy making.

Bureaucratic Politics

The president's economic policies also reflect the organizational interests of the institutions involved in the policy-making process—the Council of Economic Advisers, the Office of Management and Budget, the Treasury Department, and the Federal Reserve Board—and the beliefs of the officials whom he has appointed to manage them. The next section describes the functions and organizational perspectives of those agencies and the nature of their relationship with the president.

The Economic Subpresidency

The president's macroeconomic policy-making role entails discharging statutory duties and responsibilities and meeting popular and elite expectations that his actions will result in a prosperous economy. In his role as economic manager, the president must develop and implement policies and build support for those policies in the public and within the Washington community. To accomplish this complex and demanding task, he needs information, advice, and administrative assistance to focus energy on major issues, integrate the policies of his administration, take account of all important interests, and maintain the cohesion of his administration. This advice and assistance is provided by certain organizations and processes, located in the presidency and within the executive branch, which James Anderson and Jared Hazleton call "the economic subpresidency." The use of the economic subpresidency varies among presidents and with economic conditions, but it is central to policy making and presidential management of the economy.

The economic subpresidency comprises all those who are engaged in making, defining, communicating, and implementing economic policy decisions, "whether they act personally or as part of an institution." [21] Activities of the economic subpresidency include direct advisory relationships with the president and interaction between other advisers with respect to economic policy. The economic subpresidency consists of four major administrative units—the CEA, OMB, the Treasury Department, and the Fed—and various intragovernmental committees and councils, presidential assistants, and other advisers.

The Council of Economic Advisers

The Council of Economic Advisers has three members who are appointed by the president and subject to Senate confirmation, plus a small staff of approximately thirty-five divided evenly between professional economists and support personnel. Traditionally, most CEA members and professional staffers have had extensive experience in business or government. The CEA's chair is responsible for administration of the council, hiring staff, representing it on other government councils and committees, and reporting to the president. He or she establishes the council's orientation according to the president's overall objectives. The chair's relationship with the president largely determines the CEA's influence in shaping economic policy.

The CEA has no operational responsibility but serves entirely in a staff capacity. Its principal functions are to gather information, make economic forecasts, analyze economic issues, and prepare the president's annual economic report to Congress. Its primary role has been to provide the president with expert economic advice. On occasion CEA members have acted as public spokespersons for the president. The council usually has not performed coordinating or brokerage functions, although its members tend to reflect the theories and policy views of professional economists who share the president's perspectives. In general, Democratic presidents have had Keynesian CEA members, and Republicans have selected classical conservative and monetarist economists. Reagan, for example, appointed a conservative economist to chair the CEA at the start of his presidency and added a monetarist and a supply-sider. All three were committed to free trade, reduced government spending, a balanced federal budget, and limited federal intervention in the economy.

The CEA's relationship with the president is a function of how he perceives the need for economic expertise. If he feels such a need—and most presidents have when confronted with the seriousness and complexity of economic issues—and if he and the CEA members share basic interests and values, then the council plays an important role in economic policy making. Its expertise enhances presidential policies, and its analyses and forecasts acquire political significance through association with the presidency. However, the council can do only what the president asks and allows it to do.

Carter's and Reagan's relationship to the CEA illustrates the range of uses that can be made of the council and of its influence on policy. The chairman of Carter's CEA was Charles Schultze, who had served as director of the budget under President Johnson. Schultze played a major role in shaping the Carter administration's economic policies, and the CEA was very much at the center of the economic subpresidency. In contrast, the two CEA chairmen in Reagan's first term, Murray Weidenbaum and Martin Feldstein, were overshadowed by the budget director, David Stockman, and Secretary of the Treasury Donald Regan, neither of whom were economists. Weidenbaum's influence was primarily in regulatory policy. Feldstein, a distinguished academician, quickly fell out of favor with the president and the White House because of his dire predictions of the probable consequences of administration policies. The CEA was at the periphery of the economic subpresidency during Reagan's first term. Indeed, when Feldstein returned to Harvard in July 1984, the president delayed appointing a successor for almost a year. The council's professional staff shrank in size, and rumors circulated in Washington that Reagan wanted to abolish the unit. He finally named Beryl Sprinkel, a supply-side economist who had served for four years as undersecretary of the Treasury for monetary affairs, as chairman in April 1985. Sprinkel rebuilt the council's staff and moved it back into the mainstream of the economic subpresidency.[22]

Under President Bush the CEA played a more significant role with respect to the deficit than it did under Reagan. Its chairman, the monetarist economist Michael Boskin, enjoyed the president's confidence and often acted as a spokesman for the administration.

President Clinton appointed Laura D'Andrea Tyson of Stanford University, who was an expert on trade policy and not a professional macroeconomist, to chair his CEA. Her selection, like Sprinkel's during the Reagan administration, indicated continuation of "the recent pattern of emphasizing policy orientation over professional reputation in CEA appointments." [23] During the development of Clinton's 1993 economic plan, Tyson and the other CEA members, Alan Blinder and Joseph Stiglitz, cautioned against placing too much emphasis on deficit reduction.[24]

The council's forecasts help to set the boundaries of the president's legislative program and budget proposals. It is to the president's advantage for the council to approach its advisory task deductively, fitting program pieces together within the framework of his overall objectives. As the former CEA chairman Paul McCracken observed, "An economic adviser does his most effective work when he is positioned to look at the general interest." [25] The council's contribution to policy making is, then, primarily conceptual and not in the realm of implementation or coordination.

The Office of Management and Budget

Presidents receive economic advice of a different sort from the office of Management and Budget. While the CEA's primary concern is with controlling the business cycle and achieving sustained economic growth, OMB's major focus is the allocation of resources to administrative agencies and their programs through the annual preparation of the president's budget. Its institutional bias is toward holding down spending. It is the principal instrument through which the president fashions the expenditure component of fiscal policy. In addition, OMB provides economic forecasts to the president and acts as a "legislative and regulatory gatekeeper" by conducting detailed policy analysis of proposed bills and agency rules.[26]

The Office of Management and Budget was originally a presidential staff agency comprising an elite group of government careerists devoted to serving the presidency and the president. Since President Nixon reorganized it in 1970, OMB has been more actively involved in serving the political needs of the president. Beginning in the Nixon administration, OMB directors have actively participated in developing presidential policies and in building support for them. The budget has become as much a political weapon as a managerial tool or an instrument of fiscal policy.

The politicization of OMB and the political utilization of the budget were never more apparent than during the Reagan administration and David Stockman's tenure as budget director (1981–1985). Stockman dominated federal budgeting in a manner unknown before him. He centralized the executive budget process in OMB and involved himself extensively in the congressional budget process through direct negotiations and bargaining with congressional committees.

Under Stockman's successor, the economist James C. Miller III, OMB continued to serve Reagan's political interests, but much less visibly. During the Bush presidency OMB was a major player in the economic subpresidency. Its director, Richard Darman, and the White House chief of staff, John Sununu, were the major negotiators with Congress concerning fiscal policy. (Darman dealt primarily with spending and Sununu with taxes.) OMB also became the dominant agency for economic forecasting.

The budget remained the primary instrument for the achievement of the president's policy goals during the Clinton administration. Clinton named Leon Panetta, chairman of the House Budget Committee, as his first OMB director. Panetta was a "deficit hawk" Democratic loyalist who possessed parliamentary acumen and budgetary expertise.[27] He played a major role in shaping Clinton's 1993 economic plan and selling it to Congress. Panetta's successor, when he became Clinton's chief of staff in June 1994, was the economist Alice Rivlin, who had previously served as director of the Congressional Budget Office and was even more hawkish on the deficit than Panetta. Their presence "ensured that deficit reduction would command considerable attention" as the administration shaped economic policy.[28]

The Treasury Department

The third institutional participant in the economic subpresidency is the Treasury Department, which is responsible for collecting taxes, managing the national debt, controlling the currency, collecting customs, and handling international monetary affairs, including management of the balance of payments and the value of the dollar in relation to other currencies. It is the primary government source of information on revenues, the tax system, and financial markets. It also takes the lead in developing tax bills and steering them through Congress.[29]

The primary concerns of the Treasury Department traditionally have been the adequacy of revenues, the soundness of the dollar, and the cost of financing the debt. To finance the debt, the department has advocated either low interest rates or a balanced budget. Since 1951, however, it has opposed easy credit and usually has acted as a restraint on expansionary fiscal policies. Before the Reagan administration, a situation in which high interest rates accompanied a large deficit was anathema to the institutional interests of the Treasury. Its position altered substantially under President Reagan and Donald Regan, secretary of the Treasury during Reagan's first term. An avowed believer in supply-side economics, Regan argued that temporary deficits resulting from tax-cut incentives would lead ultimately to economic growth, expanded revenues, and balanced budgets. He opposed efforts to reduce the deficit by raising taxes. His concern was much more with the supply of money in the domestic economy than with the exchange value of the dollar. Regan's successor as secretary of the Treasury, James A. Baker III, concentrated heavily on exchange rate problems.

Secretary of the Treasury Nicholas Brady played a rather marginal role in the economic subpresidency under President Bush. As noted, Darman and Sununu dominated administration negotiations over the deficit. One veteran White House observer and analyst suggests that the "patrician" Brady was no match for the "pit bull approach of his two economic policy colleagues." [30]

President Clinton's two secretaries of the Treasury, Lloyd Bentsen and Robert Rubin, were central participants in the economic subpresidency. By appointing Bentsen, a moderate Democrat with business experience who chaired the Senate Finance Committee, Clinton sought to reassure the business community.[31] The appointment of Rubin, a Wall Street investment banker who first served as chair of the National Economic Council (see below), served a similar purpose. Both men were deeply involved in shaping the 1993 economic program.[32]

Organizationally, the Treasury Department is divided between large units with major line responsibilities, such as the Internal Revenue Service, and policy-related units, such as the office of the undersecretary for monetary affairs. The policy-related units, located in the office of the secretary, never have provided coordination of economic policy for an administration, although the potential to do so exists.[33]

The Federal Reserve Board

The Federal Reserve Board is an independent agency charged with responsibility for regulating the money supply and the banking system. Its seven members are appointed by the president to fourteen-year terms with the consent of the Senate. The president designates one member of the board to act as its chair for a four-year term. The Fed has three means by which it controls the money supply: the rediscount rate, reserve requirements, and open-market operations.

The rediscount rate is the interest rate charged commercial banks to borrow from the Federal Reserve. An increase in the rediscount rate tightens the availability of credit because it forces banks to charge more to their borrowers.

Reserves are liquid assets that banks hold to meet demands for ready cash from their depositors. The Federal Reserve requires commercial banks belonging to it to maintain a certain percentage (usually ranging from 10 to 20 percent) of their deposit liabilities in the form of cash in their vaults or on account with the regional reserve bank for this purpose. A reduction in the reserve requirement increases the amount of money banks may loan to their borrowers, while an increase in the reserve requirement decreases the availability of bank credit.

Open-market operations are the major instrument through which the Fed manages the money supply, through the purchase and sale of U.S. government securities by regional Federal Reserve Banks. When the Fed wants to expand the supply of money, it orders its regional banks to buy government securities on the money market. The regional reserve banks pay for the securities by drawing checks on themselves. The checks are cashed by the Treasury Department at commercial banks, and as a result the Treasury's account balances are increased. The commercial banks present the checks to regional reserve banks on which they were drawn for redemption. The regional reserve banks credit the checks to the commercial banks' reserve accounts with the Federal Reserve. The commercial banks may then lend money according to the reserve requirement. If the reserve requirement is, say, 10 percent, the banks can lend to private borrowers ten times the original amount of the securities purchased. Conversely, sale of government securities by the Federal Reserve in the open market contracts the money supply in a similar manner.[34]

Although neither the president nor Congress can tell the Fed how to conduct monetary policy, the board traditionally has been responsive to political pressures. One critic charges that the Fed has shown far greater responsiveness to political timing than to cyclical fluctuations in the economy. He maintains that the formal independence of the Fed is a myth and that its policies are designed primarily to maintain its internal cohesion and reduce its external vulnerability.[35]

In some respects the independence of the Fed has political value to the president and Congress because it can serve as a convenient scapegoat for adverse economic conditions. Traditionally, expansionary monetary policy has been attacked as a major cause of inflation, and restrictive policy has drawn fire for contributing to economic stagnation and unemployment. In 1981–1982 presidential and congressional frustration over efforts to improve the economy resulted in criticism from the White House and Capitol Hill that ultra-high interest rates were causing unemployment, pushing up prices, and increasing the size of the budget deficit. After 1982 the sharp drop in inflation and the prolonged recovery from the 1981–1982 recession enabled the Fed to reduce interest rates. Political attacks on the Fed largely ceased as it gauged the money supply to the needs of an expanding economy not plagued by inflation. Also, as Reagan appointees began to serve on the board (by 1986 they were a majority), the White House criticized the Fed less often. President Bush pushed the Fed to reduce rates during the recession that began in 1990. The Fed responded slowly, after assuring itself that to do so would not stimulate inflation. During the Clinton administration the Fed frequently received criticism from members of Congress and Wall Street for being quick to raise interest rates at the first sign of inflation and slow to reduce them when the economy lagged. Relations between the president and the Fed chairman, Alan Greenspan, were generally cordial, however, and the White House seldom attacked the Fed. What was perhaps the strongest clash between the Clinton administration and the Fed occurred in 1994 when Greenspan, with help from the banking industry, torpedoed a Treasury Department proposal to create a Federal Banking Commission that would consolidate bank regulation in a single agency.[36] The proposal would have combined the responsibilities shared by the Treasury Department's Office of the Comptroller of the Currency and its Office of Thrift Supervision, the Fed, and the independent Federal Deposit Insurance Corporation.

Presidents and Economic Policy Coordination

The independence of the Fed, the operational needs and organizational interests of the Treasury Department, and the institutional perspectives of other departments and agencies have led presidents to seek various ways of coordinating economic policy. For reasons explained in Chapter 6, the cabinet has not been a satisfactory vehicle for collective

leadership. Instead, presidents have developed a variety of intragovernmental councils and committees designed to provide a cohesive macroeconomic policy and to integrate it with other policy objectives. Most of
these entities failed to survive the administrations of their creators, for
subsequent presidents sought mechanisms more compatible with their
own operating styles. However, a brief review of these undertakings
reveals common patterns in their approaches and indicates the essential
requirements for a minimal amount of coordination.

President Eisenhower displayed a preference for sharply focused
groups, which, although they met often, were too numerous to bring
about effective coordination. In keeping with his preference for a less
formal structure in policy-making processes, President Kennedy abolished most of the groups his predecessor had established and worked
primarily with groups created to address specific problems, such as
housing credit and labor-management relations. The most significant
development for macroeconomic policy making during the Kennedy
administration was the creation of the "troika," an informal committee
consisting of the chair of the CEA, the secretary of the Treasury, and the
director of the budget. The troika's original purpose was to coordinate
economic forecasting, but it quickly became a mechanism for developing cooperation within the economic subpresidency in formulating fiscal policy and, when joined by the chair of the Fed, for coordinating
monetary policy. (When the group included the chair of the Fed, it was
known as the "quadriad.")

Working with staff support from the CEA, the Treasury Department,
OMB, and occasionally the Fed, the troika/quadriad has helped many
presidents formulate macroeconomic policy in a rapid, adaptive manner
with some measure of protection from political and bureaucratic pressures. Not all presidents have made extensive use of the troika, but it is
a natural institutional grouping that continues to operate, with the
Treasury Department assuming responsibility for revenue estimates,
OMB generating estimates of federal expenditures, the CEA forecasting
economic trends, and the Fed (when involved) projecting money supply requirements. Under Lyndon Johnson, the troika operation became
regularized, and it emerged as the principal mechanism for the development of fiscal policy advice and alternatives.[37] The troika's proposals,
arrived at through discussion and debate, usually resulted in a consensus, which Johnson accepted. He had other sources of advice, but most
of them were informal. He listened to other cabinet members and a
wide variety of outsiders. The loosely structured informality of the troi-

ka operation and the use of informal channels of advice were characteristic of Johnson's ad hoc approach to policy formulation generally.

President Nixon was uncomfortable with attempts to make policy by cabinet-level committees. In early 1971 he designated Secretary of the Treasury John Connally as his economic "czar" with the responsibility for making major decisions. Connally worked through the troika, which he dominated. His successor as Treasury secretary, George Shultz, inherited Connally's title but operated in a more collegial manner. At the start of his second term, in January 1973, Nixon made Shultz assistant to the president for economic affairs and named him to chair a new cabinet-level coordinating body, the Council on Economic Policy. Shultz soon became the dominant figure in making and expounding economic policy for the Nixon administration. He worked primarily through interdepartmental committees focused on specific problems rather than through the council.

Gerald Ford moved quickly to replace the Nixon machinery with a more formal and structured process that would operate openly and comprehensively and reflect Ford's intense interest in economic affairs. In September 1974 President Ford established the Economic Policy Board (EPB) and assigned it responsibility for coordinating domestic and foreign economic policy. The secretary of the Treasury chaired the EPB, which also included the secretaries of labor, commerce, and state, the chair of the CEA, the director of OMB, and the assistant to the president for economic affairs, who also directed the small EPB staff, which was housed in the Executive Office of the President. Departments and agencies provided information, analysis, and expertise. Roger Porter, who served as executive secretary to the EPB throughout its existence, has described it as providing systematic advice to the president by exposing him to competing arguments "in a group discussion that permitted exchange and argument among the advocates before the president." [38]

President Carter replaced the EPB with the Economic Policy Group (EPG), cochaired by the secretary of the Treasury and the chair of the CEA. The EPG was a large, unwieldy body. It had no staff, was accessible to a wide range of interested officials, and was not organized as a formal advisory body to the president. Attempts to focus its work led to the creation of a steering committee, chaired by the secretary of the Treasury and including the chair of the CEA, the director of the budget, and the presidential assistants for domestic affairs and for national security affairs. However, its operations remained so unstructured that it was unable to coordinate even major policy initiatives. [39]

President Reagan replaced the Economic Policy Group with the Cabinet Council on Economic Affairs (CCEA). Like its predecessor in the Nixon administration, the CCEA was a forum for discussion of issues and alternatives. Roger Porter was its secretary and informally coordinated its operations. The council served to establish consensus within the administration. In addition to the council, the troika met regularly to coordinate economic forecasting.

Against the backdrop of the relatively smooth operation of the CCEA, economic policy making during Reagan's first term involved a struggle for influence within the economic subpresidency. The major participants were Donald Regan, David Stockman, and the presidential assistants James Baker and Edwin Meese. The administration had clearly defined macroeconomic policy goals: to reduce the role of the federal government in the U.S. economy, thus reducing taxes and spending, and to increase productivity, savings, and investment, thus ensuring vigorous and sustained economic growth and full employment. There was, however, sharp disagreement over the means to that end. That conflict reflected competition among classical conservative, monetarist, and supply-side theories and focused on the significance of federal budget deficits. The winners in the conflict were Regan and Meese. Stockman was the principal loser.[40]

During Reagan's second term, the content of macroeconomic policy changed very little. This absence of change suggests that a carefully managed economic policy process, designed along the lines of Ford's Economic Policy Board, would not have made much difference in Reagan's economic policy decisions, which were based more on an unyielding commitment to a theory (supply-side economics) than on carefully reasoned analysis or on accurate economic forecasts.

President Bush continued the Economic Policy Council. Its activities were managed by Roger Porter, as assistant to the president for economic and domestic affairs, with the help of his staff in the Office of Policy Development.[41] However, the council met irregularly and did not establish an effective round-table process for preparing issues for presidential decision. Nor did the troika, which fell into disuse during Reagan's second term, acquire its former importance.

In addition, the Bush White House tended to bypass both the cabinet council system and the interagency process.[42] The major players in shaping economic policy in the Bush administration were the OMB director, Darman, and the chief of staff, Sununu. But no single individual or group had responsibility for defining for the economic subpresidency how policies were to be integrated. This apparently was due, at least in part, to the lack of any change in the basic direction of policy as set in the Reagan administration. Although not ideologically committed to the policy, President Bush refused to deviate substantially from it. He opposed new taxes (except for those approved as part of the 1990 budget agreement with Congress), proposed no new major spending programs, and advocated reductions in discretionary nondefense spending.

Given the high priority that President Clinton placed on economic issues during the 1992 campaign, it is not surprising that he was deeply involved in making economic policy. One of his first acts was to establish a National Economic Council (NEC) to coordinate domestic and international economic policy in a manner similar to the National Security Council in foreign and military policy making.[43] Operating with a professional staff of twenty, the NEC's first chair, Robert Rubin, established an open, collegial, and nonhierarchical process that incorporated a wide and balanced range of economic considerations into the issue recommendations sent to the president.[44] The NEC's effectiveness became apparent during the 1993 budget battles; cabinet members worked through the budget and refrained from infighting and leaks that have plagued previous administrations.[45] All was not well, however, because Clinton's economic advisers frequently clashed with his political advisers, who had managed his campaign. These conflicts concerned the primary focus of the administration's economic program and were fought both within the presidency and publicly.[46] The economic advisers stressed the importance of deficit reduction and the impact of policy on financial markets. The political advisers wanted to emphasize the populist issues that had helped to elect Clinton.[47] Although Clinton's management of the economy featured impressive structural and procedural innovations, the conflict between his political and economic advisers produced a mixed message that increased the difficulty of securing congressional approval of his proposals.[48]

As in other areas of policy, the nation is heavily dependent on presidents' attitudes, values, and operating styles for economic leadership. Congressionally established advisory mechanisms, such as the CEA, are helpful, and presidents can take other measures to assist them in identifying issues and achieving policy coordination; but there is no guarantee that the president will adopt effective policies or achieve his objectives. There is, moreover, an important check on presidential economic policy making—the powers of Congress over taxing, spending, and the monetary system.

The Congressional Role in Macroeconomic Policy

Most of the executive branch agencies and processes that involve macroeconomic policy and the president's economic role were established by statute: the Federal Reserve Act of 1914, the Budget and Accounting Act of 1921, and the Employment Act of 1946. Traditionally, Congress has dealt with economic policy through separate consideration of tax legislation and annual appropriations. Tax bills have entailed redistributive issues—that is, questions of who bears the burdens, and efforts of special interests to secure favorable provisions, or "loopholes." The congressional tax-writing committees (House Ways and Means and Senate Finance) have jealously guarded their powers and been unwilling to propose new tax legislation that did not accommodate special interests. The 1986 tax reform act departed substantially from traditional revenue legislation that contains numerous advantages and benefits for a wide range of interests. The two tax-writing committees responded positively to President Reagan's call for simplification and reform of the federal tax code.[49]

Appropriations decision making, centered in the House and Senate Appropriations committees, traditionally focused on incremental changes in budget requests of departments and agencies. The politics of the budget process was a highly stylized game in which the institutional participants played specific roles. The primary consideration in Congress was the amount of increase or decrease in each agency's base, which was the previous year's appropriation. The total level of expenditures was the sum of the thirteen major appropriations bills that are passed annually.[50]

Neither through its taxing nor its spending legislation did Congress attempt consciously to shape fiscal policy. Rather, its money decisions were the product of its fragmented structure of authority, as reflected in the multiplicity of powerful committees and subcommittees, the weakness of its party organizations, and the strong constituency orientation of its members because of their constant concern with reelection.

Although the Budget and Accounting Act of 1921 required the president to prepare an annual budget, a comprehensive plan for spending, and the Employment Act of 1946 required an annual economic report that projected revenues and expenditures in light of economic forecasts, Congress imposed no such requirements on itself. Fiscal policy was whatever remained of the president's program after it emerged from "a piecemeal and haphazard legislative process." [51] The inability of Congress to participate rationally on an equal basis with the presidency in shaping fiscal policy led to conflict during the Nixon administration when federal spending became a politically significant issue. Spending grew rapidly in response to previously enacted statutory "entitlements" that could not be disregarded without revising the original authorizing legislation. Entitlements include Social Security benefits, federal retirement payments, farm price support payments, welfare payments, and food stamps. Most entitlement payments to individuals increase automatically with the cost of living.[52] The problem was compounded by "off-budget" spending through loan guarantees and tax credits.

Nixon challenged Congress to curb spending; when it did not do so, he frequently vetoed spending bills and made extensive use of impoundment. The primary response of Congress to this controversy with Nixon and to frustration over its inability to shape policy was the Budget and Impoundment Control Act of 1974, which created a procedure for handling impoundments. More important, that statute established a congressional budget process, created House and Senate Budget committees, and provided Congress with independent staff support for macroeconomic forecasting and budget analysis in the form of the Congressional Budget Office.

Central to the congressional budget process in its present form are the budget resolution and the reconciliation legislation.[53] The budget resolution must be approved by both House and Senate but does not require the president's signature. As such it does not have the force of law, but it serves as the vehicle for changes in budget policy, allocates available money to congressional appropriations committees, and may activate reconciliation legislation. The extent to which the budget resolution changes budget policy, as opposed to reflecting existing policies, determines its importance. Usually the budget resolution is merely the means by which Congress organizes its action, but on three occasions it has set in motion major changes in fiscal policy. Presidents Reagan in 1981 and Clinton in 1993, each with sharply differing objectives, used the congressional budget process to change tax and spending policy. In 1995, Republican congressional leaders used the budget process to impose far-reaching policy changes that Clinton strongly opposed.

Each budget resolution contains totals for revenues, expenditures, the deficit or surplus, and the national debt for the next fiscal year. Congress must adhere to these totals as it makes taxing and spending decisions. The budget resolution also contains target totals for the next four fiscal years and allocations of new budget authority for the next year to the major areas of federal spending—for example, defense, agriculture, and interest on the national debt.[54] It may also include reconciliation instructions.

Reconciliation is the process that Congress uses "to bring revenue and spending under existing law into conformity with the levels set in the budget resolution." [55] It proceeds in two stages. First, Congress incorporates in the budget resolution binding instructions to specific committees—those that have jurisdiction over revenues and mandatory spending programs—to recommend statutory changes that will achieve the spending and revenue levels set in the resolution. Next, the committees' recommendations are enacted by the House and Senate in a reconciliation bill. Reconciliation is an optional process that has tended to be used when either the president's budget or Congress seeks a multiyear deficit reduction agreement. Reconciliation legislation has become the major means of reducing the deficit. The 1995 reconciliation bill stalled in January 1996 after a protracted battle between President Clinton and Congress over how to achieve a balanced budget by 2002. Although not far apart on the amount of savings needed, they disagreed fundamentally over spending priorities and the congressional insistence on removing entitlement status from Medicaid and welfare.

The creation of the congressional budget process did not substantially change "the established process in Congress for raising and spending money." [56] Nor did it make Congress more fiscally responsible. What the congressional budget process did produce was a change in executive-legislative budget relationships. [57]

The increased centralization of budgetary decision making in Congress enhanced its ability to influence presidential budget policies while providing the president with greater leverage over congressional budget decisions. Congress and the president became, as Schick put it, "more interdependent: each [was] more vulnerable than before to having its budget preferences blocked or modified by the other." [58]

Since 1981, Congress has been locked in protracted conflict with Presidents Reagan, Bush, and Clinton over fiscal policy and the deficit. Reagan and Bush attempted to control the deficit through spending cuts and resisted tax increases while Congress fought to protect pork barrel projects that benefited its constituencies and entitlements and other programs that enjoyed wide popular or strong interest group support. In 1993, with the thinnest of congressional majorities, Clinton achieved a five-year $486 billion deficit reduction by balancing tax increases and spending cuts. Two years later, a transformation occurred in the politics of budget making. Congress seized the initiative from the president. The Republican majority broke the pattern of ritualistic denunciation of deficits that was traditionally accompanied by deceptive accounting practices ("blue smoke and mirrors") and changes in budgetary rules that enabled members to avoid the political consequences of raising taxes or cutting spending. Congress passed, but Clinton vetoed, a balanced budget bill that substantially reduced taxes; made major reductions in the growth of entitlements, including Medicare, Medicaid, and welfare; removed entitlement status from Medicaid and welfare and funded them through block grants to the states; and sharply cut spending on several popular discretionary programs. Cutting the budget deficit has not been a winning issue in recent years, as Bush and Clinton found out in 1992 and 1994. By January 1996 Clinton and Congress agreed that the budget should be balanced by 2002, but were unable to agree on how to do so. Although compromises produced agreements on the 1996 and 1997 budgets, prospects for resolving the conflict over how to reach the 2002 goal appeared bleak as Clinton's second term began.

Conclusion

Can the president bring order and cohesion to macroeconomic policy? Can the presidency serve as the instrument for effective management of the economy? Such questions have become increasingly important since 1970 as the U.S. economy has matured, interdependence with other economies has increased, and the ability to increase productivity, sustain economic growth, and keep inflation and unemployment at acceptably low levels has faltered from time to time. Clearly, the challenge to presidents posed by macroeconomic policy is of continuing importance. Presidents face formidable obstacles and problems as they respond to that challenge.

Three major obstacles confront presidents in the performance of their economic policy role: expectations are inordinately and unrealistically high; they have limited authority to meet those expectations; and the base of knowledge on which they act is often limited and unreliable. The problem of unrealistic expectations is not peculiar to macroeconomic policy. Modern presidents have tended to make sweeping promises in order to be elected, and the American people have developed a deep faith that a strong, capable president can provide solutions to their most pressing problems.

As presidents attempt to develop policies that will produce outcomes to meet popular expectations, they encounter problems. Bush discovered as the recession of 1991 dragged on into 1992 that the public is impatient for tangible results, and the pressure for actions that can provide a "quick fix" is great. Approaching elections heighten the search for measures that will produce immediate results. Also, fulfillment of one set of expectations, such as curbing inflation, may lead to consequences, such as increased unemployment and high interest rates, that dampen others. Pressure for action is usually strong, and the popular bias against inaction runs deep; yet inaction may be the most prudent course to follow. In short, exaggerated popular expectations that the president will manage the economy effectively may limit his capacity to do so. Even an ostensibly healthy economy may not satisfy or ease the apprehensions of the public, as Clinton discovered in 1994. In that midterm election, many voters, "driven by perceptions of job insecurity and sluggish wage growth," were concerned about the future of the economy and their family finances.[59]

In striving to meet the unrealistic expectations of a public eager to place its trust in executive leadership, presidents discover that their authority to act is quite limited. In the area of macroeconomic policy three factors restrict presidential ability to act: congressional prerogatives, the independence of the Federal Reserve Board, and the absence of coordinating power within the executive branch. Presidents must collaborate with Congress in making fiscal policy. Their success depends on congressional responsiveness to their leadership, to their effectiveness as communicators and persuaders. They do not have independent authority to increase or reduce taxes or spending.

Although fiscal policy leadership is a difficult task under the best of circumstances because of congressional prerogatives, monetary policy is equally confining because of the independence of the Fed. The only resources the president has available to influence the Fed are persuasion and the periodic opportunity to appoint new members to the board and to designate its chair. Although presidents have regularly exerted pressure on the Fed, and it has taken political factors into consideration, there is no assurance that monetary policy will be compatible with fiscal policy or that it will not impede the achievement of other policy objectives. Presidents lack the authority to coordinate fiscal and monetary policy. They must rely instead on persuasion and on ad hoc committees to coordinate their economic policies and to integrate economic policy goals with those of other policies.

Presidents also discover that economics provides a rather shaky foundation for recommending policies that directly affect the operation of the entire economy. Economic forecasting is an inexact science and is subject to considerable margins of error. The validity of the projections of the Council of Economic Advisers, the Office of Management and Budget, the Treasury Department, and the Federal Reserve Board depends on the assumptions that underlie them and on the quality and quantity of information available. The assumptions vary with the institutional orientation of the agency making the forecast, the theories of the economists on the agency's staff, and political pressures on the agency. The Fed's assumptions, for example, reflect the influence of monetarism; OMB's, a traditional concern with budget balancing. As Stockman's account of his tenure as OMB director indicates, there is also pressure on forecasters to resolve budget problems by adopting best-case or "rosy" scenarios of economic performance.[60] If the assumptions underlying a forecast prove wrong, then policies based on the forecast may lead to unanticipated outcomes. For example, the record deficits incurred during his administration initially caught President Reagan by surprise because he enthusiastically accepted OMB's rosy scenario.

The nation has moved from a conservative consensus on economic policy in the 1920s and early 1930s to a Keynesian consensus in the 1950s and 1960s to a lack of consensus in the 1980s and 1990s. Policies have shifted from Nixon's imposition of wage and price controls to Reagan's embrace of supply-side theory, Bush's pragmatism, and Clinton's emphasis on long-term growth and investment in human capital. Despite all these changes, presidents still lack the capacity to control the economy even though rapidly changing economic conditions, in the United States and elsewhere, would seem to require a maximum amount of adaptiveness. The president's ability to respond to new situations, such as a sudden, large increase in the price of oil, is very limited. Institutional arrangements, both statutory and constitutional, restrict the president's actions and dictate that he rely primarily on persuasion to accomplish his objectives. Moreover, experience with different processes for economic policy making and coordination suggests that the internal structure of the presidency has little effect on policy outcomes in this area. Beyond economic conditions, over which the president has little control, the factors that appear to affect economic policy making and outcomes most substantially are the president's ideology and leadership.

NOTES

1. John P. Frendreis and Raymond Tatalovich, *The Modern Presidency and Economic Policy* (Itasca, Ill.: Peacock Publishers, 1994), 300.

2. Edward R. Tufte, *Political Control of the Economy* (Princeton, N.J.: Princeton University Press, 1978).

3. A. James Reichley, "A Change in Direction," in *Setting National Priorities: The 1982 Budget,* ed. Joseph A. Pechman (Washington, D.C.: Brookings, 1981), 236–240.

4. Alan Stone, *Regulation and Its Alternatives* (Washington, D.C.: CQ Press, 1982), 262.

5. Lester M. Salamon and Alan J. Abramson, "Governance: The Politics of Retrenchment," in *The Reagan Record,* ed. John L. Palmer and Isabel V. Sawhill (Washington, D.C.: Urban Institute Press, 1984), 47.

6. Marshall R. Goodman, "A Kinder and Gentler Regulatory Reform: The Bush Regulatory Strategy and Its Impact" (Paper presented at the annual meeting of the Midwest Political Science Association, Chicago, April 1991).

7. David S. Cloud, "Industry, Politics Intertwined in Dole's Regulatory Bill," *Congressional Quarterly Weekly Report,* May 6, 1995, 1219–1224; Bob Benenson, "GOP Sets the 104th Congress on New Regulatory Course," *Congressional Quarterly Weekly Report,* June 17, 1995, 1693–1697.

8. David S. Cloud, "Dole's Bill: An 'Aggressive' Position," *Congressional Quarterly Weekly Report,* May 6, 1995, 1221.

9. Walter W. Heller, *New Dimensions in Political Economy* (New York: Norton, 1966).

10. Jackie Calmes, "The Voracious National Debt," *Congressional Quarterly Weekly Report,* March 24, 1990, 896.

11. George Hager, "Deficit Shows No Gain from Pain of Spending Rules," *Congressional Quarterly Weekly Report,* July 20, 1991, 1963.

12. "Fiscal 1993 Budget by Function," *Congressional Quarterly Weekly Report,* Feb. 1, 1992, 245; "Fiscal 1994 Budget by Function," *Congressional Quarterly Weekly Report,* Apr. 10, 1993, 901.

13. Frendreis and Tatalovich, *The Modern Presidency and Economic Policy,* 314.

14. "Administration Economic Assumptions," *Congressional Quarterly Weekly Report,* Feb. 11, 1995, 430; John R. Cranford, "White House Sees Solid Growth Leading to 'Soft Landing,'" *Congressional Quarterly Weekly Report,* Feb. 11, 1995, 412.

15. George Hager, "Time Is Ripe for Agreement but Gridlock Dies Hard," *Congressional Quarterly Weekly Report,* Nov. 16, 1996, 3280–3281.

16. Pat Towell, "Conflict Looms over B-2 and F-22 As Bill Heads to House Floor," *Congressional Quarterly Weekly Report,* July 29, 1995, 2292.

17. Tufte, *Political Control of the Economy,* 143.

18. Paul E. Peterson and Mark Rom argue that there is little incentive for presidents to "manipulate the economy for either electoral or partisan reasons." In their view, presidents can best achieve their diverse objectives through economic policies that maintain a balance between steady economic growth with minimal rates of unemployment and inflation. "Macroeconomic Policymaking: Who Is in Control?" in *Can the Government Govern?* ed. John E. Chubb and Paul E. Peterson (Washington, D.C.: Brookings, 1989), 149.

19. George Hager and David S. Cloud, "Democrats Tie Their Fate to Clinton's Budget Bill," *Congressional Quarterly Weekly Report,* Aug. 7, 1993, 2122–2129.

20. David R. Beam, "New Federalism, Old Realities: The Reagan Administration and Intergovernmental Reform," in *The Reagan Presidency and the Governing of America,* ed. Lester M. Salamon and Michael S. Lund (Washington, D.C.: Urban Institute, 1984), 440; Paul E. Peterson, *The Price of Federation* (Washington, D.C.: Brookings, 1995), 69.

21. James E. Anderson and Jared E. Hazleton, *Managing Macroeconomic Policy: The Johnson Presidency* (Austin: University of Texas Press, 1986), 14.

22. Dick Kirschten, "Sprinkel Finds a Better Market for Advice in Second Reagan Term," *National Journal,* Mar. 22, 1986, 714–715. According to Reagan CEA member William Niskanen, Feldstein's assumption of a public role destroyed his effectiveness. His successor, who had no ties to academia, was "comfortable with a short leash" and thus more effective. William A. Niskanen, *Reaganomics* (New York: Oxford University Press, 1988), 295, 296.

23. Frendreis and Tatalovich, *The Modern Presidency and Economic Policy,* 55.

24. Bob Woodward, *The Agenda* (New York: Simon & Schuster, 1994), 263–264, 269–271.

25. Paul W. McCracken, "Reflections on Economic Advising" (Paper presented at the Princeton University Conference on Advising the President, Princeton, N.J., Oct. 31, 1975), 4.

26. Joseph A. Davis, "Policy and Regulatory Review: Growth in Legislative Role Sparks Concern in Congress," *Congressional Quarterly Weekly Report,* Sept. 14, 1985, 1809.

27. M. Stephen Weatherford and Lorraine M. McDonnell, "Clinton and the Economy: The Paradox of Policy Success and Political Mishap" (Paper presented at the annual meeting of the American Political Science Association, Chicago, Aug. 31–Sept. 3, 1995), 21.

28. Ibid., 28.

29. Anderson and Hazleton, *Managing Macroeconomic Policy,* 27.

30. Colin Campbell, "The White House and the Cabinet under the 'Let's Deal' President," in *The Bush Presidency: First Appraisals,* ed. Colin Campbell and Bert A. Rockman (Chatham, N.J.: Chatham House, 1991), 211.

31. Frendreis and Tatalovich, *The Modern Presidency and Economic Policy,* 56.

32. Weatherford and McDonnell, "Clinton and the Economy," 20–21.

33. Colin Campbell, *Managing the Presidency: Carter, Reagan and the Search for Executive Harmony* (Pittsburgh: University of Pittsburgh Press, 1986), 123–135.

34. Robert J. Shapiro, "Politics and the Federal Reserve," *The Public Interest* 66 (Winter 1982): 122.

35. Ibid., 120.

36. Paul Starobin, "One-Two Punch," *National Journal,* Apr. 2, 1994, 768–883.

37. Anderson and Hazleton, *Managing Macroeconomic Policy,* 83.

38. Roger B. Porter, *Presidential Decision Making: The Economic Policy Board* (New York: Cambridge University Press, 1980), 176.

39. Campbell, *Managing the Presidency,* 138.

40. David A. Stockman, *The Triumph of Politics: Why the Reagan Revolution Failed* (New York: Harper & Row), 1986.

41. Campbell, "The 'Let's Deal' President," 210.

42. Ibid., 211.

43. Frendreis and Tatalovich, *The Modern Presidency and the Economy,* 70.

44. Paul Starobin, "The Broker," *National Journal,* Apr. 16, 1994, 878–883.

45. Weatherford and McDonnell, "Clinton and the Economy," 21.

46. Woodward, *The Agenda.*

47. Weatherford and McDonnell, "Clinton and the Economy," 39.

48 Ibid., 42.

49. Jeffrey H. Birnbaum and Alan S. Murray, *Showdown at Gucci Gulch: Lawmakers, Lobbyists, and the Unlikely Triumph of Tax Reform* (New York: Random House, 1987).

50. Each year Congress passes thirteen major appropriation bills that finance the operations of the government that are conducted by departments and agencies. The appropriations do not include entitlement programs, such as Social Security, Medicare, and Medicaid, or interest on the national debt.

51. James L. Sundquist, *The Decline and Resurgence of Congress* (Washington, D.C.: Brookings, 1981), 199.

52. R. Kent Weaver, *Automatic Government: The Politics of Indexation* (Washington, D.C.: Brookings, 1988).

53. This discussion follows Allen Schick, *The Federal Budget: Politics, Policy, Process* (Washington, D.C.: Brookings, 1995), chap. 5.

54. Schick defines budget authority as "legislation that enables an agency to incur obligations. Obligations occur when agencies take any action ... that commits the government to the payment of funds." Ibid., 19.

55. Ibid., 82.

56. Allen Schick, "The Evolution of Congressional Budgeting," in *Crisis in the Budget Process: Exercising Political Choice*, ed. Allen Schick (Washington, D.C.: American Enterprise Institute, 1986), 8.

57. Ibid., 15.

58. Ibid.

59. Alfred J. Tuchfarber, Stephen E. Bennett, Andrew E. Smith, and Eric W. Rademacher, "The Republican Tidal Wave of 1994: Testing Hypotheses About Realignment, Restructuring, and Rebellion" (Paper presented at the annual meeting of the American Political Science Association, Chicago, Aug. 31–Sept. 3, 1995), 20–21.

60. Stockman, *The Triumph of Politics*, 97–98, 329–332.

READINGS

Anderson, James E., and Jared E. Hazleton. *Managing Macroeconomic Policy: The Johnson Presidency*. Austin: University of Texas Press, 1986.

Collender, Stanley E. *Guide to the Federal Budget: Fiscal 1996*. Washington, D.C.: Urban Institute Press, 1995. Published annually.

Fisher, Louis. *Presidential Spending Power*. Princeton, N.J.: Princeton University Press, 1975.

Frendreis, John P., and Raymond Tatalovich. *The Modern Presidency and Economic Policy*. Itasca, Ill.: Peacock Publishers, 1994.

Kettl, Donald F. *Leadership at the Fed*. New Haven, Conn.: Yale University Press, 1986.

Mills, Gregory B., and John L. Palmer, eds. *Federal Budget Policy in the 1980s*. Washington, D.C.: Urban Institute Press, 1984.

Niskanen, William A. *Reaganomics*. New York: Oxford University Press, 1988.

Pfiffner, James P., ed. *The President and Economic Policy*. Philadelphia: Institute for the Study of Human Issues, 1986.

Porter, Roger B. *Presidential Decision Making: The Economic Policy Board*. New York: Cambridge University Press, 1980.

Schick, Allen. *The Federal Budget: Politics, Policy, Process*. Washington, D.C.: Brookings, 1995.

Schick, Allen. *The Capacity to Budget*. Washington, D.C.: Urban Institute Press, 1990.

Stein, Herbert. *Presidential Economics: The Making of Economic Policy from Roosevelt to Reagan and Beyond*. 2d rev. ed. Washington, D.C.: American Enterprise Institute, 1988.

Stockman, David A. *The Triumph of Politics: Why the Reagan Revolution Failed*. New York: Harper & Row, 1986.

Tufte, Edward R. *Political Control of the Economy*. Princeton, N.J.: Princeton University Press, 1978.

Wildavsky, Aaron. *The New Politics of the Budgetary Process*. 2d ed. New York: HarperCollins, 1992.

10 THE POLITICS OF NATIONAL SECURITY POLICY

To comply with national security policies instigated by the Reagan administration, the U.S. Air Force has begun dismembering B-52 bombers, which are then left for ninety days so that Russia can confirm the destruction with satellite photos.

FOLLOWING WORLD WAR II THE United States and the Soviet Union were the dominant countries in world affairs. Cast in the role of adversaries, they led two armed camps of nations—one democratically governed, the other ruled by Communist Party dictatorships. The industrial democracies and the communist bloc coexisted in an uneasy peace, maintained in part by the threat of mutual nuclear annihilation. At the same time, each power grouping actively courted the support of the "uncommitted" nations of the so-called Third World. These countries, most of which faced enormous economic and social problems, varied in their orientations toward Washington and Moscow.

Superimposed on the basic pattern of U.S.-Soviet competition was the twentieth-century technological revolution in communications, transportation, and weaponry, which had the effect of shrinking the world and making the risks of military confrontation greater than ever. In addition, the United States grew more economically dependent on other countries, especially suppliers of basic raw materials, such as oil. In an environment characterized by military precariousness and economic interdependence, national security policy—foreign affairs and military policy—claimed most of the president's attention. No chief executive could focus primarily and indefinitely on domestic policy. Sooner or later, presidents found themselves caught up with national security issues.

Modern presidents from Franklin D. Roosevelt to George Bush were drawn almost irresistibly to concentrate on national security policy rather than domestic policy. The reasons were at least twofold: first, the crucial importance of the United States in the international community; and second, the political advantages that presidents normally derived from devoting much of their energy to national security.[1]

Reagan came into office in 1981 committed to bringing about a conservative revolution in domestic and economic policy but found himself drawn toward national security policy issues. His successor, George Bush, was preoccupied with foreign and military policy from the start of his administration and only reluctantly turned his attention home when the economy faltered and his reelection campaign approached. In that campaign Bill Clinton successfully attacked Bush for neglecting the health of the economy and serious domestic problems and promised that, if elected, he would concentrate on them. Much to his dismay, Clinton discovered upon taking office that the end of the cold war brought new conflicts and greater uncertainty to international affairs. Like his predecessors, he too had to involve himself extensively with foreign policy.

This chapter examines the president's role in making and directing national security policy. It reviews the major concepts and issues that have dominated national security policy since World War II. It then defines the national security policy-making problem as one in which the president is both the solution and the problem. It explains this situation by analyzing (1) the relationship between the president and Congress with respect to national security and (2) the problem of organizing an effective policy-making system for national security.

Issues and Conflicts in National Security Policy

From the end of World War II until March 1968, when the North Vietnamese Tet offensive precipitated Lyndon Johnson's decision to end the escalation of American involvement in the Vietnam War, U.S. national security policy rested on a single overarching concept or doctrine, which was supported by a broad consensus: the necessity for military *containment* of communism. That goal was pursued consistently, and differences of opinion within the policy-making elite and in the mass public were accommodated by compromises. Bipartisan support for the consensus in Congress gave presidents a free hand in formulating and implementing foreign and military policies. The only effective constraints imposed on presidential actions were the boundaries of the consensus, which began to break up in 1968, when it became apparent that containment could be preserved only through an indefinite, limited war in Vietnam or greatly expanded U.S. involvement that carried risks of conflict with the Soviet Union.

Even after the United States failed to "contain" communism in Vietnam, presidents continued to employ single, overarching concepts to build domestic political support for their national security policies. They found that "selling programs to Congress and the American people in the postwar era was always made easier if they could be clothed in one garment." [2] In 1972 and 1973 President Nixon told the American people that a policy of détente would ease, if not end, the precarious Soviet-American tensions of the cold war. Détente was to be implemented through actions such as cultural exchanges, increased trade between the two countries, and negotiations to limit strategic nuclear weapons. Established attitudes and behavior patterns are not easy to change, however, and Nixon and his successor, Gerald Ford, found it convenient to seek support for their policies by citing threatening Soviet actions in various parts of the world, such as Africa, Latin America, and the Middle East.

Jimmy Carter effectively campaigned on the pledge, which he reaffirmed at the outset of his administration, that morality, manifested in universal commitment to the defense of human rights, would be the cornerstone of U.S. foreign policy. However, Carter's human rights focus failed to provide the basis for a new consensus because it would not be consistently applied. The United States found it easier to protest and threaten to take action against human rights violations in countries not vital to its interests, like the Soviet Union and its allies, than in those that were vital, like South Korea and South Africa. Indeed, misguided application of the human rights doctrine hastened the downfall of the shah's friendly but authoritarian government in Iran and contributed to the establishment of the equally oppressive, but virulently anti-American, Islamic republic of Ayatollah Ruhollah Khomeini. Nor did the United States have the capacity to enforce the doctrine against powerful violators.

Carter's inability to establish a new foreign policy consensus based on human rights illustrates the contradictions that have become inherent in the international environment of the United States. From an American perspective, that environment has become more and more unmanageable because of the decline in the relative economic power of the United States, which stems from continued dependence on imported oil and from economic interdependence with other industrial democracies. In addition to the contradiction between the commitment to human rights and the need for stable allies, serious dilemmas for the United States are embodied in many issues: devotion to Israel versus the need for Arab oil; the desire for military strength sufficient to protect vital U.S. interests versus domestic political pressures (for example, the drive, following the collapse of communism and the end of the cold war, to use part of the defense budget to reduce the budget deficit and fund domestic programs); and the preference for imported goods, such as Japanese automobiles and electronics equipment, versus the demand to preserve the health of domestic industries. The intermingling of new international issues, predominantly economic, with domestic social and macroeconomic policy issues further complicates the president's efforts to present national security policy in terms of an overarching framework. These new issues include the leverage exerted on the United States by foreign producers of oil and other natural resources, the management of the international monetary system, international sales of U.S. agricultural products, and international trade policy. These issues have immediate and powerful effects on important domestic constituencies and must be dealt with through negotiations. In addressing such issues presidents do not enjoy the discretion or broad support that traditionally has been accorded them in foreign and military policy.

The Reagan administration's handling of national security policy exemplifies the issues and conflicts presidents face in this area of policymaking. Reagan took office proclaiming belligerently that his administration's framework for national security policy was continued opposition to and competition with the Soviet Union,[3] which he once called "the evil empire." In practice, his anti-Soviet stance was less than doctrinaire. In November 1981, for example, facing a growing peace movement in Western Europe, Reagan offered to cancel plans to place additional land-based intermediate-range missiles in West Germany and in several other North Atlantic Treaty Organization (NATO) countries in exchange for the withdrawal of comparable Soviet SS-20 missiles from Eastern Europe and the western part of Russia.

The pattern of strong anti-Soviet rhetoric and restrained conduct continued through the Reagan administration. The president, however, who throughout his political career had steadfastly proclaimed opposition to accommodating the Soviet Union, found it difficult to build a successful national security policy on that position. For example, negotiations to limit nuclear weapons and curtail the arms race, although initially unsuccessful, eventually produced the Intermediate Range Nuclear Forces Treaty, the first arms *reduction* agreement of the cold war.

Throughout the Reagan administration, journalists and political critics questioned its interpretation and explanation of its actions. The critics also raised questions about the president's knowledge of the details of events and the role of the State Department, the Central Intelligence Agency (CIA), and the National Security Council (NSC) and its staff in handling them.

The Reagan administration's foreign policy surged out of control with the disclosure of the Iran-contra affair.[4] In November 1986 the administration acknowledged that it had sent arms to Iran, but stated that only a small number of obsolete weapons had been involved. It maintained that the shipments were designed to establish contact with and encourage moderate elements in Iran. Reagan refused to acknowledge that selling arms to Iran had been an error, and he vigorously denied that there had been any explicit exchange of arms for hostages, although each hostage's release had been preceded by an arms shipment. The seriousness and complexity of the affair snowballed in late November 1986 when the president acknowledged, through Attorney General Edwin Meese, that profits from the arms sales ($10 million–$30 million) had been diverted to the Nicaraguan contras through a numbered Swiss bank account.

The Iran-contra affair raised questions about the content of the policies involved, the appropriateness and even legality of certain actions by the president and members of his staff, and the president's credibility and competence. The selling of arms to Iran in apparent exchange for American hostages called into question the commitment of the United States to resisting terrorism and isolating countries, such as Iran, that support terrorism. It also undermined the U.S. position of neutrality in the seven-year war between Iran and Iraq and damaged its relations with moderate Arab states such as Saudi Arabia. Several members of Congress charged that the arms sales apparently violated laws requiring "the administration to report on covert operations and other diplomatic and military operations overseas."[5] (The president exempted himself from the legislation and the embargo against arms sales to Iran that had been in effect since the 1979–1980 hostage crisis by formally making a finding, on January 17, 1986, that the sales were necessary to national security.)

The diversion of profits from the arms sales to the contras was in direct conflict with the Boland Amendment of 1984, which prohibited use of government funds to support covert operations against the government of Nicaragua, and the decision of Congress not to authorize military aid to the contras in 1986. To the surprise of many, when Reagan disclosed that funds had secretly been diverted to the contras, he stated that he had not been fully informed about the matter. His biographer, Lou Cannon, observes that Reagan had "a difficult time keeping his story straight" because of mental confusion and his desire to "claim credit for helping the contras even while distancing himself from the diversion."[6]

Questions about Reagan's competence in managing foreign policy focused on his detached administrative style, which entailed extensive delegation and a disdain for factual details. His supporters explained that he took care of "the big picture" and left the rest to subordinates. Until late 1986 this approach seemed to serve him quite effectively. The Iran-contra affair emboldened critics to point out that regardless of how little Reagan may have known, he was accountable for the actions of his administration. The operation of the foreign policy process, especially the role played by the NSC staff, contributed a great deal to Reagan's political difficulties and did little to protect him from foreign policy mistakes.

In contrast to Reagan, Bush was a hands-on president deeply engaged in the formulation and implementation of national security policy. He concerned himself with its details and participated actively in negotiations with foreign leaders. In addition, he approached foreign policy with a pragmatic, rather than ideological, orientation. All of this resulted, however, in the criticism that his administration's foreign policy was purely tactical and lacked a strategic design.[7]

In general, the Bush administration's national security policies met with popular approval, although the administration's refusal to retaliate against the government of China for the June 1989 Tiananmen Square massacre of students pressing for democratic reforms drew sharp criticism. Many members of Congress questioned the administration's conduct of relations with Panama and Iraq, but the public remained supportive. For the most part, Bush continued the policies of the late Reagan years but with greater flexibility and adaptiveness.[8] As Terry Deibel put it, "Bush has provided just what the American people seemed to want when they elected him: a kind of competent Reaganism." He "restore[d] professionalism to the conduct of foreign policy."[9] In the Persian Gulf War, for example, Bush skillfully mobilized domestic and world opinion behind the most effective international coalition since World War II. He demonstrated the ability of the United States to project its power far from its home base. However, by not removing Iraqi president Saddam Hussein from power and bringing peace and stability to the Middle East, the United States failed to realize fully the fruits of victory.

Despite its success, the Bush foreign policy was essentially reactive. Even its major initiatives—the invasion of Panama and the gulf war—were responses to crises. The absence of a strategic framework led to an emphasis on individual problems and to policies that lacked cohesion. While Bush spoke grandly of a "new world order," he gave little indication of its shape and dimensions. His administration was unable to develop a strategic design for the post–cold war world or a replacement for the Soviet threat as the unifying force that held the NATO countries and Japan together. Moreover, the absence of a strategic focus for national security may have left the Bush administration with little sense of how to counter growing domestic pressures for reduced international involvement or to cope with the increasing impact of international factors on the domestic economy.

The national security policies of the Clinton administration, often described as "ad hocracy," reflect a confusion of means and ends unresolved by a central vision or overarching conceptual framework.[10] From the outset it expressed a wide array of goals, including the expansion of democracy and human rights; the alleviation of disease, hunger, and poverty; free markets within states and free trade between them; and control of weapons of mass destruction. It also embraced both multilateralism and unilateralism as means to achieve its ends, and it rejected isolationism.

The most extensive statement of the administration's strategy, which eventually appeared in July 1994, identified three central themes: domestic renewal, engagement abroad to enlarge market democracies, and multilateralism as a primary mode of operation.[11] Domestic purpose provided the dominant orientation for the national security policy: market democracies would be extended and threats contained in order to achieve renewal at home.[12] Two of Clinton's biggest foreign policy successes—enactment of legislation implementing the North American Free Trade Agreement (NAFTA) and renewing and expanding the General Agreement on Tariffs and Trade (GATT)—were justified as improving the American economy. Even so, a national security strategy grounded in domestic purpose could not furnish a rationale or guidance for handling specific situations involving the potential use of force or imposition of economic sanctions.

In its application, this strategy was replete with indecision, inconsistencies, and policy reversals and often seemed to be formulated in response to domestic political interests and pressures rather than guided by its inner logic. In no case were these difficulties more apparent than with respect to the civil war in Bosnia. As a presidential candidate, Clinton had criticized the Bush administration for not taking action to end the fighting. As president, he initially advocated lifting the embargo on arms to the Muslim-led government forces and supporting them with air strikes against their Serbian opponents. After sharp criticism from France and Great Britain, contributors of most of the troops to a United Nations peacekeeping force, he abandoned "lift and strike" in favor of working through NATO and the United Nations. Clinton agreed, in November 1995, to commit U.S. ground forces to participate in a NATO peacekeeping force to enforce a settlement to the conflict agreed to by the warring Serbs, Croats, and Muslims. This action encountered sharp domestic criticism from Congress and the media, and polls showed little support for military involvement in Bosnia. The United States under Clinton appeared reluctant to use its considerable military power. Public opinion had played a major role in the abrupt end to the humanitarian mission of U.S. forces in Somalia after eighteen servicemen were killed fighting the forces of a local warlord. Criticism from congressional conservatives hampered efforts to negotiate an end to North Korea's nuclear weapons development program.

The clash of ends (humanitarianism versus free trade) and means (multilateralism versus unilateralism) in Clinton's foreign policy appeared dramatically in controversies with China and Japan, respectively. In early 1993 Clinton informed China that unless it significantly improved its human rights record he would not renew most-favored-nation status for it a year later. (The granting of this status assures a country that it will receive the same tariff concessions that are extended to all other states.) When the deadline arrived without appreciable improvements in human rights, Clinton extended the status, rationalizing that so much was at stake economically that ending it would do more harm than good. In May 1995, Clinton threatened to impose 100 percent tariffs on Japanese luxury cars unless Japan agreed within six weeks to restructure its markets to permit increased sales of U.S. automobile and auto parts manufactures. Japan and several European countries sharply criticized the United States for threatening unilateral action instead of taking its complaint to the World Trade Organization, a multilateral entity established in the 1994 GATT agreement. Ironically, the United States played a major role in creating the World Trade Organization. Eventually, at the last minute, the two countries signed a face-saving agreement that changed little.

The National Security Policy-Making Problem

When the Soviet Union collapsed in 1991, and with it the threat posed by international communism, isolationist forces long dormant in the United States reawoke to challenge the dominant internationalism of the post–World War II era. This development made any prospect of a national security policy built on a broad consensus beyond reach in the foreseeable future. Isolationism and the end of bipartisan congressional support for administration policies, which resulted from the Vietnam War, have made the need for effective international leadership in the United States all the more critical. The governmental structure established in the Constitution—separate institutions sharing power—creates continuing tension between the president and Congress over the control of national security policy. Edward S. Corwin observed that the Constitution "is an invitation to struggle" between the two branches "for the privilege of directing American foreign policy."[13] Although the struggle continues, and power over foreign policy is divided, the president has played the dominant role in shaping national security policy through most of the nation's history.

Dependence on presidential leadership carries risks, however. The idiosyncrasies of individual presidents' operating styles and personalities can be sources of uncertainty and lack of cohesiveness in policy and can reinforce the institutional tensions between Congress and the president.(To some extent this happened during the Iran-contra affair.) The nation needs in its national security policy "institutions that provide continuity" and "structures and processes that promote coherence."[14] The problem is that if institutions, structures, and procedures respond to the short-term needs and whims of individual presidents, discontinuity in policy is likely to multiply. National security policy making presents the United States with a circular and seemingly inescapable problem: the country's dependence on the president for central policy leadership, born of constitutional arrangements and operational imperatives, leads to discontinuity in policy and a lack of cohesiveness that result from a policy-making system geared to presidential domination.

The President, Congress, and National Security

The powers of the United States in international affairs are "inherent, plenary, and exclusive." [15] They are not granted expressly by the Constitution; rather they derive from the nation's existence as a sovereign entity in the international community. To say that the national power over international affairs is inherent means that it does not depend on an affirmative grant of power in the Constitution. The exclusive and plenary character of that power means that it cannot be exercised by the states or anyone else and that its exercise is not limited by the reserved powers of the states.

The Constitution, however, is ambiguous in its assignment of the power to control foreign relations. That both the president and Congress have formal constitutional powers in that sphere indicates that the Founders intended control to be shared. In a 1793 debate with James Madison in the *Gazette of the United States*, Alexander Hamilton argued that direction of the nation's foreign policy is inherently an executive function.[16] Madison's position—that since the power to declare war is vested in Congress, presidential powers in this regard are merely instrumental—has not been borne out by subsequent events. Long-standing usages and the practical aspects of the conduct of foreign relations have combined to make the president the sole organ of the United States in the conduct of its external affairs. Negotiations and communications with other governments have been from the early years of the Republic a presidential monopoly.

Congress, however, has retained considerable ability to influence the substantive content of the foreign and defense policies that the president implements. Policies formulated by the president cannot remain viable for long without congressional support in the form of implementing legislation and appropriations. Nevertheless, throughout most of U.S. history the president has been and is today the "most important single factor in the determination of American foreign policy." [17] The reasons can be understood, at least in part, through examination of the powers of the president and Congress in national security matters.

The Powers of the President

In addition to the inherent powers of the executive derived from the involvement of the United States in the international community, the president's powers over national security stem from two sources: formal powers granted by or implied from specific constitutional provisions and powers delegated to the executive branch by Congress. The specific constitutional provisions on which the president's dominant national security policy role is based include the power to receive ambassadors and ministers, the power to negotiate treaties, the clause designating him as commander in chief of the armed forces, the general grant of executive power, and the clause enjoining him to "take care that the laws be faithfully executed." Operationally, these provisions result in four major areas of presidential authority over national security: recognition and nonrecognition of other governments; making, implementing, and terminating international agreements; the appointment of personnel to conduct foreign and military policy; and the use of military force as a means of achieving policy goals.

Recognition and Nonrecognition of Foreign Governments. The president's power, granted in Article II, Section 3, of the Constitution, to "receive Ambassadors and other public Ministers" is the source of the power of recognition and nonrecognition of foreign governments. Because foreign diplomats are accredited to the president, the decision whether to receive them and thus recognize their governments is exclusively the president's. Congress may formally pressure the president to grant or refuse recognition, but it has no direct involvement in the decision. Because the president can grant recognition, by implication he can also refuse to grant it or withdraw it.

Traditionally, under international law, governments grant recognition to other governments provided they are stable, have effectively established their authority, and are meeting their international obligations. The United States has expressed its approval or disapproval of foreign regimes through recognition and nonrecognition. This weapon is particularly effective when exercised by a nation as powerful and influential as the United States. Nonrecognition by the United States connotes a lack of respectability, if not a lack of legitimacy, in the international community. The prospect of U.S. recognition and the threat of its withdrawal can be used to influence the conduct of another nation. Although the leverage gained through use of the recognition power is limited, its considerable symbolic significance makes it an important presidential instrument in international politics. But recognition or nonrecognition is not a casual decision. Once recognition is granted or relations are broken, much of the leverage that the power provides is lost.

Some well-known instances involving use of the recognition power illustrate its value as well as its limitations. After the Russian Revolution in 1917–1918, the United States refused to recognize the communist government of the Soviet Union on the grounds that it had obtained power illegally, expropriated foreign-owned property without compensation, and oppressed its citizens. Although the disapproval of the Soviet regime implied through nonrecognition did not end, FDR established diplomatic relations with the Soviet Union in 1933; he believed that practical considerations made recognition advantageous to the United States. In contrast, immediately following the proclamation of the new state of Israel in 1948, President Harry Truman granted it recognition, making the United States the first nation to do so. The support of the United States has been vital to the survival of Israel under precarious conditions.

When a communist regime took power in China in 1949 after a revolutionary struggle, the United States refused to recognize it and persisted in regarding the nationalist government on the island of Taiwan as the legitimate government of China. Not until 1979 did the United States establish diplomatic relations with the People's Republic of China. Recognition of the PRC symbolized a resumption of the historic friendship between the two countries. It was made possible by a relaxation of ideological rigidity by the Chinese regime, U.S. acceptance of the regime as the legitimate government of China, and mutual awareness of the policy and economic advantages that would accrue to each nation. At the same time, however, the United States did not recognize PRC sovereignty over Taiwan.

The United States broke diplomatic relations with the Islamic Republic of Iran in December 1979 because of that government's support of the seizure of the U.S. embassy by radicals a month earlier. The damage to United States-Iranian relations resulting from the hostage crisis that ensued and the continued anti-Americanism of the Islamic regime have prevented resumption of diplomatic relations between the two countries.

In 1991 the United States granted recognition to the three Baltic republics of Estonia, Latvia, and Lithuania, which had declared their independence from the Soviet Union in 1990. Although sympathetic to the Baltics, the Bush administration had delayed recognition because it did not wish to upset the precarious position of the Soviet president, Mikhail Gorbachev, in his efforts to reform that country. Following the failure of a coup against Gorbachev in August 1991, the United States moved cautiously by delaying recognition of several more Soviet republics that had declared their independence. Its major concern was that the collapse of the Soviet Union would leave control of its vast arsenal of 27,000 nuclear weapons in the hands of local political leaders and military commanders. In December 1991, as several member republics led by Russia and Ukraine dissolved the Soviet Union, the Bush administration voiced support. However, it delayed recognition of all but one of the component republics until early 1992, when their viability and popular support were established. When the Clinton administration recognized the government of Vietnam in July 1995, it sought to achieve economic gain for both countries and an end to the conflict over the Vietnam War (1965-1973) that had divided this country for thirty years. It risked renewed bitterness and resentment on the part of those who had supported the war and many of those who fought in it.

In these instances, and in other cases involving the recognition power, presidents are legally free to act without regard to Congress. However, congressional views and public opinion effectively limit the range of presidential discretion. President Clinton's recognition of Vietnam was politically difficult for him because he had avoided military service in the war and his action was certain to be criticized as self-serving. On another front, he resisted pressures from Canada, most Latin American countries, and many of his own liberal supporters to improve relations with Fidel Castro's Cuba and move toward eventual recognition. Although there were strong economic arguments for doing so, Clinton apparently concluded that the domestic political costs would be excessive.

② *International Agreements.* The Constitution provides a second influential presidential power in foreign affairs: the authority to conduct negotiations with other nations that result in treaties or binding executive agreements. The constitutional basis for the treaty-making power is found in Article II, Section 2, which declares that the president "shall have power, by and with the Advice and Consent of the Senate, to make treaties, provided two thirds of the Senators present concur." The authority to make executive agreements is not mentioned explicitly, but its constitutionality is "universally conceded." [18] That authority may be implied from the president's function as the nation's official organ for the conduct of foreign relations or as a convenient means of implementing a recognized executive power, such as the commander-in-chief power and the "take care" clause of the Constitution.[19] In addition, executive agreements may be concluded pursuant to provisions of valid treaties and of existing legislation.

The principal distinction between treaties and executive agreements is that Senate approval is required for treaties. The Senate's role in the treaty-making process has been limited by a precedent established in 1789, when the Senate refused George Washington's request to advise him on provisions of a treaty under negotiation. The Senate may, however, amend or attach reservations to treaties submitted for its approval. Amendments change the content of a treaty and thus require additional negotiations; reservations merely clarify the Senate's understanding of the treaty's provisions. The requirement of a two-thirds vote for approval gives the Senate substantial leverage over the executive in the treaty-making process.[20]

As an alternative to the formal treaty process, modern presidents have relied on executive agreements to conclude understandings with other governments. The distinction between treaties and executive agreements is unclear because the latter are not specifically mentioned in the Constitution. In practice, any international agreement the president submits to the Senate for approval as a treaty is a treaty. All other agreements are executive agreements. Congress repeatedly has expressed its disapproval of the use of executive agreements in lieu of treaties, but the only limitation it has imposed, in the Case-Zablocki Act of 1972, is to require that it be notified of all such agreements. Although Congress is free to take action against executive agreements to which it objects, it has been unable to impose effective limits on the president's power to make them.[21]

Presidents have continued to submit international agreements for Senate approval as treaties because of domestic political considerations. Approval by the Senate gives an international agreement a degree of legitimacy that otherwise would be lacking. For instance, President Carter chose to submit to the Senate as a treaty the agreement providing for gradual termination of U.S. control of the Panama Canal. Carter apparently knew that such action would be difficult to defend publicly in any case, and avoidance of Senate approval could impose unacceptable political costs on his administration. For similar reasons, Carter submitted the second Strategic Arms Limitation Talks agreement to the Senate as a treaty even though approval was doubtful.

On several occasions, however, modern presidents have taken important action through executive agreements: in 1940 Franklin Roosevelt exchanged fifty "over-age" destroyers for ninety-nine-year leases on bases in British possessions in the Western hemisphere; in 1973 the United States and North Vietnam ended hostilities and exchanged prisoners of war through an executive agreement; and in 1981 the United States and Israel negotiated an agreement for strategic cooperation in the Middle East.

The decision to designate an international agreement as a treaty is the president's.[22] Such a decision is political rather than legal. But Congress is not without influence, especially if the agreement is not self-executing. In other words, if a treaty or an executive agreement requires legislation or an appropriation for its implementation, Congress can require the executive to take note of its views. During the Clinton administration, two important agreements, NAFTA and GATT, required legislation to become effective. In considering the legislation, Congress conducted an extensive debate over the merits and demerits of the agreements. Clinton had to seek the support of congressional Republicans because a majority of Democrats opposed both bills. Congress has no constitutional duty to implement a treaty or an executive agreement. Moreover, even though treaties and executive agreements have the force of law, they cannot contravene specific provisions of the Constitution.

Although the president's power to negotiate international agreements is subject to political and constitutional limitations, the power to terminate such agreements is not. Clearly, the president can cancel an agreement that did not receive Senate approval. The Constitution is silent, however, about whether approval of the Senate is required to terminate a treaty. The Supreme Court ruled in 1979 that the president could unilaterally abrogate a defense treaty with Taiwan that was part of the agreements establishing diplomatic relations between the United States and the People's Republic of China.[23] Although the Court based its decision on the recognition of foreign governments, it has been interpreted as authorizing unilateral presidential breaking of treaties in accordance with their terms. President Reagan, for example, terminated without congressional approval U.S. acceptance of the jurisdiction of the International Court of Justice, a bilateral commercial treaty with Nicaragua, and U.S. membership in the United Nations Educational, Scientific, and Cultural Organization.[24] Since the Vietnam War, presidents also have expanded their power in the treaty area through reinterpretation. The Reagan administration provides the best example: in 1985 it broadened the terms of the 1972 Anti-Ballistic Missile Treaty, over the objections of the Senate and the Soviet Union, to accommodate development of the strategic defense initiative.[25]

The power to negotiate international agreements is an important aspect of the president's role in foreign affairs. It has a firm constitutional basis and as a practical matter is almost solely an executive function. However, the constitutional role of the Senate in the treaty approval process and the necessity for congressional action to implement most international agreements ensure that congressional influence will be felt in making and implementing such agreements.

Appointments. As noted in Chapter 6, the power to appoint subordinates is an important part of presidential control over policy. It is a power that the president shares with the Senate, however, in naming high-ranking officials. Although the general considerations affecting presidential appointments also apply to national security policy makers, specific concerns in this sphere warrant attention here.

The most important appointments affecting national security are the positions of secretary of state, secretary of defense, the director of central intelligence, and the president's assistant for national security affairs. With these appointments, the president indicates the direction and orientation of the foreign and military policy of his administration. The appointment of the secretary of state is significant for procedural and substantive reasons. The choice of a well-known figure with definite policy views, such as the selection of Gen. George C. Marshall by President Truman, John Foster Dulles by President Eisenhower, or Gen. Alexander Haig by President Reagan, reflects the intention to rely heavily on the secretary for advice and guidance. The choice of a relatively unknown individual, such as President Kennedy's designation of Dean Rusk or president Nixon's selection of William P. Rogers, indicates that the president intends to play the dominant role in foreign policy formulation and to relegate to the secretary the management of the foreign affairs bureaucracy. President Clinton's selection of Warren M. Christopher, a soft-spoken lawyer with a reputation as a shrewd negotiator, appeared to indicate that the president, in keeping with his campaign focus, did not intend to emphasize foreign policy or to involve himself extensively with it. Clinton signaled an increase in foreign policy emphasis at the start of his second term when he named Madeleine K. Albright to replace Christopher. As United Nations ambassador (1993–1996) she had acquired a reputation for firmness and strong policy views.

The appointment of the secretary of defense also can indicate the president's plans for the department. Kennedy's choice of Robert S. McNamara, the president of the Ford Motor Company, signified his determination to make the armed forces more efficient through application of modern management techniques. Nixon's selection of Rep. Melvin Laird of Wisconsin, a powerful Republican leader, symbolized his intention to give greater weight to congressional views in the operation of the department. Clinton reinforced the signal that he intended to leave most national security matters to subordinates when he named a highly regarded defense intellectual, Rep. Les Aspin, D-Wis., as secretary of defense.

The position of director of central intelligence involves managing the CIA and coordinating the activities of the intelligence community.[26] The directorship was often politically controversial during the cold war because of charges that the CIA and other intelligence agencies had engaged in covert activities designed to assassinate foreign political leaders and overthrow foreign governments. Critics also charged the CIA with ineffective intelligence work, such as the failure to anticipate the Iranian revolution of 1978–1979 or Iraq's invasion of Kuwait in 1990. CIA directors have tended to be either intelligence professionals, such as William Colby and Robert Gates, or experienced politicians, such as George Bush and William Casey. The latter, Reagan's first CIA director, apparently played a major role in the Iran-contra affair. His involvement could not be proved, however, because he became ill with cancer and died before the congressional investigation into the affair.[27] Casey's successor was FBI director William Webster, a former federal judge. Reagan appointed him to remove the aura of illegality and scandal that Casey's freewheeling activities had cast upon the agency. President Bush's first nominee to head the CIA was Robert Gates, whose nomination drew substantial opposition in the Senate because of his connection with the Iran-contra affair. After lengthy hearings and floor debate, the Senate confirmed Gates, 64–31, in November 1991.[28] The appointment was significant because Gates would have the task of

422 THE PRESIDENT AND PUBLIC POLICY

reshaping the role of the CIA and the rest of the intelligence community in the post–cold war era. President Clinton's replacement for Gates, R. James Woolsey, a former army officer, attracted little notice until 1994, when the nation was shocked by a revelation that a sensitive CIA operative had been a Soviet mole for nine years.[29] Although Woolsey was not personally responsible for the Ames affair, he was held accountable for the agency's ineffectiveness and resigned in early 1995.[30]

In making high-level executive and diplomatic appointments, the president must be attentive to senatorial attitudes and concerns, although the Senate normally defers to presidential choices even in the face of doubts about the competence of the nominee. Reagan's nomination of William P. Clark, a longtime political associate and California Supreme Court justice, as deputy secretary of state brought strong criticism from the press and several senators when Clark revealed a dreadful lack of knowledge of foreign affairs during his confirmation hearing before the Foreign Relations Committee. Nevertheless, the committee recommended his approval and the Senate complied.[31]

One of the most important national security appointments, that of the national security assistant, is not subject to Senate approval. The president also is free to designate personal representatives to conduct negotiations or perform specific missions without the requirement of confirmation. President Carter used distinguished career diplomats Ellsworth Bunker and Sol Linowitz to negotiate with the governments of Panama and several Middle East countries, respectively. W. Averell Harriman, a prominent Democratic statesman, served as a roving ambassador without portfolio under several presidents beginning with FDR.

The appointment power is essential to presidential control of direction and implementation of foreign and military policy. It is a means whereby the president can shape both the conduct and the content of policy. He enjoys wide latitude in exercising the power, but he must be sensitive to the limits imposed by international and domestic politics and by the Senate.

The Use of Military Force. The Constitution states, "The President shall be Commander in Chief of the Army and Navy of the United States" and of the state militia when they are called into federal service (Article II, Section 2). It does not, however, define the nature of the president's powers and duties as commander in chief. In fact, extensive powers pertaining to the use of military force are found in Article I, the legislative article. Most important, Congress is empowered to declare war. Constitutionally, then, the power to use military force is shared between Congress and the president. Historical practice, however, has resulted in a vast expansion of presidential authority to use force at the expense of the powers of Congress. The dominance of the president in this regard has been almost total in wartime; in times of peace Congress has partially reclaimed the ground it lost. Nonetheless, the result has been the continual aggrandizement of presidential power.[32]

The war powers of the president are sweeping and have their basis in the Constitution, in statutory delegations of authority by Congress, and in judicial interpretations. The constitutional foundation of the president's war powers was laid early in the Civil War when Abraham Lincoln married the commander in chief clause to the "take care" clause.[33] He used the resulting war powers to justify a wide range of actions to suppress the rebellion. These included activation of state militias, expenditure of appropriated funds for unauthorized purposes, suspension of the writ of habeas corpus in militarily insecure areas, and the imposition of a naval blockade of Confederate ports. The Supreme Court upheld the legality of the blockade in the *Prize Cases*, in which it declared that the president had a duty to defend the nation by appropriate means, including military action.[34] The refusal of the Court to overturn any of Lincoln's actions until after the war set a precedent of judicial deference that would be followed in future wars.

Lincoln's actions demonstrated that the war powers of the president extend far beyond mere military command. During World War II the president's powers as commander in chief expanded exponentially under FDR. Among other things, Roosevelt ordered the internment of all persons of Japanese ancestry, including both naturalized and native-born U.S. citizens, who were residing in the Pacific Coast states. The Supreme Court acquiesced in this deprivation of basic civil liberties.[35] Roosevelt also created by executive order emergency agencies, such as the War Labor Board, and endowed them with sweeping regulatory powers and accompanying sanctions. In his most dramatic assertion of the war power, FDR demanded of Congress on September 7, 1942, that it repeal certain sections of the Emergency Price Control Act. If Congress did not act by October 1, he threatened to act on his own authority. Congress responded as the president wished, thus avoiding a constitutional showdown.

Congress has further contributed to the development of the president's war powers through extensive delegations by statute. During

World War I, Congress enacted laws that authorized the president to regulate, requisition, and purchase a wide range of materials and products, to prohibit exports, to license trade, to censor international communications, to regulate enemy aliens in the United States, and to seize and operate the railroads. These powers were expanded during World War II through passage of legislation such as the Lend-Lease Act, which authorized the procurement and leasing of war materials to countries regarded as vital to the defense of the United States; the Emergency Price Control Act, which established the Office of Price Administration and authorized it to fix prices and ration a wide range of goods and services; and a host of other statutes. Many congressional delegations of authority to the president were open-ended and not revised or withdrawn until passage of the National Emergencies Act of 1976.

In short, once war is declared, presidential powers are vast. To ensure national survival, whatever the president says must be done is done without regard to constitutional considerations and with the acquiescence, if not full approval, of the Supreme Court and Congress. Some leading constitutional scholars have charged that the Constitution is suspended in wartime and the president becomes a de facto dictator.[36]

The president's power to use military force in peacetime, or even in periods of undeclared war, is less clear-cut. Although the Supreme Court has been reluctant to resolve questions in this area, Congress has been more assertive of its prerogatives. However, the president still has substantial responsibilities and concomitant powers to protect American lives and property abroad, discharge international obligations, and preserve national security. Constitutional language is vague, and statutory enactments are an incomplete guide to the exercise of this authority.

Between the two world wars Congress circumscribed the president's military powers through enactment of the Neutrality Acts. However, the failure of Congress to declare and implement a foreign policy of isolation from world conflicts became manifest in the 1930s when Germany, Italy, and Japan aggressively expanded their territorial holdings and began a war into which the United States inevitably was drawn. Following World War II successive presidents fashioned an internationalist foreign policy, with bipartisan congressional support, based on the military containment of communism. Presidents were expected to take the initiative, and Congress reviewed their actions through the passage of necessary legislation and appropriations.[37]

The most sensitive issue during this period, which ended in 1968 with the failure of U.S. military involvement in Vietnam, was the authority of the president to commit U.S. troops to fight abroad. On several occasions between 1945 and 1965, presidents sent U.S. forces into combat or placed them in situations that could easily result in combat.[38] These included the Korean War, the dispatch of four divisions to Western Europe as a permanent commitment to NATO, Eisenhower's responses to Chinese pressures on Taiwan and to increased tensions in the Middle East, the 1965 intervention in the Dominican Republic, as well as the Vietnam War.

Vietnam produced the most extensive and controversial instances of presidential war making in the post–World War II era. Beginning with Truman, presidents made commitments of military aid and provided military advisers to the government of South Vietnam. By the end of 1963, more than 16,000 military advisers were in that country, many of them actively participating in combat although not formally authorized to do so. In August 1964 the Johnson administration reported a confrontation in the Gulf of Tonkin between a North Vietnamese gunboat and a U.S. destroyer. At Johnson's request Congress passed the Gulf of Tonkin Resolution, which authorized the president to "take all necessary steps including use of armed force" to assist nations belonging to the Southeast Asia Treaty Organization (to which the United States was a signatory) in defense of their freedom. Only two negative votes were cast against the resolution, both in the Senate. The resolution did not distinguish between powers the president already possessed and newly delegated authority. On the authority of the Constitution, the Southeast Asia Treaty, and the Gulf of Tonkin Resolution, Johnson ordered a vast increase in the strength of U.S. forces in Vietnam, so that by late 1967 they exceeded 500,000. He also authorized military commanders to conduct air raids against military targets in North Vietnam.[39] President Nixon extended the scope of military operations even while trying to negotiate an end to U.S. involvement in the war. In 1970 he ordered a covert invasion of Cambodia to destroy enemy supply and staging areas, and in December 1972 he authorized the bombing of the North Vietnamese capital city of Hanoi and the major port city of Haiphong. These actions were taken without consulting Congress.

Initially, Congress backed administration efforts to contain communism in Southeast Asia through the use of military force. As the war dragged on, however, popular support began to wane, a widespread domestic protest movement began to take shape, and opposition to U.S. policy developed abroad from its allies and from Third World nations. Many members of Congress questioned the wisdom and the legality of placing the decision to use military force entirely in the president's hands. As long as presidential use of force appeared to be successful, congressional opposition was minimal; but when the use of force appeared to be failing, or the risks increased and the costs in popular support became too great, Congress reasserted its constitutional authority to participate as an equal partner with the president in determining where and under what conditions the United States would wage war.

The Assertion of Congressional Powers

Congress has substantial constitutional powers that enable it to claim parity with the president in shaping national security policy. As noted in the discussion of the president's powers, the Senate is directly involved in the treaty approval process and the confirmation of appointments; congressional action in the form of authorizations and appropriations is necessary to implement all presidential decisions that are not self-executing; and the power to declare war rests solely with Congress and implies a congressional prerogative over the use of military force. However, operational realities and a bipartisan foreign policy consensus led to presidential domination of national security policy during the cold war.

The failure of the Vietnam War—essentially a presidential war—ended, at least temporarily, Congress's deference to White House domination of national security policy. During the 1970s Congress limited presidents' ability to wage undeclared war, reduced unrestrained use of executive agreements, restored the treaty as the principal means of making international agreements, reassessed its sweeping delegations of authority to presidents in past wars and emergencies, and curbed secrecy and covert activities in the conduct of foreign and military affairs.

The most important congressional attempt to reclaim powers lost or given to the executive was the War Powers Resolution of 1973. Passed over Nixon's veto, House Joint Resolution 542 provided that the president may commit the armed forces to combat only in the event of a declaration of war, specific statutory authorization, or a national emergency created by an attack on the United States or its armed forces. The resolution urged the president to consult with Congress in "every possible instance" before committing forces to combat abroad, and it required consultation after such commitment. Specifically, it required a written report to Congress within forty-eight hours of a commitment and required ending the commitment within sixty days unless authorized by Congress. The commitment could be extended for thirty additional days if the president certified to Congress that military conditions required continued use of the forces to ensure their safety. Finally, it stated that, through use of a concurrent resolution that would not be subject to presidential veto, Congress may order the disengagement of U.S. forces before the end of the first sixty days.[40]

The effectiveness of the War Powers Resolution as a congressional means of controlling presidentially initiated military action is unclear. Presidents had submitted thirty-seven reports under the resolution through April 1994.[41] In only one of these, the rescue of the *Mayaguez,* a merchant ship that had been seized by Cambodian gunboats in 1975, did the president trigger the sixty-day clock. President Ford submitted four reports, Carter one, Reagan fourteen, Bush six, and Clinton eleven through April 1994. Since its passage, all presidents have regarded the War Powers Resolution as an unconstitutional encroachment on their powers, and their reports have carefully avoided any acknowledgment of its constitutionality. In addition, they have been able to circumvent the intent of the resolution by not activating the sixty-day clock, by stating that they were reporting "consistent with the War Powers Resolution," and by holding that merely informing Congress meets the resolution's requirement of consultation. The position of the executive has been consistent across administrations, while Congress has been unable to formulate a "unitary position or statement of institutional interest."[42] Nor has Congress challenged the president by starting the sixty-day clock. Congress did trigger the sixty-day clock in 1983, in legislation involving the multinational force in Lebanon, but at the same time it authorized U.S. participation in the force for eighteen months. This was done after an agreement was reached with the White House.[43]

President Bush's actions during the Persian Gulf War of 1990–1991 are typical of how presidents deal with the War Powers Resolution.[44] Before sending U.S. armed forces to the gulf in response to Iraq's August 2, 1990, invasion of Kuwait, Bush notified congressional leaders of the planned deployment on August 8. The next day he sent the Speaker and the president pro tem a letter in which he stated that the report was "consistent with" the War Powers Resolution. During the next six months there was a massive buildup of U.S. forces in the gulf area, the U.S. and Iraq exchanged bellicose threats, and the United Nations adopted a resolution imposing a deadline for Iraq to withdraw from Kuwait. At no point, however, did either the president or Congress begin the sixty-day countdown. Rather, the president argued that he had the authority to force Iraq to leave Kuwait without congressional approval. Nevertheless, on January 8, 1991, one week prior to the UN deadline, Bush asked Congress to approve a joint resolution authorizing the use of force. Congress did so four days later by votes of 52–47 in the Senate and 250–183 in the House.[45] When Bush signed the resolution, he reasserted his position that the War Powers Resolution is unconstitutional. The resolution approved on January 12, 1991, has been recognized as the functional equivalent of a declaration of war. Whether Bush weakened his position, that he already had the authority to initiate hostilities, is an unanswered question.

The effect of the War Powers Resolution on the constitutional roles of the president and Congress in making decisions about war and peace is unclear. At the very least, the legislation was a symbolic victory for Congress, serving notice that sustained military commitments outside the country could no longer be made by presidential fiat but required congressional approval and, by implication, popular support. Destler observed, "It is hard to conceive of a formula better crafted to balance the need for presidential capacity to respond quickly to foreign emergencies and the need—as a matter of right *and* effective policy—for democratic judgment on the deployment of troops in combat." [46]

However, most commentary on the War Powers Resolution has been negative. There is "growing consensus" that it "has not worked as Congress envisioned." [47] Presidents have neither consulted Congress in "any meaningful manner" nor have they sought to make the law work by invoking its provisions.[48] Instead, they have sought to circumvent it. For its part, Congress has been unwilling to challenge presidential nonresponsiveness to the War Powers Resolution, and the courts have been unwilling to intercede until it does so.[49] Michael Glennon summarized the effectiveness of the resolution: "Whatever congressional intent underlay the War Powers Resolution, any expectation that its procedures would actually lead to collective legislative-executive judgment in the war-making process was mistaken." [50] Presidential evasion, congressional acquiescence, and judicial deference have combined to accomplish this result.[51]

Can anything be said in defense of the War Powers Resolution? Congress is certainly aware of its deficiencies, as is evidenced by extensive hearings on it, frequent proposals for its amendment, and the efforts of some Republican members in 1995 to restrict U.S. support for and participation in multilateral peacekeeping operations.[52] If the resolution is so fatally flawed and revision has not been possible, why has it not been repealed? [53] The reason may be that the resolution suits congressional purposes. It "allows Congress the luxury of being politically comfortable with its decisions regarding a military action while providing a convenient forum for criticizing the President." [54] Congress can use the War Powers Resolution to force the president to end an unpopular military operation, or it can criticize presidential failure to comply with the procedural requirements of the resolution when public opinion is supportive or divided. Either way, Congress cannot lose. [55] From this perspective, the War Powers Resolution constrains presidential war making by forcing presidents to take it into account and to recognize the possibility, albeit distant, of congressional action. The resolution reminds the president that, under the Constitution, he shares with Congress the crucial decision to lead the nation into war. That Congress has not vigorously applied the War Powers Resolution or buttressed it by denying funding for military action does not mean it is of little consequence.

The ambiguities surrounding the resolution could be clarified by tightening its language and subjecting it to Supreme Court interpretation, but neither Congress nor the president has so far been willing to take such action, perhaps because the outcome is uncertain. Citing as precedent the history of presidential war making, the Court could sustain the resolution. Or, noting that since it was forced on the presidency at a time of institutional weakness, it "undercuts the legitimacy of the executive branch," the Court might choose to overturn it. [56]

Increased congressional participation in national security decision making may not be constitutionally mandatory, but it has become necessary on political grounds. The impact of international issues on domestic politics and the entry of domestic political interests, such as the Israel lobby, into the policy-making process force presidents to seek congressional support to protect their own political positions.

It is somewhat ironic, however, that Congress's desire to share in making national security policy and increased knowledge and competence on the part of individual members and expanded committee staffs have not been accompanied by congressional capability to assume the added responsibility. [57] Congressional reforms during the 1970s, especially in the House, and additional changes in the 1980s further fragmented power and made it more difficult for Congress to speak authoritatively with one voice. The proliferation of subcommittees and the growing interdependence of domestic and foreign policy issues have added to the number of congressional participants in national security policy matters. Congressional staffs have grown in size and influence so that they, too, are drawn into negotiations between the branches. These developments, along with expanded pressures from interest groups and other domestic constituencies, make more elusive the achievement of interbranch consensus.

The difficulty that Congress currently faces in assuming a more active and constructive role in national security policy should not obscure its positive contributions. Among other things, it has curbed unrestrained presidential war making; it has forced reconsideration of extensive if not excessive overseas commitments and imposed caution on assuming new obligations; it has broadened the popular base of U.S. foreign policy; and it has instituted more careful scrutiny of agencies involved in national security. Following the exposure of the Iran-contra affair, Congress moved through its relevant committees to find the facts so that responsibility could be affixed and recommendations made for changes in procedures. In sum, Congress has expanded the base of legitimacy for foreign and military policy.

The constitutional "invitation to struggle" is still present. Congress has open to it alternative approaches for developing its national security policy role in the complex international environment of the 1990s. At times it will be tempted to revert to the pattern of acquiescence in presidential domination that prevailed from World War II until 1973. On other occasions Congress may be tempted to take matters into its own hands, because of popular pressures or distrust of the president's policies and capabilities. A third path is that of collaboration tempered by a sense of constitutional and political responsibility to be constructively critical. Although the president must provide leadership, and only the executive branch can conduct and implement national security policy, Congress has a vital role to play in refining, legitimating, and reviewing all policies.

Organizing and Managing National Security

Beyond dealing with the constitutional issues and political considerations involved in national security policy, the president also confronts a formidable administrative task: organizing the presidency and the executive branch for the formulation and implementation of policy and managing the processes that have been established. The organizational task entails establishing and changing structures and processes. As the Iran-contra investigation revealed, a lax approach to these tasks can be costly.

One of the soundest observations on these problems came from the Commission on the Organization of the Government for the Conduct of Foreign Policy (the Murphy Commission). It opened its 1975 report with the observation that "good organization does not insure successful policy, nor does poor organization preclude it." [58] The commission went on to assert, however, that organizational arrangements have a continuing and powerful impact on the content of public policy and the effectiveness with which it is implemented.[59] Organization determines the level of government (national, state, or local) and the agency that will deal with a problem. Government organization performs three primary functions: it "creates capabilities" for performing tasks that are beyond the reach of individuals; it "vests and weighs particular interests and perspectives" by increasing or reducing the probability of their inclusion in decision making; and it "legitimates decisions" by ensuring that relevant parties are consulted and that decisions are made by proper authorities.[60]

Although there is no specific model to which national security organization must conform, two considerations are paramount: it must be capable of adapting to changing events and conditions, and it must be able to accommodate the operating style of the president, whose constitutional roles make him the focal point of the policy-making process. Congress has enacted legislation, such as the National Security Act of 1947, establishing organizational units to aid the president in the conduct of national security policy. The principal units are the National Security Council and its staff, the departments of State and Defense, the joint chiefs of staff, and the Central Intelligence Agency. Congress cannot, however, effectively prescribe how the president uses those units or the processes by which the president develops broad policy goals and strategies for carrying them out; nor can it prescribe how he manages and coordinates the complex and far-reaching activities of the military establishment, the foreign policy bureaucracy, and the intelligence community. The president needs help to discharge these responsibilities, and he has the authority to obtain it—from staff, cabinet, and independent agencies. How he does so is the essence of his management of national security.

Although the National Security Council, which is the basic structure for the management of national security affairs, has remained substantially unchanged since its creation in 1947, presidents have used it in various ways. Congress established the council in response to the pressures of the cold war and in reaction, at least in part, to the administrative confusion that often characterized Franklin Roosevelt's freewheeling approach to management.

The experience of presidents from Truman through Clinton substantiates Alexander George's observation that every chief executive, upon taking office, must define his role in the national security policy-making system before he can design and manage the roles and relationships of other major participants in it.[61] According to conventional wisdom, the basic choice the president must make is whether to manage the system through the secretary of state and the State Department, as Truman did, or to centralize it in the White House, as Nixon did, with the national security assistant playing the major role. Failure to decide on either approach is likely to result in confusion over policy goals and lack of cohesion in policy implementation, as was the case with Clinton.

Having come to office committed to focus on the economy and domestic problems, Bill Clinton paid little attention to the organizational and operational aspects of the national security process. He staffed the major positions with "brokers and bureaucrats" and reserved the important decisions for himself.[62] Neither the national security assistant and the NSC staff nor the secretary of state and the State Department were clearly in charge. There was little indication of conceptual thinking at any location. The result was a series of ad hoc reactions to crises, problems, and domestic pressures. The decision made on August 18, 1994, reversing the long-standing policy to admit Cuban refugees exemplifies the haphazard and disorganized nature of Clinton's decision making.[63]

Cecil Crabb and Keven Mulcahy have developed a typology for analyzing presidential management of national security that is based on responsibility for policy making and for implementation of policy.[64] They identify four presidential management styles—department-centered, formalized, collegial, and palace guard—with accompanying roles for the national security assistant—administrator, coordinator, counselor, and agent (see Figure 10-1). A president, such as Truman, who has limited interest in the formation and implementation of foreign policy, deputizes the secretary of state to act and speak for him (while making final decisions himself), and relies primarily on the State Department for analysis and implementation has a *department-centered* style. The national security assistant, in the corresponding role of administrator, acts primarily as a high-level staff aide who supervises the advisory process and facilitates the presentation of views to the president. He or she does not act independently or function as a primary policy adviser.

Figure 10-1   Presidential Management Styles and National Security Assistant's Roles

Implementation Responsibility

	Low	High
Low *Policy-Making Responsibility*	Department-centered administrator	Formalized coordinator
High	Collegial counselor	Palace guard agent

Source: Cecil V. Crabb, Jr., and Kevin V. Mulcahy, *American National Security: A Presidential Perspective* (Pacific Grove, Calif.: Brooks/Cole, 1991), 189.

Adm. Sidney Souers, Truman's executive secretary for the National Security Council, functioned in this capacity.

Dwight Eisenhower looked to the national security bureaucracy—the departments of State and Defense and the intelligence community—for policy recommendations, carefully examined a wide range of proposals and plans, and retained control over policy making and implementation. He exemplifies the *formalized* management style. His national security assistant, Robert Cutler, functioned as a coordinator. The coordinator acts in a staff role but may have considerable influence. His principal task is to facilitate the making of national security policy by defining options and managing the flow of ideas and information. He also reviews policy, but the president and the secretary of state make the final decisions.

The *collegial* management style, typified by Kennedy and Johnson, involves an informal national security process. In this model, the president operates with ad hoc working groups, tends to distrust the national security bureaucracy, and seeks to centralize decision making in the White House with the NSC staff performing independent analysis and policy review functions. The counselor role of the national security assistant, exemplified by McGeorge Bundy under Kennedy and Walt Rostow in the Johnson administration, entails a close personal relationship with the president in which the assistant is a major policy adviser and acts to safeguard the president's interests. Clinton's ad hoc management of national security policy most closely approximated the collegial style. The role of his national security assistant, Anthony Lake, was to keep foreign policy from overshadowing the president's focus on economic and domestic affairs while not appearing weak and ineffectual.[65]

In the *palace guard* management style, associated with Richard Nixon, the president centralizes policy making in the White House and maintains a tight rein on implementation. The State Department and other units of the national security bureaucracy are "virtually excluded" from an active policy-making role and "relegated" to implementing the decisions of the president and the national security assistant.[66] Nixon's national security assistant, Henry Kissinger, acted as the president's agent. In that capacity he directed the policy-making process, served as the president's closest policy adviser, and on occasion actively implemented policy—in Kissinger's case by conducting negotiations with foreign governments.

Crabb and Mulcahy argue that experience since 1947 reveals that neither the administrator nor the agent roles for the national security assistant are to be recommended. By implication, they suggest that the president adopt either the formalized or collegial management style for national security. The administrator role is likely to be ineffective unless the president and the secretary of state are capable, hands-on administrators. The agent role carries the risk that the national security assistant may go into business for himself, acting without presidential knowledge or approval as Reagan claimed was the case with Adm. John Poindexter and his assistant, Lt. Col. Oliver North, in the Iran-contra affair. Whether the president chooses the coordinator or counselor role for his national security assistant should be determined by his management style. The president also must exercise care to select a national security assistant whose personality is compatible with the designated role.[67] Jimmy Carter encountered considerable difficulty in managing national security because of conflict and competition between Secretary of State Cyrus Vance and Zbigniew Brzezinski, the national security assistant. At least part of the problem stemmed from Carter's apparent failure to recognize that Brzezinski was an ambitious, assertive individual more suited to the role of agent than that of administrator, which Carter apparently wished him to play.

A president, such as Reagan, who vacillates in establishing a preferred management style and defining the national security assistant's role, is almost certain to experience trouble formulating a coherent foreign policy and implementing it effectively. That six individuals served as national security assistant during the Reagan administration highlights the instability in the president's management of national security.

Except for ideological rhetoric castigating the Soviet Union, the president demonstrated little interest in foreign policy and was notably detached from the national security process.

By Reagan's second term, the administration had developed a national security policy system characterized by turmoil in the relationship between the State Department and the White House. Secretary of State George Shultz was the principal foreign policy spokesperson, but he was not privy to some of the covert operations conducted by North and other members of the NSC staff, and his views on the arms sales to Iran were rejected. One national security assistant, Robert McFarlane, acted as a policy advocate rather than as an honest broker coordinating policy making by departments and agencies, and he even carried out special missions for the president. Mulcahy describes the system as a "collegial arrangement for the management of foreign affairs with the White House acting as umpire." [68] It may well have been, but it could not keep the president from the major blunder that was the Iran-contra affair. An unanswered question is whether any conceivable system for managing foreign policy could have overcome Reagan's deliberate disengagement from policy making and his lack of interest in and concern with policy implementation.

In marked contrast to Reagan, George Bush was a hands-on president deeply engaged in the formulation and implementation of national security policy. He concerned himself with its details and was actively involved in negotiations with foreign leaders. Bush adopted a collegial management style and prescribed a counselor's role for Brent Scowcroft, his national security assistant. He organized the national security process in a manner that most resembled Lyndon Johnson's.[69] He made little use of a formal process to identify and analyze options and relied instead on a small group of intimate advisers. There was little evidence of conflict within Bush's national security inner circle, and it received high marks for its cohesiveness and competence.[70]

Bill Clinton's management of national security policy making suffered from two factors: his lack of interest in foreign and military policy and a preference for domestic and economic policy, and his lack of knowledge of or concern about the importance of staffing and organization.[71] His participation in the national security policy-making process was episodic and nonsystematic.[72] Moreover, no one else was authorized to speak with a strong and forceful voice for the administration.[73] These factors resulted in haphazard decision making and the appearance of weakness and inconstancy in policy.

Conclusion

National security is the president's most important substantive policy responsibility; it presents him with major and complex problems of leadership and management. For the nation, the effectiveness of foreign and military policy in preserving and protecting its sovereignty and independence is of paramount interest. That interest stands or falls to a large extent on the president's performance. He must interpret and exercise his powers within constitutional and statutory limits. He finds it imperative to consult with Congress, and to be effective he must have congressional cooperation. Yet, operational realities require that he be accorded ample latitude to act independently and often secretly. Tensions inevitably arise between Congress and the president over national security policy, although Barbara Hinckley suggests that the conflict between them is primarily symbolic and is staged to convince the public that both institutions are alert and active and that policy making is democratic.[74] However, the tasks involved are primarily executive in nature, and executive control of foreign and military policy persists in spite of Congress's major constitutional role.[75] The Constitution and political prudence require "shared power and balanced institutional participation" as norms in national security decision making.[76]

Perhaps the most important lesson in this regard is that since 1945 most of the nation's successful foreign policies—the Truman Doctrine, the Marshall Plan, NATO, the Panama Canal treaty, arms control, and the Persian Gulf War—"have been adopted by Congress and the people after meaningful debate." [77] For the most part, the major failures— FDR's Yalta agreements with Stalin, the Bay of Pigs invasion, the Vietnam War, and the Iran-contra affair—have been initiated and implemented unilaterally by presidents.

Presidents also discover that resolution of national security issues must be coordinated with the handling of domestic and economic concerns because major issues tend to overlap and solutions cannot be compartmentalized. Presidents no longer can fashion national security policies without regard to domestic political and economic pressures. Such pressures in turn lead presidents to seek ways of managing national security policy that provide them with flexibility in action and protect their personal political stakes.

The principal institutional means that modern presidents have used to manage national security—a White House–centered national security system directed by a national security assistant heading a professional NSC staff—has served this purpose, but often at the expense of long–range continuity and cohesion in policy. The alternative organizational strategy—a State Department–centered system with the secretary of state playing a dominant policy-making and advisory role—has attracted support from some students of national security policy and from political outsiders as a means of obtaining the desired degree of continuity and integration. Presidents since Eisenhower, however, have found such an arrangement unsuitable to their style of operation.

Neither Reagan's, Bush's, nor Clinton's approaches to managing national security provide an answer to the question of the extent to which organizational arrangements can contribute to making those efforts effective. Reagan's approach was eclectic. At first, he enhanced the role of the secretary without strengthening the State Department, and he downgraded the position of the national security assistant and the NSC staff. When that arrangement resulted in conflict within the administration, criticism from outside, and confusion everywhere, Reagan then adopted a more collegial system centered neither in the State Department nor in the White House and dominated by neither the secretary of state nor the national security assistant. That system served him fairly well until the Iran-contra affair erupted. But it is not clear whether Reagan would have avoided that fiasco had he made the organizational choice that analysts assumed was inescapable. Bush's informal but more professional approach had several successes and avoided failures but left a sense of unfilled potential and the absence of direction. Victory in the cold war came during Bush's term of office but not as a consequence of his management of the foreign and military policy of the United States. When it happened, his administration was singularly unprepared for it. Clinton, like Reagan, had an eclectic approach to managing national security policy. In contrast to Reagan, however, he was deeply engaged in the process when the situation required his participation, even though he was much more interested in economic and domestic policy. Although it is not manifest, it seems probable that a less haphazard and more systematic process and a higher level of presidential interest on Clinton's part would have resulted in more coherent and consistent policies.

What is clear is that in the emerging international system the United States is the world's major power. Its people and the rest of the world are deeply affected by the policy preferences, personality, and operating style of its presidents. The statecraft they employ and how they view and exercise national power will critically affect the shape of that system.

NOTES

1. The "two presidencies" thesis holds that presidents enjoy relatively greater success with Congress in foreign than in domestic policy. According to Terry Sullivan, modern Republican and Democratic presidents have had approximately equal success with foreign policy proposals, but Democratic administrations have done better with domestic policy because of their party's domination of Congress. See Sullivan, "A Matter of Fact: The `Two Presidencies' Thesis Revitalized," in *The Two Presidencies: A Quarter Century Assessment*, ed. Steven A. Shull (Chicago: Nelson Hall, 1991), 143-157.

2. James Chace, "Is a Foreign Policy Consensus Possible?" *Foreign Affairs* (Fall 1978): 30.

3. Strobe Talbot, *The Russians and Reagan* (New York: Vintage Books, 1984).

4. The most comprehensive and informative account of the Iran-contra affair is by Theodore Draper, *A Very Thin Line: The Iran-Contra Affairs* (New York: Hill & Wang, 1991). For the perspective of two participants in the congressional hearings, see William S. Cohen and George J. Mitchell, *Men of Zeal* (New York: Viking, 1988). The role of the CIA and its director William Casey receive careful attention by Bob Woodward in *Veil: The Secret Wars of the CIA, 1981–1987* (New York: Simon & Schuster, 1987). Also essential to a full understanding of Iran-contra is the report of the Tower Commission (John Tower, Edmund Muskie, and Brent Scowcroft). President's Special Review Board, *Report of the President's Special Review Board* (Washington, D.C.: Government Printing Office, 1987).

5. John Felton, "Secret Weapons Sale Stirs Up Legal Questions," *Congressional Quarterly Weekly Report*, Nov. 22, 1986, 2929.

6. Lou Cannon, *President Reagan: The Role of a Lifetime* (New York: Simon & Schuster, 1991), 717.

7. Terry L. Deibel, "Bush's Foreign Policy: Mastery and Inaction," *Foreign Policy* (Fall 1991): 20-22; Steven V. Roberts, "The Second Sin of George Bush," *New Leader*, Mar. 11–15, 1991, 3.

8. Daniel P. Franklin and Robert Shepard, "Analyzing the Bush Foreign Policy" (Paper presented at the annual meeting of the American Political Science Association, Washington, D.C., Aug. 29–Sept. 1, 1991), 2–3.

9. Deibel, "Bush's Foreign Policy," 3–4.

10. David C. Hendrickson, "The Recovery of Internationalism," *Foreign Affairs* (Sept./Oct. 1994): 26–43. For similar criticisms see Richard N. Haas, "Paradigm Lost," *Foreign Affairs* (Jan./Feb. 1995): 43–58; and Larry Berman and Emily O. Goldman, "Clinton's Foreign Policy at Midterm," in *The Clinton Presidency: First Appraisals*, ed. Colin Campbell and Bert A. Rockman (Chatham, N.J.: Chatham House, 1995), 290–324.

11. William J. Clinton, *A National Security Strategy of Engagement and Enlargement* (Washington, D.C.): Government Printing Office, 1994).

12. Berman and Goldman, "Clinton's Foreign Policy," 302–303.

13. Edward S. Corwin, *The President: Office and Powers*, 4th ed. (New York: New York University Press, 1957), 171.

14. Ibid.

15. Joseph E. Kallenbach, *The American Chief Executive* (New York: Harper & Row, 1966), 485.

16. Corwin, *The President*, 179.

17. Ibid., 185.

18. Ibid., 213.

19. Ibid.; Kallenbach, *The American Chief Executive*, 502.

20. The treaty-making process entails three distinct stages: negotiation, Senate approval, and ratification by the president. Contrary to popular understanding, the Senate does not ratify a treaty—it approves the treaty negotiated by the president. The president may refuse to sign, that is, to ratify, a treaty approved by the Senate, either because of amendments or reservations or because it was negotiated by a previous administration.

21. Cecil V. Crabb, Jr., and Pat M. Holt, *Invitation to Struggle: Congress, the President, and Foreign Policy*, 4th ed. (Washington, D.C.: CQ Press, 1991), 6.

22. Harold Hongju Koh argues, however, that Congress should create by statute its own procedures for determining when international agreements should be submitted to the Senate for approval. See Koh, *The National Security Constitution: Sharing Power after the Iran-Contra Affair* (New Haven, Conn.: Yale University Press, 1990), 195.

23. *Goldwater v. Carter*, 444 U.S. 996 (1979).

24. Koh, *The National Security Constitution*, 44.

25. Ibid., 43.

26. The intelligence community consists of the Central Intelligence Agency; the National Security Agency; the Bureau of Intelligence and Research in the Department of State; the Defense Intelligence Agency and the intelligence offices of the army, navy, air force, and marine corps; and intelligence offices in the departments of Energy and Treasury. Crabb and Holt, *Invitation to Struggle*, 25.

27. Woodward, *Veil*, chap. 25.

28. Pamela Fessler, "Gates Confirmed to Lead CIA into Post-Soviet Era," *Congressional Quarterly Weekly Report*, Nov. 9, 1991, 3291–3292.

29. Aldrich Ames was the Soviet branch chief of the CIA's counterintelligence group. From 1985 through 1993 he sold sensitive information, including the names of the entire network of spies that the United States had established in the Soviet Union during the cold war, to the KGB. Most of those agents were executed. For accounts of the Ames case, see Tim Weiner, David Johnson, and Neil A. Lewis, *Betrayal* (New York: Random House, 1995); and David Wise, *Nightmover* (New York: HarperCollins, 1995).

30. Donna Cassata, "Congress Jumps to CIA's Aid in Its Quest for Identity," *Congressional Quarterly Weekly Report*, Jan. 7, 1995, 41–42.

31. Clark subsequently proved to be a quick learner and a person of great administrative ability. Within a year he was receiving praise from many of his former critics.

32. Corwin, *The President*, chap. 6; Arthur M. Schlesinger, Jr., *The Imperial Presidency* (Boston: Houghton Mifflin, 1989), chaps 1–7.

33. Corwin, *The President*, 229.

34. *Prize Cases*, 67 U.S. (2 Black) 635 (1863).

35. *Korematsu v. United States*, 323 U.S. 214 (1944).

36. Clinton Rossiter, *Constitutional Dictatorship: Crisis Government in Modern Democracies* (New York: Harcourt, Brace & World, 1963).

37. James L. Sundquist, *The Decline and Resurgence of Congress* (Washington, D.C.: Brookings, 1981), 107.

38. Such actions have numerous precedents, including Jefferson's dispatch of the navy to stop the Barbary pirates from seizing U.S. merchant ships and holding their crews for ransom, and Theodore Roosevelt's contribution of U.S. Marines to the international expeditionary force that put down the Boxer Rebellion in China in 1904.

39. Larry Berman, *Planning a Tragedy: The Americanization of the War in Vietnam* (New York: Norton, 1982). For a comparative analysis of how Eisenhower and Johnson dealt with pressures to intervene militarily in Vietnam, see John P. Burke and

Fred I. Greenstein, *How Presidents Test Reality: Decisions on Vietnam, 1954 and 1965* (New York: Russell Sage Foundation, 1989).

40. The Supreme Court's decision in *Immigration and Naturalization Service v. Chadha*, 462 U.S. 919 (1983), which held that the legislative veto was unconstitutional, made this provision inoperative. Congress subsequently substituted a joint resolution for the concurrent resolution; however, the former is subject to a presidential veto.

41. U.S. House of Representatives, Subcommittee on International Security, International Organizations and Human Rights, *The War Powers Resolution: Relevant Documents, Reports, Correspondence*, 103d Cong., 2d sess., 1994, Committee Print.

42. Robert A. Katzman, "War Powers: Toward a New Accommodation," in *A Question of Balance: The President, Congress, and Foreign Policy*, ed. Thomas E. Mann (Washington, D.C.: Brookings, 1990), 55.

43. Ibid., 66.

44. Joshua Lee Prober, "Congress, the War Powers Resolution, and the Secret Political Life of 'a Dead Letter,'" *Journal of Law and Politics* 7 (1990): 177–229.

45. Carroll J. Doherty, "Bush Is Given Authorization to Use Force Against Iraq," *Congressional Quarterly Weekly Report*, Jan. 12, 1991, 65–70.

46. I. M. Destler, "The Constitution and Foreign Affairs," *News for Teachers of Political Science* (Spring 1985): 16.

47. Katzman, "War Powers," 35; Thomas M. Franck, "Rethinking War Powers: By Law or by.'Thaumaturgic Invocation'?" *American Journal of International Law* 83 (1989): 768.

48. John M. Hillebrecht, "Ensuring Affirmative Congressional Control Over the Use of Force: Two Proposals for Collective Decision Making," *Stanford Journal of International Law* 26 (1990): 511.

49. See *Lowry v. Reagan*, 676 F. Supp. 333 (D.D.C. 1987), and *Dellums v. Bush*, 752 F. Supp. 1141 (D.D.C. 1990). In *Lowry*, the district court rejected the request of 110 members of Congress that it issue a declaration that President Reagan was required to file reports under the War Powers Resolution concerning two incidents in the Persian Gulf. The court held that it could not act because Congress had not acted on the issue. In *Dellums*, the court rejected the request of 45 Democratic members of Congress that it enjoin President Bush from conducting military operations in the Persian Gulf without a declaration of war by Congress. The court held that the issue was not ripe for decision because a majority of Congress had not sought relief and the executive had not committed itself to a course of action that made war imminent.

50. Michael J. Glennon, *Constitutional Diplomacy* (Princeton, N.J.: Princeton University Press, 1990), 102–103.

51. Koh, *The National Security Constitution*.

52. Dick Kirschten, "A Contract's Out on U.N. Policing," *National Journal*, Jan. 28, 1995, 231–232.

53. On June 7, 1995, the House rejected, by a 217–201 vote, a proposal by Rep. Henry Hyde, R-Ill., to repeal the War Powers Resolution. Carroll J. Doherty, "House Approves Overhaul of Agencies, Policies," *Congressional Quarterly Weekly Report*, June 10, 1995, 1655.

54. Prober, "Congress, the War Powers Resolution," 229.

55. Ibid., 223–226, 229.

56. Destler, "The Constitution and Foreign Affairs," 15.

57. Sundquist, *The Decline and Resurgence of Congress*, 270.

58. *Report of the U.S. Commission on the Organization of the Government for the Conduct of Foreign Policy* (Washington, D.C.: Government Printing Office, 1975), 1.

59. Also see Burke and Greenstein, *How Presidents Test Reality*, esp. chap. 13.

60. Graham T. Allison and Peter Szanton, "Organizing for the Decade Ahead," in *Setting National Priorities: The Next Ten Years*, ed. Henry Owen and Charles Schultze (Washington, D.C.: Brookings, 1976), 232–233.

61. Alexander L. George, *Presidential Decisionmaking in Foreign Policy: The Effective Use of Information and Advice* (Boulder, Colo.: Westview, 1980), 146.

62. Burt Solomon, "When It Comes to Geopolitics ... Who's Painting the Big Picture?" *National Journal*, Mar. 5, 1995, 550–551.

63. Burt Solomon, "Clinton's Fast Break on Cuba ... Or Foreign Policy on the Fly," *National Journal*, Sept. 3, 1995, 2044–2045.

64. Cecil V. Crabb, Jr., and Kevin V. Mulcahy, *American National Security: A Presidential Perspective* (Pacific Grove, Calif.: Brooks/Cole, 1991), chap. 9. The discussion relies on Crabb and Mulcahy.

65. Elizabeth Drew, *On the Edge* (New York: Simon & Schuster, 1994), 28, 138.

66. Crabb and Mulcahy, *American National Security*, 189–190.

67. Ibid.

68. Kevin V. Mulcahy, "The Secretary of State: Foreign Policymaking in the Carter and Reagan Administrations," *Presidential Studies Quarterly* (Spring 1986): 296.

69. Burt Solomon, "Making Foreign Policy in Secret May Be Easy, But It Carries Risks," *National Journal*, Jan. 12, 1991, 90–91.

70. Larry Berman and Bruce W. Jentelson, "Bush and the Post–Cold–War World: New Challenges for American Leadership," in *The Bush Presidency: First Appraisals*, ed. Colin Campbell and Bert A. Rockman (Chatham, N.J.: Chatham House, 1991), 99–103.

71. Bruce W. Nelan, "The No-Guts, No-Glory Guys," *Time*, Nov. 22, 1993, 48–50; Bert A. Rockman, "Leadership Style and the Clinton Presidency," in *The Clinton Presidency*, 352–355.

72. Solomon, "When It Comes to Geopolitics"; Solomon, "Clinton's Fast Break on Cuba."

73. Mortimer B. Zuckerman, "The Limits to Leadership," *U.S. News & World Report*, Sept. 12, 1994, 96.

74. Barbara Hinckley, *Less than Meets the Eye: Foreign Policy Making and the Myth of the Assertive Congress* (Chicago: University of Chicago Press, 1994), 175, 193.

75. Paul E. Peterson, "The International System and Foreign Policy," in *The President, the Congress, and the Making of Foreign Policy*, ed. Paul E. Peterson (Norman: University of Oklahoma Press, 1994), 12–14.

76. Koh, *The National Security Constitution*, 207.

77. Stephen E. Ambrose, "The Presidency and Foreign Policy," *Foreign Affairs* (Winter 1991–1992): 136.

READINGS

Berman, Larry. *Planning a Tragedy: The Americanization of the War in Vietnam*. New York: Norton, 1982.

Burke, John P., and Fred I. Greenstein. *How Presidents Test Reality: Decisions on Vietnam, 1954 and 1965*. New York: Russell Sage Foundation, 1989.

Crabb, Cecil V., Jr., and Pat M. Holt. *Invitation to Struggle: Congress, the President, and Foreign Policy*. 4th ed. Washington, D.C.: CQ Press, 1991.

Crabb, Cecil V., Jr., and Kevin V. Mulcahy. *American National Security: A Presidential Perspective*. Pacific Grove, Calif.: Brooks/Cole, 1991.

Draper, Theodore. *A Very Thin Line: The Iran-Contra Affairs*. New York: Hill & Wang, 1991.

Fisher, Louis. *Presidential War Power*. Lawrence: University Press of Kansas, 1995.

George, Alexander L. *Presidential Decisionmaking in Foreign Policy: The Effective Use of Information and Advice*. Boulder, Colo.: Westview, 1980.

Glennon, Michael J. *Constitutional Diplomacy*. Princeton, N.J.: Princeton University Press, 1990.

Henderson, Philip G. *Managing the Presidency: The Eisenhower Legacy—From Kennedy to Reagan*. Boulder, Colo.: Westview, 1988.

Henkin, Louis. *Democracy and Foreign Affairs*. New York: Columbia University Press, 1990.

Hinckley, Barbara. *Less than Meets the Eye: Foreign Policy Making and the Myth of the Assertive Congress*. Chicago: University of Chicago Press, 1994.

Koh, Harold Hongju. *The National Security Constitution: Sharing Power after the Iran-Contra Affair*. New Haven, Conn.: Yale University Press, 1990.

Mann, Thomas E., ed. *A Question of Balance: The President, the Congress, and Foreign Policy*. Washington, D.C.: Brookings, 1990.

Peterson, Paul E., ed. *The President, the Congress, and the Making of Foreign Policy*. Norman: University of Oklahoma Press, 1994.

President's Special Review Board (Tower Commission). *Report of the President's Special Review Board*. Washington, D.C.: Government Printing Office, 1987.

Schlesinger, Arthur M., Jr. *The Imperial Presidency*. Rev. ed. Boston: Houghton Mifflin, 1989.

Spanier, John, and Steven W. Hook. *American Foreign Policy Since World War II*. 13th ed. Washington, D.C.: CQ Press, 1995.

11 THE PRESIDENCY AT CENTURY'S END

WOW. THE BAD NEWS IS MOST OF THEM AREN'T CONNECTED TO ANYTHING.

ACTUALLY, THEY'RE CONNECTED TO CONGRESS, BUT THE DIFFERENCE IS ONLY TECHNICAL.

This cartoon depicts an awestruck Bill Clinton facing a machine representing presidential power—and its restrictions. The president may be the head of a large and complicated bureaucracy, but he has limited powers.

AS THE TWENTIETH CENTURY draws to a close, students of the presidency are reflecting on how the institution and its context have changed in the past as a way to understand what to expect in the future. It is particularly critical to examine the two features identified at the beginning of this book as central to the modern presidency: politics and change. How have the political conditions confronting the presidency changed? What changes in the institution and its environment will shape presidential conduct as the nation enters the twenty-first century? This chapter is different from the others in the book. It is a brief interpretive essay that integrates many observations and arguments touched upon previously.[1] Ultimately, we return to the central problem that has perplexed the nation since its creation—how to empower the president without endangering the system.

The Presidency Since Midcentury

The twentieth century could well be termed the "presidential century." Throughout the nineteenth century, the federal government was dominated by Congress and its closely associated political parties whose power was based on the distribution of jobs and local benefits. Bold presidential leadership, as evidenced by Thomas Jefferson, Andrew Jackson, and Abraham Lincoln, stands out precisely because it was so rare. During the present century, particularly since World War II, the presidency went through a sweeping transformation: national politics now hinge on assertive presidential leadership that draws its strength from direct links with the public.

Changes in the presidency and its role in the larger political system accompanied several long-term developments, including a shift in responsibility for public action from state governments to the federal government, the political mobilization of citizens, and the emergence of the United States as a world power. Franklin D. Roosevelt is credited most often with ushering in a "modern presidency" that contrasts with the "traditional presidency." [2] One group of scholars has challenged this analytic convention by reexamining the presidency's historical roots and suggesting that nineteenth-century presidents were not as passive or peripheral to public affairs as they are sometimes depicted. Still other observers suggest that the presidency has moved into a new, "postmodern" era consistent with changes in the domestic and international environments. We remain convinced that traditional presidents played a far less critical role in the life of the nation than even the least active twentieth-century presidents. Later in this chapter we examine the claims for a postmodern presidency.

In an essay that was later expanded into his influential book, *Presidential Power,* Richard Neustadt described "The President at Mid-Century." Neustadt was principally concerned with the imbalance between the "demands and expectations pressing in upon the President" and his limited capacity to respond to them.[3] By midcentury the presidency had become the focal point for initiative in government with responsibility for action routinized and institutionalized in units and processes within the Executive Office of the President. But the president lacked the authority to implement his initiatives; the Constitution forced him to share powers with other institutions—Congress, the judiciary, and the states. In terms of formal powers the presidency was a weak institution hindered by constitutional, and consequently political, restraints. The presidency had become a "clerkship" whose services were needed by others, but whose influence over them was limited because none of them shared his obligations or outlook.[4] The major problem confronting the American political system at midcentury was that presidents would fail because of restraints imposed by other participants in the political system.

Presidents could overcome the weakness of their office through the exercise of leadership skills, primarily the power to persuade. In the American system of fragmented power, presidents had to function as the preeminent bargainer. Governing rested on acts of persuasion, not commands. Presidents could help themselves by consciously making choices that maximized their power to persuade.[5]

From the "Mid-century" essay and *Presidential Power* emerged a prescriptive model for presidential leadership. This model was persuasive because of its accurate portrayal of how the American political system had become dependent on a single leader. Power (defined as influence) is at the core of Neustadt's model. Presidents should understand its nature and guard their power prospects at all times. In making choices they must recognize the power stakes involved in those choices. Others cannot do it for them; they must be their own power experts, and they must be sensitive to the power stakes of others, the targets of their persuasive efforts. Persuasion, which is where real presidential power lies, entails bargaining. The president has three resources for bargaining: vantage points, which are the formal powers of the office; his reputation among Washington insiders; and popular prestige, which is based on public approval of his performance. Presidents should be professional politicians who understand power and know how to bargain. This is no job for an amateur.

Two Decades of Reappraisal and Reform

Neustadt's model reflected and shaped the dominant themes in the scholarship and textbooks of the 1950s and early 1960s, which stressed that only the president truly represented the American people and that heroic presidential leadership was a necessary and sufficient means to deal with the domestic and international problems confronting the nation.[6] With few exceptions, weakness was regarded as the principal problem with the presidency, not its potential for the abuse of power.

Vietnam and Watergate drastically altered the public and elite perspective. Fewer people believed that an omnipotent president would benevolently lead the nation to a resolution of its problems. The major concern of scholars and politicians shifted from the weakness of presidential power to its abuse. The historian Arthur M. Schlesinger, Jr., a biographer of heroic presidents, led the way by renouncing his earlier advocacy of aggressive presidential leadership and by charging that the presidency was out of control.[7] Congress acted to reestablish constitutional parity with the presidency, asserting legislative prerogatives in the areas of war powers, spending, budget control, executive agreements, national emergencies, and confirmation of presidential aides.[8]

Congress, however, lacked the ability to provide an effective substitute for presidential leadership. It could block presidential initiatives but could not establish broad policy goals and provide policy coordination and integration on its own. By 1980 James Sundquist predicted that because of the "crisis of competence" in the national government "the same fundamental forces that brought about the modern strong presidency in the first place will again reassert their influence."[9]

Much of the concern with competence was prompted by the difficulty Gerald Ford and Jimmy Carter experienced in adjusting to major changes in the larger political environment. Even before the publication of *Presidential Power,* the House Democratic Study Group, a caucus of northern liberal Democrats founded in 1958, set in motion a push for internal reform that thoroughly revamped the U.S. Congress.[10] Some of the congressional reforms adopted during the 1970s responded to presidential aggrandizement, but others reflected dissatisfaction with internal legislative conditions. What developed was a legislature where power was far more broadly distributed among members than in the past and where traditional norms, such as the seniority rule, were rejected or made less stringent. Leadership, it has been argued, was the principal casualty as individualism ran rampant in the halls of Congress.

Congress was not, however, the only part of the president's environment to undergo change. The early 1960s witnessed the beginning of substantial changes in the media that carried through into the following decade. These included the expansion of the television evening news to its current half-hour format, a dramatic rise in public reliance on television as the major source of news, a startling proliferation of Washington correspondents, and a shift in professional norms toward aggressive investigative reporting. Political parties underwent massive change. The Democrats' national convention of 1968 served as the launch pad for a wide-ranging series of internal reforms that transformed the presidential nominating process; the Democrats also have been blamed for accelerating party decline. Simultaneous changes in the electorate made citizens candidate-centered rather than party-centered. Finally, social movements that arose during the 1960s and 1970s—civil rights, women's rights, consumer protection, the elderly, gay rights, and environmental protection—began to transform American politics. They were joined by a new surge of organizational representatives in Washington as lobbying efforts multiplied, became more sophisticated, and were supplemented by the creation of political action committees.[11]

The reforms of Congress and political parties, industry trends in the media, and changes in interest representation contributed to an unsettled environment, which gave rise to discussion of how these new conditions would affect the presidency. Fred Greenstein termed it an "intractable environment"; Neustadt characterized it as "atomization"; Samuel Kernell considered the cumulative changes tantamount to a restructuring of American politics from "institutionalized" to "individualized" pluralism, necessitating that presidents shift from bargaining to going public.[12] Ronald Reagan's entry on stage seemed to offer a test of the new imperatives.

The Reagan-Bush Era

The Reagan presidency brought to an end the intentional reduction of presidential power that followed Vietnam and Watergate, and the reluctance to impinge on presidential power extended into George Bush's term. Although these presidents reclaimed a number of powers lost by their predecessors, the Reagan and Bush years by no means restored the imperial presidencies of Lyndon Johnson and Richard Nixon.[13] Congress remained, for the most part, assertive and jealous of the prerogatives and independence it had acquired during the 1970s and was determined not to surrender them to a popular president.

Elsewhere in this book, we review the important institutional and policy changes brought about during the Reagan presidency. Centralized control of executive and judicial appointments provided Reagan and Bush with substantial power over policy. Reagan was the first president to implement broad administrative and judicial strategies for pursuing domestic policy objectives outside legislative action. His principal policy legacy was a large structural budget deficit that has curtailed the growth of existing federal domestic programs and discouraged the creation of new programs, a trend that promises to continue for years to come. Although the largest peacetime military expansion in the nation's history, initiated under Reagan, came to a halt under Bush, both administrations demonstrated a willingness to use their enhanced power in

Grenada (1983), Libya (1986), Panama (1989), and the Persian Gulf (1990–1991). More important, Reagan abandoned his confrontational rhetoric toward the Soviet Union during his second term, moved toward major arms reduction agreements, and substantially improved relations prior to the unexpected demise of the Soviet system that occurred under Bush.

Reagan's failure, in the Iran-contra affair, "both of method and policy was so resounding as to cast enduring doubt on the utility of combining ignorance with insistence." [14] According to Neustadt, Iran-contra demonstrated anew his 1960 precepts that the president can protect his prospects for future influence only through present choices and that he can rely only on himself to gauge those prospects.

Bush succeeded in avoiding any single misstep as grand as the Iran-contra incident, but he was criticized for lacking vision and a sense of direction. Exhibiting a far more engaged approach to the office than his predecessor, Bush garnered broad praise for an exemplary performance during the Persian Gulf War, which came on the heels of democracy's triumph in Eastern Europe and the former Soviet Union. But in struggling to overcome the budget deficit, Bush was far less adept in projecting the kind of optimistic symbolic leadership at which Reagan excelled. Moreover, the economic recession of 1991–1992, although far milder than that of 1981–1982, came at the end of Bush's term, whereas Reagan's bout with recession was well behind him before his campaign for reelection began. A political malaise seemed to grip the Bush administration, particularly on domestic issues. Some commentators saw this development not as a reflection of Bush's personal limitations, but as the inevitable problem of an administration whose ideological and programmatic agenda was exhausted after twelve years in office.

The Reagan and Bush presidencies did not cause Neustadt to abandon or substantially revise his model of leadership. Although Neustadt recognizes that there have been substantial changes in the political and institutional setting since midcentury, he contends that the president's "power problem" remains "roughly what it was then, if not more so," something he would not have expected in 1960.[15] But Neustadt may assign insufficient importance to changes in the presidential environment that have overtaken the ability of one individual to achieve government effectiveness through personal action. If so, Neustadt's advice on presidential leadership could prove disastrous for the nation. Moreover, continued adherence to the "personal solution"—finding a president whose skills and temperament are commensurate with the demands of the position—may inhibit the pursuit of alternative avenues for achieving effectiveness, what Theodore Lowi terms the "institutionalist approach." [16]

The Clinton Presidency

Bill Clinton came to the White House committed to major policy change. His presidency—not completed as of this writing—was one of moderate achievement during the 103d Congress (1993–1994) and wide-ranging conflicts with a Republican-controlled Congress after that. In 1995, House Republicans, led by Speaker Newt Gingrich, seized control of the domestic and economic policy agendas, without protest from the president. Clinton and the congressional Republicans disagreed sharply over fiscal policy, the proper role of government, and their respective institutional prerogatives, especially the authority to use military force to achieve foreign policy objectives.

The Clinton presidency as we have described and analyzed it demonstrates that presidential performance depends on both personality and context. A complex individual, Clinton is highly intelligent, ambitious, energetic, politically experienced, and knowledgeable about domestic and economic policy. In his two campaigns, he demonstrated the ability to overcome adversity, adapt to changing conditions, and communicate effectively with the public.

Other personal factors, however, counterbalanced these positive traits. Because of a lack of interest, he distanced himself from foreign and military policy but did not delegate authority to a surrogate who could speak for him. Only when events forced him to do so, as in the cases of Somalia and Bosnia, did he become involved. The resulting impression of ineptitude on the part of the administration in this crucial policy area has not been fully overcome. His eagerness to please and his tendency to ruminate publicly about pending decisions resulted in the perception of inconstancy with respect to his basic beliefs and goals, reinforcing the "slick Willie" image that carried over from his days in Arkansas politics. Allegations of scandal—marital infidelity and the Whitewater real estate affair—contributed to a lack of public trust in him. His open political partnership with his wife, Hillary, and her leading role in developing the ill-fated health care reform proposal brought about resentment in Washington and elsewhere. Disorganization in the Clinton White House reflected an overly engaged leadership style that on occasion resulted in failures of coordination and communication.

The economic, political, and institutional contexts in which he governed also contributed to Clinton's mixed performance. Although the economy grew, unemployment fell, and inflation was under control, Clinton received little credit from the public. Despite improved aggregate economic indicators, Clinton could not overcome the widespread impression among the middle class that it had not shared in the prosperity and its jobs were not secure. Even though the 1992 election resulted in unified party control of the government, Clinton's mandate for change—with 43.3 percent of the vote—was questionable. Moreover, he experienced great difficulty holding the support of liberals and conservatives among the congressional Democrats, while Republicans were strongly united in their opposition. Clinton's efforts to reconcile divergent views within his own party often reinforced perceptions of his inconstancy. Democratic party leaders and committee chairs, accustomed to dealing with Republican presidents for the previous twelve years, were not particularly accommodating.

The 1994 election changed the political and institutional contexts dramatically. (Some observers believe that a party realignment may have occurred in the electorate, with the Republicans in the majority.) The new Republican congressional majority, led by Gingrich, demonstrated an unusually high degree of party unity in preempting policy leadership from the presidency for the first time since the administration of Herbert Hoover. Party government reappeared in the House after an absence of eighty-five years.

Clinton, however, proved to be resilient. He convinced a majority of the public that the Republicans were to blame for the standoff over the 1996 budget, which twice resulted in shutting down the federal government. Through vetoes and veto threats he moderated the content of a Republican plan to transfer responsibility for welfare to the states. In foreign policy, he vetoed a bill that would have forced an end to U.S. participation in the embargo on selling arms to participants in the civil war in Bosnia, and he persisted, despite congressional opposition, in his commitment of U.S. forces to help enforce a peace agreement in that conflict.

As Clinton began his second term, congressional Republican leaders awaited his proposals for balancing the budget by 2002 and solving the financial problems of Medicare and Social Security before announcing theirs. Although Clinton's presidency appeared unlikely to be one of achievement,[17] neither would it be one of preparation for a conservative revolution led by the Republicans.

Table 11-1 Recurrent Structures of Presidential Authority

Previously established commitments	President's political identity	
	Opposed	Affiliated
Vulnerable	Politics of reconstruction (Reagan)	Politics of disjunction (Carter)
Resilient	Politics of preemption (Clinton)	Politics of articulation (Bush)

Source: Stephen Skowronek, *The Politics Presidents Make: Leadership from John Adams to George Bush* (Cambridge, Mass.: Harvard University Press, 1993), 36.

Stephen Skowronek's historical institutional analysis in *The Politics Presidents Make* provides another framework for explaining Clinton's performance and the significance of the Clinton presidency.[18] Skowronek maintains that what presidents do is a function of political context. That context is embodied in "recurrent structures of presidential authority" that he calls "political time." He develops a typology *(Table 11-1)* of those structures based on two factors: a president's political identity, which is defined by his opposition to or affiliation with the established political regime, and whether the governing commitments of the established regime, as embodied in its ideology and policies, are "resilient or vulnerable." The typology contains four patterns of politics: the *politics of reconstruction* (president opposed, commitments vulnerable); the *politics of disjunction* (president affiliated, commitments vulnerable); the *politics of articulation* (president affiliated, commitments resilient); and the *politics of preemption* (president opposed, commitments resilient).

Clinton's presidency has been one of preemption, which followed Carter's presidency of disjunction, Reagan's reconstructive leadership, and Bush's politics of articulation. President Carter confronted the Hobson's choice inherent in the politics of disjunction—he could either affirm the vulnerable commitments of the established regime and thus become the symbol of its failure or he could repudiate them and lose the backing of his political supporters and be rendered impotent. President Reagan transformed the political regime. He took office opposed to the old regime, whose commitments were vulnerable, and seized the opportunity to define a new conservative public philosophy, reformulate the political agenda, and change the relationship between the state and society. President Bush was an affiliated leader who functioned as an "orthodox-innovator." He promised to preserve the gains of the Reagan revolution and continue its work.

Clinton's place in political time prevented him from exercising reconstructive leadership. He came to office opposed to a recently established regime with strongly resilient commitments. A self-proclaimed New Democrat with technocratic skills, committed to a change of course, willing to work with his party and Congress, and seeking cooperation rather than confrontation with established interests, Clinton appeared well equipped for the politics of preemption. But political constraints and his inability to persuade the public and Congress of the viability of his alternatives hampered his efforts to bring about changes. Ultimately, as we noted in Chapter 1, Clinton did not preempt the Republican opposition but was preempted by it.

The Presidency at Century's End

Three aspects in particular of the presidency's contemporary condition have attracted scholarly attention: presidents' relationships with the public, changes in the international position of the United States, and divided party control of the presidency and Congress. In each case, scholars have evaluated the significance of recent changes and their implications for the future. We examine each of these areas, with reminders of themes raised earlier in the book.

The People's Tribune

Central to the contemporary presidency is its unique relationship with the public. Today's president serves as the tribune of the people—their champion. Presidents have come to personify the federal government for millions of citizens, and the public's support for presidential initiatives has become the principal weapon in a chief executive's political arsenal. To assess this development and its significance for the future, we explore its origins as well as its continuing importance.

Far from viewing the change in the president's relationship with the public as a new development, Jeffrey Tulis in *The Rhetorical Presidency* stresses doctrines of governance and constitutional understandings that emerged early in the twentieth century. Before entering public office, Woodrow Wilson offered a constitutional reinterpretation that called for presidents to expand their use of public rhetoric as a way to provide the kind of inspirational leadership pioneered by Theodore Roosevelt. Wilson, in essence, designed and implemented a de facto "second Constitution" that rested on "active and continuous presidential leadership of public opinion" as a means to provide the political system with the energy it requires.[19] In his role as "leader-interpreter," a Wilsonian president would interact directly with the people, shaping as well as responding to their desires. With Wilson's example and justification, subsequent presidents have sought to exercise personal leadership over an otherwise balky institutional system, although Tulis suggests that such efforts are likely to succeed only under limited conditions. Nonetheless, presidents, other political elites, and the public have accepted the new doctrine, thereby encouraging efforts at inspirational leadership even when conditions are not right.

Barbara Hinckley also regards the Constitution as lying at the heart of the symbolic presidency, but with markedly different effects: because the presidency is an undefined office, "presidents become what people want them to be"; "the office is open to become what people say it is and expect it to be." [20] As a result, the presidency has become shrouded in symbolism reflecting the traits projected onto it by American culture. By portraying themselves as one with the people, presidents claim to serve as true representatives of the nation as well as champion of the people's cause, precisely what the people want.

Theodore Lowi offers yet another long-term view of the special relationship that has developed between the presidency and the people, but his view rests on more tangible foundations. The public, Lowi suggests, is engaged in a collective exchange relationship with its leader: the citizenry will invest the presidency with power and accept presidents as the embodiment of their hopes and fears so long as they receive tangible benefits in return. When presidents fail to provide peace and prosperity, the public withdraws its support. Because it is not always possible to deliver economic and international security, successive presidents, regardless of partisan and personality differences, have engaged in similar "pathological" behaviors: seeking to maintain initiative by centralizing power, using illusions of success or outright deception as a means to cover their shortcomings, and relying on charisma and "plebiscitary aspects" of the office to "mobilize the electorate in order to unify the elite." [21] The "personal presidency," which Lowi dates from 1961, is "an office of tremendous personal power drawn from the people" and resting "on the new democratic theory that the presidency with all powers is the necessary condition for governing a large, democratic nation." [22] With the impossibility of meeting such daunting expectations, each president is doomed to failure.

Of these three scholars, only Lowi locates the beginning of the new public-presidency relationship in the midcentury period.[23] All three, far from viewing Reagan's presidency as a turning point, see it as wholly consistent with the trends they identify. From the perspective of these authors, Reagan illustrates the maturing of long-term trends that are not especially welcome. Far from endorsing "the people's tribune" as a solution to the system's search for effective leadership, each regards the development as unhealthy for the larger political system and concludes by calling for the public to become educated on the presidency's limitations as well as its potential for leadership.[24]

Some scholars, however, have been more positive about the modern president's public prominence. Bert Rockman suggests that a more plebiscitary office—one deriving power from public support—might strengthen political accountability; and Samuel Kernell concludes that "as one looks to the future, the prospect for the continued use of going public as presidential strategy shines bright."[25] Kernell seems to endorse going public as a necessity, driven partly by technological innovation and partly by the disappearance of alternatives. With power broadly dispersed in the public and Congress, bargaining provides an insufficient answer to the problem of leadership. But in the long run, Kernell recognizes that presidents encounter problems in going public. Not only is it difficult to control public opinion, but also presidents discover that the advantages they once enjoyed are likely to evaporate as other elites, particularly in Congress and the media, as exemplified by Speaker Newt Gingrich and the conservative talk show host Rush Limbaugh, adopt the same techniques.

A Postmodern Presidency

Evaporation of American advantages in the international system is the starting point for Richard Rose's discussion of the postmodern president. Far from rejecting Neustadt's model, Rose takes it a step further: bargaining is now necessary abroad as well as at home. Victory in World War II meant that the United States emerged as the sole economic and military superpower. Operating from a dominant position, presidents found international bargaining largely unnecessary. The disappearance of American hegemony removes an advantage that citizens and presidents have taken for granted.

In the future, Americans must contend with interdependence, the effect that other nations can have on domestic policies, and a decline in national influence. The imbalance between responsibility and capability afflicting the modern presidency will become even greater for postmodern presidents. "International responsibilities remain great, but the

United States can no longer be sure that other nations will fall into line once decisions are taken in Washington." [26] Moreover, external shocks ranging from oil embargoes to currency adjustments will have a direct impact on domestic policies.

The transition to interdependence will be especially painful for the United States because the nation is so ill-prepared for the shift. "While the traditional President did not participate in the international system and the modern President could dominate it, the postmodern President has no choice but to cooperate and compete." [27] Under these conditions, the president has a new imperative: "going international" (foreign bargaining) is now more critical and more difficult, whereas "going Washington" (domestic bargaining) and going public used to be sufficient.[28]

The international hegemony that the United States enjoyed after World War II began to erode during the Johnson administration and the Vietnam War. Carter was the first president forced to contend fully with the new forces, and Reagan followed suit. During the Persian Gulf crisis, Bush demonstrated that he was the first postmodern president to meet Rose's criteria of "world leader," exerting influence on policy and having other major nations reinforce his actions by their own.[29] Clinton experienced the realities of the postmodern presidency most directly in his efforts to end the civil war in Bosnia. He had to deal with three warring factions (Muslims, Serbs, and Croats) who were driven by six centuries of hostility; reconcile differences with Britain and France, the countries whose troops comprised the bulk of the UN peacekeeping force; and contend with a Russia beset by resurgent nationalism. In addition, he had only limited public and congressional support for the use of military force to help secure U.S. objectives. Rose makes a convincing case for how altered conditions in the international environment now impinge on presidential calculations, but he identifies no particular changes in the presidency, as an office, that would distinguish it from the modern presidency of the last half century.[30]

Leadership of Divided Government

Since January 1969 the presidency and both houses of Congress have been controlled by the same political party in only two periods, the Carter administration and the first two years of the Clinton administration. Unified party government prevailed during only 21 percent of those twenty-eight years (to January 1997), while it existed 88 percent of the time from 1900 to 1969. The four earlier instances of divided government in the twentieth century occurred for periods of two years each when William Howard Taft, Woodrow Wilson, Herbert Hoover, and Harry S. Truman lost majorities in the second half of a term. With the exception of Clinton in 1994, the other modern cases are strikingly different. Nixon and Bush assumed office with partisan majorities in neither house of Congress, a situation confronted by Dwight D. Eisenhower during the last six years of his presidency, and by Gerald Ford, as well. Reagan enjoyed a Republican majority in the Senate during his first six years, but the House remained solidly Democratic.

From 1968 to 1992 divided control of the government was persistent rather than brief. Going into the 1992 election, Republicans had won five of the previous six presidential elections and seven of the previous ten, and the Democrats had dominated Congress, serving as the majority party in the House of Representatives since 1954 and in the Senate for all but six years, 1981–1987, over the same period. The 1994 and 1996 elections reversed the partisan division, giving control of Congress to the Republicans during a Democratic presidency.

What has divided party control of government meant for the presidency? Does it constitute a permanent feature of it that will carry over into the next century? What results will it produce with the partisan division reversed (that is, a Republican Congress and a Democratic president)? Divided government has raised serious problems for customary models of presidential leadership. James Sundquist notes that "the dominant school of the midcentury" believed "in party government and presidential leadership," holding "that in the long run a government that is able to act, even if it makes mistakes, is less dangerous than one that is rendered impotent by deadlock and division." [31] Since 1969, however, the dominant pattern has been a system of "forced coalition government" made necessary by the accidents of the electoral process.[32] The results of this experiment have not been heartening, Sundquist argues. Rather, divided government produced stalemate over domestic issues under Eisenhower, deadlock on both foreign and domestic fronts during the Nixon-Ford era, and immobility for seven of the eight years under Reagan, even when a consensus existed on the need to address the burgeoning national debt. The same inertia on the budget afflicted Bush and Clinton. Sundquist therefore issues an urgent call for political scientists to address the problem and either develop a new theory to replace the party responsibility model or seriously confront the need for constitutional reform.

Charles O. Jones finds that "separated presidents" have adopted distinctive styles in seeking to provide leadership within this constrained setting. Even Carter adopted a "trusteeship" style that separated him from members of his own congressional party, just as he had pursued and won the presidency as an outsider. But Jones believes that presidents are locked into a new dynamic in Washington. As described by Neustadt in 1960, the Constitution's separation of powers was better understood as "separated institutions sharing powers," but for the contemporary period Jones suggests that the formulation should be "separated institutions competing for shared power," with "each institution protecting and promoting itself through a broad interpretation of its constitutional and political status, even usurping the other's power when the opportunity presents itself." [33] To further complicate matters, the separation based on divided electoral outcomes has coincided with the new assertiveness of a Congress that reformed itself to regain power lost to the executive. The Clinton presidency, especially after 1994, provides additional evidence that supports Jones's separated system perspective.

The persistence of divided government represents a fundamental alteration in the strategic conditions confronted by presidents since midcentury. Eisenhower experienced six years of "separation," just as Truman was tested for two. Sundquist suggests that these episodes of divided government were regarded as exceptions, and observers expected that presidential leadership would be restored through traditional party structures. The situation has proved anything but temporary. The weakening of party organization, degeneration of partisanship in the electorate, and growth of split-ticket voting contributed to a persistent pattern of divided partisan control of the presidency and Congress.

Can presidents cope with the consequences of divided government? Only marginally, says George C. Edwards III, and the constraints on presidents imposed by the decline of political parties and divided government should force us to reconsider broadly held models of presidential leadership. Edwards concludes that none of the president's three sources of influence—party leadership, public leadership, and personal legislative skills—enables him to do anything more than influence congressional actions at the margins. The first two constitute the "principal underpinnings" of presidential influence but are subject to only limited presidential control.[34] The most important skill presidents can have is to recognize and exploit opportunities for leadership offered by the conditions they confront. In the game of politics, presidents' strategic and tactical decisions may be more or less astute, but they can play only with the hand they are dealt. Edwards agrees with Lowi and Tulis that going public is not a cure-all: while "the public relations skills of Reagan's administration were impressive . . . they could not by themselves create or sustain goodwill." [35] Reagan's greatest resource flowed from the 1980 election when his victory changed the terms of policy debate. In sum, Edwards's principal advice to presidents would be simple: seek an electoral mandate. But what if, as is often the case, presidential elections do not produce a mandate but are uncertain? And, because even a clear mandate has a limited life, how is the president to govern in its absence?

Presidents, argues Edwards, are better thought of as facilitators who "help others go where they want to go anyway" than as directors "leading others where they otherwise would not go." [36] A facilitator operating at the margins sounds very much like Neustadt's model of the president as bargainer, a prospect that observers concerned with policy effectiveness, like Sundquist, are likely to view with dismay. Short of an electoral solution, there appears to be little likelihood of overcoming the institutional competition that has characterized end-of-the-century governance.

Not all analysts take a negative view of divided government. Morris Fiorina views it as an American form of coalition government flowing from the absence of third party options at the polls. Ticket-splitting resembles voting for a third party and produces similar patterns of governance. [37] Jones offers a "diffused responsibility perspective" to supplant the more familiar party responsibility model articulated in the early 1950s. [38] Under this view, the president certifies the nation's policy agenda by triggering proposals and helping Congress to set priorities, but each party attempts to preserve and protect its existing strengths. This perspective does not offer a solution to the impasse but provides a realistic basis for evaluating the current political agenda.

The Presidency at Century's End: An Assessment

What, then, is the condition of the presidency as the twentieth century draws to a close? In many respects, the position of contemporary presidents is more isolated and precarious than ever. If the world seemed lonely from the perspective of Neustadt's executive at midcentury, it must seem even more so now that political parties have lost support in the electorate and reforms have weakened them organizationally while a revitalized Congress aggressively challenges presidents over policy and institutional prerogatives. As Washington folklore has it, Eisenhower could conduct business with Sam Rayburn and Lyndon

Johnson—who epitomized midcentury broker-style leadership—while they sat around sipping bourbon and branch water. Today's president must contend with more assertive and ideological congressional leaders who are less willing to compromise than their predecessors. Hinckley's research demonstrates that contemporary presidents go to great lengths to portray themselves as above party, and, when Congress is mentioned, it is largely to criticize its abilities as a governing institution. Presidents project themselves as governing alone, thereby reflecting the image of heroic leadership that the public has come to expect. Problems arise when the solitary would-be hero cannot fill the bill.

At the same time, modern presidents desperately need to mobilize support and now do so through presidency-centered techniques rather than traditional party structures. White House aides construct "presidential parties" to serve as electoral and governing coalitions, but the new structures are less stable and less useful than traditional party coalitions.[39] Public relations, a high presidential priority, is made necessary by the need to generate "mass" support through direct and mediated appeals. Ironically, the media, on which presidents now depend for reaching the public, are far more independent and critical than the political parties they partially replaced. While they help presidents broadcast appeals to general audiences, the media have reduced the latitude within which presidents must operate.

Finally, presidents have less control than ever over policy outcomes, both domestic and international. Leadership of domestic policy has always been difficult, but the constraints of massive structural budget deficits and the stresses of divided government have further complicated the task. The proliferation of interest groups and the mobilization of new population groups into politics have made policy making even more difficult. In the past, it was sometimes suggested that modern presidents turned to the international system, perhaps out of frustration, as an area where policy making was more likely to succeed. But Richard Rose predicts that foreign policy will no longer offer relief, international problems will prove less easy to resolve than in the past, and they will assume new urgency and new forms as interdependence makes itself felt into the next century. Therefore, the policy area over which presidents traditionally have held the greatest constitutional authority has become more complex and less subject to executive influence.

Despite these changes, Americans seem more firmly rooted in their conception of heroic leadership than ever before. For more than twenty-five years, political scientists have labored long and hard to revise their own textbook version of the presidency, but the readers of this revised standard version were unconvinced. Moreover, the scholarly consensus may be disintegrating. New justifications have emerged for presidents' use of politicized and centralized decision making as a means to pursue "responsive competence" rather than "neutral competence." [40] And in his reflections on presidents since Nixon, Arthur Schlesinger seems to have returned to a search for heroic qualities. [41]

Nevertheless, concerns about executive power persist. Thomas Langston calls for a diminished constitutional rather than a personal presidential leadership on the ground that the heroic model is appropriate only in times of extreme crisis, such as the Great Depression and the two world wars. [42] Charging that the Bush administration employed a strategy to govern without Congress, Charles Tiefer argues that only the legislature can restore the constitutional balance between the branches. [43] Michael Lind fears that the imperial presidency, although temporarily in suspension, will soon return and questions whether the resurgence of Congress under Republican leadership can be sustained against parochial and centrifugal forces within the institution. Speaker Gingrich, Lind argues, was able to gain power only by borrowing the techniques of the plebiscitary presidency. [44]

We are left, then, with the traditional quandary of presidential leadership: Can presidents fulfill their responsibilities without endangering the separated system? End-of-the-century presidents, it might be argued, confront a gap between demands and capabilities that has widened since midcentury. Recent presidents' reliance on appeals to the public as an answer to their power problem lends new vibrancy to concerns expressed at the Constitutional Convention about the danger of executive demagoguery. Expressions of the need for strong executive leadership and concern about presidential effectiveness contend with fears of excessive executive power that were engendered by the Vietnam and Watergate experiences. Reform proposals search for ways to balance institutional power within the system or to reduce popular expectations and demands.

Institutional stalemate and deadlock have not yet become the permanent state of affairs, but they occur with sufficient frequency to encourage efforts to reform the system. Proposals have been made to limit congressional terms and do away with PACs, actions that are likely to reduce the power of incumbents and the institutional power of Congress. There have also been suggestions to link presidential and congressional elections by making their terms coincide.

Scholars are especially attracted to proposals for reeducating the public and enhancing civic consciousness and responsibility as ways to make public expectations of presidential performance more realistic. However, it is probably more reasonable to expect either the Democrats, the Republicans, or a new party to emerge as a majority party between now and the beginning of a new century than to expect a massive transformation in deeply ingrained and widely reinforced public expectations of government and politics. A party realignment would not make it any easier for presidents to meet performance expectations, but it might possibly ease the institutional gridlock that has become increasingly commonplace.

In the absence of realignment, political analysts and practitioners should give serious consideration to their continued adherence to the party responsibility model. If divided government has become the normal state of political affairs during this final decade of the twentieth century and is a condition resulting from free electoral choice, then a new conceptual basis for establishing political accountability is needed. Jones's diffused responsibility perspective accepts a diminished presidential role and suggests a new way to evaluate presidential, congressional, and party performance in coping with the policy agenda. It will not remove policy deadlocks or institutional conflict, but it promises to make them more understandable. Prospects for such understanding through popular acceptance of a diffused responsibility perspective are limited. Dissatisfaction with government performance and presidential leadership seems likely to remain high so long as public expectations of the national government remain unrealistic, analysts continue to think in terms of the party responsibility model, and presidents are regarded as the principal agents of collective action.

This, then, is the condition of the presidency at the conclusion of the twentieth century. It remains at least as weak an office as Neustadt described at midcentury. Increased capacity to generate popular support and expanded institutional resources have not been sufficient for presidents to overcome the combined effects of party decay, a more assertive and independent Congress, greater international interdependence, and persistently unrealistic public expectations of presidential performance. Constitutional reform proposals abound, but serve only as a basis for discussion and analysis of the deficiencies of the present system. There is little likelihood of their adoption any time soon. Bargaining remains necessary even if no longer sufficient for success; power stakes are ignored only at enormous risk. In some respects, Neustadt's model may actually have gained relevance as constitutional relations became more strained and political conditions more fragmented since the mid-1950s. In this regard, it remains a helpful guide for making governance viable.

At midcentury, Neustadt reflected a scholarly consensus on the kind of leadership the nation required, but at century's end, the confidence derived from that agreement has vanished. End-of-the-century presidents find themselves in an ambiguous position, and scholarly opinion is appropriately ambivalent. The conditions that gave rise to Neustadt's classic interpretation remain no less a limitation on presidential leadership than they were more than three decades ago and probably impose even greater constraints on executive initiative than they did earlier. But Neustadt's personality-based answers to the president's power problem as well as those provided by his critics have proved unable to close the gap between performance and expectations. Until the conditions confronted by presidents change further, as eventually we believe they will, the end-of-the-century presidency can best be described as still functioning but unable to govern single-handedly, precisely what the Framers of the Constitution intended.

NOTES

1. The argument in this chapter follows closely that found in our article "The Presidency Since Mid-Century," *Congress and the Presidency* 19 (Spring 1992): 29–46. We wish to thank the editors of *Congress and the Presidency* for allowing us to use portions of the article.

2. Fred I. Greenstein, "Change and Continuity in the Modern Presidency," in *The New American Political System,* ed. Anthony King (Washington, D.C.: American Enterprise Institute, 1979), 45–46.

3. Richard E. Neustadt, "The Presidency at Mid-Century," *Law and Contemporary Problems* 21 (1956): 613.

4. Richard E. Neustadt, *Presidential Power* (New York: Wiley, 1960), 6–8.

5. Neustadt, "The Presidency at Mid-Century," 617–619.

6. Thomas E. Cronin, "The Textbook Presidency," in *Perspectives on the Presidency: A Collection,* ed. Stanley Bach and George T. Sulzner (Lexington, Mass.: D. C. Heath, 1974), 54–74.

7. Arthur M. Schlesinger, Jr., *The Imperial Presidency* (Boston: Houghton Mifflin, 1973).

8. James L. Sundquist, *The Decline and Resurgence of Congress* (Washington, D.C.: Brookings, 1981).

9. James L. Sundquist, "The Crisis of Competence in the National Government," *Political Science Quarterly* 95 (1980): 205.

10. A comprehensive list of reform efforts can be found in Charles O. Jones's essay, "Congress and the Constitutional Balance of Power," in *Congressional Politics,* ed. Christopher J. Deering (Chicago: Dorsey, 1989), 335.

11. For discussions of these developments, see Samuel Kernell, *Going Public: New Strategies of Presidential Leadership,* 3d ed. (Washington, D.C.: CQ Press, 1997); Nelson W. Polsby, *Consequences of Party Reform* (New York: Oxford University Press, 1983); Martin P. Wattenberg, "From a Partisan to a Candidate-Centered Electorate," in *The New American Political System, Second Version,* ed. Anthony King (Washington, D.C.: American Enterprise Institute, 1990); Jack L. Walker, "The Origins and Maintenance of Interest Groups in America," *American Political Science Review* 77 (June 1983); and Robert H. Salisbury, "The Paradox of Interest Groups in Washington—More Groups, Less Clout," in *The New American Political System, Second Version.*

12. Greenstein, "Change and Continuity in the Modern Presidency," 70–75; Richard E. Neustadt, *Presidential Power: The Politics of Leadership from Roosevelt to Reagan* (New York: Free Press, 1990), 234, 237; Kernell, *Going Public,* 11–30.

13. In the second edition of *The Imperial Presidency* (1989), however, Arthur M. Schlesinger, Jr., suggests that Reagan moved two-thirds of the way toward restoring an imperial presidency. Reagan meets two of the three "tests" posited by Schlesinger (page 441)—assertion of presidential war-making powers and heavy reliance on secrecy—but unlike Nixon, Reagan did not direct his powers against administration critics (page 457).

14. Neustadt, *Presidential Power* (New York: Free Press, 1990), 269–270.

15. Ibid., xiv.

16. Theodore J. Lowi, *The Personal President: Power Invested and Promise Unfulfilled* (Ithaca, N.Y.: Cornell University Press, 1985), 137.

17. Erwin C. Hargrove and Michael Nelson, *Presidents, Politics, and Policy* (New York: Knopf, 1984).

18. Stephen Skowronek, *The Politics Presidents Make: Leadership from John Adams to George Bush* (Cambridge, Mass.: Harvard University Press, 1993). The discussion here follows Chaps. 2 and 8 of Skowronek's book.

19. Jeffrey K. Tulis, *The Rhetorical Presidency: The Pursuit of Popular Support* (Princeton, N.J.: Princeton University Press, 1987), 18.

20. Barbara Hinckley, *The Symbolic Presidency: How Presidents Portray Themselves* (New York: Routledge, 1990), 8, 148.

21. Lowi, *The Personal President,* 165.

22. Ibid., 20.

23. This seems largely an artifact of Lowi's desire to present Neustadt's *Presidential Power* as the work that redefined the presidency's role within the constitutional order. See Lowi, *The Personal President,* 9–10. The incidence of presidential failures, one might argue, are the truly defining indicators of Lowi's analysis, and here he includes Truman while recognizing that Eisenhower was the only "clear exception" to his dynamic of failure (page 10).

24. Tulis, *The Rhetorical Presidency* (page 9), explicitly rejects the fascination with effectiveness found in the presidency literature. He distinguishes his own concerns from those of most analysts who adopt the stance of "institutional partisanship," taking "the side of the presidency in the executive's contests with other institutions." Understanding the political order is the explicit purpose of his work rather than contributing to presidential effectiveness, although he recognizes the potential for integrating skillful rhetoric into a bargaining perspective (pages 11–12). The discussions on public education can be found in Tulis, *The Rhetorical Presidency,* 204; Hinckley, *The Symbolic Presidency,* 148; and Lowi, *The Personal President,* 212.

25. Bert A. Rockman, "The Modern Presidency and Theories of Accountability: Old Wine and Old Bottles," *Congress and the Presidency* 13 (Autumn 1986): 135–156; Kernell, *Going Public,* 264.

26. Richard Rose, *The Postmodern President: The White House Meets the World,* 2d ed. (Chatham, N.J.: Chatham House, 1991), 73.

27. Ibid., 28.

28. Ibid., 40.

29. Ibid., 57, 332–336.

30. Michael Nelson makes a similar point in his review of Rose's book. "Is There a Postmodern Presidency?" *Congress and the Presidency* 16 (Autumn 1989): 155–162.

31. James L. Sundquist, "Needed: A Political Theory for the New Era of Coalition Government in the United States," *Political Science Quarterly* 103 (Winter 1988): 632, 633.

32. Ibid., 626.

33. Charles O. Jones, "The Separated Presidency—Making It Work in Contemporary Politics," in *The New American Political System, Second Version,* 3. Jones also sets forth eight different combinations of party control, ranging from Republican control of all three institutions to Democrats enjoying threefold control. Since World War II the system has experienced five of the eight combinations.

34. George C. Edwards III, *At the Margins: Presidential Leadership of Congress* (New Haven, Conn.: Yale University Press, 1989), 217.

35. Ibid., 215–216.

36. Ibid., 5, 4.

37. Morris P. Fiorina, "Coalition Governments, Divided Governments, and Electoral Theory" (Paper presented at the annual meeting of the American Political Science Association, San Francisco, Aug. 30–Sept. 2, 1990).

38. Charles O. Jones, "The Diffusion of Responsibility: An Alternative Perspective for National Policy Politics in the U.S.," *Governance* 4 (April 1991); American Political Science Association, Committee on Political Parties, "Toward a More Responsible Two-Party System," *American Political Science Review* 44 (1950).

39. Lester G. Seligman and Cary R. Covington, *The Coalitional Presidency* (Chicago: Dorsey, 1986).

40. Terry Moe, "The Politicized Presidency," in *The New Directions in American Politics,* ed. John E. Chubb and Paul E. Peterson (Washington, D.C.: Brookings, 1985).

41. This is most evident in Schlesinger's discussion of Ford and Carter. *The Imperial Presidency,* 2d ed., 437–438.

42. Thomas S. Langston, *With Reverence and Contempt: How Americans Think About Their President* (Baltimore: Johns Hopkins University Press, 1995).

43. Charles Tiefer, *The Semi-Sovereign Presidency: The Bush Administration's Strategy for Governing Without Congress* (Boulder, Colo.: Westview, 1994).

44. Michael Lind, "The Out-of-Control Presidency," *New Republic,* Aug. 14, 1995, 18–23.

READINGS

Hinckley, Barbara. *The Symbolic Presidency: How Presidents Portray Themselves.* New York: Routledge, 1990.

Jones, Charles O. "The Diffusion of Responsibility: An Alternative Perspective for National Policy Politics in the U.S." *Governance* 4 (April 1991).

———. *The Presidency in a Separated System.* Washington, D.C.: Brookings, 1995.

Kernell, Samuel. *Going Public: New Strategies of Presidential Leadership.* 3d ed. Washington, D.C.: CQ Press, 1997.

Langston, Thomas S. *With Reverence and Contempt: How Americans Think About Their President.* Baltimore: Johns Hopkins University Press, 1995.

Lowi, Theodore J. *The Personal President: Power Invested and Promise Unfulfilled.* Ithaca, N.Y.: Cornell University Press, 1985.

Moe, Terry. "The Politicized Presidency," in *The New Directions in American Politics.* Ed. John E. Chubb and Paul E. Peterson. Washington, D.C.: Brookings, 1985.

Neustadt, Richard E. "The Presidency at Mid-Century." *Law and Contemporary Problems* 21 (1956).

———. *Presidential Power.* New York. Wiley, 1960.

———. *Presidential Power: The Politics of Leadership from Roosevelt to Reagan.* New York: Free Press, 1990.

Rose, Richard. *The Postmodern President: The White House Meets the World.* 2d ed. Chatham, N.J.: Chatham House, 1991.

Schlesinger, Arthur M., Jr. *The Imperial Presidency.* 2d ed. Boston: Houghton Mifflin, 1989.

Sundquist, James L. *The Decline and Resurgence of Congress.* Washington, D.C.: Brookings, 1981.

———. "Needed: A Political Theory for the New Era of Coalition Government in the United States." *Political Science Quarterly* 103 (Winter 1988).

Tulis, Jeffrey K. *The Rhetorical Presidency: The Pursuit of Popular Support.* Princeton, N.J.: Princeton University Press, 1987.

APPENDIX A

RESULTS OF PRESIDENTIAL CONTESTS, 1912–1996

Year	Republican nominee (in *italics*) and other major candidates	Democratic nominee (in *italics*) and other major candidates	Election winner	Division of popular vote[a] (percent)	Division of electoral vote[b]
1912	*William Howard Taft* (incumbent president)	*Woodrow Wilson* (governor of New Jersey)	Wilson (D)	42–23	435–8
	Theodore Roosevelt[c] (former president)	James Champ Clark (representative from Missouri and Speaker of the House)			
1916	*Charles Evans Hughes* (justice, U.S. Supreme Court)	*Woodrow Wilson* (incumbent president)	Wilson (D)	49–46	277–254
	Elihu Root (former secretary of state)	None			
1920	*Warren G. Harding* (senator from Ohio)	*James Cox* (governor of Ohio)	Harding (R)	60–34	404–127
	Leonard Wood (general)	William McAdoo (former secretary of the Treasury)			
	Frank Lowden (governor of Illinois)	A. Mitchell Palmer (attorney general)			
	Hiram Johnson (senator from California)				
1924	*Calvin Coolidge* (incumbent president)	*John W. Davis* (former solicitor general)	Coolidge (R)	54–29	382–136
	Hiram Johnson (senator from California)	Alfred Smith (governor of New York)			
		William McAdoo (former secretary of the Treasury)			
1928	*Herbert Hoover* (former secretary of commerce)	*Alfred Smith* (governor of New York)	Hoover (R)	58–41	444–87
	Frank Lowden (governor of Illinois)	James Reed (senator from Missouri)			
		Cordell Hull (representative from Tennessee)			

Year	Republican nominee (in *italics*) and other major candidates	Democratic nominee (in *italics*) and other major candidates	Election winner	Division of popular vote[a] (percent)	Division of electoral vote[b]
1932	*Herbert Hoover* (incumbent president) Joseph France (former senator from Missouri)	*Franklin D. Roosevelt* (governor of New York) Alfred Smith (former governor of New York) John Garner (representative from Texas and Speaker of the House)	Roosevelt (D)	57–40	472–59
1936	*Alfred Landon* (governor of Kansas) William Borah (senator from Idaho)	*Franklin D. Roosevelt* (incumbent president) None	Roosevelt (D)	61–37	523–8
1940	*Wendell Willkie* (Indiana lawyer and public utility executive) Thomas E. Dewey (U.S. district attorney for New York) Robert Taft (senator from Ohio)	*Franklin D. Roosevelt* (incumbent president) None	Roosevelt (D)	55–45	449–82
1944	*Thomas E. Dewey* (governor of New York) Wendell Willkie (previous Republican presidential nominee)	*Franklin D. Roosevelt* (incumbent president) Harry Byrd (senator from Virginia)	Roosevelt (D)	53–46	432–99
1948	*Thomas E. Dewey* (governor of New York) Harold Stassen (former governor of Minnesota) Robert Taft (senator from Ohio)	*Harry S. Truman* (incumbent president) Richard Russell (senator from Georgia)	Truman (D)	50–45	303–189
1952	*Dwight D. Eisenhower* (general) Robert Taft (senator from Ohio)	*Adlai Stevenson* (governor of Illinois) Estes Kefauver (senator from Tennessee) Richard Russell (senator from Georgia)	Eisenhower (R)	55–44	442–89
1956	*Dwight D. Eisenhower* (incumbent president) None	*Adlai Stevenson* (previous Democratic presidential nominee) Averell Harriman (governor of New York)	Eisenhower (R)	57–42	457–73
1960	*Richard Nixon* (vice president) None	*John F. Kennedy* (senator from Massachusetts) Hubert Humphrey (senator from Minnesota) Lyndon B. Johnson (senator from Texas)	Kennedy (D)	49.7–49.5	303–219

Year	Republican nominee (in *italics*) and other major candidates	Democratic nominee (in *italics*) and other major candidates	Election winner	Division of popular vote[a] (percent)	Division of electoral vote[b]
1964	*Barry Goldwater* (senator from Arizona)	*Lyndon B. Johnson* (incumbent president)	Johnson (D)	61–39	486–52
	Nelson Rockefeller (governor of New York)	None			
1968	*Richard Nixon* (former Republican presidential nominee)	*Hubert Humphrey* (incumbent vice president)	Nixon (R)	43.4–42.7	301–191
	Ronald Reagan (governor of California)	Robert F. Kennedy (senator from New York)			
		Eugene McCarthy (senator from Minnesota)			
1972	*Richard Nixon* (incumbent president)	*George McGovern* (senator from South Dakota)	Nixon (R)	61–38	520–17
	None	Hubert Humphrey (senator from Minnesota)			
		George Wallace (governor of Alabama)			
1976	*Gerald R. Ford* (incumbent president)	*Jimmy Carter* (former governor of Georgia)	Carter (D)	50–48	297–240
	Ronald Reagan (former governor of California)	Edmund Brown, Jr. (governor of California)			
		George Wallace (governor of Alabama)			
1980	*Ronald Reagan* (former governor of California)	*Jimmy Carter* (incumbent president)	Reagan (R)	51–41	489–49
	George Bush (former director of Central Intelligence Agency)	Edward M. Kennedy (senator from Massachusetts)			
	John Anderson (representative from Illinois)				
1984	*Ronald Reagan* (incumbent president)	*Walter F. Mondale* (former vice president)	Reagan (R)	59–41	525–13
	None	Gary Hart (senator from Colorado)			
1988	*George Bush* (vice president)	*Michael Dukakis* (governor of Massachusetts)	Bush (R)	53–46	426–111
	Robert Dole (senator from Kansas)	Jesse Jackson (civil rights activist)			
1992	*George Bush* (incumbent president)	*William Clinton* (governor of Arkansas)	Clinton (D)	43–37	357–168
	Patrick Buchanan (journalist)	Paul Tsongas (former senator)			
1996	*Robert Dole* (senator from Kansas)	*William Clinton* (incumbent president)	Clinton (D)	49–41	379–159
	Patrick Buchanan (journalist)	None			

APPENDIX B

PERSONAL BACKGROUNDS OF U.S. PRESIDENTS

President	Age at first political office	First political office / Last political office[a]	Age at becoming president	State of residence[b]	Father's occupation	Higher education[c]	Occupation
1. Washington (1789–1797)	17	County surveyor / Commander in chief	57	Va.	Farmer	None	Farmer, surveyor
2. Adams, J. (1797–1801)	39	Surveyor of highways / Vice president	61	Mass.	Farmer	Harvard	Farmer, lawyer
3. Jefferson (1801–1809)	26	State legislator / Vice president	58	Va.	Farmer	William and Mary	Farmer, lawyer
4. Madison (1809–1817)	25	State legislator / Secretary of state	58	Va.	Farmer	Princeton	Farmer
5. Monroe (1817–1825)	24	State legislator / Secretary of state	59	Va.	Farmer	William and Mary	Lawyer, farmer
6. Adams, J. Q. (1825–1829)	27	Minister to Netherlands / Secretary of state	58	Mass.	Farmer, lawyer	Harvard	Lawyer
7. Jackson (1829–1837)	21	Prosecuting attorney / U.S. Senate	62	Tenn.	Farmer	None	Lawyer
8. Van Buren (1837–1841)	30	Surrogate of county / Vice president	55	N.Y.	Tavern keeper	None	Lawyer
9. Harrison, W. H. (1841)	26	Territorial delegate to Congress / Minister to Colombia	68	Ind.	Farmer	Hampden-Sydney	Military
10. Tyler (1841–1845)	21	State legislator / Vice president	51	Va.	Planter, lawyer	William and Mary	Lawyer
11. Polk (1845–1849)	28	State legislator / Governor	50	Tenn.	Surveyor	U. of North Carolina	Lawyer
12. Taylor (1849–1850)	None	None / a	65	Ky.	Collector of internal revenue	None	Military
13. Fillmore (1850–1853)	28	Stale legislator / Vice president	50	N.Y.	Farmer	None	Lawyer
14. Pierce (1853–1857)	25	State legislator / U.S. district attorney	48	N.H.	General	Bowdoin	Lawyer
15. Buchanan (1857–1861)	22	Assistant county prosecutor / Minister to Great Britain	65	Pa.	Farmer	Dickinson	Lawyer

Personal Backgrounds of U.S. Presidents *(Continued)*

President	Age at first political office	First political office / Last political office[a]	Age at becoming president	State of residence[b]	Father's occupation	Higher education[c]	Occupation
16. Lincoln (1861–1865)	25	State legislator / U.S. House of Representatives	52	Ill.	Farmer, carpenter	None	Lawyer
17. Johnson, A. (1865–1869)	20	City alderman / Vice president	57	Tenn.	Janitor-porter	None	Tailor
18. Grant (1869–1877)	None	None / a	47	Ohio	Tanner	West Point	Military
19. Hayes (1877–1881)	36	City solicitor / Governor	55	Ohio	Farmer	Kenyon	Lawyer
20. Garfield (1881)	28	State legislator / U.S. Senate	50	Ohio	Canal worker	Williams	Educator, lawyer
21. Arthur (1881–1885)	31	State engineer / Vice president	51	N.Y.	Minister	Union	Lawyer
22. Cleveland (1885–1889) 24. (1893–1897)	26	Assistant district attorney / Governor	48	N.Y.	Minister	None	Lawyer
23. Harrison, B. (1889–1893)	24	City attorney / U.S. Senate	56	Ind.	Military	Miami of Ohio	Lawyer
25. McKinley (1897–1901)	26	Prosecuting attorney / Governor	54	Ohio	Ironmonger	Allegheny	Lawyer
26. Roosevelt, T. (1901–1909)	24	State legislator / Vice president	43	N.Y.	Business-man	Harvard	Lawyer, author
27. Taft (1909–1913)	24	Assistant prosecuting attorney / Secretary of war	52	Ohio	Lawyer	Yale	Lawyer
28. Wilson (1913–1921)	54	Governor / Governor	56	N.J.	Minister	Princeton	Educator
29. Harding (1921–1923)	35	State legislator / U.S. Senate	56	Ohio	Physician, editor	Ohio Central	Newspaper editor
30. Coolidge (1923–1929)	26	City councilman / Vice president	51	Mass.	Storekeeper	Amherst	Lawyer
31. Hoover (1929–1933)	43	Relief and food administrator / Secretary of commerce	55	Calif.	Blacksmith	Stanford	Mining engineer
32. Roosevelt, F. (1933–1945)	28	State legislator / Governor	49	N.Y.	Business-man, landowner	Harvard	Lawyer
33. Truman (1945–1953)	38	County judge (commissioner) / Vice president	61	Mo.	Farmer, livestock	None	Clerk, store owner
34. Eisenhower (1953–1961)	—	None / a	63	Kan.	Mechanic	West Point	Military

472

Personal Backgrounds of U.S. Presidents *(Continued)*

President	Age at first political office	First political office / Last political office[a]	Age at becoming president	State of residence[b]	Father's occupation	Higher education[c]	Occupation
35. Kennedy (1961–1963)	29	U.S. House of Representatives / U.S. Senate	43	Mass.	Business-man	Harvard	Newspaper reporter
36. Johnson, L. (1963–1969)	28	U.S. House of Representatives / Vice president	55	Texas	Farmer, real estate	Southwest Texas State Teacher's College	Educator
37. Nixon (1969–1974)	34	U.S. House of Representatives / Vice president	56	Calif.	Streetcar conductor	Whittier	Lawyer
38. Ford (1974–1977)	36	U.S. House of Representatives / Vice president	61	Mich.	Business-man	U. of Michigan	Lawyer
39. Carter (1977–1981)	38	County Board of Education / Governor	52	Ga.	Farmer, business-man	U.S. Naval Academy	Farmer, business-man
40. Reagan (1981–1989)	55	Governor / Governor	69	Calif.	Shoe salesman	Eureka	Entertainer
41. Bush (1989–1993)	42	U.S. House of Representatives / Vice president	64	Texas	Business-man, U.S. senator	Yale	Business-man
42. Clinton (1993–)	30	State attorney general / Governor	46	Ark.	Car dealer	Georgetown	Lawyer

[a] This category refers to the last civilian office held before the presidency. Taylor, Grant, and Eisenhower had served as generals before becoming president.
[b] The state is where the president spent his important adult years, not necessarily where he was born.
[c] Refers to undergraduate education.

APPENDIX C

THE CONSTITUTION
ON THE PRESIDENCY

ARTICLE I

Section 3. ... The Vice President of the United States shall be President of the Senate, but shall have no Vote, unless they be equally divided.

The Senate shall chuse their other officers, and also a President pro tempore, in the Absence of the Vice President, or when he shall exercise the Office of President of the United States.

The Senate shall have the sole Power to try all Impeachments. When sitting for that Purpose, they shall be on Oath or Affirmation. When the President of the United States is tried the Chief Justice shall preside: And no Person shall be convicted without the Concurrence of two thirds of the Members present.

Judgment in Cases of Impeachment shall not extend further than to removal from Office, and disqualification to hold and enjoy any Office of honor, Trust or Profit under the United States: but the Party convicted shall nevertheless be liable and subject to Indictment, Trial, Judgment and Punishment, according to Law.

Section 7. ... Every Bill which shall have passed the House of Representatives and the Senate, shall, before it become a Law, be presented to the President of the United States; If he approve he shall sign it, but if not he shall return it, with his Objections to that House in which it shall have originated, who shall enter the Objections at large on their Journal, and proceed to reconsider it. If after such Reconsideration two thirds of that House shall agree to pass the Bill, it shall be sent, together with the Objections, to the other House, by which it shall likewise be reconsidered, and if approved by two thirds of that House, it shall become a Law. But in all such Cases the Votes of both Houses shall be determined by yeas and Nays, and the Names of the Persons voting for and against the Bill shall be entered on the Journal of each House respectively. If any Bill shall not be returned by the President within ten Days (Sundays excepted) after it shall have been presented to him, the Same shall be a Law, in like Manner as if he had signed it, unless the Congress by their Adjournment prevent its Return, in which Case it shall not be a Law.

Every Order, Resolution, or Vote to which the Concurrence of the Senate and House of Representatives may be necessary (except on a question of Adjournment) shall be presented to the President of the United States; and before the Same shall take Effect, shall be approved by him, or being disapproved by him, shall be repassed by two thirds of the Senate and House of Representatives, according to the Rules and Limitations prescribed in the Case of a Bill.

ARTICLE II

Section 1. The executive Power shall be vested in a President of the United States of America. He shall hold his Office during the Term of four Years, and, together with the Vice President, chosen for the same Term, be elected, as follows. Each State shall appoint, in such Manner as the Legislature thereof may direct, a Number of Electors, equal to the whole Number of Senators and Representatives to which the State may be entitled in the Congress: but no Senator or Representative, or Person holding an Office of Trust or Profit under the United States, shall be appointed an Elector.

[The Electors shall meet in their respective States, and vote by Ballot for two Persons, of whom one at least shall not be an Inhabitant of the same State with themselves. And they shall make a List of all the Persons voted for, and of the Number of Votes for each; which List they shall sign and certify, and transmit sealed to the Seat of the Government of the United States, directed to the President of the Senate. The President of the Senate shall, in the Presence of the Senate and House of Representatives, open all the Certificates, and the Votes shall then be counted. The Person having the greatest Number of Votes shall be the President, if such Number be a Majority of the whole Number of Electors appointed; and if there be more than one who have such Majority, and have an equal Number of Votes, then the House of Representatives shall immediately chuse by Ballot one of them for President; and if no Person have a Majority, then from the five highest on the list the said House shall in like Manner chuse the President. But in chusing the President, the Votes shall be taken by States, the Representation from each State having one Vote; a quorum for this Purpose shall consist of a Member or Members from two thirds of the States, and a Majority of all the States shall be necessary to a Choice. In every Case, after the Choice of the President, the Person having the greatest Number of Votes of the Electors shall be the Vice President. But if there should remain two or more who have equal Votes, the Senate shall chuse from them by Ballot the Vice President.] [1]

The Congress may determine the Time of chusing the Electors, and the Day on which they shall give their Votes; which Day shall be the same throughout the United States.

No Person except a natural born Citizen, or a Citizen of the United States, at the time of the Adoption of this Constitution, shall be eligible to the Office of President; neither shall any Person be eligible to that Office who shall not have attained to the Age of thirty five Years, and been fourteen Years a Resident within the United States.

In Case of the Removal of the President from office, or of his Death, Resignation, or Inability to discharge the Powers and Duties of the said Office,[2] the Same shall devolve on the Vice President, and the Congress may by Law provide for the Case of Removal, Death, Resignation or Inability, both of the President and Vice President, declaring what officer shall then act as President, and such Officer shall act accordingly, until the Disability be removed, or a President shall be elected.

The President shall, at stated Times, receive for his Services, a Compensation, which shall neither be increased nor diminished during the Period for which he shall have been elected, and he shall not receive within that Period any other Emolument from the United States, or any of them.

Before he enter on the Execution of his Office, he shall take the following Oath or Affirmation: — "I do solemnly swear (or affirm) that I will faithfully execute the Office of President of the United States, and will to the best of my Ability, preserve, protect and defend the Constitution of the United States."

Section 2. The President shall be Commander in Chief of the Army and Navy of the United States, and of the Militia of the several States, when called into the actual Service of the United States; he may require the Opinion, in writing, of the principal Officer in each of the executive Departments, upon any Subject relating to the Duties of their respective Offices, and he shall have Power to grant Reprieves and Pardons for Offenses against the United States, except in Cases of Impeachment.

He shall have Power, by and with the Advice and Consent of the Senate, to make Treaties, provided two thirds of the Senators present concur; and he shall nominate, and by and with the Advice and Consent of the Senate, shall appoint Ambassadors, other public Ministers and Consuls, Judges of the supreme Court, and all other officers of the United States, whose Appointments are not herein otherwise provided for, and which shall be established by Law: but the Congress may by Law vest the Appointment of such inferior Officers, as they think proper, in the President alone, in the Courts of Law, or in the Heads of Departments.

The President shall have Power to fill up all Vacancies that may happen during the Recess of the Senate, by granting Commissions which shall expire at the End of their next Session.

Section 3. He shall from time to time give to the Congress Information of the State of the Union, and recommend to their Consideration such Measures as he shall judge necessary and expedient; he may, on extraordinary Occasions, convene both Houses, or either of them, and in Case of Disagreement between them, with Respect to the Time of Adjournment, he may adjourn them to such Time as he shall think proper; he shall receive Ambassadors and other public Ministers; he shall take Care that the Laws be faithfully executed, and shall Commission all the officers of the United States.

Section 4. The President, Vice President and all Civil Officers of the United States, shall be removed from office on Impeachment for, and Conviction of, Treason, Bribery, or other high Crimes and Misdemeanors.

ARTICLE VI

... This Constitution, and the Laws of the United States which shall be made in Pursuance thereof, and all Treaties made, or which shall be made, under the Authority of the United States, shall be the supreme Law of the Land; and the Judges in every State shall be bound thereby, any Thing in the Constitution or Laws of any State to the Contrary notwithstanding.

The Senators and Representatives before mentioned, and the Members of the several State Legislatures, and all executive and judicial Officers, both of the United States and of the several States, shall be bound by Oath or Affirmation, to support this Constitution; but no religious Test shall ever be required as a Qualification to any Office or public Trust under the United States.

AMENDMENT XII *(Ratified June 15, 1804)*

The Electors shall meet in their respective states and vote by ballot for President and Vice-President, one of whom, at least, shall not be an inhabitant of the same state with themselves; they shall name in their ballots the person voted for as President, and in distinct ballots the person voted for as Vice-President, and they shall make distinct lists of all persons voted for as President, and of all persons voted for as Vice-President, and of the number of votes for each, which lists they shall sign and certify, and transmit sealed to the seat of the government of the United States, directed to the President of the Senate; — The President of the Senate shall, in the presence of the Senate and House of Representatives, open all the certificates and the votes shall then be counted; — The person having the greatest number of votes for President, shall be the President, if such number be a majority of the whole number of Electors appointed; and if no person have such majority, then from the persons having the highest numbers not exceeding three on the list of those voted for as President, the House of Representatives shall choose immediately, by ballot, the President. But in choosing the President, the votes shall be taken by states, the representation from each state having one vote; a quorum for this purpose shall consist of a member or members from two-thirds of the states, and a majority of all the states shall be necessary to a choice. [And if the House of Representatives shall not choose a President whenever the right of choice shall devolve upon them, before the fourth day of March next following, then the Vice-President shall act as President, as in the case of the death or other constitutional disability of the President—][3] The person having the greatest number of votes as Vice-President, shall be the Vice-President, if such number be a majority of the whole number of Electors appointed, and if no person have a majority, then from the two highest numbers on the list, the Senate shall choose the Vice-President; a quorum for the purpose shall consist of two-thirds of the whole number of Senators, and a majority of the whole number shall be necessary to a choice. But no person constitutionally ineligible to the office of President shall be eligible to that of Vice-President of the United States.

A M E N D M E N T   X X *(Ratified Jan. 23, 1933)*

Section 1. The terms of the President and Vice President shall end at noon on the 20th day of January, and the terms of Senators and Representatives at noon on the 3d day of January, of the years in which such terms would have ended if this article had not been ratified; and the terms of their successors shall then begin.

Section 2. The Congress shall assemble at least once in every year, and such meeting shall begin at noon on the 3d day of January, unless they shall by law appoint a different day.

Section 3.[4] If, at the time fixed for the beginning of the term of the President, the President elect shall have died, the Vice President elect shall become President. If a President shall not have been chosen before the time fixed for the beginning of his term, or if the President elect shall have failed to qualify, then the Vice President elect shall act as President until a President shall have qualified; and the Congress may by law provide for the case wherein neither a President elect nor a Vice President elect shall have qualified, declaring who shall then act as President, or the manner in which one who is to act shall be selected, and such person shall act accordingly until a President or Vice President shall have qualified.

Section 4. The Congress may by law provide for the case of the death of any of the persons from whom the House of Representatives may choose a President whenever the right of choice shall have devolved upon them, and for the case of the death of any of the persons from whom the Senate may choose a Vice President whenever the right of choice shall have devolved upon them.

Section 5. Sections I and 2 shall take effect on the 15th day of October following the ratification of this article.

Section 6. This article shall be inoperative unless it shall have been ratified as an amendment to the Constitution by the legislatures of three-fourths of the several States within seven years from the date of its submission.

AMENDMENT XXII *(Ratified Feb. 27, 1951)*

Section 1. No person shall be elected to the office of the President more than twice, and no person who has held the office of President, or acted as President, for more than two years of a term to which some other person was elected President shall be elected to the office of the President more than once. But this Article shall not apply to any person holding the office of President when this Article was proposed by the Congress, and shall not prevent any person who may be holding the office of President, or acting as President, during the term within which this Article become operative from holding the office of President or acting as President during the remainder of such term.

Section 2. This Article shall be inoperative unless it shall have been ratified as an amendment to the Constitution by the legislatures of three-fourths of the several States within seven years from the date of its submission to the States by the Congress.

AMENDMENT XXIII *(Ratified March 29, 1961)*

Section 1. The District constituting the seat of Government of the United States shall appoint in such manner as the Congress may direct:

A number of electors of President and Vice President equal to the whole number of Senators and Representatives in Congress to which the District would be entitled if it were a State, but in no event more than the least populous State; they shall be in addition to those appointed by the States, but they shall be considered, for the purposes of the election of President and Vice President, to be electors appointed by a State; and they shall meet in the District and perform such duties as provided by the twelfth article of amendment.

Section 2. The Congress shall have power to enforce this article by appropriate legislation.

AMENDMENT XXV *(Ratified Feb. 10, 1967)*

Section 1. In case of the removal of the President from office or of his death or resignation, the Vice President shall become President.

Section 2. Whenever there is a vacancy in the office of the Vice President, the President shall nominate a Vice President who shall take office upon confirmation by a majority vote of both Houses of Congress.

Section 3. Whenever the President transmits to the President pro tempore of the Senate and the Speaker of the House of Representatives his written declaration that he is unable to discharge the powers and duties of his office, and until he transmits to them a written declaration to the contrary, such powers and duties shall be discharged by the Vice President as Acting President.

Section 4. Whenever the Vice President and a majority of either the principal officers of the executive departments or of such other body as Congress may by law provide, transmit to the President pro tempore of the Senate and the Speaker of the House of Representatives their written declaration that the President is unable to discharge the powers and duties of his office, the Vice President shall immediately assume the powers and duties of the office as Acting President.

Thereafter, when the President transmits to the President pro tempore of the Senate and the Speaker of the House of Representatives his written declaration that no inability exists, he shall resume the powers and duties of his office unless the Vice President and a majority of either the principal officers of the executive department or of such other body as Congress may by law provide, transmit within four days to the President pro tempore of the Senate and the Speaker of the House of Representatives their written declaration that the President is unable to discharge the powers and duties of his office. Thereupon Congress shall decide the issue, assembling within forty-eight hours for that purpose if not in session. If the Congress, within twenty-one days after receipt of the latter written declaration, or, if Congress is not in session, within twenty-one days after Congress is required to assemble, determines by two-thirds vote of both houses that the President is unable to discharge the powers and duties of his office, the Vice President shall continue to discharge the same as Acting President; otherwise, the President shall resume the powers and duties of his office.

NOTES

1. The material in brackets has been superseded by the Twelfth Amendment.
2. This provision has been affected by the Twenty-fifth Amendment.
3. The part in brackets has been superseded by Section 3 of the Twentieth Amendment.
4. See the Twenty-fifth Amendment.

Index

Greenspan, Alan, 391
Greenstein, Fred, 8, 22, 33, 35, 98, 104,
    162, 167, 188, 447
Grenada, 447–448
    media role in, 36–37, 120–121
    support and public opinion of Reagan,
        Ronald, 98, 102, 113
Gridlock. *See* Compromise
Grossman, Michael Baruch, 122, 128,
    129, 294–295
Guinier, Lani, 187
Gulf of Tonkin Resolution, 425

H
Hadley, Arthur, 58
Hagelin, John, 60
Hagerty, James, 120
Haig, Alexander
Haiti, 110, 186, 332
Hamilton, Alexander, 5, 16, 24, 44, 290,
    291, 414
Hammerschmidt, John Paul, 178
Harding, Warren, 32, 53, 153, 157, 160,
    165, 366
Harkin, Tom, 63
Harlan, John Marshall, 316
Harlow, Bryce, 226
Harriman, W. Averell, 422
Harrison, Benjamin, 87, 89, 153, 156,
    158
Harrison, William Henry, 153, 156, 157
Hart, Gary, 56, 61, 64
Harvard University, 156
Hayes, Rutherford B., 31, 87, 153, 155,
    156, 158
Haynsworth, Clement, Jr., 300, 302, 303
Hazleton, Jared, 385
Health care reforms. *See also*
        Medicaid/Medicare
    Carter, Jimmy and, 353
    Clinton, Bill and, 332, 336, 346, 350,
        359
    failure of, 13, 116, 125, 212, 213, 224,
        226, 234, 346, 355–356, 359
    Gergen, David and, 127
    public opinion of, 335
Heclo, Hugh, 247, 251
Hepburn v. Griswold (*First Legal Tender Case*)
    (1870), 310–311
Heroic presidency, 4–6, 11, 445–446,
    459–460. *See also* Presidency
Hess, Stephen, 274
Higher Education Act, 352
Hill, Anita, 289
Hinckley, Barbara, 35, 36, 101–103, 107,
    113, 125, 436, 453, 459
Hinckley, John, Jr., 109

Hodgson, Godfrey, 9
Holt, Frank, 176
Homosexual issues, 116, 355
Hoover Commission (1949), 270, 278
Hoover, Herbert
    background of, 155, 156, 157, 158–159
    Congress and, 455–456
    economic policies, 367
    judiciary and, 301–302
    personality, 163, 167, 168
    presidency of, 31, 164
House of Representatives. *See also* Con-
        gress
    elections and, 45, 46, 68, 87, 88
    Jay Treaty, 24
    Republican takeover of 1994, 343
Hume, Brit, 129
Humphrey, Hubert, 52, 54, 61
Humphrey, William, 314
Huntington, Samuel P., 204

I
ICC. *See* Interstate Commerce Commission
Illinois, 72
*Immigration and Naturalization Service v.
    Chadha* (1983), 269, 273, 440n40
Impeachment. *See* Bureaucracy; Nixon,
        Richard M.; Presidents
Imperial presidency, 6–12, 242n85, 447,
    460. *See also* Johnson, Lyndon,
        Baines; Nixon, Richard M.
Impoundment, 207, 223, 225, 272–273,
    397
Incumbents. *See* Candidates
Independent voters. *See* Political parties
Industrial era, 27
Inflation. *See* Economic issues
Intelligence activities, 272, 421, 439n26.
    See also Covert activities
Interest groups
    budget issues and, 250, 384
    growth of, 447
    health care reform, 356
    policy making and, 340–342
    political issues, 381–384
    presidents and, 114–116, 208, 219–220,
        282, 384, 459
Interest rates. *See* Economic issues
International Court of Justice, 420
Interstate business, 370
Interstate Commerce Commission (ICC),
    27, 371
Interstate Highway System, 352
Iowa caucuses, 57, 62, 63–64
Iran
    hostage crisis, 83, 106, 108, 416–417
    intelligence in, 421

ACKNOWLEDGMENTS

78 *Gallup Report,* November 1988, pp. 6–7. © 1988 by The Gallup Reports; *The Gallup Poll Monthly,* November 1992, page 9. Used by permission. **108** Harold W. Stanley and Richard G. Niemi, *Vital Statistics on American Politics,* 5th ed., p. 262. © 1995 by CQ Press, Washington, D.C. Used by permission of the publisher. **123** Harold W. Stanley and Richard G. Niemi, *Vital Statistics on American Politics,* 5th ed., p. 53. © 1995 by CQ Press, Washington, D.C. Used by permission of the publisher. **149** Reprinted by permission of Greenwood Publishing Group, Inc. Westport, Conn., from *The Leadership Question,* by Bert A. Rockman. © by Praeger Publishers, 2004. Fred 1. Greenstein, *Personality and Politics,* p. 27. © 1975 by W. W. Norton. Used by permission of the author. **151** Henry J. Abraham, *Justices and Presidents: Appointments to the Supreme Court,* 2d ed., pp. 380–385. © Henry J. Abraham, 1994, 2005. Reprinted by permission of Oxford University Press, Inc. Harold W. Stanley and Richard G. Niemi, *Vital Statistics on American Politics,* 5th ed., pp. 240–243. ©1995 by CQ Press, Washington, D.C. Used by permission of the publisher. **154** Edward Pessen, *The Log Cabin Myth: The Social Backgrounds of the Presidents,* p. 68. © 1984 by Yale University Press, New Haven, Conn. Used by permission of the publisher. **216** Michael Nelson, ed., *Guide to the Presidency,* p. 451. © 1989 by Congressional Quarterly Inc. Reprinted by permission of the publisher. **218** Stephen J. Wayne, Richard L. Cole, James F.C. Hyde, "Advising the President on Enrolled Legislation," *Political Science Quarterly* 94 (Summer 1979): 310. © 1979 by Political Science Quarterly. Used by permission of the publisher. **236** George C. Edwards III, *At the Margins: Political Leadership in Congress,* pp. 177, 180, 185, 186. © 1989 by Yale University Press, New Haven, Conn. Used by permission of the publisher. **Chap. 10** A small portion of this material was originally written for a chapter in LEADERSHIP AND THE BUSH PRESIDENCY, Ryan J. Barilleaux and Mary Stuckey, eds. (Praeger Publishers, an imprint of Greenwood Publishing Group, Inc, Westport, Conn., forthcoming October 1992). © 1992 by Ryan J. Barilleaux and Mary Stuckey. Reprinted with permission of the publisher. **433** Cecil V. Crabb, Jr., and Kevin V. Mulcahy, *American National Security: A Presidential Perspective,* p. 189.© 1991 by Wadsworth Publishing, Belmont, Calif. Used by permission of the publisher.

PHOTOGRAPHS AND CARTOONS

3 The White House/Bill Fitz-Patrick; **43** Fred Sons; **96** Library of Congress; **147** The White House; **199** R. Ellis; **244** Tom Toles © 1993 *The Buffalo News.* Reprinted with special permission of Universal Press Syndicate. All rights reserved; **288** Reuters/Bettmann; **327** The White House; **365** National Archives; **405** Alex S. MacLean; **443** Tom Toles © 1993 *The New Republic.* Reprinted with special permission of Universal Press Syndicate. All rights reserved.